A HISTORY OF THE BLACK WATCH [ROYAL HIGHLANDERS] IN THE GREAT WAR, 1914–1918

VOLUME TWO

VOLUME ONE: REGULAR ARMY
1st, 2nd and 3rd (Special Reserve) Battalions

VOLUME TWO: TERRITORIAL FORCE
4th, 5th, 4/5th, 6th, 7th and the Reserve Battalions
and Allied Regiments
The Royal Highlanders of Canada
and The Sydney Scottish Rifles

VOLUME THREE: NEW ARMY
8th, 9th, 10th, 11th, 12th, 13th and 14th Battalions

WAR MEMORIAL AT KILLIN TO MEN OF THE BLACK WATCH BATTALIONS

A HISTORY OF THE BLACK WATCH
[ROYAL HIGHLANDERS]
IN THE GREAT WAR, 1914–1918

EDITED BY
MAJOR-GENERAL A. G. WAUCHOPE, C.B.
Author of
"The Black Watch, 1725–1907"

AM FREICEADAN DUBH

LONDON
THE MEDICI SOCIETY LIMITED
MCMXXVI

Printed and bound by Antony Rowe Ltd, Eastbourne

TO
THE MEMORY OF
THE EIGHT THOUSAND MEN
OF THE
REGULAR, TERRITORIAL AND SERVICE BATTALIONS
OF
THE BLACK WATCH
WHO GAVE THEIR LIVES IN THE GREAT WAR
THIS HISTORY IS DEDICATED

"Without labour there is no coming to rest, nor without fighting can the victory be obtained."

PREFACE

THIS record of The Black Watch during the Great War shows how some thirty thousand men served in the Regiment in France, Belgium and Salonika, in Palestine and Mesopotamia, of whom eight thousand were killed and over twenty thousand were wounded.

The long days in the trenches encouraged a very close understanding between officers and men, and many hours were spent talking over what might best be done for the good of the Regiment after the war. Serving in the earlier part of the war as a company officer, I gathered from these discussions that there were three schemes which great numbers of our men hoped might, one day, be realized.

The first of these schemes entailed the reorganization of the Regimental Association, in order that help might be given to the large number of men, who, it was feared, would find themselves in difficulties or in distress after the war. This first object has been achieved through the labours of many officers of The Black Watch, among whom I must mention the names of the Earl of Mansfield, Colonel S. A. Innes and Major L. Gibson.

The second scheme often spoken of was that of a War Memorial, which should not only be a visible monument to those who fell, but, at the same time, be of help to those who had suffered through the war, and to all widows and children.

This object has also been achieved by the establishment of the Dunalistair Home, the successful foundation of which was so largely due to the labours of the late Brigadier-General W. McL. Campbell and of Colonel H. H. Sutherland.

The third object which I found so many of our men were anxious to see fulfilled was that a history of The Black Watch during the war should be written and published at such a price as would render its purchase possible by all ranks and their relatives. It was hoped that this history would form a true record of the main achievements of our Regular, Territorial and Service Battalions, that is to say, a record of the gallantry of all those men who bore the Red Hackle and crossed the seas in the service of the Regiment; and further, that this account, written by those who shared equally in the hardships and in the fighting, might also furnish a picture of the life led by our men in various lands and campaigns throughout these years of trial and danger.

It has been, therefore, in the endeavour to realize this last object that this history has been written. In these volumes the work of each separate battalion is described mainly by officers who took part in the actual actions and scenes here set out; and the thanks of the Regiment are due to those who have given so much time and labour to this end. But as these accounts have

PREFACE

been revised, and in many parts re-written by me, I accept full responsibility for the whole.

Our Territorial Battalions, direct descendants of The Black Watch Volunteer Battalions, had long held a fine reputation in Scotland for discipline and soldierly bearing. The conduct of their contingents which served as reinforcements to the Second Battalion during the South African War, served but to enhance this reputation and to knit all units of the Regiment yet more firmly together. It was no surprise therefore that our four Territorial Battalions were among the earliest ready to take the field, and among those who earned the highest praise for gallant deeds and unstinted good work.

Unlike the Territorial Battalions, the Service Battalions had no organization and no history, yet from the first day that they went into battle till the end of the war they nobly upheld the traditions of The Black Watch. This was partly due to their well-trained officers, to the splendid quality of the recruits who came so very largely from our 42nd Regimental District, and, above all, to the fine spirit—of which the Red Hackle is the symbol—that enheartened every man and, though unseen, was felt by every man to be the link that binds together each platoon, company and battalion of The Black Watch.

The task of editorship has at times seemed almost beyond my powers. As editor I am conscious of many defects, both of omission and commission. None the less I believe that this history, which describes the many gallant deeds and cites the names of those who fell in action, gives a faithful record of all those Battalions whose spirit and achievement have brought yet more honour and glory to The Black Watch. I believe also that this history shows that the same spirit of trust and good fellowship which has united all ranks of the Regiment since its earliest days still flourishes: that this spirit which inspired The Black Watch in the great victories of the Peninsula, Waterloo and Seringapatam, and sustained the heroes of Fontenoy and Ticonderoga, is the same spirit which filled the hearts and strengthened the resolve of those who in this last war gave their lives in the service of their King, their Country and their Regiment.

It is impossible for me to thank all those officers, non-commissioned officers and men who have given their help in the writing of this history, but I well know that they gave their help willingly and for the good of the Regiment. I must, however, take this opportunity to thank Colonel John Stewart and Captain G. S. M. Burton for their assistance in revising proofs and arranging the appendices of these volumes.

It is therefore with the hope that the great deeds described

PREFACE

in these pages will serve as an example and an encouragement to all those who in future years join The Black Watch and wear the Red Hackle that I am emboldened to publish this history.

I am greatly indebted to Sir William Orpen, to Mr. Charles Payne ("Snaffles"), and also to Sir Bruce Seton (the owner), and Mr. J. Beadle, the painter of the "Pipes of War," who have been good enough to grant me permission to reproduce certain pictures as illustrations to this history.

I ask all readers who detect errors in the text, or who are in possession of additional material or facts dealing with the history of the Regiment in the Great War, to send any information or corrections to the Officer Commanding, The Black Watch Depot, Perth.

A. G. WAUCHOPE,
Major-General.

BERLIN,
November, 1925.

Note.   The two months delay in the publication of Volumes II and III has been due to Strikes and other unforeseen causes, and although unavoidable is very greatly regretted.

CONTENTS OF VOLUME TWO

	PAGE
EDITOR'S PREFACE.	vii
BATTLE HONOURS OF THE BLACK WATCH.	xviii
FOREWORD BY GENERAL THE RIGHT HON. SIR JOHN G. MAXWELL, G.C.B., K.C.M.G., C.V.O., D.S.O.	xix

THE FOURTH BATTALION

CHAPTER I—From the Date of Mobilization to the Battle of Loos, September 25th, 1915.   3

CHAPTER II—September 24th, 1915—March 7th, 1916.
1. The Battle of Loos.   15
2. Givenchy.   22
3. Amalgamation with the 5th Battalion.   24

LIST OF APPENDICES—
   I. Record of Officers' Services.   25
   II. Summary of Casualties.   28
   III. Casualties—Officers.   29
   IV. Nominal Roll of Warrant Officers, Non-Commissioned Officers and Men Killed in Action or Died of Wounds or Disease in the Great War, 1914–18.   31
   V. Honours and Awards.   35
   VI. List of Actions and Operations.   36

THE FIFTH BATTALION

CHAPTER I—From the Date of Mobilization, August 4th, 1914, to the Date of Amalgamation with the 4th Battalion, March 15th, 1916.   39

LIST OF APPENDICES—
   I. Record of Officers' Services.   53
   II. Summary of Casualties.   56
   III. Casualties—Officers.   57
   IV. Nominal Roll of Warrant Officers, Non-Commissioned Officers and Men Killed in Action or Died of Wounds or Disease in the Great War, 1914–18.   58
   V. Honours and Awards.   61
   VI. List of Actions and Operations.   64

CONTENTS

THE FOURTH—FIFTH BATTALION

CHAPTER I—From the Amalgamation of the Two Battalions in March, 1916, to November, 1916.   PAGE
1. The Trenches near Festubert.   67
2. The Fighting on the Somme.   74

CHAPTER II—November 19th, 1916—July 31st, 1917.
1. Ypres: Holding the Line.   78

CHAPTER III—July 31st, 1917—January 21st, 1918.
1. Passchendaele and After.   84

CHAPTER IV—January–May, 1918
1. The German Attack.   91

CHAPTER V—May, 1918—April, 1919.
1. Buzancy and the Final Advance.   97

LIST OF APPENDICES—
I. Record of Officers' Services.   105
II. Summary of Casualties.   111
III. Casualties—Officers.   112
IV. Nominal Roll of Warrant Officers, Non-Commissioned Officers and Men Killed in Action or Died of Wounds or Disease in the Great War, 1914–18.   113
V. Honours and Awards.   119
VI. List of Actions and Operations.   122

THE SIXTH BATTALION

CHAPTER I—August, 1914—May, 1915.
1. Mobilization at North Queensferry.   125
2. Dundee and the Tay Defences.   127
3. Move to Bedford to join 51st (Highland) Division.   128

CHAPTER II—May to December, 1915.
1. The Move to France.   129
2. In the Line near Festubert.   130
3. The Somme Area.   132

CHAPTER III—Christmas, 1915—July, 1916.
1. With the 30th Division at Maricourt.   135
2. Four months in the Labyrinth near Arras.   136

CONTENTS

CHAPTER IV—July to October, 1916.   PAGE
  1. The Attack on High Wood.   139
  2. Armentières.   141
  3. At Bailleul.   142
  4. Return to the Somme.   142

CHAPTER V—October and November, 1916.
  1. The Battle of Beaumont Hamel.   144

CHAPTER VI—November, 1916—May, 1917.
  1. Courcelette.   154
  2. New Year at Aveluy.   155
  3. The Battle of Arras.   158
  4. Attack on Greenland Hill.   159

CHAPTER VII—June to November, 1917.
  1. The Third Battle of Ypres.   163
  2. Attack near the Steenbeek River.   164

CHAPTER VIII—November, 1917—January, 1918.
  1. The Battle of Cambrai.   170

CHAPTER IX—February to June, 1918.
  1. The German Offensive, 1918.   176
  2. Battle of the Lawe.   187
  3. Move to Vimy Ridge.   188

CHAPTER X—July, 1918.
  1. Move to Champagne.   189
  2. Battle of Rheims.   190
  3. Bois de Courton.   192
  4. Citation in French Army Orders.   196

CHAPTER XI—August, 1918—October, 1919.
  1. Capture of Greenland Hill.   198
  2. Cambrai Area.   199
  3. Crossing of the Ecaillon.   199
  4. Fighting near Mount Huoy.   201
  5. Iwuy.   201
  6. Move to Belgium and the Cologne Area.   201
  7. The March Past in Paris.   202
  8. Back to England.   203
  9. Demobilization.   203

CONTENTS

LIST OF APPENDICES—

		PAGE
I.	Record of Officers' Services.	205
II.	Summary of Casualties.	216
III.	Casualties—Officers.	217
IV.	Nominal Roll of Warrant Officers, Non-Commissioned Officers and Men Killed in Action or Died of Wounds or Disease in the Great War, 1914–18.	219
V.	Honours and Awards.	229
VI.	List of Actions and Operations.	234

THE SEVENTH BATTALION

CHAPTER I—AUGUST, 1914.
1. Mobilization. — 239
2. Early Days at Kinghorn. — 241

CHAPTER II—APRIL, 1915.
1. At Kinghorn. — 245
2. With the Highland Division at Bedford. — 247

CHAPTER III—MAY TO JUNE, 1915.
1. The First weeks in France. — 249

CHAPTER IV—AUGUST, 1915, TO JUNE, 1916.
1. Near Albert and Maricourt — 255
2. The Labyrinth. — 258

CHAPTER V—JULY, 1916
1. The Somme. — 264

CHAPTER VI—AUGUST TO NOVEMBER, 1916.
1. Armentières and Beaumont Hamel. — 268

CHAPTER VII—NOVEMBER, 1916, TO JANUARY, 1917.
1. Courcelette and a Rest in Millencourt. — 275

CHAPTER VIII—FEBRUARY TO JUNE, 1917.
1. The Battle of Arras. — 279

CHAPTER IX—JUNE TO SEPTEMBER, 1917.
1. Ypres. — 288

CHAPTER X—OCTOBER AND NOVEMBER, 1917.
1. Attack on the Hindenburg Line. — 294

CONTENTS

CHAPTER XI—DECEMBER, 1917, TO THE END OF APRIL, 1918.　PAGE
   1. The German Offensives.　298

CHAPTER XII—MAY TO AUGUST, 1918.
   1. Roclincourt and Champagne.　306

CHAPTER XIII—AUGUST, 1918, TO APRIL, 1919.
   1. The Final Offensive and Demobilization.　311

LIST OF APPENDICES—
   I. Record of Officers' Services.　315
   II. Summary of Casualties.　324
   III. Casualties—Officers.　325
   IV. Nominal Roll of Warrant Officers, Non-Commissioned Officers and Men Killed in Action or Died of Wounds or Disease in the Great War, 1914–18.　326
   V. Honours and Awards.　334
   VI. List of Actions and Operations.　337

THE RESERVE BATTALIONS

2/4th Battalion　342
2/5th Battalion　342
2/6th Battalion　343
2/7th Battalion　344
Third Line Battalions　344

THE ROYAL HIGHLANDERS OF CANADA　347
   APPENDICES　369

THE SYDNEY SCOTTISH RIFLES　373

INDEX　375

ILLUSTRATIONS TO VOLUME TWO

MEMORIAL AT KILLIN TO MEN OF THE BLACK WATCH
BATTALIONS. *Frontispiece*

THE FOURTH BATTALION.
Facing page
FOURTH BATTALION OFFICERS AFTER THE BATTLE OF
NEUVE CHAPELLE. From a painting in the Albert Gallery,
Dundee. 10
COLONEL HARRY WALKER, C.M.G. 21

THE FIFTH BATTALION.
OFFICERS BEFORE EMBARKATION TO FRANCE, 1st NOV.,
1914. 40

THE FOURTH-FIFTH BATTALION.
SKETCH OF THE BUZANCY WAR MEMORIAL. 100

THE SIXTH BATTALION.
COLONEL SIR ROBERT MONCREIFFE. BART. C.B., C.M.G.,
V.D., T.D. 127
OFFICERS IN FRANCE, 1915. 127
SIXTH BATTALION COLOURS WITH THE CROIX DE
GUERRE AWARDED AFTER THE BATTLE OF TAR-
DENOIS, JULY, 1918. 196

THE SEVENTH BATTALION.
"THERE CAM A PIPER OOT O' FIFE." By "Snaffles." 237
SERGEANTS OF THE SEVENTH BATTALION, NEAR ST.
OMER, JULY, 1917—PRIOR TO THE THIRD BATTLE
OF YPRES. 290
WOUNDED MEN OF THE SEVENTH BATTALION WAITING
TO BE TRANSFERRED TO HOSPITAL AT MERVILLE,
APRIL, 1918. 302

RESERVE BATTALIONS.
194 OFFICERS OF THE BLACK WATCH (TERRITORIAL
BRIGADE)—BRIDGE OF EARN, 1915. 341

ALLIED REGIMENT OF CANADA.
"PIPES OF WAR." After the painting by J. Beadle. 349
THE ROYAL HIGHLANDERS OF CANADA. INSPECTION
BY H.R.H. THE DUKE OF CONNAUGHT ON THE CHAMP
DE MARS, MONTREAL, 28th MAY, 1915, BEFORE EM-
BARKATION TO FRANCE. 351

LIST OF MAPS TO VOLUME TWO

	Facing page
NEUVE CHAPELLE, MARCH 10th–12th, 1915.	100
BUZANCY, JULY, 1918.	100
BEAUMONT HAMEL.	152
BATTLE OF CAMBRAI.	174
THE GERMAN OFFENSIVE, EAST OF BAPAUME, MARCH, 1918.	186
THE GERMAN OFFENSIVE, RIVER LAWE, APRIL, 1918.	188
THE BATTLES OF ARRAS, APRIL, 1917, AND AUGUST, 1918.	286
THIRD BATTLE OF YPRES.	292
CHAMPAGNE OFFENSIVE.	308
GENERAL MAP OF FRANCE.	End of Volume

Note. *The Map of the Third Battle of Ypres illustrates the operations of the 4/5th, 6th and 7th Battalions. The remainder, except the first two serve both the 6th and 7th Battalions.*

BATTLE HONOURS OF THE BLACK WATCH

The Royal Cypher within the Garter. The badge and motto of the Order of the Thistle. In each of the four corners the Royal Cypher ensigned with the Imperial Crown. The Sphinx, superscribed " Egypt."

" GUADALOUPE, 1759," " MARTINIQUE, 1762," " HAVANNAH," " NORTH AMERICA, 1763-64," " MANGALORE," " MYSORE," " SERINGAPATAM," " CORUNNA," " BUSACO," " FUENTES D'ONOR," " PYRENEES," " NIVELLE," " NIVE," " ORTHES," " TOULOUSE," " PENINSULA," " WATERLOO," " SOUTH AFRICA, 1846-7, 1851-2-3," " ALMA," " SEVASTOPOL," " LUCKNOW," " ASHANTEE, 1873-4," " TEL-EL-KEBIR," " EGYPT, 1882-4," " KIRBEKAN," " NILE, 1884-5," " PAARDEBERG," " SOUTH AFRICA, 1899-1902."

The Great War—25 Battalions.—" Retreat from Mons," " MARNE, 1914, '18," " Aisne, 1914," " La Bassée, 1914," " YPRES, 1914, '17, '18," " Langemarck, 1914," " Gheluvelt," " Nonne Bosschen," " Givenchy, 1914," " Neuve Chapelle," " Aubers," " Festubert, 1915," " LOOS," " SOMME, 1916, '18," " Albert, 1916," " Bazentin," " Delville Wood," " Pozières," " Flers-Courcelette," " Morval," " Thiepval," " Le Transloy," " Ancre Heights," " Ancre, 1916," " ARRAS, 1917, '18," " Vimy, 1917," " Scarpe, 1917, '18," " Arleux," " Pilkem," " Menin Road," " Polygon Wood," " Poelcappelle," " Passchendaele," " Cambrai, 1917, '18," " St. Quentin," " Bapaume, 1918," " Rosières," " LYS," " Estaires," " Messines, 1918," " Hazebrouck," " Kemmel," " Béthune," " Scherpenberg," " Soissonnais-Ourcq," " Tardenois," " Drocourt-Quéant," " HINDENBURG LINE," " Épéhy," " St. Quentin Canal," " Beaurevoir," " Courtrai," " Selle," " Sambre," " France and Flanders, 1914-18." " DOIRAN, 1917," " Macedonia, 1915-18." " Egypt, 1916." " Gaza," " Jerusalem," " Tell 'Asur," " MEGIDDO," " Sharon," " Damascus," " Palestine, 1917-18," " Tigris, 1916," " KUT AL AMARA, 1917," " Baghdad," " Mesopotamia, 1915-17."

The list of Honours given above shows that The Black Watch had won 28 Battle Honours before 1914, and gained 69 Battle Honours during the Great War. As it was impossible to emblazon all these Honours on the King's or Regimental Colours, the Army Council decided that only ten Great War Honours selected by the Regiment should be emblazoned on the King's Colour. A committee therefore was appointed, under the Chairmanship of Sir John Maxwell, Colonel of the Regiment, which selected the following ten Honours to be borne on the King's Colour :—

(1) MARNE, 1914, '18
(2) YPRES, 1914, '17, '18
(3) LOOS
(4) SOMME, 1916, '18
(5) ARRAS, 1917, '18
(6) LYS
(7) HINDENBURG LINE
(8) DOIRAN, 1917
(9) MEGIDDO
(10) KUT AL AMARA, 1917

These 10 Honours were chosen as being the most representative of the various Campaigns in which the twelve Battalions of the Regiment who fought overseas took part.

The Regimental Colour still bears the 28 Honours won before the Great War, and the 10 Honours chosen by the committee are emblazoned on the King's Colour.

FOREWORD

BY

GENERAL THE RIGHT HON. SIR JOHN G. MAXWELL,

G.C.B., K.C.M.G., C.V.O., D.S.O., COLONEL, THE BLACK WATCH

THIS year, 1925, is the 200th Anniversary of the formation of the Independent Companies from which, in 1725, The Black Watch originated. The commissions of the six Captains of these Independent Companies are dated 1725, therefore it seems very appropriate to publish this year *The History of The Black Watch in the Great War.*

I, as its Colonel, have been asked to write this " Foreword," a task rendered no easier by the admirable Preface of Major-General A. G. Wauchope, the editor of this history.

In no part of the Empire was there a more hearty response to the call for men than in Scotland. We, of The Black Watch, are not given to boasting unduly of our deeds: we prefer to rest assured that every man who had the honour of wearing the Red Hackle acted up to and, collectively, enhanced the glorious traditions of our Regiment. No less than twenty-five Battalions served in the Great War, and eight thousand men of The Black Watch laid down their lives for their King and Country.

The official record of the battles and engagements in which these Battalions served shows that in whatever theatre of war the Regiment was represented, the traditions of The Black Watch were most worthily upheld. It is therefore right and proper that, as far as possible, a complete and true story of the exploits of each Battalion, in the various theatres of war, is recorded and incorporated in this history.

I desire to emphasize what General Wauchope has said, that no matter its shortcomings, if there be any, this history is written by the Regiment for the Regiment and for the countless friends of The Black Watch all the world over. No outside aid has been evoked. Every endeavour has been made, consistent with the design of the work, to keep within certain limits, so that the history can be published at such a price to bring it within the reach of all. One would like to know that a copy is in the hands of all past and present Black Watch men, as well as the relatives of those whose loss we mourn.

We are proud of our Regiment, and of the fact that His Majesty the King is our Colonel-in-Chief. We are justly proud of our records, both of the past and of the Great War. We hope that this history will be kept as a treasured heirloom and handed down to future generations of Black Watch men in order that they may emulate the valour and devotion of their predecessors.

FOREWORD

Our thanks are indeed due—and I offer them in the name of the Regiment—to Major-General Wauchope, and all who have assisted him in the compilation of this history. It has been an onerous task, though one of love and pride, and we congratulate them on having accomplished so successfully that which they set out to do.

J. G. Maxwell

COLONEL, THE BLACK WATCH.

THE FOURTH
BATTALION

CHAPTER I

FROM THE DATE OF MOBILIZATION TO THE BATTLE OF LOOS, 25TH SEPTEMBER, 1915

THE 4th Battalion The Black Watch is the lineal descendant of the 1st and 2nd Volunteer Battalions of The Black Watch. The citizens of Dundee were among the first to give practical shape to the proposals born of the Volunteer movement in 1859. In that year the 1st Forfarshire (Dundee) Rifles were formed, and in 1881 were joined to The Black Watch under the Territorial system, and given the title of the 1st (City of Dundee) Volunteer Battalion The Black Watch.

The 2nd (Angus) Volunteer Battalion was formed from the independent Volunteer companies raised in Forfarshire in 1859 and organized a year later into two administrative battalions. In 1874 these two battalions were amalgamated, and in 1881 this Battalion became the 2nd Volunteer Battalion The Black Watch.

It would be out of place in this history to relate the doings or to dwell on the efficiency of these two battalions before the outbreak of the Great War. It is sufficient to recall the fine services rendered by the officers and men of this Battalion who joined the three Black Watch Service companies that served and fought with the 2nd Battalion The Black Watch in the South African war.

In the history of the Regiment during the Great War the 4th Battalion holds a notable position, since it represented a Scottish city at war. The other three Territorial battalions of The Black Watch were recruited from the counties of Forfar, Perth and Fife; but the 4th Battalion stood for the city of Dundee, from which alone it drew its recruits, and consequently, as the Battalion was successful or otherwise, so in great measure did the fortune of war fluctuate in the opinion of the citizens of Dundee. The Battalion had in it the spirit and local patriotism which is the basis of so much that is best in Scottish character and in Scottish history.

It is a far cry back to those days of August, 1914, when war still suggested colour and romance and not khaki, mud and hardship in every form. The difficulties of mobilization, of equipping the Battalion and of arranging its administration were considerable. But the good spirit of the 4th, the hard work and efficiency of Colonel Walker and his staff soon overcame them all.

The Battalion was able to take up its duties as a coast defence unit immediately on mobilization in a fully armed condition. Before the end of August two companies were sent to guard the approaches to and south end of the Tay Bridge, and one company the north end. Two companies were stationed at Broughty Ferry and provided all sentry duties in connection with the Garrison Artillery there and at the Naval Air Station on the Tay. Three companies were stationed in Dundee and provided detachments to guard the city's water supply, the docks and the submarine dry dock. Training and musketry at Buddon were so arranged as to fit in with the coast defence duties. The men were drilled incessantly under Sergeant-Majors Charles and McNab in various parts of the city, being housed in Bell Street Drill Hall at night.

Three hundred and fifty men, the full number required to complete the establishment, were all attested within two weeks of mobilization, and were all Dundee men. The formation of a second battalion was begun as soon as the 1/4th had been brought up to strength, and the ranks of the second battalion were also filled with men from Dundee in September and October, 1914.

In September the Battalion moved to Buddon under canvas, where, gradually, under its Commanding Officer, Colonel H. Walker, and the Adjutant, Captain F. R. Tarleton, it was soon welded into a well-organized unit, conscious of its strength, proud of its past history and traditions, and eager to join in battle against the enemy across the seas.

The 1/4th were in possession of their full war establishment of rifles and ammunition. The Battalion had a boot contract running for peace-time supplies, and this was easily and rapidly adapted to supply the new demands on mobilization. Uniform was fairly quickly obtained from the Territorial Force Association, though there was some delay in providing greatcoats. There was, however, a much greater delay in clothing the second line. A natural keenness to serve in France soon began to show itself, and officers and men hoped eagerly for a more active sphere than the peaceful links of Buddon or the Tay Bridge, with its monotonous round of guard duties; but the days of service overseas were still far distant.

Under the wise leadership of Colonel Walker, than whom no man in all Dundee was more loved or respected, the Battalion performed its duty, continued the course of military training, and took over, on the north side of the Tay, the various guards and duties that the 5th Battalion The Black Watch had been performing. So the monotonous round went on until at last on the morning of the 23rd of February, 1915, the Battalion received the long-hoped-for order to move to France on active service.

The 4th paraded at Dudhope Castle, and in three detachments moved to Tay Bridge Station. Before moving off, Colonel Walker addressed the Battalion in the following words:

FAREWELL TO DUNDEE

"Men of the 4th Royal Highlanders, the chance has come for you to show in the field those high qualities which have always made the 4th Black Watch a Territorial battalion with which it is an honour to be associated. Men, you belong to a great Regiment, one whose battalions of the line have gathered glory and reaped fame in every quarter of the globe. You have a great tradition to sustain, and I trust that when you proceed on active service, to whichever destination you may be sent, you will remember that tradition and do your best to garner fresh laurels for The Black Watch. I myself have every confidence that you will do nothing to tarnish the fair name of the Regiment. I think, indeed, you may be trusted to conduct yourselves in the way you should do as a Battalion of Scotia's premier Highland Regiment—the 42nd Highlanders."

On the march to the station the enthusiasm of both troops and spectators knew no bounds. It was a wonderful expression of a city's feeling. Dundee was giving, and giving freely, of her best. The pipers of the 6th Black Watch had come to play the Battalion out, and to the strains of "Hielan' Laddie" and "Happy we've been—a thegither," the 4th set out on the Great Adventure. Brigadier-General McKerrell bade the Battalion "Good-bye."

The officers who left with the Battalion were:

Lieut.-Colonel Harry Walker, T.D., Officer Commanding.
Major E. Tosh.
Captain F. R. Tarleton, Adjutant.
Major J. B. Muir, Officer Commanding B Co.
Major J. S. Y. Rogers, R.A.M.C.
Captain E. L. Boase, Officer Commanding D Co.
Captain N. C. Walker, Officer Commanding A Co.
Captain F. W. Moon, Officer Commanding C Co.
Captain E. V. Campbell.
Captain S. B. Gowans, Transport Officer.
Captain J. L. Rettie.
Captain C. M. Couper.
Captain R. W. McIntyre.
Lieutenant W. B. Gray.
Lieutenant W. L. Robertson.
Lieutenant A. J. Stewart.
Lieutenant B. H. Gladstone.
Lieutenant I. M. Law.
Lieutenant K. L. Miller.
Lieutenant J. W. H. Robertson.
Lieutenant S. H. Steven.
Second Lieutenant D. M. Shepherd.

THE FOURTH BATTALION THE BLACK WATCH

Second Lieutenant C. B. Sherriff.
Second Lieutenant P. D. Weinberg.
Second Lieutenant G. W. Cox.
Second Lieutenant B. S. Sturrock.
Second Lieutenant T. Stevenson.
Second Lieutenant J. L. Pullar.
Second Lieutenant J. R. Philip.
Quartermaster and Hon. Lieutenant D. McLachlan.

On arrival at Southampton the Battalion embarked on the s.s. *Rossetti*, which for a night and a day lay anchored opposite Netley Hospital, but at 6 p.m. on February 25th she sailed for Havre. A draft of 300 Scots Guardsmen was also on board. The following morning Havre was reached, and at 9.30 a.m. the 4th disembarked in France. Without delay the Battalion fell in and with skirling pipes and waving tartans marched up the long, steep hill to the rest-camp on the outskirts of the town.

One little incident is worthy of record. As B company marched past a small school, the schoolmaster called his children to their feet, and the voices of the French bairns were heard singing the well-known air of " God save the King." It was a great welcome, and contained a happy suggestion of the thanks of that next generation for which, in its own small part, the 4th were striving to save a birthright.

After one day in camp outside Havre the Battalion entrained and moved to Lillers, a small village some twelve miles behind the Armentières–La Bassée sector of the British front. From there the Battalion marched to Calonne, on the Lys Canal, ten miles behind the firing line, and on March 4th proceeded to Richebourg-St. Vaast, where it joined the Bareilly Brigade, part of the 7th Meerut Division of the Indian Army Corps. The Corps Commander was Lieutenant-General Sir James Willcocks; Lieutenant-General C. A. Anderson commanded the 7th Division, the Brigade Commander being Brigadier-General W. M. Southey.

Each brigade of the Indian Corps consisted of one British and three Indian battalions. Officers and men of the 4th were glad to find the 2nd Battalion The Black Watch in the Bareilly Brigade, and there were many meetings of old friends serving in the two battalions. The Indian battalions of the Brigade were the 2/8th Gurkhas, 41st Dogras and 58th Rifles. The Indian Corps had had some very hard fighting during the previous four months, and all battalions had suffered heavily, but the coming battle was soon to prove that the fighting spirit was high and esprit de corps strong in the Bareilly Brigade.

It was a strange experience for men of the 4th Battalion to live alongside the Indian battalions. But in spite of serving under

ARRIVAL IN FRANCE, FEBRUARY, 1915

the most difficult conditions of a foreign country and a cold and uncongenial climate, in spite too of fighting far from their homes and after many of their British officers had been killed, the Indian battalions fought well and proved themselves in France, as they did later in Syria and Mesopotamia, to be fighting units of great value in a brigade strengthened by the presence of two British battalions.

In the annals of the Battalion, March 5th was a proud day, for it was then that certain companies of the 4th proceeded into the line. B company, at that time commanded by Major Muir, sent up Nos. 5 and 7 platoons into the line, while platoons 6 and 8 remained in readiness to proceed into the trenches when required. Until the morning of the 10th of March, A, B and C companies, with Headquarters in Richebourg-St. Vaast, performed the duty of supplying working and carrying parties for the line.

It is but natural that all the incidents occurring at the beginning of a battalion's career in the fighting line should be deeply impressed on the minds of the men, and although there were to be many dates of much greater general sadness, none had more tragic significance than March 5th, 1915, for on that morning the first man of the Battalion gave his life for his country. Corporal Ralph Dick had accompanied his platoon into the line, where they were being instructed in trench duties by the 2nd Black Watch. Dick had proceeded to an advanced post in No Man's Land, and at two o'clock in the afternoon a bullet had taken the war's first levy from the 4th. Near the entrance to the Crescent and Port Arthur trenches, Corporal Dick was laid to rest, and a wooden cross was raised above his grave.

On the morning of March 10th the Battalion, less D company, which was already in the trenches, moved up to a breastwork named Windy Corner, facing the shell-battered village of Neuve Chapelle. By 7 a.m. 500 British guns had opened fire on the German positions.* The Battle of Neuve Chapelle had begun, and the 4th was taking part in its first general action. During the bombardment the three companies lay outside Richebourg. Cover was scanty, and many casualties occurred when the German counter-fire commenced. At eleven o'clock the order to advance was given and, led by that most gallant gentleman and fine soldier, Colonel Harry Walker, the 4th moved into battle under heavy fire, arriving in the British front line after the whole of the village of Neuve Chapelle had been captured, and at a time when two brigades of the Meerut Division were consolidating the captured German trenches.

At this time part of the Dehra Dun Brigade, supported by the Jullunder Brigade of the Lahore Division, was assaulting

* See Map facing page 100.

THE FOURTH BATTALION THE BLACK WATCH

the enemy lines around the Bois de Biez (a wood south-east of Neuve Chapelle village). A, B and C companies of the 4th were ordered to support the battalions holding the captured positions and moved over No Man's Land, passing the trench held by D company, on their right; No. 1 platoon of A company, under Lieutenant S. H. Steven, and No. 2 platoon, under Lieutenant C. B. Sherriff, arrived first in the German trenches. Lieutenant Steven and his platoon moved along the captured trench until they arrived at a portion retained by the Germans, and delivered a bombing assault. In the meantime Lieutenant Sherriff, with No. 2 platoon, had moved on to the left of the German position.

The Germans were, however, strongly dug in around a fortified house and opened heavy machine gun fire on the two platoons of A company; while another assault was being prepared, intense artillery fire was opened by the British guns on the position. The gunners knew that the place was in German hands but, owing to the telephone wires being cut by shell fire, were unaware of the presence of the A company men.

Under this fire the 4th withdrew, and, after the bombardment ceased, the position was carried with the bayonet. Lieutenant Steven was then ordered to advance on a ruined house. The men moved forward in open order, suffering several casualties. Sergeant Macdonald, of No. 1 platoon, did splendid work during these operations. Owing to the cool gallantry and able leadership of Lieutenant Steven the objective was gained, in spite of the heavy enfilade fire to which he and his platoon were exposed.

A section of A company (No. 3 platoon) was ordered to take possession of an old house supposed to be a stronghold of German snipers. Sergeant Thomas Bowman with fifteen men of the section and five others advanced into a hail of bullets. At once four men were shot down, Private Gray, of Hilltown, being killed. After twenty yards had been covered, Sergeant Bowman ordered the men to halt and lie down, so intense was the enemy fire. In a moment or two they were up, Sergeant Bowman rushing ahead, and with a cheer the section doubled forward to the assault. Two hundred yards of open ground in full view of the enemy had to be covered, and only a few of the gallant section reached the objective. The men at once proceeded to put the house into a state of defence. Loopholes were constructed, barricades erected and all preparations made to meet a counter-attack. B company at one time lay for a considerable period in No Man's Land and lost a lot of men. Finally, they advanced to the foremost captured German trenches to support the Seaforths and Gurkhas in the event of a German counter-attack. During the

NEUVE CHAPELLE, MARCH, 1915

advance of C company on the German trenches Lieutenant W. B. Gray, who had done splendid work, was badly wounded.

Many gallant deeds were performed in this action, but none finer than that of Private Dolan. While his company was lying on open ground under heavy fire he saw a comrade, Private Rafferty, badly wounded in both legs. Private Rafferty was in an exceptionally dangerous position, but Private Dolan left his shelter and crossed the exposed ground to Rafferty's side. Here with the bullets whistling around he attended to his comrade, and remained by his side until Pipe-Major Low and Piper Donaldson came to his assistance.

Another brave deed was that of Captain Leslie Boase. While at Port Arthur this officer saw two badly wounded men. One of them was a man of the Meerut Division, the other a German. Captain Boase crept out to where they were, and under heavy fire bandaged them and gave them water. Later he returned to the trench, and with the assistance of four men, selected from the number who volunteered for the hazardous task, the two wounded men were brought into safety.

At midnight the 4th was relieved, and by the evening of the 12th was back on the duties of working parties. The British at this time were firmly dug in around Neuve Chapelle; but the troops of the Indian and IV Corps, exhausted by the strain of thirty-six hours' continuous heavy fighting, were unable to advance any farther.

Two sections of B company came in for a particularly rough time during the action. Twenty-eight men of "B," under Sergeant Milne, had been isolated for three days and nights near an old brewery at Port Arthur. The trench was in a terribly battered condition, with broken parapets that offered no protection from the fierce artillery and machine gun fire of the enemy. So heavy was the fire that it was impossible to rebuild the parapet, and the men crouched low in the shallow trench. Throughout the three days and nights, without food or water, the little party stuck to its post, and when at last it was relieved, only eight men were left unwounded, including its gallant commander.

No. 10 platoon of "C," commanded by Lieutenant G. W. Cox, with Sergeants W. Robb and C. Craig, had also been isolated in a very hot corner of the firing line for three days and nights. It was observed that a strong party of Germans had dug themselves in on the right flank of this platoon, opposite the 2nd Black Watch. Captain Gilroy, of the 2nd, a well-known Broughty Ferry officer, with a corporal and six men of his regiment, immediately attacked this position with hand grenades, and the Germans at once surrendered. Ceasing fire, the Highlanders approached to bring the men in, when two Germans snatched up their rifles and fired. Captain Gilroy fell at once, badly wounded, and later died of his wounds; the second shot killed one of his party. Needless to say, this treachery was at once summarily avenged.

On the 14th of March the Bareilly Brigade was relieved and marched back from Neuve Chapelle to billets in the village of Paradis, some two and a half miles from the little town of Merville. Here the Battalion rested for eight days, and during this period was inspected by Lieutenant-General Sir James Willcocks, when both he and Lieutenant-General C. A. Anderson, the Divisional Commander, addressed the Battalion, complimenting all ranks on having come through this baptism of fire with such credit.

After this brief period of rest the 4th was employed holding the line in and around Neuve Chapelle until the beginning of May. The usual routine was for two companies to be in the line for three days, with two companies in support. After three days the support companies, who usually found the ordinary working parties, relieved those in the front line, and at the end of a spell of six or nine days the whole Battalion came out for a brief rest; then the old routine began anew. During one of these periods of rest, khaki bonnets were served out to all ranks in place of the glengarry.

During this period out of the line Colonel Walker carried out much valuable military training. Trench warfare was new to the 4th, and there was much to learn both as regards tactics and ways and means by which to lessen the discomfort and hardships of the men. The 2nd Battalion were now old hands at trench warfare and were able to help in many ways. Major A. G. Wauchope was lent to assist in training; parties of bombers, scouts and snipers were formed in each company, and arrangements for the issue of rations and cooking in the trenches were made. Colonel Walker's energy was visible in every direction, whether as regards drill, discipline or dress. Boots and half-putties were soon found to be far more serviceable than shoes and spats, and the khaki bonnets now issued proved a better headdress than the glengarry. Colonel Walker was at first doubtful whether the Battalion should wear the red hackle with the bonnet; but Major Wauchope strongly urged that all battalions of The Black Watch were entitled to and should wear that prized distinguishing mark.

On April 10th, when the 4th occupied billets in Paradis, Sir John French, accompanied by Sir Douglas Haig, inspected the Battalion and addressed them as follows:

" Fourth Battalion The Black Watch, I must address you in
" a somewhat different manner from that which I have spoken

FOURTH BATTALION OFFICERS AFTER BATTLE OF NEUVE CHAPELLE, 10TH MARCH, 1915

After a painting by Joseph Gray in the Albert Gallery, Dundee

NAMES OF OFFICERS

*1. Lt.-Col. Harry Walker, C.M.G.
2. Major J. B. Muir
*3. Major E. Tosh
4. Major J. S. Y. Rogers
*9. Lt. Talbert Stevenson
5. Capt. E. L. Boase
6. Capt. F. R. Tarleton
*10. Bn. Sergt.-Major Charles
*7. Lt. P. D. Weinberg
*8. Lt. Sidney Steven, M.C.

This picture was given to Colonel J. B. Muir, D.S.O., Commanding The Fourth Black Watch, who presented it in February, 1922, on behalf of the Officers of the Battalion, to the Corporation of the City of Dundee.

* Killed in Action.

Vol. II

BATTLE OF AUBERS RIDGE, MAY 9TH

"to the other battalions. They are Regulars—you are Terri-
"torials. I cannot find words to express my admiration for the
"courage, the self-denial and the splendid fighting spirit of the
"Territorials in this war. I only hope that the people at home
"understand and appreciate your sacrifice and your usefulness
"as we do out here. We are proud of you, we are proud to
"belong to the same country as you do. You stood up at Neuve
"Chapelle in one of the most severe battles of the war under the
"command of Sir Douglas Haig, whom I am glad to have with
"me this afternoon, in a manner for which I cannot find words
"to express my admiration. I am sure that in the future you
"will do as splendid service as you did then. I have come here
"this afternoon just to thank you most warmly, your Command-
"ing Officer and the Battalion, for the tremendous help you gave
"us in the successful conduct of the battle."

On the 29th of April news came of the first honours awarded to the Battalion. Lieutenant S. H. Steven was awarded the Military Cross; while Sergeants Thomas Bowman and John Macdonald were each awarded the Distinguished Conduct Medal for their gallant work at the Battle of Neuve Chapelle. Sergeant Macdonald unfortunately died a day or two after the news of his decoration arrived. At this period arrived the first draft from home, and they were to have a rough breaking in. Once more the 4th was to go into battle, and on the night of the 8th of May the Battalion again moved up behind the line in fighting order.

It was a glorious spring night, stars shining. The Battalion assembled in an orchard in the vicinity of Richebourg-St. Vaast, the roads of which were thronged with troops on the move. But by 3 a.m. all movement of troops had ceased, and in silence the Battalion lay listening to the faint rumble of transport on the paved roads behind the German lines. At daybreak on the 9th the bombardment began. The attack was to be launched from the line Festubert–Neuve Chapelle–Fromelles, the objective being to drive the enemy off Aubers Ridge from the gently rising slopes of which they were able to command the British positions alike by fire and observation.

Although in proportion to the front of attack more guns were employed for this assault than at the battle of Neuve Chapelle, the bombardment was much less effective; indeed, speaking in general, the artillery work on the 9th of May was not very successful. This, however, was in no sense due to bad guidance or lack of skill on the part of the personnel of the Royal Artillery. Far from it, for at that time the British gunners were, without doubt, the finest in the field. But many guns were much worn

THE FOURTH BATTALION THE BLACK WATCH

by the fighting round Ypres and at Neuve Chapelle. The proportion of shrapnel to high-explosive shell was too high to get the best results in a bombardment against a well-entrenched enemy. In many instances also the ammunition was defective. Hence, shells which should have burst upon the German wire exploded harmlessly in No Man's Land or, sad to relate, amongst our own men, Major Muir being wounded by a fragment from one of them, though fortunately not seriously.

The first attack of the Indian Corps had been made by the Dehra Dun Brigade at 6 a.m. The enemy machine gun fire had swept the lines of the assaulting companies, and in a few minutes the attack had ended in a complete failure. The 1st Division on the right had attacked at the same time; their troops had displayed the same gallantry, but the task had proved equally impossible, and this attack also failed.

Orders were then issued that the bombardment was to be renewed and that a second attack would be made in the afternoon. The Bareilly Brigade was ordered to relieve the Dehra Dun Brigade and to prepare to deliver the second assault at 4 p.m. At 10.50 a.m. the Battalion was ordered to go forward and occupy Blackadder and Crescent Trenches, but the whole of the communication trench up which the 4th had to move was so blocked by the troops of the Dehra Dun Brigade, many of whom were wounded, that it was found impossible to complete the movement until 2.25 p.m.

The 58th Rifles, one of the finest Indian battalions in the whole Corps, was the assaulting battalion on the front of the 4th, and at about 3 p.m. two companies of the 4th moved up to act as support to that regiment. One company of the Battalion was ordered to join in the assault with the 58th Rifles. But the whole attack proved a complete failure. Before reaching the enemy trenches the attacking platoons had to cross some 300 yards of flat open ground, through which ran a small stream too deep to wade. The only means of getting over this obstacle were a few narrow bridges, some of which were hidden; others broken, and others blocked with the bodies of those who had been killed and wounded in the earlier assault. Over the whole of No Man's Land the Germans concentrated a deadly machine gun fire. Most of the attackers were either killed or wounded before they had advanced many yards from their own trench. The two 4th Battalion officers who were with the assaulting company soon realized that most of their men were either killed or wounded, and that the attack had failed. They therefore ordered their men to lie down until dark, when those who were unwounded were able to crawl back to the British line. Among many others, the big drummer, Troup, was killed that day.

BATTLE OF AUBERS RIDGE, MAY 9TH

The position of the Battalion during and after the assault was peculiarly trying. It could neither advance nor move to right or left, but had to lie still and endure a trying bombardment from the German guns. No one in the Battalion deserves more credit for his unflagging devotion to duty during the terrible hours of that Sunday than Major Rogers, the medical officer, who, with great coolness and utter disregard for personal safety, continued dressing the wounded under very heavy fire. So numerous were the wounded that the stretcher bearers were unable to cope with the task of evacuation, and many gallant men had to lie exposed to the German bombardment until, with the coming of night, it was possible to get them carried back across the open.

Lieutenant Weinberg was killed as, holding his platoon's flag, he gallantly waved his men forward. When he fell, the flag was picked up by Donald Pyott, son of Sergeant-Major Pyott, but he too was killed at once. The flag was again lifted by Private J. Ross, who ran forward through the deadly stream of lead till he also was killed. Lieutenant Weinberg was the first officer of the 4th to be killed. Six officers were wounded, amongst them Captain Boase, who was killed later in the war at High Wood on the Somme while serving with the 7th Black Watch.

On the night of the 9th/10th the Battalion was relieved and went back to Lansdowne Post, the battalions of the Bareilly Brigade requiring some days to reorganize after the severe losses incurred on this day.

On the night of the 15th the Garhwal Brigade made a third attack over the same ground, and met with the same fate. Without a far heavier bombardment than was possible with the guns available, no troops could succeed in attacking over the 300 yards of open ground that separated the enemy trenches from the British lines.

Shortly after the action of May 9th a pathetic ceremony took place. This was the erection of memorial crosses for some of the fallen. The fact that Sergeant-Major Pyott, who lost his son in the action, and Private John Troup, whose father was also amongst the fallen, took part in the ceremony renders it almost unique in the annals of the Regiment. A cross was erected for:

Sgt. W. D. Brown.	Pte. Coghill.
Corpl. Mulligan.	„ J. Diamond.
„ Stewart.	„ Donnachie.
L/Cpl. Taylor.	„ Kelman.
„ Whyte.	„ Kennedy.
Pte. Allan.	„ Masterton.
„ Angus.	„ McAvoy.
„ W. Brown.	„ Montague.

THE FOURTH BATTALION THE BLACK WATCH

Another cross for:

Sgt. H. Jarron.
L/Cpl. Smith.
Pte. Glenday.

Pte. Grant.
,, McIntosh.
,, Ross.

Sergeant-Major Pyott put a white cross for his boy, and Private John Troup erected the cross on his father's grave. It bore the simple inscription:

"456 Sergeant, H. Coy., 4th Black Watch, killed in action "9th May, 1915."

On the stand of the cross was the one word "Archie," by which name Sergeant Troup was known to all.

From the 9th until the 25th of May the 4th remained in the firing line and reserve trenches, while the battle was carried on by fresh divisions on the right and left.

After the attack on the 9th the Battalion took part in no severe action until the Battle of Loos, which was fought on the 25th of September, 1915. During the intervening months the Battalion spent many long and arduous spells in the trenches holding the line. When out on the short rests, training was continued, and the gaps in the sadly depleted ranks were filled by drafts from Scotland.

The 2nd and 4th Battalions had now been closely associated for some months. A firm friendship had grown up between Colonel Walker and Colonel Wauchope, the two Battalion Commanders, and both felt that a day devoted to sports and games would give the many friends in the two battalions a chance to meet. The arrival of the 5th Battalion of The Black Watch, under Colonel Blair-Imrie, added to the zest of the proposed meeting.

The suggestion was adopted with great keenness by all three battalions, and two days before the Battle of Loos, inter-regimental games were held on the grassy meadows near the Lys Canal at Estaires between the 2nd, 4th and 5th Battalions of The Black Watch. The pleasant little French town of Estaires was for twenty-four hours filled with officers and men of the Regiment. Wherever one looked were the dark tartans and red hackles of Scotland's oldest Highland regiment. As far as the writer can recollect, the honours of the day went decidedly to the 2nd Battalion. But whoever may have been the victors in the games, there were many men of all three battalions who felt that quiet and sunny day was one of the happiest and most peaceful spent in 1915.

CHAPTER II

SEPTEMBER 24TH, 1915—MARCH 7TH, 1916

The Battle of Loos—Givenchy—Amalgamation with the 5th Battalion

THE Battle of Loos will ever be remembered as a particularly glorious page in Scottish military history. In it those magnificent Scottish divisions, the 9th and 15th of the New Armies, were to cover themselves with glory. Practically every Scottish regiment in France was engaged in the Battle of Loos and subsidiary operations, in which all did magnificent work, but the cost was terrible and, like other battalions of the Regiment, the 4th lost very heavily.

The battles of Neuve Chapelle and the 9th of May had made great gaps in the ranks of the Battalion, which, added to the casualties incurred in ordinary trench warfare and those caused by sickness, had brought down the strength of the Battalion to such an extent that, although it had received large drafts of men from home, its fighting strength on September 24th, 1915, was only 423 bayonets as opposed to 900 who had originally arrived in France. The ration strength was actually 540, but this included all employed men and those in the Battalion transport. Many changes had also taken place among the personnel of the officers ; only thirteen of those who had landed in France now remained with the Battalion.

The following is a list of officers who were with the 4th at this time and took part in the Battle of Loos. An asterisk indicates that the officer proceeded to France with the Battalion:

*Lieutenant-Colonel Harry Walker, C.M.G.
*Major and Adjutant F. R. Tarleton.
*Major Elmslie Tosh.
*Major J. S. Y. Rogers, Medical Officer.
A Company. *Captain Walker, *Captain McIntyre, Lieutenant A. B. Watson, Lieutenant L. Wilson.
B Company. *Captain E. V. Campbell, Captain P. F. Duncan, Lieutenant R. C. Cunningham, Lieutenant J. P. Bruce.
C Company. Captain O. S. Moodie, Captain S. L. Watson, *Lieutenant S. H. Steven, Second Lieutenant T. Williamson.
D Company. *Captain C. M. Couper, Captain C. Air, *Lieutenant B. S. Sturrock, Lieutenant Colin Methven.
*Lieutenant A. J. Stewart, Machine Gun Officer.
Lieutenant T. H. Anderson, " T.M." Battery.

THE FOURTH BATTALION THE BLACK WATCH

Lieutenant I. M. Law, with Brigade Headquarters.
*Captain Gowans (Transport) and *Lieutenant Pullar were at depot in reserve, where also was Quartermaster McLachlan.
The Battalion Sergeant-Major Charles was senior N.C.O.

The French attack in Champagne was the main effort of the Allies' offensive in the autumn of 1915; the other operations had as one of their chief objects the holding of enemy troops from the Champagne battle, though it was also hoped to gain important results from the subsidiary operations. The scene of the principal of these was between La Bassée and Arras; the share of the British Army was the Battle of Loos.

Though the main object of the attack was to draw the enemy reserves from the districts east of Loos and to distract the attention of the German Staff, the task set the Indian Corps was an ambitious one. The Indian Corps was ordered to seize the Aubers Ridge, and then, by advancing south-east to turn the German defences of La Bassée from the north. The attack was made by the Meerut Division, with the Garhwal Brigade on the right and the Bareilly Brigade on the left, the Dehra Dun Brigade being in Divisional reserve. Each of the assaulting brigades had three battalions in the front line and two in reserve. The Bareilly Brigade was formed for attack with the 4th Black Watch on the right, 69th Punjabis in the centre and the 2nd Black Watch on the left. The 33rd Punjabis and 58th Rifles were held at first in support.

The left flank of the Brigade was to be protected by troops of the 60th Brigade, but detailed arrangements were hard to make and these troops suffered very severe losses when crossing No Man's Land, consequently the left flank of the Bareilly Brigade was without any adequate protection. Unfortunately, as the attack developed the right flank also was left unguarded, for the reason that the troops of the Garhwal Brigade were held up by uncut wire, and one company of the 2/3rd Gurkhas alone penetrated the German lines.

In following the fortunes of the 4th in the Battle of Loos it must be remembered, therefore, that both flanks of the Bareilly Brigade were open to counter-attacks by the enemy. Major-General Claud Jacob was now in command of the Meerut Division, and Brigadier-General Charles Norie commanded the Bareilly Brigade. Both officers were experienced soldiers and had the full confidence of all ranks. Fine weather is a great help towards the success of any assault, especially in trench warfare, and it was more especially important on this occasion, for gas and smoke clouds were to be released by British troops

BATTLE OF LOOS, SEPTEMBER 25TH

for the first time. Unfortunately, on the 24th, a good deal of rain fell, but the sky cleared towards evening just as the Battalion paraded to move off to its assembly position.

Nothing untoward occurred during the move into the front trenches, and long before Zero hour the Battalion was in position as follows: C and D companies in the front line under Captains Moodie and Couper, with A and B companies under Captains N. C. Walker and E. V. Campbell in support. The Brigade machine gun company and the Brigade bombing section had also moved up into the forward trenches, and with each was a detachment from the 4th; the Battalion machine gun section being commanded by Lieutenant A. J. Stewart.

Rain was falling when the order to " Stand to " was passed down the lines early on the morning of the 25th, and all ranks adjusted their gas masks. On each man's back was strapped or sewn a piece of red cloth about eighteen inches square, the object of these being that troops and observing officers in rear might distinguish their own men from the Germans.

Zero hour was at 5.50 a.m., at which moment the British bombardment opened; a large mine was successfully exploded under the enemy's position in front of the 2nd Battalion The Black Watch, and gas and smoke were released. The enemy lines were partly hidden by the clouds of smoke, but the wind was not favourable for the employment of gas. Whether the enemy were much affected by the gas discharged from the lines of the Meerut Division is uncertain, but the light wind was constantly changing after dawn, and many British and Indian troops were put out of action before they had put on their gas masks.

The assault was made at 6 a.m. Led by Major Tarleton, the officers and men of C and D companies left their trenches and advanced at a steady double across No Man's Land, and at the same time the two other assaulting battalions of the Brigade swept forward across the open. The assaulting troops had barely left their trenches when they were met by steady rifle fire from the German lines. Major Tarleton fell almost at once badly wounded in the face, and officers and men fell on every side. Soon the enemy's rifle fire grew in volume, and when their artillery opened heavy shrapnel fire on the advancing troops the losses became heavy. Men stopped in their stride to pitch forward and lie motionless on the ground. Many others were wounded, and either lay where they fell or, if still able to walk, struggled on until their strength gave out and they too fell.

The leading companies of the 4th, magnificently led by their officers and non-commissioned officers, having secured the German front line, swept forward and captured the support trenches, while the British artillery lengthened its range and put down a heavy barrage to cut off the German reinforcements. There were few Germans found alive in their front line. Dead lay all around, many buried in the fallen debris, while others, still alive but badly wounded, lay huddled together; few put up any resistance, but those who did were soon silenced.

The first line was captured in a few minutes, and the assaulting waves swept forward carrying all before them. By this time the supports, including A and B companies of the 4th, with Colonel Walker, Major Tosh and Battalion Sergeant-Major Charles, were advancing across No Man's Land and came under heavy German artillery fire which now swept that area and the captured front line. Major Tosh fell hit by a bullet, but was at once lifted up by Sergeant Petrie, who was assisting him to cover when he was again hit, this time mortally. The support companies pushed forward and reinforced the leading companies, who by this time had stormed and captured the enemy's second position half a mile ahead.

The 4th Black Watch, working in conjunction with the other battalions of the Brigade, now advanced under a heavy fire towards the Moulin de Piètre and the surrounding fortified positions on the right of that building. There they occupied the trenches from which they had just driven the Germans, and made every effort to consolidate this new position. The losses had been severe, but every man in the 4th had the feeling of victory achieved, and that the assault had added further honour to his Battalion.

Up to this time the attack, both of the 4th Battalion and of the whole Bareilly Brigade, had been most successful, but the danger of the situation was obvious. It has already been shown that both flanks of the Brigade were unprotected, and consequently open to counter-attacks by the enemy. Communication with Brigade Headquarters was difficult and slow, but the four Battalion Commanders consulted together, and Colonel Walker, on the right, and Colonel Wauchope, on the left, made every effort to establish posts and so protect the exposed flanks of the Brigade.

But the losses in all four battalions had been heavy, and reinforcements were urgently demanded. Brigadier-General Norie's whole Brigade was already committed, and the Dehra Dun Brigade was the only reserve available. This Brigade the Divisional Commander ordered to advance, but owing to the condition of the communication trenches, crowded with wounded and prisoners moving to the rear, and to the intense German artillery fire, its advance was unavoidably slow, and the need for reinforcements was urgent. By this time the 4th had lost very heavily; all its officers had been either killed or wounded with

MOULIN DE PIÈTRE, SEPTEMBER 25TH

the exception of Colonel Walker, Captain Air and Lieutenant Cunningham, and the whole Brigade line was in an exceedingly dangerous position owing to the situation on the flanks and the distance advanced. Both flanks were exposed and parties were detached to cover them, Colonel Walker making every effort to join up with the company of the 2/8th Gurkhas, the only party of the Garhwal Brigade that had been able to advance on the right flank.

Meantime the enemy were fast bringing up their reserve troops, and concentrated a strong force opposite each flank of the Bareilly Brigade. Communication between Battalion and Brigade Headquarters was now cut off, and although great efforts were made to re-establish it by the Battalion's Signal Section, under Sergeant Gardiner, these were in vain.

Further progress against the Moulin de Piètre was out of the question. Colonel Walker therefore gave orders that the Battalion should occupy and consolidate the captured German trenches and make all preparations possible to resist a counter-attack.

The German bombardment now increased in intensity; and a ceaseless rain of shells fell not only on the attackers, but also on the British lines more than half a mile in rear, and little of what was happening in front could be seen from Brigade Headquarters. All contact with the rear was lost, and although runner after runner endeavoured to take back information, all were hit and no messages got through. The intensity of the enemy shelling clearly showed that a counter-attack was about to be delivered, and officers and men worked their hardest to organize and strengthen their new position. On the right flank of the Battalion, and slightly to the rear, Lieutenant A. J. Stewart, Sergeant Craig, Corporal Proctor and 14 men were working two machine guns; a heavy shell burst among them, killing one man and wounding Lieutenant Stewart and four others.

Had the Garhwal Brigade been able to make good the ground on the right, the successful advance of the Bareilly Brigade would not have formed so pronounced and narrow a salient, and it would not have been possible for the enemy to move unseen along the unoccupied trenches towards the position now held by the Brigade. But of this advantage the Germans were not slow to avail themselves.

About 11 a.m. enemy bombing parties attacked the posts on the right, and were only held back with difficulty, as the numbers of the attackers increased every moment, and the Battalion was already reduced to about half its strength. Half an hour later it was found that other parties of the enemy had managed to gain some trenches on the right rear of the Brigade, and slowly, holding trench after trench with great steadiness, the

4th was forced to withdraw from its forward position. Stand after stand was made, the men of the 4th halting and firing as they retired, and inflicting considerable losses on the German attackers whenever their snipers or bombers could be seen.

Colonel Walker, who throughout the battle had conducted operations with great valour and coolness, realized that unless reinforcements arrived all ground gained would be lost. Owing to the breakdown of communications, he was unaware that none were immediately available, and he set out on a gallant attempt to cross the open and reach Brigadier-General Norie. Unfortunately, he had proceeded only a short distance when he fell mortally wounded.

The enemy bombing parties never ceased their vigorous attacks, and by this time there were but few bombs left in the Battalion, many men were running short of ammunition, and only one officer, Lieutenant Cunningham, was unwounded. Still, the retirement was never hurried, and it was only when the enemy had succeeded in working far in on both flanks of the hard-pressed Brigade, only when the last line of retreat was almost cut, that three officers and 199 men, the remnants of the Battalion that had so gallantly captured three lines of German trenches earlier in the morning, were forced to recross No Man's Land and reoccupy the British lines.

But the 4th had played its part manfully and received the highest praise from both Brigade and Divisional Commanders. The main object of the attack had been not to gain ground, but to draw German reserves from more vital parts of the battlefield, and thus give assistance to the British divisions fighting near Loos. The success of the assault, although but temporary, had done much to achieve this purpose, as a failure would have added to the power of German resistance elsewhere.

But if the gallant part played by the Battalion on the 25th had brought fresh and lasting honour to the 4th, the losses were very heavy. Out of 20 officers and 420 men who actually took part in the attack, 19 officers and 230 men were killed and wounded. The other battalions had also suffered heavily; the Brigade therefore was relieved in the trenches, and marched back to billets in the neighbourhood of Pont du Hem on the 26th to refit and reorganize.

Special mention should be made of the Battalion Medical Officer, Major J. S. Y. Rogers, whose personality and devotion to duty had earned for him the affection of all officers and men in the 4th. His gallant work and good organization in relieving and tending the wounded during the operations were of the greatest service to the Battalion.

The chief and irreparable loss suffered by the 4th during

COLONEL WALKER
Killed at the Battle of Loos, 1915, when commanding the Fourth Battalion The Black Watch

DEATH OF COLONEL WALKER, SEPTEMBER 25TH

the fighting was the death of Lieutenant-Colonel Walker—
"Colonel Walker, our finest type of civic soldier." Such was
the brief phrase in which someone, writing of the City of
Dundee Battalion of The Black Watch on the morrow of the
25th of September, 1915—singled out for special mention its
gallant leader. Never were words more happily chosen, and never
was the spirit of the man more aptly portrayed. His natural
talent and high character, supplemented by a widely educated
mind, bade fair to carry him far on the road to fame. His fellow-
citizens had hoped to place him in a position of responsibility
in the councils of the nation, but he felt that the path of duty,
for him, lay with the men of the 4th, whose call in the defence
of freedom and liberty even in those earlier days of peaceful
occupations was clear to one of his vision and foresight.

It was said of one of Nelson's captains that he was "ever
willing to go out in all weathers." Such a man was Colonel Harry
Walker. In peace or in war he had no thought of self, but only
a high sense of duty and of what was right. His successful com-
mercial career gave promise of a yet more brilliant future in the
public service. But this was not to be, and he died in action at
the head of his men, commanding the Battalion that he loved so
well. To the success of the 4th Black Watch he had given much
time, labour and thought, and it was largely due to his strong
character and personal energy that the Battalion had earned the
high esteem of all soldiers and civilians, and had acquitted itself
so well in the fiery test of war.

The losses on the 25th had been so severe and the Battalion
was so weak, especially in officers, that it was now organized into
two companies and temporarily amalgamated with the 2nd Battalion The Black Watch. Of these companies, now known as
No. 5 and No. 6, one was commanded by Lieutenant T. Stevenson and the other by Lieutenant R. C. Cunningham. Colonel
A. G. Wauchope commanded the whole Battalion of six companies, and appointed Lieutenant L. Pullar, of the 4th, acting
Adjutant of the Battalion until after the arrival of Captain
Hamilton-Johnston at Givenchy. With hard work and good
will this organization was completed within three days at Pont
du Hem, and on the 29th of September the Battalion moved
to the neighbourhood of La Gorgue.

These days of reorganization were sad ones not only for the
Battalion, but for the city of Dundee, its home. There had been
many families represented by more than one member in the ranks
of the 4th, very few of whom had come through the recent fighting without at least one casualty. The following incident will
give a true idea of many that took place at this time.

Lieutenant Harvey Steven joined the Battalion from the

THE FOURTH BATTALION THE BLACK WATCH

Depot during the battle, and as it was then engaged he was detained at the transport lines. When the survivors of the fight came back, he learned that his brother, Lieutenant S. H. Steven —who had been awarded the M.C. for conspicuous gallantry at Neuve Chapelle—had been killed but, putting his private grief aside he, like all others, set himself to the task of helping to reorganize and enhearten the battle-worn survivors. A week later Harvey Steven himself was killed gallantly leading his men at Givenchy.

But the operations near Loos were not yet ended, and the Battalion was not left for long at La Gorgue. It is interesting to note that in these operations the two Regular battalions, the 1st and 2nd, two Territorial battalions, the 4th and 5th, and two Service battalions, the 8th and 9th, six battalions of The Black Watch, all took part and most worthily upheld the traditions of the Regiment.

The little hill of Givenchy proved to be a point of importance in the lines opposite La Bassée throughout the war. The defence of this position was now entrusted to two British battalions, the 1st Seaforth Highlanders and the battalion now composed of the 2nd and 4th Black Watch. On October 1st the Battalion took over the trenches round Givenchy which had lately become the centre of great mining activity.

The duties were arduous; the German shelling was severe and his snipers most daring. No Man's Land was covered with old mine craters, and from the edges of these craters a constant battle was waged between the German and Black Watch snipers. Nothing could exceed the energy and power of leadership displayed by Lieutenants Cunningham and Stevenson, commanding the two companies of the 4th, in organizing the defence.

On October 7th it was discovered that enemy mines had reached almost up to the parapet of the trench held by The Black Watch battalion. By vigorous counter-mining the British Tunnelling Company succeeded in blowing up one of these mines, but on the morning of the 8th two other German mines exploded and destroyed part of The Black Watch parapet, and temporarily buried some of the defenders. The parapet was hastily built up again, but another section in Lieutenant Cunningham's line was destroyed by very heavy shell fire, and several German parties were seen advancing from the cover of the old craters. It was only good organization and steady machine gun and rifle fire that prevented the enemy from reaching this trench.

After this the enemy's efforts became less persistent, and the Battalion was relieved from its duty of holding Givenchy and was allowed some much needed rest in billets in rear. Strong drafts of officers and men from Scotland, and the return of

THE 4TH ATTACHED TO THE 2ND BLACK WATCH

others from hospital who had been previously wounded, once again brought up the strength of the 4th. Before the end of October, Colonel Wauchope reported that the 4th was now ready to be organized as a complete unit, and early in November this was accomplished.

It was fortunate that the drafts had arrived so speedily, as the 2nd Battalion was now under orders to leave France for Mesopotamia. Throughout 1915 the friendship between officers and men of the two battalions had been close, and the many hardships and test of battles shared together had only served to knit this friendship all the more firmly. Colonel Wauchope had no praise too high for Lieutenants R. C. Cunningham and T. Stevenson, who took over command of the two companies of the 4th at this most difficult time, and in an official letter which he subsequently wrote to the Commanding Officer of the 4th, he expressed his unstinted admiration for the power of leadership, the high character and devotion to their Regiment shown by these two officers. Both were awarded the M.C. for gallantry in France; Lieutenant Stevenson was wounded twice in 1916, and was killed in action in 1917. Lieutenant Cunningham was the only officer of the Battalion who came through the Battle of Loos unwounded, but he also was subsequently killed in action. Colonel Wauchope also referred in his letter to the good work done by Lieutenant L. Pullar when acting Adjutant to the Battalion.

The 4th Black Watch was now attached to the 44th Brigade, 15th Division, IV Corps. The remainder of November and the whole of December was spent with the 15th Division, after which, at the end of the month, the Battalion was withdrawn from the line and given a period of rest preparatory to joining the 51st (Highland) Territorial Division, at that time holding the line at Fricourt, in the Somme area.

By this time the Battalion had received many drafts of both officers and men and was almost up to fighting strength, the fourth company being formed on Christmas Day, 1915; while earlier in December, Lieutenant-Colonel G. McL. Sceales, 1st Argyll and Sutherland Highlanders, took over the command of the Battalion from acting Captain R. C. Cunningham.

On January 1st, 1916, the 4th was resting at Allouagne attached to the 44th Brigade, and six days later it entrained at Lillers and, after a long train journey and night march, reached its billets at Rainneville, about seven miles from Amiens. Strength, 28 officers and 685 other ranks.

It now formed part of the 154th Brigade of the 51st (Highland) Division, commanded by Major-General Harper, the Brigade Commander being that fine soldier and most gallant

THE FOURTH BATTALION THE BLACK WATCH

Highland gentleman, Brigadier-General Charles Edward Stewart (The Black Watch), whose Brigade was composed as follows:

>4th Black Watch from Meerut Division.
>5th Black Watch from the 8th Division.
>4th Seaforth Highlanders from the 7th Division.
>4th Cameron Highlanders from the 7th Division.

January, and the first few days of February, were spent at Rainneville training and resting, during which period, on January 11th and 25th, the Battalion was inspected by the Brigade and Divisional Commanders respectively. On February 6th the 154th Brigade moved to Corbie and the following day to La Neuville, where news was received that the 4th and 5th Battalions were to be amalgamated, and that the new unit would join the 118th Brigade, 39th Division, which had just arrived in France.

In order to carry out the amalgamation the Battalion marched to Renescure, near St. Omer. The weather was bad, the march of some ten kilometres being carried out in a blinding snowstorm. So heavy, indeed, was the fall of snow that the roads became almost impassable for transport but, by the untiring efforts of Transport Sergeant Cruickshanks and his men, the waggons reached their destination safely. There had also been some mistake regarding billeting arrangements, and it was with difficulty that accommodation was found for the Battalion. Regarding this the following incident is recorded:

At that time there were about twenty " prisoners " in the Battalion, undergoing punishment for various small offences, and in the confusion of the night march through the snow some of these were lost. The following morning the Commanding Officer received a message from these " prisoners," stating that they had formed a guard-room for themselves at a place some two miles away and would be exceedingly obliged if their rations and letters were forwarded to them!

By the end of February the weather had improved, and on March 7th the 4th moved to La Belle Hôtesse, where the work of amalgamation with the 5th commenced.

Such is the story of the 4th as an independent unit. The remainder, showing the soldierly conduct and gallant deeds its survivors performed in conjunction with those of the sister Battalion—both later to absorb the 9th (Service) Battalion—will be found in subsequent chapters of this volume which relate the history of the 4/5th Battalion The Black Watch.

APPENDIX I

Record of Officers' Services

Abbreviations :—" K."—Killed. "D. of W."—Died of Wounds. "W."—Wounded.

THE FOURTH BATTALION

Air, C. A. Capt. Joined 25th May, 1915. *w.* 3rd June, 1915. *k.* 25th Sept., 1915.
Anderson, F. K. 2nd Lieut. Joined 21st July, 1915. *k.* 25th Sept., 1915.
Andrews, T. F. 2nd Lieut. Joined 14th Nov., 1915. Awarded M.C. 26th June, 1916.

Berry, J. L. 2nd Lieut. Joined 9th Oct., 1915. Transferred to 13th Battn. Gloucesters, 25 Aug., 1916.
Bethune-Duncan, W. B. Lieut. With Battn. to France, Feb., 1915. *k.* 3rd Sept., 1916.
Blair, D. Lieut. Joined 12th May, 1915. *w.* 29th June, 1915. Seconded to Army Dental Corps 23rd Oct., 1916.
Boase, E. L. Capt. Joined 24th Feb., 1915. *w.* 9th May, 1915. Rejoined 13th Feb., 1916. *k.* (with 1/7th Battn.) 31st July, 1916.
Bruce, J. P. 2nd Lieut. Joined 21st July, 1915. *w.* 25th Sept., 1915.

Campbell, E. V. Capt. *k.* 26th Sept., 1915.
Couper, C. M. Capt. Missing 25th Sept., 1915. *d. of w.* in German hands 28th Sept., 1915.
Cox, W. A. M. 2nd Lieut. Joined 9th Oct., 1915. *w.* 3rd Sept., 1916.
Cox, G. W. 2nd Lieut. Joined 9th May, 1915.
Cunningham, R. C. 2nd Lieut. Joined 6th May, 1915. Awarded M.C. 25th Sept., 1915. Promoted Capt. *k.* 3rd Sept., 1916.
Cunningham, T. F. 2nd Lieut. Joined 9th Oct., 1915. Seconded M.G.C. 24th March, 1916.
Currey, R. F. Lieut. Joined 12th Nov., 1915. Awarded M.C. 6th Jan., 1917. *w.* 23rd Oct., 1917.
Cuthbertson, A. A. 2nd Lieut. Joined 13th May, 1915. *w.* 14th Aug., 1915. Rejoined 25th January, 1917. *w.* 11th July, 1917.

Donald, G. R. Lieut. Joined 23rd Oct., 1915. Promoted Capt. To U.K. for duty War Office, 5th Oct., 1916.
Duncan, J. O. Capt. Joined 5th Feb., 1915. To Base 18th Nov., 1916.
Duncan, P. F. Capt. Joined 24th Feb., 1915. *w.* 25th Sept., 1915.

Finlayson, F. W. H. 2nd Lieut. Joined 12th Nov., 1915. To 154th Brigade M.G.C. 14th Jan., 1916.

Gibson, C. M. 2nd Lieut. Joined 25th Oct., 1915. *k.* 14th Oct., 1916.
Gladstone, B. H. Lieut. Went to France with Battn. Invalided about April, 1915.
Glover, V. 2nd Lieut. Joined 13th Feb., 1916. Seconded M.G.C. 24th April, 1916.
Gowans, Capt. Went to France with Battn. as Transport Officer. Invalided home Nov. 1915.
Gray, W. B. Lieut. Joined 24th Feb., 1915. *w.* 10th March, 1915.

Harley, N. 2nd Lieut. Joined 18th Feb., 1916. To U.K. for duty 26th Dec., 1917.

THE FOURTH BATTALION THE BLACK WATCH

James, H. 2nd Lieut. Joined 12th Nov., 1915. *w.* 3rd Sept., 1916.

Kennedy, J. Capt. and Adj. Left Battn. to command 13th Welch Regiment, 13th July, 1916.

Law, I. M. Lieut. Went out with Battn. to France. To U.K. sick 31st Oct., 1915. Rejoined Battn. 4th July, 1916. *w.* 14th Oct., 1916.

McCririck, C. S. 2nd Lieut. Joined 6th Feb., 1916. *w.* 20th July, 1916. *w.* 13th Nov., 1916. Awarded M.C. 6th Jan., 1917.

McIntyre, R. W. Capt. Joined 22nd Feb., 1915. *w.* 25th Sept., 1915. Mentioned in Despatches 1st Jan., 1916. Awarded M.C. 14th Jan., 1916. Rejoined 21st June, 1916. Gassed 7th Nov., 1917.

McMaster, J. 2nd Lieut. Joined 27th Sept., 1915. To 154th Brigade M.G.C. 14th Jan., 1916.

McLachlan, D. Lieut. and Q.M. Joined 24th Feb., 1915. Promoted Capt. 1st July, 1917. Transferred to 9th Battn. 18th May, 1918.

Menzies, J. D. S. 2nd Lieut. Joined 14th Nov., 1915.

Methven, C. M. Lieut. Joined 9th July, 1915. *w.* 25th Sept., 1915.

Mill, R. C. K. Lieut. Joined 28th Jan., 1916. *k.* 3rd Sept., 1916.

Miller, K. L. Lieut. Went to France with Battn. Seconded for special duties, June, 1915.

Mitchell, A. 2nd Lieut. Joined 12th Nov., 1915.

Moodie, O. S. Capt. Joined 24th Feb., 1915. Missing 25th Sept., 1915. Officially reported Prisoner of War 20th Nov., 1915.

Moon, F. W. Capt. Joined 24th Feb., 1915. To 191st Inf. Bde. 23rd Aug., 1917.

Moon, P. M. Capt. Joined 9th Oct., 1915. *w.* 5th Nov., 1915.

Moser, G. R. 2nd Lieut. Joined 12th Nov., 1915. To R.F.C. 16th Jan., 1916.

Muir, J. B. Major. *w.* 9th May, 1915. *w.* 5th July, 1915. Rejoined 25th Nov., 1915. Left Battn. to command 2/1st Battn. Ox. and Bucks L.I. 5th Aug., 1916.

Osborne, E. C. 2nd Lieut. Joined 14th Nov., 1916. *w.* 7th May, 1918.

Philip, J. R. 2nd Lieut. *w.* 9th July, 1915. Rejoined 21st June, 1916. Mentioned in Despatches 25th May, 1917. *w.* 31st July, 1917. Rejoined 23rd Jan., 1918. *w.* 28th March, 1918. Awarded M.C. 8th June, 1918.

Plimpton, R. A. Lieut. Joined 12th Nov., 1915. Awarded M.C. 17th Nov., 1916. Awarded Bar to M.C. 6th Jan., 1917. Promoted Capt. *k.* 27th Sept., 1917.

Prain, J. C. Lieut. Joined 9th Oct., 1915. *w.* 25th April, 1916.

Pullar, J. L. Lieut. Joined 21st Feb., 1915. Appointed Adjutant 26th Sept., 1915. To U.K. 16th Feb., 1916.

Rettie, J. L. Capt. *w.* 26th April, 1915. Rejoined 4th July, 1916. *w.* 3rd Sept., 1916.

Robertson, J. W. H. Lieut. *w.* 9th May, 1915.

APPENDIX I

Robertson, W. L. Lieut. Went to France with Battn. To U.K. sick Aug., 1915. Rejoined Battn. 20th Aug., 1916. *w.* 3rd Sept., 1916.

Robertson, W. S. Lieut. Joined 14th Nov., 1915. Awarded M.C. 6th Aug., 1916. *k.* 3rd Sept., 1916.

Rogers, J. S. Y. Major. R.A.M.C. *w.* 9th May, 1915. Mentioned in Despatches 1st Jan., 1916. Awarded D.S.O. 14th Jan., 1916. To U.K sick 23rd Sept., 1916. Rejoined 23rd Jan., 1917. Transferred to 9th Black Watch Training Staff 8th June, 1918. Rejoined 24th July, 1918. Awarded Croix de Guerre 12th August, 1918.

Sceales, G. A. McL. Major. Joined Battn. and assumed command 7th Nov., 1915. Promoted Lieut.-Col. 22nd December, 1915. Awarded D.S.O. 1st Jan., 1917. Mentioned in Despatches 4th Jan., 1917. To Tank Corps 28th Oct., 1917.

Scratton, G. H. 2nd Lieut. Joined 12th Nov., 1915. Appointed Adj. 13th July, 1916. Awarded M.C. 6th Jan., 1917. *k.* 1st Aug., 1917.

Shepherd, D. M. Lieut. Went to France with Battn. *w.* June, 1915.

Shepherd, E. A. Capt. Joined 9th Feb., 1916. *k.* 3rd Sept., 1916.

Steven, H. S. Lieut. Joined 27th Sept., 1915. *k.* 7th Oct., 1915.

Steven, S. H. 2nd Lieut. Joined 27th Aug., 1915. Awarded M.C. 29th April, 1915. *k.* 25th Sept., 1915.

Stevenson, T. 2nd Lieut. *w.* 9th June, 1915. Rejoined 9th Oct., 1915. Promoted Capt. *w.* 13th Nov., 1916. Awarded M.C. 1st Jan., 1917. Rejoined Battn. 17th July, 1917. *k.* 14th Nov., 1917.

Stewart, A. J. Lieut. *w.* 25th Sept., 1915. Rejoined 24th Feb., 1916. Promoted Capt. Awarded Croix de Guerre 11th Feb., 1917. Mentioned in Despatches 18th Dec., 1917. Promoted Major. Awarded D.S.O. Left Battn. 28th Sept., 1918.

Sturrock, B. S Lieut. Joined 24th Feb., 1915. *k.* 26th Sept., 1915.

Tarleton, F. R. Capt. and Adj. *w.* 25th Sept., 1915.

Thomson, S. C. 2nd Lieut. Joined 6th Feb., 1916. Transferred M.G.C. 24th March, 1916.

Tosh, E. Major. Joined 24th Feb., 1915. *w.* 9th May, 1915. *k.* 25th Sept., 1915.

Walker, H. Lieut.-Col. T.D. Joined 24th Feb., 1915. *w.* 25th Sept., 1915. Awarded C.M.G. 23rd June, 1915. *d. of w.* 27th Sept., 1915.

Walker, N. C. Capt. Joined 24th Feb., 1915. *k.* 25th Sept., 1915.

Watson, A. B. 2nd Lieut. *w.* 25th Sept., 1915. Rejoined Battn. 22nd Jan., 1917. Mentioned in Despatches 18th Dec., 1917.

Watson, S. L. Lieut. Joined 17th July, 1915. *k.* 25th Sept., 1915.

Watt, A. Capt Joined 23rd Oct., 1915. *w.* 10th June, 1916. *d. of w.* 20th June, 1916.

Weinberg, P. D. 2nd Lieut. Joined 24th Feb., 1915. *k.* 9th May, 1915.

Wilkie, W. F. 2nd Lieut. Joined 9th Oct., 1915. To U.K. 10th Oct., 1917. Promoted Capt. Rejoined Battn. Left Battn. 24th July, 1918.

Williamson, T. C. 2nd Lieut. Joined 9th July, 1915. *k.* 26th Sept., 1915.

APPENDIX II

SUMMARY OF CASUALTIES. THE FOURTH BATTALION

The discrepancy between these figures and those given by the war diaries is accounted for by the fact that, save in the case of regular battalions, the diaries seldom give a record of casualties other than those suffered in main actions.

OFFICERS

Killed.	Wounded.	Missing.	Prisoners.	Total.
53	47	—	6	106

OTHER RANKS

Killed.	Wounded.	Missing.	Prisoners.	Total.
370	552	—	110	1032

APPENDIX III

Casualties—Officers

Abbreviations :—* Killed in action.   † Died of wounds.

THE FOURTH BATTALION

Name.	Rank.	Date.
Air, C. A.	Capt.	*25.9.15.
Anderson, F. K.	2nd Lieut.	*25.9.15.
Barnet, J. H.	2nd Lieut.	*1.8.18.
Bethune-Duncan, W. B.	Lieut.	*3.9.16.
Boase, E. L.	Capt.	*30.7.16.
Brown, J. T.	2nd Lieut.	†27.4.18.
Brown, W.	2nd Lieut.	*5.10.17.
Campbell, E. V.	Capt.	*26.9.15.
Couper, C. M.	Capt.	†28.9.15. In German hands.
Crosbie, W. R.	Lieut.	*12.4.18.
Cunningham, R. C.	Capt.	*3.9.16. M.C.
Delahunt, P. G.	2nd Lieut.	†28.8.18.
Dobson, G.	Lieut.	*11.4.18.
Ferrier, R. E.	2nd Lieut.	*15.10.16.
Fraser, J.	2nd Lieut.	†28.3.18.
Gibson, C. M.	2nd Lieut.	*14.10.16.
Greenless, G. C.	2nd Lieut.	*1.12.17.
Haggart, J.	2nd Lieut.	†3.1.18.
Hill, W. R.	2nd Lieut.	†24.8.18.
Kent, C. S.	2nd Lieut.	*24.10.18.
Kimber, J. W.	Lieut.	†11.5.18.
Lakeman, A. F.	2nd Lieut.	*5.8.18. And Tanks.
Levie, P. Mc.L.	Capt.	*24.10.18. M.C.
Logan, G. C.	Lieut.	*31.7.17.
Lundie, J. E.	2nd Lieut.	†29.3.18.
Marshall, J.	Lieut.	*24.10.18.
McGregor, A.	2nd Lieut.	*11.4.18.
McVicar, T. G.	2nd Lieut.	*28.3.18.
Musgrove, J. W.	2nd Lieut.	*19.7.18.
Paisley, G. W.	2nd Lieut.	*27.12.17.
Peebles, P.	2nd Lieut.	*19.7.18.
Prosser, J.	Lieut.	*28.9.18.
Robb, W. J. M.	2nd Lieut.	*20.7.18.
Rorie, T. H. B.	Capt.	*18.8.16.
Shepherd, E. A.	Capt.	*3.9.16.
Sheriff, L. F. D.	2nd Lieut.	*13.11.16.
Smith, H. H.	2nd Lieut.	*19.9.18.
Smith, W. T.	2nd Lieut.	*14.10.16.
Stevenson, T.	Capt.	*14.11.17. M.C. and Bar.
Steven, H. S.	Lieut.	*7.10.15.
Steven, S. H.	Lieut.	*25.9.15.
Sturrock, B. S.	Lieut.	*26.9.15.
Swinton, J. G.	2nd Lieut.	*25.3.18.

THE FOURTH BATTALION THE BLACK WATCH

Name.	Rank.	Date.
Tosh, E.	Major	*25.9.15.
Walker, H., C.M.G.	Lt.-Col.	†27.9.15.
Walker, N. C.	Capt.	*25.9.15.
Watson, S. L.	Capt.	*25.9.15.
Watt, A.	Capt.	†20.6.16.
Weinberg, P. D.	Lieut.	*9.5.15.
Wilkes, S. A.	2nd Lieut.	*24.8.18.
Wilson, J. C.	2nd Lieut.	*17.10.16. And R.F.C.
Williamson, T. C.	2nd Lieut.	*26.9.15.
Young, G. W.	Lieut.	†8.4.18. In German hands.

APPENDIX IV

NOMINAL ROLL OF WARRANT OFFICERS, NON-COMMISSIONED OFFICERS AND MEN KILLED IN ACTION OR DIED OF WOUNDS OR DISEASE IN THE GREAT WAR, 1914-18

Abbreviations—* Killed in action. † Died of wounds. ‡ Died at home.

THE FOURTH BATTALION

Adam, J., L/Cpl., 1497	*25.9.15	Campbell, P., Cpl., 202150	† 6.9.17
Alcorn, W. J., L/Cpl., 200435	*14.10.16	Campbell, W. G., Pte., 6224	*13.11.16
Allan, J., Pte., 2670	†30.10.15	Carberry, J., Sgt., 3795	*29.9.16
Allan, T., Pte., 2462	* 9.5.15	Cassidy, J., Cpl., 201325	* 3.9.16
Allday, T., Sgt., 1045	*25.9.15	(M.M.)	
Anderson, C., Pte., 2489	†28.3.15	Chalmers, A., Pte., 3240	* 2.8.16
Anderson, R., Pte., 2559	†10.6.15	Chalmers, J., Pte., 4266	*23.10.16
Andrews, R., Cpl., 1093	*12.4.15	Chapman, D.H., L/Cpl., 2562	*25.9.15
Angus, J., Pte., 1414	* 8.5.15	Charles, W., Sgt.-Major, 9507	*25.9.15
Auld, D., Pte., 2534	* 3.9.16	Clark, C., Pte., 1323	* 8.8.15
		Clark, E., Cpl., 4704	*30.8.16
Bald, R., Pte., 202904	‡ 8.6.17	Clark, W., Pte., 4094	*23.10.16
Barclay, J., Pte., 2587	‡ 4.1.16	Clements, W. J., Pte., 1359	† 4.10.15
Barnett, D., Pte., 2135	‡25.9.14	Cochrane, J., Pte., 6346	† 7.12.16
Barron, J., Pte., 201364	* 3.9.16	Coghill, G., Pte., 3183	* 9.5.15
Barrie, A., Pte., 3439	*5.12.15	Coleman, H., Pte., 4093	* 2.7.16
Beat, W., Pte., 1430	†3.10.15	Colquhoun, G., Pte., 2110	*25.9.15
Bell, G., Pte., 3496	*25.9.15	Connell, J., Pte., 2478	*25.9.15
Berry, G., Pte., 3760	*25.9.15	Connelly, A., Pte., 2924	* 3.9.16
Berry, J., Pte., 1787	* 7.6.15	Cook, W. J., Pte., 4868	†20.10.16
Bertie, J., Pte., 2461	‡3.10.15	Coupar, T., Pte., 2275	* 9.5.15
Bertram, W., Pte., 6228	†25.1.17	Couttie, J., Pte., 3257	†17.9.16
Black, A., Pte., 4476	† 5.9.16	Coyle, F., Pte., 2787	*30.7.16
Black, J., Pte., 2947	* 9.5.15	Craig, G., Sgt., 3155	†28.2.16
Blues, J., Pte., 3379	*22.5.15	Crawford, P., Pte., 3855	*25.9.15
Boath, D., Pte., 2771	*25.9.15	Croll, W. L., Pte., 202247	*13.11.16
Bogue, A., Pte., 4052	*30.7.16	Crossan, P., Pte., 4635	* 3.9.16
Bonnett, P., Pte., 3901	† 1.8.16	Cuthill, W., Pte., 1602	*25.9.15
Boyd, R., Pte., 3877	*25.9.15		
Boyle, P., Pte., 6357	*23.10.16	Dair, W., Pte., 2068	†11.5.15
Brown, A., Pte., 2631	*10.3.15	Dalgleish, D., Sgt., 1213	*25.9.15
Brown, A. C., Pte., 2510	*16.5.15	Davidson, J., Pte., 2651	*15.4.15
Brown, D., Pte., 3113	* 9.5.15	Davie, J., Pte., 2022	*25.4.15
Brown, G., Pte., 241096	‡ 8.7.17	Diamond, J., Pte., 2049	* 9.5.15
Brown, J., Pte., 2477	†12.3.15	Dick, J., Pte., 2869	*23.10.16
Brown, W., Pte., 2745	*25.9.15	Dick, R. A. Y., Cpl., 1871	* 6.5.15
Brown, W., Pte., 1370	* 9.5.15	Dickson, J., Pte., 2102	‡20.12.14
Brown, W. D., Sgt., 892	* 9.5.15	Dingwall, H., L/Cpl., 200782	*14.10.16
Bruce, W., Pte., 4740	*25.9.15	Dodds, G., Pte., 2967	* 2.4.15
Burgess, E., Pte., 201193	‡17.5.17	Doig, J., Pte., 3404	*25.9.15
Burgess, J., Pte., 4114	*24.7.16	Dolan, H., Pte., 2421	*25.9.15
Burnett, J., Pte., 2334	* 3.9.16	Donachie, J., Pte., 2365	* 9.5.15
		Donlan, M., Pte., 1643	‡13.9.14
Cairney, J., Pte., S/20762	‡19.4.17	Downton, P., Pte., 201370	*25.10.16
Cairns, J., Pte., 2498	*25.9.15	Drumm, M., Pte., 6415	*30.12.16
Cameron, A., Pte., 3539	*29.9.15	Duff, J., Pte., 3099	*25.9.15
Campbell, G. W., Pte., 6421	*12.1.17	Duncan, J., Pte., 3351	*25.9.15

31

THE FOURTH BATTALION THE BLACK WATCH

Duncan, W. E., Pte., 4101	†15.10.16	Hanley, A., Pte., 2154	*21.7.16
Dunn, M., Pte., 4153	* 5.12.15	Harper, A., Pte., 2265	†26.3.15
		Harper, W., Pte., 3492	*24.10.16
Elder, R. T., Cpl., 961	*25.9.15	Harrow, R., Sgt., 566	*11.3.15
Eltome, W., Pte., 2389	* 9.5.15	Harrow, W., Pte., 3860	*25.9.15
		Henderson, J., Sgt., 2878	†23.10.16
Fairweather, D. G., Pte., 201478		Henderson, W., Pte., 201188	* 3.9.16
	*14.10.16	Hendry, H., Pte., 3527	*14.10.16
Farrell, F., Pte., 4310	* 3.9.16	Hendry, T., Pte., 1896	*25.9.15
Fenwick, D., Cpl., 1434	*14.11.16	Higgins, S., Pte., 200759	*30.7.15
Ferguson, F. R., L/Sgt., 4235	*27.10.16	Houston, D., Pte., 3120	* 3.9.16
Ferguson, J., Pte., 3002	* 4.9.16	Howie, J., Pte., 1564	*10.3.15
Ferguson, J., Pte., 3725	*29.6.15	Hutchinson, J., L/Cpl., 200080	
Ferguson, W., Pte., 1789	*25.9.15		*15.3.17
Findlay, W., Pte., 3164	† 3.7.15	Hutchinson, T., Pte., 3759	† 6.11.16
Finlay, R., Pte., 4743	‡19.4.16	Hutchinson, W., Cpl., 1259	*24.3.15
Fisher, A., Pte., 4004	*24.10.16	Hutton, D., Pte., 200564	* 3.9.16
Fitzpatrick, J., Pte., 1736	†12.8.15		
Fitzsimmons, P., Sgt., 1203	*25.9.15	Jarran, H., A/Sgt., 845	* 9.5.15
Fleming, R., Pte., 4855	‡29.2.16	Johnston, D., L/Cpl., 3598	*23.10.16
Foley, W., Sgt., 2384	†15.10.16	Johnston, J. A. K., L/Cpl., 5064	
Forbes, W., Pte., 6517	† 5.1.17		†13.10.16
Forbes, W., Pte., 4164	* 3.9.16	Jones, D., Pte., 200903	*14.10.16
Forgan, J., Pte., 4679	† 5.9.16		
Fraser, A., Pte., 1644	*25.9.15	Keenan, J., Pte., 2406	* 9.5.15
Fullerton, J., Pte., 1699	*25.9.15	Kelly, D., Pte., 1864	*29.6.15
		Kelly, J., Pte., 2792	* 3.9.16
Galbraith, D., Pte., 6216	*12.1.17	Kelly, P., L/Sgt., 2202	*14.11.16
Gardiner, J., Pte., 5672	‡27.11.16	Kelly, T., L/Cpl., 3436	†24.1.17
Garty, T., Pte., 3311	*25.9.15	Kelman, J., Pte., 2576	* 9.5.15
Geddes, J., Pte., 1321	*25.9.15	Kennedy, E., Pte., 3696	* 9.5.15
Gellatly, D., Pte., 2847	† 9.5.15	Kidd, G., Sgt., 3736	*25.9.15
Gellatly, J., Pte., 2375	* 8.6.15	Kidd, J., Pte., 2901	†25.9.15
Gemmell, W., Cpl., 2248	*30.3.15	King, W., Pte., 2399	* 3.9.16
Gentle, N., Pte., 6379	*14.11.16	Knox, J., Pte., 1535	* 3.9.16
Gibson, A., Pte., 201402	†26.3.17		
Glen, D., Pte., 3261	*12.4.15		
Glenday, G., Pte., 2505	* 9.5.15		
Glover, W., Pte., 3818	*13.11.16	Lamb, S., Pte., 4954	*21.9.16
Gordon, J., Pte., 202079	*14.11.16	Lamond, A., Pte., 1888	*25.9.15
Gould, G., Pte., 2736	* 3.9.16	Lamont, P., Cpl., 1503	*25.9.15
Gow, D., Pte., 1495	* 3.9.16	Lamont, W., Pte., 6232	*23.10.16
Gowans, J., Pte., 3359	* 8.9.16	Lauchlin, J., Pte., 3610	*25.9.15
Gray, A., Pte., 6260	*13.11.16	Law, D., Pte., 202100	*14.10.16
Gray, E., Pte., 2551	*23.10.16	Lickley, D. D., A/C.Q.M.S., 4112	
Gray, G., Pte., 201134	*14.10.16		‡ 2.7.16
Gray, J., Pte., 2225	* 3.9.16	Linn, A., L/Cpl., 4624	‡15.5.16
Gray, J., Pte., 6222	† 3.2.17	Linnen, G., Pte., 3262	*25.9.15
Gray, R., Pte., 1889	*10.3.15	Loftus, C., Cpl., 3628	*12.3.15
Green, M., Pte., 4883	* 3.9.16	Loftus, J., L/Cpl., 2164	*25.9.15
Grieve, J., Pte., 6166	*21.9.15	Logan, R., Cpl., 2040	*12.3.15
Guthrie, W. S., Cpl., 1536	†18.1.17	Low, A., Pte., 2518	† 2.9.15
		Lowden, R., Pte., 3717	†26.4.15
Halliday, W., Pte., 3268	* 8.6.15	Lumsden, T., Pte., 292029	‡18.6.18
Hancock, G. A., Pte., 3271	*25.9.15	Lyon, A., Pte., 2881	*29.6.15

APPENDIX IV

Macdonald, A., Pte., 3291 — *23.7.16
Macdonald, J., Pte., 4773 — ‡10.2.16
Macdonald, S., Pte., 200923 — ‡ 9.3.17
McArthur, J., Pte., 202474 — *20.6.17
McAvoy, T., Pte., 1493 — * 9.5.15
McBain, W., Pte., 201225 — * 3.9.16
McBride, J., Pte., 6272 — †14.11.16
McCann, J., Pte., 2803 — *25.9.15
McCarran, J., Pte., 3346 — † 8.9.16
McCumiskey, W., Pte., 201301 — * 3.9.16
McDermot, T., Dmr., 3200 — *25.9.15
McDonald, G., Pte., 4853 — ‡ 6.2.16
McDonald, H., Pte., 200164 — * 3.9.16
McDonald, J., Pte., 2738 — * 7.10.15
McDonald, J., Pte., 2751 — * 9.5.15
McDonald, J., Pte., 200471 — * 4.9.16
McDonald, J., Sgt., 2056 (D.C.M.) — * 8.5.15
McDonald, M., Pte., 1598 — † 6.12.15
McDougall, W. T., Pte., 3625 — †30.12.15
McEwan, P., A/Cpl., 201399 — ‡ 3.5.18
McFarlane, J., L/Cpl., 2126 — *25.9.15
McFarlane, T., Pte., 1897 — *25.9.15
McGhee, J., Pte., 2495 — ‡28.11.15
McGhee, W., L/Sgt., 2579 — *25.9.15
McGonigal, R., Pte., 2503 — *25.9.15
McGregor, R., Pte., 3103 — *10.3.15
McGregor, W., Pte., 2016 — †29.3.15
McInroy, J., Pte., 2485 — * 9.5.15
McIntosh, A., Pte., 1477 — *25.9.15
McIntosh, A., Pte., 3000 — * 9.5.15
McIntosh, C., Pte., 1792 — *25.9.15
McKay, A. M., Pte., 3849 — *25.9.15
McKay, A., Pte., 6323 — *13.11.16
McKillop, J., Pte., 3507 — * 5.9.15
McLachlan, C., Pte., 2106 — *30.3.15
McLaren, A., Pte., 3297 — *30.7.16
McLauchlan, J., Sgt., 3391 (M.M.) — † 3.1.17
McLaughlan, J., L/Cpl., 3651 — *25.9.15
McLean, P., Pte., 2753 — *25.9.15
McLean, T., Pte., 1463 — *16.7.16
McLeod, A., Pte., 200400 — * 3.9.16
McMahon, J., Pte., 3407 — *25.9.15
McManus, J., Cpl., 316892 — ‡18.5.18
McNair, T., L/Cpl., 1435 — *15.9.15
McNally, T., Pte., 2761 — *25.9.15
McNaughton, D. C., Pte., 1501 — * 4.8.16
McNeil, J., Pte., 4884 — ‡25.12.16
McQueen, C., Pte., 2088 — *29.9.15
McRitchie, A., Pte., 3723 — *25.9.15
McVicar, A., L/Cpl., 1499 — *25.9.15
Magee, D., Pte., 200567 — *14.10.16

Maguire, J. R., Pte., 3595 — *25.9.15
Mainds, G., Sgt., 4028 — †20.11.16
Maitland, G. M., Pte., 4090 — *14.10.16
Martin, F., Cpl., 2941 — *25.9.15
Martin, P., Pte., 2951 — *12.7.15
Masson, P., Pte., 4292 — * 3.9.16
Masson, A. R., Pte., S/28707 — ‡15.10.18
Masterton, G., Pte., 2583 — * 9.5.15
Meekison, T., Pte., 2622 — * 3.9.16
Meldrum, J. D., A/Q.M.S., 290326 (East Africa) — †19.11.17 (*a*)
(*a*) Attached 1st/3rd K.A.R.
Mellis, R., Cpl., 4216 — *30.7.16
Methven, D., Pte., 1286 — * 5.8.15
Middleton, D., Pte., 2898 — *25.9.15
Middleton, J. D., Sgt., 2846 — *21.9.15
Middleton, J. J., Pte., 20062 — * 3.9.16
Middleton, N., Pte., 203060 — ‡22.7.17
Millar, G., C.S.M., 3/3627 — ‡16.3.16
Millar, J., Pte., 3763 — *25.9.15
Millar, J., Pte., 4040 — †16.9.16
Miller, A., Pte., 3989 — * 3.9.16
Mills, F., Pte., 4196 — † 4.9.16
Mills, J., Pte., 4377 — *25.9.15
Milton, T., Pte., 2974 — *20.9.16
Mitchell, A., Pte., 3878 — †10.9.16
Mitchell, J., Pte., 6186 — *13.11.16
Mitchison, N., Pte., 6191 — *14.10.16
Moncur, D., Pte., 200988 — *14.10.16
Money, R., Pte., 1830 — * 3.9.16
Montague, J., Pte., 3027 — * 9.5.15
Montgomery, H., Pte., 3304 — * 8.9.16
Morrison, A., Pte., 2627 — *25.9.15
Morrison, J., Pte., 2556 — †28.5.15
Mowat, F., Pte., 3435 — † 7.6.15
Mugie, D., Pte., 4061 — *14.10.16
Mulligan, C., Cpl., 2001 — * 9.5.15
Murphy, T., Pte., 6257 — *13.11.16
Murray, D., Pte., 2142 — * 3.9.16
Myles, R. L., Pte., 2377 — †25.9.15

Nairn, J., Pte., 2822 — * 9.6.16
Naismith, T., Sgt., 1422 — *25.9.15
Napier, H., Pte., 202000 — *14.10.16
Nicholson, J., Pte., 2253 — *13.7.15
Nicol, J., Cpl., 2391 — *25.9.15
Nicolson, D., Pte., 4241 — †21.6.16
Niven, J., Pte., 200927 — *25.9.15
Norrie, T., Pte., 1997 — *25.9.15

O'Brien, J., Pte., 2764 — * 9.5.15
Orr, R., Pte., 4473 — * 6.11.16
Osborne, C., Cpl., 291029 (M.M.) — ‡24.10.18

THE FOURTH BATTALION THE BLACK WATCH

Palk, J. W. McK., Pte., 5120	†16.11.16	Steven, W., Pte., 3076	†21.5.15
Paton, T., Cpl., 2744	*14.10.16	Stevenson, R. B., Pte., 6510	†17.1.17
Paterson, C., Pte., 4021	*29.9.16	Stewart, A., Pte., 201305	*30.7.16
Paul, A., Pte., 201110	*14.10.16	Stewart, G. A., Pte., 3749	*25.9.15
Philip, J., Pte., 201261	*14.10.16	Stewart, J., Cpl., 857	* 9.5.15
Piggott, J., Pte., 2030	*23.7.16	Stewart, J., Pte., 3362	*25.9.15
Potter, R. S., Pte., S/28546	‡16.10.18	Stewart, R., Pte., 2671	* 2.7.15
Pyott, D., Pte., 1844	* 8.5.15	Stirton, H. C., Sgt., 3574	†11.9.16
		Stirton, J. C., L/Cpl., 1098	*25.9.15
Rae, W., Pte., 1500	†18.5.15	Stormont, J., Cpl., 4227	*3.9.16
Ramsay, W., Pte., 1874	*25.9.15	Strachan, A., Pte., 2063	*10.3.15
Reid, W., Pte., 1992	*28.7.15	Strachan, G., Pte., 2758	*29.7.15
Reith, G., Pte., 6206	*14.10.16	Strachan, P., Pte., 2804	* 3.9.16
Rennie, N., Pte., 4248	† 5.8.16	Strang, G., Pte., 6198	*29.9.16
Ritchie, G. A., Pte., 4942	†29.6.16	Sullivan, H., Pte., 1420	*25.9.15
Robertson, G., L/Cpl., 1460	† 2.5.15		
Robertson, J. P., Sgt., 1523	*25.9.16	Tarbet, W., Pte., 4940	*23.10.16
Robertson, J. L., L/Cpl., 4066		Taylor, J., L/Cpl., 202631	†20.3.17
	†23.7.16	Taylor, T. S., Pte., 202115	*14.10.16
Robertson, P., Pte., 2058	†12.5.15	Taylor, W., L/Cpl., 2131	* 9.5.15
Ross, A., Pte., 6208	*13.11.16	Tennant, W., L/Cpl., 1641	† 6.9.16
Ross, A., Pte., 201022	*14.10.16	Thomson, D., C.S.M., 882	*25.9.15
Ross, J., Pte., 1845	* 8.5.15	Thomson, W., Pte., 4918	*14.11.16
Ross, T., Pte., 200654	* 3.9.16	Thomson, W. A., C.S.M., 171	*25.9.15
Ryan, A., Pte., 5140	†16.11.16	Thornton, J., Pte., 1642	*25.9.15
		Timmons, T., L/Cpl., 2232	*25.9.15
Sandeman, A., Pte., 2486	*25.9.16	Tracey, J., Pte., 200749	‡29.4.17
Sangster, A., Pte., 3080	† 5.9.16	Troup, A. B., Cpl., 456	* 9.5.15
Scott, J., Pte., 2168	†18.5.15		
Scott, T., Pte., 2275	*10.3.15	Walker, A., Pte., 6337	* 9.2.17
Simpson, A., Pte., 200613	* 3.9.16	Walker, A. McA., L/Cpl., 4858	
Sinclair, A., Pte., 6147	*23.10.15		*14.10.16
Skerry, E., Cpl., 2258	*25.9.15	Wallace, C., Pte., 2143	* 9.5.15
Smeaton, A., Pte., 4638	* 2.7.16	Watson, G., Sgt., 827	*25.9.15
Smith, A., Pte., 2521	*25.9.15	Watts, R. L., Pte., 3619	‡26.12.16
Smith, J., Pte., 923	*25.9.15	Weir, J., Pte., 3315	†20.5.15
Smith, J., Pte., 3331	*25.9.15	White, A., Pte., 4493	* 6.8.16
Smith, J., Pte., 3519	* 9.5.15	Whyte, C. R., L/Cpl., 1431	* 8.5.15
Smith, N., Pte., 200551	* 3.9.16	Will, D., Pte., 3300	*14.10.16
Smith, P., L/Cpl., 2986	* 9.5.15	Williamson, J., Pte., 4753	* 8.9.16
Smith, T., Pte., 2210	*29.9.16	Williamson, W., Pte., 2138	*10.3.15
Sneddon, T., Pte., 202113	*14.10.16	Wilson, A., Pte., 201273	*30.6.16
Spalding, J., L/Cpl., 1988	†16.6.15		
Spalding, J., L/Cpl., 2034	*15.9.15	Yeaman, T., Pte., 1822	† 8.5.15
Steel, D., Pte., 2585	* 3.9.16	Young, A., Pte., 202128	*13.11.16

APPENDIX V

HONOURS AND AWARDS

The Fourth Battalion

C.M.G.
Lieut.-Colonel H. Walker.

D.S.O.
Major J. S. Y. Rogers.

M.C.
Capt. R. W. McIntyre.
2nd Lieut. R. C. Cunningham.
2nd Lieut. S. H. Steven.

Mentioned in Despatches
Major J. S. Y. Rogers.
Capt. R. W. McIntyre.
Lieut. T. Stevenson.
R.S.M. W. Charles.

APPENDIX VI

List of Actions and Operations

The Fourth Battalion

1915. Landed in France. 26th February.

BATTLE OF NEUVE CHAPELLE. (Windy Corner.) 10th March.

BATTLE OF AUBERS RIDGE. (Rue des Berceaux.) 9th May.
Trench warfare. Rue du Bois, Rue Tilleloy, Winchester Road. May–September.

BATTLE OF LOOS. (Fauquissart.) 25th September.
Trench warfare. Givenchy, Locon, Rue du Bois, Hohenzollern Redoubt. September–December.

1916. Trench warfare. January–March.
Amalgamated with 5th Battalion. March, 1916.

THE FIFTH
BATTALION

CHAPTER I

FROM THE DATE OF MOBILIZATION, AUGUST 4TH, 1914, TO THE DATE OF AMALGAMATION WITH THE 4TH BATTALION, MARCH 15TH, 1916

THE 1st Forfarshire (Dundee) Rifles were first formed in 1859. In 1860 additional companies were raised and amalgamated into one unit for administrative purposes, with regimental headquarters at Dundee.
In 1881 the Battalion was affiliated to The Black Watch under the Territorial system, and some years later was given the title of the 5th (Dundee Highland) Volunteer Battalion The Black Watch. The Battalion sent a strong contingent with each of the three Volunteer Service companies that joined and fought with the 2nd Battalion The Black Watch during the South African War.

In 1909 the 5th Battalion was under the command of Lieutenant-Colonel H. Scrymgeour-Wedderburn and consisted of eight companies, with headquarters situated as follows:

A company	Kirriemuir.
B company	Forfar.
C company	Montrose.
D company	Brechin.
E and F companies	Arbroath.
G and H companies	Dundee.

Before the Great War the Battalion did not form part of any division, but was allotted to the Coast Defences, under which scheme eight officers and 200 other ranks formed a Special Service Section and undertook definite obligations to man the Tay defences in the event of any national emergency.

On July 28th, 1914, while the Battalion was undergoing annual training in camp at Monzie, near Crieff, this special section was called up for duty and at once proceeded to its war stations at Dundee and Broughty Ferry.

The remainder of the Battalion, on completion of the annual training on August 2nd, was not disbanded, but the men proceeded to their homes on leave. Two days later orders were received for the Battalion to mobilize, and, in accordance with a scheme prepared beforehand, the various companies and detachments assembled at their drill stations throughout Forfarshire at 9 o'clock the following morning, and by early afternoon all ranks had reported to a man at their war stations.

The right half Battalion was billeted in the vicinity of Broughty Castle, the Battalion Headquarters being at Ferry House; while the left half occupied Hawkhill School, Dundee. Until the end of October the Battalion was employed in erecting defences, building blockhouses, constructing defensive

THE FIFTH BATTALION THE BLACK WATCH

works in the vicinity of Broughty Ferry and on Spiers Hill, Tayport, and in patrolling their areas, at the same time continuing war training. From the date the Special Service Section went on duty, recruits enlisted in such large numbers that great difficulty was found in providing them with the necessary arms and equipment; many of them, indeed, carried out their training in civilian clothing.

The obligations of members of the Territorial Force did not then include their service overseas, but in this emergency a call was made for volunteers, and practically the whole Battalion gladly volunteered to undertake this responsibility. Following this, late in September, instructions were received to form a second or reserve battalion, and with this in view about 300 other ranks, who had in the majority of cases not reached the age standard, were, with a proportion of officers, drafted to Forfar on September 26th, 1914, to form a nucleus for the new unit which, later, came under the command of Lieutenant-Colonel P. S. Nicoll, T.D., D.L., and was brigaded as one of the Home Defence units.

On October 24th the Battalion, which now came to be known as the 1/5th Battalion, received orders to proceed overseas and, five days later, on the 29th, entrained for Southampton, the officer personnel of the Battalion being as under:

Commanding Officer	Lieutenant-Colonel H. Scrymgeour-Wedderburn.
Second-in-Command	Major Lord Glamis.
	Major H. F. Blair-Imrie.
Adjutant	Captain G. F. Bowes-Lyon.
Lieutenant and Quartermaster	A. Hall.
Machine Gun Officer	Captain A. W. Duke.
Transport Officer	F. N. E. Kitson.
Medical Officer	Major G. F. Whyte, M.B., R.A.M.C. (T.F.).
Regimental Sergeant-Major	J. Robertson.
Regimental Quartermaster-Sergeant	J. Peffers.

No. 1 Company

Officer Commanding	Captain J. B. McNab.
Second-in-Command	Captain T. Aubertin.
Lieutenant	R. F. D. Bruce.
,,	J. W. N. Gordon.
,,	I. M. Bruce-Gardyne.
Second Lieutenant	The Hon. J. H. Bowes-Lyon.
Company Sergeant-Major	V. Glass.

OFFICERS OF THE FIFTH BATTALION BEFORE EMBARKATION TO FRANCE ON NOVEMBER, 1ST, 1914

Back Row: Lt. J. McP. S. Duke, Lt. and Q.M. A. Hall, Lt. Morris, R.A.M.C., Hon. Capt. G. S. Rae, Lt. T. Aubertin, Lt. A. H. M. Wedderburn, Lt. Coutts, Lt. Hon. H. R. C. Arbuthnott, Lt. A. W. Duke, Lt. T. Lyell, 2nd Lt. J. Gordon, 2nd Lt. Pithie

Centre Row: Capt. J. B. McNab, Capt. H. F. Blair Imrie, Major P. S. Nicoll, Major Lord Glamis, Lt.-Col. H. Scrymgeour Wedderburn, Chaplain the Rev. Dr. Coats, Capt. and Adjt. the Hon. G. F. Bowes-Lyon, Capt. T. Maule Guthrie, Capt. J. A. Wilson, Hon. Major J. F. Dickson

Front Row: 2nd Lt. J. Murray, 2nd Lt. J. H. Campbell, 2nd Lt. I. M. Bruce-Gardyne, Lt. R. F. D. Bruce, 2nd Lt. H. R. McCabe, 2nd Lt. G. M. Adams

BATTALION LEAVES FOR FRANCE, NOVEMBER, 1915

No. 2 Company

Officer Commanding	Captain T. Lyell.
Second-in-Command	Captain A. H. M. Wedderburn.
Lieutenant	J. F. Dickson (late Major), V.D.
,,	J. H. Campbell, of Stracathro.
,,	H. S. Queckett.
,,	G. M. Adams.
Company Sergeant-Major	J. Marnie.

No. 3 Company

Officer Commanding	Captain J. D. Duncan.
Second-in-Command	Captain J. A. Wilson.
Lieutenant	J. Murray.
,,	W. C. O. Barrie.
,,	L. A. Elgood.
Company Sergeant-Major	G. Low.

No. 4 Company

Officer Commanding	Captain J. Cruickshank.
Second-in-Command	Captain W. L. Mitchell.
Lieutenant	A. Dickie.
Second Lieutenant	H. R. McCabe.
,,	R. M. Leslie.
Company Sergeant-Major	W. Milne.

The Battalion embarked on Sunday, November 1st, on the s.s. *Architect* for Le Havre, disembarking there the following morning and proceeding to an adjacent rest-camp for completion of equipment up to field scale, there having been no time to issue this before leaving Scotland. Unfortunately, owing to the fact that the 5th had been, like other Territorial units, included in reinforcements of the original Expeditionary Force during the critical stages of the First Battle of Ypres, it was found impossible to complete this equipment before the Battalion was required at the front; therefore, at an hour's notice, on the day after arrival, and before there was time to issue everything required, the Battalion was ordered to move up to the front line. This journey in 1914 was somewhat tedious, it taking twenty-four hours to travel a distance usually completed in four.

The Battalion arrived at St. Omer on November 4th, where it was met by the D.A.D.R.T., whose cheery shout of welcome was at once recognised in the darkness as coming from the large and cheerful form of Captain A. S. Grant, D.S.O.,The Black Watch, a former Adjutant of the Battalion. Detraining and unloading transport and stores was at once carried out in pouring rain and inky darkness, and in a silence which could only be " heard " between the *sotto voce* remarks of the Second-in-Command and Quartermaster, to say nothing of those of Captain Grant himself.

From St. Omer the Battalion marched to billets at Blendeques, where it remained one week, moving thence by march route to Thiennes, where it joined the 24th Infantry Brigade under Brigadier-General F. C. Carter, C.B., forming part of the 8th Division under Major-General F. Davies, and on November 14th moved into billets in Estaires.

The following day General Rawlinson, commanding the IV Corps, welcomed the Battalion to his command and on parade gave a general appreciation of the existing conditions under which the 5th would be employed. At this time the 24th Brigade comprised the 1st Battalion Worcester Regiment, 2nd Battalion Northamptonshire Regiment, 2nd Battalion East Lancashire Regiment, 1st Battalion Sherwood Foresters and 5th Battalion Black Watch.

Shortly before the arrival of the Battalion the Brigade had taken over the sector of the trench line opposite Neuve Chapelle, and the first duty of the 5th was to improve the existing temporary defences, which consisted mainly of old roadside ditches and hastily constructed breastworks, the low-lying nature of the country precluding any deep trenches.

After a very short period devoted to instruction, the Battalion took over a section of the front line, and on November 18th experienced its first casualty. The first tour under instruction was very trying, owing partly to the bad weather, but mainly to the lack of all ordinary comfort. It should be remembered that few of the arrangements, so well organized later on in the war, could then be made for the men's health and well-being. The trenches were seldom drained, duck-boards were unknown, and it was common for men to stand hour after hour over their ankles in mud and water. There were few " dug-outs," and little overhead cover of any sort. In these early days it was sometimes found that communication trenches had not yet been constructed, and the companies had to march by night to relieve their comrades. Sanitary arrangements in the trenches were this autumn of the most primitive kind. It was only after the New Year that material was made available and time could be given to add to the comfort of the troops as well as to the security of the line.

Billets were very welcome after a period in the trenches, but it was only later in the winter that a good system of hot baths and steam laundries was provided. Men were often billeted

IN THE TRENCHES, WINTER, 1914

in farm buildings and greatly appreciated the cafés and *estaminets* common in all the villages visited by the Battalion. Separate company messes were usually formed, and from the start to the finish of the war the rations were excellent, though often supplemented by purchases of coffee and milk, vegetables and wine. In no war has the feeding and clothing of the troops been carried out so efficiently or on so lavish a scale, and after this autumn the health of the men bore witness to the excellence of the medical and sanitary arrangements. But it was inevitable that in this the first winter the troops should find that comforts were few and hardships many. However, this period of initiation to active service was made considerably easier by the cameraderie and good fellowship shown by all ranks of the Regular battalions in the Brigades.

The first experience of actual warfare the 5th met with after the training period was on the 20th of December, when the Battalion stood to arms for forty-eight hours behind the system of trenches known as Port Arthur in anticipation of an enemy attack which, however, never took place. The month of December was passed in the line under appalling weather conditions. A certain number of men became casualties from enemy fire, but a far larger number were admitted to hospital suffering from the effects of the extreme cold, from being constantly wet in the trenches and from the trying conditions under which they had to live; in fact, when the right half Battalion left the trenches on December 9th they could only muster some 150 men, on account of the large numbers who at this time were temporarily unfit for duty.

The first reinforcements reached the 5th on December 25th, when Captain Arbuthnott, Lieutenant Taylor, Sergeant-Major Burgess and 191 other ranks arrived, Lieutenant Taylor and Sergeant-Major Burgess being posted to No. 4 company, Sergeant-Major Milne becoming Regimental Quartermaster-Sergeant.

On January 3rd, 1915, Company Quartermaster-Sergeant W. Garden left the Battalion to take a combatant commission with the 1st Black Watch. He was the first non-commissioned officer of the 5th who received a commission, and his rank at the close of the war was Major in the Machine Gun Corps, having been also awarded the D.S.O. and Military Cross.

The Battalion War Diary for January and February contains little of interest to the general reader. Day after day appear paragraphs such as:

> "Nos. 1 and 2 companies at C lines."
> "Nos. 3 and 4 companies at A lines."
> "One man wounded."

THE FIFTH BATTALION THE BLACK WATCH

During this time the 5th lost 16 other ranks killed and 61 wounded; one officer killed and one wounded. Owing to illness, Lieutenant-Colonel H. S. Wedderburn was invalided to England at the end of January, Major H. Blair-Imrie succeeding him in command.

On February 26th the Battalion was relieved and proceeded to La Gorgue for a few days' rest to prepare for a projected attack on Neuve Chapelle which was to take place on March 10th. On the 9th, just before dark, the Battalion moved up to advanced billets to the south of Richebourg-St. Vaast, and the following morning went forward as support to the 24th Infantry Brigade, having been detailed to carry out the following duties.

The Battalion machine gun section, under Lieutenant A. Duke, was attached to the 1/4th Cameron Highlanders in C lines, under Captain Porter of the 60th, the Brigade Machine Gun Officer; while the grenadier section, under Lieutenant Bruce-Gardyne, was also brigaded and took part in the original assault on the German lines. Incidentally they were the only grenadiers of the 24th Brigade who did not have an officer, non-commissioned officer or man killed in this action, and consequently they earned the soubriquet of the " Bullet-proof Jocks." No. 1 company, Captain McNab, moved to Pink Farm for the purpose of guarding German prisoners. One platoon of No. 2 company occupied " B " Redoubt, another was employed escorting prisoners, and the remaining two supplied a working party for digging trenches. Nos. 3 and 4 companies furnished parties to connect the old British and German front lines. The Battalion Headquarters and such men of Nos. 3 and 4 companies not employed were located in Sign Post Lane.

Although the Battalion was not actively employed in the actual assault, the 5th suffered a number of casualties, Captain A. L. Watt being killed, Captains H. R. C. Arbuthnott and J. A. Wilson, Lieutenant McP. S. Duke and Second Lieutenant F. N. E. Kitson being wounded, in addition to 13 other ranks killed and 67 wounded, during the fighting between the 10th and 12th of March. In addition to the work already detailed, the Battalion was employed in salvage work and bringing up R.E. stores, and also, on the 14th and 15th, it was employed in the unpleasant but necessary work of burying the dead.

During this fighting the Battalion lost one of its most popular characters in Piper Howie, a stretcher bearer. His coolness and daring throughout the action, to say nothing of his tenderness to the wounded, set a wonderful example to all his party, who with him worked unceasingly throughout the first day and night of the battle. He finally fell, shot through the heart, in the act of bearing a badly wounded man to the rear.

IN THE TRENCHES, MARCH–APRIL, 1915

In the course of this fighting, considerable disorganization was experienced in keeping the front line troops supplied with various requirements, but thanks to the initiative of the Quartermaster (Lieutenant A. Hall) and the Transport Officer (Second Lieutenant Kitson) the Battalion received its rations, letters and parcels without a hitch. The gallantry of these officers was specially noticeable, and Second Lieutenant Kitson was afterwards awarded the Military Cross; while Lance-Corporal Anderson, the Transport corporal, received the D.C.M. and Cross of St. George.

When the front line troops of the 24th Infantry Brigade were withdrawn from the Neuve Chapelle action, the 5th was attached to the 25th Infantry Brigade as support when that Brigade resumed the attack, and on the evening of March 11th, when it in turn was withdrawn, the Battalion occupied the trenches at Neuve Chapelle, and was employed under the 23rd Infantry Brigade in clearing the battlefield, consolidating the position captured and holding certain strong points.

The Battalion remained on this duty for four days, when it was relieved by the 2nd Black Watch and withdrew to reserve billets for rest after being in action for six consecutive days, during which it had lost five officers and 80 other ranks killed and wounded. For service during this operation Lieutenant-Colonel H. Blair-Imrie received the C.M.G., and one Military Cross and eight D.C.M.'s were awarded to the Battalion (see Appendix V).

On March 16th the Battalion moved from the line to La Gorgue, and thence, on the 21st, to La Flinqué and various other places before it returned to the line once more at La Boutillerie on the 26th, relieving the 1st British Columbian Regiment in the 8th Division area. On the whole, April, which the Battalion spent holding the line in various places, with the usual few days' intervals of rest, was a quiet month. Preparations, however, were now being made for an attack on Aubers Ridge early in May, in support of operations by the French Army farther south.

During this time, and while the Battalion was in Divisional reserve at Bac St. Maur, on April 21st, the 24th Brigade was inspected by the Commander-in-Chief, Sir John French, who addressed all battalions and expressed his admiration for the patriotic spirit shown by Territorial units in volunteering for duty overseas; he also expressed admiration for their courage and soldierly bearing, and thanked the Battalion for their services during the recent operations at Neuve Chapelle.

While at Bac St. Maur, Captain J. Kennedy, M.C., D.C.M., 2nd Black Watch, was appointed Adjutant vice Captain G. F. Bowes-Lyon, who had been invalided in November, 1914.

Captain Kennedy was a man of outstanding character. He

THE FIFTH BATTALION THE BLACK WATCH

had long served as Company Sergeant-Major in the 2nd Black Watch, in Major Wauchope's company, an officer who had the highest esteem and regard for Kennedy both as a man and as a soldier, and who recommended him for his commission soon after the 2nd Battalion had landed in France. Kennedy earned his D.C.M. in 1914 for his gallant conduct when leading half Major Wauchope's company in a counter-attack made in order to help an Indian battalion to recover a trench captured by the Germans near le Plantin. His services throughout the war were marked by exceptional ability, and in 1917 he was appointed Lieutenant-Colonel and received command of a battalion.

While the preparations for the coming attack were proceeding, a working party of 50 other ranks under Second Lieutenant Elgood was attached for duty to the 2nd Field Company Royal Engineers. This party was engaged almost every night cutting and clearing the wire on the Brigade front in preparation for the assault, and was later complimented by the Division Commander on its work, Second Lieutenant Elgood being awarded the M.C.

The 5th moved into the line again on the 27th, and on May 4th it was withdrawn, with the 24th Brigade, to Divisional reserve in the vicinity of Sailly sur la Lys to prepare for the coming attack on the 9th. The general scheme of the 24th Brigade attack was as follows: The 2nd East Lancashire Regiment and the 2nd Northamptonshire Regiment were ordered to attack a portion of the enemy's line astride the Petillon–Fromelles road, with the 1st Battalion Worcestershire Regiment and the 1st Battalion Sherwood Foresters in support, the 5th Black Watch moving up behind them to the first German line (when captured) in Brigade reserve.

The night of the 8th was clear and starlit, the roads were in good condition and the Brigade had no difficulty in reaching its assembly positions, although it suffered somewhat from machine gun fire, the assembly trenches being in an exposed position and not affording complete protection.

The preliminary bombardment opened at 5 a.m. on the 9th, and forty minutes later the assault began. Unfortunately the bombardment did little damage to the enemy front line, and the assaulting troops at once came under heavy enfilade rifle and machine gun fire from a salient on the right flank, which brought the advance to a standstill.

According to instructions received beforehand, the Battalion had started to move up at the moment of assault following the 1st Battalion Worcestershire Regiment. But owing to the failure of the assault, the forward trenches were filled with troops, and the crowding grew worse and worse as great difficulty was experienced in bringing the wounded back from the front line.

BATTLE OF AUBERS RIDGE, MAY, 1915

A second attempt was made about 9 a.m., but again without success, and another at 1 p.m. had the same result. By this time casualties had been heavy throughout the Brigade, and orders were received to stand fast.

During the whole day, and particularly in the afternoon, the enemy from his point of vantage on the Aubers Ridge was able to keep up a heavy and accurate shell fire on the whole of the Brigade front, which considerably damaged it and increased the number of casualties. About 10 p.m. the 5th received orders to withdraw to a point in the vicinity of Rouge de Bout, from which, early the following morning, the whole Brigade was withdrawn into Divisional reserve. Although the Battalion had not taken part in the actual assault on May 9th, the casualties were fairly heavy, eight officers being wounded, 31 other ranks killed and 106 wounded.

It is not necessary to describe the attacks made by other divisions on the right and left of the 24th Brigade on the 9th of May, but it may be said that the same factors—namely, the strength of the enemy's position and the lack of the necessary guns to give an effective preliminary bombardment—caused the failure of each of the several attacks which were made on that day in the neighbourhood of the Aubers Ridge.

The Battalion spent the next six days at Pont du Hem and Estaires, from which, on the 15th, it moved to Wangerie and there occupied a series of posts for two days, after which it proceeded to billets on the La Flinqué–Laventie road. On the 20th, the 5th was organized into two companies and, with the 2nd Battalion Northamptonshire Regiment, which had been similarly organized, this new Battalion came under command of the Officer Commanding the Northamptonshire Regiment. On the same day, however, this officer was wounded, and Lieutenant-Colonel Blair-Imrie assumed command. This amalgamation, however, only lasted for one tour in the trenches, near Neuve Chapelle, after which the two battalions were again reorganized as separate units.

From now onwards throughout the summer the Neuve Chapelle sector was singularly quiet, and no action of importance took place. The French attack on the Somme front was then in progress, and nearly every part of the British line was, in consequence, comparatively peaceful.

By the month of June, however, the 5th was greatly under strength, the numbers on the 14th having fallen to 14 officers and 369 other ranks. Few reinforcements were received throughout the summer, only 16 men in June, 11 in July and 14 in August; while the casualties during the same period, even in this quiet sector, were 59 in June, 68 in July and 85 in August.

September was much the same, one draft of 50 men being received; while the losses for that month amounted to 56, the total strength on September 24th being 20 officers and 400 other ranks. In October, however, larger drafts arrived, and on the 31st of that month the Battalion strength, as given in the War Diary, was 32 officers and 575 other ranks.

The only incident as regards fighting in which the 5th took part during the summer was that in which, on September 25th, the bombing platoon was engaged in an attack near Chapel Farm, the remainder of the Battalion being in Brigade reserve at Limit Post. This operation was one of the many designed to draw attention from the main point of the British attack—namely, Loos and the French operations just south of that village.

The grenadier platoon (bombers), under Second Lieutenant Macintyre, was ordered to report to the Officer Commanding 2nd Battalion Berkshire Regiment, one of those battalions destined to lead the 8th Division attack on the German trenches in the vicinity of Bois Grenier, its task being to clear a strong point, Angle Fort. This was done successfully, and, having expended all its bombs, the platoon was withdrawn and rejoined the Battalion. For services on this occasion, Lance-Corporal A. Ogilvie was awarded the D.C.M., and Sergeant W. Murray the M.M.

On the 18th of October orders were received that the 5th was to become a Pioneer Battalion, Divisional troops, and would be employed under the orders of the Chief Engineer 8th Division. The change took place at once, and, after a farewell inspection by the Officer Commanding 24th Brigade, the Battalion took up its new duties.

Although all ranks regretted the change, still officers and men could not fail to appreciate the reason. In order to counteract the growing mining activities of the enemy, the need for miners of experience was very great. In the Battalion there were large numbers of trained miners, and consequently it was an easy matter to organize the 5th as an expert mining battalion.

The Battalion War Diary states:

" The Battalion was to become Divisional troops employed
" under the orders of the C.R.E. 8th Division in various duties,
" chiefly in the erection of winter quarters and in mining, having
" been selected for this duty on account of the large number of
" skilled tradesmen in its ranks."

No. 1 company of the new Pioneer Battalion was sent to assist the 15th Field company R.E. at Avesnes; No. 2 was sent to work on roads in the Divisional area; No. 3 went to the 181st Tunnelling company; and No. 4 to the 2nd Field company R.E. at Croix Biance.

IN THE TRENCHES, AUTUMN, 1915

On October 31st, Major R. B. Millar took over command from Lieutenant-Colonel H. Blair-Imrie at Rue de Bruges, the latter proceeding to England for the purpose of superintending the training of the 2/5th Reserve Battalion at Ripon, Yorkshire, owing to the unsatisfactory numbers in the drafts recently received by the Battalion.

The 5th was thus employed for the remainder of the time the 8th Division spent in the Neuve Chapelle area, and, on November 24th, it moved to Point Sec Bois, and the following day to Steenbecque, the Division being then in Corps reserve. The Battalion strength on November 30th was 32 officers and 565 other ranks. A period of rest and training followed, during which the Battalion took part in Divisional manœuvres. Christmas, 1915, and New Year, 1916, passed without any special mention being made in the Diaries. The weather was wet, and conditions, even in Corps reserve, were not good.

On January 4th the Battalion, having previously received orders to join the 154th Brigade, 51st (Highland) Division, was inspected by Major-General H. Hudson, C.I.E., commanding the 8th Division, who complimented all ranks on their work whilst under his command. The same day, and at the same place—Steenbecque—the III Corps Commander, General Pulteney, also inspected the 5th and said " Good-bye."

In General Hudson's farewell address to the Battalion he referred in glowing terms to the work it had done during its service with his Division, and cordially thanked all ranks for their cheerful response to all demands made upon them. It was with many regrets that the Battalion left the 8th Division, tempered, however, with a certain amount of satisfaction that it was joining the 51st (Highland) Division, in the ranks of which it had many friends.

On January 6th the 5th left Steenbecque and, entrained at Thiennes, arrived at Lonseau, near Amiens, that evening and marched to Coisy, where it joined the 154th Brigade, 51st (Highland) Division—Major-General G. M. Harper, C.B., D.S.O.—the other battalions in the Brigade being the 4th Black Watch, 4th Seaforth Highlanders and 4th Cameron Highlanders. The Brigade was commanded by a Regular Black Watch officer, Brigadier-General Charles Edward Stewart, C.M.G., who had come direct from the command of the 1st Battalion.

At this time the 51st Division was in the I Corps reserve, training and reorganizing. Shortly after the arrival of the Battalion Lieutenant-Colonel Blair-Imrie resumed command, and the 5th was inspected by General Allenby, the Corps Commander, who congratulated the Battalion on the state of its transport. The majority of the horses were those that had accompanied the

THE FIFTH BATTALION THE BLACK WATCH

Battalion from Scotland, and the Corps Commander spoke very highly of the horse-mastership of the Transport Officer, Lieutenant Kitson, and Sergeant Spence. In point of fact, no requisition for replacements had been made since the Battalion arrived in France, a record few units could show after fourteen months' war service, and in spite of the fact that the Battalion had considerably more animals of the heavy draught type than it was entitled to by Regulation. At the 8th Division Horse Show held in September, 1915, at Estaires, the 5th carried off the championship for heavy draught horses, after a very keen competition with the shire horses of the Divisional Train and R.A.S.C., the winning animal being a Clydesdale horse of Montraive (Fife) breeding. The 5th also won the championship for pack ponies with an animal that came from Invermark Deer Forest.

The 5th was not destined to remain long with the 51st Division, for, on February 25th, it proceeded by train to St. Omer and marched to Renescure, joining the 118th Brigade, 39th Division. Before this occurred, however, whilst at Coisy, the first break-up in the Battalion took place.

By this time it had been realized by higher authority that specially organized formations, consisting entirely of machine guns, were necessary, and in order to form these the trained machine gunners of battalions were transferred to the newly formed Machine Gun Corps. Thus it came about that most of the original machine gunners of the 5th, together with Lieutenant A. W. Duke, who was promoted Captain, and Sergeant Burnett, promoted Company Sergeant-Major, were posted to the 154th Machine Gun Company, in which they were joined by Lieutenant Mill and other machine gunners who came out with a draft from the Reserve Battalion.

Another, and a much more vital, change was contemplated, and definite instructions for this reached the Battalion towards the end of February. At this period of the war great difficulty was experienced in maintaining Territorial units at war strength, and, with a view of economizing man power and tending to greater efficiency, the Army Council decided that the amalgamation of certain Territorial battalions was necessary. It has already been pointed out that the 5th had experienced great difficulty in maintaining its strength throughout the latter part of 1915, and it was, therefore, not astonishing that the Battalion was one of those selected for amalgamation. In pursuance of this scheme, it was directed that the 4th and 5th Territorial Battalions would be merged into one unit as a war-time measure, and would be known as the 4/5th Battalion.

On March 7th the Battalion moved to La Belle Hôtesse, and on the 5th the amalgamation took place.

AMALGAMATION WITH FOURTH BATTALION, 1916

The amalgamation of the two battalions entailed a considerable amount of work and care, but it was most amicably carried out by both the 4th and 5th, and the newly formed unit came into being under the command of Lieutenant-Colonel G. A. McL. Sceales, D.S.O., Argyll and Sutherland Highlanders.

Under the amalgamation the 4/5th was composed of two reorganized companies from each battalion, the 4th Battalion forming A and B companies, and the 5th Battalion forming C and D companies. C company in the new battalion was formed from the officers, non-commissioned officers and men of Nos. 3 and 4 companies of the 5th, with Major J. Cruickshank in command and Captain T. Aubertin, Second-in-Command. The platoon commanders were Lieutenant J. Murray and Second Lieutenants J. Husband, J. Leslie and K. G. Yarrow, the Company Sergeant-Major being D. Burgess. D company was formed from Nos. 1 and 2 companies, with Captain T. Lyell, M.C., in command and Captain A. H. M. Wedderburn, Second-in-Command, the platoon officers being Lieutenants D. Guthrie, I. Bain, W. D. MacBeth and R. M. Ritchie, and J. Baird as Company Sergeant-Major. Captain J. Kennedy, D.S.O., M.C., was appointed Adjutant, and Lieutenant J. Paterson, Transport Officer.

The combined unit was posted to the 118th Infantry Brigade, 59th Division, which, less one brigade, had just arrived from home. The 118th was made up entirely of Territorial units withdrawn from other formations, and comprised the 1/1st Hertfordshire Regiment, 1/6th Battalion Cheshire Regiment, 1/1st Cambridgeshire Regiment and the 4/5th The Black Watch.

After the amalgamation the balance of personnel from both the 4th and 5th, when the new Battalion had been completed to war strength, proceeded to Etaples and Boulogne under Lieutenant-Colonel Blair-Imrie, there to form a Base Depot for the purpose of receiving drafts from home, and for testing and completing any training found necessary before despatching them as reinforcements to the Battalion in the front line.

So ends the story of the 5th Battalion The Black Watch as a separate unit; the remainder of its history and its deeds will be found in the account of the 4/5th Battalion given in the subsequent chapters of this volume.

APPENDIX I

Record of Officers' Services

Abbreviations :—" K."—Killed.   " D. of W."—Died of Wounds.
" W."—Wounded.

THE FIFTH (ANGUS AND DUNDEE) BATTALION

Adam, G. M. 2nd Lieut. With Battn. Nov., 1914. *w.* 7th Dec., 1914. To Base (Boulogne) 6th April, 1915.

Arbuthnott, H. R. C. Capt. Joined 25th Dec., 1914. *w.* 10th March, 1915.

Aubertin, T. Capt. Joined 11th Nov., 1914. *w.* 9th May, 1914. Rejoined 7th Oct., 1915. Joined 4/5th (Composite) Battn. 15th March, 1916.

Bain, I. McP. 2nd Lieut. Joined 22nd March, 1915. Joined 4/5th Battn. 15th March, 1916. To hospital sick February, 1917.

Barrie, W. C. O. 2nd Lieut. Joined 1st Nov., 1914. *w.* 4th Dec., 1914. (At duty.) *w.* 5th June, 1915.

Bowes-Lyon, G. F. Capt. Went out with Battn. To hospital sick 15th Dec., 1914.

Bowes-Lyon, J. H. Hon. 2nd Lieut. With Battn. Nov., 1914. *w.* 9th May, 1915.

Bruce, L. 2nd Lieut. With Battn. Nov., 1914.

Bruce, R. F. D. Lieut. Joined 1st Nov., 1914. Sick 10th Jan., 1915 to 26th March, 1915. *w.* 9th May, 1915. Rejoined 13th July, 1915. With 9th Battn. 30th June, 1916, to 15th Sept., 1916. Sick to U.K. 15th Sept., 1916. Promoted Capt. 1st June, 1916.

Bruce-Gardyne, I. M. Lieut. With Battn. Nov., 1914. Mentioned in Despatches 22nd June, 1915. Awarded M.C. 23rd June, 1915. Promoted Lieut. 2nd Nov., 1914. Capt. 19th July, 1915. To 24th Infantry Bde. Headquarters 25th Sept., 1915.

Campbell, J. H. 2nd Lieut. With Battn. Nov., 1914. Left for U.K. Feb., 1915.

Clark, J. M. Capt. C.F. Joined 15th Sept., 1915.

Coats, J. D. O. 2nd Lieut. With Battn. Nov., 1914. Left Battn. (No record when left Battn. in Mesopotamia, 1918.)

Coutts, F. Capt. With Battn, Nov., 1914. Promoted Major 22nd April, 1916.

Cruickshank, J. Capt. With Battn. Nov., 1914. Joined 4/5th (Composite) Battn. 15th March, 1916.

Dickie, A. D. Lieut. With Battn. Nov., 1914. *w.* 9th May, 1915.

Dickson, J. F. Capt. With Battn. Nov., 1914. Transferred to U.K. 30th May, 1915.

Duke, A. W. Lieut. With Battn. Nov., 1914. *w.* 9th May, 1915. Rejoined Battn. 7th Oct., 1915.

Duke, McP. S. J. Lieut. With Battn. Nov., 1914. *w.* 10th March, 1915. Rejoined Battn. 26th July, 1915.

Duncan, J. D. Capt. With Battn. Nov., 1914. To Base (Boulogne) 6th April, 1915.

THE FIFTH BATTALION THE BLACK WATCH

Elgood, L. A. 2nd Lieut. With Battn. Nov., 1914. Mentioned in Despatches 22nd June, 1915. Awarded M.C. 10th July, 1915. O.B.E. 3rd June, 1919. Mentioned in Despatches 9th July, 1919. Promoted Lieut. 9th April, 1915. Capt. 5th Sept., 1917.

Forsyth, J. C. 2nd Lieut. Joined 30th Aug., 1915.

Glamis, Lord. Major. With Battn. Nov., 1914. *w.* 29th Jan., 1915.
Gordon, J. W. N. Lieut. With Battn. Nov., 1914. *k.* 22nd Jan., 1915.
Grant, G. A. 2nd Lieut. Joined 28th April, 1915. To U.K. sick 25th Sept., 1915. Awarded M.C. 18th Jan., 1916.
Grant, H. A. Capt. Joined 12th March, 1915. Joined 9th Battn. 16th June, 1916.
Guthrie, D. S. 2nd Lieut. Joined 13th July, 1915. Joined 4/5th (Composite) Battn. 15th March, 1916.
Guthrie, T. M. Capt. With Battn. Nov., 1914. With 4th (Reserve) Battn. 30th Oct., 1917.

Hall, A. Lieut. and Q.M. Joined XIII Corps Cyclist Battn. (no date given in Diaries).
Handyside, A. 2nd Lieut. Joined 26th July, 1915. Joined 9th Battn. 6th June, 1916.
Husband, J. W. 2nd Lieut. Joined 28th Aug., 1915. Joined 4/5th (Composite) Battn. 15th March, 1916.

Imrie Blair, H. F. Major. With Battn. Nov., 1914. Mentioned in Despatches 22nd June, 1915. Awarded C.M.G. 23rd June, 1915. Transferred to U.K. 2nd Nov., 1915. Rejoined Battn 24th Feb., 1918.

Kennedy, J 2nd Lieut. Joined Battn. 24th April, 1915. Promoted Capt. To hospital accidentally injured 2nd Sept., 1915. Rejoined Battn. 24th Feb., 1916. Joined 4/5th (Composite) Battn. 15th March, 1916.
Kitson, F. N. E. 2nd Lieut. With Battn. Nov., 1914. *w.* 12th March, 1915.

Laird, A. C. 2nd Lieut. Joined Battn. Feb., 1916. Joined 4/5th (Composite) Battn. 15th March, 1916.
Leslie, R. M. 2nd Lieut. With Battn. Nov., 1914. To No. 2 Training Camp March, 1915.
Lyell, T. Capt. With Battn. Nov., 1914. *w.* 1st Dec., 1914. To U.K. 7th July, 1915. Rejoined Battn. 1st March, 1916. Joined 4/5th Battn. 15th March, 1915.

MacBeth, W. D. 2nd Lieut. Joined 13th July, 1915. Joined 4/5th (Composite) Battn. 15th March, 1915.
McCabe, H. R. Lieut. With Battn. Nov., 1914. *w.* 9th May, 1915.
McIntyre, W. 2nd Lieut. Joined 13th July, 1918. Transferred to 1st Battn. 16th June, 1916.
McNab, J. B. Capt. With Battn. Nov., 1914. To U.K. 28th December, 1915. Mentioned in Despatches 1st Jan., 1916.
McPherson, R. S. L. Capt. Joined 22nd March, 1915.

APPENDIX I

Mill, R. C. K. 2nd Lieut. Joined Jan., 1916. Transferred to 154th Bde. M.G.C. 14th Jan., 1916. Joined 4/5th (Composite) Battn. 15th March, 1916.

Millar, R. H. Major. Joined 31st Oct., 1915. Assumed Command of Battn. 2nd Nov., 1915. Promoted Lieut.-Col. Transferred to U.K. 24th Feb., 1916.

Milne, F. W. Lieut. R.A.M.C. Joined 27th March, 1915. To No. 18 General Hospital 3rd Aug., 1915.

Mitchell, W. L. Capt. With Battn. Nov., 1914. To 8th Div. Signal Coy. 7th Oct., 1915.

Moffat, J. A. Capt. Joined 26th July, 1915. Transferred to U.K. 17th Nov., 1915.

Murray, J. Lieut. With Battn. 1914. Joined 4/5th (Composite) Battn. 15th March, 1916.

Nicoll, P. S. Major. With Battn. Nov., 1914.

Paterson, I. S. 2nd Lieut. Joined 13th July, 1915. Joined 4/5th (Composite) Battn. 15th March, 1916.

Quekett, H. S. 2nd Lieut. With Battn. Nov., 1914. *w.* 9th May, 1915.

Rae, G. S. Capt. Joined Battn. 15th April, 1915.
Ritchie, R. M. 2nd Lieut. Joined 31st March, 1915. *w.* 9th May, 1915. Rejoined Battn. 29th Jan., 1916. Joined 4/5th (Composite) Battn. 15th March, 1916.

Taylor, N. R. Lieut. Joined 25th Dec., 1914.
Thompson, G. Capt. C. F. Left Battn. for U.K. 15th Sept., 1915.
Thornton, R. Major. R.A.M.C. Joined 8th Aug., 1915.

Vaughan, C. S. C. Lieut. Joined 29th Jan., 1916. To U.K. sick, Oct., 1916.

Watt, A. L. Capt. With Battn. Nov., 1914. *k.* 10th March, 1915.
Wedderburn, A. H. M. Capt. Went out with Battn. Nov., 1914. *w.* 15th Feb., 1915. Rejoined 23rd July, 1915. To 4/5th Battn. 16th March, 1916.
Wedderburn, H. S. Succeeded to command of 5th Battn. in Sept., 1909; to France with the Battn. Nov. 1914. Invalided home Jan. 1915.
Whyte. Major. To hospital sick 27th March, 1915.
Wilkie, G. S. M. 2nd Lieut. Joined 13th July, 1915. *w.* 2nd Aug., 1915. *d. of w.* 4th Aug., 1915.
Wilson, J. A. Capt. With Battn. Nov., 1914. *w.* 12th March, 1915.
Wilson, W. Capt. With Battn. Nov., 1914.

Yarrow, K. G. 2nd Lieut. Joined 13th July, 1915.

APPENDIX II

Summary of Casualties. The Fifth Battalion

The discrepancy between these figures and those given by the war diaries is accounted for by the fact that, save in the case of regular battalions, the diaries seldom give a record of casualties other than those suffered in main actions.

OFFICERS

Killed.	Wounded.	Missing.	Prisoners.	Total.
36	16	—	—	52

OTHER RANKS

Killed.	Wounded.	Missing.	Prisoners.	Total.
247	239	—	—	486

OFFICERS, 1914–18

Year.	Killed. D. of wounds. D. on service.	Wounded.	Missing.	Total.	Year.
1914	—	3	—	3	1914
1915	3	13	—	16	1915
Totals:	3	16	—	19	

OTHER RANKS, 1914–18

Year.	Killed. D. of wounds. D. on service.	Wounded.	Missing.	Total.	Year.
1914	—	1	—	1	1914
1915	36	190	1	227	1915
Totals:	36	191	1	228	

TOTAL:

Officers, 19.   Other Ranks, 228.

Note.—The *Red Hackle* gives the number as being 19 officers, 329 other ranks.

APPENDIX III

Casualties—Officers

* Killed in action.   † Died of wounds.   § Died.

THE FIFTH BATTALION

Name.	Rank.	Date.
Anderson, W. K.	A/Capt.	*22.7.18.
Barr, J. W.	2nd Lieut.	*24.3.18.
Barrie, W. C. O.	Lieut.	*14.10.16.
Begg, W.	2nd Lieut.	*13.11.16.
Bell, W.	2nd Lieut.	*3.5.17.
Blair, A. N.	Lieut.	§13.3.17.
Brown, A.	Capt.	†21.4.18.
Butler, C. H.	2nd Lieut.	*23.4.17.
Cumming, G.	2nd Lieut.	*21.3.18.
Don, T. D.	2nd Lieut.	*21.7.18.
Dunn, M.	2nd Lieut.	*16.5.17.
Gordon, J. W. N.	Lieut.	*22.2.15.
Grassie, J. A. A.	2nd Lieut.	*21.3.18.
Hollis, B.	Lieut.	*31.7.17.
Johnstone, R. J. L.	Lieut.	*26.9.17.
Kitson, F. N. E.	Lieut.	†15.8.17.
Laird, A. C.	2nd Lieut.	*22.11.16.
Leitham, H. W.	2nd Lieut.	†17.10.18.
Leslie, G. C.	Lieut.	†15.8.17.
MacBeth, W. D.	2nd Lieut.	*23.4.17.
Maxwell, D.	Capt.	†3.8.18. M.C.
McNicoll, G. R.	2nd Lieut.	*20.11.17.
Mill, R. C. K.	Lieut.	*3.9.16.
Nicoll, L. O.	2nd Lieut.	*26.9.17.
Paterson, I. S.	Lieut.	*1.11.17. M.C.
Quekett, J.	2nd Lieut.	*31.7.17.
Renny, J.	2nd Lieut.	*26.9.17.
Sim, W. G.	2nd Lieut.	*14.10.18.
Stuart, J. O. G.	Capt.	*30.3.18. M.C.
Taylor, N. R.	Capt.	*3.5.17. M.C.
Watson, J. F.	2nd Lieut.	§22.1.16.
Watt, A. L.	Capt.	*10.3.15.
Whiteley, L.	Lieut.	*31.7.17. M.G.C.
Whyte, W.	Lieut.	*28.9.18.
Wilkie, D.	Major	*24.4.17.
Wilkie, J. S. McL.	2nd Lieut.	†4.8.15.

APPENDIX IV

NOMINAL ROLL OF WARRANT OFFICERS, NON-COMMISSIONED OFFICERS AND MEN KILLED IN ACTION OR DIED OF WOUNDS OR DISEASE IN THE GREAT WAR, 1914–18

* Killed in action.   † Died of wounds.   § Died.   ‡ Died at home.

THE FIFTH BATTALION

Name	Date	Name	Date
Adam, J. G., Pte., 2279	†14.3.15	Crawford, D., Pte., 843	§ 4.7.15
Addison, W., Cpl., 2559	* 3.9.16	Crawford, J., C.Q.M.S., 2312	†14.11.16
Alcorn, R., Pte., 1860	* 9.5.15	Cruickshanks, W., Pte., 1549	†15.10.16
Alexander, H., Pte., 240893	* 3.9.16	Culman, W., Pte., 3780	‡25.9.15
Allan, J., Pte., 240470	*27.5.18	Cunningham, P., Pte., 240413	* 3.9.16
Anderson, A., Pte., 2051	* 6.5.15		
Anderson, J., Pte., 2498	* 9.5.15	Davidson, J., Pte., 2025	*14.10.16
		Davidson, J., Cpl., 460	*14.10.16
Balfour, D., Pte., 1819	*10.3.15	Davie, A., Pte., 2329	* 3.9.16
Ballantine, D., Pte., 240490	*14.10.15	Dinnie, G., Pte., 3155	†13.9.16
Barker, W., Pte., 3187	†28.7.16	Donaldson, D., Pte., 2603	†11.5.15
Beaton, J., L/Cpl., 1273	* 9.5.15	Donaldson, G., Pte., 2668	* 8.3.15
Beattie, F., Cpl., 240743	*14.10.16	Doran, A., Pte., 2143	* 9.1.15
Beattie, J., Pte., 2626	* 2.1.17	Doyle, R., Pte., 3744	†16.10.16
Begg, A., Pte., 3177	*29.9.16	Duff, H., Pte., 240940	*14.10.16
Begg, C., Pte., 2186	† 9.9.15	Dunbar, A., Pte., 1777	* 3.9.16
Bell, G., Pte., 1980	* 6.12.14	Duncan, D., Pte., 3229	*14.10.16
Bissett, H., L/Cpl., 240198	*14.10.16	Duncan, H., Pte., 1597	* 1.11.14
Bowman, C., Pte., 2091	* 3.9.16	Duncan, J., Pte., 2331	* 3.9.16
Boyd, J., Pte., 2395	* 3.9.16	Duncan, J., Pte., 2646	*10.5.15
Brady, P., Pte., 3764	*14.10.16	Duncan, R., Pte., 240796	*14.10.16
Brand, A., Pte., 1762	† 5.9.16	Dundas, J., Pte., 2229	*10.3.15
Brand, D., Pte., 240165	*14.10.16	Dunn, W., Pte., 2062	* 8.3.15
Bremner, G., Pte., 1728	*22.4.16	Dunn, W., L/Cpl., 2196	†23.1.15
Bruce, A., Pte., 3506	*14.10.16	Dutch, G., Pte., 240361	*14.10.16
Bruce, W. A., Sgt., 2063	*20.6.15		
Burgess, R., Pte., 240912	*14.10.16	Edward, J., Pte., 1863	‡21.9.16
Burgess, S., Pte., 3182	§ 5.11.16	Evans, W., Pte., 1543	* 6.12.14
Butchart, J., Pte., 240842	*14.10.16		
		Fawns, D., Pte., 1694	† 6.2.15
Calder, A., Pte., 1766	* 8.2.15	Fenton, A., Pte., 1751	*23.7.16
Campbell, J., Pte., 1736	‡21.4.15	Ferguson, D., Pte., 4062	†16.11.16
Cargill, A., Pte., 240719	*14.10.16	Ferguson, J., L/Cpl., 240821	* 3.9.16
Cargill, D., L/Cpl., 2756	*14.11.16	Fitchett, J., Pte., 2098	§21.4.15
Cargill, J., Pte., 1148	†24.2.15	Fox, A., Pte., 2497	*23.10.16
Cargill, J., Pte., 240723	*14.10.16	Fraser, R., L/Cpl., 307	* 9.5.15
Cargill, W., Pte., 241026	* 3.9.16	Fraser, R., Pte., 240629	§24.5.18
Christie, H., Pte., 3771	*14.10.16		
Clark, C., Pte., 241017	* 3.9.16	Galloway, J., Pte., 240822	*14.10.16
Clark, W., Pte., 1348	* 5.2.15	Gibb, R., Pte., 241120	*14.10.16
Cömitz, J., Pte., 1486	* 9.5.15	Gill, R., Pte., 241112	*14.10.6
Conning, W., L/Cpl., 804	*16.6.16	Glen, A., Pte., 3254	†16.10.16
Coupar, F., Cpl., 241322	*14.10.16	Gordan, A., L/Cpl., 2281	†15.10.16
Coutts, W., Pte., 1631	* 9.5.15	Gordon, J., Pte., 1557	* 9.5.15
Cowans, P., Pte., 3778	*14.10.16	Gordon, W., Pte., 2246	*14.10.16
Craig, G., Pte., 241095	* 3.9.16	Gourlay, W., L/Cpl., 3283	†14.10.16
Crawford, C., Pte., 3756	*21.9.16	Gove, W., Pte., 3259	*30.7.16

APPENDIX IV

Grant, A., Pte., 1458	*14.10.16	McLaren, H., Pte., 2790	* 3.9.16
Gray, A. M., Pte., 3502	*12.10.16	Mackie, J., Pte., 3295	* 3.9.16
Grewar, S., Pte., 240874	* 3.9.16	McLeish, G., Pte., 1672	†19.5.15
Guthrie, D., Pte., 457	*14.10.16	Marchbank, W., Pte., 240857	* 3.9.16
		Martin, A., Pte., 1008	*21.2.15
Hagan, J., Cpl., 34	†10.5.15	Martin, D., Sgt., 240174	* 3.9.16
Hannay, G., Pte., 1973	* 3.9.16	Martin, D. C., Cpl., 241085	*26.3.17
Hardie, A., Pte., 1705	*13.3.15	Maxwell, J., Pte., 1369	* 9.5.15
Harris, J., Sgt., 2176	† 9.1.17	Meekham, J., Pte., 3030	* 3.9.16
Howie, A., Pte., 1568	*10.3.15	Meldrum, G., Pte., 240446	* 7.9.16
Howie, J., Pte., 3794	†31.10.16	Melville, W., Pte., 1499	*10.3.15
Hutchison, G., Pte., 467	*10.10.16	Miller, G. E., A/Sgt., 2309	* 9.5.15
Hutchison, H., Pte., 1959	†10.5.15	Miller, W. E., L/Cpl., 630	† 6.8.16
Hutchison, J., Pte., 821	* 9.5.15	Milne, A., Pte., 2618	†23.8.16
		Milne, J., Pte., 1756	*14.10.16
Irvine, T., Pte., 573	†12.6.15	Milne, J., L/Cpl., 2014	* 9.5.15
		Milne, J., Pte., 2657	*9.5.15
Jack, J., A/Sgt., 240152	*14.10.16	Milne, J., Pte., 3298	*12.10.16
Jack, R. L. I., Pte., 2029	†13.2.15	Mitchell, A. B., Pte., 3217	* 3.9.16
Jack, W. D., Pte., 2319	† 7.3.16	Mitchell, C., Pte., 1654	*6.12.14
Johnstone, H., Pte., 1879	*28.12.14	Mitchell, J., Pte., 241125	*14.10.16
		Moir, C., Sgt., 2633	*23.10.16
Keen, W., Cpl., 2406 (M.M.)	*30.7.16	Moonie, C., Pte., 2499	* 9.5.15
Keillor, J., Pte., 3201	* 7.9.16	Morris, J., Pte., 2215	*23.7.16
Kilcullan, T., Pte., 1707	*27.3.15	Mostyn, P., Pte., 1989	* 9.5.15
Kydd, D., Pte., 2181	*25.8.15	Mowat, G., Pte., 240726	* 3.9.16
Kydd, J., Pte., 2875	† 7.8.16	Mugg, R., Pte., 3318	*23.10.16
		Muir, D., Pte., 2580	* 9.5.15
Laird, J., Sgt., 240218	* 3.9.16	Mundin, D. S., Pte., 240971	*14.10.16
Lamb, D., Pte., 2162	†15.3.15	Murray, C., Pte., 2121	*11.2.15
Lamond, W., Pte., 2425	*29.1.15	Murray, D., Pte., 2292	* 3.9.16
Lauder, G., Pte., 2262	† 4.3.15	Murray, J. K., Pte., 1501	† 5.1.15
Law, J., Pte., 2013	‡28.3.15		
Lindsay, J., Pte., 766	* 9.5.15	Nairn, J., Pte., 240972	*14.10.16
Lindsay, P., Pte., 2393	§ 8.6.15	Ness, A., Pte., 825	* 9.3.15
Louran, J., Pte., 968	*30.7.16		
Lowe, D., Pte.,1036 (M.M.)	†17.11.16	O'Brien, E., Sgt., 2407	*14.10.16
Lundie, J., Pte., 1657	* 3.9.16	Old, H., Pte., 2534	*30.7.16
Lyall, D. C., Pte., 3633	‡23.10.16	Ormond, J., Pte., 1632	†12.3.15
Lyell, G., Cpl., 3256	*14.10.16		
Lynch, J., Pte., 240343	*23.10.16	Park, J., Pte., 240853	*30.7.16
		Parker, B., Pte., 15	† 7.9.15
Macgregor, G., Pte., 1254	*11.3.15	Paton, W. D., Pte., 241238	*14.10.16
Macgregor, T., Pte., 2155	*31.1.15	Patrick, R. S., Pte., 241236	*14.10.16
McAulay, J., Pte., 2535	*12.1.17	Paul, A., Pte., 3365	§15.8.16
McCulloch, J., Pte., 241231	*14.10.16	Payne, W., Pte., 1237	*11.3.15
McCulloch, T., Pte., 3807	†17.10.16	Peters, J., Pte., 3377	‡15.10.16
McDonald, B., Pte., 3037	†19.2.18	Petrie, A., Pte., 240696	*14.10.16
McDonald, J., Pte., 240820	* 3.9.16	Pyott, J., Sgt., 447	†15.11.16
McGregor, J., Pte., 1920	†30.12.16		
McKenzie, W., Pte., 2077	*11.2.15	Rae, R., Pte., 1960	*25.9.15
McKinnes, H., Pte., 241229	†14.10.16	Ramsay, R., Sgt., 240332	‡22.7.17
McKinnon, J., Pte., 2516	* 1.9.16	Rankine, G. F., Sgt., 812	†10.5.15
McLagan, M. W., Pte., 241230		Rattray, A., Sgt., 1427	* 9.5.15
	*14.10.16	Rattray, A., Pte., 2789	†14.11.16

59

THE FIFTH BATTALION THE BLACK WATCH

Rea, W., L/Sgt., 240861	* 3.9.16	Stewart, R., Pte., 2459	† 4.5.15
Reid, F. F., L/Cpl., 406	*13.3.15	Strachan, P., L/Sgt., 557	† 8.5.15
Reid, J., Pte., 2210	†13.4.15	Strachan, R., L/Cpl., 240664	*14.10.16
Robert, J. L., Pte., 1779	*14.10.16	Syme, W., Pte., 3841	*14.10.16
Robertson, H., Pte., 3478	*13.11.16		
Robertson, J., Pte., 2227	*14.10.16	Tait, R., Pte., 240817	* 3.9.16
Robertson, J., Pte., 240781	* 3.9.16	Taylor, G., Pte., 3580	* 9.11.16
Robertson, J. T., Pte., 2426	*30.7.16	Taylor, J., Pte., 1941 (M.M.)	*30.7.16
Robertson, R., Pte., 3818	*21.9.16	Thomson, A., Pte., 3454	‡22.1.16
Robertson, R., Pte., 1651	*14.10.16	Thomson, E., Cpl., 2265	†12.3.15
Ross, G., Pte., 2271	† 8.5.15	Thomson, F., Pte., 3526	‡25.10.16
		Thomson, J., L/Cpl., 240753	*14.10.16
Savage, H., Pte., 2230	* 5.2.15	Thomson, R., Pte., 3341	* 3.9.16
Scott, F. S., Pte., 1537	* 1.3.15	Thornton, R., Pte., 2750	* 7.9.16
Scott, W., Pte., 2391	† 8.9.16	Thwaites, C. B., Pte., 3833	*29.9.16
Shepherd, W., Pte., 2374	*11.3.15	Toner, E., Pte., 1525	*24.7.16
Sheridan, J., Pte., 1353	*23.7.15		
Simpson, A., Pte., 747	* 2.8.16	Walker, W., L/Cpl., 1968	†21.9.16
Simpson, A., Sgt., 1562	* 3.9.16	Walker, W., Pte., 3417	*11.9.16
Simpson, K., Pte., 785	* 9.5.15	Wallace, A., Pte., 1885	† 9.5.15
Skea, W., Pte., 2166	†21.3.15	Wallace, W., Pte., 2983	†15.10.16
Smith, A., Pte., 2485	*13.3.15	Webster, J., Sgt., 1214 (D.C.M.)	* 1.11.14
Smith, D., Sgt., 820	†23.6.16	Weir, C., Pte., 2282	*14.10.16
Smith, H., Pte., 2884	* 3.9.16	White, R., Pte., 677	* 9.5.15
Smith, H., Pte., 3570	*17.8.16	Whyte, J., Pte., 2102	* 3.9.16
Smith, J., Pte., 918	† 6.2.15	Wilson, D., Pte., 1607	†24.2.15
Smith, N., Pte., 2370	†11.4.15	Wilson, R., Pte., 3206	* 3.9.16
Smith, W., L/Sgt., 2276	*12.1.17	Wright, D., Pte., 2818	† 8.9.16
Smith, W. L., Pte., 3419	* 3.9.16		
Snowball, B., Cpl., 2310	* 9.5.15	Young, W., Pte., 2323	†10.5.15
Speirs, A., Pte., 1656	* 9.5.17	Young, W. B., Pte., 240812	*14.10.16
Spink, H., Pte., 2605	* 9.5.15		
Stewart, J., Pte., 2691	* 3.9.16		

APPENDIX V

HONOURS AND AWARDS

The Fifth Battalion

C.M.G.
Major H. F. Blair-Imrie.

M.C.
R.S.M. J. Baird.
Lieut. I. M. Bruce-Gardyne.
2nd Lieut. L. A. Elgood.
2nd Lieut. G. A. Grant.

Bar to D.C.M.
C.S.M. W. Stewart.

D.C.M.
L/Cpl. G. Anderson.
L/Cpl. J. Anderson.
Sgt. M. G. Beverley.
Sgt. A. Christie.
Pte. J. Davidson.
Sgt. W. Finlay.
Pte. R. Graham.
C.S.M. J. Marnie.
Sgt. G. G. McFarlane.
Sgt. S. S. B. Milne.
Pte. T. Myles.
Pte. J. Nicoll.
C.S.M. Pattison.
C.S.M. J. A. Pattison.
C/Sgt. C. S. Reid.
Pte. D. Smart.
C.S.M. W. Stewart.
L/Cpl. G. Watson.
Sgt. J. Webster.
Sgt. W. Webster.

Bar to M.M.
Pte. A. Bennet.
Pte. A. Drury.
Pte. A. Leuchars.

M.M.
L/Cpl. J. Beattie.
Pte. A. Bennet.
L/Cpl. H. R. Brown.
Sgt. W. Byars.

THE FIFTH BATTALION THE BLACK WATCH

M.M.

A/Cpl. J. Cairns.
L/Cpl. J. Cassidy.
Pte. T. Cattro.
Pte. W. R. F. Deas.
Pte. A. Drury.
Pte. C. Duncan.
Pte. S. Easton.
Pte. A. Ferrier.
L/Cpl. W. Galgetty.
Sgt. J. Gibb.
Cpl. J. Gordon.
Pte. G. Gouk.
Cpl. C. Graham.
Sgt. G. Guthrie.
A/Sgt. J. Harris.
Pte. W. High.
L/Cpl. C. L. Horne.
Pte. J. Hutcheson.
Pte. R. S. Hutcheson.
L/Cpl. M. Jamie.
Pte. J. Jolly.
Pte. F. Kelly.
Pte. A. Leuchars.
Pte. D. Lowe.
Sgt. R. Martin.
Cpl. P. McGovern.
Pte. W. McPherson.
Sgt. W. Munro.
Sgt. W. Murray.
Cpl. W. Nicol.
Pte. C. Petrie.
Sgt. W. Porter.
L/Cpl. W. Ramsay.
Pte. A. Redford.
C/Sgt. J. Reid.
Pte. G. Shepherd.
L/Sgt. J. Shepherd.
Pte. D. Smart.
Sgt. G. Soutar.
Sgt. J. Stephen.
C.S.M. W. Stewart.
L/Cpl. J. Taylor.
Pte. G. Turnbull.
L/Cpl. G. Watson.
L/Cpl. J. Watson.
Cpl. W. Watson.
Pte. D. Yarrow.
Pte. A. Young.

APPENDIX V

Mentioned in Despatches
Major H. F. Blair-Imrie.
Capt. J. B. McNab.
Lieut. I. M. Bruce-Gardyne.
2nd Lieut. L. A. Elgood.

C.S.M. D. Burgess.
Pte. J. Davidson.
Pte. A. Ferrier.
Pte. W. High.
Pte. A. Howie.
Sgt. J. Laird.
C.S.M. J. A. Pattison.
Pte. A. Redford.
Pte. D. Smart.
L/Cpl. J. Taylor.
Sgt. H. J. Y. Tevendale.

FOREIGN DECORATION
Cross of St. George
L/Cpl. G. Anderson.

APPENDIX VI

List of Actions and Operations

The Fifth Battalion

1914.   Landed in France. 2nd November.
  Trench warfare. Estaires, Neuve Chapelle. November–December.

1915.   Trench warfare. Neuve Chapelle. January–March.

  BATTLE OF NEUVE CHAPELLE. 10th March.
  Trench warfare. La Gorgue, La Boutillerie.

  BATTLE OF AUBERS RIDGE. 9th May.
  Trench warfare. Wangerie, Neuve Chapelle. May–September.

  BATTLE OF LOOS. 25th September.
  Trench warfare. Convent Wall, Neuve Chapelle. October–December, 1915.

1916.   Trench warfare. January–March.
  Amalgamated with 4th Battalion. March, 1916.

THE FOURTH-FIFTH BATTALION

CHAPTER I

FROM THE AMALGAMATION OF THE TWO BATTALIONS IN
MARCH, 1916, TO NOVEMBER, 1916

*The Trenches near Festubert—The Fighting
on the Somme*

EARLY in 1916, owing to the difficulty in raising a sufficient number of men to maintain the Territorial units up to fighting strength, it was decided to amalgamate certain Territorial battalions, amongst them being the 4th and 5th Territorial Battalions The Black Watch.

In order to carry out the amalgamation both Battalions proceeded to La Belle Hôtesse on March 7th, and here by the 15th it had been completed and the 4/5th Battalion was formed under the command of Lieutenant-Colonel Sceales. It was no light task which rested upon the Commanding Officer's shoulders, but, possessing as he did those qualities which make a successful leader, he carried the amalgamation through with brilliant success. A and B companies of the 4/5th were formed from the 4th, and C and D were made up from the sister Battalion.

The following is a list of the officers who were transferred to the new Battalion, the remainder proceeding to the Base Camp on March 22nd.

Commanding Officer	Lieutenant-Colonel G. A. McL. Sceales.
Second-in-Command	Major J. B. Muir.
Adjutant	Captain J. Kennedy, M.C., D.C.M.
Bombing Officer	Lieutenant G. H. Scratton.
Signalling Officer	Lieutenant F. H. Currey.
Medical Officer	Major J. S. Y. Rogers.
A Company	Captain R. C. Cunningham, M.C.
	Captain E. Shepherd.
	Lieutenant F. H. H. Buchanan.
	Lieutenant R. A. Plimpton.
	Lieutenant E. C. Osborne.
	Second Lieutenant C. M. Gibson.
	Second Lieutenant W. A. Cox.
B Company	Captain T. Stevenson.
	Captain L. Watt.
	Lieutenant W. S. Robertson.
	Lieutenant Bethune-Duncan.
	Lieutenant T. F. Andrews.
	Second Lieutenant H. James.

FOURTH-FIFTH BATTALION THE BLACK WATCH

C Company	Major J. Cruickshank.
	Captain T. Aubertin.
	Lieutenant J. R. Murray.
	Second Lieutenant J. W. Husband.
	Second Lieutenant R. C. K. Mill.
	Second Lieutenant A. C. Laird.
D Company	Captain T. Lyell.
	Captain A. H. M. Wedderburn.
	Lieutenant I. McP. Bain.
	Second Lieutenant C. S. McCririck.
	Second Lieutenant M. W. Nicoll.
Transport Officer	Second Lieutenant I. S. Paterson.
Quartermaster	Hon. Lieutenant and Quartermaster McLachlan.
Chaplain	Rev. E. J. Hagan.

In March, 1916, a new Army Division, the 39th, arrived in France short of one brigade, and in order to complete it to strength and stiffen its ranks with experienced men it was decided to put a Territorial brigade into it. This, numbered 118th, under the command of Brigadier-General Bromielaw, was composed as follows: The 1/6th Battalion Cheshire Regiment from the 7th Division, the 4/5th Battalion The Black Watch from the 51st Division, the 1/1st Battalion Hertfordshire Regiment from the Guards Division and the 1/1st Cambridgeshire Regiment from the 27th Division.

On the 14th and 15th respectively the Battalion was inspected by the General Officer Commanding 39th Division and by the First Army Commander, moving on the 24th to Caudescure: strength, 37 officers and 1051 other ranks. A fortnight was spent here in organizing the new Battalion, and on April 4th it moved into the front line at Moated Grange in the sector just north of Neuve Chapelle.

The next five months were spent in this area, the Battalion being engaged in the usual trench warfare in the various parts of the Festubert, Givenchy and Richebourg-St. Vaast areas. The trenches and breastworks, especially those in the Givenchy sector, which was the most difficult one to hold, were not in good order. No Man's Land was a series of mine craters, along the edge of which ran the saps and trenches which were held as the front line. In this area there had been continuous heavy fighting since the earliest days of the war. In addition, the enemy were exceedingly active with rifle grenades and heavy trench mortars, and casualties in the Battalion were numerous.

Early in June the Adjutant, Captain Kennedy, left the Battalion to take command of the 13th Welch Regiment. Lieutenant

G. H. Scratton succeeded him, and about the same time Major Muir left to take command of a battalion of the Oxford and Buckinghamshire L.I.

On the night of the 17th of June a party of B company, under Lieutenants T. Andrews and H. James, carried out a highly-successful raid on the German trenches near La Basseé Canal. The scheme of attack was as follows: A heavy artillery barrage was to fall on the enemy front and support lines at a fixed hour; shortly after the barrage started a mine was to be exploded some distance away with the idea of attracting enemy attention from the area to be raided. Immediately after the mine went up, the barrage was to lift and the raiding party was then to rush in through the enemy wire, kill or capture as many as they could and return at a given time to their own lines.

Everything went off without a hitch, and the party returned with eight men wounded, and one German prisoner, in addition to which they claimed to have killed at least twenty. The arrangements for this raid were made by Captain T. Stevenson of B company. On the following day the Battalion was congratulated on its success by the Division and Corps Commanders, Lieutenant Andrews, later, being awarded the M.C.; whilst Private Low received the D.C.M. and Lance-Corporal Adam the Military Medal.

Just before this raid, on June 10th, the Battalion lost a valuable officer in Captain Watt of C company; he was badly wounded by a rifle grenade, and died in hospital in Bethune on the 20th.

On July 1st the great British offensive on the Somme began, its main object being to relieve the pressure on Verdun, where the Crown Prince's army was making a great attack on the French line. Again, as at Loos, there was much activity all along the British front in order to keep enemy troops pinned to their ground and prevent them reinforcing their attack further south. On the Festubert–Neuve Chapelle front the 116th Brigade, 39th Division, made a determined attack on the enemy line. Unfortunately this was a failure, in spite of the great gallantry of the Sussex battalions which composed the assaulting troops. The shelling was severe both at the time the Battalion was holding the line and also during the attack.

During the remainder of the month operations on the Division front were confined to heavy artillery bombardment of the German lines, to which the reply was feeble, possibly because the enemy had diverted his guns to the Somme front.

About this time rumours reached the Battalion that the Division would soon move south, and all ranks realized that it was only a matter of weeks before they would take part in the Somme battle. On August 9th, while the 4/5th were resting at Riez de Vinage, orders were received that the Division was to undergo special training, after which it would proceed to the Somme area, and two days later the Battalion moved, by march route, to Auchel, the first stage of its journey south. Moving by Magnicourt, the Battalion reached Bethonsart on the 13th, where the next ten days were spent in hard training and preparation for the coming attack. In addition to training, time was also found for company sports during the long summer evenings.

On August 23rd, Lieutenants Philip and Murray, together with two non-commissioned officers from each company, proceeded by motor bus to the Somme area in order to reconnoitre the front which the Battalion was to take over. On the same date the 4/5th marched to Guoy en Ternois; and on the following day to Lucheux, where it entered the V Corps, Fifth Army. On the 25th the Battalion reached Bus, and eventually arrived at its destination, Inglebelmer, ten miles behind the firing line, on the 26th. As a result of the constant hard training and marching it had done prior to the move the Battalion was hard and fit, and during these long and trying marches only ten men fell out.

At Inglebelmer, which was empty of civilians, the Battalion realized the heavy fighting in progress not far away. Gunfire was incessant, and the sky was lurid with constant flashes from exploding shells. The roads were crowded with transport, guns and limbers; while at night endless streams of pack animals carrying rations and ammunition left the village for the front area.

On the night of the 28th the 39th Division received their preliminary orders for an assault on the German positions opposite the village of Hamel in the valley of the Ancre, and the next few days were spent in preparing for the assault, issuing field dressings and extra ammunition and organizing carrying parties. On September 1st the strength of the Battalion was 30 officers and 1016 other ranks. In this fighting the 4/5th was attached to the 116th Brigade; the task of the Battalion was to clear and hold the ground between the Ancre and the Beaucourt road, its position being on the extreme right of the 39th Division front.

The Beaucourt–Hamel railway ran along the north-east bank of the Ancre, cutting British and German lines at right angles. This railway cut the centre of the Battalion front, the line itself giving the general direction of attack. The Battalion front was narrow, being only some fifty yards wide; it was joined on the left by a steep bluff running parallel to the railway, and on the right by the marshy ground on the north-east bank of the Ancre River.

On the night of September 2/3rd the Battalion moved up to its assembly position in the trenches, Giant's Causeway, Dollie's

ATTACK ON BEAUMONT HAMEL, SEPTEMBER, 1916

Brae and a trench close to the railway which connected the two. The congestion was great, but all difficulties were overcome and by midnight the Battalion was in position.

At dawn on the 3rd the attack was launched, A and C companies—Captains Cunningham and Rettie—leading the assault from Giant's Causeway. The advance was successful at first, and the three waves of A company reached their objective without difficulty, but when there they came under heavy machine gun fire and were compelled to withdraw about fifty yards and became mixed up with the company that followed. This caused some disorganization, added to which the company commander and his two second lieutenants became casualties, leaving only one officer, Second Lieutenant Edwards, with the company. About this time the 11th Battalion Royal Sussex Regiment was forced back, leaving the left of the 4/5th front exposed; but Second Lieutenant Edwards was able to bring forward a Lewis gun and so covered the retirement of the Sussex men and kept down the German fire until that Battalion again advanced.

In the meantime A and C companies, now reorganized into two waves, went forward again in conjunction with the Sussex men. By now it was broad daylight, and machine gun fire from some enemy dug-outs on the left and in front became very heavy, causing many casualties, and the line became somewhat disorganized in consequence.

It is difficult to say with certainty what point was reached during this advance, but it appears that the Battalion reached the German support line, where A and C companies dug themselves in, while B and D constructed a support line about fifty yards in rear. By this time Second Lieutenant Edwards was the sole surviving officer of the two forward companies and did exceedingly good work in reorganizing the line, posting Vickers and Lewis guns where they could be best used.

The Battalion remained in this position all day subjected to heavy trench-mortar and rifle grenade fire from the German support line and to sniping and machine gun fire from the farther side of the Ancre River. About 8 a.m. Captain Lyell, with the remainder of the reserve company D, sent one platoon up to the front German line, keeping the remainder in the old British front line.

About noon an order was received to retire; by this time the 4/5th were in a very precarious position owing to the attack by the troops on their left flank having broken down before the weight of hostile fire; still, outnumbered and isolated, the Battalion fought on until about 4 p.m., when the survivors withdrew to the old British line.

The fighting on this occasion was of a peculiarly grim and

determined nature, men on both sides firing point-blank at each other at twenty yards range. By the middle of the afternoon the railway gully, the only route by which wounded could be evacuated, was a death trap, and the Battalion stretcher bearers, particularly Privates Davidson and Smart, did most gallant service when rescuing the wounded, although constantly exposed to heavy fire.

During this fighting the 4/5th lost three officers killed, five wounded and two missing; 34 other ranks killed, 157 wounded and 17 missing. Many acts of gallantry were performed by men of the Battalion throughout the day, but perhaps none is more deserving of mention than that of Sergeant Laird of D company. Two platoons of his company had been sent forward to the front line by Colonel Sceales in the course of the forenoon, Sergeant Laird being platoon sergeant of one of them. Throughout the day this gallant non-commissioned officer led and encouraged his men under most trying conditions, exposing himself with utter disregard for his own safety while dragging wounded men to cover. Immediately before the withdrawal was ordered, Sergeant Laird, while carrying in a wounded officer, was hit himself for the second time, this time mortally. When the few men left in the Battalion withdrew down the railway gully, Laird's body was left behind, but was brought in two nights later by a patrol of B company.

The Roman Catholic padre, Northcote, rendered gallant aid to the stretcher bearers throughout the day. He took up his position in the most dangerous part of the railway gully, where he coolly succoured the wounded and comforted the dying until he himself was hit by a fragment of a shell. Fortunately, although he lost the sight of one eye, the wound did not prove fatal. Major Rogers, the Battalion medical officer, also did most gallant work assisted by Lance-Corporals McLiesh and Dick, and by dusk that evening he had dressed over 400 wounded men, having worked for fourteen hours under continuous and heavy shell fire. The 4/5th were relieved that night by a battalion of the Rifle Brigade, and, few in numbers, many of whom were wounded and all utterly exhausted, the Battalion returned to Inglebelmer, where it spent the next day.

On the night of the 5th, when the officers who had not taken part in the battle had come up, the Battalion took over the front line in the Hamel sector, remaining there until the 12th, when it went back to rest in Mailly Wood, some two miles behind Inglebelmer. While resting here, Major Rogers and Captain Lyell were sent down the line, and the Battalion received a draft from home, including some officers.

The brief breathing space the Battalion now enjoyed was much needed. The weather was glorious and the countryside

SCHWABEN REDOUBT, OCTOBER, 1916

well wooded and beautiful. By night and day the heavy artillery fire in front never slackened. Looking from the high ground above Mailly Wood towards the line at night, the whole horizon seemed to blaze with bursting shells, and it was easy to gauge from the intensity of the fire when infantry attacks were in progress.

The 4/5th went into the line again at Hébuterne on the 19th, where it remained for a week. This tour was uneventful. The trenches held by the Battalion lay on the high ground on the north-east side of the Ancre some half a mile north of Beaumont Hamel and commanded a splendid view of the Thiepval battle area on the other bank of the river. After relief on October 6th, the Battalion marched back to a rest-camp at Senlis, where it remained until the 10th, on which day it moved into the line in the Thiepval area.

At this period Colonel T. D. Murray joined the Battalion. Colonel Murray had seen much service in Egypt, where he had commanded a battalion of the Hampshire Regiment, but his heart had always been with his own Regiment, and at this, the first opportunity, Colonel Murray gladly reverted to the rank of Major in order to serve once more with a battalion of The Black Watch. He was first posted as Second-in-Command, but when Colonel Sceales left the Battalion in December, 1917, Colonel Murray succeeded him in command.

For three days the Battalion held the south face of Schwaben Redoubt, which portion of it had been captured a day or two before. In this sector the trenches were blown to pieces, and the shell-torn ground and numerous dead bore testimony to the severity of the recent fighting. The position was an exceedingly difficult one to hold, as the enemy occupied the north face of the Redoubt on the high ground and dominated the trenches held by the Battalion; in addition, the German shell fire was particularly heavy, which not only caused many casualties, but also made the work of bringing up rations and water exceedingly difficult. Great credit is due to the Quartermaster (McLachlan) and Sergeant Cruickshank for the way in which supplies were always brought up.

After two days' rest in shelters and dug-outs behind Thiepval Wood and one night spent in Senlis, the 4/5th moved into huts in Martinsart. On October 10th it moved again into the line preparatory to an attack on the north face of the Schwaben Redoubt, due to take place at 2 p.m. on the 14th.

The Thiepval Spur was the one portion of the high ground between the Somme and the Ancre which had successfully resisted capture since July 1st. Its defences consisted of two main portions—the cellars and dug-outs of Thiepval itself and the two redoubts, Schwaben and Stuff, on the crest of the ridge commanding the Ancre valley. On September 29th the 18th Division captured Thiepval village and the south face of the Schwaben Redoubt; Stuff Redoubt was captured on October 9th by the 25th Division, but an attack on the remainder of Schwaben the same day failed. From the British face of the Schwaben Redoubt two old German communication trenches, the Strassburg line, led to the valley of St. Pierre Divion on the west, and Lucky Way on the east, both trenches being much damaged by British artillery fire. Prisoners captured during the night of the 12th stated that the moral of the enemy troops holding the north face of the Redoubt was low, but, as far as the front attacked by the 4/5th was concerned, this proved wrong, the enemy being evidently determined to hold on to their positions at all cost.

The original orders laid down for the attack were that the Battalion should be drawn up in assembly trenches in columns of platoons in four lines, with fifty yards distance between platoons. Colonel Sceales, however, obtained permission, in the event of hostile shelling during the assembly, for platoons to close up on the leading waves and lie down in shell holes with five yards between platoons, opening out to intervals of fifty when the assault commenced.

The Battalion moved up to its assembly position in single file via Wood Post and Blighty Valley and, as a barrage was being put over the south face of the Redoubt, Colonel Sceales ordered Major G. F. Bowes-Lyon, who was in charge of the assembly, to close up the companies, and by so doing all casualties were avoided during the move. Zero hour was fixed for 2.46 p.m. The attack was made by B company on the right, C in the centre and D on the left, with A in close support.

The British barrage was punctual, and at Zero hour the assault commenced. From the start casualties were very heavy, especially among the officers. In the two leading waves these were partly caused by the British barrage, due to the eagerness of the men to go forward. Major Bowes-Lyon, Captain Moffat and Second Lieutenant Dickson were the only officers who reached the German lines unwounded. In addition to these losses many others were caused by the heavy rifle fire from the right, where the enemy exposed themselves above the parapet and fired on the advancing troops. These Germans, however, were soon forced to take cover by machine gun fire which was brought to bear on them by a team of the 118th Machine Gun company under Second Lieutenant T. F. Cunningham— a Black Watch officer—who took his gun out into No Man's Land and continued firing until he and most of his team became casualties, the gun itself being blown up at 3.50 p.m.

From the moment of entering the German trenches the com-

SCHWABEN REDOUBT, OCTOBER, 1916

panies got mixed up, and, owing to all the officers by that time having become casualties, it is somewhat difficult to say exactly what took place. It is known, however, that on the left the enemy put up slight resistance, many of them surrendering before the leading wave reached the trench. On the right, Major Bowes-Lyon, Second Lieutenant Dickson and Sergeant D. Hutton and 10 men of B company went well through the German line, killing a large number and making many prisoners. Finally, when Major Bowes-Lyon, Second Lieutenant Dickson and several of the men had been wounded, the party decided to return to its original objective.

During this movement Sergeant Hutton conducted himself with great gallantry, carrying in Major Bowes-Lyon and supervising the evacuation of the wounded, after which he, with the remaining men, joined a party of the Cambridgeshire Regiment and helped to bomb dug-outs in the north face of the Redoubt. In the centre the advance of C company was held up by barbed wire, and all the officers became casualties. On the left D company took its objective, Captain Moffat being wounded soon after reaching the German line.

At 7 o'clock that night two companies of the K.R.R.C. arrived in the front line to reinforce and help to consolidate the ground gained. At 10 p.m. Captain Millar, R.A.M.C., the Battalion medical officer, had gone round the front line and made arrangements for the collection and evacuation of the wounded, which had been impossible to complete before, owing to the front line and all its approaches being so heavily shelled.

At 10.50 p.m. orders were received to send up the reserve company to assist in holding the line, in conjunction with two K.R.R.C. companies. This move was carried out shortly afterwards, when the remaining men of the three assaulting companies—only thirty in all—were sent back to dug-outs in the south face of the Redoubt.

With the exception of a small enemy counter-attack early in the morning of the 15th no fighting took place, and the day was spent by the front line troops in improving their positions and completing the evacuation of the wounded. Shelling was continuous throughout the day and culminated with a very heavy barrage about 9 p.m., after which the enemy attacked in force against the extreme left of the line held by the 118th Brigade. This attack failed, the Germans retiring in disorder, but heavy shelling continued for an hour, then becoming desultory and, with the exception of an unsuccessful flammenwerfer attack at 1.25 a.m. on the 16th, nothing of note took place, and at 5 a.m. the front line troops were relieved by the 12th Battalion Sussex Regiment, the 4/5th moving to Wood Post on the main Authuile road, and a few hours later to Martinsart Wood.

The attack on the 14th was a soldier's battle. At the beginning of the fight nearly all the officers of the attacking companies were either killed or wounded, and it says much for the grit and endurance of the men that the 4/5th never wavered; it carried its attack forward with great gallantry and determination, hung on for hours under heavy German shell fire, repelled all enemy counter-attacks and, finally, having consolidated the captured position, handed it over intact to the relieving platoons of A company.

Where all did so well it would be invidious to single out the name of any individual man, yet mention must be made of the magnificent work rendered by the regimental stretcher bearers and runners; it was due to their devotion and self-sacrifice that the wounded were brought in and that the Commanding Officer was able to direct and control operations throughout the whole day.

An amusing story is told of one of the runners of the Battalion. He was rather a character, and inclined to be talkative. One wild, rainy night he put his head inside the dug-out where the Colonel was sitting. The dug-out was dripping wet and the floor ankle-deep in mud, while outside the German shells were falling quite close. With a sudden burst of confidence born, no doubt, of the rum ration, the runner, shaking his head sadly from side to side, said to the Commanding Officer, " Ye ken, sir, I'm sorry fur ye. I aye think ye must hae been accustomed tae something better at hame."

While at Martinsart Wood the Battalion received a draft of officers and men who were badly wanted to fill the ranks thinned by the recent fighting, in which it had lost four officers killed and nine wounded; 27 other ranks killed, 220 wounded and 30 missing—a total of 13 officers and 277 other ranks.

On the 22nd the 4/5th moved to the Bluffs and on the following day took over the captured trenches at Schwaben Redoubt. This tour was the worst so far experienced by the Battalion owing to the terrible weather conditions and heavy shelling, from which, in thirty-six hours, the 4/5th losses amounted to well over a hundred.

On the 25th the Battalion moved to Senlis and again into the line at Thiepval on the 29th, after which, on November 3rd, it moved to St. Authuille Bluffs, on the 8th again into the line on the River Ancre, and on the 12th it occupied the front line at Schwaben Redoubt in preparation for an attack the following day.

The fighting during these last six weeks was by far the most severe the 4/5th experienced in France. During this period the

ST. PIERRE DIVION, NOVEMBER, 1916

Battalion had been almost continuously in action; it had taken part in two frontal attacks, in each of which the losses suffered were very heavy, amounting to nearly 40 officers and over 1000 men.

About the beginning of November rumours that the Division was to go into rest were freely circulated, but, as usual, these proved false, for, on November 3rd, the Battalion moved up to dug-outs on the North Bluff, behind Thiepval Wood, in readiness for a coming attack on St. Pierre Divion. This operation had originally been intended to take place early in November, but the weather broke and heavy rain made the battle area impassable, with the result that it did not take place until the 13th. On this occasion the 4/5th was the left Battalion on the Division front, the River Ancre separating it from the Naval Division on its left.

The assault took place early in the morning of the 13th under cover of a thick mist which, although it somewhat hampered the movements of the British troops, also prevented the enemy from seeing the leading waves until the men were upon them. From the outset the attack was a complete success, and what was left of the village was soon captured. Little resistance was met with, probably due to the fact that the enemy were caught in the middle of a relief.

By 10 a.m. the 4/5th had captured the great tunnels at St. Pierre Divion together with many prisoners, and having taken all its objectives the Battalion spent the remainder of the day reorganizing, clearing dug-outs and evacuating prisoners and wounded. During the night of the 13th the 4/5th, together with a battalion of the Cambridgeshire Regiment, moved further forward and, under cover of a heavy barrage, dug in behind the "Hansa" line—the German third line.

Throughout the 14th the enemy shelled the new British line heavily and constantly, but did not make any counter-attack, and that night the Battalion was relieved and marched back to Warloy.

In the recent fighting the 4/5th had, once again, done well, and on this occasion its casualties were light—one officer killed and three wounded; eight other ranks killed, 124 wounded and 16 missing—a total of four officers and 148 other ranks.

From Warloy the Battalion moved to Candas, stopping one night at Vauchel, and there entrained for an unknown destination. The rumours of a move had materialized, but far from being to a "rest" area, the destination proved to be the "Sinister Salient"—Ypres.

CHAPTER II

NOVEMBER 19TH, 1916—JULY 31ST, 1917

Ypres: Holding the Line

THE 4/5th was destined to spend the next thirteen months in Flanders, mostly in or near the Ypres Salient. Arriving at Wormhoudt on the 19th, the remainder of November was spent there resting and training. The Division was now in the V Corps (Second Army), commanded by General Sir Aylmer Hunter-Weston, and never in its history had the Battalion met a General Officer who took a keener interest in all its affairs. No matter was so small, no affair apparently so trifling that it failed to arouse the interest and invite the inspection of the Corps Commander. The strain of continuous fighting during the past three months may have caused a certain easing in the surface discipline and order of the Battalion, and doubtless the energetic methods of the indefatigable Corps Commander made for efficiency; certainly no man in the whole corps worked harder or spared himself less than did its commander.

After ten days' rest at Wormhoudt the Battalion went into the support trenches at Boesinghe, near Elverdinge, on the extreme north of the Ypres Salient, where it relieved a French battalion, moving into the front line a few days later. At this point the British trenches ran along the southern bank of the Yser Canal, and those of the enemy were on the opposite bank. Apparently the sector had been a peaceful one when occupied by the French, judging from the way in which they had lived in wooden huts in the front line; but the 39th Division had not been in long before this changed, rifle grenades, trench-mortar bombs, etc., being showered on the enemy, who retaliated in kind.

About December 15th the 4/5th was relieved by a Battalion of the 38th Division and moved back to camp near Poperinghe, returning to the front line on Christmas Eve, the sector being that of Irish Farm, in the salient proper. The move was carried out after dark, the Battalion being taken by train to the Asylum just behind Ypres, whence it marched through the town via the canal bank to the front line.

This first march through the ruined city was one full of interest to both officers and men. Even in the darkness the ruins of what had been tall and stately houses could be made out, and the chaos and desolation of the whole city was most impressive. Fortunately that night enemy artillery fire was light, and the Battalion passed through the city without casualties.

The front line in the Irish Farm sector was in a shocking condition of disrepair and consisted only of breastworks, owing to the low-lying nature of the ground and the impossibility of digging deep without meeting water. The country had been so blasted with shell fire that for miles there was nothing to be seen but a brown lifeless plain marked by thousands of water-logged shell holes, the whole area being covered with grim traces of the countless fights which had taken place during the past two years. A and D companies were the first to occupy the front line, with C and B in support near La Brique, and after a week the latter went up, relieving A and D.

On the night of December 31st the enemy attempted to raid the line held by the 4/5th, but was driven off without difficulty, leaving one of their number behind as a prisoner. On this occasion the Battalion was prepared for the raid; for some days it had been noticed that the enemy was registering a "box barrage" on the 4/5th front, and this was taken by the Commanding Officer as an indication that a raid might take place. The Divisional artillery was warned, and for two nights the gunners stood to arms ready to give the Battalion heavy supporting fire if called on; each night Lewis guns were sent out into No Man's Land with the object of firing down the British wire, and it was also arranged that the support companies should reinforce the front line, moving over the open.

About 11 p.m. on New Year's night the German barrage came down in earnest and the S.O.S. signal went up from the Battalion front. Within a minute a terrific British artillery fire fell on the German front line opposite The Black Watch position, cutting off the enemy raiders' line of retreat. All these arrangements worked admirably, and it is not surprising that the enemy were beaten off easily, the Battalion loss being slight—one officer missing, four other ranks killed and 11 wounded, including Second Lieutenant Paul of C company, and Sergeant McLaughlan of B company.

Weather conditions in January, 1917, were appalling, heavy rain alternating with brief spells of frost, and in order to move about the water-logged trenches the men were issued with gum boots. These certainly kept out the wet, but were bad for the feet, with the result that there were many cases of trench feet in the Battalion. The question of rations and their transport to the front line was also a problem. The whole salient was overlooked by the enemy from one point or another, and it was impossible to light fires anywhere near the front line, at any rate, by daytime, with the result that food had to be cooked some way behind the line and brought up in containers, which might or might not keep it hot during the journey.

On the night of the 12th the Battalion, after a short rest on the canal bank, went into the line in the Potijze sector, the relief taking place under intense hostile shelling. Considering the crowded condition of the trenches, owing to the relief and to the fact that two companies were in the open on the Menin road during this bombardment, the casualties were surprisingly light. The 4/5th was relieved in the front line by the 6th Battalion Cheshire Regiment on the 18th and marched back to billets in the prison at Ypres, where officers and men occupied what had once been the cells. Though most of the roof of the main building had gone, the majority of these cells were intact and, on the whole, the prison made a good billet. While here a big draft of men from the Scottish Horse joined the Battalion—a splendid type of man. It was here, too, that Major Rogers, the medical officer, returned from sick leave and met with a great welcome from all ranks.

While the Battalion was occupying the prison the enemy shelled it heavily on the 24th, obtaining two direct hits by which two men were killed and three wounded. On the night of the 24th the 4/5th was relieved by the 16th Battalion K.R.R.C. and moved back by train to a camp near Vlamertinghe.

By this time all ranks had recovered from the hard times they had gone through on the Somme. The drafts from home had been exceedingly good, and the Battalion was still a Volunteer unit with no gaps in its ranks. As regards sport, the 4/5th had a fine football team and a magnificent pipe band, due mainly to the efforts of Pipe-Major McLeod and Drum-Major Low.

During one of the tours in Ypres prison the following amusing incident occurred. Lieutenant Murray's servant was acting batman for Major Murray, as the latter's servant was on leave. The servant in question unfortunately partook too freely of Headquarter's rum ration one morning and, falling downstairs, was being carried by stretcher bearers to the aid-post. Lieutenant Murray met the procession and, suspecting the cause of the injury, diverted it into the guard-room. While in the guard-room Major Murray sent over an orderly to ask the servant where his belt was. "Hi!" said the orderly, "Where's Major Murray's belt?" The dazed servant murmured sleepily, "Major Murray, Lieutenant Murray, Major Murray, Lieutenant Murray. There's far too many o' these . . . Murrays about!"

On February 4th the Battalion again took over the front line, this time in the Wieltje sector, and after a quiet tour in the line returned on the 9th to the Ypres prison. The weather by this time turned to hard frost, which lasted for nearly two months and added to the discomfort of the troops holding the front line.

On the 16th the 4/5th relieved the 6th Battalion Cheshire Regiment in the Potijze sector. Each time the Battalion went

TRENCH WARFARE NEAR YPRES, FEBRUARY, 1917

into the line it was noticed that the enemy shell fire had increased in violence since the last tour, and on this occasion the Battalion suffered severely from it, especially Battalion Headquarters. During this tour Lieutenant Milne and Sergeant Waugh one night not only entered the enemy front line, but explored it for some way without meeting any Germans. Apparently the enemy, fearing raids, held the line lightly at night.

On the 18th, when the Division was being relieved, the Germans put down a heavy barrage on all roads and communication trenches behind the British line. An inter-Divisional relief was in progress, and on each side of the Potijze–Ypres road stood long lines of waiting transport belonging to the two divisions concerned in the relief. Along the narrow space between these lines came the infantry in single file, and down on this mass of men and animals fell the German barrage; but, although the fire was exceedingly heavy, casualties were marvellously few.

After relief the Battalion occupied its old billets in the prison for a few days. This period was an exciting one. By some chance a battery of heavy guns occupied the prison courtyard, and the enemy were constantly engaged in trying to locate it with heavy shells, finally succeeding in getting a direct hit on one of the guns and landing another shell on the ammunition dump, scattering the contents all over the courtyard, but fortunately few shells exploded. A German shell also landed in the 4/5th guard-room, causing several casualties and killing the sentry.

On the 24th the Battalion was relieved by the 5th Battalion Lancashire Regiment and went back by train to " B " Camp near Poperinghe, where it remained until the 27th, when it marched to Montreal Camp and joined the X Corps under General Morland, the Battalion strength then being 33 officers and 716 other ranks.

The following week was spent in Montreal Camp, where the Battalion was inspected by the Corps Commander, who expressed himself well pleased with its turn-out. On March 3rd the 4/5th relieved the 13th Battalion Sussex Regiment at Zillebeke Bund, the position being at the Ypres end of the lake whence the water supply of Ypres was drawn. Here the Battalion witnessed a curious sight. An enemy aeroplane suddenly fell from the clouds and smashed into the lake without any sign of its having been attacked by British 'planes or fired at by anti-aircraft guns.

After three days in this support position the 4/5th relieved a battalion of the Cambridgeshire Regiment in the front line in the Observatory Ridge sector. This was a most uncomfortable place, dominated by the enemy holding Hill 60; it was so dangerous that the Battalion only spent three days in the line at one time, but, short as this time was, casualties were numerous.

FOURTH-FIFTH BATTALION THE BLACK WATCH

On relief by the 13th Battalion Sussex Regiment on the 10th the 4/5th moved back to billets in the cavalry barracks at Ypres, which, like the prison, was one of the principal targets of the enemy artillery.

The next sector occupied by the Battalion was in the Hooge area, another wretched part of the line. Here the Battalion Headquarters came in for a good deal of shelling which on one occasion led to the following incident. Major Murray received a parcel from home in which was a notebook sent by his small son with instructions that his father was to draw an animal on each page. During a particularly heavy artillery bombardment, Major Murray, in order to occupy his mind, proceeded to draw in the notebook lions, tigers, etc., as requested by his son. While thus engaged the Adjutant came in and looked over his shoulder, started, became very white and went away. Later the Signalling Officer and the Medical Officer arrived and asked Major Murray what he was doing. When he told them they seemed relieved. "Thank God, sir," said the Signalling Officer. "Scratton [the Adjutant] told us you had gone mad and were drawing all kinds of wild animals in your notebook."

The next tour in the front line was in the Zillebeke sector. On the night of the 26th the enemy attempted to raid The Black Watch line, but without success. On March 27th the Battalion moved to the infantry barracks at Ypres for three days, and from there to Montreal Camp on the 3rd, the latter move being carried out in a blizzard.

From Montreal Camp the 4/5th marched back to billets in Houtkerque on April 5th, and after a few days spent in Battalion training it moved to Vlamertinghe on the 9th and was employed in that neighbourhood on railway construction for nearly three weeks. The time spent on this work was a real rest from the strain of the front line and was fully enjoyed by all ranks.

On April 21st the Brigade Boxing Competition was held, in which the Battalion not only won the Cup, but four firsts out of six contests. On the 27th the 39th Division was transferred to the VIII Corps, and the next day moved up to Ypres, whence, on May 6th, it went into the front line in the Hilltop sector.

May, June and July, 1917, were quiet months for the 4/5th, most of the time being spent in ordinary trench warfare in various parts of the Salient, the Battalion being in reserve in "D" Camp at Vlamertinghe during the attack on the Messines Ridge, after which it moved back with the 39th Division in order to train for what is now known as the Third Battle of Ypres. This training was carried out at Seninghem, Serques, Moulle and St. Jan Ter Biezen, in which place, favoured with good weather, training and recreation proved of great value. During this period the

IN THE TRENCHES NEAR YPRES

Battalion went once into the line, on July 10th, for a few days, at La Brique, where a party consisting of two officers, Second Lieutenants Bell and Robertson, and 10 men encountered some Germans in No Man's Land, with the result that both the officers and two men were wounded.

Rumours of a coming British attack had grown definite some time before the Battalion reached St. Jan Ter Biezen, and when billeted there the 4/5th received orders and drew battle stores for the coming fighting. When this had been done the Battalion moved up to assembly positions on the canal bank near Ypres, the trench strength being 20 officers and 512 other ranks.

CHAPTER III

JULY 31ST, 1917—JANUARY 21ST, 1918

Passchaendale and After

THE main object of the forthcoming series of attacks now known as the Third Battle of Ypres was to drive the enemy from the high ground overlooking Ypres, and by so doing rid the town and the ground round it from observed enemy artillery fire and greatly widen the Salient. It was also intended, if possible, to push the attack further and gain possession of the Belgian coastal towns and German submarine bases in that country.

The attack which began on July 31st had been planned on a very wide front. The area over which the attack took place was completely dominated by the enemy. The drainage system had been obliterated, and the former green fields had been changed into a sea of mud where all landmarks such as roads, houses and woods had been utterly destroyed by shell fire. Consequently the concentration of men and guns for the coming attack was an operation of extreme difficulty.

The conception of this attack was brilliant and the arrangements whereby the concentration was carried out were excellent, but one disastrous incident may go far to ruin the most carefully planned schemes. A few days before the actual assault took place the enemy captured a British non-commissioned officer. This traitor—the Battalion Diary calls him an unmitigated blackguard—had had many opportunities to learn the plans for the assault, and after he was captured he gave the enemy full information regarding the coming attack, including the positions of brigades and battalions with their objectives, the wood in which the British tanks were concealed and, worst of all, the position of many British batteries. The result of this will be seen later.

The disposition of the 39th Division in the coming attack was as follows: The 116th and 117th Infantry Brigades were to attack from the front line in the Hilltop and Wieltze sectors, their first objective being the German front line systems and later a position from the left corner of Kitchener Wood to Corner Cot, just behind the village of St. Julien. After these had been captured the 118th Brigade, starting from the canal bank and advancing in artillery formation at first, was then to extend and, having passed through the 116th and 117th Brigades, was to push on through Kitchener Wood and St. Julien, cross the Steenbeek River and finally dig in on the far bank. From the front line trenches to the Steenbeek was a distance of about two miles, and here the Battalion was to join up with the 55th (Lancashire) Division on the right and 51st (Highland) Division on the left.

THIRD BATTLE OF YPRES, JULY, 1917

The 118th Brigade was disposed as follows: The 1/6th Battalion Cheshire Regiment on the right, the 1/1st Battalion Hertfordshire Regiment (centre) and 4/5th The Black Watch on the left; the 1/1st Battalion Cambridgeshire Regiment in support.

The position to be attacked was a strong one and well fortified by concrete shelters, known as " pill-boxes," manned by machine guns, and the task of dealing with these was by no means an easy one. The enemy front line trenches were lightly held, the German main force being behind the Steenbeek ready for a counter-attack directly the British advance should be held up.

At 3.50 a.m. on July 31st the attack was launched, and at 8 a.m. the Battalion advanced in artillery formation, reaching its position for the final advance about ten o'clock, three companies being in the front line and one in support. The 4/5th had a comparatively easy journey through Kitchener Wood and across the Steenbeek, and although shelling was heavy there were few casualties. On the right, also, the Cheshire Battalion took the village of St. Julien; but a battalion of the Hertfordshire Regiment in the centre suffered such severe losses from machine-gun fire that the battalion was unable to advance and indeed was practically wiped out. This unfortunately exposed the left flank of the Cheshire battalion and the right flank of The Black Watch, with the result that, although the 4/5th reached its final objective, it was obliged to withdraw to the Steenbeek River in order to conform with the rest of the Division line, and in doing so lost heavily, not only from artillery fire, but also from machine gun fire on the right flank.

No counter-attack was made the next day, the enemy contenting himself with heavily shelling the new front line, and at 10.30 a.m. orders were received that the Battalion would be relieved and withdraw into support; but these could not be complied with by daylight, and it was not until nightfall that the 118th Brigade was relieved, the 4/5th Battalion moving to La Brique.

The weather had now broken and the men came down soaked through and through and plastered with mud from head to foot. The Quartermaster had sent up all the overcoats and blankets he had, and these, together with a double tot of rum, did much to relieve the wet and weary men.

The following day the 4/5th, now organized as one company, returned to Hilltop, where it occupied the old German front line. It was raining hard, the mud was appalling and the two days the Battalion—now only 200 strong—remained in the line, were about the worst ever experienced. In the afternoon of the 2nd the 4/5th advanced from the old German line across the open, past Raucovin Farm to Kitchener Wood and took up a line in front of the wood, where it remained for three days under heavy German artillery fire; by day and night the shelling never slackened, and repeated counter-attacks were repulsed. Early in the morning of the 6th the Battalion was relieved by the Oxford and Buckinghamshire Light Infantry and withdrew through a heavy hostile barrage to Reigersburg Château, which was reached at 6 p.m.

By this time the 4/5th was reduced to a mere handful; so heavy indeed had been the losses that C company only numbered one officer and six men, while the others were almost in the same condition. The behaviour of the men in the action had been magnificent; few remained, but those who did knew that they had done great work. The casualties were two officers killed, one of whom was Lieutenant Scratton, the adjutant, 14 wounded and one missing; 41 other ranks killed, 230 wounded and 48 missing, making a total of 17 officers and 319 other ranks.

Among the many cases of gallantry the following may be mentioned: Sergeant Hutton found himself in command of his company on the 31st when all its officers had been either killed or wounded. On the morning of August 1st, when German machine guns in a ruined farm in front of his position were causing much trouble, Sergeant Hutton, accompanied by Sergeant Dolan, went out to attack this machine gun nest. Dolan was hit, and Hutton carried him in under very heavy fire.

Captain A. J. Stewart, C company, was later awarded the D.S.O. for the magnificent way in which he handled his company throughout the fight. C company had a very bad time from the start of the attack, and when the Battalion went into the line for the second time, Captain Stewart did exceedingly good work. By his coolness, courage and personal example he contributed in no small measure to the defeat of the hostile counter-attack. For services on this occasion, Major Rogers, the Battalion Medical Officer, received a Bar to his D.S.O., while two officers were awarded Bars to the M.C., and three others the M.C. itself; one Bar to the D.C.M., two D.C.M.'s, four Bars to the M.M. and two M.M.'s were later awarded to other ranks for their services in this action.

On August 7th the 4/5th went back to Thieshouk, where it was inspected by the Army Commander, who addressed the Battalion and said that the Second Army was so short of men that the 4/5th, together with the rest of the 39th Division, would be required to relieve battalions in the Zillebeke area, adding, however, that they would not be used as fighting troops for some time.

On the 20th the 4/5th went up in support behind Battle Wood, just south of Hill 60. From this position there was a fine view down the valley towards Menin and Combles, which were still in the hands of the enemy. On the left the Fifth Army was still battering away at the German position with varying success, but it was not until the end of September that the Battalion was again actively engaged.

On August 23rd the 4/5th went into the front line in front of Battle Wood, by this time an awful scene of desolation, as it was in this neighbourhood that some of the hardest fighting of the war had taken place. The line held by the Battalion was a curious one. It was part of the area recently captured from the Germans and the front trench was by no means good. There was no wire in front and the exact location of the enemy was uncertain; the Germans also seemed to have little idea as to the position of the British line, and though they shelled the railway embankment and Battle Wood, the front line itself was seldom touched. An illustration of this uncertainty regarding the British positions may be mentioned. One morning two Germans carrying mail bags jumped into one of the trenches held by the Cambridgeshire Battalion under the impression that it was their own.

After a few tours in the line and short periods of rest behind it the Battalion moved up to Beggar's Rest Camp near Vermoozeele, on September 18th, in order to support a successful attack in the Shrewsbury Forest sector made by the 117th Brigade on the 20th. On the following day, together with the rest of the 118th Brigade, it relieved the 117th in their newly-won positions. In this fighting the 41st Division had also taken part and had sustained severe losses, with the result that by the 25th it was compelled to fall back all along the line, and, in order to help them, the 118th Brigade was directed to take over from the 41st Division and try to recover the lost ground.

On the morning of September 26th the 118th Brigade attacked the ridge to the left of Tower Hamlets, the 4/5th being on the right of the 118th Brigade. The attack was not entirely successful; no definite advance was made, since the state of the ground made the maintenance of communications under heavy hostile artillery fire extremely difficult. The result of thirty-six hours' fighting was that the British line was pushed forward a little in some places, but it was found impossible to form a definite line on the position won.

Once more the 4/5th lost heavily, one officer being killed, four wounded and three missing; 19 other ranks killed, 114 wounded and 95 missing—a total of eight officers and 228 other ranks. Captain Plimpton, commanding A company, was the officer killed, and among those wounded was Major Rogers, R.A.M.C. On relief on the night of September 27th the 4/5th went back to rest in a camp near Westhoutre, where, on October

2nd, it was inspected by the G.O.C. 39th Division. Strength, 19 officers, 837 other ranks.

October and November were the worst months experienced by the Battalion during the whole period spent in the neighbourhood of Ypres. The weather had definitely broken and the condition of the battle area is indescribable. The main object of the Passchendaele attack had failed, with the result that the enemy were more alert than ever. Holding the line, which in the vicinity of Dumbarton Lakes and Gheluvelt was merely a series of shell-hole posts, all of them in a shocking condition and many ankle-deep in mud, was a terrible strain, and casualties both from wounds and sickness were numerous. Gas shells were now being used by the enemy in large quantities, and the losses from these, and other causes, were many. The Medical Officer, Stokes, who was acting for Major Rogers, was blinded in both eyes, and Sergeant Hutton, by this time Company Sergeant-Major, was badly gassed, and went down the line never to return. After one tour in the front area the 4/5th sent back 200 casualties suffering from gas, and, in addition, nearly the whole Battalion seemed affected by it.

On October 28th, Lieutenant-Colonel Sceales left the 4/5th to take command of a Tank Brigade. His departure was a great loss to the Battalion, and only those who served under him can understand what an inspiration he was to officers and men alike. He had taken over command of the Battalion when it had consisted of two distinct parts, and he left it a composite unit with a fine regimental spirit of its own. All survivors of the old 4/5th who fought under Colonel Sceales on the Somme or at Ypres will remember that gallant gentleman with genuine affection and admiration, and his loyalty to his own officers and men will never be forgotten. He was succeeded by Major Murray, the Second-in-Command.

Early in November, Colonel Murray was badly gassed and lost the sight of both eyes for a time. On the 1st, Captain Peterson, commanding B company, was shot through the heart by a German sniper. This officer was one of the finest in the Battalion, and his loss, like that of Captain Plimpton, was one of the worst the Battalion experienced during this most trying period. Later in the month, on the 14th, the Adjutant, Captain Stevenson, was also killed; and the same day a German party raided the Battalion line and captured a Lewis gun team. This raid the enemy repeated at 5.30 on the following morning; this last attack, however, was quickly beaten off, the raiders leaving three prisoners in the hands of the Battalion.

By this time the Division was much reduced in number. The 4/5th could only muster 200 rifles for the trenches, and when

CORPS RESERVE, NOVEMBER, 1917

relieved on November 25th by the 2nd Battalion Royal Scots Fusiliers and moved back to comfortable billets near Stenvoorde, it was hoped that the whole Division would be given a rest; but four days later the Battalion moved up once more to a wretched camp near Brandhoek. This camp was a collection of rotten, rain-soaked, leaking tents without floor-boards, and, as the weather was very bad, with hard frost and a bitterly cold wind, the discomfort can hardly be imagined. On December 7th the Battalion moved to Goedaersveldt, where it entrained and travelled to Selle, a distance of about thirty miles.

The long-looked-for rest had come at last, and on the 9th the 4/5th went into billets—A and B companies in the village of Bellebuene, and C and D in Cremarest in the XI Corps, Fourth Army area. After the terrible experiences of the past few months the rest in these peaceful billets was much enjoyed by all ranks. New Year's Day, 1918, was seen in by the officers in B company mess. Breakfasts were eaten when the New Year was only fifteen minutes old, and an hour later the Battalion moved off to entrain once again for the front area. There was a hard frost and the roads were like ice, with the result that the ten miles march to the station proved trying to everyone.

At 2 p.m. that day the 4/5th arrived at Irish Farm once more and found it a maze of huts, tents, railway roads and R.E. dumps. It was exceedingly interesting to see this place again, for the first time the Battalion was near it the enemy lines were only a few hundred yards away; and now, ten months later, the place was like a fair, with masses of men moving about where formerly the enemy's activity had made all movement impossible.

After two brief and uneventful tours in the line the 4/5th came out again to Houtkerque on January 21st and moved that day by train to Watteau, having seen the last of the Salient for some time.

No division had ever spent a longer period fighting in the Ypres Salient than did the 39th. For fourteen months the 4/5th The Black Watch was in the neighbourhood of Ypres, and the losses had been very severe; it may be safely said that more Forfarshire and Dundee men were buried round Ypres than in any other part of Belgium or France.

During the whole time in the Salient no part of the Battalion performed its duties more gallantly or more efficiently than did the transport. From the peculiar nature of the line the work of bringing up rations and water was a task of great difficulty and danger at all times. McLachlan, the Quartermaster, and Lieutenant Paterson, the Transport Officer, both rendered good and gallant service in bringing up their supplies night after night over shell-swept roads and through villages which at all times were little more than death traps. Sergeant Cruickshank, the Battalion Transport Sergeant, lost his life while in charge of waggons near Hill 60; the shell which killed him narrowly missed Lieutenant Paterson, whose brother, Captain I. Paterson, had been killed the same day. McLachlan was a veteran soldier with much fighting experience in Egypt and elsewhere, and time after time gave evidence of his courage and ability in facing the dangers and meeting the difficulties of his task.

One of the best features of Colonel Sceales' period of command had been the pleasant comradeship which existed throughout the Battalion between all officers and men, but by the end of the period in the Ypres Salient the happy family which had formed the Battalion in the early days of 1917 was no more; many were dead and many others had returned home to recover from their wounds. Here and there in the companies a few veterans of the Somme and Ypres remained, but in the Officers' Mess, Colonel Murray, Major Stewart and Major Rogers were all who remained of the older hands. Many of the finest officers in the Battalion had laid down their lives in the Salient, and—to name but a few—men like Plimpton, Scratton, Stevenson and Paterson could hardly be replaced.

CHAPTER IV

THE GERMAN ATTACK, JANUARY–MAY, 1918

THE Division was now back in General Gough's Fifth Army. It formed part of the VII Corps, commanded by General Congreve, V.C., the other Divisions being the 9th and 21st. On January 29th the Battalion marched via Bray to Plateau Station, where it entrained for Peronne, moving thence to Haute Allaine and next day to Guilia Wood.

On the 31st, after a short move by a light railway to Tyke Dump, the 4/5th went into the line in the Guedecourt sector, relieving a battalion of the South African Brigade of the 9th Division. This part of the line was in good order, and although the enemy shelled the sector pretty severely, they were very methodical in their bombardments and seemed to pay particular attention to certain portions of the line, with the result that by avoiding these danger spots the Battalion was able to live more or less peaceably.

By this time special orders had been issued as to salvage, and every man on leaving the trench area was expected to bring back some salved article with him. A Divisional Order was published weekly giving the value of the articles salved by each unit, and it says much for the industry of the Battalion that during its tour in the line the salvage collected by the 4/5th was valued at more than all brought in by the remainder of the Division; there was certainly no lack of material, as the whole front was littered with rifles, overcoats, tents, bicycles, blankets, ammunition, Lewis guns, etc., the debris left behind by the British on their retirement two months before.

On the night of February 5th two men of C company, Petrie and Watson, were in a sap leading out towards the enemy from the left flank of the Battalion front. They spotted a party of Germans approaching the British line who apparently did not know of the existence of this particular sap. The enemy lay down in No Man's Land, and one of them crawled forward to examine the British wire. Petrie and Watson quickly made their plans and the former crawled out of the sap and lay down, covering the German near the wire. When the remainder of the enemy party began to advance towards the wire, Petrie emptied his magazine into them at a few yards' range, while Watson did the same from the sap. The latter then rushed gallantly at the Germans and, single-handed, made four of them prisoners, and, judging from the screaming of the others, the fire of these two men had good effect. Both received an immediate award of the Military Medal for this gallant deed.

The 4/5th was relieved by the 6th Battalion Cheshire

FOURTH-FIFTH BATTALION THE BLACK WATCH

Regiment on February 6th and went into support at Queen's Cross, about 2000 yards behind Gouzeaucourt. It was now fairly well known that the enemy were concentrating a very strong force opposite the British Fifth Army front, and had brought up fresh divisions from the Russian front to take part in a coming attack.

About this time, owing to lack of reinforcements, one battalion was taken from each brigade, the men from it being dispersed among the other units to fill up the ranks, as it was not possible to obtain a sufficient supply of men from Scotland or England.

On February 9th men of the Cheshire Regiment brought in a few wounded Germans they found lying in No Man's Land. These turned out to be prisoners who had escaped from the French and having travelled over twenty miles of country had crawled through the wire under cover of darkness, only to be caught once more when crossing No Man's Land, as they found it impossible to gain their own trenches owing to a heavy German barrage.

On the 19th, Major Naden, of the Cheshire Regiment, joined the 4/5th as Second-in-Command. He had fought in practically every corner of the world—Ashanti, Benin, Madagascar, the Indian Frontier and South Africa—and rapidly became a great favourite with all ranks. He succeeded in going right through the war to the finish, winning the D.S.O. with three Bars and the M.C. with one Bar, and, by the irony of fate, was badly injured in a motor-car smash after the Armistice, an accident that has rendered him a cripple for life.

On February 22nd the 4/5th came out of the line and proceeded to Dessart Camp, near Fins, where, two days later, it was so heavily shelled that the Battalion had to evacuate the camp for a few hours. The beginning of March found the 4/5th once more in the line at Gouzeaucourt, awaiting the expected attack. The weather was at this time very cold, the ground being covered with snow, but raids by both sides were frequent, one being carried out by the Battalion. The raiders, under command of Captain J. R. Philip, entered the enemy's trenches, found them empty of men but full of barbed wire, and were therefore unable to bring back any prisoners.

The 39th Division was relieved by the 9th on March 14th, when the 4/5th went back to camp at Moislains, a village which had been thoroughly destroyed by the enemy in their retirement in 1917. While here, the 39th Division was in support and under orders to move at any time; but in spite of this the usual football competitions and boxing contests were held, and on the 17th a Divisional Horse Show and jumping competition took place at Moislains.

THE GERMAN OFFENSIVE, MARCH, 1918

The long-expected enemy attack on the Fifth Army front began at 3.30 on the morning of March 21st under cover of a thick mist. The enemy shelling was very heavy at first, and was not confined to the British trench system, all roads, approaches and strong points in the back areas being heavily shelled. The Battalion stood to arms at once, and it was an eerie job waiting in the thick mist listening to the German shells falling on all sides and knowing nothing of what was taking place in front.

After an hour or two, orders were received that the men could take off their equipment, but were to be ready to move at a moment's notice. Reports filtered through that the 9th Division on the immediate front was standing firm, but late in the afternoon bad tidings was received. It appeared that there had been a break through further south and, in consequence, the 39th Division were ordered to assist the 21st, and the Battalion moved off in motor buses, the men being in great form and laughing as if off for a holiday. Little did they know what was to come.

The buses took the 4/5th to Longairnes, where, with the remainder of the Brigade, it proceeded to dig a line on some rising ground about 500 yards in front of the village. The orders the Brigade received were to hang on to this position and resist the advancing enemy to the last. That night the Germans gave no trouble save for a little intermittent shelling, and by dawn on the 22nd the Battalion had constructed a mile of excellent trench complete with fire-steps and traverses. On the left of the 118th Brigade were the 117th and 116th Brigades; on the right the remainder of the 16th Division.

On the forenoon of the 22nd the Germans advanced in force covered by screens of smoke, and the 4/5th was withdrawn from the trench to a position 300 yards behind it, in order to counter-attack should the enemy succeed in taking the trench system from the Cambridgeshire and Cheshire Battalions. It was now a beautiful sunny day, and the 4/5th had just cleared the village when the enemy put down a most astounding barrage on it, chiefly with 8-inch shells, under cover of which they attacked, and by the sound of the firing in front it seemed as if every second German had a machine gun.

Later in the day orders were received that the 118th Brigade was to retire to Tincourt Wood as the Divisions on both flanks were falling back. The move was carried out in column of route with 200 yards interval between companies, and during the march several enemy aeroplanes swooped down over the retiring columns and brought machine gun fire to bear on them, but without causing many casualties. C company, under Captain J. D. Stewart, was left behind to fight a rearguard covering action, and was engaged in heavy fighting, with the result that few men of the company rejoined the Battalion that night, and Captain Stewart himself was wounded and taken prisoner.

There was a thick mist on the morning of the 23rd, and although the enemy made no further attack during the night, it was certain that they were in great force. An hour or two after dawn orders were received to fall back to St. Denis, near Peronne, as a Division on the right had once more been forced to retire and the enemy had almost surrounded the 118th Brigade. Fortunately the companies of the 4/5th were able to withdraw, although the enemy were practically on their heels. A company had actually to fight its way back until it came under shelter of the 116th Brigade, who were covering the withdrawal of the rest of the Division.

The march to St. Denis was about ten miles, and on the way the Battalion passed a deserted battery position where there was a heap of gunners' rations which were taken over by the men. On reaching the end of their journey the Brigade once more got into a good position on the high ground between Mont St. Quentin and Peronne, and again all ranks looked forward to holding it against the oncoming Germans.

A few hours later the Germans advanced in dense masses towards Peronne, and the grey-coated men could be seen pouring through the town on the right of the 118th Brigade, whose machine guns took heavy toll of the advancing enemy, but so great were the numbers that the casualties inflicted had little or no effect on their advance. Orders were now received that the Brigade would withdraw to Clery, and the 4/5th, less A company, who remained behind to cover the withdrawal, retired across the valley, losing heavily all the way. On reaching the new position it was found that the Battalion now consisted of only about 150 men out of the 600 who had gone into action on the 21st.

That night the position had become so serious that the men of the Battalion who had been left behind before it went into action rejoined. Every man—Pioneers, Salvage, Labour Corps and R.E.—fit or unfit, was now sent up to the line, in addition to which dismounted cavalry were fighting side by side with the infantry. During this period Major Cruickshank, who was in command of the Divisional Training School, did excellent work in organizing stragglers and leading them back to the fighting line.

Meanwhile the Somme bridges had been destroyed and the German attack temporarily held up. But the Fifth Army had practically ceased to exist. Yet, in spite of all losses and of the rapidity of retreat, the survivors of the Fifth Army still had full confidence in General Gough, their gallant Commander. It

THE GERMAN OFFENSIVE, MARCH, 1918

is now known that some forty German Divisions attacked fourteen weak British Divisions on March 21st, and it seems a miracle that the enemy did not break right through and gain the sea coast.

On the night of the 25th the Germans crossed the Somme at Eterpigny and occupied the Maisonette, the 39th Division withdrawing to Bois Vert behind Herbecourt, and the following day, after being nearly surrounded by the enemy, it retired to Bray. On the 27th the 118th Brigade fell back to Mortcourt and the following day to Caix, where the 4/5th strength was found to be seven officers and 53 men. That day, for the first time since the beginning of the retreat, the men of the 39th Division were allowed to attack the Germans, a composite battalion of the 118th Brigade counter-attacking and retaking Wyencourt Ridge, on which it consolidated the ground won.

By this time the strength of the German attack had weakened and the enemy infantry were becoming dispirited. They had expected to break through the British line on the first day, but as day after day passed and the British still fought on, the Germans got weary and lost their driving power. In addition to this, every mile they advanced over the devastated country made the question of supplies more and more difficult until, by the end of March, they had shot their bolt and had fought themselves to a standstill.

On the evening of the 30th the Division was relieved and the 4/5th proceeded the same night to Villers Brettoneux. The strength of the Battalion was one officer and 30 other ranks; and out of the whole Division barely 700 men could be mustered.

During this retirement it was difficult to keep any record of the countless gallant deeds performed by officers and men alike. The conduct of all ranks had been splendid throughout, and the privations and miseries they endured again brought out that calm indifference and contempt for danger which is characteristic of the British soldier. Though often outnumbered and surrounded, officers and men had fought grimly on, and at no time was there ever the slightest sign of panic.

Colonel Murray, who had handled the Battalion with coolness, decision and skill under trying circumstances during the early days of the assault, had been compelled to leave, worn out with strain and anxiety; although suffering from severe gas poisoning he carried on for three days of terrific fighting and only went back when ordered to do so. Among many others Captain Stuart, killed, and Captains Philip and Penny, wounded, had each done notable work. As usual, the Medical Officer's services were beyond all praise, and Regimental Sergeant-Major Hutton had once more proved himself a source of inspiration to all ranks. The Battalion had, however, for the moment almost ceased to exist. The Divisional Commander was dead, killed by a shell, and the Brigadier and Brigade Major were both prisoners of war, the former being wounded.

On Sunday morning, March 31st, the remnants of the 118th Brigade moved to Longeau, near Gentelles, thence to Rumaisnie by motor bus, where, on April 1st, what was left of the four battalions of the 118th Brigade was formed into one unit and eventually reached Linnier on the 3rd.

On April 8th, after a day spent at Vazenval, the Battalion moved to Meneslies, and arrived at Arques on the 10th, where a composite brigade was formed out of what remained of the battalions of the 39th Division. No. 4 Battalion consisted of men belonging to the four units of the 118th Brigade, including the 4/5th The Black Watch. On the same day that this composite unit was organized it entrained at St. Omer, detrained early the following morning at Voormezeele and proceeded to the Reninghelst–Ouderdom area, where it joined the XXII Corps and was attached to the 21st Division; the 39th Division, to which it had originally belonged, now ceased to exist, owing to the heavy casualties incurred during the recent fighting.

The 4/5th, as part of this composite battalion, experienced some further fighting in Flanders, but the period was not long nor were the actions of any special interest. The Battalion Diary says little concerning the fighting in which the 4/5th took part during this period. It is stated that on certain dates the Battalion went into the line, and that on certain others it came out. On April 26th the enemy attacked heavily, and on the following day a post manned by the composite 4th Battalion seems to have been taken by the enemy, recaptured and again lost, but no mention is made of any casualties; it appears that on the whole this period was fairly quiet.

The Diary states that orders were received on April 30th for the 39th Division composite brigade to be reorganized as two battalions by the 1st of May, and, on the 5th of May, the 4/5th, then at Ganspette, was organized as two companies and so regained its own identity.

CHAPTER V

MAY, 1918—APRIL, 1919

Buzancy and the Final Advance

BY the spring of 1918 the drain on British man power had become so great that it was found necessary to amalgamate many units. Early in May orders reached both the 4/5th and 9th (Service) Battalions The Black Watch that the latter was to be absorbed by the 4/5th and that this newly constituted Battalion would then join the 15th (Scottish) Division.

In accordance with this order, on May 14th, the 4/5th was transferred to the 15th Division where, at Madagascar Camp, the amalgamation took place. Three days later Lieutenant-Colonel R. A. Bulloch—a fine officer of many years' service in The Black Watch—took over the command of the new 4/5th Battalion, and 10 officers and 57 other ranks of the 9th went to England to re-equip and form an entirely new 9th Battalion under command of Major Cruickshank. The strengths of the two battalions which were now amalgamated were: 4/5th Battalion, 19 officers and 350 other ranks; 9th Battalion, 22 officers and 672 other ranks. Although Colonel Bulloch took over command of the 4/5th on May 17th, the amalgamation is officially recorded as having taken place on June 9th.

For the first few days the 4/5th Battalion formed part of the 46th Brigade and, on June 5th, the Battalion was transferred to the 44th Brigade, of which the old 9th had originally formed part. When the amalgamation took place the 15th (Scottish) Division was holding the front line in the Fampoux sector east of Arras, the Division then forming part of the XVII Corps.

On June 16th, while in the front line near Fampoux, the Battalion carried out a successful raid, Second Lieutenant Harvey and 32 other ranks succeeding in taking three prisoners, with a loss of three men wounded and one missing. The first fortnight in July passed quietly, the Battalion being engaged in ordinary trench warfare; but rumours of a move were rife, and on July 11th and the three following days the Division was relieved by Canadians, and the 4/5th marched to Tincques on the 16th, where, with the rest of the Division, it entrained for a new area.

In May, June and July the French had been engaged in stemming a heavy German attack in the neighbourhood of Rheims, and in July Marshal Foch asked Sir Douglas Haig to send four divisions to help to throw the Germans back. The 15th, 34th, 51st and 62nd Divisions were formed into the XXII Corps under Lieutenant-General Sir A. Godley. The original destination of this Corps was a centre some way east of Rheims,

FOURTH-FIFTH BATTALION THE BLACK WATCH

but this was changed, and the 15th Division detrained at Clermont and other places in that vicinity, and joined the French Tenth Army (General Mangin), French XX Corps (General Berdoulat), near Soissons.

On July 23rd the Battalion, having moved partly by road and partly by motor omnibus, arrived at Chaudun, where with the remainder of the Brigade it became Divisional reserve, going into the front line at La Foulerie, about a mile east of Chazelles, two days later. While here orders were received to prepare to attack on the 28th, and it was in accordance with these instructions that the 44th Brigade moved forward to Bois Gerard, about two miles north-east of La Foulerie, on the morning of the 28th.

An attack by the 45th and 46th Brigades on the 23rd had resulted in the 15th Division line being slightly advanced in places. This first attack may be termed the first phase of the Buzancy fighting, and the coming operation, in which the 44th Brigade was to take part, formed the second.

The objective of the forthcoming operation was the village of Buzancy and the high ground east of it, and Brigadier-General Thompson decided to attack in the following manner: Two companies of the 8th Battalion Seaforth Highlanders were to attack Buzancy, clear the village and link up with the French troops operating on their right. Another company of the same battalion was to attack Buzancy Château, which was well fortified and a nest of machine guns, and with this company a section of light trench mortars, half a section of flammenwerfers and one company of the 4/5th The Black Watch. On the left of these General Thompson ordered the 5th Battalion Gordon Highlanders to attack the enemy position from the Buzancy–Bois l'Evêque road to the south edge of Chivry Farm. In accordance with these directions, Lieutenant-Colonel Bulloch detailed B company for this operation, and that company, together with C company of the Seaforths, carried out the attack on the Château.

Zero hour was fixed at 12.30 p.m. on the 28th, and two minutes before that time a heavy artillery barrage fell on the German lines. At Zero the attacking troops moved forward, and a few minutes later the Seaforths had taken the Château and grounds, B Company of the 4/5th meeting with some resistance from strong points in the north-east corner of the village. These were eventually dealt with, the chief point of resistance being blown up by a party of the 91st Field Company R.E., after which Lieutenant Badenoch of The Black Watch, having collected some men near by, rushed the house and cleared the enemy out of it, eventually, with the help of the Seaforths, taking over one hundred Germans prisoners.

BUZANCY, JULY, 1918

About an hour after this, as the French troops on the right had not succeeded in getting forward, and as, in consequence, the right flank of the Seaforths was exposed, Captain Murray of that regiment ordered B company of the 4/5th to establish posts on the right flank to protect it from being turned.

During the afternoon this position, roughly running along a line north and south and just east of Buzancy, was precarious, and as the day wore on it appeared likely that the Seaforths and The Black Watch would be compelled to retire, as the Germans were seen pushing up small bodies of troops with the intention of counter-attacking from the right flank. These fears proved correct, and at about four o'clock two heavy German counter-attacks were launched, with the result that what was left of the Seaforths and The Black Watch were obliged to withdraw through Buzancy to their original line.

It was a heart-breaking failure, but no blame whatever could be attached to the Scottish troops. They took and held Buzancy and the high ground just east of it and only withdrew fighting when it became obvious that the troops on their right had not carried out their attacks, and that had they not withdrawn all would have been either killed or captured during the fierce enemy counter-attacks. In summing up the result of this fighting the *15th Division History* states :

" Although unsuccessful in retaining the ground won, the
" 15th Division that day inflicted a blow on the enemy the result
" of which was speedily apparent."

No fighting took place during the night of the 28th or the whole of the 29th, but during that day the Division extended its line somewhat farther south and received orders for an attack to be carried out the following morning, in conjunction with an effort which was to be made by the XX (French) Corps on the right.

In this operation, which consisted of a turning movement round the Bois d'Hartennes, the 44th Brigade was in support of the 45th and 46th and was detailed to take the final position, passing through the 45th and 46th when they had captured their objective. This attack, like the other, failed owing to heavy enemy machine gun and artillery fire, with the result that the Brigade was ordered to reoccupy its original position, and that night it relieved the 46th in the right sector of the front line, the 4/5th being on the right of the 5th Gordon Highlanders, with the Seaforths in support, and on this line the Brigade consolidated.

Early in the morning of August 2nd patrols reported that the enemy were retiring, and strong officer patrols were sent out by the front line battalions in order to get in touch with the retreating

Germans. Thus began the general retirement of the German Armies, and it is of interest to note that the 4/5th Battalion was one of those holding the front line when that movement first started. When it was found that the retreat was actually in progress, General Reed ordered the 44th Brigade to advance due east through Taux and get in touch with the French, and when night fell the Brigade had crossed the Crise River three miles east of the position it had occupied in the morning. On August 3rd the Division was relieved by the French and the 4/5th moved back to La Raperie.

Thus ends the story of the part played by the 4/5th in the fighting for and around Buzancy. One incident, however, remains to be told. After the fighting was over, and after the Division had returned north, the following special Order was issued by General Sir H. S. Horne, K.C.B., K.C.M.G., Commanding First Army:

" The following letter from the General Officer Commanding
" the 17th (French) Division to the General Officer Commanding
" the 15th (Scottish) Division is published for the information of
" all ranks:

"' *27th August*, 1918.

"' MON GENERAL,—After relieving your Division in the
" pursuit on the Vesle, I established my Headquarters at Buzancy.
" I found there the traces still fresh of the exploits of your Scottish
" soldiers, and the officers of my staff were able to see clearly what
" hard fighting you had to gain possession of the village, and,
" above all, the park.

" Wishing to leave on the spot some lasting tribute to the
" bravery of your soldiers, I entrusted to one of my officers,
" Lieutenant Rene Puaux, the task of erecting there, with the
" material at hand, a small monument, emblematic of the homage
" and admiration of my Division for yours.

" This monument has on it a medallion, on which are in-
" scribed thistles and roses, and beneath the words:

HERE THE NOBLE THISTLE OF SCOTLAND WILL FLOURISH
FOR EVER AMONG THE ROSES OF FRANCE.

"And beneath:

17TH FRENCH DIVISION
TO
15TH SCOTTISH DIVISION.

" This monument was erected on the highest point of the
" plateau, where we found the body of the Scottish soldier who
" had advanced the farthest (on July 28th, 1918—Buzancy).

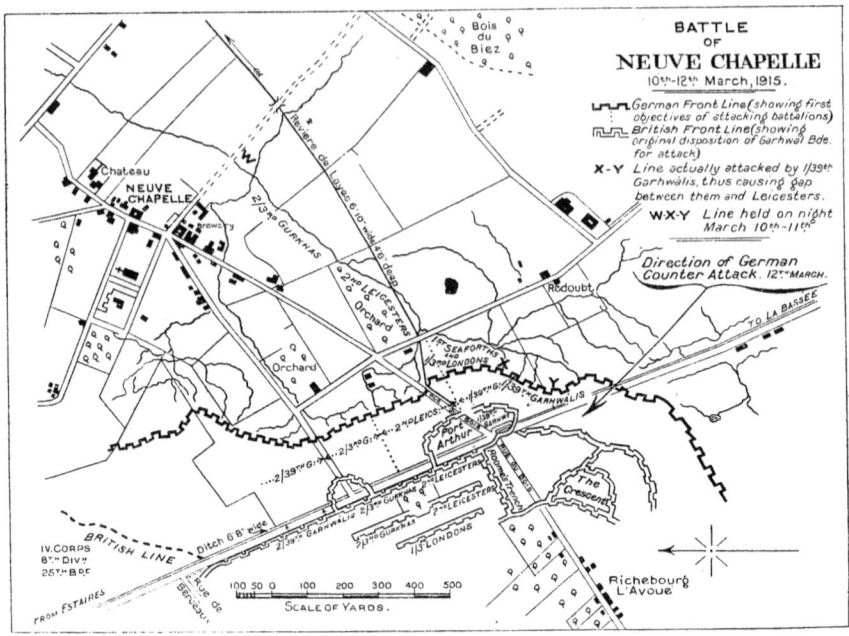

[See page 7]

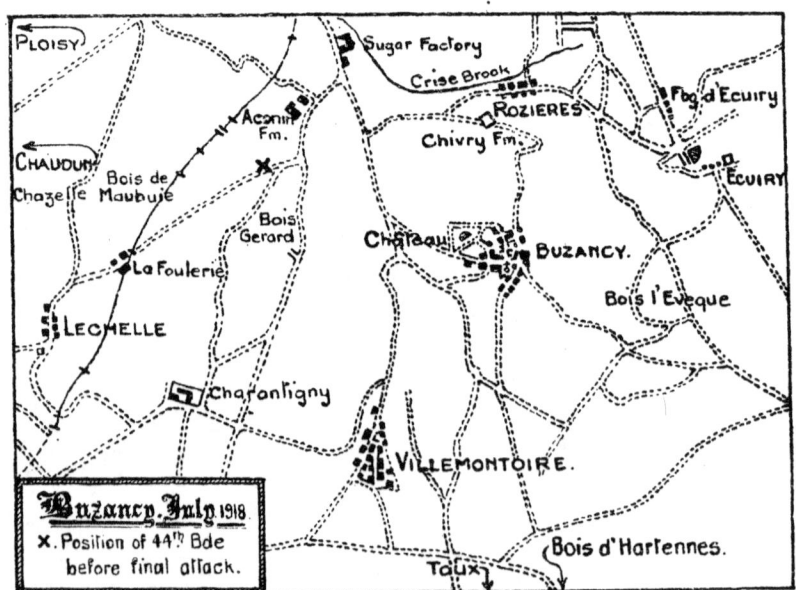

WAR MEMORIAL AT BUZANCY ERECTED BY THE 17TH FRENCH DIVISION ON THE SPOT WHERE A SOLDIER OF THE 4/5TH BATTALION FELL NEAREST TO THE ENEMY POSITION, JULY 28TH, 1918

BUZANCY, JULY, 1918

" The photograph of this monument appeared in the last
" number of the journal *L'Illustration*. I thought you would be
" glad to have a few copies of the photograph, which I send you
" herewith. They convey to you, together with the memories
" which I have kept of our short meeting at Vierzy, the expres-
" sion of my esteem and my admiration for your valiant Division.

" Will you please accept, dear General, the expression of my
" sincere regards?

"(Signed) C. GASSOUIN,

(General de Division),

" Commanding 17th (French) Division."

" I am confident that this testimony of the true feeling of
" comradeship which exists between our ally and ourselves will
" be highly appreciated by all ranks of the First Army.

"(Signed) H. S. HORNE, General,

" Commanding First Army.

" First Army Headquarters,

" 15th *September*, 1918."

It is worthy of mention that this monument is believed to be the only one erected by the French Army on any battlefield in memory of a British formation. The Scottish soldier alluded to above was a man of the 4/5th Battalion Black Watch.

On August 4th the Battalion arrived at Monneville and, proceeding via Clermont, reached Tincques the following morning. The Battalion then marched to Penin, where it remained for three days, during which time His Majesty The King passed through the village and was loyally greeted by the Battalion.

In this fighting the 4/5th lost two officers killed, eight wounded and one missing; 41 other ranks killed, 211 wounded and 31 missing—a total of 294. For services during the period officers and men of the Battalion received, in all, one Legion of Honour, 12 Croix de Guerre and one Medaille Militaire from the French Government, and four M.C.'s, three D.C.M.'s and seven Military Medals from the British.

The 15th Division was now in the First Army, and after ten days spent in rest it relieved the 56th in the right sector of the XVII Corps just south of the Scarpe River, the 4/5th moving into the line in the Neuville Vitasse sector on the 15th. The Division, however, did not remain long in this part of the line, but reached the Loos sector about the end of the month and took over the left sector of the I Corps (First Army) front from the 11th Division, the Battalion moving into the Hulluch sector in support on the 24th.

It was opposite this sector that the Division had gone into the line for the first time just over three years before, and the few men who had been there at that time saw great changes. Instead of a continuous line of trenches strongly held in front there was now a line known as the " outpost zone " consisting of strong points, behind which came a series of "defended localities" running back several thousand yards, each strongly wired and so arranged that the fire from one would flank others on its right and left. In addition, these defended localities were linked up by tunnels, thus doing away with the long and dangerous communication trenches of former days. Leading from these tunnels were large dug-outs in which the garrisons of the various posts, and support troops, lived. They were lit by electricity and so arranged that their entrances could be blocked and denied to the enemy should he capture any particular post.

September passed quietly. By this time the enemy was making preparations for withdrawal in order to conform to his line retreating farther south. Continuous pressure was kept on him by means of strong fighting patrols which went out each night, but few met with opposition, and it was only when they had proceeded some distance behind the enemy's so-called front line that they were fired on.

The 4/5th Diaries give no mention of any raid carried out by the Battalion during the period, but on October 1st it is noted that the enemy artillery fire was very heavy and every kind of shell was indiscriminately hurled on the British positions and areas behind the line. This bombardment went on all day and died down completely during the evening, the night being absolutely still as regards German gun fire. Early the following morning a German deserter gave himself up to a patrol of the 8th Seaforths and stated that his regiment had retired that night, with the result that the 44th Brigade Commander at once sent out strong patrols, and General Reed ordered all three brigades to push forward into the German lines. At this time the 44th Brigade were holding the centre sector of the Division line with the 45th on the right and 46th on the left; when the advance started the 4/5th Black Watch on the right and the 8th Seaforths were holding the Brigade front line and were able, before nightfall on October 2nd, to push forward to the eastern side of Hulluch, and the following day reached the western bank of the Haute Deule Canal.

The next few days were spent in making arrangements to force a crossing, as the enemy had destroyed all the bridges and were holding the eastern bank in strength. On the 12th the crossing

CROSSING THE SCHELDT, NOVEMBER 7TH, 1918

was effected and the 46th and 44th Brigades had established posts on the other side of the canal by nightfall. The advance now began in earnest, and on the 17th was taken up by the 44th and 46th Brigades. The Germans were now retiring as fast as they could and the Division spent the next few days following them up, the 4/5th halting at the undermentioned places:

October 17th Meurchin, 18th Carvin, 19th Bois de l'Epinoy, 20th La Roserie, 21st Hucquinville, and on the 22nd reached L'Ecuille, near the western bank of the Scheldt. Here the advance was held up for about a fortnight. The enemy had destroyed all the bridges across the canal and river, and it was evident that they intended to make a stand on the eastern bank of the Scheldt and Escaut rivers.

The crossing of these was a difficult operation for which much preparation was required. Both were wide and deep, and, to make matters worse, there was a strip of marshy ground on the western bank which, intersected by wide ditches, prevented the British troops from gaining the banks. In addition, on the eastern bank the ground sloped up abruptly and, covered as the country was with forest, the enemy artillery and infantry were screened from view, and from the high ground were able to keep their front under good observation.

In view of these difficulties it was decided that the Divisions on the right and left, in front of which the ground was easier, should advance and endeavour to outflank the enemy holding the ground opposite the 15th Division. On November 7th, as the 16th Division on the left had gained the banks of the Scheldt, orders reached the 15th to force a passage on the following day. General Reed entrusted the operations to the 44th Brigade, and Brigadier-General Thompson detailed the 8th Seaforths to cross west of Crèvecoeur, while The Black Watch were to cross at Antoing and advance through Fontenoy to Gerounde, the two battalions to form a defensive left flank should the 16th Division be unable to get forward.

Early on the 8th the crossing began, and by noon both battalions had got over and established posts on the eastern bank; although under heavy artillery fire, both battalions pushed forward, and by nightfall their line ran between Le Large and Rosoir. At dawn on the 9th the advance was continued, and a few hours later the Seaforths had occupied Vezonaucx and the 4/5th patrols had advanced to Fontenoy and Bourgeon without opposition.

On that morning news was received that the end of the war was in sight and that an Armistice would be signed within the next few days. This had a special interest to all who had served in any battalion of The Black Watch, and more particularly to those of the 4/5th, for it was here on the plains of Fontenoy,

FOURTH-FIFTH BATTALION THE BLACK WATCH

173 years before, that The Black Watch had received its "baptism of fire," and now one of the youngest of its children was engaged in following up a retreating enemy after a long and bitter war. The pursuit continued and the Battalion, reaching Blicquy on the 10th, advanced to Huissignies the following day, where news was received that hostilities would cease at 11 a.m.

Thus ends the fighting story of the 4/5th. The rest is soon told. On November 19th the Battalion was inspected by Major-General Reed, and on the 25th moved to Chièvres, where, on December 11th, demobilization began and a party consisting of twenty-six miners proceeded to Scotland. Demobilization and training occupied most of the time for the next three months, during which the Battalion moved as follows: December 17th, to Soignies; 18th, to Ronquières; 22nd, to Nivelles; and, finally, on February 24th, to Brain-le-Comte. Here it remained until reduced to Cadre strength, and after having sent 10 officers to the 6th Battalion and 167 other ranks to the 8th Battalion, both in the Army of Occupation, the Cadre was reduced to four officers and 47 other ranks, and early in April, 1919, returned to Scotland.

So ends the history of this gallant Battalion, too short to record worthily all the gallant deeds of officers and men, too short to give full praise to all those who gave their lives for their country, but a tale that shows on every page how each Battalion, whether fighting separately as the 4th, 5th or 4/5th, or when amalgamated as one unit, nobly upheld the finest traditions of The Black Watch.

APPENDIX I

Record of Officers' Services

Abbreviations :—" K."—Killed. "D. of W."—Died of Wounds. "W."—Wounded. "M."—Missing. "P. of W."—Prisoner of War.

THE FOURTH–FIFTH BATTALION

Adams, J. 2nd Lieut. Joined 20th June, 1918.
Adams, J. C. 2nd Lieut. To hospital sick 15th Oct., 1918.
Adams, J. O. 2nd Lieut. Joined 22nd Jan., 1917. *w.* 31st July, 1917.
Allison, G. 2nd Lieut. Joined 22nd Oct., 1916. To U.K. sick 9th Nov., 1916.
Aubertin, T. Capt. Joined 16th March, 1916. To II Corps School Staff 15th May, 1917.

Badenoch, K. E. Lieut. Joined 19th Oct., 1917. Awarded M.C. 31st May, 1918. Promoted Capt. 6th June, 1918.
Bain, J. McP. 2nd Lieut. Joined 16th March, 1916. Sick 14th Oct., 1916 to U.K.
Baldwin, J. Lieut. Awarded M.C. Gassed 5th Oct., 1918.
Baldwin, J. B. Lieut. M.O.R.C., U.S.A. Joined 6th Sept., 1918.
Barker, A. G. 2nd Lieut. Joined 9th July, 1918.
Barnett, J. H. 2nd Lieut. Joined 4th June, 1918. To hospital sick 19th June, 1918. Rejoined Battn. *k.* 1st Aug., 1918.
Barret, J. H. 2nd Lieut. Joined 4th Jan., 1918.
Barrie, W. C. O. Lieut. Joined 3rd Aug., 1916. *k.* 14th Oct., 1916.
Belford, C. R. 2nd Lieut. Joined 16th Dec., 1917. To hospital sick 22nd March, 1918.
Bell, D. 2nd Lieut. Joined —. *w.* 11th July, 1917.
Bell, T. C. 2nd Lieut. Joined 19th Aug., 1918. *m.* 21st Aug., 1918.
Bennett, D. McK. 2nd Lieut. Joined 28th March, 1917. Injured to U.K. 6th Aug., 1917.
Bett, M. J. 2nd Lieut. Joined 9th July, 1918.
Bowes-Lyon, G. F. Major. Joined 5th Sept., 1916. *w.* 15th Oct., 1916.
Boyers, E. Capt. To hospital 21st Jan., 1917.
Brown, J. E. 2nd Lieut. Joined 11th Jan., 1917.
Browne, P. A. 2nd Lieut. Joined 9th July, 1918. *w.* 1st Aug., 1918.
Bruce, R. F. D. Capt. Joined 28th Oct., 1918.
Bruce-Gardyne, I. M. Capt. Joined 7th Dec., 1916. *w.* 31st July, 1917. Awarded M.C. Rejoined 5th Sept., 1918.
Buchan, J. L. Lieut. D.S.O. Joined 27th Aug., 1917. Appointed Adjutant 12th Jan., 1918. Promoted Capt. Awarded the Croix de Guerre 12th Aug., 1918.
Buchanan, F. H. H. 2nd Lieut. Joined 12th Nov., 1915.
Bulloch, R. A. Lieut.-Col. D.S.O. Joined 17th May, 1918. Awarded Chevalier of the Legion of Honour and Croix de Guerre 12th Aug., 1918. To 15th Divisional H.Q. 11th Oct., 1918.

Calder, H. E. 2nd Lieut. Joined 22nd Oct., 1916. To 118th T.M. Battery 22nd Jan., 1917. Rejoined 28th Oct., 1918.
Calder, H. E. 2nd Lieut. Joined 15th Oct., 1917. *w.* 27th March, 1918.

FOURTH-FIFTH BATTALION THE BLACK WATCH

Cameron, S. 2nd Lieut. Joined 11th Jan., 1917. *w.* 31st July, 1917.
Catto, F. E. 2nd Lieut. Joined 27th Aug., 1918.
Clark, R. S. 2nd Lieut. Joined 27th Aug., 1918.
Coutts, F. 2nd Lieut. Joined 11th Jan., 1917. To U.K. sick 1st May, 1917.
Coutts, W. G. 2nd Lieut. Joined 4th Jan., 1918. Transferred to 1st Battn. M.G. Corps 21st Aug., 1918.
Cowan, R. W. 2nd Lieut. 4th July, 1916. To U.K. sick 24th Aug., 1916.
Cruickshank, J. Major. Joined 16th March, 1916. To Infantry Base Depot as Instructor 24th June, 1916. Rejoined Battn. *w.* 23rd March, 1918.
Culross, C. C. 2nd Lieut. Joined 1st Sept., 1918. Gassed 15th Sept., 1918. Rejoined 2nd Oct., 1918. *w.* 31st Oct., 1918.

Davidson, J. Lieut. Joined 5th Sept., 1918.
Davie, S. L. 2nd Lieut. *w.* 29th Oct., 1917. Rejoined 13th Dec., 1917. Transferred to 1st Black Watch 26th July, 1918.
Dickson, W. 2nd Lieut. Joined 21st Sept., 1916. *w.* 14th Oct., 1916.
Donald, H. G. 2nd Lieut. Joined 22nd Oct., 1916. Promoted Lieut. 6th Jan., 1918.
Drew, J. Lieut. Joined 3rd Aug., 1916. To Base marked P.B. March, 1917. Rejoined from Base 7th May, 1917. Transferred to Base (Calais) 8th Jan., 1918.
Dron, W. Capt. and Q.M. Joined 28th Oct., 1918.
Duncan, A. 2nd Lieut. Joined 7th July, 1917. To U.K. sick 28th Nov., 1917.
Duncan, J. N. Lieut. Joined 27th Aug., 1918. *w.* 15th Sept., 1918.

Edwards, A. L. C. 2nd Lieut. Joined 10th Aug., 1916. *w.* 10th Oct., 1916. Awarded M.C. 17th Oct., 1916.
Edwards, F. T. 2nd Lieut. Joined 30th April, 1918. *w.* 31st May, 1918.

Farrar, G. R. 2nd Lieut. Joined 4th Jan., 1918. *w.* and *m.* 26th April, 1918. Officially reported *p. of w.* 31st May, 1918. Awarded M.C. 4th June, 1918.
Fergusson, R. Mac. 2nd Lieut. Joined 21st Sept., 1916. *w.* 14th Oct., 1916.
Ferrier, R. E. 2nd Lieut. Joined 21st Oct., 1916. *k.* 1916.
Forbes, A. S. Capt. C.F. Joined 30th Aug., 1916.
Forrest-Bell, F. A. 2nd Lieut. Joined 3rd Oct., 1917. *w.* 30th March, 1918. Promoted Lieut. 25th July, 1918.
Forsyth, J. C. 2nd Lieut. Joined 16th March, 1916. Awarded M.C. 4th January, 1917. Promoted Lieut. 1st July, 1917. Seconded 1st July, 1917.
Fraser, A. 2nd Lieut. Joined 4th Jan., 1918. Awarded M.C. 14th May, 1918. Promoted Lieut. 19th June, 1918. To U.K. 18th June, 1918.
Fraser, D. D. Capt. C.F. Joined 20th May, 1917.
Fraser, J. 2nd Lieut. Joined 15th Oct., 1917. *d. of w.* 28th March, 1918.
Fullerton, G. 2nd Lieut. Awarded M.C. 31st Aug., 1918. To hospital 7th Oct., 1918. Rejoined 28th Oct., 1918.
Fyfe, D. W. 2nd Lieut. Joined 22nd Oct., 1916. To hospital, shell-shock, 27th Oct., 1916.

APPENDIX I

Gilchrist, J. S. Capt. R.A.M.C. To hospital 21st May, 1918.
Gillies, W. L. 2nd Lieut. Joined 16th Dec., 1917. *m.* 24th March, 1918.
Gould, D. 2nd Lieut. Joined 24th Oct., 1917. Gassed 7th Nov., 1917.
Grant, D. A. 2nd Lieut. Joined 22nd Oct., 1916. To U.K. 10th Oct., 1917.
Guthrie, D. S. 2nd Lieut. Joined 16th March, 1916. *w.* 3rd Sept., 1916.

Hagan, E. J. Capt. C. F. Joined 16th March, 1916. Transferred to the 30th C.C.S. 29th Aug., 1916.
Hansen, A. A. 2nd Lieut. Joined 4th Jan., 1918. To 1/6th Battn. 3rd June, 1918.
Harrison, B. A. Lieut. M.O.R.C., U.S.A. Joined 5th Oct., 1918.
Harrison, H. 2nd Lieut. Joined 21st Aug., 1918.
Harvey, J. C. T. 2nd Lieut. Joined 4th Jan., 1918. To hospital sick 20th June, 1918. To U.K. sick 18th July, 1918.
Hendry, J. 2nd Lieut. Joined 14th Aug., 1916. *w.* 3rd Dec., 1916.
Herald, J. 2nd Lieut. Joined 21st Aug., 1918.
Herbert, G. 2nd Lieut. Joined 20th June, 1918. *w.* 1st Aug., 1918.
Hollis, B. 2nd Lieut. Joined 14th Nov., 1916. *k.* 31st July, 1917.
Hunter, B. 2nd Lieut. Joined 7th March, 1917. *w.* 31st July, 1917. Rejoined 20th June, 1918.
Husband, J. W. 2nd Lieut. Joined 16th March, 1916. *w.* 22nd April, 1916. Rejoined 17th May, 1916. To A.D.C., Calais, 13th April, 1917.

Inch, R. 2nd Lieut. Joined 14th Nov., 1916. Promoted Lieut. 1st July, 1917. *w.* 31st July, 1917. Rejoined 27th June, 1918. Awarded M.C. 21st Aug., 1918.

Johnstone, R. J. H. 2nd Lieut. Joined 11th Jan., 1917. *k.* 26th Sept., 1917.

Keiller, J. M. R. Capt. Joined 5th Dec., 1917. Missing 24th March, 1918.
Keir, J. 2nd Lieut. Joined 13th Oct., 1917.
Kinnear, H. 2nd Lieut. Joined 15th July, 1918. *w.* 16th Aug., 1918.

Laing, J. C., Lieut. Joined 2nd Sept., 1918.
Laird, A. C. 2nd Lieut. Joined 16th March, 1916. Transferred to R.F.C. 14th Aug., 1916.
Law, G. 2nd Lieut. Joined 19th July, 1917. Left Battn. 9th Aug., 1917.
Lawson, D. 2nd Lieut. Joined 4th June, 1918. Transferred to 1st Black Watch 26th July, 1918.
Leslie, R. M. Lieut. Joined 25th June, 1918. To hospital sick 2nd July, 1918.
Lundie, J. E. 2nd Lieut. Joined 4th Oct., 1917. *d. of w.* 25th March, 1918.
Lyell, R. 2nd Lieut. Joined 25th Nov., 1916. *w.* 31st July, 1917. Gassed 27th Sept., 1917.
Lyell, T. Capt. Joined 16th March, 1916. Awarded M.C. 15th Oct., 1916. Transferred to 2nd Battn. 1st Aug., 1918.

FOURTH-FIFTH BATTALION THE BLACK WATCH

Macbeth, W. D. 2nd Lieut. Joined 16th March, 1916. To U.K. sick 27th June, 1916.

Mackersey, J. J. 2nd Lieut. Joined 22nd Oct., 1916. *w.* 13th Nov., 1916. Rejoined 5th Dec., 1916. To U.K. sick 6th Jan., 1917.

McCabe, H. R. Lieut. Joined 24th March, 1917. Transferred to 1/1st Cambs. Regiment 6th Dec., 1917.

MacDonald, J. P. 2nd Lieut. Joined 1st May, 1918. To Base (Calais) 3rd July, 1918.

MacDowell, J. D. 2nd Lieut. Joined 10th Oct., 1916. To U.K. sick 2nd Jan., 1917.

McGladden, J. 2nd Lieut. Joined 19th Aug., 1918.

McGrady, F. L. Lieut. Joined 1st May, 1917. Transferred to 118th Inf. Bde. 6th Sept., 1918.

McKenzie, A. McG. 2nd Lieut. Joined 15th Oct., 1917. Gassed 7th Nov., 1917.

McNicol, D. 2nd Lieut. Joined 4th Jan., 1918. *m.* 24th March, 1918.

McRitchie, R. Lieut. Joined 16th March, 1916.

McVicar, T. G. 2nd Lieut. Joined 21st Oct., 1917. *k.* 26th March, 1918.

Martin, L. G. Lieut. U.S.A. Joined 16th June, 1918. Left Battn. 24th July, 1918.

Mathewson, A. 2nd Lieut. Joined 25th Nov., 1916. Transferred to Tank Corps 12th Jan., 1917.

Maxwell, D. 2nd Lieut. Joined 14th Nov., 1916. Awarded M.C. Promoted Capt. Awarded Bar to M.C. 4th June, 1918. *w.* 1st Aug., 1918. *d. of w.* 3rd Aug., 1918.

Milne, J. I. 2nd Lieut. Joined 15th Oct., 1917. To hospital (sick).

Milne, J. J. 2nd Lieut. Joined 25th Nov., 1916. *w.* 31st July, 1917. *w.* 30th March, 1918.

Moffat, J. A. Capt. Joined 3rd Aug., 1916. *w.* 14th Oct., 1916.

Munro, J. McK. 2nd Lieut. Joined 15th Oct., 1917. *m.* 24th March, 1918.

Murray, J. R. Lieut. Joined 16th March, 1916. Awarded M.C. 6th Jan., 1917. Promoted Capt. *w.* 26th Sept., 1917.

Murray, T. D. Major. Joined 8th Oct., 1916. Awarded D.S.O. 6th Jan., 1917. Mentioned in Despatches 25th May, 1917. Promoted Lieut.-Col. To hospital sick 4th Dec., 1917. Rejoined Battn. 16th Jan., 1918. To hospital sick 23rd March, 1918.

Naden, F. Major. D.S.O., M.C. Joined 19th Feb., 1918.

Neill, D. A. 2nd Lieut. Joined 19th Aug., 1918.

Nelson, W. 2nd Lieut. Joined 4th July, 1916. *w.* 14th Oct., 1916.

Nicoll, J. S. 2nd Lieut. Joined 11th March, 1916. Promoted Lieut. 1st July, 1917. To 191st Inf. Bde. 23rd Aug., 1917.

Nicoll, L. O. 2nd Lieut. Joined 22nd Oct., 1916. *k.* 26th Sept., 1917.

Nicoll, M. W. 2nd Lieut. Joined 4th July, 1916. *w.* 14th Oct., 1916.

Ogilvie, R. D. 2nd Lieut. Joined 2nd March, 1917. *w.* 26th March, 1918.

Orr-Ewing, H. E. D. Capt. Joined 17th Sept., 1918. To Aldershot 3rd Oct., 1918.

APPENDIX I

Paterson, G. F. 2nd Lieut. Mentioned in Despatches 18th Dec., 1917.
Paterson, I. S. 2nd Lieut. Joined 16th March, 1916. *w.* 14th Oct., 1916. Awarded M.C. 17th Nov., 1916. *k.* 1st Nov., 1917.
Paul, W. B. D. 2nd Lieut. Joined 22nd Oct., 1916. *w.* 2nd Jan., 1917. Rejoined Battn. 11th Jan., 1917. Shell-shock 22nd Jan., 1917.
Penney, C. H. P. C. 2nd Lieut. Joined 8th Oct., 1917. *w.* 28th March, 1918. Awarded M.C. 8th June, 1918. Promoted Capt. Rejoined Battn. 6th Oct., 1918.
Pilcher, W. H. 2nd Lieut. Joined 28th March, 1917. *w.* 3rd Aug., 1917.
Porter, K. W. 2nd Lieut. Joined 15th Oct., 1917.
Potts, D. S. 2nd Lieut. Joined 16th Dec., 1917. *w.* 22nd March, 1918.

Quekett, J. 2nd Lieut. Joined 22nd Oct., 1916. *k.* 31st July, 1917.
Quekett, R. S. 2nd Lieut. Joined 25th Nov., 1916. To U.K. sick 25th March, 1917.

Rae, W. 2nd Lieut. Joined 5th Sept., 1918.
Ramsay, D. P. 2nd Lieut. Joined 14th Nov., 1916. *w.* 31st July, 1917.
Renny, J. 2nd Lieut. Joined 22nd Oct., 1916. *k.* 26th Sept., 1917.
Richards, G. H. B. 2nd Lieut. Joined 5th Feb., 1917. To R.F.C. 27th Nov., 1917.
Ritchie, J. A. 2nd Lieut. Joined 21st Oct., 1917. Gassed 7th Nov., 1917. Rejoined 7th July, 1918. *w.* 1st Aug., 1918. *d. of w.* 8th Aug., 1918.
Robertson, W. G. 2nd Lieut. Joined 4th Jan., 1918. Transferred 14th Battn. 14th Jan., 1918.
Ross, J. C. 2nd Lieut. Joined 21st Sept., 1916. *w.* 14th Oct., 1916. Rejoined 9th April, 1917. *w.* 1st Aug., 1917.

Shand, F. G. Lieut. Joined 18th Aug., 1917. *w.* 30th March, 1918. Awarded M.C. 26th Nov., 1917.
Shand, W. A. 2nd Lieut. Joined 27th Aug., 1918.
Sheriff, L. E. D. 2nd Lieut. Joined 21st Sept., 1916. *k.* 13th Nov., 1916.
Skinner, A. C. 2nd Lieut. Joined 4th Jan., 1918. Awarded M.C. 8th June, 1918.
Smith, C. R. Buchanan. 2nd Lieut. Joined 16th Dec., 1917. *w.* 27th March, 1918.
Smith, J. 2nd Lieut. Joined 3rd Oct., 1917. *k.* 14th Nov., 1917.
Smith, L. P. Denrocke. 2nd Lieut. Joined 3rd Oct., 1917. *w.* 22nd March, 1918. Promoted Lieut. Rejoined 9th Oct., 1918.
Smith, W. T. 2nd Lieut. Joined 21st Sept., 1916. *k.* 14th Oct., 1916.
Stevenson, N. D. 2nd Lieut. Joined 27th Aug., 1918.
Stewart, J. D. 2nd Lieut. Joined 19th May, 1917. *w.* and *m.* 22nd March, 1918.
Stokes, K. H. Capt. R.A.M.C. Gassed 30th Oct., 1917.
Stuart, J. O. G. 2nd Lieut. Joined 22nd Oct., 1916. Promoted Capt. Awarded M.C. *k.* 30th March, 1918.
Sutherland, C. A. 2nd Lieut. Joined 15th Oct., 1917. *w.* 6th March, 1918.
Syme, D. 2nd Lieut. Joined 8th May, 1918. *w.* 3rd July, 1918. *d. of w.* 4th July, 1918.

FOURTH-FIFTH BATTALION THE BLACK WATCH

Vint, J. 2nd Lieut. Joined 20th June 1918. *w.* 1st Aug., 1918.

Wallace, J. 2nd Lieut. Joined 4th Oct., 1917. *w.* 27th March, 1918. Rejoined 9th Oct., 1918.
Wallis, B. H. Capt. Joined 18th Jan., 1918. Transferred to 1/1st Camb. Regt. 4th Feb., 1918.
Watson, P. T. 2nd Lieut. Joined 28th April, 1917. *w.* 31st July, 1917.
Watt, L. McLean. Capt. C.F. To U.K. 20th May, 1917.
Wedderburn, A. H. M. Capt. Joined 16th March, 1916. To Staff 1st Division 19th Aug., 1916.
Weir, G. R. 2nd Lieut. Joined 19th Aug., 1918.
Whyte, W. 2nd Lieut. Joined 28th Nov., 1916. Promoted Lieut. *w.* 16th Nov., 1917.
Wighton, A. N. 2nd Lieut. Joined 23rd Jan., 1917. Promoted Lieut. 1st July, 1917. Transferred to King's African Rifles 28th Jan., 1918.
Wilkes, S. A. 2nd Lieut. Joined 4th Jan., 1918. *k.* 24th Aug., 1918.
Wilkie, J. F. M. 2nd Lieut. Joined 28th March, 1917. *w.* and *m.* 26th March, 1918.
Wilson, J. 2nd Lieut. Joined 16th Dec., 1917.
Wilson, D. C. 2nd Lieut. Joined 23rd Oct., 1916. *w.* 12th July, 1917. *w.* 27th Sept., 1917.

Yair, J. S. 2nd Lieut. Joined 10th Oct., 1916. To U.K. sick 9th Nov., 1916.
Yarrow, K. G. 2nd Lieut. Joined 16th March, 1916. Transferred to R.A.S.C. 17th May, 1916.
Young, G. W. 2nd Lieut. Joined 22nd Jan., 1917. Promoted Lieut. *w.* and *m.* 26th March, 1918. *d. of w.* in German hands 8th April, 1918.

APPENDIX II

Summary of Casualties. The Fourth-Fifth Battalion

The discrepancy between these figures and those given by the war diaries is accounted for by the fact that, save in the case of regular battalions, the diaries seldom give a record of casualties other than those suffered in main actions.

OFFICERS, 1914–18

Year.	Killed. D. of wounds. D. on Service.	Wounded.	Missing.	Total.	Year.
1914	—	—	—	—	1914
1915	—	—	—	—	1915
1916	4	24	2	30	1916
1917	7	30	4	41	1917
1918	10	17	4	31	1918
Totals :	21	71	10	102	

OTHER RANKS, 1914–18

Year.	Killed. D. of wounds. D. on Service.	Wounded.	Missing.	Total.	Year.
1914	—	—	—	—	1914
1915	—	—	—	—	1915
1916	5	501	63	569	1916
1917	221	357	143	721	1917
1918	264	350	—	614	1918
Totals :	490	1208	206	1904	

TOTAL :

Officers, 102.   Other Ranks, 1904.

APPENDIX III

Casualties—Officers

Abbreviations—* Killed in action.   † Died of wounds.

THE FOURTH-FIFTH BATTALION

Name.	Rank.	Date.
Barnett, J. H.	2nd Lieut.	*1.8.18
Barrie, W. C. O.	Lieut.	*14.10.16
Ferrier, R. E.	2nd Lieut.	*14.10.16
Fraser, J.	2nd Lieut.	†28.3.18
Hollis, B.	2nd Lieut.	*31.7.17
Johnstone, R. J. H.	2nd Lieut.	*26.9.17
Lundie, J. E.	2nd Lieut.	†25.3.18
McVicar, T. G.	2nd Lieut.	*26.3.18
Maxwell, D.	2nd Lieut.	†3.8.18
Nicoll, L. O.	2nd Lieut.	*26.9.17
Paterson, I. S.	2nd Lieut.	*1.11.17
Quekett, J.	2nd Lieut.	*31.7.17
Renny, J.	2nd Lieut.	*26.9.17
Ritchie, J. A.	2nd Lieut.	†8.8.18
Sheriff, L. E. D.	2nd Lieut.	*13.11.16
Smith, J.	2nd Lieut.	*14.11.17
Smith, W. T.	2nd Lieut.	*14.10.16
Stuart, J. O. G.	2nd Lieut.	*30.3.18
Syme, D.	2nd Lieut.	†4.7.18
Wilkes, S. A.	2nd Lieut.	*24.8.18
Young, G. W.	2nd Lieut.	†8.4.18

Any other Officer casualties which occurred in the 4/5th Battalion, other than the above, will be found in the lists of either the 4th, 5th or 9th Battalions.

APPENDIX IV

NOMINAL ROLL OF WARRANT OFFICERS, NON-COMMISSIONED OFFICERS AND MEN KILLED IN ACTION OR DIED OF WOUNDS OR DISEASE IN THE GREAT WAR, 1914–18

* Killed in action.   † Died of wounds.   ‡ Died.   § Died at sea.

THE FOURTH-FIFTH BATTALION

Adams, D. C., Pte., S/22245	* 1.4.18	Brown, D., Pte., 267910	* 1.4.18
Adamson, A., Pte., S/43523	*15.1.18	Brown, W., Sgt., 240212	*31.7.17
Adamson, J., Pte., 293307	*15.9.18	Bruce, G., Pte., 201103	*31.7.17
Airlie, J., Pte., 201300	*31.7.17	Bruce, P., Pte., 200741	*31.4.18
Aitken, D., Pte., 202349	†27.4.18	Bryce, W., Pte., S/21645	* 7.11.17
Allan, A. S., Pte., 292941	* 1.8.18	Buchan, R., L/Cpl., 200924	*29.10.17
Allan, A., Pte., 240535	*14.10.16	Buchanan, B., A/L/Cpl., 202563	
Allan, G., L/Cpl., 240954	* 3.5.18		*31.7.17
Allan, J., Pte., 350445	* 3.8.17	Burgess, D., C.S.M., 240093	*31.7.17
Anderson, C., Pte., 240994	*31.7.17	Burke, J., Cpl., 202565	*16.11.17
Anderson, F., Pte., 240765	*29.10.17	Butchart, C., Pte., 240868	* 3.5.18
Anderson, G., L/Cpl., 241193	*31.7.17	Butchart, W., Sgt., 201025	*26.9.17
Anderson, J., A/L/Cpl., 240282			
	*27.9.17	Cairns, R., Pte., S/40551	‡25.7.18
Anderson, J., Pte., 202668	* 4.8.17	Calder, W., Pte., S/23324	*22.2.18
Anderson, W., Pte., 240911	*28.7.18	Cameron, A., L/Cpl., 201222	*26.9.17
Archibald, G., Pte., 202511	*31.7.17	Cameron, G. S., Pte., S/22975	* 1.4.18
Archibald, W., L/Cpl., 201185		Cameron, L., Pte., S/18280	† 8.8.18
	* 3.8.17	Campbell, A., Pte., S/43529	*15.1.18
Arnott, J., L/Cpl., 201483	*31.7.17	Campbell, A., Pte., 201505	†28.7.18
		Campbell, J. A., Pte., 202711	*26.9.17
Ballantyne, J., L/Cpl., 240849		Campbell, W., Pte., 202122	* 4.7.17
	* 1.8.18	Capon, C., Pte., 201734	†29.4.18
Barnett, J., L/Cpl., S/7478	†22.2.18	Carcary, E., Cpl., 240463	* 1.4.18
Barrie, J., Pte., 202395	*31.7.17	Cargill, J. T., Pte., 241203	† 9.5.18
Barrie, R., Pte., 201991	*26.9.17	Carr, D., Pte., 202527	† 3.5.18
Bayne, A., Pte., S/22246	*21.3.18	Carr, R., Pte., 290476	*26.9.17
Beattie, J., Pte., 202384	*31.7.17	Cayle, J., Pte., 202314	*21.3.18
Bell, J., Pte., 240478	*31.7.17	Chalmers, A., Cpl., 200127	*26.9.17
Bennett, W., Pte., 200676	*31.7.17	Chalmers, J., Pte., 202408	†24.3.18
Bentley, L., Pte., 268331	† 9.4.18	Chapman, R. S., Pte., 351147	* 1.4.18
Billing, E. J., Pte., 201798	*26.9.17	Charles, J., L/Cpl., 240997	* 1.4.18
Black, H., Pte., 202433	*14.9.18	Cherry, G., Pte., 268888	†20.9.18
Black, J., Pte., S/19540	† 2.8.18	Chivers, J., Pte., 200402	*31.7.17
Bland, J., Pte., 202151	*31.7.17	Christie, A., Pte., 201182	*31.7.17
Bloomer, W. J., Pte., 266283	* 1.4.18	Christie, T., Pte., 200443	*11.1.18
Boag, W., Pte., 202640	*26.9.17	Christieson, R., Pte., 201630	* 1.8.18
Boyle, W., Pte., S/24384	*19.8.18	Clapham, J. R., Pte., 267737	*18.9.18
Bradley, C., Pte., S/23076	*22.3.18	Clark, A., Pte., 201896	*15.2.18
Brady, W., Pte., 240802	‡15.1.18	Clark, F. J., Pte., 350467	*30.10.17
Brand, A. M., Pte., 240106	*26.8.16	Clark, J., Pte., 291951	*31.3.18
Bremner, J., L/Cpl., 202506	*21.3.18	Clark, J. McK., Pte., S/23004	*22.2.18
Breslin, M., Pte., 202279	*31.10.17	Cleveland, C., Pte., 201547	* 1.4.18
Brett, W., Sgt., 202242		Cobb, J., Pte., 240386	*27.9.17
(M.M.)	*26.9.17	Cohen, M. A., Pte., 201649	* 1.4.18
Britton, J., Pte., S/19683	† 4.8.18	Cook, J., Pte., S/9584	†30.8.18
Brodie, W., Pte., 265317	*28.7.18	Cooper, T., Pte., 202731	†11.2.18

FOURTH-FIFTH BATTALION THE BLACK WATCH

Cooper, W., L/Cpl., 201015 * 5.7.17
Cooper, W., Pte., 202354 *26.9.17
Copland, J., Pte., 202254 31.7.17
Corrall, W., Pte., 240188 *31.7.17
Coulson, N., Pte., 202251 * 9.7.17
Coupar, R., Pte., 268832 * 1.4.18
Cowan, A., Pte., S/23079 †24.4.18
Crichton, D., Pte., 202278 † 3.8.18
Crighton, A., Cpl., 240094 * 1.4.18
Crighton, P. K., Pte., 268833 *27.9.17
Croall, D. C. S., Pte., 202305 * 3.5.18
Crosthwaite, R., Pte., S/22538 †16.9.18
Cruickshanks, G. B., Sgt., 200015
 * 2.11.17
Cumming, D., Pte., 202575 *28.6.17
Cunningham, T., Pte., 290508†19.8.18
Cunningham, W. A., Cpl., 290513
 * 1.4.18

Davidson, J., Pte., S/43513 * 1.4.18
Davison, M., L/Cpl., 202145 * 1.4.18
Declat, M., Pte., 15993 ‡11.10.18
Dewar, J., Sgt., 200234 *31.7.17
Dick, A., Pte., 268836 * 3.5.18
Dick, H., Pte., S/21466 *28.7.18
Dickson, J., Pte., 202393 *31.7.17
Dillon, C., Cpl., 200914 *23.9.17
Doig, A., Pte., S/21949 * 9.2.18
Dolan, A. F., Sgt., 200593
 (M.M.) * 1.8.18
Donaldson, W., Cpl., 202175 † 5.2.18
Dougall, G., Pte., 351175 † 3.8.18
Douglas, J. C., Pte., 201849 *26.9.17
Dow, G., Pte., 202299 * 9.7.17
Dowie, W., L/Sgt., 201251 *27.9.17
Downie, W., Pte., 202588 *31.7.17
Drummond, G., Pte., 202441 *31.7.17
Duff, C. C., Pte., S/21386 † 3.9.18
Duncan, E. J., Sgt., S/13314 *14.9.18
Duncan, G. P., Pte., 201888 *19.2.18
Duncan, H., Pte., 202008 * 1.8.18
Dunn, W., A/L/Cpl., 202579 *31.7.17
Dyas, G., Pte., 267525 *18.9.18

Edwards, D. L., L/Cpl., 240909
 *22.5.18
Elder, J., Sgt., 240260 *27.9.17
Emslie, D., L/Sgt., S/14452 * 1.8.18
Endean, G. H., Sgt., S/5734 *1.8.18
Esplin, C. G., Pte., 201602 *20.7.18
Ewan, D., Pte., 202300 *27.9.17
Ewing, P., Pte., 292755 * 3.5.18

Fairweather, E. W., Pte., 268187
 (M.M.) * 1.4.18

Farish, F., Cpl., S/40362 *28.7.18
Fergus, J. B., Pte., 202722 * 9.7.17
Ferguson, D., Pte., 202400 * 2.8.17
Ferguson, D., Pte., S/6500 †30.7.18
Fieldhouse, A., Pte., 202333 *31.7.17
Findlay, R., L/Sgt., 240317 *31.7.17
Fleck, F., Pte., 235039 *19.8.18
Forbes, H., L/Cpl., 200311 † 6.9.18
Forbes, J., C.Q.M.S., 200458 † 5.8.17
Forman, L. L., Pte., 201816 *27.9.17
Forsyth, J., Cpl., 240589 †30.7.18
Forsyth, J., Pte., 8228 *21.3.18
Fraser, D., Pte., 200893 *21.7.17
Fraser, W., Pte., 201908 *26.9.17
Fulton, D., Pte., S/5644 *16.9.18
Fyfe, J., Pte., 240206 *31.7.17

Gair, D., Pte., 202490 † 7.10.17
Galloway, A., Pte., S/42153 †16.9.18
Galloway, W., Pte., 200448 †10.8.18
Garth, E. L. L., Pte., 202585 *28.6.17
Gay, G., Pte., 202583 * 5.5.17
Geekie, F. C., L/Cpl., 293074 *22.2.18
Gibb, J., Pte., 200503 *28.7.18
Gibson, O., Pte., 240813 *23.10.16
Gilfillan, T., Cpl., 265567 *21.3.18
Given, W., L/Cpl., 241219 *31.7.17
Gordon, R., Pte., 200083 * 2.8.17
Gouk, D., Pte., 240684 *27.9.17
Gow, J., Pte., 200556 *27.8.17
Graham, F., Pte., 292155 *27.9.17
Graham, J., Pte., 202081 *27.9.17
Grant, D. W., Pte., 21065 *31.7.17
Grant, W., Cpl., 202504 *27.9.17
Gray, J. E. L., Pte., 240987 * 1.4.18
Gray, J., L/Cpl., 202825 *16.11.17
Gray, J. D., Sgt., 240005 *28.7.18
Gray, W. R., L/Cpl., 265149 *28.7.18
Greenoway, A., C.Q.M.S., S/4413
 *21.7.18
Gill, J., Pte., 240215 † 6.7.17

Hammond, W., Pte., 267916 *28.7.18
Hampton, J. F., L/Cpl., 240175
 † 4.8.18
Hanna, R., Pte., 201367 *31.7.17
Hawkins, T. A., Pte., 291673 *20.7.18
Hayes, V. W., Pte., 201753 *16.11.17
Healy, T., Sgt., 200158
 (M.M.) *27.5.18
Henderson, A., Pte., 351226 *15.11.17
Henderson, D., Pte., 241220 * 3.5.18
Henderson, J., Pte., S/9199 * 1.8.18
Henderson, J., Pte., 203618 *15.9.18
Henderson, R., Pte., 268837 † 1.10.17

APPENDIX IV

Herd, W., Cpl., 202083 *21.3.18
Heron, C., Pte., 203137 *25.11.17
Heron, J., Pte., 310020 * 1.4.18
Hicks, G. H., Pte., S/40852 †23.7.18
Hill, W., Pte., S/21670 *25.11.17
Hinchliffe, T., L/Cpl., S/9574 *28.7.18
Hogan, A., Cpl., 200585 * 1.4.18
Hollington, E. H. T., Pte., 201745
　　　　　　　　　　　　*24.11.17
Hood, S., Pte., 240518 *14.10.16
Hosie, G., Sgt., 240145 * 3.5.18
How, J., Pte., 240830 *28.6.17
Hunter, J., L/Sgt., 240208 *31.7.17
Hutchison, D., Pte., 266206 * 3.5.18
Hutton, J., Cpl., 291831 †29.7.18
Hynd, J., Pte., 202512 *31.7.17
Hynd, W., Pte., S/25188 *16.9.18

Innes, J., Pte., S/25516 * 3.10.18
Innes, W., Pte., S/21615 * 1.4.18
Ireland, J., Sgt., 200761 *27.9.17

Jaffary, J. B., Pte., S/25490 *22.10.18
Jamie, M., L/Cpl., 240126
　　　　　　　　(M.M.) † 1.8.17
Jamieson, J., Pte., 293044 * 7.11.17
Japp, B. W., Pte., 240754 *14.9.18
Jaynes, J., Pte., S/18977 *28.7.18
Jeffery, L. O. D., Pte., 240226 *26.9.17
Johnston, A., Pte., 202270 *27.9.17
Johnston, H., Pte., 200905 * 3.5.18
Johnston, J., Pte., S/12791 * 7.11.17
Johnstone, J. M., Pte., 202366 *26.9.17
Jones, E. J., Pte., S/23353 * 1.4.18
Jones, O. E., Pte., 201667 *29.10.17

Kay, J., Pte., S/4043 † 5.3.18
Kearns, A. D., Pte., 200917 †28.3.18
Keay, J., Pte., 267178 † 9.2.18
Keir, J., Pte., 240878 †28.7.18
Kendall, D., Pte., 202044 * 3.5.18
Kennedy, J. H., Pte., 268839 †27.9.17
Kennedy, J. S., Pte., 202348 *31.7.17
Kennedy, J. J., Pte., S/23431 *18.6.18
Kennedy, S., L/Cpl., 240505 *27.9.17
Kennedy, W., Pte., S/40822 *18.9.18
Kerr, J., Pte., 201537 ‡30.9.18
Kidd, J. H., Pte., S/21860 *17.11.17
Kimlo, J., Pte., 241010 *27.9.17
King, W. B., Pte., 201704 * 3.5.18
Kinnison, J. K., Pte., 201893 † 5.2.18
Kirk, T., Pte., 202550 * 1.4.18
Kirkwood, D., L/Cpl., 241222‡ 2.3.18
Knowles, C. J., Pte., S/10434 * 1.4.18
Kynoch, A., Pte., 241083 *31.7.17

Laidlaw, J., Pte., S/18301 *28.7.18
Laing, G., Pte., 201298 *31.7.17
Laing, T., Pte., S/22996 * 3.5.18
Laing, W., Pte., 202269 *31.7.17
Laird, S., Pte., S/24723 †16.9.18
Lamb, J. P., Pte., S/21321 †24.8.18
Lamb, G. M., Cpl., 240926 *31.7.17
Lane, J. A., Pte., 202187 *27.9.17
Latto, J., C.S.M., 290450 *28.7.18
Leighton, W., Pte., S/22813 * 1.4.18
Leithead, A., Pte., 268840 * 3.5.18
Lenox, W. S., Pte., 268100 * 1.4.18
Leslie, J., Pte., 200092 *31.7.17
Lindsay, W., Cpl., 350043 *15.9.18
Lindsay, W. J., L/Cpl., S/16939
　　　　　　　　　　　　* 1.8.18
Low, A., Pte., 202694 *25.9.17
Low, R., Pte., 201166 *19.8.18
Lowrie, G., Pte., S/9890 *24.3.18
Lumsden, J. W., Pte., 350395 *26.9.17
Lyon, G. H., L/Cpl., 240962 † 7.8.17

MacDonald, A., Pte., 268841 *26.9.17
MacDonald, G. D., Pte., 201180
　　　　　　　　　　　　*31.7.17
MacGillivray, E., Pte., S/11061
　　　　　　　　　　　　* 3.5.18
MacGregor, D. O. H., Cpl., 202229
　　　　　　　　　　　　*31.7.17
Mackenzie, D., L/Cpl., S/7502
　　　　　　　　　　　　* 2.10.18
Mackenzie, K. A., Pte., 241122
　　　　　　　　　　　　* 1.8.17
Mackie, W., Pte., 202105 *26.9.17
McAllan, H. J., Pte., 202716 *31.7.17
McBain, J., Pte., 200820 † 1.5.18
McCaig, R., Pte., 293163 *28.7.18
McCallum, R., L/Cpl., 202317
　　　　　　　　　　　　*31.7.17
McDonald, A., Pte., 291597 †12.8.18
McDonald, A., Pte., 203217 * 3.5.18
McDonald, C., Cpl., 200792 *31.10.17
McDonald, D., Sgt., 200063 *31.7.17
McDonald, J., Pte., 3/2909 *28.7.18
McDougall, J., Pte., S/43263 *28.7.18
McDougall, J., Pte., 265876 *21.3.18
McFarlane, D. A., Pte., 350973
　　　　　　　　　　　　*15.11.17
McFarlane, J., Pte., 202171 *24.4.18
McFarlane, W., L/Cpl., 267829
　　　　　　　　　　　　*24.4.18
Macfarlane, G. Y., Sgt., 240161
　　　　　　(D.C.M.) *31.7.17
McGhie, J., Pte., 202421 * 1.4.18
McGinn, J., Pte., S/23342 * 1.4.18

FOURTH-FIFTH BATTALION THE BLACK WATCH

McGlidill, A., Sgt., 1435	* 1.4.18	Mitchell, R., Sgt., 240142	*31.7.17
McGowan, D., Sgt., 200813	*31.7.17	Mitchell, D., Pte., S/18721	‡ 1.5.18
McGregor, J., Pte., 200472	†23.11.17	Mitchell, G., Pte., 202312	*31.7.17
McGregor, T. B., Pte., 241234	* 9.7.17	Mitchell, H., Pte., S/23248	†26.3.18
		Moffat, W., Pte., 265121	*20.9.18
McGuire, J., Pte., 201490	*15.10.18	Moir, D., Pte., 240354	* 8.4.17
McHardy, W., Pte., 293103	*27.9.17	Moir, W. D., L/Cpl., 240941	* 4.8.17
McHugh, F., Pte., 200531	*28.7.18	Money, T. B., L/Cpl., 200913	*23.9.17
McIntosh, J. S., Pte., 268852	†31.7.18	Moore, R. V., L/Cpl., 241108	* 1.4.18
McIntyre, A., Pte., 350769	†27.7.18	Mortimer, R., Pte., 202149	*31.7.17
McKay, J., Pte., 202351	† 5.8.17	Mowat, G., Pte., 240726	* 3.9.16
McKechnie, C., Pte., S/40326	*28.7.18	Mulligan, W., Pte., 201351	*21.7.17
McKelvie, R., Pte., 268842	*27.9.17	Munn, R., Pte., S/23335	†17.5.18
McKenzie, D., Cpl., 240110	* 1.4.18	Munro, A. T., Pte., 203033	*27.9.17
McKenzie, E., Pte., S/23264	* 1.4.18	Murray, D., Pte., 200619	* 4.2.18
McKenzie, R., Pte., S/4517	*23.7.18	Murray, P., Pte., 202329	* 1.4.17
McKillen, J., Pte., S/43524	* 1.4.18	Myers, C., Pte., S/20466	*28.2.18
McLagan, D., L/Cpl., 350399	*27.9.17		
McLaren, A., Pte., 202607	*31.7.17	Nelson, A., Pte., 201061	*20.7.18
McLauchlan, J., Pte., 268771	*26.9.17	Nelson, D., Pte., S/23267	*16.11.17
McLaurin, D., Pte., 202657	†11.8.17	Ness, A., Pte., 291445	*26.9.17
McLean, A., L/Cpl., 202328 (M.M. and Bar)	*28.7.18	Newton, R., Pte., 202611	†13.7.17
		Nicol, A. J., Cpl., 240050	†25.11.17
McLean, A., Pte., 202606	‡17.6.17	Nicol, A., Pte., 202223	†29.7.18
McLean, W., Cpl., 265162	*21.3.18	Nicol, A., Pte., 200547	*31.7.17
McLevy, H., Sgt., 201149	*23.3.18	Nicol, W., Pte., 292788	*27.9.17
McLeod, A., Pte., 202664	*31.7.17		
McMahon, A., Pte., 200885	† 4.3.18	Ogilvy, S. R., Pte., 202221	*19.8.18
McNaght, J., Sgt., S/13100	†26.9.17	Oliver, F., L/Cpl., 202477	*31.7.17
McNeelly, J., Pte., 291202	*19.8.18		
McQuattie, J., Pte., 266700	*27.5.18	Parker, C. M., Pte., 291768	* 3.5.18
McQueen, W., Pte., 200559	* 3.5.18	Pearson, D., Pte., 202612	*26.9.17
McTigue, J., Pte., 291998	* 1.4.18	Pearson, J., Pte., 201274	*31.7.17
Mann, J. B., Pte., S/25469	* 2.10.18	Peattie, W., Pte., 202219	†18.7.18
Marshall, H., Sgt., 200260	*26.9.17	Petrie, A., Pte., 203151	*23.7.18
Martin, A., Pte., 202464	* 1.8.17	Philip, J., Pte., 266267	†28.11.17
Martin, A., Cpl., 266523	*20.7.18	Phillip, J., Pte., 240603	† 6.3.18
Martin, J., Pte., 350600	*26.7.18	Porter, R., Pte., 268846	*27.9.17
Mathieson, A., L/Cpl., S/21449	* 9.6.18	Porter, W., Sgt., 240117 (M.M.)	‡29.8.17
Meechan, F., Pte., 241228	* 1.4.18	Prentice, J., Pte., 290287	*24.11.17
Melville, C., Pte., 240921	* 5.5.17	Preston, J., Pte., 202380	* 3.5.18
Mercer, J., Pte., S/24977	*30.9.18	Pringle, A., Pte., 202368	†31.7.18
Michie, D., Pte., 201609	* 3.5.18	Pryde, D., Pte., 350159	*29.10.17
Mill, J., Pte., 201452	*31.7.17	Pryde, W., Pte., 202155	*31.7.17
Millar, C., Sgt., 200916	*14.11.17	Purvis, J. K., Pte., 266926	*26.9.17
Millar, J. H. H., Pte., 268640	*27.5.18		
Miller, G., Pte., 200996	* 9.7.17	Rae, E., Pte., 268124	†26.7.18
Mills, T., Pte., 202232	*27.4.18	Rae, H. S., Pte., 202617	*27.9.17
Milne, D., Pte., 240462	*16.11.17	Rae, R., Pte., S/9807	*28.7.18
Milne, G., Pte., 240977	† 4.4.18	Ramsay, G., Pte., 200046	† 6.3.18
Milne, J., L/Cpl., 241055	* 1.4.18	Randall, H. J., Pte., 201768	*15.11.17
Milne, J., Pte., 240060	* 1.4.18	Reid, A., Pte., 241241	* 9.7.17
Minty, A. E., Pte., 201675	*26.9.17	Reid, J. I., L/Cpl., 202391	‡ 3.11.17
Mitchell, A. R., Pte., 290077	* 6.2.18	Reid, T., Pte., 202452	* 9.7.17

APPENDIX IV

Reilly, F., Pte., 203377 — *28.7.18
Rennie, D. S., Pte., 240100 — * 3.5.18
Rice, E., Pte., 201156 — †23.9.17
Ritchie, A., Pte., 202615 — * 3.5.18
Ritchie, J., Pte., 240547 — †26.7.18
Ritchie, R. L., L/Cpl., S/18735 — * 1.8.18
Robb, J., L/Cpl., 202685 — †31.3.18
Roberts, F., Pte., 350364 — * 1.4.18
Roberts, G. B., L/Cpl., S/18106 — *1.8.18
Robertson, D., Pte., S/22974 — * 1.8.18
Robertson, H., Pte., S/21614 — *22.2.18
Robertson, J., A/L/Cpl., 241242 — *26.9.17
Robertson, N., L/Cpl., 201088 — * 1.4.18
Robertson, W., Pte., 200860 — *31.7.17
Robertson, W., Pte., 202655 — *27.9.17
Rodgers, D. H., Pte., 201829 — *27.9.17
Ross, D., Pte., 240985 — *31.7.17
Ross, T. R., Pte., 265339 (M.M.) — *19.8.18
Ross, W., Pte., 201133 — *31.7.17
Ross, W. T., C.S.M., 200460 — *31.7.17
Russell, D., Pte., S/3497 — †23.2.18
Ryans, A., L/Cpl., S/21383 — *10.6.18

Sadler, G., Pte., S43286 — * 1.8.18
Saunders, A., Pte., 292072 — *26.7.18
Scott, A., Pte., 201616 — †25.3.18
Scott, A., Pte., 267269 — *27.9.17
Scott, C., L/Cpl., 267871 — * 1.8.18
Scott, J., Pte., S/18272 — *10.6.18
Scott, J., Pte., 268849 — *30.7.18
Sharp, F. J., Pte., S/22980 — * 1.4.18
Sharp, J., Pte., 202625 — ‡ 6.4.17
Shearer, J., Pte., S/40163 — *28.7.18
Shields, H., Pte., S/25192 — * 3.10.18
Simon, W., L/Cpl., S/40590 — †27.8.18
Simpson, G., Pte., 202785 — *27.9.17
Skinner, D. C., Pte., 200365 — *26.9.17
Small, J. A., Pte., 350536 — * 1.8.18
Smith, B., Pte., S/21646 — †29.4.18
Smith, C., Pte., 202290 — *31.7.17
Smith, C., Pte., 202623 — * 3.5.18
Smith, C., Pte., S/43210 — *28.7.18
Smith, D., Pte., S/16560 — ‡ 9.11.18
Smith, G., Sgt., 240955 — *28.3.18
Smith, H. G., Pte., 350773 — *25.3.18
Smith, J., Pte., 266038 — *26.9.17
Smith, R., C.S.M., 200054 — *26.9.17
Smith, W., Sgt., 200416 — †12.1.18
Smith, W., Pte., 268895 — * 1.8.18
Snowdowne, B., Pte., 202119 — *27.9.17

Spalding, W., Pte., S/16241 — * 1.8.18
Spence, E., Pte., 240744 — *31.7.17
Steel, A., Pte., S/40834 — * 1.8.18
Stevenson, T. W. D., Pte., 267774 — *24.11.17
Stewart, J., Pte., 240038 — ‡ 3.11.18
Stewart, S., Pte., 200614 — *26.9.17
Stirton, S. S., Pte., 202195 — *27.9.17
Storie, A., L/Cpl., 240854 — *26.5.18
Strachan, L., Pte., 200991 — *27.9.17
Stratton, F., L/Cpl., 200904 — 27.9.17
Stuart, J. W. D., Pte., 268268 — † 4.8.18
Sturrock, J., L/Cpl., 240241 — *27.9.17
Summers, B. J., Pte., 241244 — *31.7.17
Sutherland, J. G., Pte., 201112 — * 1.4.18
Sutherland, J., Sgt., 200185 — *31.7.17
Swankie, D., Pte., 202360 — *31.7.17
Sweeney, N., Pte., 202640 — *31.7.17
Swinnens, A. B., Pte., 201773 — †17.1.18
Sword, G., Pte., 241129 — * 8.1.18
Sword, W., Pte., 267137 — † 3.5.18

Tasker, J., Pte., S/3012 — * 1.4.18
Tasker, R., Pte., 241148 — †26.9.17
Taylor, A., Pte., 201084 — *14.5.17
Taylor, G., Pte., 200635 — *23.3.18
Taylor, P., Pte., S/21384 — *28.7.18
Taylor, R., L/Cpl., 201255 — *28.7.18
Thom, A., Pte., S/9805 — *28.7.18
Thom, J., L/Sgt., 240533 — *26.9.17
Thompson, A., Pte., 202639 — †29.8.17
Threadgold, S. A., Pte., 202665 — *26.9.17
Timmons, A., Pte., 240427 — *21.3.18
Tuvan, A., Pte., 292058 — * 1.8.19

Vollands, H., Pte., 202632 — *27.9.17

Wade, R., Pte., 240873 — *31.7.17
Walker, A., Pte., 202053 — *31.7.17
Walker, D., Pte., 241253 — *27.9.17
Walker, J., Pte., 202689 — *26.9.17
Watters, A., Pte., S/23349 — * 3.5.18
Wateridge, W. J., Pte., S/40618 — * 1.8.18
Watson, A., Pte., S/20776 — *21.3.18
Watson, J., Pte., S/23425 — * 1.4.18
Watson, J., L/Cpl., 240481 (M.M.) — * 3.5.18
Watson, J. I., Pte., 201555 — *28.7.18
Watt, J., Pte., 240026 — *31.7.17
Webster, W., Pte., 201621 — †22.2.18
White, W., Pte., 22001 — *31.7.17
Whittet, T., Pte., 240961 — *31.7.17

FOURTH-FIFTH BATTALION THE BLACK WATCH

Whyte, D., Pte., 200461	† 2.4.18	Wylie, G., Pte., 202729	*27.9.17
Wilkie, J., Pte., 201605	† 4.9.17	Wylie, J. C., L/Cpl., S/23103	*10.11.18
Wishart, J., Pte., 201173	*31.7.17	Wylie, R., Sgt., 200065	* 5.10.18
Witty, W. G., Pte., 201777	*15.11.17		
Wolfe, A., Pte., 203403	*28.7.18	Young, A., Sgt., 200667	† 8.8.18
Wood, E. J., Pte., 292849	§30.12.17	Young, J., Pte., 200121	*31.7.17
Woolsey, G., Pte., S/40211	*26.9.17	Young, J., L/Cpl., 265728	*27.9.18
Wylie, C. F., Pte., 240858	*30.4.18	Yule, G., Pte., 241257	† 2.8.17

APPENDIX V

HONOURS AND AWARDS

The Fourth-Fifth Battalion

D.S.O.
Lieut.-Colonel G. A. McL. Sceales.
Major T. D. Murray.
Lieut. A. J. Stewart.

Bar to M.C.
Lieut. R. A. Plimpton.
Capt. D. Maxwell.

M.C.
Capt. R. C. Cunningham.
2nd Lieut. T. F. Andrews.
Lieut. W. S. Robertson.
Capt. T. Lyell.
2nd Lieut. A. L. C. Edwards.
2nd Lieut. I. S. Paterson.
Lieut. R. A. Plimpton
Capt. T. Stevenson.
2nd Lieut. J. C. Forsyth.
Lieut. R. F. Currey.
Lieut. J. R. Murray.
Lieut. and Adj. G. H. Scratton.
2nd Lieut. C. S. McCririck.
2nd Lieut. A. Fraser.
Capt. D. Maxwell
2nd Lieut. G. R. Farrar.
Capt. J. R. Philip.
Capt. C. H. P. C. Penney.
2nd Lieut. A. C. Skinner.
Capt. K. E. Badenoch.
2nd Lieut. G. Fullerton.
Lieut. R. Inch.
2nd Lieut. A. Scott.
Lieut. J. Baldwin.
Capt. I. M. Bruce-Gardyne.
Lieut. F. G. Shand.
C.S.M. J. Baird.
C.S.M. T. Bowman.

Bar to D.C.M.
Sgt. W. Stewart.

D.C.M.
Pte. J. Low.
Pte. D. Stuart.
Sgt. D. Hutton.
Sgt. W. Findlay.
Sgt. W. Webster.
Pte. T. Myles.
Sgt. G. Y. McFarlane.
Pte. P. Gethins.
Sgt. W. Stewart
Pte. J. L. Herd.
C.S.M. A. Anderson.
Pte. D. Hedley.
Sgt. I. I. Keith.
Sgt. J. Dickson.
L/Corpl. W. Somerville.
Sgt. S. Malcolm.
Sgt. T. McDonald.

M.S.M.
C.S.M. A. Anderson.

Bar to M.M.
Pte. P. Gethins.
Pte. A. Bennett.
L/Corpl. H. Brough.
Sgt. G. Cruickshank.
L/Corpl. A. Maclean.
L/Corpl. W. F. Hill.

FOURTH-FIFTH BATTALION THE BLACK WATCH

M.M.

L/Corpl. R. Adam.
Sgt. W. Henderson.
Corpl. J. Cassidy.
Sgt. J. Coltart.
L/Corpl. W. Watson.
Pte. W. Murdoch.
Pte. D. Jones.
Pte. J. Leys.
Sgt. Piper D. McLeod.
L/Corpl. J. Brisbane.
Sgt. A. Gammie.
Sgt. J. D. Petrie.
Corpl. R. Wood.
Pte. A. Ferrier.
Pte. C. Petrie.
Pte. D. Smart.
Pte. W. High.
Pte. A. Redford.
Pte. W. Hunter.
Pte. T. Cathro.
Pte. T. Healey.
Sgt. W. Munro.
Pte. D. Hamilton.
Pte. P. Gethins.
L/Corpl. C. Horne.
Pte. D. Lowe.
Pte. A. Leuchars.
Pte. A. Bennett.
Pte. A. Brown.
Pte. D. McKay.
Sgt. G. Sivewright.
Pte. J. Robb.
Corpl. J. Cairns.
L/Sgt. A. Anderson.
Sgt. W. Brett.
L/Corpl. H. M. McLeish.
Corpl. P. McHugh.
Corpl. J. McCormack.
Pte. G. Shepherd.
Sgt. G. Guthrie.
Sgt. J. Houston.
Sgt. J. Harris.
Sgt. D. Ogilvie.
Sgt. A. Waugh.
Pte. A. Drury.
Pte. G. Hutchinson.
Sgt. A. F. Dolan.

Sgt. W. Martin.
Sgt. W. Baird.
L/Sgt. J. McLaughlin.
L/Corpl. J. Montague.
Sgt. H. McGregor.
Sgt. D. Hutton.
L/Corpl. J. G. McFarlane.
Sgt. G. Cruickshank.
Corpl. C. Osborne.
Pte. J. Jolly.
Pte. A. Maude.
Pte. D. A. C. McLennan.
Pte. R. Cairnie.
Pte. J. Gordon.
L/Corpl. G. Watson.
Pte. H. Keddie.
Pte. A. Morrison.
L/Corpl. J. Spalding.
Pte. G. H. White.
Sgt. D. S. Grier.
Pte. G. Turnbull.
Pte. E. Fairweather.
Sgt. G. Soutar.
Corpl. J. McManus.
L/Sgt. J. Dempster.
C.S.M. W. Stewart.
Pte. R. S. Hutchinson.
Pte. W. McGregor.
L/Corpl. A. Maclean.
Sgt. J. Stephen.
L/Corpl. F. Willets.
Pte. W. Stewart.
Pte. W. Robertson.
L/Corpl. H. Mill.
L/Corpl. H. Brough.
Pte. F. Sayle.
Sgt. G. Paton.
Pte. J. Reid.
L/Corpl. R. Sutherland.
C.Q.M.S. W. Smith.
Corpl. J. Davidson.
Sgt. J. Higgins.
L/Corpl. W. Dalgetty.
Pte. C. Scott.
Pte. T. Rankine.
L/Corpl. W. F. Hill.

APPENDIX V

MENTIONED IN DESPATCHES

Lieut.-Colonel R. A. Bulloch.
Lieut.-Colonel G. A. McL. Sceales.
Major S. A. Innes.
Major T. D. Murray.
Capt. J. R. Philip.

Capt. A. J. Stewart.
Lieut. G. F. Paterson.
2nd Lieut. A. S. G. Loxton.
2nd Lieut. J. C. McIntyre.
2nd Lieut. A. B. Watson.

C.S.M. D. Burgess.
Pte. J. Chevens.
Sgt. A. Buchan.

Sgt. D. Hutton.
Sgt. J. Laird.

FOREIGN DECORATIONS

CHEVALIER OF THE LEGION OF HONOUR, AND CROIX DE GUERRE

Lieut.-Colonel R. A. Bulloch., D.S.O.

CROIX DE GUERRE

Major J. S. Y. Rogers.
Capt. and Adjutant J. I. Buchan.

Capt. A. J. Stewart.

Sgt. J. Cairns.
Corpl. J. Moffat.
Pte. M. Kidd.
Pte. A. Robertson.

Sgt. S. Malcolm.
Corpl. J. Davidson.
Pte. T. Ross.
Pte. J. Graham.

CROIX DE GUERRE AND MÉDAILLE MILITAIRE

Sgt. A. Dickson.

APPENDIX VI

List of Actions and Operations

The Fourth-Fifth Battalion

1915. 4th and 5th Battalions amalgamated at La Belle Hôtesse. 7th March. Trench warfare. Moated Grange, Festubert, Givenchy, Festubert, Givenchy, La Bassée Canal, Richebourg, Givenchy, Festubert. March–September.

BATTLE OF POZIÈRES RIDGE. (Beaumont.) 3rd September.
Trench warfare. Beaumont Hamel, Thiepval. September–October.

BATTLE OF THE ANCRE HEIGHTS. (Capture of Schwaben Redoubt.) 14th–16th October.
Trench warfare. Schwaben Redoubt, Thiepval, River Ancre, Hansa Line, Ypres. October–December.

1917. Trench warfare. Ypres, Wieltje, La Bugne. January–July.

BATTLE OF PILCKEM RIDGE. (Steenbeek.) 31st July–August.
Trench warfare. Klein Zillebeke, Zwartelen. August–September.

BATTLE OF POLYGON WOOD. (Zwartelen.) 27th September.
Trench warfare. Ypres, Shrewsbury Forest, Vierstraat, Polderhook, Ridgewood, Steenvoorde. September–December.

1918. Trench warfare. Alberta Sector, Gondecourt. January–March.

THE OFFENSIVE IN PICARDY. (FIRST BATTLE OF BAPAUME). (St. Denis and Clery.) 24th–25th March.

BATTLE OF POZIERES. (Herbecourt, Proyart.) 26th–27th March. Wiencourt Ridge. 28th March.

BATTLES OF THE LYS. (SECOND BATTLE OF KEMMEL RIDGE) (Voormezeele.) 26th–27th April.
4/5th Battalion absorbed 9th (Service) Battalion in Fampoux Sector. May 16th.
Trench warfare. Fampoux, Arras, Fampoux.

BATTLE OF THE SOISSONAIS. (Attack on Buzancy.) 28th July–2nd August.
Trench warfare. Neuville Vitasse, Hulluch, Loos Salient. July–October.

ADVANCE TO VICTORY. 2nd October–11th November.

THE SIXTH
BATTALION

CHAPTER I

AUGUST, 1914, TO MAY, 1915

Mobilization at North Queensferry—Dundee and the Tay Defences —Move to Bedford to join 51st (Highland) Division

IN 1859 and 1860 eighteen separate companies of Volunteers were raised in Perthshire, but were shortly afterwards formed into two Administrative Battalions. Of these companies, those belonging to Perth, Dunblane, Coupar-Angus, Crieff, Alyth, Doune, Callendar, Birnam and Auchterarder were formed in 1869 into the First Perthshire Administrative Battalion. The Battalion Headquarters was established at Perth, where it still remains.

Under the Territorial system of 1881 the Battalion was affiliated to the County Regiment, and in 1888 received the designation of the 4th (Perthshire) Volunteer Battalion (The Black Watch) Royal Highlanders.

Much of the success of the Battalion had been due to the energy and fine spirit of Sir Robert Moncreiffe, who joined in 1884 and commanded it from 1893 to 1911. Even this long period did not end his connection with the Regiment, for, on the outbreak of war, Sir Robert rejoined and commanded the Battalion in France.

During the South African War three more companies were raised in Perth, and about fifty men joined the three Volunteer Service companies who fought with the 2nd Battalion of the Regiment in South Africa.

Under the new Territorial organization in 1908, the 4th Volunteer Battalion became the 6th (Perthshire) Battalion The Black Watch, with its recruiting area over the whole county of Perth, and it was under this title that the lineal descendants of the Volunteer companies of 1859 fought as a unit of The Black Watch throughout the Great War.

In April, 1914, a small detachment, three officers and 40 men, of the 6th Battalion spent a few days at the war station, near the Forth Bridge, for the purpose of testing the mobilization scheme and railway arrangements. This proved of great value, and when the real call came the scheme of mobilization ran without a hitch.

On August 4th, 1914, a fortnight after the Battalion had completed its annual training, orders were received to mobilize. On the morning of the 5th, men were pouring into their Company Headquarters, where they were medically examined, issued with identity discs, kit bags and ammunition. By the evening of the same day the 6th had become an organized unit and went into camp at Queensferry. Here it was immediately joined

THE SIXTH BATTALION THE BLACK WATCH

by two detachments, one from Belfast and another from Dublin. It is of interest to record that this Battalion of Highland soldiers had well-organized detachments in Ireland in 1914, and that these joined with the same enthusiasm as did the men from Perthshire.

Headquarters of the Battalion occupied the Golf Club House near Carlingnose, and the eight companies were detached over a large area. On mobilization, the 6th was commanded by Lieutenant-Colonel C. E. Colville, in the absence, through illness, of Lieutenant-Colonel D. C. Campbell, who was never able to join the Battalion, but died in the autumn of 1914, to the deep regret of his many friends in the regiment.

The companies were commanded as follows;—

A company (Perth), Captain A. Innes.
B   „   (Perth), Captain G. D. Pullar.
C   „   (Dunblane), Major C. Murray-Stewart.
D   „   (Crieff), Captain L. Gibson.
E   „   (Blairgowrie), Captain W. Alexander.
F   „   (Auchterarder), Captain T. E. Young.
G   „   (Dunkeld and Pitlochry), Captain R. G. Gordon.
H   „   (Aberfeldy), Captain J. Wylie.

The Adjutant was Captain J. W. Oxley, Gordon Highlanders, and the Quartermaster an ex-regular of The Black Watch, Major B. Sadler. The Regimental Sergeant-Major, Sergeant-Major J. Wilson—better known among his countless friends as "Punch"—had also served with The Black Watch.

The first few weeks at Queensferry proved to be a time of hard work for all ranks. Block-houses, dug-outs and fortifications had to be constructed, and the approaches to the Forth Bridge, landing places and other points as far west as the dockyard at Rosyth guarded.

The Special Service section, under Captain J. Hally, maintained a continuous coast patrol from the week preceding the outbreak of war. The training, digging and construction work had a disastrous effect on uniforms, of which the supply was scanty, surplus supplies having been taken to fit out the New Armies. Months passed before the 6th were issued even with new glengarries, while constant marching, hard training and patrolling railway tracks wore out both clothing and boots, and the invariable advice sent to friends at home, who were raising money for "comforts," was to invest the funds in boots, socks and shirts. Recruits poured in and were steadily trained throughout this period, but, keen as they were, they could not perform any guard duties for lack of uniform and equipment.

Another disadvantage that all Territorial battalions suffered

COLONEL Sir ROBERT D. MONCRIEFFE, Bart., C.B., C.M.G.,
V.D., T.D., Commanding The Sixth Battalion

OFFICERS OF THE SIXTH BATTALION AT BOIS DE PACAUT (N. of Béthune), JUNE, 1915

Back Row: Capt. D. B. Calder, Capt. S. H. Marshall (slightly in front), 2nd Lt. J. B. Smith,
2nd Lt. A. F. Hill, 2nd Lt. R. G. Macnaughton
Third Row (Standing): 2nd Lt. A. B. Sadler, 2nd Lt. W. E. Coutts, 2nd Lt. T. Johnson, Lt. A. P. West,
2nd Lt. L. G. Miles, 2nd Lt. J. N. Wilson, 2nd Lt. R. G. A. Dickson, Lt. J. Craig, Capt. A. Innes,
Capt. J. MacRosty
Sitting: Capt. G. D. Pullar, Capt. W. Alexander, Major J. Wylie, Lt.-Col. C. C. MacDowell,
Col. Sir R. D. Moncreiffe, Bart., V.D., A.D.C., Capt. & Adjt. J. A. Durie, Capt. L. Gibson,
Major W. Haig, R.A.M.C.
In Front: Capt. J. Hally, 2nd Lt. R. Lynn, 2nd Lt. N. F. Dixon, 2nd Lt. W. P. Stewart,
2nd Lt. R. L. West, 2nd Lt. W. Baynham, Rev. R. Macdonald, M.A., (C.F.)

TRAINING, WINTER, 1914

from was the loss, during the first week of the war, of the few experienced soldiers they possessed, namely, the Regular Sergeant Instructors, who were sent off to train the First New Army. In one way, however, this was to the good, as it put all ranks on their mettle, and forced officers and non-commissioned officers to develop their own initiative and resource, and to overcome the many unforeseen difficulties that arose. Men with aptitude and training for particular work soon came to the front, and, whether as instructors in drill and musketry or as butchers and cooks, they were soon all fitted into their proper grooves.

About a fortnight after mobilization, Sir Robert Moncreiffe was reappointed to command the Battalion vice Lieutenant-Colonel Campbell. Sir Robert had commanded it for eighteen years—from 1893 to 1911—when he had brought the Battalion to a state of high efficiency. The greatest enthusiasm was shown by officers and men when he came back to take over command at Queensferry.

Shortly after this a second line Battalion was formed under the command of Colonel A. W. Hay-Drummond. This unit, composed mainly of men not then considered fit for service overseas, took over the defences on the south side of the Forth. This enabled the 1/6th to devote more time to training the large number of recruits now flowing into the Battalion.

In addition to work on the fortifications, the Battalion had another unusual duty to perform. When vessels came into the Forth for coaling, platoons were frequently employed in searching the coaling parties who arrived from various mining districts in Scotland, usually at night, before they embarked on the tenders which took them up the river.

Early in November the Battalion received orders to take over the Tay Defences at Dundee and Wormit. The entry of the Battalion into Dundee was a memorable sight. Few of the men were properly clothed or equipped, the greater number being clad in civilian clothes much the worse for wear. By the efforts of the Commanding Officer, however, this state of affairs was quickly put right, and the 6th soon regained its name for smartness in appearance and steadiness on parade. The duties on the Tay Defences were similar to those on the Forth. On the Dundee side, guard duties were frequent, the twenty-four hour spell at the docks, with the Custom House as Headquarters, being an experience which few will readily forget.

On the Fife side, as the spring of 1915 came in, much training was carried out, mainly under Lieutenant-Colonel MacDowell, Second-in-Command, and by the end of March the Battalion was in hard condition and fit for a twenty mile march in full kit, or

THE SIXTH BATTALION THE BLACK WATCH

a whole day of field training. This hard work stood the Battalion in good stead when it went to France.

Early in January, 1915, the eight-company organization of the Battalion was altered to four, the rearrangement being carried out as follows:—

G and H companies became No. 1 company under Major J. Wylie.

B and D companies became No. 2 company under Captain G. D. Pullar.

C and E companies became No. 3 company under Captain W. Alexander.

A and F companies became No. 4 company under Captain T. E. Young.

Captain L. Gibson was appointed Adjutant, and Major R. Stirling, Royal Army Medical Corps, took over the duties of Battalion Medical Officer, his place being taken by Major W. Haig, Royal Army Medical Corps, before the Battalion went overseas.

On April 15th the 6th was ordered to entrain for Bedford. Keen though all ranks were to get away, Dundee was left with great regret, for the many residents on either side of the river had taken endless pains in entertaining the troops and had shown them boundless hospitality. Bedford was reached next morning, where the 6th and 7th (Fifeshire) Battalion formed part of what afterwards became the 153rd Infantry Brigade of the 51st (Highland) Division, which had been training all the winter in Bedford.

Before the end of 1914 the 51st Division had sent six Battalions, besides a Field Ambulance and Field Company, to France. Their places were now taken by the 6th and 7th Battalions The Black Watch and by a Lancashire Territorial Brigade consisting of the 4th Battalion King's Own Royal Lancashire Regiment, 8th Battalion King's Liverpool Regiment, 4th Battalion Loyal North Lancashire Regiment and 2/5th Battalion Lancashire Fusiliers. The Highland Division was then under command of Major-General R. Bannatine-Allason, and consisted of the 152nd, 153rd and 154th Brigades. The 153rd was formed by the 6th and 7th Battalions The Black Watch and the 5th and 7th Battalions Gordon Highlanders, under command of Brigadier-General Douglas Campbell.

A fortnight of feverish energy followed the arrival of the 6th at Bedford, during which time the Battalion was completely re-clothed and re-equipped, and all unfit men were weeded out and replaced from the second line. A complete transport section, which up to this time had consisted of a few commandeered civilian vehicles and horses, was also organized.

CHAPTER II

MAY TO DECEMBER, 1915

The Move to France—In the line near Festubert—The Somme Area

ON the 2nd of May, 1915, the Battalion entrained at Bedford (the transport section having left two days in advance), embarked the same evening at Folkestone and reached Boulogne about midnight, where it spent a bitterly cold night under canvas in the rest camp. The following evening the Battalion entrained at Pont de Briques, joining the train in which the transport section had travelled from Havre.

After an all night journey in trucks, the 6th detrained at Berguette and went into billets at La Pierrière in the neighbourhood of Busnes. Two days later the Battalion moved to Paradis, which was reached after a long and tedious night march in thick fog, and was there held in reserve during the second battle of Neuve Chapelle. The 6th now joined the Indian Corps under Sir James Willcocks, then in the First Army commanded by Sir Douglas Haig. Returning to La Pierrière on May 12th, the Battalion marched two days later with the Division via St. Vénant and Hazebrouck to Flêtre, and remained in reserve for the Second Battle of Ypres which was then at its height. This march gave all ranks for the first time an idea of a Division on the march, and of the checks and delays inseparable from the movements of so large a body of troops. While at Flêtre the 6th saw the newly arrived 9th (Scottish) Division on the march, in the ranks of which many old friends were recognized.

From Flêtre, after almost continuous marching by day and night, and suffering greatly from the new boots served out in Bedford, the Battalion reached Le Touret on May 20th. The route lay through Rouge Croix, Bleu, Estairs and Pont Riqueul. On May 19th a party of officers went from Pont Riqueul to Festubert and there inspected the trenches which were to be taken over by the 51st Division from the 2nd; during their journey they came for the first time under shell fire at Lacouture.

On the 20th the 6th moved via Locon to Le Touret *en route* for the trenches, but were held up on the way owing to an attack being made by the Canadians immediately in front. Towards midnight, the 6th arrived in front of Indian village, near Festubert, where it took over the line from a battalion of the Coldstream Guards (2nd Division), who were not a little surprised to find a battalion of raw Territorials taking over a complicated line just captured from the enemy. The Guards, however, showed great patience in helping their successors to take over the new trenches, then a mere scrape in the ground about eighteen inches deep.

THE SIXTH BATTALION THE BLACK WATCH

All who were present will remember those first two days in the trenches. Men and officers suffered severely from thirst and had the unpleasant task of burying many enemy dead; in addition it was necessary to convert the shallow ditch which they had taken over into a well-built fire trench, working all the time under continuous fire from enemy snipers and machine guns.

On the night of the 22nd the Battalion was relieved by the 7th Black Watch and moved into reserve near Chocolat Menier Corner. A thunderstorm burst overheadth at night, and the men being in the open were immediately soaked to the skin; many, however, were so exhausted that they slept throughout the storm. A fine day of sunshine followed which soon restored everyone to a condition of comparative comfort. The day was Sunday, but several attempts to hold a Battalion Church Parade in a neighbouring orchard were frustrated by enemy shell fire. On this day an issue of blue Balmorals with khaki covers was made, the head-dress hitherto having been the glengarry. On the 24th a move was made to Le Touret, and the following day to bivouacs in the Bois de Pacaut, where the Battalion rested for several days.

On May 31st the Battalion, after a march of some nine miles, returned to the trenches in front of Festubert, where it took over from the 48th Canadian Highlanders (Toronto). Here the 6th found its right resting on a notoriously hot corner known as L 8, and in touch with the 2nd Battalion Gordon Highlanders, who astonished the 6th by their persistence in shaving every morning in the front line, even under the most adverse conditions. Many men of this fine Battalion fell in an attempted advance by the 20th Brigade on the night of June 3rd, while the companies of the 6th held the line, their duty being to give a vigorous covering fire.

Until now the 6th had been wonderfully fortunate in escaping casualties. The next tour in the same sector—June 11th to 14th—was, however, a costly one, the losses including Lieutenant R. P. Haldane, the first officer of the 6th to be killed, six men killed and 16 wounded, the shelling during Sunday the 15th being particularly heavy and accurate. It is surprising that the losses were not greater, as protection against enemy fire was very slight, consisting as it did of low breast-works and shelters constructed by the Canadians, usually with only a single layer of sandbags.

On the 17th the Lancashire Territorial Brigade attached to the Division made a gallant but unsuccessful attack on the German lines in front of Festubert, and the Battalion moved to La Touret in reserve. The same evening, working parties of the 6th, amounting practically to the whole Battalion, were sent to

TRENCH WARFARE, JUNE–JULY, 1915

the front line to dig new trenches; but the second attack having also failed, this work was not carried out. Many losses, however, were suffered from shell fire, and the Battalion moved into the front line again on the following night.

The remainder of the month was spent in this area, and on the 27th the Commanding Officer, Sir Robert Moncreiffe, was admitted to hospital, having started an old wound while attempting to rescue some men from a shell-wrecked dug-out. On the same day the Second-in-Command, Lieutenant-Colonel MacDowell, received orders to join the Royal Field Artillery, and Major Wylie, then commanding A company, took over command of the Battalion.

Relieved that night by the 2nd Battalion Bedfordshire Regiment, the 6th went into billets near Locon and furnished numerous working parties in the forward area. From there, on the 28th, the Battalion moved a few miles further north to Laventie and the breast-works in front of Fauquissart, the 51st relieving the Lahore Division of the Indian Corps.

Here conditions were different to those so far experienced; the Germans were more peaceful, and contented themselves by firing a few occasional rounds of artillery fire, whereas at Festubert the showing of a light or even the kindling of a fire at once brought down heavy shelling; at Fauquissart, under the comparative security of high breast-works, lights and fires were safely allowed by night and day. Most of the losses in this sector were incurred on patrol work, in which both sides were very active, opposing parties often meeting one another in the long corn and grass of No Man's Land. In this way, Corporals Newell and Willis of A company were shot, and for plucky work in bringing them in under fire the first decorations awarded to the 6th were received. Private Jenkins gained the Distinguished Conduct Medal, Private Deane the Croix de Guerre, and Private Macdonald was mentioned in despatches; unfortunately Newell and Willis died almost immediately, and the Battalion thus lost two very capable non-commissioned officers.

The visit to this sector ended with a stay of several days in good billets at Laventie. Much work had to be done by night, but the days passed pleasantly, a frequent afternoon entertainment being provided by Transport Sergeant Willard, who put his section through a regular circus performance every day. The 6th left Laventie on the 21st, and was scarcely clear of the village before the enemy shelled it heavily. That evening the Battalion reached Merville, where several days were spent resting and training.

On July 25th the Battalion marched through St. Vénant to Berguette, where it entrained for the south, detraining the next day at Méricourt, whence it marched to Bresle, and were the first infantry of the 51st Division to reach the Somme area.

The arrival of Highland soldiers for the first time in the neighbourhood created immense excitement amongst the inhabitants and the French troops, and the Battalion's first acquaintance with the Somme area was most pleasant. During the few days spent at Bresle the 6th was inspected by General Sir Charles Munro, Commanding the Third Army, the 51st Division having now joined the X Corps (General Morland) in that Army.

On August 1st the Battalion had the interesting experience of taking over a sector of the line from the French, when the 6th went into the firing line in front of La Boisselle. Here the trenches were dug in the chalky soil to a depth of fifteen feet and were provided with deep and roomy shelters, a great contrast to the shallow, ditch-like lines of breast-works at Festubert. With such protection it was possible for a battalion to remain for several weeks in one sector without relief, and this was to be the experience of the 6th for the next five months.

Everywhere there was evidence of the prodigious energy and ingenuity of the French engineers and infantry. Their officers took a just pride in these famous lines, and displayed an intimate knowledge not only of their own sector, but also of the enemy lines in front; this knowledge they took great pains to pass on to their successors. They were especially anxious that points to which they had clung tenaciously—such as " Ilot " and " Duhollo "—although only hopeless masses of wreckage, should not be abandoned, and they never were.

The French troops relieved by the 6th were the famous 19th Regiment of Infantry, a splendid body of men drawn from Brittany. At one point the Highlanders were addressed by a sturdy Poilu in the broadest Scotch, and later on it was discovered that in pre-war days he had been employed in selling onions in the streets of Perth!

On Sunday, August 8th, the Battalion had its first experience of the effect of enemy mines. Shortly before midnight, just as the " Ilot " sector had been taken over by C company, the Germans exploded two large mines, at the same time bombarding the whole sector with intense artillery fire and aerial torpedoes, which exploded in the trenches with a tremendous crash, causing some confusion. As the result of former mine explosions, the trenches gave little protection in some places, while in others the front line was blown out of existence. One man, Private Nicholson, was blown right out of the front trench, captured by the enemy and afterwards died a prisoner in German hands.

The most serious effect of these explosions was the collapse

THE SOMME, AUGUST–NOVEMBER, 1915

of a large dug-out occupied by a whole platoon of C company. Fortunately, willing hands soon got to work, and though many men were more or less injured, only one man was killed. Captain Pullar superintended the rescue work, while Major Alexander reorganized the defence of the position, and Captain Innes the clearing and rebuilding of damaged trenches. By daylight the work was complete, the lines restored and C company was relieved by A under Captain Marshall. It is interesting to note that the total amount of artillery ammunition available for retaliation that night was two 18-pounder shrapnel shells. For his able handling of a dangerous situation Major Alexander was awarded the Distinguished Service Order.

On the morning of the 13th the 6th had the satisfaction of seeing a large part of the enemy line in front of them destroyed by the explosion of a huge French mine, a sight not likely to be forgotten by those who witnessed it, and more especially by those who suffered from the German mine on the 8th. During this tour the 6th instructed the officers and men of the 8th Battalion Suffolk Regiment, 18th Division, of the Second " New Army," in the duties of trench warfare, and after handing over the line to them withdrew to billets in Albert.

After spending a week in Albert, the 6th moved to Buire village, on the Ancre, where Colonel Sir Robert Moncreiffe resumed command, succeeding Major Wylie. Here the time was spent in training and recreation until the beginning of September when the Battalion entered the front line at Bécourt, accompanied by the usual enemy shelling and trench-mortar fire. Now, however, the Divisional Artillery were better supplied with heavy ammunition, and were able to deal more effectively with the German fire.

While in the line here, the Battalion was visited by two working-men delegates from Tyneside who, greatly impressed by what they saw, promised to impress on their fellow workmen at home the need for speeding up the supply of munitions.

October and November were spent in various parts of this area, ten days in the line and ten days out at Hénencourt being the regular routine. On October 25th, the Battalion, chosen to represent the 153rd Brigade, was inspected by His Majesty The King near Buire.

The last tour in the trenches, at the end of November, was spent in front of Aveluy, " F " sector. The weather was bad, and to make matters worse the enemy celebrated St. Andrew's night by a four hours' bombardment of the front line held by B and C companies. This caused the garrison to be broken up into a number of small detachments, some of which became almost isolated owing to the mud and heavy going, the mud being often over three feet deep. Under such conditions it was very difficult to bring up supplies, and the men in the front line depended for some time on their emergency rations. The kilt was temporarily discarded and improvised " shorts," made out of a couple of sandbags, was the usual dress for the 6th Battalion during this period.

Early in December, the 51st Division was ordered to form the Corps reserve on relief by the 32nd, and on the 21st the Battalion handed over the Authuile sector to a Battalion of the Highland Light Infantry of that Division, and saw no more of the Ancre area until the following summer. Leaving Martinsart on the 21st and halting at Beaucourt on the 22nd, the Battalion reached the end of its journey, Vaux-en-Amienois, the following day. Here it was to spend over a month resting and training.

CHAPTER III

CHRISTMAS, 1915, TO JULY, 1916

With the 30th Division at Maricourt—Four months in the Labyrinth near Arras

ON Christmas Day the 6th suffered a severe loss when, owing to illness, Sir Robert Moncreiffe was obliged to give up the command. A farewell parade was held on that day, when it was easy to see that the regret the Commanding Officer felt on leaving the Battalion, for which he had done so much, was shared by every officer and man. He was succeeded in command by Lieutenant-Colonel C. M. Truman, 12th Lancers.

Life at Vaux seemed wonderfully peaceful and came as a welcome relief after the racket and unceasing vigilance which had been the lot of the 6th for the past seven months. Amiens was within easy distance, and the men were glad to spend their spare time in the city. At that time the town was untouched by war; it was cheerful and well lit, and, but for the sand-bagged front of the cathedral, showed no outward sign of the battle which was being fought so few miles away. Some leave was now allowed, and a number of officers and men were able to spend a few days in Scotland, for the first time since they had left it seven months earlier.

Much time was devoted to training, which included some ceremonial drill. Wet and dry canteens were opened, and this period was perhaps the most pleasant that the Battalion spent in France. New Year's Day, 1916, was celebrated in the orthodox manner, but the French villagers were always very friendly towards " les Eccossais," who, on their part, kept their rejoicings within reasonable bounds.

On February 6th, 1916, the Battalion moved to Corbie with the 153rd Brigade, lent temporarily to the 30th Division, then in the front line beyond Bray-sur-Somme. The 6th reached Corbie that night, and no sooner had it settled into billets than every available man was called out to unload a number of trucks containing shells. On the 8th, the Battalion moved to Sailly-le-Sec on the Somme, a little village chiefly noted for the streams of mud which ran down its streets. On February 12th, a march further forward was made to Grovetown Camp, beyond Bray, where the Battalion camped in tents pitched in a muddy field. Bray itself was regularly shelled by the enemy and the transport section suffered some casualties.

On the 15th, the Battalion received orders to take over the Maricourt defences, which consisted of an ill-defined system of trenches surrounding the village. Maricourt, though close to the front line, had been so seldom shelled by the enemy that the garrison was able to live in the village. But shortly before the arrival of the 6th, enemy bombardments had almost destroyed both Maricourt and the neighbouring village of Suzanne: trenches had to be dug and shelters constructed for the troops, not only as protection from shell fire, but also from the rain or snow which now fell almost continuously.

On February 19th the Battalion moved to Etinehem, in Brigade reserve, but on the 24th came back to the trenches at Maricourt in abominable weather, heavy falls of snow alternating with spells of hard frost. The days were spent with little shelter from the cold and wet of February. Hardships were not lessened by constant changes of plan. The 6th was "nobody's child" at this time as the Brigade was only temporarily attached to the 30th Division, and no one seemed to have the special duty of looking after the comfort of the men.

Towards the end of the month the 153rd Brigade received orders to move to the Corbie area and rejoin its own Division. This was carried out on the 29th, when the 6th reached Poulainville. A week later another series of marches through Doullens, Beaudricourt and Maroeuil, brought the Battalion into the Maison Blanche area, where, on the 12th, it relieved the French in reserve.

In this new sector, the 6th was to take over part of the famous Labyrinth, north of Arras, including the ruined village of Neuville-St. Vaast. It is a dreary and desolate country, especially in the winter, and was the area the French had wrested from the Germans the previous May. Here, as at La Boisselle, French troops did their utmost to assist the Highland Division when taking over the line. In both the Albert and Arras sectors, the 6th received the greatest hospitality and help from all ranks of the French army, and from the villagers behind the line. The French people did all they could to add to the comfort of the Highlanders, and they may be sure that their ancient Scottish allies will not forget the help and constant kindness they received in France.

In front of Maroeuil, and about three miles from it, lies the famous Vimy Ridge, and here the 6th was continually in the line for the next four months with only three periods of rest of six days each. These short spells were spent at Maroeuil and Bray, both of which villages were under constant shell fire.

Not only the British front line but all the country for many miles in rear of it was commanded by the enemy holding the crest line of Vimy Ridge. Major F. W. Bewsher says in the *History of the 51st (Highland) Division:*

VIMY RIDGE, MARCH, 1915

"This area can almost be called the spiritual home of the 51st (Highland) Division in France since it occupied it for three months in 1916, five months in 1917 during the battle of Arras, and returned there in May, 1918. From May onwards it remained in that part of the world, with the exception of a brief interlude in Champagne, and there it began the Advance to Victory which culminated with the Armistice."

Reconnoitring this complicated sector occupied some time, and it was not until March 21st that the 6th went into the line at Neuville-St. Vaast.

The retention of the Vimy Ridge was of vital importance to the Germans, and it was, therefore, only natural that they made every effort to hold it, and to add to the security of their position. They attempted many raids on the British line, though seldom with any success, and were very enterprising in mining operations. On one occasion after exploding a mine, the enemy heavily bombarded the sector held by Lieutenant Flett's platoon, and attempted to raid the trenches. During the ensuing fight with the raiders Flett had his ankle smashed by a grenade and later his thigh and knee were broken by two successive bombs; but he bravely continued to command his platoon and refused to leave his post until the raiders had been beaten off. For this gallant action Flett was awarded the Military Cross, but shortly afterwards died of his wounds.

The Germans, however, were no longer allowed undisputed freedom in their mining operations. The 51st Divisional tunnelling companies undermined their galleries, and in a short time were able to spring several surprises on the enemy. So effective indeed was this work that before the Division left the area, the Germans gave up mining and blew up their half-prepared mines in No Man's Land, an act which did no harm to the British, and in several instances gave the Highland Division the advantage of improved observation.

The task of the British was made easier by the great development of co-operation between infantry and artillery. It was the boast of the Division that at this period for every German shell sent into the lines held by the Highland Division, twelve were returned, with the result that in a short space of time the 51st gained absolute command of No Man's Land.

The scouts and snipers of the Battalion, under Lieutenants McLaren and Rutherford and Sergeant Wallace, showed the greatest enterprise in their different duties and few mornings passed without the snipers claiming one or more victims; the German snipers at first were also active, and on the last day of

May, after a determined duel with one of them, Lieutenant Thomas was unfortunately killed.

By the end of the month the Battalion, although reduced in numbers, had taken a further portion of the line. This was held during the determined attacks made by the Germans further north but, except for a severe bombardment with "tear-shells," the 6th was not involved in the fighting. In the Battalion sector the Royal Engineers erected a form of Camera Obscura, by means of which a careful study of the enemy lines could be made from the safety of a strong dug-out.

In June fresh activity was shown on both sides in connection with the Somme offensive further south, and was marked by an increase in the number of raids, in mining operations and by additional artillery fire. On the forenoon of the 23rd, the long expected Zivy mine exploded, but did no damage, as the front line garrison near it had been withdrawn; indeed, the only result was to give the Battalion a better view of the German line than it had before.

On the 28th Lieutenant-Colonel A. O. Jenney, Cameronians, took over command from Lieutenant-Colonel Truman, who was appointed to command the 12th Lancers. His departure was greatly regretted. On the 29th, the 2nd Battalion Queen's Westminster Rifles was sent into the line for instruction by the 6th, first by platoons and then by companies.

The Battalion left the Labyrinth finally on July 6th, after four months in the line, and proceeded to Maroeuil, where it spent five days resting and training. During this time steel helmets were replaced by Balmoral bonnets. On the 12th the Battalion moved to Bray, and the following day reached Orlencourt, where it expected to remain for a fortnight. Little did anyone realize that the Battalion was to go straight into the battle of the Somme. After only two nights at Orlencourt, the 6th moved by bus to Halloy, reached Fienvillers on the 16th, entrained at Candas on the 20th, arrived at Méricourt that afternoon, and on the following day marched to Mametz Wood in reserve.

CHAPTER IV

JULY TO OCTOBER, 1916

*The attack on High Wood—Armentières—At Bailleul—
Return to the Somme*

MÉRICOURT presented a very different scene to that which the men of the Battalion remembered when they detrained there a year earlier. The great Somme battle had now been in progress for nearly three weeks. Extraordinary activity prevailed, troops, horses, stores, guns, German prisoners, and tons of food for man and beast passed through the little country village in an endless stream. Fresh battalions arriving hourly marched almost without a pause to the front line; other battalions returning from the battle sadly reduced in numbers but still in good spirit, the men carrying countless and most varied trophies, awaited means of transport to quieter scenes. In the air, as far as the eye could see, were lines of British and French observation balloons, while countless aeroplanes were constantly on the move.

After a night in bivouacs at Dernancourt, the 6th moved on July 21st through Méaulte and the ruined village of Fricourt to Mametz Wood. Here four days were spent in reserve, and the Battalion suffered some casualties from high explosive and gas shells. During these days the Battalion was kept busy providing numerous working and carrying parties. Moving to and fro through Mametz Wood, officers and men were able to form some idea of the fierce fighting which had taken place before the enemy were driven back, and of the appalling difficulties the British troops had to overcome in forcing their way through the shell-torn wood, covered as it had been with barbed wire entanglements.

The Battalion now moved to the neighbourhood of Bazentin-le-Grand, where over fifty men were killed and wounded from shell fire. The closeness of this position to some British batteries drew the attention of the enemy, and it was no uncommon experience for the 6th to undergo an hours' continuous bombardment, during which many men were buried by showers of earth and debris.

Four days were spent in this position, when on Sunday morning, July 30th, orders were issued to the Battalion for the first definite attack it had so far been called upon to make. The assault was to be made against High Wood, and was to take place at 5.30 p.m. the same day. Little time was available for reconnaissance, bringing up ammunition and water, and for the many other preparations necessary before an attack; in addition, this organization was all the more difficult to complete since the

THE SIXTH BATTALION THE BLACK WATCH

assembly trenches—running from the southern edge of High Wood in the direction of Longueval—had to be reached in daylight.

High Wood is perched on the top of a large upland, and is the highest point in that part of the country. From the northeast corner of the wood a strongly fortified trench ran to Flers. The position had been assailed many times without success. The last effort to take it had been made on July 23rd, but although some ground had been gained, the enemy still remained in possession of the wood. During the night of July 27th, connection was established by the 6th with the 29th Division. It is stated in the *History of the 51st Division* that for the first time in this sector a continuous line of defences was now presented to the enemy.

The attack of the 153rd Brigade was to be carried out by the 6th Battalion on the right with the 7th on the left, while on the right of the 6th was a Battalion of the 29th Division. C company under Captain J. Hally and D company under Captain Innes, led the assault of the 6th, with B and A companies in support.

The attack was launched at 6.10 p.m., the leading companies following the barrage slowly, and then lying down until it lifted. The moment, however, that the companies began to renew their advance they were met by heavy machine gun fire, as the artillery barrage had been insufficient to destroy the enemy resistance, and the losses were heavy. The Battalion, nevertheless, continued to advance, and got as far as the German front line wire. Here Captain Hally was killed and Captain Innes wounded, Company Sergeant-Majors Gardiner and Cairns of C and D companies were both killed, and the advance stopped, as it was clearly evident that the enemy was holding his front line very strongly, and large numbers of Germans were plainly seen in their trenches.

Meanwhile, on the left, the 7th Battalion had been held up by a strong redoubt on the eastern corner of the wood, and on the right the 29th Division had also been unable to advance, consequently the 6th was left isolated with both flanks in the air and was thus exposed to the full force of the German fire which the British guns were unable to silence.

The two leading companies were almost annihilated, but the few men who were still unwounded dug themselves in in shell holes, where they remained until dark, when they were eventually withdrawn to the original front line during the night. Every effort was made to bring in the wounded that night and the following day, and in this task many non-commissioned officers and men, unfortunately, lost their lives. The following night, the

HIGH WOOD, JULY 30TH, 1916

companies were able to dig a new fire trench about a hundred yards in advance of their old front line, and to bring in the wounded, also to bury many of their dead comrades. The digging of this trench was no small achievement after what the Battalion had gone through, and the work was all the more arduous as the heat was extreme. At the start, the work was held up by a sudden heavy bombardment, but once on the ground, every man worked at top speed and succeeded in completing a traversed trench within two hundred yards of the German line.

It was a great disappointment to the Battalion that this, its first real attack, had ended in failure. Had it been possible to give more time for preparation and had the infantry been supported by a heavier artillery bombardment, the attack in all probability would have succeeded; but the Germans were strong both in numbers and in position, their trenches were well wired and heavily manned by machine gunners and, in addition, they had an excellent field of fire. Six weeks of hard fighting were to pass before the enemy was forced out of this position.

One of the greatest difficulties during this fight was the evacuation of the wounded, and great credit is due to Major Haig, R.A.M.C., and to the Battalion stretcher bearers for their organization and conduct in carrying out this work.

The Battalion losses in this action and in the days preceding it amounted to four officers killed (Captain Hally, Lieutenants Miller, McEwan and Roy), six wounded: 50 other ranks killed and 200 wounded.

For services on this occasion, nine Military Medals were awarded to non-commissioned officers and men of the Battalion.

The 51st Division was now withdrawn from the Somme battle, and on August 1st the Battalion, after eleven days of strenuous fighting, moved to Méaulte, and on the 6th moved further back to a camp between Buire and Hénencourt. On the 8th the transport moved by road to Poulainville, and the next day to the village of Wanel near the railway junction of Longpré, the Battalion following by train. Two days later the 6th again entrained and, travelling by night via Boulogne, arrived at Thiennes on the morning of the 11th, and marched to Wardrecques, within a few miles of St. Omer. Here a few days were spent pleasantly resting and reorganizing.

On the 16th the Battalion moved by train to Steenwerck, and marched to Armentières, where it received a cordial welcome from the New Zealanders it had come to relieve. One night only was spent in the town, the 6th taking over the front line in advance of the ruins of Houplines the following day. There had been no great activity in this sector since the autumn of 1914,

THE SIXTH BATTALION THE BLACK WATCH

and the trenches proved to be the most comfortable and well equipped of any yet occupied by the Battalion. Shortly after the arrival of the Division, however, the situation changed, for the Highland Division began its usual aggressive tactics, and the time it spent in this neighbourhood—fortunately in fine weather—was marked by the increased activity of artillery and trench mortar fire and raids.

Much useful patrol work was accomplished in continuation of the activities of the New Zealanders, who had secured complete ascendency over the enemy in this sector. The raids usually followed the release of British poison gas from cylinders sunk in the front trenches, and were undertaken with varying success; one of these carried out by the Battalion during the night of August 30th was attended by heavy casualties caused mainly by enemy artillery fire and accumulation of British gas in a low lying part of No Man's Land. Out of a specially trained force of forty all ranks, the losses on this occasion were two officers and 21 men wounded, some of whom subsequently died.

No fighting of importance took place during the time the Battalion was in this area, but hard work was done in altering trenches and preparing concrete dug-outs. During ten days spent in a rest camp west of Bailleul, the Battalion furnished a Guard of Honour[1] of three officers and 100 men for General Plumer when he visited the town of Bailleul in order to present medals to Belgian troops. On this parade the massed pipe bands of the Division, numbering 90 pipers and 70 drummers, were present. The people of Bailleul had never seen or heard anything like this mighty band before, nor, in fact, had many men of the Division.

The Divisional Horse Show at Bailleul was held on September 12th, and those who saw the spotless turn-out of horses and vehicles could scarcely believe that three weeks before that same transport had careered up and down the dusty and shell-torn Fricourt road carrying rations and ammunition during the Somme battle; the 6th secured a fair share of the prizes of this Show.

Another spell in the trenches beginning on the 19th at Chapelle d'Armentières, ended the stay of the 6th in this neighbourhood and, after spending the last five days of September in billets at Meteren, the Battalion entrained on the 30th at Bailleul for another tour of duty in the Somme area, arriving at Doullens and marching to Beauval the same day. From this date until the end of the year, the Battalion encountered the

[1] Captain A. Innes was in command of the Guard, with Lieutenants R. G. A. Dickson and W. P. Stewart as subalterns.

RETURN TO THE SOMME AREA

vilest of weather and had the poorest kind of protection; billets were unknown, trenches and soaking bivouacs being the best shelter that fell to its lot.

On October 1st, at Beauval, Lieutenant-Colonel A. O. Jenney left the Battalion and Lieutenant-Colonel J. Wylie took over command.

CHAPTER V

OCTOBER AND NOVEMBER, 1916

The Battle of Beaumont Hamel

THE Battalion spent the first few days in the new area as follows: Vauchelles, October 2nd; Louvencourt, October 4th; and Courcelles au Bois, October 8th, and moved into the line at Hébuterne on the 12th. These villages provided wretched accommodation. They were all extremely dirty and muddy and the whole area was congested by an immense concentration of troops.

A remarkable feature in the front line area here was the massing of artillery close behind the trenches, and even more noticeable was the enormous concentration of trench mortars in the front line—every bay containing at least one mortar and a pile of ammunition. On several occasions direct hits from German guns on one or other of these dumps reduced the bays to the semblance of small mine craters and seriously hampered the efforts of working parties.

After a couple of days in the line, the 6th moved to Colincamps further south, and on the 17th to Bus, arriving the following day at Forceville, some six miles behind the village of Beaumont Hamel, the capture of which was now known to be the objective of the next attack.

The Battalion had a vast amount of work to do in the area, digging assembly trenches, extra shelters, and forward gun positions; also occasionally rehearsing an attack on taped out ground in rear. Much had been learnt from the failure of the Division at High Wood, and it was determined that its next effort should be successful. While in the line facing Beaumont Hamel, the 6th carried out an immense amount of preparatory work under most depressing weather conditions, in trenches that were constantly filling in and becoming silted up with mud.

On October 24th, the Battalion went into the trenches in battle order ready for an assault planned for the following day but, owing to continuous wet weather, the attack was postponed and the 6th was withdrawn two days later to Mailly Copse. Unfortunately that very night, during a raid on the German salient near the head of "Y" Ravine, Lieutenant Q. McLaren, a daring and resourceful officer, was killed; his death was mourned by the whole Battalion and by none more than the men of the scout section, who would have followed him anywhere. While at Forceville, Lieutenant-Colonel T. M. Booth took over command from Lieutenant-Colonel Wylie.

In hourly expectation of being called on to attack, the Battalion, during the next few days, rehearsed its task on taped

BEAUMONT HAMEL, NOVEMBER 12TH, 1916

out ground in the neighbourhood. On November 5th, the Battalion moved to Rancheval, and on the 11th to Mailly Wood, going into the line opposite Beaumont Hamel preparatory to the attack now definitely fixed for the following day. The strength of the Battalion was now 29 officers and 666 other ranks.

The details of what actually happened during this memorable phase of the battle of the Ancre will probably never be exactly known, but it is possible to indicate what was intended, and a brief outline of the general plan will help the reader to visualize the situation.

The position of Beaumont Hamel was known to be one of great strength, and had defied repeated efforts to capture it during the Somme offensive in July, 1916. Four Divisions were, therefore, employed for this attack, each operating on a comparatively narrow front, the 63rd (Naval) Division on the right, the 51st (Highland) and 2nd Division in the centre and the 3rd Division on the left.

The task assigned to the Highland Division was the capture of Beaumont Hamel village and the famous " Y " Ravine to the south of it; this was a deep ravine, which stretched towards the British lines in two arms. The enemy defences between these two arms formed a marked and very strong salient in the German defences.

The Division attacked with two Brigades, the 153rd on the right and the 152nd on the left, the 154th being in reserve; the attacking battalions from right to left were the 7th Battalion Gordon Highlanders, in touch with the Naval Division, 6th Battalion The Black Watch, 5th Battalion Seaforth Highlanders, and 8th Battalion Argyll and Sutherland Highlanders, in touch with the 2nd Division.

To the 6th fell probably the toughest task of all, the taking of " Y " Ravine, in the banks of which were shelters capable of holding masses of the enemy. The futility of making a frontal attack on the ravine and its defences had been proved in the July offensive, and on this occasion the idea was to effect an entry at the north end of the salient, and by bombing, work southwards along it, making the task of its capture easier, and on these lines the operation was carefully rehearsed beforehand.

The method of attack was for the Battalion to assault in four " waves "; each wave had a definite objective, and was held responsible for the taking and " cleaning up " of the portion of the enemy line allotted to it, and for bombing up the communication trenches towards the next line. The first wave consisted of two platoons of A company on the right and two platoons of B company on the left, their duty being the taking of the enemy front line and the head of the ravine. The second wave, consisting of the two remaining platoons of A and two of B, were to pass through the first wave and take the enemy's second trench.

The third wave was composed of two platoons of C company, and two platoons of D company, their object being to pass through the first two waves and take the enemy third line. The fourth wave, the remaining platoons of C and D, were given the German fourth line and the bank beyond it.

As each wave reached its objective, its duty was to pull up trench boards and place them as bridges across the captured trench and so enable the succeeding waves to pass over. Each wave, as the trench assigned to it was captured, and the communication trenches ahead cleared, was to work forward to the next trench, the whole strength of the Battalion finally to assemble and reorganize on the " green " line (the bank beyond the German fourth trench, near the entrance to a large cave). When this was done the 5th Gordon Highlanders, who were to follow up the 6th, were then to pass through and continue the advance.

The 7th Battalion The Black Watch, the remaining battalion of the 153rd Brigade, was held in reserve and, as events proved, lent very great assistance in the later stages of the battle when many officers and non-commissioned officers of the attacking Battalions had been killed or wounded.

From the above description it will be seen that every possible preparation had been made, and on the evening of Sunday, November 12th, the Battalion moved up from Mailly Wood, leaving behind a certain number of officers, non-commissioned officers and specialists. The men, moving up by an overland route along a taped out course, laden with bombs, picks and shovels, sandbags and wirecutters, reached the assembly trenches after dark, where they spent a cheerless night in freezing mud.

The state of the ground across which the attack was made can hardly be imagined. It was knee deep in wet clay, and as the men were heavily loaded with ammunition, bombs and tools, and wearing greatcoats, it is amazing that any advance was made. One thing only was in the attackers' favour. For three weeks prior to the assault, the British guns had daily subjected the German lines to a heavy bombardment at dawn, and, although on the morning of the attack the shelling was far more severe, the enemy in many parts of the line thought it was the usual morning bombardment and remained below in their dug-outs, unconscious till too late of the fact that the men of the Highland Division were on top of them.

Zero hour was 5.45 a.m. on November 13th, and was

BEAUMONT HAMEL, NOVEMBER 13TH, 1916

notified by the explosion of a mine in front of the 152nd Brigade. This mine went up to the second, and immediately a magnificent artillery barrage fell on the German lines. The intensity and accuracy of this barrage far outstripped anything of the kind before attempted on the 51st Division front, and the earth trembled for miles around with one continuous mighty rumble, punctuated here and there by the discharge of an extra heavy gun, or the explosion of some giant shell.

The Battalion moved off without delay, but the ground was covered by a thick fog so that little could be seen even a few yards off. As the fog hid every landmark and the mud hampered every movement, it became almost from the very start impossible to maintain direction. Consequently, after the assault began the British artillery barrage was soon the only guide, and this, moving forward at the rate of a hundred yards every four minutes, got ahead of the troops, who were frequently held up; the maintaining of direction was thereafter a matter of chance. For the first half hour or so there was little artillery retaliation by the enemy, but as soon as our men showed up through the fog in front of the German lines, they were met by a heavy and destructive machine gun fire. With men dropping on every side, it was all the more difficult for the survivors to keep touch with one another in the semi-darkness and mist, but the first wave of A and B companies eventually gained the German front line, and some of the second wave also got through according to plan, and were immediately lost to sight. With the arrival of large numbers of Germans from their shelters in the ravine, the right half of the first wave had a difficult job to tackle, and a number of them were overpowered and taken prisoner. Little groups of men did their best to capture the particular part of the enemy line on to which they happened to stumble, but they had no idea how the attack was progressing, or how far they were from any of their own comrades.

Meanwhile, C and D companies on the left, who were attacking a more straightforward part of the line, had succeeded in making fair progress, and some of them gained the second and even the third German lines according to the plan of attack. Early in the battle, Captain T. Ferguson was killed leading D company. Lieutenants Cairns, MacLeod and Begg were also killed in the early stages of the fighting, and six or seven other officers were wounded, so that from start to finish the Battle of Beaumont Hamel may well be termed a " soldiers' battle."

Second Lieutenant Lindsay of B company had an unenviable experience; he got stuck fast in a mud hole from which he took nearly an hour to extricate himself, although under constant shell and rifle fire. In spite of everything, however, he kept his wits about him and was able, about 7 a.m., to report to the Commanding Officer on the progress of his company and on the general situation. In the absence of further reports, and as nothing whatever could be seen from the original Battalion front line, the adjutant, Captain Ellis, was sent out to make a reconnaissance, during which he was severely wounded and did not return.

As had been anticipated, the trenches guarding the ravine had proved the stiffest task of the whole operation, and by 8.15 a.m., a certain number of men, finding themselves " on their own," had collected back in the British front line, patrols reporting that the salient in front of the ravine was still strongly held by the enemy.

At this time the mist was still so thick that nothing could be seen at more than a few yards distance. Two machine guns from the salient and one in rear of the ravine, continuously swept No Man's Land, making progress across it extremely difficult, and the situation on this part of the line remained critical till about noon. Before one o'clock, however, Second Lieutenant Leslie with 25 men, gained an entry at the north end of the salient, and by a brilliant and determined piece of work, captured 103 prisoners and liberated a number of men of the Battalion who had been taken prisoner earlier in the day. This daring venture practically completed the capture of the ravine and made further progress possible.

At 1.30 p.m., Colonel Booth arrived in the old British front line, just as Leslie had completed the work of clearing the ravine. Here the Commanding Officer collected all the remaining men of the Battalion—about thirty—in the British front line, and joined Leslie at the west end of the ravine. The salient was now rapidly cleared of the enemy. One machine gun was captured, another knocked out by bombers, and the German snipers who had hung on persistently, were gradually silenced.

By 2.30 p.m., progress became more evident. The timely arrival of a bombing party of the 4th Gordon Highlanders greatly assisted the work, and more men of the 6th, who had been isolated in the ravine, were released and joined in the advance to the German second line. Meantime, the Commanding Officer had advanced his Battle Headquarters to the point of the German salient, in their old front line, and from there, under heavy fire, the Battalion signallers ran out a line and established telephone connection with Brigade Headquarters. This service, owing to the fog and to the impossibility of seeing what was happening, was of the utmost value, but in accomplishing the task, Stewart, the signalling sergeant, was severely wounded.

About 3 p.m., Colonel Booth went forward and found

CAPTURE OF THE RAVINE, NOVEMBER 13TH, 1916

Second Lieutenant Lindsay in the second German line reorganizing the men there, while Second Lieutenant Leslie was working forward with a small patrol to reconnoitre the third line. These two young officers deserve the highest praise for the energy and determination they displayed throughout the whole action; in fact the turning of a critical situation into a complete success was in no small measure due to their resource and fine leadership.

By this time so many officers had been killed or wounded that a message was telephoned back asking that Captain Innes and two subalterns might be sent up from those left out of the battle. Meanwhile a party of the 4th Gordon Highlanders from the Divisional reserve had arrived, and between three and four o'clock the advance became more rapid, the survivors of the 6th reaching a sunken road north-east of the ravine—just in front of the " green " line.

At 4.30 p.m., Second Lieutenant Lindsay, with all the men that could be collected, pushed on from the sunken road to the " green " line, a bank beyond the German fourth line, and joined up with the 4th Battalion Gordon Highlanders on the right, who were in turn in touch with the 7th Battalion of that regiment on their right.

By 9 p.m., the Battalion was firmly established on the " green " line, and Captain Innes with Second Lieutenants Condor and Young reported at the forward Battalion Headquarters. Second Lieutenant Young at once took over the duties of Adjutant, while Captain Innes and Second Lieutenant Condor went forward to the " green " line to organize and consolidate the position. On the way there they found two subalterns, a Lewis gun team, and about 20 men in the German third line, and took them forward to the " green " line.

After dark the enemy resistance died down, but it had been a day of tremendous effort, fighting a stubborn enemy, and operating in water-logged clay country, strewn with tangled barbed-wire and wreckage of every description. The men were thoroughly exhausted, but with the knowledge of the good work accomplished and under the inspiration of Captain Innes they set to work with the picks and shovels which had cumbered their movements all day and in a few hours had thoroughly consolidated the position they had so hardly won. By 3 a.m. on the 14th, the Battalion was in touch with the 4th Battalion Gordon Highlanders on the right, and with the 6th Battalion Gordon Highlanders on the left. The arrival of a party of Royal Engineers with bombs, rations and water was heartily welcomed.

Daybreak on the 14th brought down a heavy enemy shelling which caused further losses. In the forenoon orders were received to hand over to the 4th Battalion Gordon Highlanders, and before midday the 6th was withdrawn, and although this was done in daylight, it was accomplished without further loss.

Beaumont Hamel had cost the Battalion dearly. Captain Ferguson and Lieutenants Cairns, Macleod and Begg had been killed, and Captain Ellis and Lieutenants Strathairn and Keay died of their wounds later. Five other officers had been wounded; 71 men were killed, 141 wounded and two were returned as missing, making a total of 12 officers and 214 other ranks. Of the officers who took part in the attack that morning, only Colonel Booth, Major Young and Lieutenants Dickson, Leslie, Lindsay and Barr came back unwounded.

The foregoing account of the battle is limited to describe the doings of the 6th Black Watch, but the other Battalions of the Highland Division were also successful, and the stronghold of Beaumont Hamel, which until now both sides had regarded as impregnable, was wrested from the enemy. Owing to the fog, any attempt to control the fortunes of the day from Division or Brigade Headquarters, or even at times from Battalion Headquarters, or from the air, was impossible, and the successful outcome of the fighting must be attributed to the soundness of the scheme of attack, the thoroughness of the artillery and machine gun barrage, and most of all, to the determination of every individual to make the attack a success.

The following sentence taken from the *History of the 51st Division* gives a true picture of the ground over which the troops attacked.

" Let two teams dressed in battle order play football in the
" dark on a ploughed field in a clay soil after three weeks' steady
" rain, and the difficulties of the attacking troops might then in
" some measure be appreciated."

Early in the morning of the 13th, the streams of German prisoners who were being shepherded to the rear of the battle area, gave obvious proof that success has attended the long delayed attack. Many of the prisoners seemed highly pleased to be out of the fray, and to their credit many of them did good service in carrying down wounded on their way. A great number of these Germans had been hunted out of their dug-outs by smoke bombs thrown into them—a most effective way of urging the occupants to seek fresh air without delay.

The experiences of an eye-witness are always of peculiar interest, and the following graphic description written by Sergeant W. Mitchell, D company, gives a true picture and is well worthy of reproduction:

CAPTURE OF THE RAVINE, NOVEMBER 13TH, 1916

"About 4 p.m. on Sunday, November 12th, 1916, we
"assembled outside our huts in Mailly Wood, about three kilo-
"metres behind the line, after having been supplied with our
"tools, bombs, etc., not forgetting our special rations. The
"company commander then came on parade, and after a few
"words of encouragement from him we moved up by platoons,
"duly arriving in the reserve trenches. It was by this time about
"5.15 p.m., and we had to remain here for over five hours; about
"six o'clock we had tea, and then it was a case of each man
"making himself as comfortable as possible for the next few
"hours, as everything had already been prepared for moving up
"to the front line. At the appointed hour the order was passed
"along to get ready to move. Instead of using the communica-
"tion trenches, we went by a new route which had been taped
"out that night for our special benefit. It was a great assistance
"to us, as it saved us the labour of going along the trenches,
"laden with all the 'over the top' necessaries. When we
"arrived at our assembly position in the front line, it was about
"midnight, so after getting all the sentries posted, we got
"everything in order for jumping over. We had first to cut a
"few gaps in our own wire to enable men to get through without
"delay. In this operation we had no trouble at all. It was about
"the quietest night I ever had in the trenches. We had now
"everything arranged, so there was nothing more to do but
"wait patiently for 'Zero.' None of us slept much that night,
"but everybody was in wonderfully bright spirits. In one of
"our sections an argument was started as to who would be in
"the Hun trench first, one wee chap from the 'Pow' declaring
"his willingness to bet a whole franc on the business. About
"5 a.m. we had a hot drink served out to us. It was dignified
"with the name of 'rum-punch,' but its actual character was
"subject for some difference of opinion. 'It's rum with some
"tea in it,' said one man—'Away, man, it's tea with a little
"rum.' Whatever the concoction may have been, it was most
"enjoyable, and it put a nice heat into us. Time was meanwhile
"wearing on, and at five minutes before 'Zero' our platoon
"was ordered to take up a position in front of our own wire.
"We had no sooner lain down there when the preliminaries to
"attack began. Everything was timed to the second. On our
"left a large mine was touched off, and the artillery began to
"play on the Hun front line, together with the trench mortars
"and Stokes guns which did magnificent work. There was also
"an excellent machine gun barrage the like of which had never
"been heard before up to that date. As for weather, it was so
"misty we could hardly see ten yards in front of us. This made
"it very difficult to keep our direction, but we knew which way

"to go, so we started creeping forward, and as the barrage
"lifted we made for the enemy trenches. We had little diffi-
"culty in getting over his wire, and as he had noticed this with
"his flare lights, he started bombing us, causing some casualties.
"Our other platoons meantime had got through on the left,
"and working along the trench they came across the Hun just
"about the same time as we got through ourselves. It was our
"turn then. We cleared the trench of all that was left, and
"leaving a number of men to see that no occupants remained in
"the dug-outs, moved forward towards the second line along
"with another company. The Germans put up a little more
"resistance there, but we captured the trench after a bit of a
"struggle, and took a great number of prisoners, especially from
"their dug-outs. By this time my own company had only one
"officer left, and owing to the darkness in which the attack
"began, some of the companies had got a bit mixed. That
"did not hinder us any, however, as we all knew our final
"objective, and with a few hurried orders we moved forward
"to take the third line. It was at this time I was slightly
"wounded and became a subject for the attention of the
"stretcher bearers, but from where I was I could see our
"men getting well forward and entering the village of Beaumont
"Hamel."

Worn out after two days hard fighting, with uniforms tattered and torn, and plastered from head to foot with mud, the men marched back to camp behind Mailly Wood, comfortless at the best, but welcome as affording comparative peace and rest. Two of the weirdest figures to arrive back were the pioneer sergeant and the Padre's batman, each staggering under a huge mailbag full of "souvenirs."

With the irony of fate, immediately after the battle, a keen frost set in which hardened the ground and produced the very conditions that had been wanted for the attack.

The chaplains, Gordon and Hunter, did splendid work on the days following the fight, searching the battlefield under continuous shell fire, and so well did they carry out this work that every missing man of the Battalion was accounted for.

On the 18th the Battalion moved back to comfortable billets at Rancheval, and two days later, showing little signs of the strenuous times it had gone through, the Battalion was inspected and congratulated by Brigadier-General D. Campbell, commanding the 153rd Brigade.

The following paragraph from the *History of the 51st (Highland) Division* is of interest:—

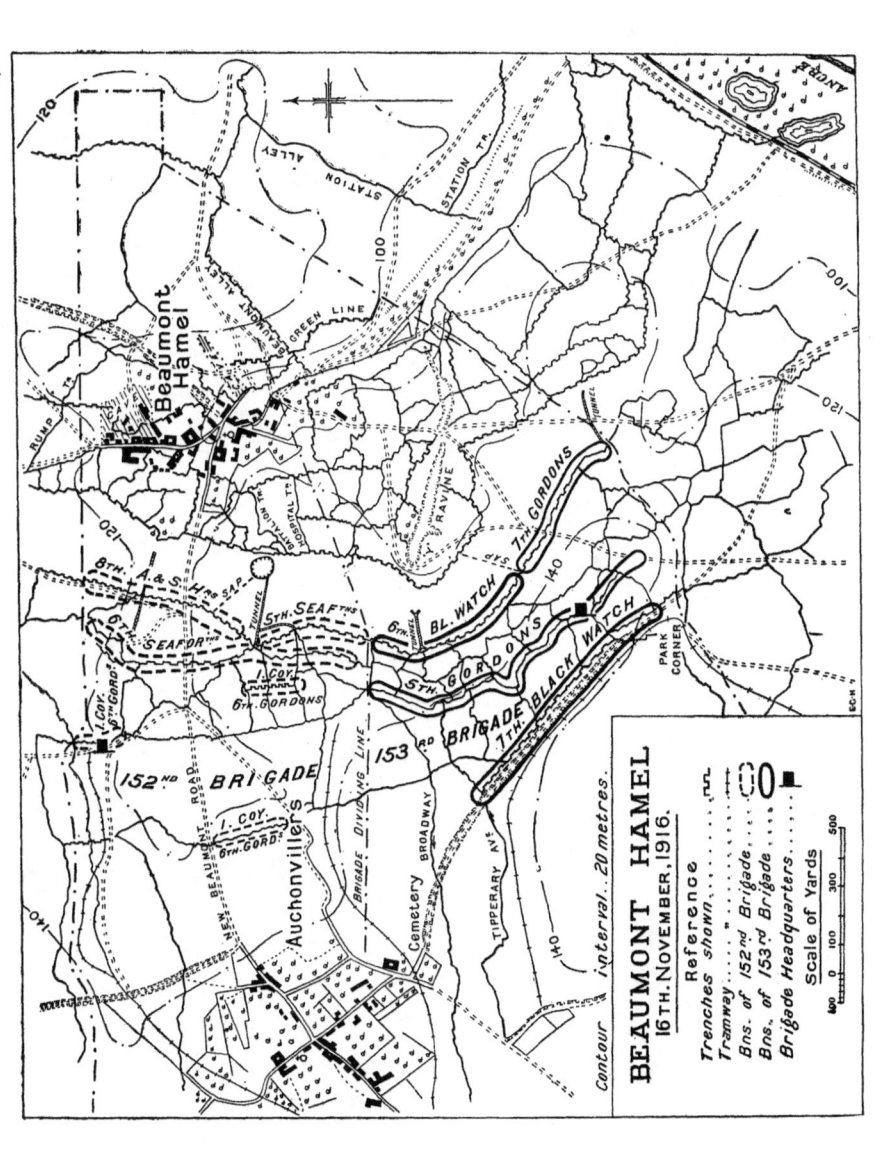

AT REST, RANCHEVAL

"The satisfactory results of these operations may be put down to the following causes:

"First, to the resolution and gallantry of the officers and men. In spite of heavy losses and of the appalling state of the ground, they pressed on to their objectives with the greatest determination. In many cases the barrage was irretrievably lost. The resistance of a courageous and cunning enemy, protected by the strongest field of defences that experience could devise, had then to be overcome by the superior fighting qualities of the infantry soldier alone. The manner in which he overcame this resistance was in accordance with the highest traditions of the Highland Regiments."

CHAPTER VI

NOVEMBER, 1916, TO MAY, 1917

*Courcelette—New Year at Aveluy—The Battle of Arras—
Attack on Greenland Hill*

(See Map facing Page 286.)

AFTER two days' rest at Rancheval, the 6th was once more on the move. All ranks had looked forward to a short rest, and it was a disappointment when, after some days of marching through Redauville on November 24th, to Ovillers on the 26th, the Battalion found itself on November 27th relieving the 73rd (Canadian) Battalion. This battalion belonged to the 4th Canadian Division and was one of the battalions of The Black Watch of Canada, wearing the correct uniform of the Regiment. The line taken over was in front of Courcelette including the Regina trench of ill fame which faced the village of Pys.

This was by far the worst front line the Battalion had ever taken over. Every inch of the country had been ploughed up time and again by shells from both sides during the latter stages of the Somme battle. The whole front area was reduced to a morass, and the trenches were mere pits often waist deep in mud, into which the men sank, their boots sometimes sucked off by the wet clay. It was impossible to get hot food up to the front line—and it was equally out of the question to change socks in these mud holes. Only those who went through this particular experience can have any idea of the miseries of it, and it was but slight consolation to know that the Germans, a hundred yards in front, were in the same plight.

During this time the 6th lost many men through exhaustion in addition to casualties from artillery fire. The whole of the area was under observation in clear weather from Loupart Wood, where the enemy had many observation posts, and as the few dug-outs available in the sector had previously belonged to the Germans, they knew the exact location of every one of them, and planted shells with exasperating accuracy right on the entrances. One lucky shot caused quite a pyrotechnic display one night by setting alight a big store of Very light cartridges and rockets at Battalion Headquarters in " Death Valley," and the conflagration was very nearly intensified by a zealous, but somewhat misguided, non-commissioned officer who attempted to pour a petrol tin of paraffin on the flames thinking it was water; fortunately a lynx-eyed Headquarter cook missed his precious tin in time, and averted a serious " blaze up."

On November 30th, after three miserable days and nights, the 6th handed over their line to the 5th Battalion Gordon Highlanders. The relief, which on first taking over had been a

TRENCH WARFARE, COURCELETTE, WINTER, 1916

very lengthy affair, was much simplified by the Second-in-Command, who laid out some eight hundred yards of white tape from the front line to Battalion Headquarters, thereby helping both the incoming and the outgoing troops to find their way across the otherwise trackless waste of mud. On relief the Battalion occupied the support position at the Chalk Pits, and three days later, on the Brigade being relieved, moved back to good billets in Senlis. Here on December 4th, Lieutenant-Colonel Wylie again took over command of the Battalion, Colonel Booth having been appointed to command the Divisional School at St. Riquier.

A week later a second spell in the cheerless and universally hated Regina trench was endured, and another wretched four days were spent there, the companies, however, holding the front line for only two days at a time. Owing to the cold and mud it was thought right to replace the kilt by trews for these four days; but as the authorities forgot to issue braces, the troubles of the men were little lessened by the change of dress. Remarkable work was done by the Battalion scouts in this sector; they kept in touch with the small groups of men posted in the line, most of their work being done in the dark, over a flat and marshy waste devoid of all landmarks.

On the 19th the Battalion was again relieved. It moved first to Wolfe Huts, and then to Bouzincourt, arriving at Senlis on the 22nd. Here Christmas was celebrated with some comfort, the men enjoying some visits to the Divisional theatre and the feasts of plum pudding and other luxuries supplied by good friends at home.

Moving to Aveluy on the 28th, the 6th spent New Year's Day in Bruce Huts overlooking the village. About midnight the enemy shelled the Battalion area with high velocity guns, but caused no losses. While in this neighbourhood many of the older hands took the chance to renew their last winter's acquaintance with La Boisselle and Authuile.

On the 6th of January, the Battalion was once more posted in the all too familiar front line at Courcelette, but fortunately for the last time. Now, however, the companies were growing used to the conditions and, with a good outfit, suitable clothing and gum boots, were fairly well off, losing only one man from sickness. They could ill afford to lose more, for at this time the strength of the Battalion had dwindled to 17 officers and 426 other ranks. Officers, non-commissioned officers and men were borrowed from the two companies in support to bring the two companies in the front line to a strength of fifty each; thus one hundred men held over a thousand yards of line, the fighting strength of the Battalion being under two hundred rifles.

THE SIXTH BATTALION THE BLACK WATCH

Frost made conditions more tolerable, and by dint of damming up short sections of the line with sandbags and baling out the mud in between, revetted hollows were cleared, enabling four to six men to stand in each in comparative dryness. Practically no wire defences existed, and one night a runner—Corporal Robertson of Aucherarder—who had missed the Battalion front line and got into No Man's Land, held up and marched in a German patrol of three armed men. For this act he received from the hands of General Harper, the Divisional Commander, an immediate award of the D.C.M.

On January 8th, 1917, the 6th bade farewell to the sector. Illness, rheumatism and trench feet, brought on by living for days under wet sodden conditions had caused more losses than were suffered by the Battalion in the Battle of Beaumont Hamel.

The forthcoming rest period was hailed with delight, and on the way back to Senlis—which was reached on the 9th—the 6th received a magnificent draft of men from the Scottish Horse which brought it nearly up to strength.

The following week was spent in marching to the rest area, halts being made at Puchevillers on the 12th, Gézaincourt on the 14th, Longvillers on the 15th, and Drucat on the following day. Here rest, reorganization and training coupled with the arrival of more reinforcements brought the 6th once more into good fighting trim; the strength, which on leaving Courcelette had been reduced to about 200 men in the trenches, was now increased to 25 officers and 1028 other ranks.

Towards the end of January, Colonel Booth again took over command, Lieutenant-Colonel Wylie proceeding to England, Major Henderson became Second-in-Command, and Captain Rutherford was appointed adjutant. In addition to Lieutenant-Colonel Wylie's departure, the Battalion lost another officer who had come to France with it, Captain Innes, who left to take command of a Cheshire battalion.

Early in February orders were received for the 6th to move to the neighbourhood of Arras, and there prepare for a forthcoming attack. The journey north, beginning on the 5th, was made by a march route in the coldest weather ever experienced by the Battalion in France. Moving via Argenvillers (February 5th), Maison Ponthieu (6th), Nuncq (7th), Croisette (8th), Ourton (9th), Villers Brulin (10th), the Battalion finally reached Louez, near Maroeuil, on the 11th, where some of the older soldiers had had many and varied experiences in the spring of 1916.

The remainder of February, 1917, and the first fortnight of March, were spent in carrying out railway construction in the

TRENCH WARFARE, ARRAS, MARCH, 1917

Anzin–St. Aubin–St. Catherine area, where the 6th replaced the 2nd Battalion Royal Fusiliers.

On March 16th, the Battalion moved into the line at Ecurie, the 153rd Brigade having taken over the Roclincourt section. Preparations for an attack on a large scale, now known officially as the Arras Offensive, were at this time in full swing. These included, amongst other work, the preparation of assembly trenches, wire cutting, raids for identification purposes, and, most important of all, practising the attack on taped-out ground behind the front area. Throughout the whole of this period the weather was atrocious, frost and snow being followed by thaw and rain, which reduced the trenches to a deplorable state, and made work in them most laborious.

The numerous raids, in which, of course, the 6th took part, and the British artillery activity at the time, naturally brought down heavy enemy retaliation, which made life in the front line still more unpleasant. In addition, the severity of the weather, and the shortness of fodder, caused a serious mortality among animals which added to the difficulties of transport in this shell-torn area.

On March 31st, the Battalion carried out a successful raid and was able to establish the fact that the 51st Division was opposed by Bavarians, who were among the most stubborn troops of the German Army. The raiding party consisting of Lieutenant R. J. Menzies in command, with Lieutenants Scott and Boyd and 64 men, was withdrawn from the line for practice ten days prior to the operation, the plan of the trenches to be attacked being laid out on the south-eastern outskirts of Maroeuil. The raid was most successfully carried out on March 31st. Three officers and 46 men of the 2nd Bavarian Reserve Infantry Regiment were either killed or captured, thus proving that this regiment was holding the line. The raiders lost one man killed, 23 wounded and one missing.* Lieutenant Scott highly distinguished himself in this raid and was awarded the M.C.; Military Medals were won by Lance-Corporal Menzies and Private Devlin.

The forthcoming operations were part of a plan designed to drive the Germans from the salient into which they had been forced as a result of the fighting on the Somme between the Ancre and Scarpe. The task allotted to the 51st (Highland) Division, XVII Corps, Third Army, in conjunction with the Canadian Corps on the left, and the 34th Division on the right, was the capture of the southern shoulder of Vimy Ridge.

* Two weeks later, during the battle of Arras, German documents were captured corroborating the casualties inflicted by the 6th.

THE SIXTH BATTALION THE BLACK WATCH

The first phase of the Battle of Arras began on April 9th, and for a week prior to this the Battalion held the line at Roclincourt, during which time it was under continuous and heavy shell fire. For the first time in the history of the 6th, the Battalion Headquarters' dug-out, in which were the Commanding Officer, the Second-in-Command, the Medical Officer, the Adjutant and Liaison Officer, was blown in by a 5·9 shell. Fortunately no one was injured. Another and more disastrous direct hit occurred on April 1st, just after the Battalion had moved into Maroeuil. A high-velocity shell smashed into a crowded billet with fatal results; 21 men were killed outright, and 28 wounded. The 6th took no part in the first phase of the battle, as the 153rd Brigade was in Divisional reserve, the Battalion being in Brigade reserve.

On the night of April 7th, the Battalion was relieved in the line by the 9th Royal Scots Fusiliers; during this relief Captain MacDowell was seriously wounded and died a few weeks later. D company lost in him a gallant and capable commander, and to all who knew him, "Micky's" death was like the loss of a brother. On relief the Battalion moved first to Ecoivres, and then to Ecurie, where it remained during the first phase of the battle. On the morning of the 10th, the 6th moved up over the ground just captured and took over the new support line which it held until relieved the following evening by the 2nd Division, when it returned to Maroeuil for a few days, during which Lieutenant Douglas Cable returned from hospital and took over the duties of Assistant Adjutant.

On the 14th, the Battalion was ordered to move on the following day with the 153rd Brigade through Arras to Blangy in the St. Laurent area, to take over the Oppy line near Fampoux. Orders were issued at once, and the 6th with transport complete, moved off before midday, reaching Blangy in the afternoon of the 15th, where it bivouacked in an old factory, going into the line at Fampoux that night, relieving the 5th Battalion Cameron Highlanders. Here orders were received that the Division would be employed in what is now known as the second phase of the Battle of Arras, planned to take place on the 23rd.

At this time the enemy held a strong position north-east of the River Scarpe on high ground known as Greenland Hill. Through a deep cutting in this hill the Arras-Douai railway ran in a straight line north-east from Fampoux. On the right of the railway were the Chemical Works and the village of Roeux, north-east of which lay Hausa and Delbar Woods, from which the enemy had magnificent observation. While the Germans had good covered approaches to their positions on the high ground,

BATTLE OF ARRAS, APRIL 23RD, 1917

the British line was entirely exposed and troops holding it were under constant artillery fire. The forthcoming attack was, therefore, planned with the object of securing Greenland Hill and the village of Plouvain, north-east of Roeux. In addition to being commanded from the German line it should be mentioned that, owing to the marshy nature of the country on the north bank of the River Scarpe, there was little ground available in which the attacking troops could be assembled.

The 51st Division attack was carried out by the 154th Brigade on the right and the 153rd on the left, the main attack being delivered by the latter Brigade disposed as follows: 7th Battalion The Black Watch on the right, 7th Battalion Gordon Highlanders on the left. In the rear of these two battalions, the 6th Gordon Highlanders (lent from the 154th Brigade) were on the right behind the 7th Black Watch, and the 6th Black Watch in support of the 7th Gordon Highlanders, on the left.

There were four objectives. The 6th Black Watch was detailed to attack the fourth, or final objective three hours and twelve minutes after Zero, with the 6th Battalion Gordon Highlanders on its right and troops of the 17th Division on its left. The first three objectives were to be taken by the 7th Black Watch and 7th Gordon Highlanders, the last being the Gavrelle–Roeux road, on reaching which the 6th Black Watch and 6th Gordons were to "leap-frog" through the leading troops and take Greenland Hill and the high ground overlooking Plouvain.

The Battalion held the line at Fampoux for five days prior to the assault, when all ranks made themselves acquainted with the position although constantly harassed by enemy shelling; Major Macdonald and Second Lieutenant Scott were wounded here. On the night of April 20th, the Battalion was relieved by the 8th Battalion Argyll and Sutherland Highlanders and withdrew to Arras for forty-eight hours' rest. Here it received its fighting equipment and moved up to assembly positions in the Oppy line during the night of the 22nd.

Zero hour had been fixed at 4.45 a.m. on April 23rd. Moving off an hour before this the Battalion advanced in artillery formation, but, on reaching the British front line, it had to extend owing to heavy machine gun fire which caused many losses in both the 6th Black Watch and 7th Gordon Highlanders. None the less the latter battalion captured the German front line, although it did not succeed in advancing much further except in isolated parties. After 6.20 a.m., the advance of the 6th became very difficult, and was only carried out by means of

THE SIXTH BATTALION THE BLACK WATCH

short section rushes from shell hole to shell hole. The Gavrelle road was reached about 9 a.m. and the next two hours were occupied in driving off repeated German counter attacks made in force. These offered magnificent targets to the British infantry machine gunners and artillery, who took heavy toll from the enemy. Further advance was consequently slow, and at 11.15 a.m. it was again held up by machine gun fire and snipers on Greenland Hill and in the Chemical Works. In the early afternoon, however, by hard fighting and persistent attack, the 6th was firmly established on the lower slopes of Greenland Hill, well east of the Gavrelle–Roeux road.

From this point enemy machine gun fire from the ridge above made any further advance impossible, and the ground captured was consolidated. While thus occupied the Battalion suffered many casualties, five officers being killed and several others wounded. Time after time during the afternoon the enemy attempted to dislodge the 6th from their position, but on every occasion their attacks were broken up by Lewis gun and artillery fire. About midnight on the 23rd, the 6th was relieved by a battalion of the 34th Division and reformed in the old German front line.

The losses suffered by the Battalion in the action included five officers killed, Second Lieutenants Butler, MacBeth, Garvie, Doe and Glass; four wounded, Second Lieutenants Condor, Mac Donald, Gyle, and Hepden; 25 other ranks killed, 123 wounded and 48 missing. Total: Nine officers and 196 other ranks.

On the afternoon of the 24th, the 6th was withdrawn from the battle and moved to billets in Arras. The following afternoon the Division began moving back to a rest area. The 153rd Brigade entrained at Arras on the 25th and moved to Ligny St. Flochel, whence the 6th marched to Marquay for a well-earned three weeks' rest and for training.

Commenting on this fighting, Major F. W. Bewsher states in the *History of the 51st Division*:

" So ended a most sanguinary encounter. From most diffi-
" cultly situated assembly trenches, an attack had been launched
" against a position of considerable strength. . . . The men had
" advanced against a stout opposition and had suffered heavy
" casualties, had then been systematically bombarded in shallow
" trenches and shell-holes, and had been repeatedly counter-
" attacked. They, however, maintained a portion of their gains
" against all comers, and had appreciably deepened the area held
" east of the Scarpe."

Shortly after being withdrawn from the battle the two

IN RESERVE, MAY, 1917

following messages were received by the Division Commander, and communicated to all ranks:

1

From the Commander-in-Chief:

"The fierce fighting of yesterday (23rd April) has carried us on another step forward. I congratulate you on the results of it, and on the severe punishment you have inflicted on the enemy."

2

From General Sir Charles Fergusson, commanding the XVII Corps:

"I wish to express to the Division through you my congratulations on the splendid work which they have done in the recent fighting, especially on Monday, 23rd April.

"Had it not been for the fine fighting spirit of the Division, the result might easily have been disadvantageous to us. I am proud and delighted with the Division, as they may be themselves with the grand fight they put up, and I know when they are rested and reorganised they will be keen to add to their reputation."

The 6th spent the next three weeks resting, training and re-fitting. Marquay was a pleasant village and had seldom been occupied by troops; the weather was delightful and altogether the rest period passed all too quickly. Attack practices, tactical schemes and musketry courses were carried out, and Regimental sports were held.

Brigadier-General D. Campbell now left the 153rd Brigade and was succeeded by Brigadier-General A. Gordon, C.M.G., D.S.O.

Meanwhile the fighting east of Arras continued with results favourable to the Allies. Between the 10th and 13th of May the British line was considerably advanced, the Roeux trenches being taken on the 12th.

In anticipation of being required in this fighting, the 51st Division began moving back to the front line east of Arras on the 10th; two days later the 6th moved up by train to Arras, and next day marched to the Oppy line near Fampoux, where it remained in support for two days, being then withdrawn to the railway embankment at Blangy St. Laurent.

On the evening of the 15th, the Battalion was ordered to hold itself in readiness to move up if required to meet an enemy counter attack. About 3.30 a.m. on the 16th, the 6th, therefore, moved up by the towpath to the Oppy line and came under orders

THE SIXTH BATTALION THE BLACK WATCH

of the 152nd Brigade Commander. This Brigade, which had relieved the whole of the 4th Division on the night of May 12th, had been subjected to a heavy enemy bombardment on the 15th which gave colour to the rumours of a coming German counter attack. Nothing, however, happened on the immediate front of the 152nd Brigade; but elsewhere desperate encounters took place with the enemy at close quarters. The fighting consisted of a series of independent contests in which platoons or half companies tackled the enemy wherever the latter tried to get a footing. Frequently the men faced round to their rear, in order to deal with the enemy who had broken in by way of the railway cutting; many of these were finally caught between the two wings of the Highland Division and few escaped.

C company of the 6th Black Watch was attached to the 5th Battalion Gordon Highlanders to clear up the situation near the Chemical Works. This was carried out late in the afternoon, and in the evening the other three companies were moved up in artillery formation to clear out any remaining parties of the enemy, and to relieve the troops of the 152nd Brigade in the front line. The relief was completed and the line securely re-established early next morning. The 153rd Brigade then took over the sector, where the Battalion was kept fully employed in clearing the battlefield and improving the defences until the end of the month. The 6th was then relieved by a battalion of the 4th Division.

CHAPTER VII

JUNE TO NOVEMBER, 1917

The Third Battle of Ypres—Attack near the Steenbeek River

(*See Map facing Page* 292.)

THE Highland Division left the Arras area on June 1st, its destination being the Ypres Salient; the 6th Battalion moved with the remainder of the 153rd Brigade by road, billeting at the following places: Marquay, Pressy, Beaumetz, Wizernes, and finally arrived at Serques on the 8th, where it remained nearly a fortnight preparing for and rehearsing a pending attack.

On the 21st, the Battalion moved to Poperinghe by train, and into the line at Lancashire Farm on the 28th. This tour was a quiet one, and on July 5th, the Battalion entrained for St. Omer and marched thence to St. Momelin, where it carried out further training for the coming attack. A practice ground, on which all the landmarks and strong points were shown, was laid out to represent the area to be attacked.

To show how thorough were these preparations, the following description is taken from the *History of the 51st Division:*

"General Maxse, the Corps Commander, took the greatest "interest in the training, visiting each Brigade and lecturing to "all the officers. Large training areas were hired, and so that "officers and men might form some impression of the German "position, which they could not see, a large model was made, "about the size of four tennis courts, in which hills, valleys, "streams, houses, roads, woods, trenches, etc., were all accurately "represented by models. Platforms were then erected at "intervals round it, from which officers could point out to their "men the appearance of the area which they would traverse "during the operations. . . .

"An exact replica of the German trenches was also marked "out with tracing tapes on the training ground full size, in "which every known trench and farm was represented. The "troops were then practised on this course until they could find "their way to their objectives according to plan, without any "officers taking part in the exercise. The men were also care-"fully trained in the manner in which each post was to dig "itself in during consolidation, and how to pile the earth as it "was excavated, so that it at no time obscured their field of fire "to their front."

The Messines–Wytschaete ridge had been taken early in June and the object of the coming offensive was to capture the Passchendaele ridge, from which the enemy had complete observation for some two thousand yards as far back as the Yser Canal. The British trenches in this area were bad, consisting mainly of dilapidated breast-works which gave little cover from view and even less protection from shell fire.

On June 23rd the Battalion moved up in motor omnibuses to " C " camp on the Proven–Poperinghe road and there completed its training and preparation for the attack. A week later, on the 30th, the 6th moved up to Windmill Camp. That very day a calamity befell the Brigade. The Brigadier, General A. Gordon, and his Brigade Major, Captain Lean, while making a final tour of the front line before the Brigade moved into assembly positions, were both hit; Captain Lean was killed outright and the Brigadier fatally wounded. General Gordon died in hospital three days later, and was succeeded in command of the Brigade by Lieutenant-Colonel H. G. Hislop, 7th Battalion Argyll and Sutherland Highlanders.

The object of the attack was the Steenbeek River, about two thousand yards behind the German front line. The attack was divided into four stages, the first objective, the " blue " line, being the enemy front trenches; the second, the " black " line, his support system; the third, the " green " line, the River Steenbeek itself; and the fourth and final objective, a line about two hundred yards north-east of the river.

The front allotted to the Division was about fourteen hundred yards in length, and General Harper decided to attack with two Brigades, the 152nd on the right, and the 153rd on the left, the 154th being in Division reserve. Each Brigade was to attack on a two Battalion front. Those from the 153rd Brigade were the 7th Gordon Highlanders on the right and the 7th Black Watch on the left. A battalion of the 38th Division was on the left of the 7th Black Watch and in rear of these battalions were the 6th Seaforth Highlanders on the right and 6th Black Watch on the left. The task to these two Battalions in reserve was to pass through the leading troops after they had taken the " black " line, and continue the advance and secure the capture of the Steenbeek River line.

The German troops on the 51st Division front consisted of the 23rd (Reserve) Saxon Division, who were actually being relieved by the 3rd German Guards Division when the attack was made. On the night of July 30th, the 6th, under command of Colonel T. M. Booth, moved up to its assembly position in rear of the British front line.

At 3.50 a.m. on the 31st, an artillery barrage came down on the German lines and the battle opened. At this early hour it was still dark, but the flashes from bursting shells and from projectiles filled with burning oil, which were thrown into the

THIRD BATTLE OF YPRES, JULY 31ST, 1917

enemy lines by trench mortars, lit up the ground. Ten minutes after Zero A company of the 6th went forward, followed by B and C companies, D company holding the original British front line.

At 6 a.m. Battalion Headquarters moved forward to Hindenburg Farm, a few hundred yards behind the original German front line. Immediately after this a report was received from Captain Lindsay, commanding B company, that he had occupied the " black " line. At 7.15 a.m., Lieutenant Hamilton, who had been wounded and was being carried down by four German prisoners, was able to report that B, C and D companies were established in the " black " line, and had gained touch with the 6th Battalion Seaforth Highlanders on the right; although at the moment of his leaving the advance was held up by machine gun fire.

At 7.30 a.m., by a joint effort of the 6th Battalion Black Watch and the 5th Battalion Gordon Highlanders, an enemy strong point was captured with about a hundred prisoners; a quarter of an hour later B company took Cane Wood, with twelve prisoners, and a few minutes later captured Rudolph Farm, midway between the " black " and " green " lines, which contained seventy more of the enemy. This company made great progress throughout the morning and within another hour, by nine o'clock, although reduced to a strength of only fifty rifles, had captured Kliest Farm.

At 9.20 a.m., Colonel Booth moved his Headquarters further forward to Gournier Farm, half-way between the " blue " and " black " lines, and from there sent forward every available man to assist in consolidating the " black " line, where A company was established in front of Cane trench in touch with the 6th Battalion Seaforth Highlanders on the right, and the 5th Battalion Gordon Highlanders on the left. From this point Colonel Booth made a personal reconnaissance of the " green " line, and, finding about forty men of D company holding some gun-pits on the road between Ferdinand and Chien Farms, he sent them over the Steenbeek River, where they were able to establish four posts under Second Lieutenant Drummond.

During the afternoon the fighting in this advanced position grew very severe; Second Lieutenant Drummond and his men drove off no less than three determined counter-attacks between 3.45 and 5 p.m., in each of which the enemy lost nearly a hundred men killed or wounded. At the same time, C company established itself on the right, between Ferdinand and Chien Farms; B company dug in at Francois Farm, and A company, with the 7th Battalion Gordon Highlanders on its right occupied the " black " line.

THE SIXTH BATTALION THE BLACK WATCH

At 6 p.m. the enemy put down a very heavy barrage on the "black" line, and five minutes later, launched another counter-attack on D company, on the far side of the Steenbeek River; this time, owing to the severe losses inflicted on his handful of men by this and the other three attacks, and to the withdrawal of the troops on his left, Second Lieutenant Drummond was forced to withdraw to the Gun Pit line south of the Steenbeek from which position he put out standing patrols to prevent the Germans crossing the river.

By this time the previous fifteen hours of continuous fighting had wellnigh exhausted British and German alike, and the night passed without further incident. The following day, August 1st, was spent in consolidating the positions won, bad weather and almost continuous rain making the task far from easy. The enemy made one more counter-attack at 8.30 p.m., but this was driven off without difficulty.

The following account, written by a man of D company, gives a vivid description of what took place in that extremely hard task, namely, the crossing of the Steenbeek River:

"On the evening of July 30th, the Battalion set out under "cover of the dark for the next day's scene of action. To D "company was assigned a position behind the British front line "trench where with the approach of Zero hour, 3.50 a.m., they "were subjected to a merciless bombardment. A scurry was "made for the front line trench. But even there things were "hot, and many casualties were suffered, amongst the number "being Captain R. J. Menzies, formerly of the London Scottish, "one of D company's most highly esteemed and deeply lamented "officers.

"At 4 a.m. A company went forward, followed by B and "C. Good progress was made despite stubborn resistance from "numerous enemy 'pill-boxes.' Here a tank proved of valuable "assistance, dealing more effectively with the hidden machine "gun nests than the ordinary infantry was able to do.

"D company advanced and collected at the Gun-pits at "Ferdinand Farm, where Colonel Booth, making a personal "reconnaissance, found between thirty and forty men assembled. "With two sergeants he proceeded over the Steenbeek and "after inspecting the position, established four posts, which "were afterwards placed under the command of Second "Lieutenant Drummond. Numerous small parties reported "to this nucleus until the force holding the bridge-head was "about 50 strong.

"For a time all went well, and attempts were made to "render the position which had been occupied beyond the

THIRD BATTLE OF YPRES

"Steenbeek a formidable one. But towards three o'clock in the
"afternoon the enemy was observed massing near Langemarck
"village. Counter-attack after counter-attack was delivered and
"repulsed. The enemy waited for further reinforcements which
"could be clearly seen coming up, again attacked and was again
"repulsed. But the plight of the mere handful of the 6th whose
"lot it had been to push forward into that advanced position
"was momentarily becoming more desperate. Ammunition was
"running short. A Welsh regiment on the left had fallen back.
"There was no connection on the right. What was to be done?
"There was nothing for it but to withdraw, temporarily at least.
"Word was passed for the men to make, one at a time, for the
"German Gun-pits on the other side of the river. Those who
"came through bear witness that it was one of the most terribly
"exciting moments of their lives. Stumbling through the mud,
"falling, rising, pressing on, while the enemy, barely 100 yards
"away, stood up and took deliberate aim at them—one of the
"memories of the Great War which no length of time will ever
"blot out.

"In one of the enemy's abandoned 'pill-boxes' at the
"Gun-pits, 'Company Headquarters' was established. The
"position, one which dominated the Steenbeek, was consoli-
"dated. Another counter-attack on the part of the Boche proved
"unavailing, being broken up mainly by a destructive barrage
"from the other side. Patrols were put out to prevent the river
"being recrossed, but no further attempt was made to renew
"the struggle.

"Thus ended one of the most courageous offensives ever
"engaged in by the 6th Battalion The Black Watch, though it
"is doubtful if the gain of it was commensurate to the losses
"sustained and the heroism displayed."

The losses suffered by the 6th in this battle were one officer, Captain R. J. Menzies, killed, and eight wounded, 50 other ranks killed and 234 wounded and nine missing.

The awards for gallantry included three Military Crosses, two Distinguished Conduct Medals, one bar to the Military Medal, and 12 Military Medals.

The Battalion was relieved on the evening of August 1st, and returned to Siege Camp, which, owing to rain, wind and mud, was far from being an ideal resting place.

Looking back on the events of these two memorable days, one point stands out clearly, namely, the great improvement made in the arrangements for sending back information. It must be borne in mind that this flat country in which the fighting took place was often obscured by bursting shells, and little or nothing of the progress of events in the battle could be seen by those behind; consequently the guiding of operations depended entirely on information sent back by runner or gleaned from the passing wounded. The fact that all through these desperate days, in weather of the vilest description, and operating over the worst possible country, a continuous stream of exact and valuable information was transmitted, shows the high state of efficiency reached as a result of the thorough training beforehand. The fact also that in spite of all difficulties it was possible to drive the enemy back to the Steenbeek River, to capture a large number of prisoners and material, and to repel no less than five counter-attacks, shows the tenacity and determination of all ranks, not only in the 6th Battalion but in the whole of the 51st Division.

The captures included 15 officers and 624 other ranks; two field guns, four trench mortars, and 29 machine guns; in addition, many other machine guns were destroyed.

On August 4th, the 153rd Brigade was relieved by part of the 154th, and the 6th Battalion moved back to St. Jan Ter Biezen, where the Brigade settled down to train under its new commander, Brigadier-General A. T. Beckwith. It was during this training period that Lieutenant-Colonel T. M. Booth relinquished command of the Battalion to take up an appointment in England, being succeeded, on the 16th, by Lieutenant-Colonel N. Campbell, 8th Battalion Argyll and Sutherland Highlanders.

On August 30th, the 6th moved up to Siege Camp, where it spent the next ten days in reserve, supplying working parties and training, moving up to the line on September 12th, when it took over trenches in the Langemarck sector.

The tour here passed with little worthy of record except that on the 16th the enemy attacked three posts, two of which had to be evacuated in order that a defensive flank might be formed so as to prevent the garrisons from being cut off altogether.

After a short period of attachment to the 152nd Brigade in the Vorna–Comedy Farm area near the Steenbeek, the 6th was withdrawn from the line and, on the 28th, moved with the 153rd Brigade to the neighbourhood of Gomiécourt and from there, on the 4th, to the Hindenburg line near Heninel. The time spent in this area was one of the most pleasant trench tours the 6th experienced; the dug-outs were exceedingly good, all ranks were comfortable and losses were few.

After a month in this neighbourhood the 51st Division was withdrawn to a rest area on the Arras–St. Pol road, the 6th Battalion being billeted in Habarcq, where men and officers

IN RESERVE, HABARCQ, SEPTEMBER, 1917

spent a very enjoyable three weeks. Here orders were received to train for a forthcoming attack on Cambrai which was to be carried out on a large scale in conjunction with tanks. Several practices were held at Wailly with the actual machines destined to be used, and on these occasions, successful liaison was carried out between the tanks and the infantry personnel. While at Habarcq the Adjutant, Captain Rutherford, M.C., left the Battalion on transfer to the Tank Corps.

CHAPTER VIII

NOVEMBER, 1917, TO JANUARY, 1918

The Battle of Cambrai

THE successes gained by the 51st Division at Beaumont Hamel in 1916, Arras in 1917, and at Ypres between July to September in that year, probably accounted for its selection to take part in the battle of Cambrai.

The intention of the Commander-in-Chief was to surprise the enemy at a point where an attack was least expected, and where, in consequence, the strength of the defending garrison had been reduced to a minimum. In addition, he proposed to employ a large number of tanks in co-operation with the infantry. These tanks eventually proved to be of immense assistance to the infantry by flattening out the broad belts of wire which protected the Hindenburg line, and also by overcoming the German strong points when machine guns held up the infantry advance. The moral effect of the tanks was also very great. The Germans had no effective means of stopping their advance, and in many instances their riflemen fled precipitately as they moved forward apparently with irresistible force. In this action a group of three tanks was allotted to every 150 yards along the whole frontage of the Division, a tactical formation that allowed of thorough co-operation with the leading infantry units.

The general idea of the plan of operations was as follows. The tanks were ordered to advance about a hundred and fifty yards in front of the leading line of infantry, and after driving their way through the enemy wire and over the front line trench, some were detailed to deal with strong points in the line while others moved forward to the second objective, to be joined by their comrades when the infantry were in full possession of the front line.

The position to be attacked was a formidable one. The famous Hindenburg line consisted of three successive systems of deep trenches protected by wide and strongly built belts of wire. The attack by the 51st (Highland) Division was to be launched from a point just north-east of Trescault village, and was to be continued in a north-easterly direction through Flesquières, in the Hindenburg support line near the Graincourt–Marcoing road, to Fontaine Notre Dame.

The Divisional Commander decided to attack on a two Brigade front, 152nd Brigade on the right, 153rd Brigade on the left and 154th Brigade in Divisional reserve. In the attack of the 153rd Brigade, the 6th Battalion The Black Watch was on the right and the 5th Battalion Gordon Highlanders on the left, the battalion on the right of The Black Watch being the 8th

BATTLE OF CAMBRAI, NOVEMBER 19TH, 1917

Argyll and Sutherland Highlanders. Behind the 6th Battalion was the 7th Battalion Black Watch and behind the 5th Battalion Gordon Highlanders their own 7th Battalion, these two being detailed for the capture of the third and fourth objectives, namely, the brown and red dotted lines, while the leading two battalions had as their objectives the Hindenburg front and support lines, the latter including the village of Flesquières.

Surprise was the essence of the whole operation. Every possible precaution was therefore taken to prevent the enemy from suspecting the British intention; by limiting movements entirely to the hours of darkness the staff were able to concentrate, unknown to the enemy, the huge forces of men and guns in camouflage shelters in Havrincourt Wood and in the ruined village of Metz by the night of November 19th.

This well arranged concentration and assembly of attacking divisions was carried out in a country which had been completely devastated by the enemy before their withdrawal to what they considered the impregnable Hindenburg line. An idea of the ground in which this concentration was carried out may be gained from the German reports. The *Local Anzeiger* of March 18th, 1917, describes the damage they did and the thorough manner in which they deliberately destroyed the homesteads and houses of the French villagers.

" In the course of these last months great stretches of French
" territory have been turned by us into a dead country. It
" varies in width from ten, twelve to thirteen kilometres, and
" extends along the whole of our new positions. No village or
" farm was left standing, no road was left passable, no railway
" track or embankment was left in being. Where once were
" woods, there are gaunt rows of stumps; the wells have been
" blown up. In front of our new positions runs like a gigantic
" ribbon, our ' Empire of Death.' "

On the night of November 19th, the Battalion moved into the front line immediately north-east of the village of Trescault, taking over from the 36th (Ulster) Division and, long before dawn, was in position of assembly.

The following graphic account of the battle is taken from Colonel Neil Campbell's official report. Narrative of events during the battle begun on 20th November, 1917. (Cambrai Front.)

" At 6 a.m. on the 19th, Battalion Headquarters with C
" company and Nos. 5 and 6 platoons of B left Metz for the
" front line north-east of Trescault and relieved a portion of
" the 8/9th Battalion Royal Irish Rifles of the 36th (Ulster)

"Division, Nos. 9, 10 and 5 platoons occupying the front line with 11, 12 and 6 platoons in support. These were the six platoons detailed to capture the Hindenburg front and support lines and they moved forward twenty-four hours prior to the actual attack in order to give all ranks an opportunity to learn the lie of the land and the various landmarks.

"The day passed quietly, the 8th Battalion Argyll and Sutherland Highlanders and 5th Battalion Gordon Highlanders coming in on our right and left respectively.

"As soon as it was dark Lieutenant Graves laid out a taped line in front of our trenches in order that every man should start at right angles to the direction of advance: flags were also put in from the support lines to this tape to show platoon flanks.

"The three platoons in the support trenches moved up to the front line two and a half hours before Zero, whilst Nos. 9, 10 and 5 moved out of that line to the taped out lines in No Man's Land half an hour before Zero.

"A company and the remaining platoons of B and D left Metz at 2.30 a.m. on the 20th before Zero hour and were in position as follows:—

"A company and Nos. 7 and 8 platoons of B were in Derby support line; D company, less two sections, were in Havrincourt Wood, the two sections being sent to the tanks, and the Battalion was in assembly position by 5.30 a.m., just half an hour before the tanks started.

"Zero was at 6.20 a.m., when the light was sufficiently clear to enable the tanks and infantry lining the tapes to be seen from the German outpost line two hundred yards away. Punctually to the second our artillery opened fire, placing a perfect barrage on the German front line, and the tanks moved forward in advance of the infantry to the German outpost position. This was quickly dealt with, the few men holding one or two sap-heads offering no resistance. The enemy artillery quickly opened fire, but it was so slight that no definite barrage line could be discerned.

"All infantry got away at their correct distance without any trouble as the advance moved off.

"Nos. 5, 9 and 10 platoons, shortly after Zero, moved forward in two lines at the requisite distance behind the tanks and captured the red line at 7.15 a.m., touch with formations on the flanks being maintained during the advance and after occupation of the red line. No resistance was offered by the enemy, who, apparently, was terrified by the appearance of such a large number of tanks, and about 30 prisoners were taken with little loss to the platoons concerned.

"Meanwhile D company, leaving Havrincourt Wood at

BATTLE OF CAMBRAI

" 7.20 a.m., had moved into the British front line and was in
" position there an hour later.

" Directly the first objective had been taken Nos. 6, 11 and
" 12 platoons, the second wave, passed through the first, but
" were held up for a short time by machine gun fire in positions
" in front of the right platoon, a tank having missed a machine
" gun which was giving trouble. Seeing what had happened,
" Sergeant N. Steele crawled forward and with a bomb settled
" the machine gun team and captured the gun. With the help
" of a tank in front of the Sapper platoon and prompt action
" by the left platoon (No. 11) the green line was reached at
" 7.45 a.m. and consolidation commenced, the garrison quickly
" surrendered and 80 Germans were captured.

" From this point the advance was taken up by Nos. 7 and 8
" platoons of B company on the right, and by the whole of A
" in the centre and on the left.

" So far the Battalion had gained its objectives without a
" hitch, casualties had been few and tanks had worked according
" to instructions. The successful advance continued and the
" brown line (Mole trench) was captured by Nos. 7, 3 and 2
" platoons, although they had been held up for a very short time
" by two machine gun posts; Sergeant Loftus in one case and
" Corporal Simpson in the other crawled forward and wiped
" out the gun teams with bombs. On the left the advance was
" also stopped, mainly by uncut wire, and here occurred a good
" example of the result of training and liaison work between the
" tanks and infantry. Captain Brown, commanding A company,
" seeing three tanks detailed to co-operate with the 7th Battalion
" Gordon Highlanders in the second phase of the fighting,
" attracted their attention by means of signals and arranged for
" the necessary gaps in the wire to be made; this was at once
" done and the capture of Mole trench completed. Here again
" only slight opposition was met with and many more prisoners
" were taken. No. 2 platoon on the left was now somewhat
" troubled by machine gun fire from Sammy trench but, with
" the aid of covering fire from Lewis guns, this platoon, by
" section rushes, gradually surrounded the enemy gun position
" and after a fierce fight with the team until the last German
" fell, captured not only the position, but also a battery of four
" guns which were posted there.

" Nos. 8, 1 and 4 platoons then advanced towards the
" Battalion's final objective and immediately came under heavy
" machine gun fire from the Grand Ravine. The 6th Battalion
" was certainly in luck that day for even here few casualties were
" sustained, this being due to the excellent manner in which
" the men took advantage of all available cover. On the right

"Private Peddie, entirely on his own initiative, crawled up close
"to an enemy post which was holding up the advance, and by
"means of rifle grenades killed five and wounded two of the
"garrison. A tank now took part in the operation and with its
"assistance the whole length of the ravine was cleared, six
"German officers and about 100 other ranks surrendering. On
"the left flank a spirited resistance was put up by a German
"post in Rowland Copse, but this was dealt with satisfactorily
"and yielded one officer and six men as prisoners together with
"three machine guns. The capture of the Battalion's final
"objective was completed by 9.15 a.m. and consolidation was at
"once commenced, touch being maintained with flanking units,
"and the 7th Battalion The Black Watch and 7th Battalion
"Gordon Highlanders passed through the front line to carry
"out the second phase of the battle."

The remainder of the day was spent by the 6th in reorganizing and preparing for the next advance, and by 7 p.m. company commanders reported their companies ready for further operations.

In compliance with orders received on the 20th the Battalion, in conjunction with the 5th Gordon Highlanders, advanced and occupied the red dotted line on the 153rd Brigade front that night, and at 3 a.m. on the 21st the leading platoons moved forward.

Zero was fixed for 6.45 a.m. when Nos. 5 and 6 platoons, B company, advanced, followed by D company, all in artillery formation. Passing through Flesquières without opposition, Nos. 5 and 6 platoons consolidated on a line north of the village, while D company passed through them and reached the dotted red line without hindrance in touch with the 8th Battalion Argyll and Sutherland Highlanders on the right and the 5th Battalion Gordon Highlanders on the left, the operation being completed with loss of only two men wounded. During the advance the Battalion took three field guns and six howitzers which had been abandoned by the enemy during the night.

About 10.30 a.m. the 154th Brigade, which had come up during the early morning, passed through the 152nd and 153rd Brigades and continued the advance towards Fontaine: the 153rd Brigade became Divisional reserve, and spent the day reorganizing.

At 6.30 a.m. on the 23rd, having received instructions to take over the whole of the 153rd Brigade front, Colonel Campbell moved A and C companies up to positions in the red dotted line, keeping B and D in reserve. Nothing more of note occurred, and the Battalion was relieved during the night by the 2nd Battalion Scots Guards, and moved back to bivouacs at Trescault.

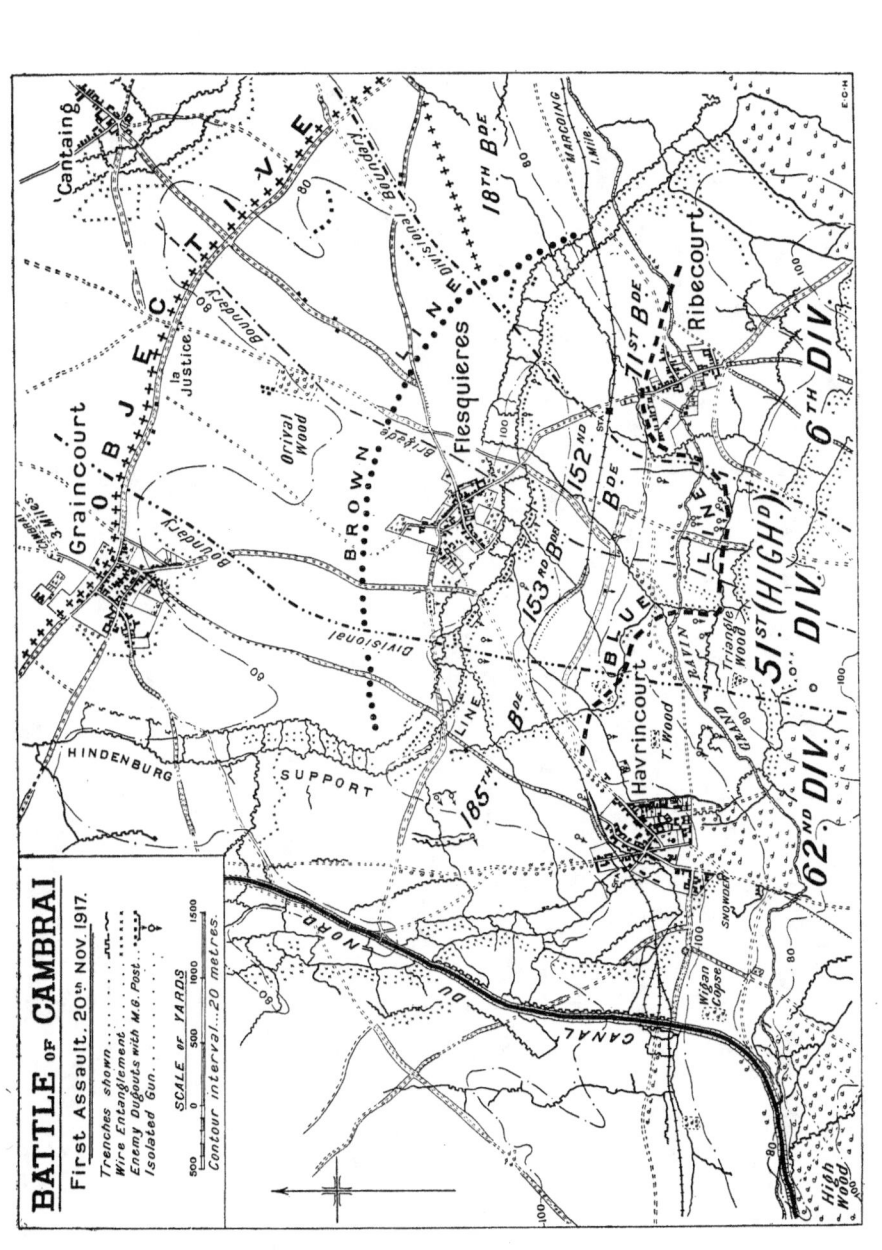

TRENCH WARFARE, SPRING, 1918

Thus ended a most brilliant and successful operation. The success achieved was greatly due to careful training and to the keenness shown by all ranks in carrying out their various tasks. Colonel Campbell says:

"I am assured that sections moved forward exactly as though carrying out a practice attack, converging where wire had to be negotiated and extending again when possible; consolidation was carried out expeditiously and well, and I had only to rectify the siting of positions in one or two cases."

There is no doubt that D Tank Battalion, under Major Watson, had much to do with the success of the operation. During the period of training Major Watson co-operated with the 6th in a whole-hearted manner, and the smooth and successful way in which the tanks assembled was directly due to the great efforts expended by him on the night prior to the attack.

It is of interest to note that the losses suffered by the 6th during their advance of over five thousand yards were one officer killed and two wounded; eight other ranks killed and 34 wounded, which speaks highly for the standard of training in the Battalion.

"The success of the Division and its cheapness in life was due, as General Maxse put it, 'to the fact that all usual war problems had been thought out beforehand, discussed in detail, and embodied in simple doctrines well known to all ranks.'" (From the *History of the 51st (Highland) Division*).

From Trescault the 6th moved to Ytres and proceeded by train to Acheux on the 25th, eventually reaching Forceville the same day, where it hoped to be given time to rest and refit. The Germans, however, prevented this, for owing to a counter-attack on a large scale developing on November 30th, the Battalion moved to Ytres. On the following day it relieved part of a London Division in the front line between Pronville and Frémicourt where, with the usual reliefs, it remained for the rest of the month, Christmas being spent in Frémicourt and New Year in the line at Louverval.

The first three weeks of 1918 were spent in the line. On the 20th, the 6th was relieved by the 11th Battalion Essex Regiment and moved to Courcelles Le Comte, where it spent three weeks in training and musketry until February 10th.

Returning to the sector in front of Pronville, the 6th had several tours of duty in the front line, with breaks at Beugny, the third spell beginning on March 15th, just prior to the German offensive described in the following chapter.

CHAPTER IX

FEBRUARY TO JUNE, 1918

The German Offensive, 1918—Battle of the Lawe— Move to Vimy Ridge

THE 6th spent the first two and a half months of 1918 in the Flesquières area. When the 51st Division took over this part of the line, the trenches were in a poor condition, but between the beginning of December, 1917, and the middle of March, 1918, they were greatly improved and in the end were considerably stronger than those held by Divisions on the right and left. All the work was carefully organized and standard patterns and sizes fixed for fire-bays, traverses and dug-outs and no haphazard work was allowed. In January, 1918, the British front had been considerably lengthened and the 51st Division held a sector of no less than six thousand yards of front line. The whole of this long line was put in a thorough state of defence and heavily wired. In addition, an intermediate line was prepared running from north of Hermies, north of Doignies, to a point north of Louverval, and in rear of this another line was constructed under Corps arrangements. The fact that the 51st Division line was so strong was well known to the enemy, for when the German attack was launched on March 21st, no attempt was made to storm the trenches held by the Highlanders.

The War Diary contains no report of any incident of much note during the period prior to the German attack, but reading from it, it is obvious that an enemy offensive was expected on that part of the front. On March 13th, the Battalion went into the front line at Pronville, on which date Lieutenant-Colonel Campbell sprained his ankle so severely that he was sent to the Base, and Major W. P. Campbell then assumed command.

The storm broke at 5.30 a.m. on March 21st, when, after a terrific bombardment for five hours, which caused the complete destruction of many lines of trenches, the Germans attacked the Divisions on the right and left, and drove them back by sheer weight of numbers. Having achieved this, the Germans then endeavoured to cut off the 51st Division by coming in from behind on either flank and attacking with machine guns, rifle and bombs.

The enemy counted on the Highlanders holding their ground despite the merciless bombardment to which they had been subjected; and in this they were right, for they succeeded in cutting off all the troops holding the front and support lines, every man of whom was either killed or captured. The survivors of these front line battalions, located in the Intermediate line

THE GERMAN OFFENSIVE, MARCH 21st, 1918

and in rear of it, soon found themselves in a desperate position, and were forced to fall back gradually, frequently halting and forming defensive flanks to retard the enemy's advance and to avoid being cut off like their comrades in front. Indeed, every inch of ground was stubbornly contested, and only given up when further delay would have entailed being cut off.

For five days and nights the desperate struggle went on and, heavy as were the casualties in the Highland Division, the losses inflicted on the enemy must have been far more, for the fire from rifle, machine gun and field gun mowed down dense masses of Germans time after time at point blank range.

The 6th, on the extreme left of the Division, where the bombardment was perhaps heavier than at any other point, received a desperate hammering. The experiences of the Battalion are best told in the words of Major W. P. Campbell, who was in command throughout the action.

" The week preceding March 20th was notable for considerable activity on our part. Our heavy artillery kept up a continuous bombardment, and blew up a large number of enemy ammunition dumps in Pronville, and along the River Agache which lay in front of our line. Artillery positions near Bourlon Wood received attention, but drew practically no retaliation from the enemy. On one occasion a grey-green cloud followed an explosion in Pronville, suggesting the presence of a gas dump. Our field batteries searched roads and villages by night, and devoted special attention to the village of Pronville.

" All through these days the enemy infantry showed considerable activity in work behind the front line, carrying timber, making dug-outs, etc. Parties of officers were seen studying our lines with maps.

" On March 19th a large number of enemy observation balloons appeared, but only a few were up on the 20th.

" Our preparations for defence went on steadily. New wire was put out each night, and when the days were misty. A system of land mines was arranged to meet the enemy ' tanks,' and the field artillery arranged their anti-tank defences. Constant patrolling of ' No Man's Land ' up to the enemy outpost line gained information that the enemy was working nightly at wire, and possible machine gun or trench mortar emplacements. No enemy patrols were met by us, and the Battalion secured no prisoners for identification. The Division, however, got identification elsewhere.

" A few days before March 20th, the General Officer commanding Third Army, and his Chief of Staff, visited the

"line. Major-General Sir G. M. Harper, K.C.B., who had so
"long commanded the Highland Division, was promoted to
"the IV Corps, and was succeeded by Major-General Carter
"Campbell, D.S.O., as Divisional Commander.

"Enemy aircraft were very quiet, and little photography
"was done. The weather was fine, but heavy ground mists made
"observation difficult. On March 20th there was a thick mist
"till well on in the day, but it suddenly lifted in the afternoon,
"and large bodies of enemy troops were seen moving into
"Pronville and about the enemy lines. The night of the 20th
"was dark, with a heavy ground mist. There was little artillery
"activity and no patrol encounters.

"At 5 a.m. on the 21st, our artillery opened heavy fire on
"enemy lines and immediately the enemy put down an in-
"tense barrage on our system. Battalion Headquarters was
"under a barrage of heavies, with high-explosive and gas.
"Communication with our front lines by wire was maintained
"for about an hour, and the front companies reported heavy
"barrage with a considerable amount of gas, but no sign of an
"enemy advance.

"Shortly after 6.30 a.m. all communication was cut, both
"forward and back, and the ground mist and smoke and dust pre-
"vented successful visual signalling. Runners were unable to get
"forward, but succeeded in reaching Brigade Headquarters, which
"was under a heavy barrage, with considerable gas shelling.

"Observers at Battalion Headquarters were unable to see
"more than a few yards beyond our wire, until about 10 a.m.,
"when the bombardment lifted off the Intermediate Line and
"Battalion Headquarters, and, the mist clearing, the enemy
"infantry was seen moving about our support line.

"Visibility was very poor, but the enemy could be seen
"dribbling up the valley (Central Avenue) through the 6th
"Division area on our left, and on the ridge across the valley.
"Enemy scouts and snipers reached our wire, but were checked
"and driven back by rifle and Lewis gun fire.

"The enemy was reported to be concentrating in the dead
"ground in front of our wire, at Posts 26 and 27 on Intermediate
"Line. The 7th Battalion The Black Watch on our right
"reported that the enemy had broken into Post 26, but that
"Post 27 was still holding out. The enemy had been steadily
"pushing up the valley on our left, and soon appeared within a
"few hundred yards of Battalion Headquarters in small groups.

"The post on the left of Battalion Headquarters reported
"the enemy pushing up the trench from the left, and a defen-
"sive flank and line to cover retirement was formed in rear
"of the Intermediate Line, with its centre on the junction of

THE GERMAN OFFENSIVE, MARCH, 1918

"Lagnicourt road and Strand. Captain Coutts, of A company, "reported the enemy pressing in Post 27, and working up Strand "in strength.

"I then went along Lagnicourt road to confer with "Lieutenant-Colonel McClintock, commanding the 7th Batta- "lion The Black Watch. The enemy was behind each Battalion "Headquarters and, with the Intermediate Line broken, and "threatened seriously from Strand, we decided that further "resistance in the present position was futile, and ordered a "withdrawal to the Beaumetz–Morchies Line. I gave Captain "Coutts the order, and was moving back with Captain D. Cable, "Adjutant, when he saw that the medical officer, Captain J. G. "Anderson, M.C., had not been warned, and he left me to go "to him.

"With Lieutenant-Colonel McClintock I was moving down "a shallow trench when I saw Second Lieutenant J. Thomson "being attended to by a stretcher bearer on the Strand, and I "went to him. I could find no trace of either Captains Cable or "Anderson until I reached the Beaumetz-Morchies Line, where "I was informed that Captain Cable had been hit by a bullet "from a low-flying enemy plane.

"The retirement was covered by two half platoons of "A company, under Captain Coutts and Second Lieutenant "J. R. B. Cassie. The Beaumetz–Morchies Line was held by "the 7th Battalion Gordon Highlanders, one company of the "7th Battalion The Black Watch, and D company, 6th Battalion "The Black Watch, under Captain MacRosty.

"All the walking wounded were sent on to Beugny, and the "remains of the Battalion, about 40 men, were put in dug-outs "in the sunken road, west of the Beaumetz–Morchies Line. "The officers remaining were Major W. P. Campbell, in com- "mand, Captain W. E. Coutts and Second Lieutenant J. R. B. "Cassie. Captain MacRosty, officer commanding D company, "reported that he had been ordered to reinforce Post 29 in the "6th Division area, and that he had advanced two hundred "yards in front of the Beaumetz–Morchies Line. There he "discovered a line of gun pits which still had one gun of the "battery in action, with about twenty shells. The battery had "been very heavily dealt with in the morning's shelling, and had "three guns with their entire teams knocked out. The survivors "of the battery amounted to one officer, one battery sergeant- "major, and four men. Captain MacRosty advanced some fifty "yards beyond this battery but found the enemy in large "numbers lining the Strand Ridge about four hundred yards "in front and well on our side of the point he had been ordered "to reinforce. Having lost a large number of his men as a

THE SIXTH BATTALION THE BLACK WATCH

"result of heavy machine gun and aimed rifle fire, he fell back
"on the gun-pits, reporting his position to Battalion and Brigade
"Headquarters.

"At that time the enemy was coming over the Strand Ridge
"in mass formation, and was engaged over open sights by the
"remaining gun of the battery already referred to, and by every
"available machine gun. The effect at that range was, of course,
"very good, and any further attempt at an advance by the
"enemy was stopped for the moment.

"After firing all available ammunition, the surviving gun and
"also one gun of the battery that had not been seriously damaged
"were pulled out by the survivors of the gun-teams, assisted by
"the men of D company, 6th Battalion The Black Watch, and
"both guns and teams ultimately reached Beugny in safety.

"On receiving Captain MacRosty's report of the foregoing,
"and as I was very doubtful if Post 29 could be still holding out,
"particularly in view of the fact that the line of the Strand,
"which was a hundred yards on the British side of all the posts
"in the Intermediate Line, was strongly held by the enemy, I
"ordered him to hold on to the gun-pits at all costs. Captain
"MacRosty had been wounded through the shoulder in the
"morning, but held his command until nightfall, when he
"handed over to Second Lieutenant A. G. Drummond, M.C.
"Lieutenant R. B. Shaw, who had brought his men back and
"joined Captain MacRosty, was also hit and thought dead, but
"he came in after dark, and went to hospital.

"The enemy tried all the afternoon to force the Beaumetz–
"Morchies Line, but was well held, D company in particular
"doing good work.

"The night was quiet, with a thick haze, and I visited
"D company to see Second Lieutenant Drummond. He re-
"ported all well, but his position was isolated, and I realised his
"danger. The gun-pits, however, were vital to us, as an enemy
"frontal attack could not succeed while they remained in our
"possession. I, therefore, ordered him to hold on.

"The morning of the 22nd opened dull and misty, but
"cleared about 10 a.m., when the enemy aircraft came over,
"and an intense heavy artillery fire was opened on the Beaumetz–
"Morchies Line and on the sunken road in rear.

"Our aircraft were not to be seen, and the enemy observers
"regulated the heavy fire with too perfect accuracy. While the
"artillery pounded us, the infantry was steadily trying to work
"up to our wire and line, but the defence held, in spite of heavy
"casualties.

"One entrance of our Headquarters dug-out was blown in.
"A small arms ammunition column of the 7th Battalion The

THE GERMAN OFFENSIVE, MARCH 22ND, 1918

" Black Watch was smashed up, but the horses escaped. Corporal
" Martin and Lance-Corporal Smeaton, of our transport section,
" brought up another convoy of ammunition, under heavy fire,
" and succeeded in delivering their loads and getting away
" without loss. Their gallantry was rewarded by the granting of
" Military Medals.

" D company had reported numerous small parties of the
" enemy working round their left flank, and I knew the danger
" lay on that side, as the next Division had been pushed back,
" but how far I did not know, nor if our flanks were ' in the air.'
" Captain Coutts, who had command of the remaining men of
" A, B and C companies, was slightly shell-shocked, and I ordered
" him to rest in the Headquarters' dug-out.

" Communication with Brigade Headquarters had become
" impossible. My runners had got through, but not back again,
" and the necessary removal of Brigade Headquarters further
" back made touch difficult until after dark.

" About 5 p.m. the enemy barrage lifted, and immediately
" his infantry poured over the ridge on our left, rushing up the
" sunken road, along and behind the Beaumetz–Morchies Line,
" and, of course, cut off D company.

" Parties of the enemy were also pushing up the valley
" towards Bapaume and we were almost surrounded. One party
" leading the enemy rush, and consisting of an officer and about
" eight men, was well up the sunken road when Colonel McClin-
" tock, of the 7th Battalion The Black Watch, and I got out of
" the dug-out and climbed up on to the bank to try to stop the
" rush.

" Colonel McClintock had a rifle and shot the leader, but
" his men came on. We then saw the parties working round our
" rear, and immediately decided to try to hold the Cambrai road
" as a left flank, to protect the 152nd Brigade on the south side
" of the road. Earlier in the afternoon a party of Loyal North
" Lancashires had been sent forward to reinforce the Beaumetz–
" Morchies Line, and, with a mixed force, very few non-
" commissioned officers, and almost no officers, we had difficulty
" in getting the line formed. We extended towards Beugny in
" an endeavour to hold the enemy who had passed us, but
" unfortunately when we moved towards the vital spot the line
" we had formed broke and fell back. About 25 men of our
" Brigade were left, with Colonel McClintock, his Adjutant,
" Captain Reid, and myself, and we settled down to fight two
" parties of the enemy who tried to surround us. One officer
" followed by a dozen men, turned back down the Bapaume
" road, and indicated by signs his desire that we should sur-
" render. He waved a revolver in one hand, and his cool

"impertinence so puzzled me—I was standing up to try to see
"enemy movements—that I ordered 'Cease fire' lest he be
"one of ours. Realizing my mistake, I flattened down with
"celerity and we at once fired on the party. I missed that
"officer but got one of his men.

"We decided to fall back on Beugny village and successfully
"carried out a small withdrawal in the approved fashion, two
"parties covering each other. Second Lieutenant Cassie had
"become separated from us, and fell back earlier, endeavouring
"to hold together a mixed party. We took up shell-hole positions
"outside the village, found some ammunition, and waited for
"the Boche, but he did not seem to come on, perhaps realizing
"that a thistle is a nasty thing to grasp!

"After a council of war, Colonel McClintock sent off a
"patrol, and we got in touch with the 6th Battalion Seaforth
"Highlanders, who still held the Beaumetz–Morchies Line
"south of the Cambrai road. Colonel McClintock went off to
"see the 6th Battalion Seaforth Highlanders, while I disposed
"our small party in a shell-hole defensive flank, facing the
"Cambrai road. This flank was later extended by a platoon of
"the 8th Battalion Royal Scots. In the village we found traces
"of a hurried exit by heavy gunners, and in a haversack there
"was an unopened parcel from home, containing salmon, bread
"and butter, which provided a welcome supper.

"*23rd March.* About 1.30 a.m. Colonel McClintock and
"I decided that we ought to go to Brigade Headquarters at
"Frémicourt, to report on the situation. Passing through the
"5th Battalion Seaforth Highlanders, who were digging a line
"before Lebecquière, we reported to Brigade about 4.30 a.m.
"After two hours rest, we moved to a camp on the west side of
"Frémicourt, collected details and secured some breakfast.
"Orders then came to move to Bancourt and prepare to defend
"that village. Second Lieutenant Cassie rejoined about 7 a.m.,
"and Quartermaster Wilson, who had brought up rations, also
"reported for duty, but I sent him back to keep up the ration
"supply. We found a poor line of trenches already dug around
"Bancourt, and we at once set to work improving them, and
"putting out all available wire. The enemy had not yet passed
"the Beugny Line, east of Frémicourt, and the day passed quietly.
"After dark, the Quartermaster brought up good rations, and
"Lieutenant J. G. A. Hewat, with Lieutenant F. S. McNicoll,
"arrived to report that echelon 'B,' consisting of these two
"officers, with Second Lieutenant A. M. Dobbie and 30
"men (pioneers, tailors, shoemakers and men returned from
"leave) had been sent up, with the details of the 153rd Brigade,
"to hold the 'Red' line, in rear of Bancourt village. Some

THE GERMAN OFFENSIVE, MARCH 24TH, 1918

"hours that night were vainly spent in a search for wiring
"materials. The Quartermaster and transport had been ordered
"back to Grevillers. The night was cold but quiet.

"*24th March.* The enemy attacked the Beugny Line, and
"an English Division moved up, but was soon ordered back.
"Enemy balloons and aeroplanes observed this movement, and
"we were shelled, but suffered no casualties.

"We were without Lewis guns, but secured one from the
"6th Battalion Gordon Highlanders, which proved to be too
"new and stiff, and would only fire single shots. In the afternoon,
"parties of the enemy could be seen moving into Frémicourt
"on our left front, and also on our right, apparently employing
"the usual flanking tactics. The dispositions at this time were
"as follows: 7th Battalion Gordon Highlanders, about 200 men;
"7th Battalion The Black Watch, about 40 men; 6th Battalion
"The Black Watch, 40 men; and 8th Battalion Royal Scots,
"about 300 men, whose left rested on the Cambrai road

"About 5 p.m. our right suddenly fell back, and after
"surveying the situation, I ordered a withdrawal to the 'Red'
"line, after notifying the Royal Scots on our left. At first
"I feared I had acted too soon, but the enemy soon opened
"heavy and accurate machine gun fire from our right, showing
"that he was endeavouring to push round and get behind us,
"which he almost succeeded in doing. Night fell, to find us
"tired and hungry, but there could be no thought of rest, and
"the Brigade Details fell back through Bapaume, down the
"Albert road. Our hopes of a respite were soon dispelled, as we
"got orders to take up a position in defence of Loupart Wood.

"*25th March.* With me were Lieutenants Hewat and
"McNicoll, Second Lieutenants Dobbie and Cassie, and a newly
"joined officer, Second Lieutenant E. Garvie. The Quarter-
"master brought up rations, and, in our shell-holes, we snatched
"a short sleep before 8 a.m. The day cleared, and with two
"lines of English troops in front of us, we awaited the enemy.
"The troops ahead of us shortly began to retire, although we
"could not actually see the enemy in the distance. We were
"ordered to hold on, and if forced, to retire through the other
"troops, who had taken up a line in rear of us. Then word
"came that a fresh Division was coming up (joyous news) and
"that we must hold on.

"This gave us fresh strength, and we hung on till 2 p.m.,
"an hour after the relieving troops were due. By this time our
"flanks were hopelessly 'in the air.' and we were obliged to
"move back, but found no one behind us. Fortunately the
"enemy did not press us hard, as we were then in a thoroughly
"exhausted condition after the experiences of the last few days.

THE SIXTH BATTALION THE BLACK WATCH

"With Lieutenant Hewat I had gone to the left side of
"the wood to see that flank of our line, and while away Lieu-
"tenant-Colonel McClintock had been wounded in the leg.
"Not knowing that the Headquarters of the 7th Battalion The
"Black Watch had moved off, we went round to their side of
"the wood, but could not find them. At this point I saw a
"most interesting situation. From my corner of the wood
"I observed a British force (not the Highland Division) moving
"up one side of a long slope, while coming up the other side
"was a Boche column. Neither force was aware of the presence
"of the other, neither appeared to have scouts out, and each
"made a glorious target. We were keen to stay to see the upshot
"of this move, but knowing that the enemy snipers were pushing
"into the wood behind us, we were obliged to come away.
"Picking up a few odd men, we took up a line in an old German
"communicating trench running towards Irles, and there
"awaited the enemy scouts. They soon appeared at the edge
"of the wood, and we gave them a few rounds. The enemy was
"plainly pushing round westwards towards Irles, and, with our
"dozen men, Lieutenant Hewat and I fell back. Lieutenant
"McNicoll, Second Lieutenants Dobbie, Cassie and Garvie
"were similarly falling back with their men, and reported to
"me later.

"Crossing the Irles–Grévillers road we halted on the ridge
"opposite Loupart Wood to rest and await developments. The
"two English battalions which had moved up, came back under
"heavy machine gun fire, and the enemy soon appeared coming
"down the road and valley. How it was managed I cannot tell
"but the enemy sent down a cloud of gas which darkened the
"sky, but an expert told us we need not put on respirators.
"Not having any word of the 7th Battalion The Black Watch
"Headquarters, Lieutenant Hewat and I decided to attempt
"to return to the wood, and were in the act of moving down
"the valley, when the enemy advance turned us back.

"On the ridge were Brigadier-General A. T. Beckwith, of
"the 153rd Brigade, and other officers of mixed units, who
"placed a line of troops in a shallow trench to await the enemy
"advance. About a hundred yards in rear of this line was a deep
"communication trench, and it was decided to get part of the
"force back there to form a support. Several Divisions and
"many battalions were mixed up, and I feared trouble. The
"Boche had appeared on the ridge, and already we were under
"a heavy and accurate machine gun fire. On top of this they
"gave us several rounds of 'whizz-bangs' from four field guns
"brought up behind the advanced infantry, at point blank
"range, and like one man the line moved back. Major Keir

THE GERMAN OFFENSIVE, MARCH 26TH, 1918

"and Captain Reid of the 7th Battalion The Black Watch, "with Lieutenant Hewat and myself, did our utmost to hold "the men, but failed, the men by this time being utterly "worn out, and the enemy, seeing the target offered, gave "them heavy shelling from these four guns.

"The Headquarters of the 6th and 7th Battalions The "Black Watch were then in the awkward position of being alone "in front, and when the men had taken cover and the enemy "fire ceased, we crossed the open, one at a time, getting to the "next trench without casualty. Here we found about 250 men, "mostly of the Highland Division, very undecided, and we "called on them to stand fast and to remember the Division "they belonged to. I have always been proud of our men, but "that moment showed me how they could answer the call of "an officer. Many were 8th Battalion Royal Scots, whose "Commander, Colonel Gemmell, had been killed that morning, "and all had been in action several days. As we were alone, and "in a bad position, I allowed the men to move back, and behind "Achiet Le Petit, Major Newson, Second-in-Command of the "7th Battalion Gordon Highlanders, had collected a number "of men before we reached that point. Major Keir and I, "with two or three other officers, made a dejected party as we "followed the retiring troops. We were not at the moment "under fire, and we could only follow in the hope that further "back someone would collect the men. Major Newson, who "was senior present, reported to 62nd Division, and we were "given a line of slits and shell-holes to hold. Major Newson "left to go to Brigade and did not return. I had then about 200 "men of the Highland Division under my command. Major "Keir, of the 7th Battalion The Black Watch, went off to try "to locate Brigade Headquarters, but returned about midnight, "having failed to find them. Having supped off part of a salved "emergency ration, we made our Headquarters in the butt of a "rifle range, and rested awhile, hearing with indifference an "occasional gas shell passing over.

"*26th March*. About 1 a.m. I got orders from 62nd Division "to move back, as we were not wanted, and I ordered the "Details of the 152nd Brigade to form an advance guard. We "moved through Puisieux East, Puisieux-au-Mont, Hébuterne, "and Colincamps to Courcelles. At Colincamps I secured some "tins of biscuits from a Labour company, and all ranks welcomed "the food.

"Reaching Courcelles about 5 a.m. (I slept twice while "actually marching) we found temporary billets. About 9 a.m. "I marched the 153rd and 154th Brigade parties to Acheux, "and there got more biscuits and frozen rabbits from the area

"commandant. Not being able to locate where our Divisional
"Headquarters were, Major Keir and I decided to march to
"Marieux, hoping to get in touch there with the IV Corps.
"Off we set again, and finding Major Gibson, D.S.O., of the
"6th Battalion The Black Watch, then on the Corps Staff, we
"gave him an account of the fighting. Unable to billet in
"Marieux, we marched to Doullens, and at last found a resting
"place in Sarton. Corps Headquarters had directed me to
"report on the morrow to Divisional Headquarters at Neuvilette,
"north of Doullens. The two Headquarters slept that night on
"straw on a kitchen floor.

"*27th March.* The men had little food and everyone was
"done up, but we pegged away, hoping for rest soon. On we
"marched through Doullens and Neuvilette to Barly. A few
"stragglers kept dropping in, and the Quartermaster, with his
"usual resource, managed to provide some food for all. I could
"no longer keep my feet and had to turn in early. So ended
"a big week."

Thus ends Major Campbell's clearly told narrative of the fortunes and misfortunes of the 6th during its terrible ordeal; it shows with what tenacity efforts were made at every stage of the fight to check and hamper the progress of the Germans. It also shows the determined efforts made whenever possible to reorganize the Battalion and preserve the identity of all units, however much reduced in numbers, and so maintain their fine esprit de corps.

The cost to the Battalion during these five days was 20 officers and 620 other ranks. The greater number of these were lost during the first day's fighting when, owing to the retirement of the Divisions on the right and left, practically the whole of the front line garrison was either killed or captured.

For services on this occasion the Battalion received three Military Crosses, one Bar and 14 Military Medals.

The 6th had scarcely emerged from the trying ordeal of the German offensive in front of Albert, when it was plunged into an equally desperate encounter further north. The survivors of the Battalion assembled at Barly, behind Doullens, on March 27th, and two days later moved to Frévent and thence by train to Lillers, and then into billets at Burbure. Here large drafts of officers and men, most of them very young soldiers, arrived, and the work of reconstructing the Battalion began at once. Lieutenant E. D. Nicoll was appointed Adjutant, and the training of fresh Lewis gunners, signallers and stretcher bearers began. At Burbure, Lieutenant-Colonel Campbell rejoined the Battalion and resumed command, although still lame from his accident.

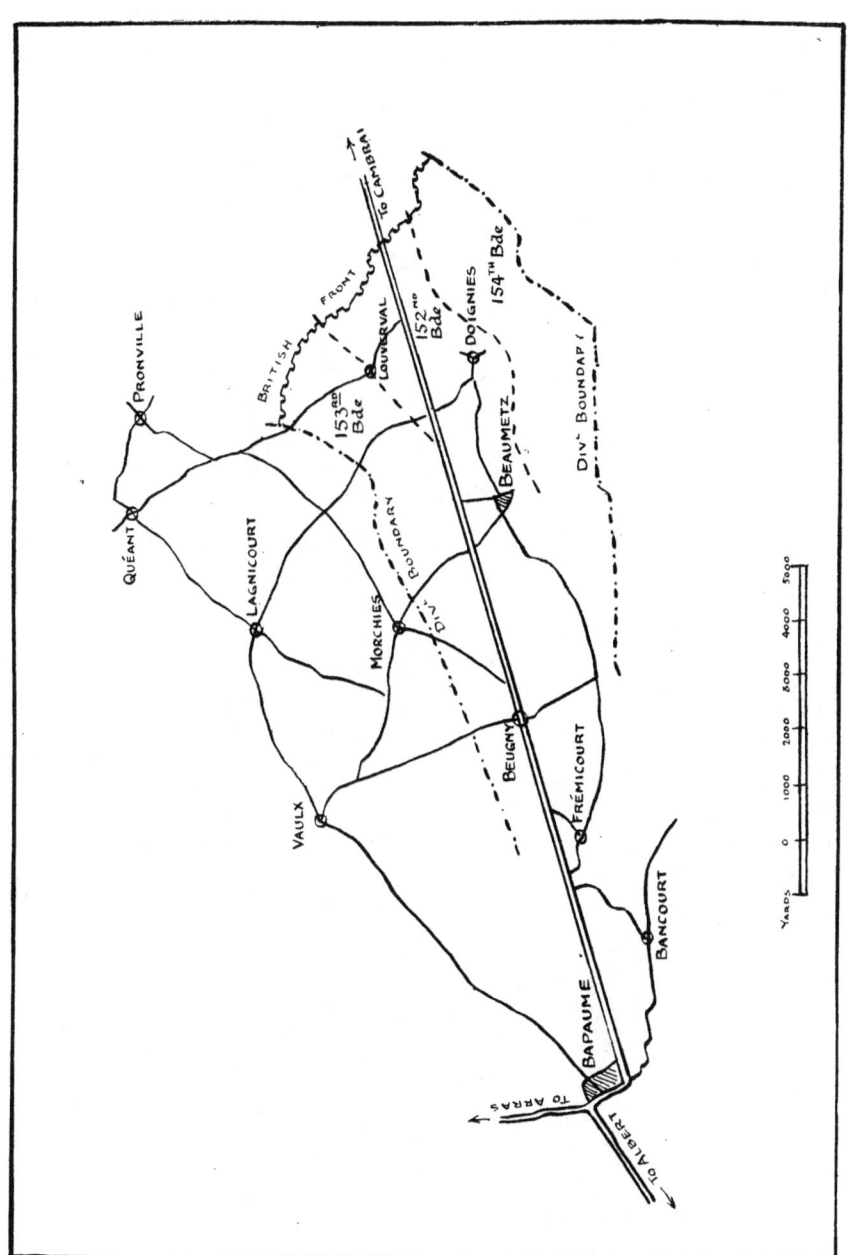

THE GERMAN OFFENSIVE EAST OF BAPAUME, MORNING OF 21ST MARCH, 1918

GERMAN ATTACK ON PORTUGUESE LINE

The Battalion had been in Burbure barely a week before the enemy attacked the Portuguese troops then holding the sector between La Bassée Canal and Armentières. The action began at 4.30 a.m. on April 8th and was so heavy that the Portuguese troops holding the front line were driven back in confusion. Every available man in reserve was needed and, consequently, the 51st Division was once again ordered into the battle. On April 8th the Battalion moved to Robecq, and the following day to Pacaut, going into the line that day on the west bank of the Lawe River with the 7th Battalion Gordon Highlanders on its right.

Action followed action in the neighbourhood of Lestrem, Paradis and Pacaut for the next forty-eight hours. The fighting was very severe and the Battalion lost heavily. The enemy greatly outnumbered the Allies, and the nature of the country, intersected as it was by a river, marshes and small canals, made organized resistance extremely difficult. Though the men were mostly fresh and untried, and though they fought under officers whom they had only known for a few days, their conduct and steadiness were exemplary.

During the fighting on April 12th, Colonel Campbell and Lieutenant Dobson were killed, and Captain Brown and Lieutenants Dobbie and Hewat were mortally wounded. When Lieutenant Dobbie was hit, his men seized a French " gig," and laying him in it, coolly wheeled him down the road under hot fire from the enemy, who were then only a few hundred yards away. That same afternoon the Battalion was withdrawn from the action to rest.

There was no cessation in the enemy's efforts during the next few days, and in consequence a mixed force of two composite battalions, under Major Steyn, Gordon Highlanders, and Major Campbell, 6th Battalion The Black Watch, the whole commanded by Lieutenant-Colonel Fleming, C.R.E., known as " Fleming's Force," was moved up east of Robecq. Here, supported by some tank gun crews, they held the line until the 154th Brigade took over on the 15th, when the 6th moved back to St. Hilaire.

Large drafts now joined and the Battalion was reorganized once again. Lieutenant-Colonel F. R. Sworder, Gordon Highlanders, took over command of the Battalion on the 19th and handed it over to Lieutenant-Colonel F. R. Tarleton, The Black Watch, on the 23rd, the day before it moved to billets near Ham En Artois.

The fighting around the forests of Nieppe and Pacaut was still in progress, and the 51st Division was disposed in depth behind the line. On May 4th the Battalion moved by train

THE SIXTH BATTALION THE BLACK WATCH

from Lillers to Maroeuil, and the next day renewed its acquaintance with the Labyrinth for the third time, taking over the line well in front of Vimy Ridge from the Canadians.

The 6th remained in this part of the line for the rest of the month, when it received orders to side-step southward for a considerable distance and take up a position opposite Oppy and Gavrelle. The relief of the front line was difficult. It was impossible to withdraw over the ridge in view of the enemy, so orders were issued that the movement should be made under cover of darkness. That night, however, the incoming relief of the Battalion, instead of arriving at 10 p.m., did not get up until about 3 a.m., and therefore, by the time all positions had been handed over, dawn had broken and it seemed impossible that the move could be effected unobserved by the enemy. It was, however, successfully accomplished in broad daylight, the men moving in small parties of three or four at a time, and the relief was achieved without a single casualty, the Battalion arriving at its destination at Ecurie at noon on the 29th. May and June were spent between Ecurie and the front line in the Oppy and Gavrelle sectors. The tour was a quiet one, marred only by one unfortunate incident. The forward transport was parked at Ecurie while the Battalion was in the trenches, and their lines near the Arras–Béthune road were shelled one day by high velocity guns; the first shell did little damage, but the second burst right in a trench, where a party of the transport men had taken cover; 14 men were killed and three severely wounded. Three horses also were killed and several others wounded by the same shell.

Early in July coming events began to cast their shadows over this area, and the Canadians returned to hold the Vimy Ridge while the 51st Division went back to the Aubigny–St. Pol area for training.

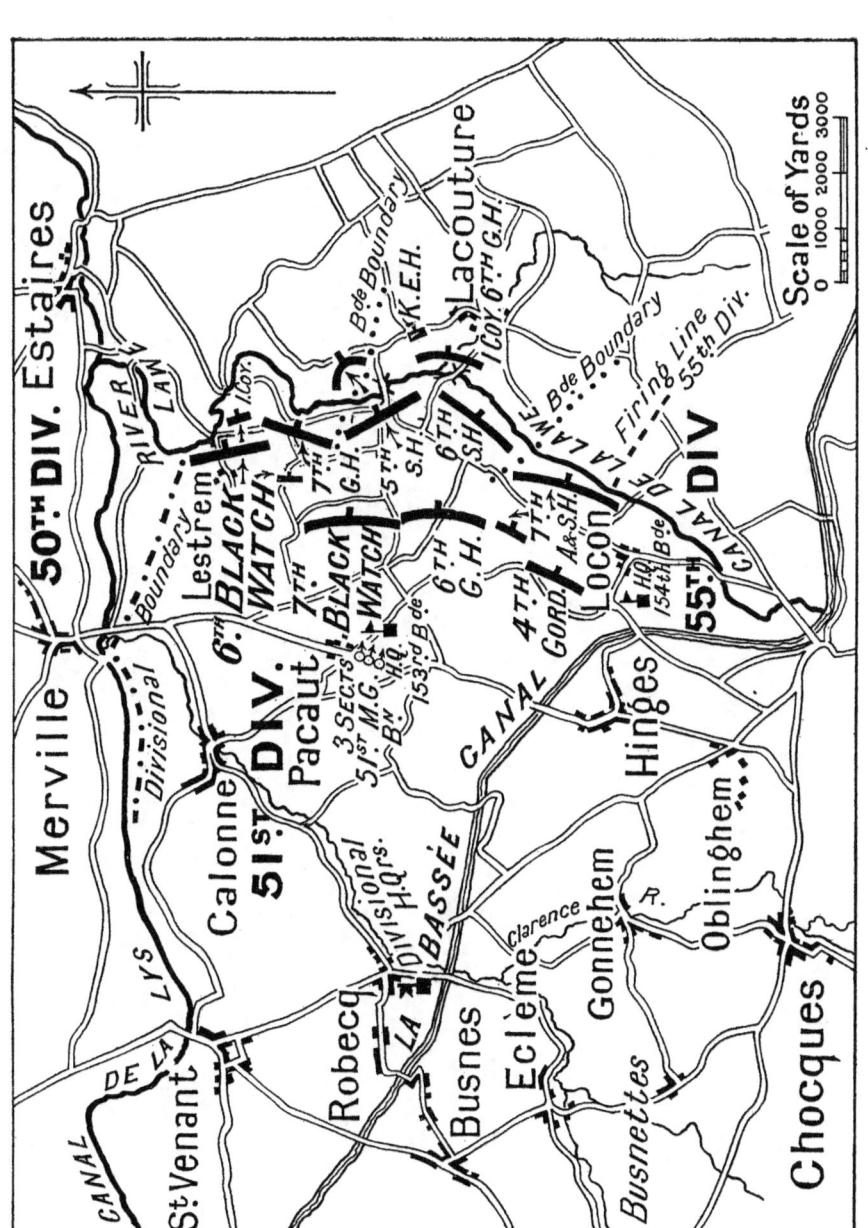

THE GERMAN OFFENSIVE: THE BATTLE OF THE RIVER LAWE, APRIL, 1918

CHAPTER X

JULY, 1918

*Move to Champagne—Battle of Rheims—Bois de Courton—
Citation in French Army Orders*

(See Map facing Page 308.)

AFTER so much hard fighting and after suffering such heavy losses the Battalion was in need of a long period out of the trenches in order to train and reorganize the new drafts, and it was hoped that the next two months might be spent in comparative quiet; but on July 14th, the second day after arrival in billets, orders reached the Battalion to entrain that night at Tincques, taking with it forty hours' rations. This gave rise to all kinds of rumours. No destination was mentioned in the orders and the general opinion was that the Division would be ordered to Italy.

Leaving Tincques during the afternoon of the 14th, the Battalion passed round the outskirts of Paris, and when near Versailles, the German gun " Big Bertha " was heard shelling the capital. Here, too, the Battalion had its first sight of the American army; trainloads of United States troops bound for Château-Thierry passed the regiment, and loud were the cheers by the American soldiers when they caught sight of the Highlanders.

Early on the 16th the train stopped at Herme, where orders were received to detrain. Outside the station a large number of French motor lorries were waiting, and the officer in charge explained that he had orders to send the Battalion off as soon as possible, but it was not until 1 a.m. on the 17th that the move began.

A long, hot and dusty journey followed. The lorries travelled at full speed through country that was entirely new to the Battalion, and evidently far from the area held by British troops. Most of the French countrymen and troops in this new area had never seen a Highlander before, which accounts for the question of an inquisitive Poilu, who asked the driver of the motor conveying the Commanding Officer and Adjutant if his passengers were Portuguese !

After five hours in the lorries, the Battalion arrived at Tours-sur-Marne, where the men spent a pleasant day resting and refreshing themselves by bathing in the canal and basking in the sunshine, little suspecting the terrific days that lay before them in the immediate future. It is necessary to explain the reasons for this move. In the beginning of July, the French General Staff believed that the Germans were about to attack in force in the neighbourhood of Rheims. To meet this danger they withdrew the French forces—eight Divisions in all—from Flanders and, in addition, asked Sir Douglas Haig to send four Divisions to ensure connection between the French and British armies about Amiens, and thus enable them to move four French Divisions further east. Sir Douglas Haig agreed to this and sent the 15th, 34th, 51st and 62nd Divisions, forming the XXII Corps, under Lieutenant-General Sir A. Godley, to the French front.

While this move was actually in progress, the enemy made their attack near Rheims and, in consequence, the XXII Corps was split up, the 51st and 62nd Divisions being sent to the neighbourhood of Rheims, while the other two went to Soissons.

To continue the story. At midnight on the 16th, orders were received to march at once to Pierry, and an hour later the Battalion was on the move. Pierry was reached about 8 a.m. on the 17th, and here the 6th first learnt that all was not going well on that part of the front. The situation was indeed serious; the Germans had broken through on the Marne, and it was not known then whether their advance could be stopped or whether in a few hours they would not be shelling Pierry. The town was occupied by French and Italian troops, amongst whom, and the unfortunate inhabitants, the greatest excitement prevailed; women and children were hurried into lorries and carts of every description and evacuated by orders of the French authorities. The place, too, was honeycombed with cellars containing vast quantities of champagne, and in order to prevent looting, strenuous measures were necessary. Strong picquets, each under an officer, were mounted over each cellar with orders to shoot troops of any nationality who might try and force their way in.

The 6th remained at Pierry until the morning of the 19th, when it moved to Epernay, some six miles away. The village had been shelled recently, and few of the houses in the main street had escaped without a crack or two; dead mules and horses encumbered the streets, but the citizens, though scared, still hesitated to quit their homes. Passing through the town, the Battalion crossed the Marne, ascended the heights on the other side, and eventually arrived at the Bois de Rheims about 4 p.m. At eight o'clock that night orders were received to start in an hour for Bois de Courton, and to be prepared to attack at 6 a.m. next morning from the line then held by the French.

This sudden move was necessary because the actual line from which the attack was to be made was merely a battle line running through the forest, and not a well defined trench system from which an attack is ordinarily made.

The journey up to the front was one of great difficulty. Only one French guide was available to lead the 6th and the 7th Battalions to the French Brigade Headquarters. The night was

BATTLE OF RHEIMS, JULY 20TH, 1918

pitch dark, and it was no easy matter to pass through the endless streams of guns and waggons, the congested traffic being still further dislocated by overturned motor lorries. At times, indeed, it was only possible for the Battalions to move in single file through this crush, and therefore it is not surprising that instead of arriving at its destination at midnight, it was 3 a.m. before the various companies, led by French guides, began moving off to their respective positions. It is interesting to note that the Battalion reached its position for assault without a single casualty, and apparently unnoticed by the Germans, who, in some places, were lying in an exhausted state barely sixty yards in front. Everything was in correct order, and companies were in position an hour and a half before the time appointed for the attack.

The frontage over which the 62nd Division on the right, and the 51st on the left, were to attack was about eight thousand yards astride the Ardre stream, which ran northwards to the Vesle River. The country was open, but on both sides of the stream thick woods covered the slopes of the hills that formed the valley of the Ardre. The Ardre formed roughly the dividing line between the 62nd and 51st Divisions, while the left Division boundary between the 51st and 14th (French) Divisions ran in a north-westerly direction from a point about a thousand yards east of Neuville to the village of Chambrecy.

When the fighting began, the opposing lines ran through the Bois de Courton, a dense wood through which it was exceedingly hard to force a way. In addition, there were various hamlets, such as Espilly, Les Haies and Nappes, which had been fortified by the enemy and were in truth strong points. The first objective, the "blue" line, ran some three miles from the position of assault, and the final objective, the "brown" line, was about three miles further north. The 51st Division attacked on a two-Brigade front, the 154th on the right and the 153rd on the left, the 152nd being in Divisional reserve.

Each Brigade advanced on a single battalion front, the objective being a line running, roughly, from Chaumuzy to the north-west corner of the Bois de Courton. When this line had been captured, it was arranged that the support battalion of each Brigade should pass through the leading troops and capture the "blue" line, after which the third battalion should continue the advance and capture the "brown" line.

Three enemy Divisions opposed the 51st, namely, the 123rd (Saxon) Division on the German right, the 103rd Hessian Division in the centre, and the 22nd (Sachsen-Meinigen) Division on the left.

The 6th Battalion led the attack of the 153rd Brigade.

THE SIXTH BATTALION THE BLACK WATCH

Three companies were in the front line, A on the right, C in the centre, and B on the left, D company being in support. At 6 a.m. the attack was launched. The men advanced with great dash, following the barrage, and in a few moments had disposed of a large number of the enemy. After advancing about six hundred yards, the leading platoons found that the wood became very dense, and the attack was held up for a short time by heavy machine gun fire; undeterred, however, the companies pushed on and fought their way forward with great gallantry, and by 10 a.m. the 6th had reached its objective.

Here the Battalion remained practically all day exposed to heavy machine gun and artillery fire. The 6th Seaforths, who originally had been detailed to carry on the advance, had been withdrawn elsewhere, although no information of this change ever reached the 6th Black Watch.

The fighting on the 20th was exceptionally fierce and was carried out under great natural difficulties. Foot by foot the men fought their way through the thick wood and undergrowth of the Bois de Courton until they reached the open country beyond, but by that time the ranks had been greatly thinned, and the companies were reduced to groups of men still organized and still undaunted. On the left the 6th were in touch with some French Colonial troops, and here Lieutenant McCorquodale with some French Senegalese troops attempted to push on into the open country beyond the wood but were unable to do so, and eventually fell back on their former position. Shortly after this the French on the right retired and, as little was known of the situation on this flank, the position became rather precarious; the companies, therefore, were reorganized and the line withdrawn a short distance into the wood.

Throughout the whole of the 20th, enemy aeroplanes, flying low over the wood, fired at every target they could see. During the evening, the 6th Seaforth Highlanders took over the line, and the Battalion was withdrawn to a position in the wood some little way back.

It should be mentioned that, owing to congestion of the roads prior to the operation, no rations had been issued, and the men went into action carrying only their emergency rations; the same thing happened on the 20th, and when dawn broke on the 21st the officers and men had had nothing to eat for twenty-four hours, except their iron rations, and had no water except what they carried in their bottles; the Battalion was, in consequence, in an exhausted condition. While an attempt was being made during the early hours of the 21st to withdraw the companies in order to give the men some food, orders were

BOIS DE COURTON, JULY 21st, 1918

received that the 152nd Brigade would continue the attack, and the 6th Battalion was to support it on the left flank in an hour's time. Colonel Tarleton speedily mustered all available men, such as signallers, runners and stretcher bearers at Battalion Headquarters, and by means of stretchers carried up both rations and water to the companies before they left their positions in the wood. This was successfully done, but there was no time to allow the men to eat before getting into their positions for the fresh attack; the Commanding Officer therefore ordered all ranks to drink what water they required, and follow him in order that the Battalion should be in time to support the 152nd Brigade. This order was readily obeyed; the companies at once turned about and moved forward to their positions, rations being carried in rear on stretchers. Such action by men seriously weakened by hunger, showed a fine soldierly spirit and a high standard of discipline.

The attack of the 152nd Brigade on the 21st was held up by machine gun fire and the Battalion, therefore, remained in support all day. As time went on, the opposition of the enemy, now heavily reinforced, increased, and no progress was made; the day was thus passed under most trying conditions, the attacking troops being exposed to heavy machine gun and artillery fire.

That night rations and water arrived safely, fortunately just before a heavy barrage fell round Battalion Headquarters. The situation remained unchanged until the afternoon of July 22nd, when, at 5 p.m., instructions were received that the French troops on the left would attack Paradis, and in conjunction with this attack the 6th was ordered to push through the 152nd Brigade and reoccupy the position it had held on the 20th, a task which the 152nd Brigade had failed to achieve after two days' hard fighting.

The task of reoccupying the line was allotted to D company, which had been in reserve on the 20th. Unfortunately, just as all preparations had been made, a shell landed close to a conference of officers. Captain Willison, who was to have led the attack, was wounded, and the command devolved on Lieutenant Anderson. D company was ordered to advance as soon as possible in order to gain ground before the French attack on Paradis developed. Many gallant attempts were made to carry out these orders, but without success; Lieutenant Anderson was shot through the head the moment he rose to lead his men; time after time the men pressed forward only to be driven back by heavy machine gun fire. On the left the French had also encountered strong opposition, and Paradis remained untaken, the Battalion line being heavily shelled throughout the night.

THE SIXTH BATTALION THE BLACK WATCH

Early in the morning of July 23rd, the survivors of the Battalion were relieved by the 7th Battalion The Black Watch and withdrew through the Bois de Sarbruge and thence to Nanteuil. This brought to an end the fierce fighting the 6th had experienced in this area.

On the 24th the Battalion moved to St. Imogé, where the following day it was inspected and congratulated on its performance by General Godley, the XXII Corps Commander.

During the two days the 6th were out of the line, the fighting had continued without cessation, constant pressure being kept on the enemy. It was, therefore, not surprising that, on the 26th, the Battalion was ordered to return at once to the Bois de Courton and take part in an attack the following morning.

That afternoon the 6th moved forward, taking all the men of echelon B, with the exception of the band and signallers, and advanced to the south of Nanteuil, whence it was led by guides to a position in the wood. The roads through the village of Nanteuil and also through the Bois de Courton, were heavily shelled; the battalion in front of the 6th suffered about forty casualties from this fire but, under the capable guidance of the Intelligence Officer of the 4th Seaforth Highlanders, the 6th reached its post without loss. That night the Battalion lay in battle positions under a downpour of rain, subjected to incessant shelling and machine gun fire until about 2 a.m., when a sudden quiet prevailed which gave rise to the suspicion that the Germans were withdrawing.

The object of the coming attack was to clear the enemy out of the Bois de Courton and into the open country north of it. The plan of battle was as follows:

The 51st Division was to attack on a three-Brigade front, the 152nd on the right, the 187th, from the 62nd Division, in the centre, and the 153rd on the left, the 154th being in reserve. Two objectives were given, the first a line between Moulin de Voipreux and La Neuville, and the second between a line from Chaumuzy to a point about a thousand yards north of La Neuville. The 153rd Brigade attack was led by the 6th Battalion, the 7th Black Watch and the 7th Gordon Highlanders being detailed to pass through the 6th when it had captured the first objective.

The operation proved entirely successful and was accomplished with little loss. The Battalion War Diary says:

"At 6 a.m. on July 27th, the Battalion attacked, D company
" on the right and A on the left, B and C being in support. By
" 7 a.m. the 6th had taken its objective with comparatively little

CAPTURE OF CHAMBRECY, JULY 28TH, 1918

"opposition. The 7th Black Watch and 7th Gordon Highlanders passed through to continue the advance, the 6th then consolidated its position and remained there that night. Next day, July 28th, the Battalion continued its advance and at 4.30 p.m. attacked the village of Chambrecy, thereby entering its last and most desperate battle in this sector."

Before relating the events which occurred during the next two days, it may not be out of place to quote the following instruction which appeared in the 6th Battalion Orders on July 19th, before the first fighting in this area.

"All ranks will be warned that the attack will be made before the eyes of the French army, and it is expected that they will maintain the prestige of the British army."

It may fairly be said that every man in the Battalion carried out the spirit of this order.

By this time the enemy had been driven into more or less open country and it appeared that the whole of the German defence was on the point of breaking. That "constant pressure"—which is so hard to maintain for any length of time—had succeeded in almost breaking the German line, and it was now within the bounds of possibility that a resolute attack would achieve the aim of Marshal Foch, and drive the enemy out of France.

The objective given to the Battalion was the village of Chambrecy, the assault on which was timed to begin at 4.30 p.m. on the 28th. Moving forward through the Bois des Eclisses, the 6th deployed the attack on more or less open ground, on a two-company front, with patrols well out in front and in touch with the 7th Battalion Gordon Highlanders on the right and French troops on the left, on the other side of the valley.

When the advance began, things were absolutely quiet, although on the left the French had apparently met with heavy artillery fire. After the Battalion had advanced some eight hundred yards, a heavy German barrage came down and machine gun fire poured into the valley from each side of Chambrecy, causing the Battalion many losses. Undaunted by this, however, the Battalion continued to advance straight in the face of this terrific fire, and not only captured the village of Chambrecy, but passed through to the north of it and established themselves just outside the north-east outskirts of the village, where they remained holding on to the ground they had gained so brilliantly, although the left flank was entirely exposed, and the situation on the right obscure.

THE SIXTH BATTALION THE BLACK WATCH

By this time all four companies had been reduced to mere groups of men, small in numbers but still resolute in spirit; night was falling, the Germans were reported to be again entering the village of Chambrecy, and it seemed as though they were contemplating a determined counter attack. The 6th had now withdrawn and taken up a position along a small hedge which crossed the previous line of advance, where it was relieved during the night by the 4th Battalion Gordon Highlanders. In the early hours of July 29th, the Battalion withdrew under cover of darkness to a position near the village of Nappes, where it remained for a day and a night enjoying uninterrupted rest, except for the constant shooting of a single sniper, who had been left behind when the Germans retired.

This brief account of the action of the 6th in the recent fighting fails to do justice to the gallantry and determination shown by every man and to the fine leadership of all commanders, which alone made the achievement of the Battalion possible. The fact that it was now reduced to less than 140 all ranks, tells eloquently how faithfully the order issued on July 19th had been obeyed.

The casualties in Champagne were five officers killed, 20 wounded and one missing; of other ranks 45 were killed, 350 wounded and 33 missing.

On the 30th the 6th moved back to Nanteuil, passing over the ground where so many of their fallen comrades were still lying, and the following day moved to the Bois de Rheims, from which it had originally started on the 19th.

On August 1st, a march past General Guillaumat, commanding the Fifth (French) Army, ended the work of the Battalion in this area. The enemy were now in full retreat and, as the French no longer needed British assistance, the withdrawal of the 51st Division then began.

For its services during this fighting, the 6th Battalion The Black Watch received the highest distinction which the French army could offer, namely, a Citation in Army Orders, which invariably carries with it the Croix de Guerre, a fitting tribute to the leadership of the officers and dash and endurance of all ranks which the Battalion displayed under the most trying conditions.

The following is the text of the Citation in French Army orders:

Extrait de l'ordre général, No. 430.

" Le Général Commandant la Vme Armée cite a l'ordre
" de l'Armée: Le 6me. Bataillon du ROYAL HIGHLANDERS.
" Unité d'élite; sous le commandement énergique du Lieutenant-

THE SIXTH BATTALION COLOURS WITH CROIX DE GUERRE AWARDED AFTER
THE BATTLE OF TARDENOIS, JULY, 1918

FRENCH ARMY ORDER

" Colonel Francis Rowland Tarleton, D.S.O., a fait, preuve d'un
" entrain et d'un mordant admirables au cours des durs combats
" du 20 au 30 Juillet, 1918. Après sept jours de combats
" acharnés, malgrè les fatigues et les pertes serieuses causées par
" le feu intense des mitrailleuses adverses s'est emparé d'un bois
" fortement organisé et opiniâtrement défendu par l'ennemi.
　" (Décision G.H.Q. No. 22389 en date du 16 Octobre, 1918.)
　　　" Le Général Commandant la Vme Armée.
　　　　　　　　　　　　　　　　　" GUILLAUMAT."

Translation.

　" This distinguished Battalion, under the energetic command
" of Lieutenant-Colonel Francis Rowland Tarleton, D.S.O., has
" given splendid proof of spirit and dash in the course of the
" hard fought battles between the 20th and 30th July, 1918.
" After seven days of bloody fighting, in spite of the exhaustion
" and the heavy losses caused by intense enemy machine gun
" fire, it successfully stormed a wood, strongly fortified and
" stubbornly defended by the enemy.
　　　　　　　" (signed)　GUILLAUMAT,
　　　　　　　　" General Officer Commanding,
　　　　　　　　" The Fifth (French) Army."

　Among the many congratulations received by the 6th from various sources, the two which were possibly more prized than any others, were those sent by the 7th Battalion and by the Perthshire Territorial Association.

CHAPTER XI

AUGUST, 1918, TO OCTOBER, 1919

Capture of Greenland Hill—Cambrai Area—Crossing of the Ecaillon—Fighting near Mount Houy—Iwuy—Move to Belgium and the Cologne Area—The march past in Paris—Back to England—Demobilization.

THE day after the 6th had been reviewed by the French Commander, the Battalion moved by train to Calonne, and marched to billets at Château de la Haie, which was reached on the 4th. Here a fortnight was spent resting and, as usual, reorganizing. For the third time in five months the Battalion was rebuilt and large drafts of new men arrived; a well contested football match between teams of the newcomers showed old members of the 6th that the new drafts were as good as had been their predecessors.

On August 17th, the 6th returned to a familiar area, the Fampoux sector, where the 51st Division relieved the 57th in that part of the line. By this time there were unmistakable signs of a German collapse and, as in Champagne, so at Fampoux, "continuous pressure" was kept on the enemy and it was decided to attack the German positions on and around Greenland Hill, and drive the enemy into the flat country to the east of it.

At 6 a.m. on August 20th, the Battalion was once more thrown into attack, its objective being the trenches between the Towy and Chili Avenues on the north-west slopes of Greenland Hill. The 6th gained these trenches about eight o'clock and, after consolidating the position, remained there all day. Early on the 26th orders were received that the Division would form the left flank of an attack on Monchy-le-Preux, south of the Scarpe River.

This operation was to be carried out in three phases and was to extend over two days; the first phase was to begin at 10 a.m. on the 26th, and the second at 7 p.m. the same day. Both were successful, and by noon on August 26th, British troops had occupied and consolidated the old British front line lost the previous March.

The third phase began the following morning at 10 a.m., and the 6th succeeded in capturing its objective, namely, some trenches north-west of Greenland Hill, a position which had been so often struggled for throughout the war. The captures by the Battalion in this fighting included four machine guns and five trench mortars; happily, the losses were not heavy; three officers were wounded, five men killed, 74 wounded and

ADVANCE TO VICTORY, OCTOBER, 1918

eight missing. Fighting continued during the whole of the following day, and many bombing attacks were driven off, but the Battalion made no further advance in this sector.

The 6th was relieved on the 29th, and moved to Roclincourt, after which it again went into the line on Greenland Hill, in which sector it spent the whole of September. On the 29th the Battalion finally returned to Roclincourt, where a week was spent in training and practising advanced guard formations.

On October 8th, the 6th moved to a new area near the Hindenburg line, close to Quéant, and the survivors of the March offensive were able to see the great strength of the German trenches from which they had attacked. On the 10th the 153rd Brigade marched through Pronville and Moeuvres to bivouacs west of Bourlon Wood. The pursuit of the German army had now indeed begun and next day the Battalion, skirting Cambrai, spent that night in an enemy shell dump. Crossing the Canal d'Escaut, the 6th found good billets in Tun–St. Martin. On the left the Canadians were constantly in action, and the Highland Division, south of the canal, made a big bid for Valenciennes.

The 14th was spent at Iwuy, which had been heavily shelled and was full of gas, the effects of which caused heavy losses among the civilians who had remained behind after the Germans had left the area.

On the 19th the 153rd Brigade, with the 154th on its right and the Canadians on the left, attacked the retiring enemy with the object of gaining a line south of the road running through Thiant and Monchaux. The 7th Battalion The Black Watch and the 6th Battalion Argyll and Sutherland Highlanders were ordered to lead the attack of the 153rd Brigade, with the 6th Battalion The Black Watch in support. The morning was foggy, and the enemy retired before the assault took place. The pursuit was then continued through a country admirably suited for rear-guard action, till at last the Germans stood their ground on a strong line south of the Cambrai–Valenciennes road running through the villages of Thiant and Monchaux.

Here the pursuit was held up for two days. The Battalion was once more in the front line near Douchy, when orders were received to renew the attack. The main objective of this assault was the crossing of the Ecaillon River and the capture of the village of Maing and the high ground south-east of it. The frontage allotted to the Division was three thousand yards; the ground sloped down on both sides to the river and was absolutely devoid of cover; the 153rd Brigade was detailed to lead the attack on the whole Division front. The 6th and 7th Black Watch Battalions were detailed for the attack, the 6th on the right on a two-company front, and the 7th on the left on a one-company front.

To facilitate the crossing of the Ecaillon, temporary bridges had been built and sent down during the night of the 23rd. These bridges proved to be heavier than had been anticipated and large numbers of men were required to carry them.

The Battalion was in position by 2 a.m. on the morning of October 24th, and two hours later, carrying their bridges with them, the two leading companies advanced in the dark down the slope towards the river. But as they drew near, the enemy opened heavy machine gun fire from the opposite bank, and both companies suffered severely, in fact two platoons were almost destroyed. In spite of this fire, however, and of the difficulties of the river crossing, the 6th resolutely pushed forward and, largely due to Second Lieutenant J. M. Walker's successful leadership, achieved the crossing. Realizing that the bridges were useless, Walker dashed forward with the survivors of his platoon and by joining hands these men struggled across the river. After cleaning his Lewis gun under cover of the opposite bank, Walker disposed of a machine gun post in a house near by. He then pushed forward round the village on the right, taking seventy-eight prisoners. With the coming of daylight enemy resistance grew less, and the Battalion gained its objective. For his action that day, Walker was awarded a well merited D.S.O.

The left company of the 6th had no difficulty in crossing the river, and was able to carry out its task without much fighting. The enemy, having retired from the banks of the river, made their next stand in the neighbourhood of Maing village. Here heavy fighting took place, but before evening most of the village had been captured. Heavy fighting went on throughout the 25th, but the 6th was not engaged. On the 26th, however, the Battalion again attacked and, as events proved, for the last time in the war.

The objectives were Famars and Mont Huoy; the 51st Division attacked with the 152nd Brigade on the right, and the 153rd on the left; the 6th Battalion The Black Watch leading the attack of the latter Brigade. The advance started at 10 a.m. on the 26th. The Battalion advanced with three companies in the front line and one in support, and although good progress was made, many losses were suffered through machine gun fire. For many hours prior to the attack the Germans had shelled the whole area with gas, the result being that every house and cellar and the entire countryside reeked with poison, in addition to which great care had to be taken to avoid the numerous "booby traps" which the Germans had left behind them.

Throughout the morning the 6th advanced steadily, and by

THE ARMISTICE, NOVEMBER, 1918

11.30 a.m. the leading companies were close to Mont Huoy. Here there was some fighting, but the left company was able to reach Le Poirier station, where its advance was brought to a standstill by machine gun fire.

Heavy fighting continued round Mont Huoy until evening, when, finding the Germans were working round its left flank, the Battalion was compelled to fall back on a line between Famars and La Fontenelle. Fighting continued until nightfall, and early on the 27th the 6th was relieved by the 4th Battalion Seaforth Highlanders, and marched back next day to Buchain and reached Iwuy on the 30th.

The losses during this fighting were two officers killed and six wounded, 37 other ranks killed, 185 wounded and one missing.

During these operations the 51st Division advanced ten miles and captured 661 prisoners, 164 machine guns, four trench mortars, three minenwerfers and six anti-tank guns. These were the last operations in which the 6th was engaged in the Great War. On November 11th the troops were told that the Armistice had been signed, and all fighting ended.

The Battalion remained at Iwuy for over two months and several drafts from Scotland brought it once more up to strength. It was a quiet and uneventful period, very welcome to officers and men after the strain of the past months. On November 14th the Battalion paraded on the occasion of the decoration of the British Commander-in-Chief by General Pershing, commanding the American Expeditionary Force in France.

Throughout November and December the Battalion was employed on salvage work on the surrounding battlefields, and on January 9th, 1919, it moved to Seneffe in Belgium, passing through Mons on its way. On January 29th, the 6th was honoured by a visit from His Royal Highness the Prince of Wales, and early in February the honorary Colonel, Sir Robert Moncrieffe, came out to see his old Battalion and received a tremendous welcome.

During all this time demobilization was proceeding throughout the whole Army. Suddenly, however, orders were received that the 6th had been selected to proceed to Germany; all officers and men earmarked for demobilization were, therefore, attached to the 7th Battalion and the remainder, about two hundred strong, prepared to move to Cologne. On February 21st, the 6th saying "Good-bye" to the 51st Division, entrained at Manage, and joined the 186th Brigade, 62nd Division, the next day at Mechernich.

The move to the Rhine, however, did not take place, and the 6th remained at Mechernich until, on March 12th, it proceeded to Merzenich, where it remained for some months.

THE SIXTH BATTALION THE BLACK WATCH

On April 16th, Colonel W. Green, C.B., D.S.O., a well known officer of the First Battalion, took over command from Lieutenant-Colonel F. R. Tarleton, D.S.O. The departure of the latter was greatly regretted and his farewell order was much appreciated by men and officers:

"Officers, non-commissioned officers, and men of the 6th Battalion The Black Watch, on relinquishing the command of the Battalion, I wish to thank you all for your loyal co-operation and the fine services you have rendered during the year I have had the honour to be your Commanding Officer. The Battalion has taken part in every battle throughout that period. It has never once failed in its duty, but has always covered itself with distinction, making for itself a history which can be surpassed by no other battalion of any regiment in the British Army."

July 12th, 1919, remains a red-letter day in the history of the 6th Battalion The Black Watch, for on that day a small detachment took part in the peace rejoicings in Paris and received the rare honour of having the French Croix de Guerre pinned on the Regimental Colours.

The party consisted of Colonel W. Green, C.M.G., D.S.O., Lieutenant J. B. Cable, M.C., Lieutenant H. W. Renton, M.C., Regimental Sergeant-Major Ross, D.C.M., Company Quartermaster-Sergeant McNeill, M.M., Lance-Corporal West, M.M. and Lance-Corporal Sutherland, M.M. A tumult of cheering greeted the appearance of the detachment of Highlanders as they passed through the Arc de Triomphe on their way to the ceremony, when the Military Governor of Paris, General Berdoulet, presented the decoration in the presence of the French and Colonial troops assembled for the Victory March.

Drawn up in three sides of a square, with The Black Watch colour party in the centre and the pipe band of the 4th Battalion Seaforth Highlanders and massed bands of the Welsh and Irish Guards in rear, the troops presented arms as the French General approached. General Berdoulat then made a tour of the ranks, accompanied by Lieutenant-General Butler, commanding the British troops, and Brigadier-General Lambert. Proceeding with the ceremony, he paid a high tribute to the valour of the Scottish troops during the war. Pinning the Croix de Guerre to the Regimental Colour of the 6th Battalion and kissing the Colour, the General shook hands with Colonel Green; the troops then presented arms while the Guards' band played the "Marseillaise," followed, at the special request of General Berdoulat, by "God save the King," which ended the parade.

RETURN TO SCOTLAND, OCTOBER 21ST, 1919

All officers and men of the Battalion now wear the ribbon of the Croix de Guerre on the sleeve of the jacket.

Little remains to be told of the doings of the 6th except the final moves before demobilization was completed. On July 19th the Battalion moved to Bruck and on August 9th to Düren. On the following day it moved to England and arrived at Brockton Camp on August 12th, the Battalion strength being 29 officers and 795 men.

On October 20th the Battalion, reduced to Cadre strength, entrained for Perth, arriving there the following morning. The same day officers and men were given a public reception and dinner in the City Hall, where they were joined by about a thousand former members of the Battalion who had come together from all parts of Scotland.

It was a most happy gathering of old comrades and will live long in the memory of those who took part in it. Two days later the Cadre was finally demobilized.

Thus ends the story of the 6th Battalion The Black Watch. But its identity has not been lost and all who fought in that Battalion, indeed, all who served with the Regiment, are proud to know that both the title and the spirit of the old 6th still survive in the present 6/7th Battalion The Black Watch, and that there the memories and traditions of these two Battalions, the 6th and 7th, who fought side by side in so many battles of the Great War are still honoured and upheld.

APPENDIX I

Record of Officers' Services

Abbreviations :—" K. in A."—Killed in Action.   " D. of W."—Died of Wounds.
" W."—Wounded.   " M."—Missing.   " P. of W."—Prisoner of War.

THE SIXTH BATTALION

Adam, J. N. 2nd Lieut. Joined 28th April, 1918. *w.* 28th July, 1918. Awarded M.C. Aug., 1918.

Aitken, A. 2nd Lieut. Joined 14th July, 1917. To U.K. Aug., 1917. Promoted Lieut. 25th July, 1918. Rejoined Battn. 9th Aug., 1918. Left Battn. Sept., 1918.

Alexander, W. Capt. Went out with Battn. May, 1915. Promoted Major 12th Aug., 1915. Awarded D.S.O. 18th Jan., 1916. To Ministry of Munitions Dec., 1917.

Allison, J. J. Lieut. Died Sept. 18th, 1917.

Anderson, G. A. 2nd Lieut. Joined 7th July, 1917. Promoted Lieut. 26th March, 1918. *p. of w.* 19th April, 1918.

Anderson, J. G. Capt. *m.* 21st–26th March, 1918.

Anderson, W. K. Lieut. Joined 19th April, 1918. *k. in a.* 22nd July, 1918.

Barr, A. 2nd Lieut. Joined Battn. from Depot 11th Sept., 1916. *w.* 13th Nov., 1916.

Barron, J. M. Capt. Wounded July, 1918. Awarded M.C. 29th July, 1918.

Baynham, W. J. 2nd Lieut. Went out with Battn. May, 1915.

Begg, W. 2nd Lieut. Joined 2nd Oct., 1916. *k. in a.* 13th Nov., 1916.

Bell, F. V. F. 2nd Lieut. Joined 9th Aug., 1918.

Black, D. J. 2nd Lieut. Joined 19th June, 1918. *w.* 20th July, 1918.

Blackmore, E. W. H. 2nd Lieut. Joined 10th Dec., 1916. Promoted Lieut. 26th July, 1917. To U.K. sick 10th Aug., 1917.

Booth, T. M. Lieut.-Col. Gordon Highlanders, D.S.O. Took over command of Battn. 31st Oct., 1916. To 51st Divl. School St. Riquier 4th Dec., 1916. Resumed command of Battn. 23rd Jan., 1917. Awarded Bar to D.S.O. 5th Feb., 1917. Mentioned in Despatches June, 1917. Relinquished command 16th Aug., 1917.

Bowie, H. Lieut. Joined 28th April, 1918. *k. in a.* 28th July, 1918.

Boyd, N. K. 2nd Lieut. Joined from B.E.F. Cadet School 24th Dec., 1916. *w.* 31st July, 1917.

Brown, A. Lieut. Joined 23rd Jan., 1915. *w.* (subsequently *d. of w.*) 12th April, 1918.

Brown, W. 2nd Lieut. Joined 14th July, 1917. *k. in a.* 5th Oct., 1917.

Buchanan, R. B. 2nd Lieut. Joined 23rd Aug., 1918.

Butler, C. H. 2nd Lieut. Joined Battn. 26th Oct., 1915. *k. in a.* 23rd April, 1916. Body recovered on battlefield 26th May, 1916.

Butler, J. W. 2nd Lieut. Joined 26th March, 1917. Left Battn. 24th Dec., 1917.

Byers, T. 2nd Lieut. Joined from 3rd Line 1st June, 1916. *w.* 28th July, 1916. Awarded M.C. 18th July, 1917. Mentioned in Despatches 18th July, 1917.

Cable, D. 2nd Lieut. Joined from Depot 10th Aug., 1916. *w.* 1st Sept., 1916. To hospital sick 12th Nov., 1916. Rejoined 18th Nov., 1916.

THE SIXTH BATTALION THE BLACK WATCH

To hospital sick 3rd Feb., 1917. Rejoined 5th April, 1917. Appointed Capt. and Adj. 13th Nov., 1917. *w.* and *m.* (*p. of w.*) 21st–26th March, 1918. Awarded M.C. 26th July, 1918. Mentioned in Despatches 18th Feb., 1918.

Cairns, G. M. 2nd Lieut. Joined from Depot 9th Sept., 1916. *k. in a.* 13th Nov., 1916.

Calder, D. B. Lieut. Went out with Battn. May, 1915. Transferred to M.G.C. 22nd June, 1915. Mentioned in Despatches 4th Jan , 1917.

Calvert, H. S. 2nd Lieut. Joined from 4th (Reserve) Battn. 24th Aug., 1917. *w.* 16th Sept., 1917. Rejoined 22nd Nov., 1918.

Calvert, T. 2nd Lieut. Joined May, 1915. *w.* 13th Nov., 1916. Awarded M.C. (date unknown) and Mentioned in Despatches.

Campbell, D. C. Capt. Joined from 13th Battn. 18th Sept., 1917.

Campbell, E. E. 2nd Lieut. Joined 31st Aug., 1918. To hospital 1st Oct., 1918.

Campbell, N. D. Lieut.-Col. In command of Battn. vice Lieut.-Col. Booth, D.S.O., 16th Aug., 1917. *k. in a.* April, 1918.

Campbell, R. D. 2nd Lieut. Joined 4th Feb., 1916. *w.* 30th March, 1916 Rejoined 26th March, 1917. To hospital 28th March, 1917.

Campbell, W. L. W. 2nd Lieut. Joined 21st Aug., 1916. To U.K. 25th Oct., 1917.

Campbell, W. P. Lieut. Went out with Battn. May, 1915. Promoted Capt. 31st July, 1916. Accidentally *w.* 4th Nov., 1916. To hospital. Rejoined 15th Dec. Promoted Major 1st Nov., 1917. Awarded M.C. March, 1918. Mentioned in Despatches 26th July, 1918.

Cargill, W. S. G. 2nd Lieut. Joined from 4th Battn. 8th Jan., 1918. *w.* 21st–26th March, 1918.

Carr, S. G. 2nd Lieut. Joined from 4th (Reserve) Battn. 2nd Oct., 1916. *w.* 13th Nov., 1916.

Cassie, J. R. B. 2nd Lieut. Joined from 9th Royal Scots 2nd Jan., 1918. Awarded M.C. 28th April, 1918. Attached Divl. Signals 12th Aug., 1918.

Chapman, H. E. 2nd Lieut. Joined from Depot 24th Aug., 1917. Transferred to R.F.C. 13th March, 1918.

Chapman, P. A. 2nd Lieut. Joined from 3rd Line 1st June, 1916. *w.* 31st July, 1916.

Christison, A. F. P. Capt. M.C. Joined Sept., 1918.

Clark, I. M. Capt. C.F. Left for U.K. on completion of engagement 5th Sept., 1916.

Clark, W. 2nd Lieut. Joined 23rd Nov., 1916. Promoted Lieut. 1st July, 1917. To U.K. 28th Sept., 1917.

Coats, E. R. 2nd Lieut. Joined 6th July, 1917. To U.K. 6th Nov., 1916.

Condor, A. C. 2nd Lieut. Joined from Depot 10th Aug., 1916. Accidentally *w.* 4th Nov., 1916. *w.* 23rd April, 1917.

Cordner, A. N. 2nd Lieut. Joined Battn. 2nd May, 1915. *w.* accidentally 4th Nov., 1916. *w.* 31st July, 1917.

Coutts, W. E. Capt. Joined from 4th (Reserve) Battn. 7th Nov., 1917. *k. in a.* 25th March, 1917.

Cowans, A. D. S. 2nd Lieut. *w.* 31st July, 1916.

Craig, J. Capt. Went out with Battn. May, 1915. To U.K. 27th April, 1916.

APPENDIX I

Cruickshanks, L. W. 2nd Lieut. Joined from 4th (Reserve) Battn., 14th April, 1917. To hospital sick 17th April, 1917.

Daly, T. P. 2nd Lieut. Joined July, 1915. To U.K. 17th March, 1918.
Davidson, J. 2nd Lieut. Joined Battn. from Depot Sept., 1918.
Davies, R. 2nd Lieut. Joined from Depot 18th Aug., 1916. To hospital 21st Sept., 1916.
Dickens, W. R. 2nd Lieut. Joined from Base 17th Feb., 1917. To U.K. 3rd Oct., 1917.
Dickson, G. H. M. 2nd Lieut. Joined 31st Aug., 1918. *k. in a.* 26th Oct., 1918.
Dickson, J. D. H. 2nd Lieut. Joined 14th July, 1917. Transferred to 1/5th Gordon Highlanders 9th Sept., 1917.
Dickson, R. G. A. 2nd Lieut. Went out with Battn. May, 1915. *w.* 13th June, 1915. To hospital sick 19th Sept., 1916. Rejoined 17th Oct., 1916. To hospital sick 19th Oct., 1916.
Dixon, N. F. 2nd Lieut. Went out with Battn. May, 1915. Transferred to Brigade M.G.C. and promoted Lieut. 13th Jan., 1916. *k.* 5th Oct., 1917. Mentioned in Despatches 7th Nov., 1917.
Dobbie, A. M. 2nd Lieut. Joined from 4th (Reserve) Battn. 24th Aug., 1917. *w.* (subsequently *d. of w.*) 12th, April, 1918.
Dobson, G. 2nd Lieut. Joined 7th July, 1917. *k. in a.* 12th April, 1918.
Doe, A. B. 2nd Lieut. Joined from Base 10th Dec., 1916. *k. in a.* 23rd April, 1917. Body found on battlefield 19th May, 1917.
Douglas, A. S. 2nd Lieut. Joined 27th Aug., 1918. *w.* 24th Oct., 1918.
Drummond, A. G. 2nd Lieut. Awarded M.C. August, 1917. *m.* 21st-26th March, 1918.
Duff, C. E. 2nd Lieut. Joined from Base 10th Dec., 1916.
Dykes, R. 2nd Lieut. Joined 10th Aug., 1918. *w.* 24th Oct., 1918.

Ellis, R. B. Lieut. Went out with Battn. May, 1915. Promoted Capt. Appointed Adj. Jan., 1916. *w.* 13th Nov., 1916. *d. of w.* 21st Nov., 1916. Awarded M.C. 4th Dec., 1916. Mentioned in Despatches 31st Dec., 1915.
Everett, A. B. 2nd Lieut. Joined 19th April, 1918. *w.* 28th July, 1918.

Falconer, C. M. Lieut. Joined Battn. 18th April, 1918. *w.* 28th July, 1918.
Farrell, S. K. 2nd Lieut. Joined Battn. 24th April, 1918. *k. in a.* 20th July, 1918.
Ferguson, T. Capt. Joined from Depot 21st Aug., 1916. *k. in a.* 13th Nov., 1916.
Ferris, W. T. 2nd Lieut. Joined May, 1915. *w.* 28th July, 1916.
Flett, W. H. 2nd Lieut. Joined from 3rd Line 15th Jan., 1916. Awarded M.C. 3rd April, 1916. *w.* 3rd April, 1916. *d. of w.* 19th April, 1916.
Fraser, A. 2nd Lieut. Attached 9th Black Watch. Awarded M.C. 16th Sept., 1918.
Fulton, L. M. Lieut. Joined Battn. 30th April, 1918. To U.K. sick 12th July, 1918. Rejoined 5th Oct., 1918. Awarded M.C. 18th Feb., 1918.
Fyfe, C. C. 2nd Lieut. Joined from 4th Battn. 8th Jan., 1918. *k. in a.* 21st March, 1918.

THE SIXTH BATTALION THE BLACK WATCH

Garvie, A. C. 2nd Lieut. Joined from Base 16th Feb., 1917. *k. in a.* 23rd April, 1917. Body recovered on battlefield 19th May, 1917.
Garvie, E. E. 2nd Lieut. Joined 24th March, 1918. *w.* 20th July, 1918. Awarded Croix de Guerre with Gold Star Jan., 1919.
Gibson, L. Capt. Went out with Battn. as Adj. May, 1915. Appointed Staff Capt. 1st July, 1915. Awarded Croix de Guerre July, 1919. Mentioned 15th June, 1916. D.S.O. 1st Jan., 1918.
Gilroy, A. Lieut. Joined 12th Nov., 1918.
Girvin, I. W. 2nd Lieut. Joined 9th Aug., 1918. *w.* 24th Oct., 1918. Awarded M.C. Dec., 1918.
Gladwyn, F. W. M. 2nd Lieut. Joined Battn. 8th June, 1918. *w.* 28th July, 1918.
Glass, W. G. 2nd Lieut. Joined from Base 11th Jan., 1917. *k. in a.* 23rd April, 1917.
Good, A. Lieut. Joined 18th April, 1918. Attached T.M. Battery 26th June, 1918. Awarded M.C. Dec., 1918.
Grassie, J. H. A. 2nd Lieut. Joined from 4th (Reserve) Battn. 22nd Jan., 1918. *m.* 21st–26th March, 1918.
Graves, H. S. Lieut. Joined 14th July, 1917. *k in a.* 20th Nov., 1917.
Gray, E. P. S. Lieut. Joined 4th Jan., 1917. Reported *w.* (attached 2/2nd Scottish Horse) 21st–26th March, 1917.
Greenway, H. 2nd Lieut. Joined 23rd Aug., 1918.
Gunter, J. E. 2nd Lieut. Joined 20th Nov., 1918.
Guthrie, H. S. 2nd Lieut. Joined from 4th (Reserve) Battn. 21st–26th March, 1917. *m.*
Guthrie, J. M. 2nd Lieut. Joined 10th Jan., 1916. To hospital sick 22nd Aug., 1916. Rejoined Battn. Promoted Capt. *k.* 28th July, 1918. Awarded posthumous M.C. Aug. 1918.

Haig, W. Major. Went out with Battn. May, 1915. Awarded D.S.O. 5th Feb., 1917. Mentioned in Despatches 13th June, 1916.
Haldane, R. P. Lieut. Went out with Battn. May, 1915. *k. in a.* 13th June, 1915.
Hale, E. N. Capt. *w.* 11th June, 1916. (At duty.) *w.* 31st July, 1916. Rejoined 6th Oct., 1916. Mentioned in Despatches Dec., 1916. Attached to R.F.C. 21st May, 1918.
Hally, J. Capt. Went out with Battn. May, 1915. *k. in a.* 31st July, 1916.
Hally, P. 2nd Lieut. Joined from 3rd Line 1st June, 1916. *w.* 31st July, 1916.
Hamilton, A. L. G. 2nd Lieut. M.C. Joined from 8th Battn. 8th June, 1917. *w.* 21st July, 1917.
Hamilton, D. L. 2nd Lieut. Joined Battn. 31st Oct., 1917. *m.* 21st–26th March, 1917.
Hanna, B. 2nd Lieut. Joined from Base 24th March, 1917. *w.* 31st July, 1917.
Hansen, A. A. 2nd Lieut. Joined 8th June, 1918. *w.* 28th July, 1918.
Harwood, W. R. 2nd Lieut. Joined from 3rd Line 30th May, 1916. To hospital sick 23rd October, 1916.
Hay-Drummond, A. W. H. Lieut.-Col. Mentioned in Despatches 24th Feb., 1917.

APPENDIX I

Hewat, J. G. A. 2nd Lieut. Joined from Base 10th Dec., 1916. Appointed Lieut. and Adj. 1917. Transferred to 10th Royal Scots 28th March, 1918. Rejoined 27th Nov., 1918.

Hill, A. F. 2nd Lieut. Went out with Battn. May, 1915. w. 25th June, 1915.

Hodge, G. R. D. 2nd Lieut. Joined 9th Aug., 1918 Awarded M.C. Dec., 1918. Mentioned in Despatches.

Hollinshead, A. Sgt., No. 952. Gazetted 2nd Lieut. in Battn. 1st Feb., 1916. w. 22nd April, 1916.

Horne, W. H. Lieut. Joined from 3rd Battn. 9th Jan., 1918. w. 21st–26th March, 1918.

Howard, I L 2nd Lieut. Joined 9th Aug., 1918. To hospital 23rd Sept., 1918.

Howarth, R. C. L. 2nd Lieut. Joined 25th Aug., 1918. To hospital 17th Oct., 1918.

Hunter, J. M. Capt. C.F. Joined 10th Sept , 1916.

Hunter, P. C. Capt. Joined 19th April, 1918. w. 28th July, 1918.

Inglis, J. A. Capt. Joined 28th April, 1918.

Innes, A. Capt. Went out with Battn. May, 1915. w. 31st July, 1916. Awarded M.C. 5th Feb., 1917. Mentioned in Despatches 31st Dec., 1915.

Jameson, M. S. Lieut. Joined from R.A.S.C. 22nd Jan., 1918.

Jarman, R. 2nd Lieut. Joined 9th Aug., 1918. w. 28th Aug., 1918. Mentioned in Despatches.

Jenney, A. O. Lieut.-Col. (The Cameronians). Joined from 6th Royal Scots and assumed command 28th June, 1916. Left to command No. 33 Prisoners of War Camp, Oct., 1916.

Johnston, F. H. 2nd Lieut. Joined 25th Aug., 1918. Awarded M.C. Dec., 1918.

Johnston, J. R. 2nd Lieut. Joined 28th March, 1918. To Base 23rd June, 1918.

Keay, R. N. 2nd Lieut. Joined from Depot 7th July, 1916. w. 21st Nov., 1916. d. of w. 30th Nov., 1916.

Keltie, K. W. 2nd Lieut. Joined 26th Oct., 1918.

Kent, C. S. 2nd Lieut. Joined 9th Aug., 1918. k. in a. 24th Oct., 1918.

Knight, H. J. Capt. Joined 10th Dec., 1917. k. in a. 21st March, 1918.

Langland, N. A. 2nd Lieut. Joined from 4th (Reserve) Battn. 16th Oct., 1917. Wounded Dec., 1918. m. 21st–26th March, 1918.

Laughland. 2nd Lieut. Wounded 22nd Dec., 1917. Missing 24th–26th March, 1918.

Lawson, A. 2nd Lieut. Joined 19th April, 1918. w. 20th July, 1918.

Lawson, W. 2nd Lieut. Joined 23rd Aug., 1918. w. 26th Oct., 1918.

Lely, C. A. 2nd Lieut. Joined from 4th (Reserve) Battn. 24th Aug., 1917. w. 21st–26th March, 1918.

THE SIXTH BATTALION THE BLACK WATCH

Leslie, J. R. 2nd Lieut. Joined 26th March, 1916. *w.* 21st Nov., 1916. Promoted Lieut. Nov., 1916. Awarded M.C. 7th Dec., 1916. To U.K. sick March, 1917. Rejoined Battn. 3rd May, 1918. Mentioned in Despatches 10th Jan., 1917.

Lindsay, J. 2nd Lieut. (Scottish Horse). Joined Sept., 1918. Awarded M.C. 10th Jan., 1917.

Lindsay, J. 2nd Lieut. Joined 24th March, 1916. *w.* 13th Nov., 1916. Awarded M.C. 4th Dec., 1916. Rejoined 24th April, 1917. Promoted Lieut. 1st June, 1916. Promoted Capt. 17th Feb., 1917. *m.* 22nd March, 1918.

Lindsay, W. H. 2nd Lieut. Joined 7th July, 1918. *w.* 20th July, 1918.

Low, P. 2nd Lieut. *w.* 31st July, 1917. Rejoined 26th Oct., 1918.

Lumsden, I. L. Major. Joined from Fife and Forfar Yeomanry 20th Aug., 1917.

Lynn, R. 2nd Lieut. Joined May, 1915. To U.K. sick 11th Feb., 1916.

MacDonald, T. A. 2nd Lieut. Joined from B.E.F. Cadet School 10th Jan., 1917. *w.* 23rd April, 1917.

MacDonald, W. Capt. Joined from 1/6th Seaforth Highlanders 24th Jan., 1917. *w.* 17th April, 1917. Promoted Major.

MacDougall, C. 2nd Lieut. Joined 22nd May, 1916. Accidentally *w.* 22nd July, 1916.

MacDowell, Lieut.-Col., C. C. Went out with Battn. May, 1915. To 51st Div. Artillery 27th June, 1915.

MacDowell, C. M. V. Lieut. Went out with Battn. May, 1915. *w.* 1st Sept., 1915. Promoted Capt. 14th Nov., 1916. *w.* 7th April, 1917. Mentioned in Despatches 9th April, 1917. *d. of w.* 28th April, 1917.

Mackintyre, C. C. 2nd Lieut. Joined from 4th (Reserve) Battn. 22nd Jan., 1918. *m.* 21st–26th March, 1918.

MacLean, K. 2nd Lieut. Joined 9th Oct., 1917. To Third Army Musketry School as Instructor 26th Feb., 1918.

MacNaughton, W. D. 2nd Lieut. Joined from 2nd Line 2nd Jan., 1916. Transferred to Brigade M.G.C. 10th Jan., 1916. Mentioned in Despatches 5th June, 1917. Awarded M.C. 19th Nov., 1917.

MacPherson, R. S. L. Lieut. Joined from 6th Entrenching Battn. 16th Oct., 1917. To U.K. 17th March, 1918.

Macrosty, J. Capt. Went out with Battn. May, 1915. *w.* 20th May, 1916. Injured 27th July, 1916. Rejoined 20th Jan., 1918. *w.* 21st–26th March, 1918. Mentioned in Despatches 15th June, 1916.

McAdam, J. L. T. 2nd Lieut. Joined 2nd July, 1917. *w.* 31st July, 1917. Awarded M.C. Aug., 1917.

McBeth, W. M. 2nd Lieut. Joined from Base 10th Dec., 1916. To hospital sick 3rd Feb., 1917. Rejoined 7th March, 1917. *k. in a.* 23rd April, 1917. Body recovered on battlefield 26th May, 1917.

McEwan, D. F. 2nd Lieut. Joined 16th March, 1916. *k. in a.* 31st July, 1916.

McEwan, W. R. 2nd Lieut. Joined 24th April, 1918. Gassed 26th May, 1918.

McFarlane, B. M. 2nd Lieut. Joined 24th April, 1918. *w.* 28th July, 1918.

APPENDIX I

McGregor, R. S. Lieut. Joined from A. and S. Highlanders 22nd Feb., 1918.

McIntyre, R. W. Capt. M.C. Joined 17th May, 1918. Attached 153rd Brigade 4th June, 1918.

McIntyre, W. Lieut. Joined 27th May, 1918.

McKay, H. G. S. Major. M.C. Joined 5th Nov., 1918.

McKenzie, J. C. 2nd Lieut. Joined 26th Sept., 1918.

McLaren, Q. 2nd Lieut. Joined from 3rd Line 2nd Dec., 1915. *w.* 10th April, 1916. Gassed 31st Aug., 1916. Rejoined 4th Sept., 1916. *k. in a.* 26th Oct., 1916. Mentioned in Despatches 4th Jan., 1917.

McLean, D. 2nd Lieut. Joined from Base 10th Dec., 1916. To U.K. 21st Feb., 1918.

McLeod, M. P. 2nd Lieut. Joined from Depot 9th Sept., 1916. *k. in a.* 14th Nov., 1916.

McNaughton, W. D. Lieut. Mentioned in Despatches 9th April, 1917 and 25th May, 1917. M.C. 19th Nov., 1917. Bar to M.C. 18th Feb., 1918.

McNicoll, F. S. 2nd Lieut. Joined 10th Dec., 1916. To hospital sick 23rd Dec., 1916. Rejoined 13th Jan., 1917. To XVIII Corps School as Instructor 28th June, 1917.

McNicoll, G. R. 2nd Lieut. Joined from Depot 11th Sept., 1916. To hospital sick 12th Dec., 1916. Rejoined 6th July, 1917. *k. in a.* 20th Nov., 1917.

McPhie, J. J. 2nd Lieut. Joined from Base 10th Dec., 1916. *w.* 12th Dec., 1916.

McRae, K. S. Capt. Joined 28th April, 1918. To XVIII Corps School June, 1918. Rejoined 4th Oct., 1918. Transferred to 4th Royal Scots 11th Oct., 1918.

McRosty, J. Capt. Mentioned in Despatches 15th June, 1916.

Marshall, S. H. Capt. Went out with Battn. May, 1915. To U.K. 27th April, 1916.

Martin, A. W. D. 2nd Lieut. Joined 7th July, 1918. Awarded M.C. Aug., 1918. To hospital 13th Oct., 1918.

Menzies, R. J. Capt. Joined from Base 11th Jan., 1917. *k. in a.* 31st July, 1917. Mentioned in Despatches Dec., 1917.

Miller, H. W. W. 2nd Lieut. Joined from 3rd Line 18th Jan., 1916. *k. in a.* 31st July, 1916.

Milligan, J. M. Major. Joined from 6th Royal Scots 7th July, 1916. Transferred to 1/7th Black Watch 12th Aug., 1916.

Milne, S. A. 2nd Lieut. Joined 26th Oct , 1918.

Milnes, H. 2nd Lieut. Joined 14th July, 1917. *w.* 28th July, 1917. Rejoined Battn. Sept., 1918.

Moncrieff, R. M. Capt. Mentioned in Despatches. O.B.E.

Moncreiffe, Sir Robert D., Bart., V.D., D.T. Lieut.-Col. Went out in command of Battn. May, 1915. Invalided to U.K. 28th June, 1915. Reassumed command 13th Aug., 1915. Invalided to U.K. 5th Dec., 1915. C.B., C.M.G. 3rd June, 1916. Mentioned in Despatches 15th June, 1916, and 24th Feb., 1917.

Morgan, A. J. 2nd Lieut. Joined from 3rd Line 1st June, 1916. *w.* 18th July, 1916.

THE SIXTH BATTALION THE BLACK WATCH

Muir, A. D. 2nd Lieut. Joined 15th January, 1915. Promoted Lieut. 1st Aug., 1916. To U.K. 11th Feb., 1917.

Nicoll, E. D. 2nd Lieut. Joined 6th July, 1917. Appointed Adj. 1918. Awarded Croix de Guerre Silver Star Jan., 1919.
Nisbet, A. F. 2nd Lieut. Joined 16th Aug., 1918. To hospital 25th Aug., 1918.

Oxley, Capt. J. W. (Gordon Highlanders). Adj. Went out with Battn. May, 1915.

Paton, G. D. 2nd Lieut. Joined from 3rd Line 1st June, 1916. *w.* 31st July, 1916. Mentioned in Despatches 23rd Oct., 1918.
Patrick, J. 2nd Lieut. Joined from Base 17th Feb., 1917. *m.* 21st–26th March, 1918.
Pennington, J. Joined 7th May, 1918. Attached Divl. Wing R.F.C. 10th May, 1918.
Philip, W. P. Lieut. Awarded M.C. 29th July, 1918.
Phillips, J. M. 2nd Lieut. Joined from Base 17th Feb., 1917. Transferred to R.F.C. 12th Sept., 1917.
Porter, W. 2nd Lieut. Joined 26th Oct., 1918.
Pullar, G. D. Major. O.B.E., 1918.

Quarton, F. 2nd Lieut. Joined 1916. To U.K. Dec. 1916.

Rae, W. A. 2nd Lieut. Joined 6th July, 1917. *k. in a.* 31st July, 1917.
Ramsay, A. L. 2nd Lieut. Joined 6th July, 1917. *w.* 31st July, 1917. Awarded M.C. Aug., 1918. To hospital 21st Aug., 1918.
Ramsay, I. G. Capt. Joined 30th Aug., 1918. Left Battn. Oct., 1918.
Raynor, K. 2nd Lieut. Joined from Depot 21st Aug., 1916. *w.* 13th Nov., 1916.
Reekie, H. L. Lieut. Joined 19th April, 1918. Detached to T.M. Batty. 26th April, 1918. *w.* 28th July, 1918.
Reid, A. 2nd Lieut. Joined 14th July, 1917. *w.* and *m.* 21st–26th March, 1918.
Reid, C. C. 2nd Lieut. Joined 16th Oct., 1917.
Renton, H. W. H. 2nd Lieut. Joined from B.E.F. School 24th Dec., 1916. To hospital 1st Jan., 1917. Rejoined 18th Jan., 1917. *w.* 31st July, 1917. Rejoined 19th April, 1918. Promoted Capt. Aug., 1918. Awarded M.C. Oct., 1918. Croix de Guerre Bronze Star Jan., 1919. Mentioned in Despatches.
Rich, F. Lieut. Joined 20th July, 1916. Accidentally *w.* 26th March, 1917.
Richard, J. E. M. Capt. Joined 12th Nov., 1918, from 1st Battn.
Robb, W. J. M. 2nd Lieut. Joined 14th July, 1917. *w.* 21st Dec., 1917. Rejoined 7th July, 1918. *k. in a.* 20th July, 1918.
Roberts, H. S. 2nd Lieut. Joined 16th June, 1916. *w.* 31st July, 1916.
Robertson, A. P. A. 2nd Lieut. Joined 3rd Nov., 1918.

APPENDIX I

Robertson, A. S. 2nd Lieut. Joined 16th Oct., 1917. To U.K. 18th Jan., 1918.

Robertson, C. J. 2nd Lieut. Joined from B.E.F. Cadet School 10th Jan., 1917. *k. in a.* 22nd March, 1917.

Robson, W. 2nd Lieut. Joined 6th July, 1917. *w.* April, 1918.

Rogers, W. M. 2nd Lieut. Went out with Battn. May, 1915. To U.K. 15th Dec., 1915. Rejoined 15th Dec., 1916. To U.K. 11th April, 1917.

Rope. 2nd Lieut. *w.* 22nd Dec., 1917.

Roy, J. W. 2nd Lieut. Joined from 3rd Line 1st June, 1916. *k. in a.* 31st July, 1916.

Rutherford, J. Lieut. Went out with Battn. May, 1915. Mentioned in Despatches June 1917. Promoted Capt. 1st July, 1917. Appointed Adj. 3rd Aug., 1917. Awarded M.C. 24th Aug., 1917. To Tank Corps 3rd Nov., 1918.

Rutherford, J. F. 2nd Lieut. Joined 14th Aug., 1916. Promoted Lieut. 1st July, 1917. To hospital 26th Oct., 1916. Rejoined 24th Dec., 1916. To U.K. 31st Oct., 1917.

Sadler, A. B. 2nd Lieut. Went out with Battn. May, 1915. To U.K. Aug., 1916.

Scott, A. C. 2nd Lieut. Joined 27th Aug., 1918.

Scott, G. 2nd Lieut. Joined from Base 12th Feb., 1917. Awarded M.C. 14th April, 1917. To hospital (shell shock) 16th April, 1917. Mentioned in Despatches 13th April, 1917.

Scott, J. 2nd Lieut. Joined 11th Sept., 1916. Gassed (to hospital) 13th Nov., 1916. Rejoined 15th Dec., 1916. Wounded 31st July, 1917. Rejoined 24th April, 1918. To hospital sick 14th July, 1918.

Scott, J. D. R. 2nd Lieut. Transferred to R.F.C. 12th Oct., 1916.

Seaton, A. W. 2nd Lieut. Joined 28th Aug., 1918.

Shaw, R. B. Lieut. Joined from 2/6th Battn. 22nd Feb., 1918. *w.* 21st–26th March, 1918.

Shearer, C. 2nd Lieut. Joined 1st Aug., 1915. Relinquished commission 19th Feb., 1916.

Smith, J. B. 2nd Lieut. Went out with Battn. May, 1915. Transferred to R.F.C. 12th April, 1917.

Smythe, P. C. Lieut. Joined from 3rd Reserve Battn. 25th Sept., 1917.

Starforth, H. W. 2nd Lieut. Joined from 2nd Scots Guards 21st Oct., 1915. To U.K. 6th Dec., 1916.

Steel, G. McL. 2nd Lieut. Joined from Base 10th Dec., 1916. *w.* 23rd April, 1916. Rejoined 22nd April, 1918. *w.* 28th July, 1918. Awarded M.C. Aug., 1918.

Stevenson, T. Lieut. M.C. Joined 11th July, 1917. Transferred to 4/5th Battn. Black Watch 17th July, 1917.

Stocker, T. T. 2nd Lieut. Joined 19th April, 1918. Left Battn. June, 1918.

Strachan, W. H. 2nd Lieut. Joined 7th July, 1918. *w.* and *m.* 20th July, 1918.

Strathairn, H. W. 2nd Lieut. Joined 16th March, 1916. *d. of w.* 16th Nov., 1916.

THE SIXTH BATTALION THE BLACK WATCH

Sutherland, G. D. 2nd Lieut. Joined from 3rd Line 15th Jan., 1916. To T.M. Batty. 14th April, 1916.

Sworder. Lieut.-Col. (Gordon Highlanders). Assumed command of Battn. April 19th, 1918, vice Lieut.-Col. Campbell *k. in a.* Relinquished command April 23rd, 1918.

Tait, T. S. 2nd Lieut. Joined 26th Oct., 1918.

Tarleton, F. R. Lieut.-Col. Assumed command of Battn. vice Lieut.-Col. Sworder 27th April, 1918. *w.* 20th July, 1918. Awarded D.S.O. Aug., 1918. Awarded Croix de Guerre with Palms Jan., 1919. Legion of Honour, 1918.

Tarrel, W. 2nd Lieut. Joined 11th Feb., 1916 *w.* 31st Aug., 1916.

Taylor, C. S. Joined 22nd April, 1918. *w.* 22nd May, 1918.

Thomas, A. J. G. 2nd Lieut. Joined 1st Aug., 1915. *k. in a.* 1st June, 1916.

Thomson, J. 2nd Lieut. Joined 2nd Nov. 1917. *w.* and *m.* 21st–26th March, 1918.

Tovani, W. R. 2nd Lieut. M.C. Joined Sept., 1918. Awarded Bar to M.C. Dec., 1918.

Truman, C. M. Lieut.-Col. (12th Lancers). Assumed command of Battn. vice Sir R. Moncreiffe 25th Dec., 1915. Left Battn. to command 12th Lancers 25th June, 1916.

Turnbull, M. 2nd Lieut. Joined 16th Aug., 1918. To hospital 13th Oct., 1918.

Uthwatt, W. R. E. A. Lieut. Joined Battn. 28th April, 1918. *w.* 20th July, 1918.

Waddell, G. 2nd Lieut. Joined from Depot 21st Aug., 1916. To hospital sick 23rd Dec., 1916. Rejoined 11th July, 1916. Severely *w.* whilst engaged in filling grenades 21st July, 1916.

Walker, J. M. 2nd Lieut. Joined 27th Aug., 1918. Awarded D.S.O. Dec., 1918.

Wallace, W. 2nd Lieut. Joined 23rd Aug., 1918. Hospital 30th Aug., 1918. Rejoined Oct., 1918.

Watt, J. J. 2nd Lieut. Joined from Depot 22nd Aug., 1916. To hospital 1st Dec., 1916. Promoted Lieut. Rejoined 19th April, 1918. Awarded M.C. Aug., 1918. To hospital 20th Sept., 1918. Rejoined Oct., 1918. Mentioned in Despatches.

Webber, R. 2nd Lieut. Joined 19th April, 1918. *w.* 24th July, 1918. To hospital 31st July, 1918.

Weir, J. 2nd Lieut. Joined 24th Oct., 1916. *w.* 13th Nov., 1916.

West, A. H. P. Lieut. Went out with Battn. and attached Brigade Headquarters May, 1915. To hospital sick 4th Oct., 1916.

West, R. L. Lieut. Joined 1st May, 1915. Promoted Lieut. 24th Feb., 1916. *w.* 13th Nov., 1916.

Williamson, G. M. 2nd Lieut. Joined 9th Jan., 1918.

Willison, C. Capt. Joined 5th Dec., 1915. *w.* 22nd July, 1918. Rejoined Aug., 1918. Awarded M.C. Aug., 1918. To hospital 15th Oct., 1918. Awarded Croix de Guerre with Palms Jan., 1919. Mentioned in Despatches.

Wilson, A. R. 2nd Lieut. Joined 9th Aug., 1918. *w.* 26th Oct., 1918.

APPENDIX I

Wilson, H. N. 2nd Lieut. Joined 3rd Nov., 1918.
Wilson, J. A. Capt. Joined 17th May, 1918. To hospital 12th Aug., 1918.
Wilson, J. C. Hon. Lieut and Q.M. Awarded M.C. 13th May, 1918. Mentioned in Despatches 7th April, 1918; 21st May, 1918; 4th Jan., 1918.
Wilson, J. N. Lieut. *w.* 2nd July, 1917. *d. of w.* 3rd July, 1917.
Winship, H. N. 2nd Lieut. Joined 3rd Nov., 1918.
Wrathall, W. P. Capt. Went out with Battn. 2nd May, 1915. *w.* 31st July, 1916. Mentioned in Despatches 13th Nov., 1916. Awarded M.C. 1st Jan., 1918. D.S.O. 16th Sept., 1918. Mentioned in Despatches 31st Dec., 1915; 4th Jan., 1917; 20th Dec., 1918. Awarded Croix de Guerre 7th Jan., 1919.
Wylie, J. Major. Went out with Battn. (commanding A Coy.) May, 1915. Assumed command of Battn. 28th June, 1915. Reverted to Second-in-Command 22nd Aug., 1915. Lieut.-Col. Assumed command of Battn. 1st Oct., 1916. To U.K. 23rd Jan., 1917. Mentioned in Despatches 15th June, 1916.

Young, F. E. 2nd Lieut. *w.* 11th June, 1916. To hospital sick 1st Dec., 1916. Promoted Lieut. Rejoined Battn. 19th June, 1918. *w.* 28th July, 1918.
Young, J. R. J. 2nd Lieut. Joined 19th April, 1918. *w.* 24th Aug., 1918.
Young, T. E. Major. Joined from 3rd Line 9th July, 1916. To hospital sick 21st Nov., 1916.

APPENDIX II

SUMMARY OF CASUALTIES. THE SIXTH BATTALION

(*b*) The discrepancy between these figures and those given by the war diaries is accounted for by the fact that, save in the case of regular battalions, the diaries seldom give a record of casualties other than those suffered in main actions.

OFFICERS, 1914–18

Year.	Killed. D. of Wounds. D. on Service.	Wounded.	Missing.	Total.	Year.
1914	—	—	—	—	1914
1915	1	2	—	3	1915
1916	15	28	—	43	1916
1917	21	18	—	39	1917
1918	17	42	14	73	1918
Totals:	54	90	14	158	

OTHER RANKS, 1914–18

Year.	Killed. D. of Wounds. D. on Service.	Wounded.	Missing.	Total.	Year.
1914	—	—	—	—	1914
1915	61	14	—	75	1915
1916	246	371	2	619	1916
1917	263	454	58	775	1917
1918	385	796	593	1774	1918
Totals:	955	1635	653	3243	

TOTAL:

(*b*) Officers, 158.   Other Ranks, 3243.

APPENDIX III

Casualties—Officers

* Killed in action. † Died of wounds. § Died.

Name.	Rank.	Date.
Allison J. S.	Lieut.	§18.9.17.
Anderson, W. K.	Lieut.	*22.6.18.
Begg, W.	2nd Lieut.	*13.11.16.
Bowie, H.	Lieut.	*28.6.18.
Brown, A.	Lieut.	†12.4.18.
Brown, W.	2nd Lieut.	*5.10.17.
Butler, C. H.	2nd Lieut.	*23.4.16.
Cairns, G. M.	2nd Lieut.	*13.11.16.
Campbell, N. D.	Lieut.-Col.	*-.4.18.
Coutts, W. E.	Capt.	*22.3.18.
Dickson, G. H. M.	2nd Lieut.	*26.10.18.
Dixon, N. F.	Capt.	†5.10.17. And M.G.C.
Dobbie, A. M.	2nd Lieut.	†13.4.18.
Dobson, G.	2nd Lieut.	*12.4.18.
Doe, A. B.	2nd Lieut.	*23.4.17.
Elder, J.	2nd Lieut.	*21.3.18.
Ellis, R. B.	Capt.	†21.11.16. M.C.
Farrell, S. K.	2nd Lieut.	*20.7.18.
Ferguson, T.	Capt.	*13.11.16.
Fleet, W. H.	2nd Lieut.	†19.4.16. M.C.
Fyfe, C. C.	2nd Lieut.	*21.3.18.
Garvie, A. C.	2nd Lieut.	*23.4.17.
Glass, W.	2nd Lieut.	*23.4.17.
Gowans, A. D. S.	2nd Lieut.	†27.4.17.
Graves, H. S.	Lieut.	†24.11.17.
Guthrie, J. M.	Capt.	*28.7.18.
Haldane, R. P.	Lieut.	†13.6.15.
Hally, J.	Capt.	*30.7.16.
Hebden, A.	2nd Lieut.	*8.5.17.
Hewat, J. G. A.	Capt.	†16.4.18.
Keay, R. N.	2nd Lieut.	†30.11.16.
Kent, C. S.	2nd Lieut.	*24.10.18.
Knight, H. J.	Capt.	*21.3.18.
Macdowell, C. M. V.	Capt.	†28.4.17.
McBeth, W. M.	2nd Lieut.	*23.4.17.
McCash, J. W.	Lieut.	*22.11.16. And R.F.C.
McEwan, D. F.	2nd Lieut.	*30.7.16.
McLaren, Q.	2nd Lieut.	*26.10.17.
McLeod, M. P.	2nd Lieut.	*14.11.16.
McNicoll, G. R.	2nd Lieut.	*20.11.17.
Menzies, R. J.	Capt.	*31.7.17.
Miller, H. W. W.	2nd Lieut.	*30.7.16.
Rae, W. A.	2nd Lieut.	*31.7.17.
Ritchie, J.	2nd Lieut.	*25.4.17. And M.G.C.

THE SIXTH BATTALION THE BLACK WATCH

Name.	Rank.	Date.
Robb, W. J. M.	2nd Lieut.	*20.7.18.
Robertson, C. J.	2nd Lieut.	*22.3.17.
Roy, J. F.	2nd Lieut.	*30.7.16.
Smith, J.	2nd Lieut.	*14.11.17.
Smith, J. B.	2nd Lieut.	*15.8.17.
Strathairn, H. W.	2nd Lieut.	†16.11.16.
Syme, D.	2nd Lieut.	†4.7.18. M.M.
Thomas, A. J. G.	Lieut.	*31.5.16.
Turnbull, D. S.	Lieut.	*15.4.17. And R.F.C.
Wilson, J. N.	Capt.	†4.7.17.

APPENDIX IV

NOMINAL ROLL OF WARRANT OFFICERS, NON-COMMISSIONED OFFICERS AND MEN KILLED IN ACTION OR DIED OF WOUNDS OR DISEASE IN THE GREAT WAR, 1914–18

* Killed in action. † Died of wounds. ‡ Died at home. § Died. ¶ Died at sea.

Adams, W. G., Pte., 265537	*31.7.17	Beachill, J., Pte., 266315	*29.3.17
Adkins, W. J., Pte., 22503	*20.7.18	Beaton, J. R., Pte., S/18088	*21.3.18
Aitken, J., Pte., 203141	*22.9.17	Bennett, J., Pte., S/25561	*24.10.18
Alexander, C., Pte., 267956	*31.7.17	Berrie, A., Pte., 241307	*31.7.17
Alexander, J., Sgt., 265048		Berry, P., Pte., 203220	†12.11.18
(M.M.)	¶17.4.17	Betchette, J., Pte., 3666	† 1.8.16
Alexander, W., Pte., 267953	† 1.8.17	Bett, G. D., Pte., S/25577	†24.10.18
Allan, I., Pte., S/8209	*21.3.18	Bett, R. W., Pte., 266063	§30.7.18
Allan, J., Pte., 265433	*30.7.16	Beveridge, D., Pte., 291037	*21.3.18
Allan, J., Pte., S/40179	†21.4.18	Beveridge, J., L/Cpl., S/40504	*31.7.17
Allan, R., Pte., S/41068	*10.4.18	Beveridge, R., Pte., S/40126	†21.6.18
Allardice, E. S., Pte., 267729	*23.4.17	Biggs, W., L/Cpl., 266766	†27.5.18
Anderson, E., Pte., S/20744	*20.7.18	Birney, J., Pte., 266247	*30.7.16
Anderson, G. W., Pte., S/24602		Bissett, A., Pte., S/9085	†22.7.18
	*20.7.18	Bissett, P., Pte., 267897	*21.3.18
Anderson, J., Pte., S/41637	*20.7.18	Bissett, T., L/Cpl., 268229	† 2.4.17
Anderson, J., Pte., 266680	*18.10.18	Black, A., L/Cpl., 265294	*30.7.16
Anderson, J. M., Pte., 265884	†12.8.18	Black, J., L/Sgt., 2187	*13.11.16
Anderson, J., Pte., 267954	*20.9.17	Black, J., Pte., 265785	*31.3.17
Anderson, T., Pte., 265958	*23.4.17	Black, W., A/L/Cpl., 1871	†14.11.15
Anderson, W., Pte., S/9012	*24.10.18	Blacklock, J., Pte., 1553	† 4.4.16
Anderson, W., L/Cpl., S/3685	§ 7.10.18	Blacklock, J., Pte., 265251	*23.4.17
Anderson, W. R., Sgt., 265147		Bogan, F., Pte., 266931	*31.7.17
(M.M.)	†28.7.18	Bolt, T., Pte., 3270	†31.5.16
Angus, R., Pte., 267952	§ 9.7.18	Bonthron, D., Pte., 293206	*20.7.18
Archer, L. R., Pte., 268405	* 7.4.17	Bonthrone, T., Pte., 3832	†13.8.16
Archibald, J., Pte., 266296	*30.7.16	Botfield, J., Pte., 267960	*31.7.17
Armit, A., Pte., S/25136	*10.9.18	Bowie, W. R., Pte., S/41079	†22.7.18
Armstrong, J., Pte., 1504		Boyd, J., L/Cpl., 2953	*30.7.16
(M.M.)	*13.11.16	Boyd, J., Cpl., S/40188	*20.11.17
Armstrong, W., Pte., 267264	*21.3.18	Boyter, A. S., Pte., 268226	*16.9.17
Auchterlonie, J., Pte., 3391	§ 9.1.16	Bradshaw, J., Pte., 267972	*26.5.18
		Brady, J., Pte., 6180	*13.11.16
Baillie, G., Pte., 3991	*30.7.16	Brock, W., Pte., S/18714	*31.1.17
Bain, J., L/Cpl., 2426	†22.8.16	Brodie, S., L/Cpl., 3489	†19.11.16
Bain, W., Pte., 266995	*31.7.17	Brooke, E., Pte., 266344	*30.7.16
Baldie, J., Pte., 2819	*26.9.15	Brooks, G. V., Pte., 292139	*21.3.18
Bamford, J., Pte., S/23860	*10.4.18	Brough, G., L/Cpl., 1921	*28.7.16
Barclay, D. U., Pte., 2982	* 8.9.16	Brown, C., Sgt., 265638	*31.7.17
Barclay, J. M., Pte., 3587	† 8.8.16	Brown, J., Pte., S/25516	†25.10.18
Barker, J., Pte., 267730	*21.3.18	Brown, J., Pte., 267869	*23.4.17
Barrett, W., Pte., S/40892	*10.4.18	Brown, J. H., L/Cpl., 1797	*22.7.16
Batchelor, D., Pte., 200371	* 1.7.17	Brown, J. T., L/Cpl., 267661	
Batchelor, G., Pte., 4325	†21.11.16	(M.M.)	*21.3.18
Bates, F., Pte., S/41940	*24.10.18	Brown, W., Pte., 1600	§ 6.12.16
Bawtree, D. E., Pte., 293008	§29.6.18	Bruce, J., Pte., 267263	*21.3.18
Bayne, A. McG., Pte., 1740	†31.7.16	Bruce, T., Pte., 267735	*21.3.18
Bayne, J., Cpl., 265666	*30.7.16	Bruce, W. B., Pte., 265981	* 8.9.16

THE SIXTH BATTALION THE BLACK WATCH

Bryce, A., Pte., 268355	*31.3.17	Collie, W. C., L/Cpl., 265419	
Buchannan, M., Pte., 265607	*31.7.17		†14.10.17
Burdett, J., Pte., 350321	†28.4.18	Collins, D., Pte., 265756	*17.5.17
Burt, R. R., Pte., S/19656	§20.7.18	Collins, F., Pte., 267975	*24.10.18
Bushfield, C., Pte., 267961	* 2.7.17	Collyer, W. J., Pte., S/43580	*26.10.18
Butchart, A., Pte., 200049	* 2.7.17	Conlin, H., Pte., 2011	†18.7.15
Byers, G. E., A/Sgt., 265205	*21.3.18	Connell, S., Pte., 2125	*30.7.16
		Connelly, J., Pte., 3062	* 8.9.16
Cairns, H. K., Pte., 1365	*12.8.15	Conway, J., Pte., 266793	*17.5.17
Cairns, W., Pte., 268298	*16.4.18	Cooper, A., Pte., 1970	*30.7.16
Cairns, W. K., C.S.M., 98	†31.7.16	Cooper, W., Pte., 285028	* 2.7.17
Cameron, A., Pte., 266666	† 2.5.17	Copland, W. S., Pte., S/41815	† 2.11.18
Cameron, A., Pte., 268120	§10.7.18	Courmack, R., Pte., S/41097	‡20.10.18
Cameron, I., Pte., 3341	*30.7.16	Coulter, T., L/Cpl., 267106	*28.5.18
Cameron, J., Pte., 2471	* 3.11.16	Coutts, S., Pte., 3422	*30.7.16
Cameron, J., Pte., 267988	† 5.4.17	Coutts, W. C., Cpl., 265536	*24.10.18
Cameron, J. K., Pte., 1877	†11.8.15	Cowan, R., Pte., S/41291	*28.9.18
Cameron, N., Pte., 265824	*31.7.17	Cowan, S., Pte., S/22769	*20.7.18
Cameron, R., Pte., 266075	*17.4.17	Cowan, T., Pte., 266824	*23.4.17
Cameron, W. G., Pte., 292740		Cowie, A., Pte., 268166	*21.3.18
	*20.7.18	Cowie, G., Pte., 265441	*28.5.18
Campbell, A. B., Pte., 265052	*30.7.18	Cowie, G. G., Pte., S/41596	§25.8.18
Campbell, D., Cpl., 1496	*14.6.16	Cownie, J. S., L/Cpl., 265102	*21.5.18
Campbell, D., Pte., 266754	*10.4.18	Craig, P., Pte., 1949	*23.6.16
Campbell, J., Pte., 202330	*23.4.17	Craig, W., Pte., 3248	† 3.9.16
Campbell, J., L/Sgt., 265343	* 2.7.17	Cramb, R., Cpl., 201426	*27.7.18
Campbell, N., Pte., 3337	† 7.9.16	Crerar, W., Pte., 267181	*28.5.18
Campbell, P., Cpl., 2017	†14.6.16	Cresswell, A. E., Pte., 288099	*24.10.18
Campbell, P., Pte., 203323	*28.7.18	Crichton, A., Pte., 202816	*20.7.18
Campbell, P., Cpl., 265090	*23.4.17	Crichton, J., Pte., 201220	*10.4.18
Cargill, J., Pte., 267876	*23.4.17	Crockart, D., L/Sgt., 265612	*21.3.18
Cargill, T., Pte., 4269	† 4.11.16	Cross, J., Pte., 265939	*23.4.17
Carmichael, D. C., Pte., S/24096		Crotty, R. A., Pte., 265795	*21.3.18
	* 2.3.18	Cruickshanks, G., L/Sgt., 267205	
Carnegie, J., Pte., S/25606	†27.12.18		*21.3.18
Carnochan, A., Pte., S/41959	*24.10.18	Cumming, R., Pte., 1934	*29.10.15
Carroll, T., Pte., S/41968	†28.8.18	Cumming, T., Pte., 1192	† 5.9.16
Cation, T., Pte., 266143	†29.3.18	Cunningham, T., Pte., 267855	
Chalmers, J., A/Sgt., 10696	§10.4.18		*24.10.18
Christie, D., Pte., 3589	*30.7.16	Currie, J. M., Pte., S/41051	†12.11.18
Christie, W., Pte., 2018	*30.7.16		
Chrystall, W., Pte., S/41092	*10.4.18	Dale, W. W., Pte., 2782	*13.11.16
Clark, A., Pte., 3986	*13.11.16	Dalgity, W., Pte., 265281	†13.4.17
Clark, A. H., Pte., S/25608	*26.10.18	Dall, R., Pte., S/25013	*10.5.18
Clark, D., Pte., S/41326	†29.9.18	Davidson, C. G., Pte., S/41052	
Clark, G., Pte., 3426	*13.11.16		†12.4.18
Clark, J., Pte., 266107	†24.4.17	Davidson, J., Pte., 25529	*24.10.18
Clark, J. S., Pte., 267022	* 2.7.17	Davidson, J. A., Pte., 265133	*30.7.16
Clark, J., Pte., 268376	† 6.5.18	Davidson, P., Pte., 265450	*16.5.17
Clark, P., Pte., 1726	*30.7.16	Davidson, W., Pte., 266485	*31.7.17
Clews, J. J., Pte., 285026	* 2.7.17	Dean, E., Pte., 267998	†31.7.17
Clogg, W., Pte., 265474	* 1.6.17	Delaney, J., Pte., S/25165	*26.10.18
Clouston, J., Pte., 266613	†31.7.17	Dempster, J., Pte., 268000	*21.3.18
Cluness, L., Pte., S/18036	*21.3.18	Dempster, W., Pte., 268192	† 2.4.17
Cochrane, A., Pte., S/41341	†14.5.18	Dewar, G., Pte., 265512	*30.7.16

APPENDIX IV

Dewar, J., Pte., 265114	† 2.4.17	Ferguson, G., L/Cpl., 1874	*13.11.16
Dewar, R., Pte., 268349	*31.7.17	Ferguson, J., Pte., 1933	*13.11.16
Dick, A., Pte., 290347	*10.4.18	Ferguson, J., Pte., 202076	*20.7.18
Dickson, J., Pte., S/25661	†25.10.18	Ferguson, P., Pte., 1723	*13.11.16
Dingwall, J., Pte., 267942	†19.4.17	Fernie, J., Pte., S/25712	*26.10.18
Dingwall, J., Pte., 3887	*25.7.16	Fernie, R., Pte., S/14586	*10.4.18
Dixon, G., Pte., 292121	*15.8.18	Ferrier, J. P. D., Pte., 267309	*16.9.17
Dodds, H. W., Pte., S/12511	*31.7.17	Findlay, D., Pte., S/25604	*24.10.18
Doig, W., Pte., 1882	*30.7.16	Findlay, J., Pte., S/41664	*20.7.18
Don, G., Pte., 1143	*30.7.16	Findlay, J. N., Pte., 3141	* 8.9.16
Donaldson, A., Pte., 292620	†21.7.18	Findlay, J., Pte., S/25723	*24.10.18
Donaldson, J., Cpl., 1816	*30.7.16	Finlayson, A., Pte., S/43256	*21.3.18
Donaldson, M., Pte., S/41102	*10.4.18	Fitchett, J., Pte., 268012	† 5.8.17
Donnelly, A., Pte., 203020	*10.4.18	Fleming, A. R., Cpl., 267819	* 1.7.17
Dott, S. McP., Pte., 2786	*26.6.15	Fleming, R., Pte., 268015	†21.5.17
Douglas, J., Pte., 1863	†11.8.15	Flynn, J., Pte., 3641	†30.6.16
Douglas, R., Pte., S/25715	*24.10.18	Forbes, A., Pte., 267819	
Douglas, W., Pte., S/41103	†29.8.18	(M.M.)	*10.4.18
Dow, J., Pte., S/41293	*27.7.18	Forbes, A., Pte., 265267	*23.12.17
Downie, G., L/Cpl., 201334	*21.3.18	Forbes, C., Pte., 1858	*29.6.16
Dreghorn, J., Pte., 267997	*21.3.18	Forbes, D., Cpl., 265925	*20.4.17
Drew, J. S., L/Sgt., 265077		Forbes, D.F., Pte., 266705	†25.4.17
(M.M.)	*31.7.17	Forbes, J. D., Pte., S/41109	*10.4.18
Duff, A. J., Pte., S/41658	* 6.6.18	Forbes, J. S., Pte., S/40948	*29.7.18
Duff, W., Pte., 1094	†31.8.16	Forbes, T., Bugler, 1218	*30.7.16
Duff, W., Pte., 265362	*31.7.17	Forbes, W., Pte., 5974	†20.12.16
Duffus, J. F., Pte., 268358	†26.10.18	Ford, G., Pte., 3594	*30.7.16
Duffy, J., Pte., 203081	*28.7.18	Forrester, W., Pte., S/41319	*20.7.18
Duffy, J., Pte., 265299	*30.7.16	Foster, D., Pte., 265641	*30.7.16
Dugan, D. W., Pte., S/41055	*10.4.18	Frame, J., Pte., S/41110	*18.10.18
Drummond, G., Pte., S/40690		Fraser, A., Pte., 3499	*30.7.16
	*21.3.18	Fraser, G., Pte., 1745	*23.6.16
Dunbar, G., Pte., 267937	† 3.5.17	Fraser, J., Pte., S/41873	*26.10.18
Duncan, A., Pte., 268007	*21.3.18	Fraser, J. R., Pte., S/19535	*21.3.18
Duncan, G., Pte., S/25718	†28.10.18	Freer, J., Pte., 268013	† 9.8.17
Duncan, J., Pte., 265404	*28.5.18	Fulton, R. E., Pte., S/41116	*28.7.18
Duncan, J. F., Pte., 266994	†25.3.18	Fyfe, D.A.S., Pte., S/14546	*21.3.18
Duncan, W., Pte., S/41311	†12.5.18	Fyffe, A., Sgt., 959	*30.7.16
Dunlop, W. K., Pte., 267698	†20.4.17		
Dunn, J., Pte., S/41960	†15.9.18	Galbraith, J., Pte., 266003	*31.7.17
Durie, G., L/Cpl., S/19516	†20.7.18	Gallacher, J., Pte., 266791	*23.4.17
Durward, G., L/Cpl., 265347	* 1.4.17	Gallacher, J., Pte., 266873	*21.3.18
Dye, R., Pte., 267994	*21.3.18	Gardiner, J., L/Cpl., 265414	†11.9.17
		Gardiner, J. W., Sgt., 265615	*21.3.18
Eadie, J., Pte., 912	†28.10.15	Gardiner, P., C.S.M., 700	*30.7.16
Edwards, C., Pte., 3768	*30.7.16	Gardiner, J. A., Pte., 268019	*23.4.17
Eggs, R. S., Pte., 265097	*23.4.17	Garson, J. R., Pte., S/41118	*10.4.18
		Gascoigne, T., Pte., 266335	*30.7.16
Fairley, J., Pte., 266871	*21.3.18	Gathercole, H., Pte., 268386	*21.3.18
Fallon, P., L/Cpl., 351	†27.6.15	Gatherum, D., Pte., 4047	†30.9.16
Farquhar, D., Pte., 6178	†24.11.16	Gebbie, T., Pte., S/41300	*10.4.18
Farquharson, G., Pte., 267742	†29.6.17	Geekie, J., Pte., 203009	† 1.4.18
Feeley, J., Pte., 1652	†25.6.16	Gehrke, C., Pte., 266999	†28.5.18
Fender, T., Pte., 1587	†19.12.15	Gellatly, F., L/Cpl., 268127	*20.11.17
Ferguson, A., Pte., 267811	*31.7.17	Gellatly, T., Pte., 266620	*21.3.18

THE SIXTH BATTALION THE BLACK WATCH

Gibb, C., Pte., 203154	*20.11.17	Hegarty, T. H. G., Pte., 2935	§ 11.9.16
Gibb, W., Sgt., 1028	*30.7.16	Heggie, D., Cpl., 1927	*13.11.16
Gibson, J., Pte., S/22125	† 3.8.18	Henderson, A., Pte., S/24093	*21.3.18
Gibson, N., L/Cpl., S/41119	*26.5.18	Henderson, J. B., Pte., 266014	
Gibson, R., Pte., S/24610	*20.7.18		*21.3.18
Gillatly, R., L/Cpl., 1857	*27.7.16	Hendry, W., Pte., 3277	*13.11.16
Gillespie, J., Pte., S/40709	†21.7.18	Herd, G. L., L/Cpl., 290302	*29.7.18
Gillies, D., Pte., 1227	‡23.7.15	Herd, J., L/Cpl., 265350	*21.3.18
Gilmour, J., L/Cpl., 267744	*31.7.17	Heron, K., Pte., 265937	*30.7.16
Gilroy, J., Pte., 292178	*20.7.18	Higgins, C. H., Pte., 3451	‡ 6.9.15
Glass, G., A/L/Cpl., 1619	*15.7.15	Hill, G. E. C., Pte., 201662	*21.3.18
Glennie, A., Pte., 285118		Hindle, P. U., Cpl., 267936	*23.4.17
(M.M.)	*25.8.18	Hoatson, W., Pte., S/20757	†28.3.18
Goodfellow, J., Pte., 4272	*13.11.16	Hogg, G., Pte., 265531	*28.5.18
Gordon, D., Pte., 265687	*30.7.16	Holleyhead, J., Pte., S/43639	*24.10.18
Gordon, J., Pte., 267881	*16.5.17	Holmes, A., L/Cpl., 267935	†29.4.17
Gordon, R. J., Pte., 5233	*13.11.16	Hood, H., Pte., 267007	† 6.9.17
Gorrie, A., Pte., 267743	*29.6.17	Hood, J., Pte., 2056	*24.6.15
Gow, A., Pte., 291553	*21.3.18	Hopkins, A., Pte., 268366	*16.5.17
Gow, J., Pte., 2926	† 5.12.15	Hopkins, R., L/Cpl., 267467	
Gow, W., Pte., S/24564	*20.7.18	(M.M.)	† 4.8.18
Gowrie, J., Pte., 1091	†29.1.17	Hosie, W., Pte., S/25662	*24.10.18
Grahame, C., Cpl., 241344		Housley, E., Pte., 292637	†26.3.18
(M.M.)	*28.7.18	Houston, J., Pte., 266721	§19.8.18
Graham, J., Pte., 726	† 6.8.15	Houston, W. C., Pte., S/20944	
Graham, W., Pte., 293263	*21.3.18		*10.4.18
Gray, D., Pte., S/8023	§15.10.17	Hovell, D. N., Pte., 265468	§22.7.18
Gray, D., Pte., 202938	*10.4.18	Hozier, J., Pte., 267719	†24.4.17
Gray, J. D., Pte., S/24497	†29.7.18	Hughes, R., Pte., 285030	* 2.7.17
Gray, R., Pte., 291558	*20.7.18	Hughes, T., Pte., 266609	*10.4.18
Greaves, G. W., Pte., S/11860	*21.3.18	Hulme, C. M., Pte., 268399	*31.3.17
Green, G., Pte., 265529	*20.7.18	Hunter, A., Pte., 266602	*23.4.17
Gregory, C. J., Pte., S/24498	†15.5.18	Hutchison, A., L/Cpl., 1179	*13.11.16
Grieve, J., Pte., S/41125	*10.4.18	Hutton, J. S., Sgt., 265075	*31.7.17
Groome, W., Pte., S/24499	*27.7.18		
Grundy, D., Pte., S/12487	*10.4.18	Imrie, A., Pte., 266978	*30.7.16
Guthrie, J., Pte., 4400	‡22.1.17	Imrie, R. G., Pte., 265533	*23.4.17
Guthrie, W., Pte., 267521	*21.3.18	Inkster, A. J., Pte., 265620	*18.4.17
		Innes, P., L/Cpl., 725	† 6.8.15
Haggart, A., Pte., 418	*26.6.15	Ireland, M. T., Pte., S/41135	† 8.5.15
Hall, W.E., A—/Cpl., S/20465	†21.7.18	Irvine, D., Pte., 268032	† 1.4.17
Halley, B. C. T., Sgt., 3284	*13.11.16	Irvine, D. A., Pte., 1895	* 3.4.16
Halliday, J., L/Sgt., 1525	*30.7.16	Irvine, J., Pte., S/41269	†23.8.17
Hallyburton, A. D., Pte., 265849		Irvine, W., Pte., 292281	*21.3.18
	§ 24.7.18		
Hamilton, W., L/Cpl., 203441		Jack, A., Pte., 267602	*19.9.17
	*28.8.18	Jackson, J., Sgt., 265092	*30.7.16
Harbridge, G. V., Pte., 2525	*13.11.16	Jackson, P. H., L/Cpl., S/41308	
Harper, J. R., Piper, 265290	†25.12.17		*29.7.18
Harrison, C., Pte., 265616	† 9.8.17	Jamieson, C. G., L/Cpl., 2099	*13.11.16
Hawker, H. J., Pte., 266564	*10.4.18	Jamieson, G., Pte., 267880	† 3.4.17
Haxton, A. F., Pte., 266253	*30.7.16	Jamieson, J. D., Pte., 1207	† 7.6.15
Hay, J. B., Pte., 285029	*21.3.18	Jarvis, W. D., Pte., S/41883	*10.9.18
Hay, T., Sgt., 1193	*30.7.16	Jennings, W., Pte., S/14627	*10.4.18
Heath, F. W., Pte., S/43638	*24.10.18	Johnston, A., Pte., 268038	* 2.7.17

APPENDIX IV

Johnston, J. A., Pte., 266277 *31.3.17
Johnston, R. B., S/41139 *10.4.18
Johnstone, J., Pte., 202178 *21.3.18
Jolly, G. B., Pte., S/25651 †31.10.18
Jones, G. R., Pte., 267946 † 2.4.17
Joyner, B., Pte., 3667 *30.7.16

Kane, J., Pte., 291132 †24.9.17
Kaye, J., Pte., 1802 *24.7.16
Keay, W., L/Cpl., 1709 *30.7.16
Keddie, A., Pte., 903 * 9.8.15
Keddie, D., Pte., 1747 *13.11.16
Keith, A., Pte., 1162 *14.4.16
Keith, A., Pte., 3353 *27.7.16
Keith, K., Pte., S/3209 *10.10.17
Kellas, R. D., L/Sgt., 267227 ‡10.11.17
Kelly, H. M., Pte., 3261 * 3.4.16
Kemp, A., L/Cpl., 1474 *13.11.16
Kennedy, H., Pte., 2411 ‡31.10.14
Kennedy, J., Pte., S/41818 *24.10.18
Kerr, A., Pte., 1641 *13.11.16
Kerr, C., Cpl., 2113 *18.9.16
Kerr, C., Pte., 268041 * 7.4.17
Kidd, D., Sgt., 240147 *27.7.18
Kidd, D., Pte., 240800 *28.7.18
Kilgour, D. A. C., Pte., 3877 *13.11.16
King, S., Pte., 267750 *17.5.17
King, W. A., Pte., 2905 *30.7.16
Kippen, J. A., Pte., 3507 * 3.7.16
Kirk, D., Pte., 265475 †19.5.17
Kirk, J., Sgt., 8103 †12.4.18
Kirk, M., Pte., S/41143 *10.4.18
Kirk, W., Pte., 290939 *31.7.17
Kirkpatrick, W., Pte., 292322 †24.10.18
Knight, W. A., Pte., S/41144 §24.6.18
Knox, W., L/Cpl., 1836 *24.6.15

Laidlaw, D. M., Pte., S/16531
   *31.7.17
Laing, D., Pte., S/41145 *10.4.18
Laing, J., Pte., 266165 *13.9.18
Laing, T., L/Cpl., 291826 *25.6.18
Lamb, A., Pte., 268051 † 2.4.17
Lamb, W., Pte., 266299 *30.7.16
Landles, J., Pte., 203534 *29.7.18
Lawrence, C., Pte., 20789 *28.7.18
Lawson, T., Pte., 202268 †29.7.18
Layton, J. M., Pte., S/43643 †28.10.18
Leach, F. H., Pte., 266349 *23.4.17
Leaver, G. F., Pte., 266530 * 8.4.17
Lee, J., Pte., S/18679 *31.1.17
Lees, S. L., Pte., 267290 †15.10.17
Leith, J., Pte., 268050 *31.7.17
Leonard, J., Pte., 268048 † 4.5.17
Lessels, G., Pte., S/19585 *10.4.18

Lilley, H. E., Pte., 2688 *30.7.16
Lindsay, G., Pte., S/13391 *10.4.18
Lindsay, G. C., Sgt., 3365 *13.11.16
Lindsay, J., Pte., 1838 *13.11.16
Lockwood, E., Pte., 266191 *30.7.16
Logan, J. M., Pte., 268396 ‡25.6.17
Low, J. B., Pte., 265918 *31.7.17
Luckie, T., Pte., 267646 * 1.4.17
Luke, D., Pte., 201813 *28.7.18
Lyall, W., Pte., 266597 *18.4.17

Macdonald, T., Pte., 266440 *21.3.18
Macfarlane, W. R., Pte., 3943 †18.8.16
Mackay, K. W., Pte., S/41892 *24.10.18
Mackay, J., Pte., 266060 *31.7.16
Mackenzie, R. K., L/Cpl., S/11940
   † 2.7.17
Mackie, J., Pte., 265636 †28.5.18
Mackie, R., L/Cpl., S/17818 *21.3.18
Mackintosh, A., Pte., S/41307 *10.4.18
MacLachlan, G., Pte., 2796 * 4.9.15
Maclaren, I., Cpl., 1961 *13.11.16
Macpherson, A., Pte., 268357 *23.4.17
Macpherson, R., Pte., 2022 † 4.3.16
Macquhae, W., Pte., 266441 † 6.4.17
McAdam, H., Pte., 1932 *13.11.16
McAinsh, J., Pte., 201580 *21.3.18
McAlpine, A., L/Cpl., 265083 *21.3.18
McAra, A., Pte., 24567 †21.7.18
McAra, J., Pte., 3466 ‡ 8.8.16
McArthur, D. M., Sgt., 265385
   †28.5.18
McBay, J., Pte., S/40724 *16.9.17
McBean, J., Pte., 265859 *20.7.18
McBride, T., Pte., 266829 †31.3.17
McBride, W., A/Cpl., 268430
   (East Africa) §20.4.18
McCafferty, J., Pte., 266934 *31.7.17
McCallum, D., Pte., 2904 *13.11.16
McCallum, P., L/Sgt., 268092
   †11.4.18
McClumpha, C. A., Pte., S/43717
   *24.10.18
McClymont, S., Pte., 1309 *26.6.15
McColl, D., L/Cpl., 265034 * 2.7.17
McCormick, J., Pte., 351270 * 8.9.18
McCready, R., L/Cpl., S/41154
   *10.4.18
McCready, T., Pte., S/41155 *10.4.18
McCulloch, D. C., Pte., 351158
   *28.7.18
McCulloch, T., Pte., 3992 *30.7.16
McDavid, J. R., Pte., S/41156 †12.4.18
McDonald, E., Pte., S/24568 †24.10.18
McDonald, J., Pte., S/11519 *21.3.18

223

THE SIXTH BATTALION THE BLACK WATCH

McDonald, J., Pte., 267896 †19.4.17
McDonald, J., Pte., 285031 * 2.7.17
McDonald, N., Pte., 1049 *13.6.15
McDonald, T., L/Cpl., 265142 *23.4.17
McEwan, D., Pte., 285032 *31.7.17
McEwan, J., L/Sgt., 406 † 5.6.15
McEwen, T., Pte., S/25521 *26.10.18
McFarlane, J., Pte., 269017 †14.9.18
McFarlane, P., L/Cpl., 266163 *20.11.17
McFarlane, J., Pte., 3349 † 9.9.16
McFaul, J., Pte., 3823 *25.7.16
McGibbon, J., Pte., 266612 *23.4.17
McGlashan, A., Pte., 266290 †20.5.18
McGregor, A., Pte., 2385 *26.6.15
McGregor, A., Pte., 5210 *13.11.16
McGregor, D., Pte., 3278 *30.7.16
McGregor, D., Cpl., 2801 *13.11.16
McGregor, G., L/Cpl., S/11403 *21.3.18
McGregor, J., Pte., 2186 (D.C.M.) *21.3.18
McGregor, J., Pte., 2196 *30.7.16
McGregor, P., Pte., 3845 * 3.4.16
McGregor, W., Pte., 1310 ‡ 1.8.15
McHugh, T., Pte., 260802 ‡29.4.17
McInnes, D., Pte., 268291 *23.4.17
McIntosh, A., L/Cpl., 265262 *30.7.16
McIntosh, F., Pte., 266513 *23.4.17
McIntosh, L., Pte., 3922 † 8.8.16
McIntyre, C., Pte., 3979 *30.7.16
McIntyre, J., Cpl., 1104 † 4.8.16
McIntyre, J., Pte., 1685 *30.7.16
McIntyre, J., Pte., 1275 *13.11.16
McKay, J., L/Cpl., 265462 *20.7.18
McKay, J., L/Cpl., S/16759 *20.7.18
McKay, J., Pte., 202301 *20.7.18
McKay, W. T., Pte., S/16864 *10.4.18
McKean, R. A., Pte., S/24645 *30.7.16
McKendrick, A., Pte., 203043 *31.7.17
McKendrick, A., Pte., 266783 * 7.4.17
McKenzie, A., Pte., 3221 †11.9.16
McKenzie, C., Pte., 1518 †31.8.16
McKenzie, J., Pte., 265370 *28.5.18
McKenzie, J. S., Pte., 268077 * 2.7.17
McKillop, P., Pte., 3429 *29.6.16
McKinlay, J., Pte., 265668 *21.3.18
McLachlan, J., Pte., 2208 * 3.8.15
McLachlan, R., Pte., S/5232 *28.7.18
McLaren, C., Pte., 265400 † 7.4.18
McLaren, G. D., Pte., 265201 *30.7.16
McLaren, J., Pte., 265297 *20.7.18
McLaren, J., Pte., 266051 *23.4.17
McLaren, J., Pte., 266868 †27.4.17

McLaren, J., Pte., 265997 *23.4.17
McLaren, J. W., Pte., 265341 *23.4.17
McLaurin, D., Pte., 4418 † 5.9.16
McLean, J. S., Pte., 266217 *30.7.16
McLean, V., Pte., 1307 *26.6.15
McLeish, D., Pte., 266218 *29.7.18
McLeish, R., L/Sgt., 202451 (D.C.M.) *26.5.18
McLellan, A., Pte., 4126 ‡ 7.1.16
McLennan, D. F., Pte., S/41292 *20.7.18
McLennan, J., Pte., 266906 * 7.4.17
McLeod, J., Pte., S/24646 *29.7.18
McLeod, J. A., Pte., 268090 *31.7.17
McLeod, L., Pte., 1659 † 1.12.15
McMahon, W., Pte., S/40576 *10.4.18
McMillan, A., Pte., S/5883 *21.3.18
McMullen, E. N., Pte., 2061 * 3.6.15
McNab, G. M., Pte., 1259 *28.6.15
McNab, J., L/Cpl., 1155 *13.11.16
McNaughton, D., Pte., 1973 *30.7.16
McNaughton, P. K., Pte., 2032 * 1.6.15
McNeill, A. S., Pte., S/5904 *20.7.18
McNeill, P., Pte., 266566 *24.5.17
McNeill, P., Pte., 267179 *20.11.17
McPhail, D. S., Pte., 4798 *30.7.16
McPherson, A., Pte., 1695 ‡18.9.16
McPherson, A., Pte., 267699 *27.7.17
McPherson, A., Pte., 1420 *26.6.15
McPherson, A., Pte., 266450 * 7.11.18
McPherson, D., Pte., 266653 *23.4.17
McPherson, R., L/Cpl., 266090 *21.3.18
McPherson, W., Pte., S/40499 *10.10.17
McPherson, W., Pte., 268080 * 1.4.17
McQuattie, W. H., L/Cpl., 266699 *24.3.18
McQuillan, A., Pte., 268100 *21.3.18
McRae, T., L/Cpl., 265786 †28.5.18
McTavish, J., Pte., 1835 †24.6.15
McVinnie, W. J., Pte., 266846 † 6.4.17
McVitie, M., Pte., 291643 *21.3.18
McWhinnie, J., Pte., 2699 ‡ 2.2.15
McWilliam, J., Pte., 268081 *21.3.18
Makemson, F., Pte., 2812 *27.7.16
Malcolm, A., L/Cpl., 265402 *31.7.17
Malcolm, W., L/Cpl., S/18136 *28.7.18
Maley, J., Sgt., 266294 † 1.7.17
Maley, T., Pte., 1602 *14.6.16
Mann, G., Pte., 268155 * 2.7.17

APPENDIX IV

Manning, M., Pte., 1370	†13.8.15	Mitchell, R. McK., C.S.M., 265005	
Marr, W., Pte., 267011	*30.7.16	(D.C.M.)	*20.1.18
Marshall, D., Pte., 267378	*21.3.18	Mitchell, W., Pte., 265386	*30.7.16
Marshall, G., Pte., 267711	†16.9.17	Moir, A., Pte., S/41346	*10.4.18
Marshall, P., Pte., 3509	*30.7.16	Moir, J., Pte., 1679	†29.5.15
Martin, D. H., Sgt., 3463	*13.11.16	Moncrieff, P., Pte., 5241	¶21.11.16
Martin, J., Pte., 3912	§15.5.16	Moncrieff, T., Pte., 78	‡ 1.12.15
Martin, W. J., Pte., 2290	‡17.8.15	Montague, C., Pte., 267915	*31.7.17
Mason, W., Pte., 1471	*13.6.15	Montgomery, L., Pte., 4117	‡26.12.15
Massie, L., Pte., 6244	†14.11.16	Moran, J., Pte., 1383	†14.4.16
Matley, P., Pte., S/41915	*24.10.18	Morris, J., Pte., 268227	*31.7.17
Matthew, W., L/Cpl., 241259	†20.7.18	Morrison, C.M., Pte., 267827	*31.3.17
Matthew, W. D., Pte., 315430		Motherwell, J., Sgt., 266141	†31.7.17
	† 9.8.18	Mould, T. S., Pte., 291004	*21.3.18
Maxwell, J., Pte., 267755	*23.4.17	Mouat, J. R., Pte., 288095	*21.8.18
Maxwell, W. J. S., Pte., 201903		Moxon, A., Pte., 266359	*30.7.16
	‡24.11.17	Muir, J., Pte., 267840	*29.3.17
May, W., Pte., 3060	* 8.9.16	Muir, W., Pte., 268371	*24.5.17
Meiklejohn, H. A., Pte., 267607		Murcar, A., Pte., 268064	*25.3.17
	*21.3.18	Murie, J., Pte., 266455	*30.7.16
Mellis, W., Cpl., 265357	*30.7.16	Murphy, J., Pte., 268139	
Melough, J., Pte., 2596	*30.11.15	(M.M.)	*31.7.17
Melville, A., Pte., 4408	*13.11.16	Murray, A., Pte., 268352	*23.4.17
Melville, G., Cpl., 1633	*30.7.16	Myles, A., Pte., 201376	†25.3.18
Menzies, J., Pte., 266910	*20.7.18		
Menzies, J., L/Cpl., 2062	*30.7.16	Napier, R., Pte., 291993	*31.7.17
Menzies, J., Pte., 3289	†31.3.16	Neill, G. B., Sgt., 290024	*21.3.18
Menzies, W., Pte., 201577	*20.7.18	Neilson, A., L/Cpl., 265742	‡ 7.10.18
Merser, R. R., Pte., S/41640	*20.7.18	Nisbet, J. B., Pte., 1236	†16.7.15
Michie, H. R., Cpl., 265534	*30.7.16	Newel, W., L/Cpl., 1765	*10.7.15
Michie, J. R., Pte., 3972	†10.10.16	Newsome, D., Pte., 200144	*18.10.18
Micklethwaite, L., Pte., 266324		Nicholson, H. D., Cpl., 266276	
	*30.7.16		*23.4.17
Middleton, A. G., Pte., 268060		Nicholson, W., Pte., 1727	§12.8.15
	*21.3.18	Nicol, R., Pte., 265259	*11.4.18
Millar, A., Pte., 267627	*21.3.18	Nicoll, P., L/Cpl., S/24594	*24.10.18
Millar, A., L/Cpl., 350442	†21.7.18	Nicolson, N., Cpl., 265321	*21.3.18
Miller, D., Pte., 268311	† 7.8.17	Niven, G., Pte., 267883	* 2.7.17
Miller, G., Pte., 266486	†22.7.18	Nixon, A., Pte., S/43404	*10.4.18
Miller, H., Pte., 3369	*30.7.16	Noble, D., Sgt., 265556	§ 6.7.18
Miller, H., Pte., S/24044	†21.7.18	Norval, T., Pte., 267429	*21.3.18
Milne, A., Pte., S/43087	*21.3.18		
Milne, A., Pte., 265571	*21.3.18	O'Brien, J., Pte., 265361	*21.3.18
Milne, A., Pte., S/9381	*21.3.18	O'Kane, R., Pte., 266933	† 8.4.18
Milne, C., Pte., 268222	*21.8.18	Ogle, W. R., L/Cpl., 2105	*30.7.16
Milne, D., Pte., 268071	*29.3.17	Oliver, C., Pte., 2744	†24.8.16
Milne, J., Pte., 200422	*20.7.18	Orr, W., Pte., 268233	*23.4.17
Milne, R., Pte., 5182	* 3.11.16	Ower, J. L., Sgt., 265515	*31.7.17
Mitchell, D. O., L/Cpl., 1277	*27.6.15		
Mitchell, H., Pte., 268067	†17.9.17	Page, D., Pte., 290638	† 1.8.17
Mitchell, J., A/Sgt., S/41056	*20.7.18	Paisley, D. G., Pte., 265817	* 1.4.17
Mitchell, J. R., L/Cpl., S/24665		Pake, A., Pte., 202853	*20.7.18
	*20.7.18	Panton, J., Pte., 266167	* 1.4.17
Mitchell, P., Sgt., 265498		Parker, T., Pte., 266599	*23.4.17
(M.M.)	*20.11.17	Parkinson, J., L/Cpl., 1990	*22.10.16

Parsons, J., Pte., 267768	*19.9.17	Robertson, G., Pte., 2518	† 2.6.15
Paterson, H., Pte., 1657	‡25.11.14	Robertson, J., L/Cpl., 267145	*21.3.18
Paterson, R., Pte., S/41310	*20.7.18	Robertson, J. C., Pte., 268008	*31.7.17
Paterson, R., Pte., 5671	*13.11.16	Robertson, J., L/Cpl., 350545	*20.7.18
Paterson, T., Sgt., 3296	*13.11.16	Robertson, J. J., Pte., S/11451	
Paton, J., Pte., S/13574	§10.4.18		†21.11.17
Patterson, A., Pte., 267767	*31.7.17	Robertson, N., Pte., 267266	*27.9.17
Patterson, J., Pte., 350428	*20.7.18	Robertson, W., Sgt., 1422	*30.7.16
Pattison, J., Pte., S/43649	†24.9.18	Robertson, W., Pte., 2067	*13.11.16
Pearson, C., Pte., 1215	* 4.9.15	Robertson, W., Pte., 266103	*28.5.18
Penney, A., L/Cpl., 266240	‡ 2.5.17	Robertson, W. W., Pte., S/41274	
Perks, H., Pte., 1815	*30.7.16		†20.8.18
Peters, J., Pte., 266787	* 2.7.17	Rodgers, P., Pte., 240659	* 2.7.17
Petrie, D., Pte., 265954	* 2.7.17	Rodgie, W., Pte., 265893	*13.11.16
Petrie, R., Pte., 268239	*31.7.17	Rogan, H. J., Pte., 2609	*30.7.16
Petty, C. G., Pte., 4093	†17.9.16	Ronaldson, J., L/Cpl., 292381	*20.7.18
✗ Philp, D., Pte., S/16346	*10.4.18	Rose, A. H., Cpl., 266250	†21.10.17
Philip, A., Pte., 265740	*21.3.18	Ross, A., Pte., 268404	§28.7.18
Phillip, W., Pte., S/25668	*26.10.18	Ross, D., Pte., 266940	* 1.7.17
Pickering, E. E., Pte., 2606	*25.7.16	Ross, D., Pte., 1548	* 7.8.15
Pilkington, I. McN., Pte., 2790		Ross, D., Pte., 267923	*20.7.18
	‡ 4.3.16	Ross, E., Pte., 265959	*31.7.17
Porter, C. W., Pte., 288113	*26.10.18	Ross, G., Pte., 2010	*24.6.15
Porter, J., Pte., 6216	§ 8.12.16	Ross, G., Pte., 310012	*20.7.18
Potter, W., Pte., 6211	*13.11.16	Ross, G. W., Pte., S/41659	*29.7.18
Potts, J., Pte., 267765	*16.9.17	Ross, H., Pte., 265199	*30.7.16
Pyott, J., Cpl., 268322	*23.4.17	Ross, J., Pte., S/43076	*21.3.18
		Ross, J., L/Cpl., 1466	*23.6.16
Rankin, F. C., Pte., S/41954	*26.10.18	Ross, T., Pte., 203022	† 1.8.17
Rattray, T. L. L., Pte., 266763	*26.10.18	Roy, R., A/L/Cpl., 290128	*21.3.18
Reader, W., Pte., 3599	*13.11.16	Russell, A., Pte., 266635	†28.4.17
Reekie, D. D., Pte., 3583	*30.7.16	Ryder, M., Pte., 1394	*30.7.16
Reekie, T., Pte., 266863	*31.7.17		
Reeves, R., Pte., S/43691	*24.10.18	Sampson, F., Pte., 266426	*28.7.18
Reid, A., Pte., 265155	*31.7.17	Saunders, J., Pte., 5689	*13.11.16
Reid, A., L/Cpl., 265176	*30.7.16	Sawyer, H., Pte., 266358	*30.7.16
Reid, J. W., Pte., 267772	*18.5.17	Scobie, J., Pte., 1449	*13.11.16
Reid, W. B., Pte., 267701	§ 7.5.18	Scobie, J., Pte., 2962	* 3.11.16
Reilly, G., L/Cpl., 2023	*14.6.16	Scobie, W. D., Pte., 266188	*31.7.17
Richardson, A., Pte., 265314	*21.3.18	Scott, A., Pte., 265611	*28.5.18
Richardson, J., Pte., 1813	*13.11.16	Scott, A., L/Cpl., 2016	†31.7.16
Richardson, T. A., Pte., 1253	*13.11.16	Scott, D., Sgt., 265108	*16.9.17
Richardson, W., Pte., 3444	§ 8.9.16	Scott, J., Pte., 266973	* 2.7.17
Riddock, R., Pte., 3965	*30.7.16	Scott, R., Pte., 266919	†23.4.17
Riley, E., Pte., S/40901	*21.3.18	Scott, W. G., Pte., S/24558	†29.8.19
Ritchie, N., Pte., 2745	*13.11.16	Seavers, T., Pte., 268252	*31.7.17
Ritchie, W., Pte., 4266	*13.11.16	Sharp, C., Pte., S/5264	*27.10.18
Robb, J., Pte., S/10462	*20.7.18	Sharpe, R., Pte., S/41359	*28.7.18
Roberts, W. A., Pte., S/24649	*20.7.18	Sharpe, T., Pte., S/41797	†11.9.18
Robertson, A., L/Cpl., 1894	* 4.6.16	Shaw, N., Pte., 268259	* 1.4.17
Robertson, A., Pte., S/12633	*20.7.18	Shaw, R., Pte., S/42175	*27.10.18
Robertson, C., Pte., 268244	*23.4.17	Shearer, A., Pte., 268262	*23.4.17
Robertson, D., Pte., 4281	‡22.3.16	Shepherd, D. D., Pte., 266224	
Robertson, D., Pte., 266741	†26.4.17		†28.10.17
Robertson, F., Cpl., 266248	*21.3.18	Sherman, A. C., Pte., S/41349	*10.4.18

APPENDIX IV

Sherriff, J., Pte., 268295 *17.5.17
Sim, J., Pte., 26693 *21.3.18
Simon, A., Pte., 5184 *13.11.16
Simpson, A., A/Sgt., 265858
    (M.M.) *10.4.18
Simpson, J., Pte., 3837 *25.7.16
Simpson, R. M., Pte., 268251 * 1.4.17
Simpson, W., L/Cpl., 268258
    (M.M.) *24.10.18
Sinclair, A., Pte., 265972 * 8.9.16
Sinclair, E. I., Pte., 265674 * 1.4.17
Sinclair, E., Pte., 266225 *30.7.16
Sinclair, M. D., Pte., S/41856 *25.8.18
Skene, R., Pte., S/25755 *24.10.18
Skilling, J., Pte., 267622 *21.3.18
Slowey, J., Pte., S/21724 *20.7.18
Smart, J., Pte., 1183 *30.11.15
Smith, A., Pte., 266691 *23.4.17
Smith, A., Pte., 266957 *21.3.18
Smith, J., Pte., 5152 *13.11.16
Smith, J., Pte., 3838 § 4.8.16
Smith, J., Pte., 285036 *29.7.18
Smith, J. McG., Pte., 1940 *13.11.16
Smith, R., Pte., S/25669 *26.10.18
Smith, T., L/Cpl., 1164 †17.11.16
Smith, W., Pte., 266577 †18.4.17
Smith, W., Sgt., 3168 †14.11.16
Smyth, C., Cpl., 265107 *23.4.17
Somerville, W., Pte., 267210 *31.7.17
Speed, J. B., Sgt., 290501 *21.3.18
Speed, J., Pte., 3338 †30.7.16
Speedy, J. W., Pte., 266654 *19.5.17
Spiers, W., Pte., 1916 *13.11.16
Steel, J., Pte., S/42038 * 4.8.16
Steel, J., Pte., 268379 *15.10.17
Steele, A., A/Sgt., 290297 *10.4.18
Steele, J., Cpl., 510 †29.11.15
Stevenson, A., Pte., S/18733 *28.5.18
Stevenson, D., Pte., 1840 *30.7.16
Stewart, A., L/Cpl., 3268 *31.8.16
Stewart, A., Pte., 266189 *10.4.18
Stewart, A., Pte., 266323 †30.7.16
Stewart, A., Cpl., 265423
    (M.M.) *21.3.18
Stewart, A. K., Pte., 267702 †21.8.18
Stewart, C., Pte., 265559 *30.7.16
Stewart, D., Pte., 4137 §26.1.17
Stewart, D., Pte., S/24621 *11.5.18
Stewart, D., L/Cpl., 266505 †11.8.18
Stewart, D., Pte., 266102 †23.4.17
Stewart, F., Dmr., 1346 *30.7.16
Stewart, J., Pte., 265274
    (M.M.) §15.7.18
Stewart, J., Pte., 5764 *30.11.16
Stewart, J., Pte., S/18286 *20.7.18

Stewart, J., Pte., 266768 §25.8.18
Stewart, M., L/Cpl., 266679 *21.3.18
Stewart, R. A., L/Cpl., 266556
    *31.7.17
Stewart, R. T., Pte., S/41811 *17.10.18
Stewart, W., Pte., 265502 *30.7.16
Stott, W., Pte., S/40889 *10.4.18
Struthers, A. R., Pte., 267848 *21.3.18
Sturrock, A., Pte., 265577 †29.4.17
Sturrock, A. J., Pte., 267873 *23.4.17
Sunderland, S. A., Pte., 268395
    * 1.4.17
Symes, T. E., Pte., 2155 †13.6.15

Tainsh, A., Piper, 265181 *23.12.17
Taylor, B., Pte., S/41354 *10.4.18
Taylor, C. B., Pte., S/41298 *29.7.18
Taylor, D., Pte., 3389 *13.11.16
Taylor, D., Pte., 266872 *31.7.17
Taylor, H., Pte., 3534 ‡28.7.16
Taylor, J. McR., Pte., 266230 *24.10.18
Thom, A. H., L/Cpl., 268381 *23.3.18
Thom, W., Pte., 266064 *23.4.17
Thomson, W., Pte., 1700 *30.11.16
Thomson, A., Pte., 265880 *17.5.17
Thomson, A. McL., Pte., 202335
    * 1.4.18
Thomson, R., Pte., 2109 † 4.8.16
Thomson, R., Pte., 3249 *13.11.16
Thomson, R., Pte., 268388 *23.4.17
Thomson, R. C., Pte., 292367 †16.8.18
Thomson, W., Cpl., 269020 *20.7.18
Thomson, W., Pte., 2628 *13.11.16
Thomson, W., Pte., S/21721 †24.3.18
Tinning, G., Pte., 268378 † 8.4.17
Todd, A. W., Pte., 2653 *13.11.16
Todd, G. M., Pte., 266932 *31.3.17
Totton, H. E., L/Cpl., 2117 †18.2.16
Towner, H., Pte., 265185 †29.7.18
Towns, J., Pte., 267776 *31.7.17
Tracey, J., Sgt., 265647 *21.3.18
Turnbull, C. S., Cpl., 1667 *30.7.16
Turnbull, D. McL., L/Cpl., 266262
    *31.7.17
Turnbull, W., Pte., 202177 *21.3.18
Turpie, J., Pte., 3558 *30.7.16

Urquhart, A., Pte., 200379 *28.7.18
Urquhart, J., Pte., S/5801 *20.7.18
Urquhart, W. Y., Pte., 3840 † 7.12.16

Valentine, J., Pte., 268149 *13.11.16
Vallance, G. L., Pte., S/41942
    †22.8.18

THE SIXTH BATTALION THE BLACK WATCH

Walker, D. C., Cpl., 1898	‡26.11.16	Whyte, J., Pte., 266278	*31.7.17
Walker, H., Cpl., 265225	† 9.8.17	Whyte, J., Pte., 266678	*23.4.17
Walker, J., Pte., 265164	*21.3.18	Whyte, W. McI., Pte., 266271	
Walker, J., Pte., 267947	*21.3.18		*30.7.16
Walker, R. T., Pte., 266066	*21.3.18	Wicks, W., Pte., S/43710	*24.10.18
Walker, W., Cpl., 265671	*20.11.17	Wilkie, A. A., Pte., S/41294	†29.7.18
Wallace, D. McH., Pte., 4315	*13.11.16	Wilkie, W., Pte., 3630	*30.7.16
Wallace, J., L/Cpl., 1751	*30.7.16	Williamson, F., Pte., 267136	*28.5.18
Wallace, J., Pte., 5251	*22.10.16	Williamson, J., L/Cpl., 265942	
Wallace, J., A/Sgt., S/8821	*20.7.18		*21.3.18
Wallace, J., C.S.M., 265460		Willis, J., L/Cpl., 2551	*10.7.15
(M.M.)	*31.7.17	Wilson, A., Pte., 291703	‡18.4.18
Wallace, P., Sgt., 265471	*20.11.17	Wilson, C. D., Pte., S/25557	*24.10.18
Wallace, R., Pte., 3537	*16.6.16	Wilson, D., Pte., 266974	*23.4.17
Warhurst, H., Pte., 2144	* 9.8.15	Wilson, E., Pte., 2614	†22.10.16
Watmough, E., Pte., 268275	*23.4.17	Wilson, J., Pte., 267856	*18.4.17
Watson, K., Pte., 268282	*18.4.17	Wilson, J., Pte., 1791	*30.7.16
Watson, R., Pte., S/41914	§30.9.18	Wilson, J. G., L/Cpl., 350806	§25.9.18
Watson, W. R., Pte., 3917	†30.7.16	Wilson, J., Pte., 268272	* 1.4.17
Watson, W., Pte., 268279		Wilson, P. M., Pte., 267778	*23.4.17
(M.M.)	† 8.8.17	Wilson, T., Pte., 268276	* 1.4.17
Watt, A., Pte., S/5926	†25.3.18	Wood, C. A., Pte., 4789	*13.11.16
Watt, W., Pte., 268277	* 2.7.17	Wood, D., Pte., 2985	*30.7.16
Watters, D., Sgt., 266543		Wood, P., Pte., 266518	†22.4.17
(D.C.M.)	*27.8.18	Woolliscroft, J. F., Pte., S/40902	
Webster, E., Pte., 266340	*28.5.18		*10.4.18
Webster, P., Pte., S/40616	*16.9.17	Wright, A. E., Pte., S/43728	‡22.1.19
Webster, W., Pte., 265282	*30.7.16	Wright, D., Pte., S/18769	† 8.8.17
Weir, P., Pte., 267212	* 1.4.17	Wright, H., Pte., 267682	§ 8.9.17
Wells, G., Pte., S/20660	*20.7.18	Wylie, D., L/Cpl., 240863	*20.7.18
Wells, R., Pte., 1195	*30.7.16		
Welsh, P., Pte., 4415	*13.11.16	Yardley, T. S., Pte., 267723	† 1.8.17
Whalan, J., Pte., 291552	*20.7.18	Young, D., Pte., 266147	§31.10.18
White, D., Pte., 266697	* 1.4.17	Young, D., Pte., 3539	*30.7.16
White, J., Pte., 269002	*20.7.18	Young, J., Pte., 202026	*10.4.18
White, R., Pte., 2041	†28.11.16	Young, J., Pte., 350818	*15.10.17
Whitlaw, J. H., Pte., 4358	‡30.7.16	Younger, P., Pte., 3024	‡ 7.4.15
Whyte, D., Pte., 266231	*23.4.17	Yule, R. P., Pte., 266541	*31.7.17

APPENDIX V

HONOURS AND AWARDS

The Sixth Battalion

C.B.
Colonel Sir Robert D. Moncreiffe, Bart., V.D., T.D.

C.M.G.
Colonel Sir Robert D. Moncreiffe, Bart., V.D., T.D.

O.B.E.
Lieut.-Colonel C. E. Colville, V.D., T.D.
Capt. R. M. Moncreiff.
Major G. D. Pullar.

Bar to D.S.O.
Lieut.-Colonel T. Booth, D.S.O.

D.S.O.
Major W. Alexander.
Major L. Gibson.
Major W. Haig.
Lieut.-Colonel F. R. Tarleton.
2nd Lieut. J. McC. Walker.
Capt. W. P. Wrathall, M.C.

Bar to M.C.
Lieut. W. D. McNaughton, M.C.
Lieut. W. R. Tovani, M.C.

M.C.
Lieut. J. N. Adam.
Capt. J. M. Barrow.
Lieut. C. R. Brown.
Lieut. T. Byers.
Lieut. and Adjt. J. R. B. Cable.
Lieut. T. Calvert.
Major W. P. Campbell.
2nd Lieut. J. R. B. Cassie.
2nd Lieut. A. G. Drummond.
Capt. J. A. Durie.
Capt. and Adjt. R. B. Ellis.
2nd Lieut. W. H. Flett.
2nd Lieut. A. Fraser.
Lieut. J. McL. Fulton.
2nd Lieut. J. W. Girvin.
Lieut. A. Good.
Capt. J. M. Guthrie.
2nd Lieut. G. R. D. Hodge.
2nd Lieut. G. R. D. Hope.
Capt. A. Innes.
2nd Lieut. F. H. Johnson.
2nd Lieut. J. R. Leslie.
2nd Lieut. J. Lindsay.
2nd Lieut. J. Lindsay.
Lieut. R. W. Macintyre.
Capt. A. W. D. Martin.
2nd Lieut. J. L. T. McAdam.
Lieut. W. D. McNaughton.
Lieut. W. P. Philip.
2nd Lieut. A. L. Ramsay.
Lieut. H. W. H. Renton.
Capt. and Adjt. J. Rutherford.
2nd Lieut. G. Scott.
Lieut. G. M. Steel.
Capt. J. J. Watt.
Capt. C. Willison.
Lieut. and Q.M. J. C. Wilson.
Capt. W. P. Wrathall.
Lieut. H. M. Wright.

THE SIXTH BATTALION THE BLACK WATCH

D.C.M.

Sgt. H. C. Allen.
Sgt. A. Auchterlonie.
C.S.M. R. Bell.
Pte. E. Black.
Pte. W. Bruce.
Sgt. P. Campbell.
L/Sgt. A. Gardiner.
L/Corpl. J. Jenkins.
Sgt. W. McPherson.
C.S.M. Mitchell.

Sgt. J. Morrison.
L/Corpl. T. Morrison.
Corpl. D. Reid.
L/Corpl. J. F. Robertson.
Sgt. J. Shaw.
Pte. J. H. Shepperd.
Sgt. P. Stewart.
Sgt. D. Watters.
Sgt. A. D. Young.

M.S.M.

R.Q.M.S. Hood.
L/Corpl. F. W. Deane.

Corpl. W. Gibb.
Piper A. Macdonald.

Bar to M.M.

Pte. R. D. Allen.
Corpl. F. Anderson.
Pte. Conachie.
Pte. A. Henderson.
Sgt. G. Howie.
Pte. W. H. Hughson.
Corpl. W. Martin.

Pte. A. W. McNaughton.
Pte. T. McRoberts.
Pte. A. Menzies.
Sgt. J. Mitchell.
Pte. J. G. Sutherland.
L/Corpl. W. Wallace.

M.M.

L/Sgt. J. Alexander.
Pte. R. D. Allen.
Corpl. R. Anderson.
Corpl. W. R. Anderson.
Pte. J. Armstrong.
Pte. J. Barclay.
Pte. W. Barrett.
C.S.M. R. Bell, D.C.M.
Pte. J. Bissett.
Pte. W. J. Blower.
L/Corpl. D. Brown.
L/Corpl. J. T. Brown.
Pte. T. Buist.
Pte. A. Cameron.
Pte. J. Cameron.
Pte. D. Campbell.
L/Corpl. J. Campbell.
Pte. J. Carter.
Pte. A. Clarke.
Pte. Connachie.

Pte. P. Conway.
Sgt. A. Cruickshanks.
Sgt. J. Cunningham.
Sgt. H. Dann.
Pte. C. Devlin.
L/Corpl. G. S. Dillon.
Pte. P. J. Don.
L/Corpl. J. S. Drew.
Sgt. C. H. Drummond.
Sgt. P. Drysdale.
Sgt. W. Duncan.
Pte. R. Dye.
L/Corpl. H. Edgar.
Pte. B. Farrow.
Pte. A. Ferguson.
Pte. E. Flood.
Pte. A. Forbes.
L/Corpl. W. Frew.
Pte. N. Fyfe.
Pte. R. Gillanders.

APPENDIX V

M.M. (*contd.*)

Sgt. W. Gilmour.
Sgt. P. Gordon.
Corpl. T. M. Gossman.
Corpl. J. Graham.
Pte. Grant.
Pte. A. Grieve.
Pte. J. Hall.
Pte. J. Handley.
Dmr. R. Hannan.
Pte. A. Haxton.
Pte. A. Henderson.
Pte. J. Hepburn.
L/Corpl. R. Hopkins.
Sgt. G. Howie.
Pte. W. M. Hughson.
Pte. D. Hunter.
Pte. J. Hunter.
Sgt. W. M. Johnstone.
Sgt. Keir.
Sgt. R. King.
Pte. T. Leatham.
Corpl. W. Leish.
Pte. F. Letts.
Corpl. A. Leuchers.
Sgt. A. D. Lindsay.
L/Corpl. W. Lindsay.
Pte. S. Livingstone.
Pte. W. Lochtie.
Sgt. J. T. Loftus.
Pte. W. Long.
Pte. J. B. Lothian.
Pte. D. C. Macrae.
Corpl. W. Martin.
Pte. J. McCarroll.
Sgt. W. McCowan.
L/Corpl. G. McCullough.
Pte. J. McDougall.
Pte. J. McFarlane.
Corpl. D. McGilvary.
Pte. D. McGregor.
Pte. R. McGregor.
Pte. G. T. McGregor.
Pte. J. McInroy.
L/Corpl. R. McKelvey.
Sgt. T. McLaggan.
L/Corpl. W. R. McLaran.
Pte. J. McLaren.
L/Corpl. J. McLean.

Corpl. J. McLean.
Pte. N. McLeod.
L/Corpl. T. McMonagle.
Pte. A. W. McNaughton.
L/Corpl. W. R. McNaughten.
Pte. J. McNee.
Pte. McNee.
Pte. J. McNeill.
L/Corpl. A. McPhail.
Pte. J. McReadie.
Pte. T. McRoberts.
L/Corpl. J. Menzies.
Pte. A. Menzies.
Corpl. R. Miller.
Sgt. J. Milne.
Sgt. J. Mitchell.
Pte. P. Mitchell.
Pte. T. Moffat.
Pte. J. A. Morton.
Corpl. A. Munn.
Pte. R. Murdoch.
Pte. J. Murphy.
Pte. Myles.
Pte. F. Nairn.
Corpl. T. Nicholson.
Pte. E. O'Neill.
Pte. G. Packman.
L/Corpl. W. J. Paterson.
Pte. H. Peddie.
Corpl. P. Peddie.
Corpl. W. Penny.
Pte. A. Prentice.
Pte. D. Prophet.
Pte. A. Punton.
L/Corpl. J. Rae.
Pte. Ramsay.
L/Corpl. W. Reid.
Corpl. J. L. Robertson.
Corpl. A. Robertson.
Pte. T. Robertson.
Pte. J. M. Robertson.
Pte. D. Ronaldson.
R.S.M., D. Ross.
Pte. W. Sandison.
Corpl. E. Simonette.
Pte. M. G. Simpson.
Corpl. W. Simpson.
Corpl. A. Simpson.

THE SIXTH BATTALION THE BLACK WATCH

M.M. (contd.)

L/Corpl. J. Sinclair.
C.Q.S.M. C. Sinclair.
L/Corpl. J. Smeaton.
Corpl. Smeaton.
Pte. H. J. Smith.
Sgt. N. Steele.
L/Corpl. A. C. Stewart.
Corpl. J. Stewart.
Pte. D. Stewart.
Pte. D. Stewart.
Sgt. J. Stewart.
Pte. J. Stobe.
L/Corpl. H. Stobie.
Pte. A. N. Storrar.
Pte. T. E. Strongman.
Pte. J. G. Sutherland.
Corpl. J. Symons.
Corpl. A. Thom.

Pte. Thomson.
Pte. J. Todd.
Pte. T. Tolmie.
Pte. R. T. Walker.
Pte. J. Walker.
L/Corpl. W. Wallace.
L/Corpl. D. Watson.
Sgt. A. Watson.
L/Corpl. D. Watson
Pte. W. Watson.
Corpl. A. Wilkie.
Pte. W. Wiseman.
L/Sgt. E. J. Wittar.
Pte. J. Woods.
Pte. J. D. G. Wylie.
Pte. G. M. Young.
Pte. A. Young.
Sgt. J. H. Young.

Mentioned in Despatches

Brig.-General W. Alexander (2)
2nd Lieut. A. Bell.
2nd Lieut. R. Bell.
Brevet Lieut.-Colonel T. M.
  Booth, D.S.O.
Lieut. C. R. Brown.
Lieut. T. Byers.
Lieut. and Adjutant D. Cable.
Lieut. D. B. Calder.
Lieut. W. P. Campbell.
Lieut. T. Clavert.
2nd Lieut. N. F. Dixon.
Capt. J. A. Durie.
Lieut. R. B. Ellis.
Major L. Gibson.
Lieut. Lord Glentanar.
Major W. Haig.
Capt. E. N. Hale.
Lieut.-Colonel A. W. H.
  Hay-Drummond.
2nd Lieut. G. R. P. Hodge.
Capt. A. Innes.

Lieut. R. Jarman.
2nd Lieut. J. R. Leslie.
Capt. C. M. V. MacDowell.
Lieut. W. D. Macnaughton (2).
2nd Lieut. R. McKelvey.
2nd Lieut. Q. McLaren.
Capt. J. McRosty.
Capt. R. G. Menzies.
Col. Sir Robert D. Moncreiffe,
  Bart. (2).
Capt. R. M. Moncrieff.
2nd Lieut. G. D. Paton.
Lieut. H. W. H. Renton.
Lieut. J. Rutherford.
2nd Lieut. G. Scott.
Lieut. D. Watson.
Lieut. J. J. Watt.
Capt. C. Willison.
Lieut. and Q.M. J. C. Wilson (3).
Capt. W. P. Wrathall (4).
Lieut. H. M. Wright.
Major J. Wylie.

Sgt. A. Brown.
Sgt. G. E. Byers.
L/Corpl. G. McCullough.

Sgt. J. Nicoll.
C.Q.M.S., C. Sinclair.
Sgt. A. D. Young.

APPENDIX V

FOREIGN DECORATIONS

Legion of Honour
Brig.-General W. Alexander, D.S.O.
Lieut.-Colonel F. R. Tarleton, D.S.O.

Médaille Militaire
Pte. G. Allan.

Croix de Guerre (Belgian)
Pte. J. Menzies.   Pte. J. C. Wylie.

Croix de Guerre (French)
L/Corpl. F. W. Deane.
2nd Lieut. E. E. Garvie.
L/Corpl. Hughson.
L/Corpl. Menzies.
Sgt. Mitchell.
Capt. E. D. Nicoll.
Lieut. H. W. H. Renton, M.C.
Capt. W. P. Wrathall, D.S.O., M.C.

With Palms
Major L. Gibson, D.S.O.
Lieut.-Colonel F. R. Tarleton, D.S.O.
Capt. C. Willison, M.C.

Gold Star
2nd Lieut. E. E. Garvie.

Silver Star
Capt. E. D. Nicoll.   L/Corpl. W. Hughson.

Bronze Star
L/Corpl. A. Menzies.
Sgt. R. Mitchell.
Lieut. H. W. H. Renton, M.C.

APPENDIX VI

List of Actions and Operations

The Sixth Battalion

1915.   Landed in France. 2nd May.
  Trench warfare. Festubert, Le Touret, Fauquissart, La Boisselle, Authuille and Ovillers. May–December.

1916.   Trench warfare. Maricourt, Maison Blanche, Neuville St. Vaast and Maroeuil. January–July.

BATTLE OF BAZENTIN RIDGE. (High Wood.) 22nd July.

BATTLE OF POZIÈRES RIDGE. (Bazentin le Petit.) 30th–31st July.
  Trench warfare. Houplines, Armentières Sector, Hébuterne and Beaumont Hamel. August–November.

BATTLE OF THE ANCRE (1916). (Beaumont Hamel.) 13th–14th November.
  Trench warfare. Aveluy and Pys. November–December.

1917.   Trench warfare. Pys, Ecurie, Roclincourt and Fampoux. January–April.

FIRST BATTLE OF THE SCARPE. (Ecurie.) 9th April.

SECOND BATTLE OF THE SCARPE. (Roeux.) 23rd–24th April.
  Trench warfare. Roeux, Chemical Works, Ypres and Lancashire Farm. April–July.

BATTLE OF PILCKEM RIDGE. (Steenbeek.) 31st July–1st August.
  Trench warfare. Ypres, Langemarck, Canal Bank and Cherisy. August–November.

BATTLE OF CAMBRAI (1917). (Grand Ravine and Flesquières.) 20th–21st November.
  Trench warfare. Longueval and Louverval. November–December.

1918.   Trench warfare. Louverval and Pronville. January–March.

FIRST BATTLE OF BAPAUME. (Beaumetz, Bancourt.) 21st–25th March.

BATTLE OF THE LYS (BATTLE OF ESTAIRES). (River Lawe, Lestrem.) 9th April.
  Trench warfare. Neuville St. Vaast, Oppy and Gavrelle. April–July.

APPENDIX VI

1918. **BATTLE OF TARDENOIS.** (Bois de Courton.) 26th–31st July.

    Trench warfare. Fampoux. August.

SECOND BATTLE OF ARRAS (1918). BATTLE OF THE SCARPE. 27th–29th August.

    Trench warfare. Greenland Hill, Plouvain and Douchy. September–October.

BATTLE OF THE SELLE. (Thiant, Monchaux.) 17th–25th October.

ADVANCE TO VICTORY. October–11th November.

"THERE CAM A PIPER OOT O' FIFE"
After the drawing by "Snaffles"

THE SEVENTH BATTALION

CHAPTER I

MOBILIZATION, AUGUST, 1914

Early Days at Kinghorn

TEN Volunteer Companies were raised in Fife in 1859, and in the following year were formed into one Battalion and called the 1st Fifeshire Rifles with Headquarters at St. Andrews. In 1881 the Territorial System was adopted, and in 1888 the title of the Battalion was changed to the 6th Volunteer Battalion The Black Watch. During the South African War the Battalion sent thirty-three non-commissioned officers and men to serve with the 2nd Battalion The Black Watch, thus earning for the Battalion the right to carry the honour "South Africa 1901–1902."

In 1908 the Volunteer Battalions were reorganized as the Territorial Force, and the 6th Battalion became the 7th (Territorial Force) Battalion The Black Watch, and was commanded by Sir Ralph Anstruther, of Balcaskie, until 1913. During these years no man did more to strengthen the strong county feeling that had always existed within the Battalion, and also, by his natural soldierly qualities, to increase its military efficiency. It was consequently with great regret that all ranks learned in 1913 of the resignation of Sir Ralph Anstruther and also that of Captain, now Colonel, Skene, of Pitlour, an officer of The Black Watch who had proved a most capable and popular Adjutant. Sir Ralph was succeeded in command by Colonel H. M. Allen, a soldier whose wide experience and strong character were destined to prove of the highest value to the Battalion in the early years of the war.

Such, in rough outline, is the origin of this Battalion, whose history in the Great War is set forth in these pages.

In the general mobilization scheme the 7th Battalion The Black Watch was detailed for Coast Defence; the war stations allotted to it were Kinghorn and Burntisland, these two towns being known as "No. 3 Section Forth Defences." The first intimation of war received by the 7th Battalion was a telegram ordering "Preparatory movement," on the evening of July 31st, 1914. This Preparatory movement consisted in sending a special service section of three officers and 117 other ranks to occupy Kinghorn Fort, which, with the island of Inchkeith, also heavily fortified, commands the entrance to the Firth of Forth. In peace time the garrison was furnished by a small detachment of Royal Garrison Artillery from Leith, but the mobilization scheme provided for this being increased on the outbreak of war to half a company, reinforced by one company of Territorial Garrison Artillery and one company of Territorial Engineers.

THE SEVENTH BATTALION THE BLACK WATCH

The "special service section" of the 7th Battalion The Black Watch was drawn from C company (Kirkcaldy) and B company (Lochgelly), and on receipt of orders this section marched under Captain G. W. McIntosh to Kinghorn, where it arrived on August 2nd.

By a curious coincidence a test mobilization of this special service section had been held earlier in the year. The section was called out and occupied the Fort for two days when, together with the regular artillery, it took part in firing practice and night manœuvres in conjunction with the Fleet. Consequently when the order for general mobilization was received, the special service section had already had some practical experience of its special duties. It is satisfactory to record that when put into operation in August, 1914, the mobilization scheme proved an unqualified success. The scheme provided for every contingency, from the supply of stores and equipment to the timing of railway trains and distribution of rations; so that, within forty-eight hours of receiving orders to move, each company with Headquarters, transport and machine gun sections found itself fully equipped and at its appointed station.

On the date of mobilization the Headquarters of the Battalion was St. Andrews, and the companies were distributed as follows:—

A company	Dunfermline.
B ,,	Lochgelly.
C ,,	Kirkcaldy.
D ,,	Cowdenbeath.
Right half E company	Cupar.
Left half E ,,	Newburgh.
F company	Leven.
Right half G company	St. Andrews.
Left half G ,,	Anstruther.
H company	Leslie.

It will be observed that though the four company system had been in operation for some little time in the Regular Army, the Territorial Infantry still retained the eight company organization. On receipt of orders to mobilize, the special service section drawn from B and C companies was already in occupation of the Fort at Kinghorn, and, by the evening of August 7th, the remainder of the Battalion, on reaching its war station, was distributed as follows:—

D company and one machine gun section	Burntisland.
The remaining companies with Battalion Headquarters, transport and one machine gun section	Kinghorn.

KINGHORN, AUGUST, 1914

Recruiting was extremely brisk. Men flocked from all parts of the county to join their local battalion, with the result that while the marching-out state, on breaking camp at Monzie, showed a total strength of 570, the corresponding state on the morning after arrival at the war station was 902.

With the exception of E and G companies from the eastern part of the county, who moved by rail, all companies proceeded to the war station by march route, and the inhabitants of all the various towns and villages through which they passed turned out to cheer them on their way. The welcome accorded the Battalion at Kinghorn and Burntisland was no less hearty and spontaneous than in other parts of the county.

On first arrival at Kinghorn, Headquarters and five companies were billeted in the Burgh School, the special service section of 117 men remaining in the Fort. A and C companies were lodged at Abden and Grangehill farms, the transport and machine gun sections occupying the disused Glue Works. D company, at Burntisland, found comfortable quarters in the school. Its principal duty was to guard the docks, and throughout its stay the company furnished numerous pickets and sentries in the neighbourhood of the quays, all excellent training for what was to follow.

During the stay at Kinghorn unoccupied buildings were available for the accommodation of the troops, and it was unnecessary to billet on private families. One advantage of this was that companies and platoons were kept together as units, which ensured thorough supervision by officers and non-commissioned officers and encouraged those habits of order, cleanliness and smartness essential in the training of the young soldier. There is little doubt that attention to these matters contributed to the high reputation for discipline which the Battalion enjoyed throughout the war.

In August the General Officer Commanding Scottish Coast Defences visited Kinghorn and announced that an attack in force by the Germans might take place at any moment. Plans for meeting such a contingency had already been prepared, and these were at once put into execution. It was assumed that any attack on the Forth could be dealt with by the Fleet and shore batteries, but it was thought possible that a landing might be effected somewhere on the east coast of Fife, with the object of taking Kinghorn Fort, the defences of Rosyth and the Forth Bridge in rear.

It was with a view, then, to frustrating an assault from the land side that defensive preparations were undertaken. These entailed the construction of a chain of defensive works in the form of a semicircle. This extended from the shore close to the Poorhouse on the east, took in the high ground to the north of the town, and ended on the Burntisland road a quarter of a mile west of the Burgh boundary.

In addition to this outer chain of defences a second line was prepared on the heights above the harbour of Pettycur, and a blockhouse was established on the promontory known as Crying Hill. Several large houses in rear of the fort were commandeered and put into a state of defence, so as to form a Keep in case the first and second lines were carried.

These preparations entailed much hard work and almost continuous digging for thirty-six hours. The nature of the soil, which in parts was composed of solid rock, gave ample scope for the Fife miner to prove his worth. So well did the coal miners of Fife take up the Territorial movement that, as originally constituted, sixty per cent of the men of the 7th Battalion were connected with the mining industry. This proved invaluable in France, when experienced men were urgently required for tunnelling work, and right well did the Fife miners carry out that difficult and dangerous duty.

The garrison at this time, in addition to the 7th, included No. 3 company, Forth Garrison Artillery, and a company of the Lowland Division Engineers. Shortly afterwards it was strengthened by the addition of a second company of the Forth Garrison Artillery and a section of a battery of Royal Field Artillery from Glasgow, and later in November by a battalion of infantry. Lieutenant-Colonel Allen was granted the local rank of Colonel and placed in command of all troops in the area.

The supposed danger of invasion was not entirely removed, nor were the trenches completely evacuated till after the New Year, but by degrees the garrison was reduced and at the end of December consisted only of detached sentry posts. For the first three months after mobilization the line was occupied in force under conditions closely approximating to those of active service. The part of the line between the coast and the Kirkcaldy road being low-lying was easily flooded in wet or snowy weather, and gave a foretaste of the mud which the Battalion first encountered at Festubert in the spring of 1915. By degrees the trenches were improved and various devices introduced to render them habitable, and the Battalion settled down to the ordinary routine of trench duties, the different companies being relieved at suitable intervals.

For convenience of command the line was divided into two sections, the right under Major Robertson, and the left under Major Wallace, with Headquarters at Abden and Grangehill farms. The fact that the men were living under service conditions was not allowed to interfere with training; parades and

TRAINING AT KINGHORN, 1914

instruction of all kinds were carried out with the same regularity as in barracks. The companies occupying the trenches left only sufficient men to furnish the minimum of sentries with their reliefs.

The strength of the Battalion gradually increased, till in the middle of September orders were received to recruit for foreign service. Then there came such a rush of recruits of the finest quality that at the end of a week no more could be taken, as it was impossible to cope with the numbers. There were neither instructors nor quarters available for so many, and by September 20th three fresh companies were formed and the strength of the Battalion was 1582.

Existing accommodation proved wholly inadequate and new quarters had to be found. The disused Candle Works had been occupied on the first alarm. Though at first a mere shell, affording very inadequate protection from the weather, the building was gradually improved, and, with the addition of a new roof and wooden floors, afforded comfortable quarters for a double company. A large three-storied factory in the High Street and a grain store were similarly dealt with, and these buildings provided shelter for nearly half the Battalion. A house was utilized for the accommodation of the regimental sick, and, under the Battalion medical officer, Captain D. E. Dickson, was soon converted into a hospital holding ten beds, a consulting room and a surgery. Two ladies placed their services at Captain Dickson's disposal and their help was of great benefit to the sick. The health of the troops was so good that in spite of the large number on the strength and the rigorous conditions under which they lived, not one man died in the Battalion until after its arrival in France.

With the sudden increase in numbers, great difficulty was experienced in obtaining the necessary clothing and equipment, especially for the new recruits, most of whom joined with only the clothes in which they stood. Owing to the enormous demand from all parts of the country, the Territorial Force Association, which was responsible for the supply of great-coats, was unable to meet the Battalion's requirements. Moreover, the men being in billets, the Ordnance Department could issue only one blanket per man, and the situation grew so serious that the Commanding Officer decided to make an appeal to private generosity for a further supply. Lady Anstruther of Balcaskie, and Mrs. Allen interested themselves in the matter, so that within forty-eight hours the first consignment had been despatched, and in less than a week seven hundred blankets had been distributed amongst the men.

The question of clothing was not so easily remedied, and

the delays seemed endless before each man was provided with even one suit of khaki. When at last, some six months after mobilization, the War Office granted Colonel Allen permission to make his own arrangements for clothing the men, all difficulties vanished and, within six weeks of placing the order, the whole Battalion was for the first time in its history able to parade in the regulation uniform of The Black Watch. Early in May, 1914, the Territorial Association had agreed to adopt the kilt as part of the uniform of the 7th; it was therefore a great satisfaction to all concerned when kilts were at last issued, and the Battalion was correctly dressed.

CHAPTER II

APRIL, 1915

At Kinghorn—With the Highland Division at Bedford

KINGHORN did not escape the rumours which were agitating the country at this time concerning the passing of a Russian force through Great Britain. On the contrary, situated as it was on the main line over which the Russians were supposed to have travelled, the tales were perhaps more insistent here than elsewhere. It was even positively stated that men on leave in Edinburgh had seen them on their way through that city. The "eye-witnesses" were summoned to Orderly Room and questioned, but nothing more definite could be elicited than that one of their number, a cook, had seen from the further side of the platform a train full of men wearing beards and bowler hats.

Meanwhile training was proceeding steadily, although the influx of so many recruits and the want of trained instructors were at first a hindrance to progress. All Regular instructors except two had been withdrawn during the first week of August, 1914. However, many of the senior Territorial non-commissioned officers, though lacking in experience, had been well grounded in the rudiments of soldiering and their zeal was beyond dispute. In addition, the recruits were of magnificent physique and most eager to make themselves proficient.

What perhaps hindered training and organization more than anything else was the long delay in the formation of the 2/7th Battalion. The order to raise a second line Battalion was received early in September and provided for the transfer to the new unit of all officers and other ranks who had not volunteered for foreign service or who, on account of age or physical shortcomings, were not up to the standard required. It was, however, fully six weeks before the transfers actually took place.

Very shortly after mobilization the Adjutant, Captain Baker Carr, was offered a Staff appointment. His successor was Captain David Beveridge, a former Territorial officer of the 7th. He had retired in 1913, but had rejoined on the outbreak of hostilities. Bringing to his new work a practical business training, combined with a sound knowledge of military duties, he proved a most efficient Adjutant, an office which he continued to hold, with a short break of about two months, until promoted in December, 1915.

The country round Kinghorn is admirably adapted for training; route marches were frequent and the high plateau of the golf links provided a good parade ground for Battalion drill and other exercises. Facilities for musketry training were, however,

THE SEVENTH BATTALION THE BLACK WATCH

lacking at Kinghorn; not only were the rifles of an obsolete pattern, but want of opportunities for practice was a further drawback. While the summer lasted, miniature practice was carried out on an extemporized range near the shore, and it was some months before a covered miniature range was constructed. But in spite of all difficulties, however, every man was put through a preliminary course of musketry on an old range near Thornton, and one company at a time went to Barry to complete the trained soldier's course. In January, 1915, the Battalion was organized on the four company system.

As suitable land was available, it was not long before each company had its own football ground, on which many keen matches were played. Concerts and other entertainments were frequently held in a hall which had been generously given by the Church of Scotland Young Men's Guild. One of the Commanding Officer's first acts after arrival at Kinghorn was to place all public-houses out of bounds, but no time was lost in opening a wet canteen. A dry canteen with grocery, tea and coffee bar was also started and added considerably to the Battalion funds.

About the middle of September the Battalion suffered a great loss when the health of the Quartermaster, Captain H. Studley, broke down and necessitated his departure on sick leave, from which he never returned. He had served with the Regiment throughout the Egyptian and South African campaigns, for which he held four medals, and before coming to the 7th had been Quartermaster to both the 1st and 2nd Battalions. Universally popular, his fine character and warmhearted disposition rendered him an outstanding personality at all the summer camps. Although greatly weakened by his severe illness, his dauntless spirit refused to rest while there was still work to be done, and against the advice of his doctor he insisted on returning to duty. At first posted to the 2/7th Battalion, he was later called upon to assist in the raising of the 3/7th, when his wide experience and mastery of detail proved invaluable. He died in February, 1916, at the age of fifty-two. Of no man can it be more truly said than of Harry Studley that he gave his life for his country. His last days were, unfortunately, clouded by the death in action in France of one of his four sons, Lieutenant Logan Studley, East Yorkshire Regiment. It is of interest to record that Captain H. Studley was given the Freedom of Berwick on his return from the South African War.

Another Black Watch soldier, Sergeant-Major Stephen Watson, proved himself to be a most capable successor. Endowed with organizing ability of the highest order, coupled with unbounded energy, Watson soon gained a reputation extending far beyond his own Battalion.

MOVE TO BEDFORD, APRIL 15TH, 1915

As the days wore on and as one Territorial unit after another was sent to France, all ranks began to chafe at the long period of inaction. It was, therefore, with deep relief that orders were received on the 13th of April, 1915, for the Battalion to hold itself in readiness to move at twenty-four hours' notice. By the morning of the 15th all was ready, kits were packed and billets vacated and left ready for the reception of the relieving Battalion, the 2/7th Battalion The Black Watch, which for some months had been in training at Hawick, under command of Colonel the Hon. Thomas Cochrane, now Lord Cochrane of Cults.

Never perhaps in its long history had the little town of Kinghorn presented a more animated appearance than when the Battalion, headed by the pipers of the 2/7th, marched to the station; the houses bright with flags, every window filled and the streets thronged with friends and relatives who had flocked from all parts of Fife to bid their lads farewell. For nearly a mile along the railway crowds had collected and continued cheering till the second train steamed off and was lost in the gathering dusk, while the strains of " Sing us a Song of Bonnie Scotland " floated back to the watchers lining the embankments.

Bedford was reached early the following morning, and the Battalion joined the Gordon Brigade of 1/1st Highland Division, then under the command of Major-General Bannatine-Allason, C.B. The Gordon Brigade was commanded by Brigadier-General Douglas Campbell, and included the 5th and 7th Battalions Gordon Highlanders and the 6th Battalion The Black Watch, the latter, like the 7th, having newly arrived from Scotland. From time to time the Division had been obliged to send one after another of its units to France, so that when its turn came to move as a Division it had to be completed by the addition of a whole Brigade from Lancashire, and by the 6th and 7th Battalions The Black Watch.

Throughout the training, the discipline of the Battalion had been excellent and serious crime unknown. The most common offence was overstaying leave, not very surprising considering that the men were those who, in civil life, were accustomed to take a day's holiday whenever they wished, for the loss of a day's pay only. The fifteen days spent at Bedford was a period of ceaseless activity, for the Battalion had to be equipped with rifles, machine guns, horses, waggons, harness and warlike stores of all kinds. When not engaged in taking over new, or in returning part-worn or obsolete equipment, the time was fully occupied by lectures, inspections and parades of every description.

With the exception of the officers' chargers, all horses had been left behind at Kinghorn, and it took several days to fit the new ones into their proper places. The animals now issued to the Battalion were a mixed lot, some never having been ridden or been in harness before, and the transport personnel did not take kindly to the Argentine, Canadian, and other breeds of animals they received. The mules were especially disliked, for there is a decided prejudice in Scotland against anything resembling a " cuddy," and mules, even more than their humbler relatives, had an evil reputation for obstinacy and vice. Even after the experience of war, when their extreme docility and usefulness were proved to be beyond dispute, this prejudice still remained.

On the 30th of April, Captain A. C. Murray, Seaforth Highlanders, joined the Battalion as Adjutant, and at last, after many false alarms, the eventful day arrived, and on Sunday, the 2nd of May, the Battalion entrained for Folkestone *en route* for France. The transport and heavy baggage moved the day before, crossing from Southampton to Havre. Boulogne was reached before midnight, and the second stage of the "Great Adventure" had begun.

CHAPTER III

MAY TO JUNE, 1915

The First Weeks in France

IMMEDIATELY after disembarkation the Battalion marched to the Rest Camp, and on the following day entrained for Berguette. The railway journey was a new experience for the men. The train consisted of cattle trucks, each bearing the legend in large white letters "Horses 8, Men 40," and into each truck forty astonished "Jocks" were duly packed. From Berguette the Battalion marched six kilometres to La Miquellerie. The billets were of the usual farm type, afterwards so familiar; it was long past midnight before the last platoon was finally stowed away.

Daylight enabled the men to take stock of their surroundings, which proved to be very attractive, and three pleasant days were spent here. The weather was fine and warm, and the men spent most of their time, when not on duty, in the open or writing their letters under the shade of the apple orchards.

On May 6th the Highland Division moved into the Lestrem–Neuve Chapelle area, to serve as a general reserve to the Indian Corps in the attack on the 9th of May, 1915. This was the 7th's first experience of marching with a Division, and the long night journey from Busnes will not easily be forgotten by those who took part in it. Reaching the point of assembly at seven in the evening, it was two o'clock on the following morning before the Battalion saw its billets, although the actual distance covered was not more than ten miles. The operation of billeting in the dark would have occupied much longer than it did but for the arrival of a consignment of "Orilux" lamps sent out by the Committee of the Battalion Comforts' Fund. This fund, organized by the ladies of Fife, under Lady Anstruther, proved of incalculable value to the Battalion throughout the war.

Though still some five miles behind the firing line, the Battalion was now within the "battle zone," and the signs of war, visible on every side, brought home to all ranks the fact that their period of probation was now over.

At 4 a.m. on the 9th of May the whole artillery of the First Army opened fire, and throughout the day, mingled with the roar of the guns, rifle and machine gun fire could be distinctly heard. British and German aeroplanes circled overhead, and many combats were witnessed. From early afternoon the procession of ambulance cars, streaming to the rear, bore testimony to the size of the casualty list; and as evening wore on the eastern horizon became lit up by flashes from hundreds of guns, and by a ceaseless shower of Very lights. In this action the 1st,

THE SEVENTH BATTALION THE BLACK WATCH

2nd and 4th Battalions The Black Watch played a gallant part, and on this day Corporal John Ripley, 1st Battalion The Black Watch, gained his V.C. His military apprenticeship had been served with the 7th, from which, little more than a year before, he had retired with the rank of Colour-Sergeant, leaving a son in the ranks to carry on the family tradition. Though forty-eight years of age, he re-enlisted on the outbreak of war in " Kitchener's Army," and was afterwards sent out with a draft to the 1st Battalion.

On May 11th the Highland Division was renamed the 51st, its Brigades being numbered 152nd, 153rd and 154th. The 7th Battalion The Black Watch, with the 5th and 7th Battalions Gordon Highlanders and the 6th Battalion The Black Watch now formed the 153rd Brigade. The following day the Battalion left Paradis, and returned to its old billets at La Miquellerie, two days later moving with the Brigade to the area Caestre–Flêtre, where it remained till the 17th.

It was here that they first met the " New Armies," represented by a Brigade of the 9th Division, one of the four Scottish Divisions which were afterwards to win immortal fame. This Brigade included the 8th Battalion The Black Watch, and was under the command of Brigadier-General E. G. Grogan, C.B., an old and highly esteemed officer of The Black Watch, well known to many senior members of the 7th. In the ranks of his present Brigade were a large number of Fife men, and many old acquaintanceships were renewed and hearty greetings exchanged.

May 17th again saw the Brigade on the move, and after another long night march Pont Riqueul was reached in the early hours of the 18th. The following afternoon the Commanding Officer, the Second-in-Command and the Company Commanders were sent forward to inspect the trenches, and ordered to report to the Headquarters of the 1st Division at Lacouture. Having been provided with a guide and joined by a similar party from the 6th Battalion The Black Watch, they proceeded to the Headquarters of the 1st Grenadier Guards in the support trench near Richebourg–l'Avoué. Here the trench system was explained and much useful information supplied by the Commanding Officer, Major Jeffreys.

On the 20th the Battalion left Pont Riqueul for billets near Le Touret, and early on the morning of the 21st information was received that the 6th Battalion The Black Watch, already in the line, was in need of support. The 7th was therefore moved up to a position in the open in rear of their trenches, where, lying in extended order, it came under enemy artillery fire. Fortunately there were no casualties.

The attack of the 9th May was renewed on the 15th, when

TRENCH WARFARE, MAY–JUNE, 1915

the 2nd Division captured the enemy's front and support lines, and on the following day the 7th Division, on the right, carried several second lines of trenches. During these operations, now known as the Battle of Festubert, ground was won on a front of four miles to an average depth of six hundred yards, and the task of the 51st Division was to consolidate the newly won position. The difficulties of this operation were increased by the nature of the land. Water was met at a depth of two to three feet, and protection from fire and view had often to be sought by erecting breastworks of earth and sand-bags.

The absence of communication trenches made movement by daylight impossible, and it was exceedingly difficult for officers or men to become thoroughly acquainted with the geography of the line. The sand-bag breastworks in the area afforded little protection against artillery fire, a direct hit bringing down a considerable length of parapet and burying any men sheltering behind it. During the night of May 21st the 7th Battalion relieved the 6th in the Festubert sector. Here the trenches ran through the uncleared battlefield, and the whole area was littered with arms, tools and the unburied bodies of both British and German soldiers. Even a few wounded men were still lying in the open, and the task of the Battalion in clearing the battlefield as well as holding the line was a heavy one.

This tour only lasted until the 26th, but heavy rain throughout the period added to the general discomfort, and companies in the front line, up to their knees in mud and water, were powerless to prevent the breastworks crumbling under the constant downpour. On the night of the 25th the 7th extended its front line to the right, taking over a portion of trench occupied by a Canadian Division. This was carried out by two platoons of D company, but on the following day the Battalion was relieved and went to Locon, where it remained four days.

On June 1st the 153rd relieved a Canadian Brigade in a sector of the line further to the south, the 7th Battalion being in reserve trenches south of Festubert with Headquarters close to Quinque Rue. The next few days were spent in strengthening the line, and at night large work parties were sent up to improve the communication trenches leading to the firing line. During the four days the Battalion was thus occupied, in addition to the ordinary enemy shelling, at least two bombardments of great violence occurred which cost the Battalion two men killed and nine wounded.

On the night of June 4th the 7th moved into the front line at Festubert for two days, during which a successful reconnaisance of No Man's Land was carried out by Captain Donaldson and Lieutenant Barclay, after which, on the 6th, the

THE SEVENTH BATTALION THE BLACK WATCH

Battalion was relieved and moved to Pacaut, where it remained until the 11th.

The next few days were spent in the line at Festubert, and on the 15th the Battalion marched to Le Touret in reserve for an attack which was to be made next day by the 154th Brigade. The objective of this operation was the north-west end of the village of Rue d'Ouvert, which formed a pronounced salient into the British line. At 6 p.m. the attack was launched and penetrated as far as the third German line. Here it was held up by uncut wire and by heavy machine gun fire. Counter-attacks in force on both flanks compelled the leading troops to fall back on the original line with heavy loss and no ground was gained. During that night the troops in the front line were relieved, and replaced by the 8th Battalion King's Liverpool Regiment and by the 7th Battalion The Black Watch.

Early on the 16th orders were received from the IV Corps to renew the attack at 4.45 a.m. These orders were not received by the 7th till less than an hour before the attack was timed to commence. There was no opportunity of explaining the details of the attack, and all that could be done by the Commanding Officer was to issue hasty orders by telephone, confirmed later by runners. The 8th Battalion King's Liverpool Regiment, supported by the 7th Battalion The Black Watch, encountered a heavy fire directly they left their trenches, and were able to make but little progress. The Liverpool Regiment gained some ground which they held throughout the day, but by 3 p.m. they were obliged to fall back to their original line.

Previous to this attack a platoon of C company, under Second Lieutenant Carnegie, had been detailed to maintain communication and to transmit messages from the front line. The men were distributed along the main communication trench at intervals of about twenty yards, but so heavy were the losses from shell fire that in a short time a messenger had to travel nearly four hundred yards before meeting the man next to him. The survivors remained at their posts with great determination, and communication between the front and reserve trenches was never lost. Carnegie had stationed himself half-way down the communication trench near its junction with the support line, and was wounded at this point while attending to a wounded man.

During this fighting the machine gun section in the front line suffered severely; Lieutenant Westwood was killed and 15 out of a total of 25 men were either killed or wounded. About eleven o'clock that night the Battalion was relieved by the 5th Battalion Gordon Highlanders, and moved back to the Reserve line near Lacouture. The losses of the Battalion on this occa-

TRENCH WARFARE, JUNE, 1915

sion were one officer killed and six wounded; 16 other ranks killed, 81 wounded and four missing.

Amongst the acts of gallantry performed that day the most notable was that of Sergeant John Lumsden of C company. During the retirement he was leading to the rear Captain Donaldson, who had been wounded in the face and had lost an eye. Just after crossing a water-course, a shell burst behind him, wrecking the bridge by which he had crossed and cutting off a party of wounded men of the 8th Battalion Liverpool Regiment on the further side. Handing over Captain Donaldson to another man, Sergeant Lumsden hastily collected planks and other material and with the help of a few other men of his platoon was able, under heavy and continuous fire, to restore the bridge and allow the men on the other side to get across. Sergeant Lumsden was afterwards killed during the attack on the High Wood in 1916.

The failure of this attack may be put down to the lack of sufficient artillery preparation and to uncut wire. At that time the number of guns and the allowance of ammunition required to give infantry a reasonable chance of success had not been fully appreciated.

After four days at Lacouture, the 7th took over the front line sector north-east of Violaines, which included a salient of special importance. This was the furthest point reached in the attack on the 16th, and had not been thoroughly consolidated. So much importance did the Germans attach to this particular point that they kept the salient under a continuous trench mortar bombardment in order still further to prevent the progress of consolidation.

The havoc wrought by these trench mortars is almost incredible; a direct hit obliterated about ten yards of the parapet, and it was exceedingly hard work to repair the damaged portions of the line night after night. In addition, the enemy had posted two field guns to command a portion of the line where many efforts had been made to construct a breastwork. These attempts were always unsuccessful, for as soon as a few feet had been built up it was immediately demolished by the fire of these guns. The Battalion was fortunate in losing only one man killed and 16 wounded during the tour.

On June 24th the 51st Division rejoined the Indian Corps, and five days later the 153rd Brigade moved to the Laventie area, the 7th being billeted in farms between Laventie and Estaires.

On July 7th, the Battalion moved into the line near Fauquissart, facing the Aubers Ridge. This area was in every way an improvement on the last. The ground in front was open and undulating, with standing corn and other crops; the county, too,

THE SEVENTH BATTALION THE BLACK WATCH

was not a swamp as was the previous area; the soil was dry and there was no difficulty in digging trenches. The front line consisted of breastworks, the second and third lines being chains of detached posts about four hundred yards apart. The first line of these posts was situated about five hundred yards behind the front line, the second roughly a thousand yards further back. On this front the enemy was much less aggressive and the three weeks spent in this area passed quietly. When not in the line, battalions furnished large working parties every night to improve the defences and to cut the long grass and standing corn in No Man's Land.

On July 21st the Battalion marched to billets in Merville. The village was full of all kinds of troops, French Territorials, Sikhs, Bengal Lancers, Gurkhas, Royal Artillery and Highlanders, a wonderful combination. Five days later the 7th went by train to Méricourt and marched from there to Bresle, where with the Division became part of the Third Army. It was about this time that leave was opened to the United Kingdom.

CHAPTER IV

AUGUST, 1915, TO JUNE, 1916

Near Albert and Maricourt—The Labyrinth

THE day after the 7th reached the new area it was inspected by the Third Army Commander, Sir Charles Munro, who praised its smart appearance and turn-out. On July 31st the Battalion moved into the line near La Boiselle, relieving the 19th (French) Regiment.

With the exception of one part of the line known as Ilot, the French considered this a quiet sector. It was certainly in exceedingly good order and all ranks were impressed by the comfort and even luxury of the trenches. The new front was a complete contrast to anything the 7th had seen before. The soil was chalk, and in this the French had constructed a most elaborate system of trenches. They had also expended great care on communication trenches which were about eight feet deep and, radiating from Battalion Headquarters to the front line, were themselves connected up by numerous lateral trenches of the same depth. So many and intricate were these trenches that it was very easy to get lost in them; every trench, of course, was named, but as this was done in French it was difficult for the Highlanders to pronounce the words. Later on some were renamed as St. Andrew's Avenue or Largo Road, familiar words more easy to pronounce and to remember.

A good deal of mining was done, and in this the Germans certainly had the upper hand. At first the Allied mining was carried on by French sappers, but towards the end of August these were replaced by the 139th Tunnelling Company. Shortly afterwards volunteers were called for from the infantry, and the 7th, largely composed of coal miners from Fife, contributed a great number of those required. In addition, Lieutenants Humphreys and Rowan—both mine managers by profession—were attached to the Tunnelling company, in which, later on, they gained distinction.

This mining work was exceedingly trying, for, apart from the uncertainty as to when an enemy counter-mine would be exploded near the galleries, there was great difficulty in disposing of the earth dug up by the Tunnelling company. This had to be passed up to the surface in sand bags and stacked on either side of the trenches. So fast did this earth accumulate that the trenches in the neighbourhood of the mine soon became almost impassable and the carrying parties, therefore, had to travel further and further as the gallery lengthened. The work would have been easy had it been possible to dump the earth behind the trenches at night, but had this been done the position of the gallery would have been "given away" to enemy airmen, and either the Germans would have counter-mined, or the area would have been heavily shelled.

Shortly after the arrival of the Division the enemy artillery and trench mortar fire increased. The British mortars were crude and, although some types were fairly effective, they could not compare either in range or accuracy with those of the enemy. At this time, also, there was a serious shortage of shells for both artillery and trench mortars, but the Germans seemed to have as many as they required, with the result that troops in the front line had for many months to endure constant shelling without being able to make an effective reply.

The most important point in this sector, and the one round which the worst fighting took place, was the "Ilot," a small salient in the British line, where the furthest point was only about ten yards from the German front line. It had been a point of honour with the French troops to hold on to this salient which, owing to mines, trench mortar bombing and aerial torpedoes, became a confused heap of chalk pits and shell-holes where constant combats with hand grenades took place. The 51st Division held it as had the French, but at great cost to themselves.

Though the fiercest fighting took place in the "Ilot," the whole of the front line suffered from artillery and trench fire mortar, and men were constantly busy repairing damage done by them. This sector had one great disadvantage, namely, that there was no water fit for either drinking or washing. Cooking had to be done some way behind the front line and the food carried up long distances by working parties. The remainder of 1915 was spent in this area, and the Battalion took part in no active fighting of great importance. It is recorded in the Battalion Diary that on one occasion the 7th took over a sector of the line from two regiments of Indian cavalry, the 19th Lancers and 36th Jacob's Horse, in front of Thiepval.

Early in November, General Harper, who had succeeded General Bannatine-Allason in command of the Division, decided to construct deep dug-outs capable of resisting the heaviest type of shell. This meant employing large working parties from all infantry battalions, and before the Division left that part of the line a sufficient number of these dug-outs had been constructed to shelter the front and support line garrisons. On November 15th the enemy put down a heavy bombardment on the Divisional front line lasting for four hours. The Diary states that the rate of fire of this so-called heavy bombardment was ten heavy shells per minute. It would be interesting to hear what the

THE SOMME, FEBRUARY, 1916

veterans of the 7th, who survived the fighting in March, 1918, thought of this "heavy" bombardment.

In this area the 7th carried out two raids, the first on September 15th, under Second Lieutenant Le Maitre, and the second on November 9th, when a party under Captain Grahame almost reached a German strong point. Discovered by the enemy, they were obliged to retire, Captain Grahame being severely wounded and others of the party were killed, wounded and missing.

Towards the end of December the Adjutant, Captain Beveridge, was promoted Major and was succeeded by Lieutenant A. Currie-Begg. The Battalion spent the periods of rest in the villages of Authuile, Aveluy, Martinsart and Millencourt, at which latter place the Battalion transport and stores were established, and where baths and canteens were available as well as a recreation hall and football ground. During these periods behind the line training was carried out and working parties were furnished for constructing a support line known as the "Bouzincourt Switch." At the end of December the 7th proceeded to Poulainville, about four miles north of Amiens, where it remained for a month.

The 51st Division was now out of the line for its first long rest since arriving in France, and training of all kinds was carried out. This was of the most comprehensive nature and included attack practices which later on helped the Division to achieve its many successes. New Year's Day was celebrated in the usual way, and as all ranks were freely given passes to Amiens during this rest period, the time passed pleasantly.

On February 6th, 1916, the 7th moved to Bray-sur-Somme, and on the 11th relieved the 2nd Battalion Bedfordshire Regiment in the front line at Maricourt. This tour, although lasting only seventeen days, was one of the most trying the Battalion had so far experienced. The Maricourt defences, which included the village, were in exceedingly bad order; moreover, the weather was miserable and intensely cold. Conditions were not much better in the support areas. There were no farm buildings or barns to serve as billets, and units had to be content with tents. These, set in a sea of mud known as Grovetown Camp, were much worn and gave little shelter from the icy gales that blew continuously. From this cheerless spot working parties of from 200 to 300 men proceeded nightly to the firing line about five miles away, for work on the defences. These parties started at dusk and it was often two or three o'clock in the morning before they returned to camp, generally wet through and thoroughly tired.

On February 27th the Battalion was relieved and moved to

THE SEVENTH BATTALION THE BLACK WATCH

Corbie, proceeding next day to Poulainville. This relief, known as "The retreat from Maricourt," will never be forgotten by those who took part in it. Some days earlier the rain had given place to snow, followed by a severe frost, and, while the relief was actually in progress, the enemy started a vigorous shelling, which caused much confusion among the transport assembled near Battalion Headquarters. During its progress a limber containing a chest, in which was the whole pay of one company, was turned over. This was not noticed in the dark, and when the search party went back the following day all they found was one ten-franc note firmly frozen to the road.

During this relief, B company, under Captain Aitken, had an unfortunate experience. It had been left behind as reinforcement to the relieving battalion, and on leaving the front line found that, instead of moving to Grovetown Camp, where it had expected to rejoin the Battalion, it had to go on to Corbie, which was reached late on the 28th. The company was under arms for twenty-four hours and marched over nineteen miles. On the 29th the 7th moved to Poulainville, where it remained until March 6th, when the 51st Division moved to a new area.

Orders had reached the Division that it would relieve the 23rd (French) Division, 12th (French) Corps, in order to allow the latter to be transferred to Verdun, where the fighting was then very heavy. The move began on March 6th, and proceeding by road and halting at Longuevillette, Doullens, Ivergny and Maroeuil, the Battalion moved into the line at Neuville-St. Vaast on the 13th, relieving French troops in the Labyrinth. The move was rather trying, the latter part of the march being carried out in a blizzard.

The new sector lay to the north of Arras and extended, roughly, from Roclincourt on the right to Neuville-St. Vaast on the left; both these villages had been reduced to ruins. So complete indeed was the destruction that when the parish priest of Neuville revisited the village after the fighting, he was unable to recognize the site of either his church or his house.

This area had been the scene of very heavy fighting in the latter part of 1915, when the French, attacking towards the Vimy Ridge, had encountered a stubborn resistance. They had been obliged to fight their way almost inch by inch, sometimes gaining, sometimes losing ground, until they finally established the line which the 7th took over. During the course of this fighting the opposing lines had become so mixed up that the whole area consisted of a mass of trenches, hence the name "The Labyrinth."

On the night of the 13th A and B companies relieved the

VIMY RIDGE, MARCH–MAY, 1916

French in the front line, while C and D companies took over the support and reserve trenches. On handing over the front line the French stated that there was a German mine under the trenches, that for some time they had been obliged to withdraw their tunnellers, and that they had only kept a few men in the listening galleries. This being the case the Germans were, of course, completely masters of the situation, and it was not until some weeks later, when the British Tunnelling companies got to work, that matters improved. Having abandoned the initiative, the French had constructed a well-sited second line trench some way behind, into which the troops holding the front line were withdrawn as soon as an explosion seemed imminent. This trench proved invaluable to the 7th, for, when later on the mine was exploded, the front line troops were safely under cover in the second line and suffered no loss. A company of the 5th Battalion Gordon Highlanders on the right, however, were less fortunate for, a few days later, a mine actually exploded under the trench in which they had been advised to take refuge, causing heavy loss.

Mining was the chief feature in this area and hardly a day passed during the three months the Division was there without at least one German mine exploding. The 7th was, however, exceptionally fortunate, and its losses from this source were few. Only once, on May 28th, was a small party of the Battalion caught by a mine, five men being killed and five wounded. Indeed, when the Division took over the line, there were very few mine craters on the whole front, but when it left in July they were so thick that an aerial photograph of the sector resembled nothing so much as a picture of a portion of the moon's surface.

When a mine exploded, a fight always arose as to which side should occupy the lip of the crater, and thus gain a good observation post of the trenches opposite. In these attacks the 7th was engaged on every occasion on which it held the front line. These attacks often developed into hand-to-hand combats in which hundreds of bombs were thrown by both sides causing many casualties. In one of these combats a party of the 7th, led by Lieutenant Davies, drove the enemy out of a crater, killing five of the defenders and bringing back a wounded German.

On May 21st a mine on the Battalion front exploded, burying a party of French Territorials in a listening gallery and destroying part of the front line. The survivors were rescued by Lieutenant A. L. Miller and two stretcher bearers, Privates Buchanan and Swan. To reach the listening gallery, these three had to cross about eighty yards of exposed ground under heavy rifle and machine gun fire. Disregarding the danger of gas in the gallery, Buchanan and Swan went down the wrecked shaft and brought up four Frenchmen, of whom one was dead and two were seriously injured. For this action Lieutenant Miller was awarded the M.C. and Buchanan and Swan the Military Medal; but unfortunately Lieutenant Miller was hit by a sniper the following day and sent to hospital.

On April 4th Major Guthrie, Second-in-Command, went to England to take up command of a Service Battalion, and on May 6th Major G. R. H. Cheape, King's Dragoon Guards, took his place as Second-in-Command.

On May 2nd, the first anniversary of the 7th's arrival in France, the Battalion received its first issue of red hackles. Formerly this mark of distinction had not been worn by Territorial Battalions of the Regiment, and this distribution was made the occasion for a ceremonial parade. After the hackles had been issued to each man by the Commanding Officer, the Battalion was drawn up in hollow square and addressed by him, the Colonel recalling the circumstances under which this distinction had been gained 122 years before.

In the Labyrinth sector the front line, instead of being a continuous trench, consisted of a series of look-out posts, connected by a sap with trenches in rear. These posts were held, as a rule, by one non-commissioned officer and three men, the number being doubled at night, while sentry groups of the same strength were posted at the rear of the sap in support. Some of these saps were old German trenches and led right through into the enemy front line; in such cases the trench was blocked by a parapet of earth and sand-bags only a few yards away from a similar block manned by the enemy. This system of defences was very trying for the front line troops, who had, in addition to holding a long line of trench, to repair damage caused by weather and enemy shelling. In this sector each battalion spent twenty-one days in the line and nine out.

On May 23rd, in consequence of troops being withdrawn to the Somme, the 51st Division line was considerably extended. The 152nd Brigade moved further to the left and took over a new sector, while the 153rd and 154th divided the line hitherto held by the Division. In fact, the Division took over the whole original frontage of the XVII Corps.

On June 3rd a successful raid was carried out by a party of seventy-five men of the 7th, under Lieutenants H. J. Herd and J. S. Finlayson. This party had carefully rehearsed the operation in Maroeuil, where a model of the area to be raided had been prepared. The model trenches, based on air photographs, were laid out exactly to scale, and thus every man learnt exactly where he had to go and what he had to do. A thorough

VIMY RIDGE, MAY, 1916

reconnaissance of the German wire defences was also made beforehand and a suitable gap in it found, while gaps were also cut in the British wire to enable the party to get through.

In preparation for this raid, the Tunnelling company drove galleries leading up to the area to be attacked. By the morning of June 3rd these had been completed, and three mines were in position ready to be exploded.

At 8.45 p.m. on the 3rd the Division artillery put down a heavy barrage on the German support line and on either flank of the position to be assaulted. At 8.50 p.m. the three mines were exploded, one on each flank of the position, and a similar one some distance away, the object of the latter being to distract the enemy's attention from the raiding party. Unfortunately, the explosion caused several casualties among the raiding party which had assembled in the front line.

The raiders were divided into three groups under Lieutenant Herd, right; Lieutenant Finlayson, left; and Sergeant McIntosh, centre. The right party got into the German trenches without difficulty and made their way down the communication trench. They were fired at from a large dug-out, but effectively silenced this by throwing bombs into it, all of which took effect. Further on they met a party of the enemy whom they attacked and captured two prisoners. The centre party, moving up the communication trench, worked round to the right, bombed two dug-outs, and attacked and killed several Germans in the front line, three being bayoneted by Sergeant McIntosh himself. After this the party effected a junction with Lieutenant Herd's party, and both then moved to the left in search of Lieutenant Finlayson's party. Unfortunately the left party had been dispersed by shell fire before reaching the enemy's lines. One shell struck a man carrying a bag of bombs and these exploded, wounding Lieutenant Finlayson and killing or wounding a number of his party. Several of the survivors, however, succeeded in reaching the enemy's front line, and there joined the other two groups.

The right and centre groups being unable to get in touch with Lieutenant Finlayson's party, moved further to the left, where they found three large dug-outs, one of which had been completely wrecked by one of the mines. The occupants of the other two were called upon to surrender, but only one man came up and he was made prisoner, after which the dug-outs were bombed. Whilst this was going on the prisoner endeavoured to escape, but was pursued and killed by Lieutenant Herd.

Before returning to their own lines the party thoroughly explored the German trenches. It was found that enormous damage had been done by the mines, many half-buried bodies and large quantities of clothing and equipment being scattered about. The leaders were satisfied that not a single German was left alive in the area they visited.

Towards the end of the time appointed for the raid the Germans put down an intense artillery and trench mortar barrage on the Battalion trenches and also on No Man's Land, with the result that when the main body returned, it was found that several men were missing. Calling for volunteers, Lieutenant Herd went out in face of the heavy fire, and with the assistance of Sergeant J. Mitchell and Private J. McNeill succeeded, after several journeys, in bringing in all the wounded, and the bodies of those killed. In this raid three men were killed and Lieutenant Finlayson and 15 men wounded; on the other hand, a German captured a few days later stated that over 60 Germans had been killed during the raid.

Telegrams of congratulation on the success of this raid were received the following day from the Corps, Division and Brigade Commanders. For their services, Lieutenant Herd was awarded the D.S.O., Sergeant McIntosh the D.C.M., and Sergeant Mitchell and Private McNeill the M.M.

During the time the 51st Division was in this sector it was subjected to many heavy bombardments. One of exceptional violence occurred on May 21st and lasted all day, the enemy paying particular attention to battery posts in rear and to communication trenches. These were deluged with lachrymatory shells, with the result that when the 7th was relieved that evening its march to billets was exceedingly unpleasant owing to this new form of shell. The fumes of chemicals hung about and were perceptible a week later.

When not in the line the 7th was billeted at either Maroeuil or Bray; the latter, a very small village on the River Scarpe, was seldom shelled, whilst Maroeuil was nearly always under artillery fire, and whenever the Battalion occupied it many casualties occurred. While the Division occupied the front line the periods of rest for battalions seldom exceeded four or five days; allowing for the day taken up by going into or coming back from the front, this gave hardly sufficient time to permit of a thorough overhaul and renewal of clothing and equipment; but in the evenings parties were able to visit the Divisional theatre and cinema at Maroeuil.

Nothing of special interest took place until June 30th, when a German raiding party, after a heavy bombardment followed by the explosion of a mine, succeeded in entering trenches held by the 7th. It was turned out after a short struggle, leaving one man behind. The Battalion lost five men killed, 18 wounded and four missing; it was subsequently ascertained that the latter

TO CORPS RESERVE, JULY 4TH, 1916

were taken prisoners—the first lost by the 7th since it arrived in France.

A few days before this raid orders had been received that the 51st Division would be relieved by the 60th (London), a second line Division recently arrived from England, and on the evening of the 29th a detachment of the 15th Battalion London Regiment was attached to the 7th for instructions. As only one week was allowed for this purpose, the training of the newcomers was carried out on an intensive system, which involved reliefs of some kind or another every night. In addition the Battalion under instruction undertook the duties of carrying up rations, ammunition and stores, nearly always under heavy enemy artillery fire and in exceptionally bad weather. On the night of July 4th the Battalion was relieved by the 7th Battalion Gordon Highlanders and moved to Maroeuil.

In the Neuville-St. Vaast sector the Battalion was fortunate in losing in three months only 23 other ranks killed, seven officers and 125 other ranks wounded and four other ranks missing, a light loss compared with that of other units who had suffered more severely from heavy artillery fire.

CHAPTER V

JULY, 1916

The Somme

ON July 6th the 7th marched from Maroeuil to Bailleul-aux-Cornailles in Corps reserve. On the 15th the Battalion moved by motor lorries to Halloy, and the following day marched to Franvillers, eventually reaching Dernancourt on the 21st.

The Battle of the Somme was at this time at its height, and the 51st Division was destined to play a great part in it. The same night the 7th arrived at Méricourt and moved into the line in Mametz Wood, relieving the 2nd Battalion Argyll and Sutherland Highlanders, 33rd Division. Passing through Fricourt, where it left its transport and surplus officers, the Battalion entered the Mametz valley on its way to the front line.

For a proper appreciation of this area known as "Happy Valley," it is best to quote the description of Major Bewsher, the historian of the 51st (Highland) Division, who writes :—

"This valley was the only line of communication through which every relief, every round of ammunition and every ration had to pass on their way to the line. . . . The enemy shelled Happy Valley mercilessly day and night, an intense barrage of high explosive, air bursts and gas shells being placed completely across it at irregular intervals, and moved backwards and forwards, up and down it. . . . The valley was traversed day and night by a constant stream of traffic. The infantry used overland tracks well clear of the road, and marched in platoon or section groups. All wheeled traffic was, however, restricted to the single road, so that periods of great congestion often occurred.

"When the German barrage opened, men, animals and motor vehicles broke into their best speed. Great columns of white dust rose up, choked everything and made seeing a matter of difficulty. Guns and limbers moved at a stretch gallop, lorries bounded from shell hole to shell hole, and every effort was concentrated on getting out of the zone involved in the barrage with as little delay as possible.

"The heavily burdened infantry man on his way to and from the line, however, carried too much on his back to make him think of doubling. He used to plod along at his regulation three miles an hour, trusting that his luck would take him through.

"It was no uncommon sight to see direct hits scored on gun teams, limbers and groups of infantry. When the barrage

MAMETZ WOOD, JULY, 1916

"ceased, and it was possible to take stock of the result, appalling "scenes were often disclosed. Teams with their riders lying in "a heap, ammunition dumps on fire, riderless and driverless "horses and waggons bolting in all directions and coming down "in the midst of old wire entanglements, were daily spectacles "in the Happy Valley. . . .

"Happy Valley, with its dust and its flies and its stench of "half-buried animals and men, will remain to all who knew it "an ineffaceable memory."

On this, its first introduction to the valley, the 7th escaped lightly. It ran into a barrage, but lost only two men killed, three wounded and three missing. The line taken over consisted of narrow and shallow trenches, and after the relief the 7th spent the remainder of that night in digging better cover. The following day a new line was sited and work on the trenches started.

Heavy shelling went on throughout the day, and at night the Germans put down a bombardment of gas shells which necessitated the wearing of gas masks during the greater part of the night. The Battalion remained in reserve in Mametz Wood until July 26th, during which time the enemy shelling was almost continuous, but fortunately the soil was light and soon the Battalion constructed deep trenches in which they were fairly safe from shell fire. Although not actively engaged in the attack on High Wood, the Battalion lost two officers wounded, three men killed and 51 wounded in the five days while they were in reserve.

The 7th took over the front line from the 4th Battalion Seaforth Highlanders on the 26th. This line ran from a point about midway between Longueval, on the outskirts of Delville Wood, to the north-western end of High Wood, the greater part of which was in possession of the enemy; but the south-eastern corner was held by the Battalion. The 7th stood to arms all that night with patrols out in front, but owing to the thick undergrowth these gained little information. The enemy shelling was particularly severe, one officer being wounded, two men killed and 11 wounded. The following day was spent in improving the line and in pushing forward bombing posts by which the 7th advanced its position about forty yards. On the right of the wood the British line ran along the Martinpuich–Longueval road, and the companies holding this part were occupied in pushing out saps to the front, the intention being to join up eventually the heads of these saps and thus form a continuous line some way in advance.

On the night of July 28th the Battalion was reinforced by

THE SEVENTH BATTALION THE BLACK WATCH

the 5th Battalion Gordon Highlanders, who took over the right sector of the line, the 7th being concentrated in the left sector with Battalion Headquarters in the south-east corner of High Wood. That night the enemy artillery was very active and concentrated a heavy fire on Battalion Headquarters which set fire to an ammunition dump, causing a stack of boxes filled with bombs to explode. This fire was prevented from spreading mainly owing to the exertions of three men of the Battalion who particularly distinguished themselves in this work. During that night the Commanding Officer and four other officers were wounded, two men were killed and 31 wounded.

On the 29th there was again heavy shelling of the area behind the front line, but during the whole period the Battalion spent in the wood the front line trenches escaped. It is probable that the German observers were unable to locate accurately the trenches in the wood, and as the Battalion posts were in many cases very close to those of the enemy, a bombardment would have caused as many casualties to their own troops as to those of the Seventh.

Orders were now received for an attack with the object of driving the enemy out of High Wood. The objective given to the 7th was the enemy front system, and the attack was carried out with C company on the right, B on the left, with A and D companies in support. Zero hour was 6.10 p.m. on July 30th. The preliminary bombardment, which lasted a quarter of an hour, was neither accurate nor sufficiently intense. There was no barrage behind which the attack could advance, with the result that when the leading companies left their trenches and had pushed some way into the wood, they were met by heavy rifle and machine gun fire, the enemy being plainly visible lining their front line trench in large numbers with fixed bayonets.

So hot was the fire that C company was held up after having gone only a few yards; B company, however, which was further from the enemy, made more progress at first, but it too came to a standstill and the attack eventually stopped. Nearly all the officers of these two companies had been killed, but the men held on for some time in shell holes between the lines until it was obvious that nothing could be gained by remaining, and the survivors withdrew to the original front line. In this attack the Battalion suffered severely, nine officers being killed and three wounded; 31 other ranks killed, 98 wounded and 14 missing. The night and day following the attack passed quietly, and most of the wounded were brought in and carried to the rear. On the evening of the 31st the Battalion was relieved, and spent the night bivouacing in Fricourt Wood.

HIGH WOOD, JULY 30TH, 1916

Thus with the close of July ended the 7th's first experience of fighting on a large scale. Unfortunately, the ground gained was disappointingly small compared to the losses incurred. The Battalion, like the rest of the Division, had come straight from the Labyrinth, and there had been no time to train behind the line before going into the fighting round High Wood.

On the morning of August 1st the transport and surplus personnel rejoined Headquarters, and the Battalion moved from the Somme area and marching via Albert arrived at Méaulte the same evening. At Méaulte Lieutenant-Colonel G. R. H. Cheape, M.C., succeeded Lieutenant-Colonel Allen, who had been wounded, and Second Lieutenant J. Reid was appointed Adjutant vice Lieutenant Begg, killed in action. Two drafts of about three hundred men, including many former men of the Battalion, brought the 7th once more almost up to strength. The Battalion spent a week at Méaulte training and refitting, after which it moved north to a new area.

CHAPTER VI

AUGUST TO NOVEMBER, 1916

Armentières and Beaumont Hamel
(*See Map facing Page* 152.)

THE Division was now sent to the neighbourhood of Armentières. The journey north was made in easy stages, partly by road and partly by rail, the Battalion finally detraining at Armentières on August 16th. During the move the weather was extremely hot, and marching in full kit, even after sundown, was trying after the long spell of trench warfare in which the Battalion had been engaged. Major J. M. Milligan, the Royal Scots, now joined the Battalion as Second-in-Command.

The day after it arrived at Armentières, the 7th relieved a battalion of the New Zealand Division in the front line, immediately north of the town. This sector in which the Division was to spend the next five weeks was one of the most quiet in the long Allied line. The front line in most places was about two hundred and fifty yards from the enemy, the nearest point being the salient known as " Fiji," where No Man's Land was only a hundred yards wide.

In appearance the defences round Armentières were very similar to those which the Battalion had first found near Festubert. Owing to the presence of water near the surface it was possible to dig only shallow trenches and to supplement these by breastworks revetted with sandbags and corrugated iron. On the whole, as the enemy's artillery activity was not great, it was comparatively easy to keep the defences in repair. The week spent in this quiet sector was invaluable to the 7th, and, indeed, to the whole of the 51st Division, as it gave good opportunities for training the large number of men who had joined after High Wood.

The New Zealanders had, by means of constant patrolling, established complete control of No Man's Land, and this was continued in a very thorough manner by the 7th—so thoroughly, indeed, that on only one occasion during its stay in the area was an enemy patrol seen on the Battalion front. The chief enemy activity in this area consisted in shelling the rest areas of Houplines and Armentières, and, at regular intervals, in bombing the front and support lines with minenwerfer and smaller trench mortars.

For some time it was thought an enemy gas attack was imminent, and this necessitated the wearing of box respirators whenever the wind blew from the direction of the German lines. The wearing of these respirators was, of course, unpleasant, but there is no doubt that the constant practice saved many lives when gas became more universally used.

ARMENTIÈRES, AUGUST–SEPTEMBER, 1916

When in reserve the 7th spent the time either in Armentières or in the adjoining suburb of Houplines. The front line trenches were only about an hour's walk from Armentières, which, although intermittently shelled, had not suffered any serious damage, most of the houses remaining intact. In these, numbers of the inhabitants lived and conducted their business in the ordinary way. The majority of the officers were usually billeted in a convent, and the men had good billets in the neighbouring houses. While the 153rd Brigade was in Divisional reserve at Bailleul it spent a week under canvas, during which time the first Divisional Horse Show was held on September 12th. Football and concerts varied the ordinary routine of parades and training.

On the night of September 15th a party under Second Lieutenant Le Maitre and Sergeant Wood went up to the front line to carry out a raid with the object of obtaining identification. Ten days previously the party had been detached to practise the attack on taped-out ground, and, in addition, the part of No Man's Land which the raiders were to cross was frequently patrolled by Lieutenant Le Maitre and his non-commissioned officers.

To help the raiders it was arranged that the artillery would put down a box barrage during the operation. The enemy's wire was cut by means of Bangalore torpedoes—long tubes containing explosives which were carried across No Man's Land by the raiding party and pushed along the ground under the wire. These torpedoes were awkward to handle and difficult to place in position, but once there they were very effective, and when exploded cleared a lane through the wire. Another advantage of this method was that, unlike an artillery bombardment, it gave the enemy no inkling of what was to take place. The raiding party left its trenches at 8.15 on the evening of September 15th, and, although its presence was detected by the enemy, it had no difficulty in placing the torpedoes in position.

Zero hour for the assault was 8.55 p.m., at which time the artillery barrage began and the torpedoes were exploded successfully, while the raiders made their way with all speed through the gap and over the parapet into the front line. In accordance with the plan, one party then worked along the trench to the left, and another to the right. Almost at once the left party met two Germans, one of whom was killed and the other taken prisoner. Advancing along the trench they bombed several dug-outs full of men and did much damage. The right party was not so fortunate. It met three Germans, but these ran away at once and the party took no prisoners. The object of the raid, however, having been attained by the capture of one prisoner, Second Lieutenant

THE SEVENTH BATTALION THE BLACK WATCH

Le Maitre gave the order to withdraw. The return journey across No Man's Land was successfully accomplished, although under considerable fire, until the raiders reached the British wire, when a shell burst amongst the party wounding Lieutenant Le Maitre and some others and killing the prisoner. Search parties from the front line brought in the body of the German for identification, and all the wounded were recovered, several of the raiders themselves gallantly going out again to make certain that no one had been left behind. The casualties were one man killed and seven wounded. For their services on this occasion Second Lieutenant Le Maitre received the M.C., Sergeant R. Wood the D.C.M. and Private J. Millar the Military Medal. It is of interest to record that Millar had been with the Battalion ever since it came to France, and had taken part in every raid and attack.

The Division was ordered to move to the Somme, and on the 25th the 7th left the quiet Armentières sector and marched back to billets between Bailleul and Meteren, where it spent the next few days. On the 30th the whole Division moved south to the Hébuterne area, and the 7th, detraining at Doullens the same day, continued the journey by march route, halting for one night at Beauval. The next ten days were spent moving towards the line, the last two nights being spent at Colincamps. The weather throughout the move was wretched, and as the area through which the Division marched was congested with troops, little shelter was obtained and no comfort was available.

At this time preparations were being made for an attack in force against Puisieux-au-Mont, and roads leading to the front line were crowded day and night with guns, munitions and stores required for the operation. Maps and plans of the area were issued, and a plan of the enemy trench system, with which the 153rd Brigade was to deal, was marked out with tapes near Léalvillers. Over this ground the 7th daily practised the assembly and the attack upon Puisieux-au-Mont, the artillery barrage being represented by men carrying flags. This was the first occasion on which the 7th had an opportunity of practising an attack in this manner; later on the method was perfected, and became part of the recognised preparation in the Division for all attacks. The proposed attack on Puisieux was eventually abandoned, but the experience gained by the Battalion was of great value.

On October 13th the Battalion was in support during the attack on Beaumont Hamel, but the next day took over the front line at Hébuterne from the 6th Battalion The Black Watch, where it was subjected to continuous artillery and heavy trench mortar fire.

BEAUMONT HAMEL, OCTOBER 13TH, 1916

Although not actually employed in the attack on Beaumont Hamel, the 7th provided large carrying parties, and during the two days it was in the line it lost two officers and 25 other ranks killed, 55 wounded and seven missing. For services on this occasion Captain Blair received the M.C., and Sergeant Jarvis the D.C.M. After three days in the line the Battalion was relieved and the 51st Division moved a few miles south to the Beaumont Hamel sector, where preparations were being hurried forward for an attack on the village. From the 18th to 22nd of October the Battalion was billeted at Forceville, some miles behind the line, but on the latter date, after church parade, it moved to camp among the woods near Mailly-Maillet. This made things easier for the working parties, who had a much shorter way to go to and from the front line.

The work on which the Battalion was now mainly employed was the formation of advance depots for battle stores in the trenches, the object being to provide munitions and rations for the attacking troops who might otherwise be cut off from their supplies by enemy artillery fire. The weather throughout was abominable, and to the parties sleeping on muddy trench boards, or wading through the clinging mud, loaded with engineer stores or munitions, it seemed as if these depots would never be filled.

On October 30th the Battalion went into the line at Auchonvillers for a week's tour. It went up in fighting kit in preparation for "Z" day, the date originally arranged for the attack on Beaumont Hamel, namely, November 2nd. Terrible weather, however, delayed the preparations to such an extent that after two or three postponements the Battalion moved back to Lealvillers on November 5th. Owing to the tension caused by the postponement of this attack, to the weather and the water-logged condition of the trenches, the weeks spent in the line had been exceedingly trying; casualties were few, but all men not actually engaged in trench duties were required to work unceasingly to keep the crumbling sides of the trenches from falling in. Sometimes sentries became so firmly fixed in the mud that they had to be dug out, and a walk round the company front line often took nearly an hour.

The 7th remained about a week at Léalvillers cleaning up and supplying working parties for clearing roads; it then returned to Mailly Wood on the 12th, and at 9 p.m. received operation orders for the attack on Beaumont Hamel, which was fixed to take place at 5.45 next morning. The other battalions of the Brigade moved up to their assembly positions, and the 7th, less two platoons, reached its post in the reserve trenches in St. John's Wood by 1.30 a.m. The two platoons referred to, one from A and one from D companies, under

Second Lieutenants Menzies and Beatson, were placed under the orders of the Officer Commanding the 6th Battalion The Black Watch for the attack and assembled with that Battalion on the parados of the front line trench, and attacked with the first wave of the 6th.

The attacking battalions of the 153rd Brigade were the 7th Battalion Gordon Highlanders on the right, and the 6th Battalion The Black Watch with two platoons of the 7th on the left. The main objective of these battalions was the "green" line, which included the station road and village of Beaumont Hamel, about six hundred yards within the enemy's position. An outstanding feature on the Brigade front was the "Y" Ravine—a deep gash in the ground almost at right angles to the line of advance, which formed a marked salient in the German position. It was anticipated that this ravine would prove troublesome, as it was known to contain many deep dug-outs and to be strongly fortified with machine guns.

The assembly was successfully carried out, and the night was spent waiting for Zero hour. An issue of coffee and rum—carried up in hot containers—was of great value during that cold and wet night. This was really the first occasion on which the Division had been given a good chance. Every man had had an opportunity of seeing for himself the careful preparations which had been made, and had also had the satisfaction of seeing British artillery thoroughly and systematically subject the German positions to a heavy and continuous bombardment for weeks prior to the attack. Moreover, it was known from patrol reports that the enemy wire had been thoroughly well cut, and every man in the Division went into the battle perfectly confident of success. In order not to alarm the enemy there was no preliminary bombardment, and up till Zero hour hardly a British gun fired.

It was still dark and a thick foggy morning when the assaulting troops, following close up to the barrage, entered the German front line to the complete surprise of its garrison, and nearly half an hour elapsed before the German artillery realized what was going on, and put down a counter barrage on No Man's Land.

With the opening of the battle the 7th practically ceased to function as a unit; the whole Battalion, with the exception of the two platoons already mentioned, being employed as carrying parties. Their chief duty was to arrange that all battle stores were safely and quickly transferred across No Man's Land, and established in depots on the ground gained.

The first of these parties followed closely behind the assaulting troops, and in many cases—where the advance was temporarily held up—they took part in the fighting, dropping their

ATTACK ON "Y" RAVINE

loads for the time being and joining in the assault. Each party consisted of a few men only, usually in charge of a non-commissioned officer, many of whom showed great determination and initiative in this very confused fighting. Sergeant H. Baptie especially distinguished himself on this day, but, unfortunately, was so severely wounded that he died later.

"Y" Ravine proved as difficult to deal with as had been feared, and the fighting in and around it for some time made the result of the whole attack uncertain. While on the right and left the 7th Battalion Gordon Highlanders and 6th Battalion The Black Watch carried out their advances according to the time-table laid down, the left of the 7th Battalion Gordon Highlanders and the right of the 6th Battalion The Black Watch were delayed by the resistance of the enemy occupying the ravine. Here the Germans had remained in their deep dug-outs until the attacking troops were upon them, when they came out in large numbers and, with machine guns, opened a heavy fire on the advancing troops. In addition to this, in other parts of the enemy lines insufficient attention had been given to " mopping up " the captured trenches, with the result that isolated posts of the enemy remained in rear of the assaulting troops and caused many casualties. Runners suffered very severely, with the result that messages failed to reach Battalion and Brigade Headquarters, and the position in front was for some time obscure.

About 9 a.m. the snipers of the 7th were sent up to engage these isolated posts, and at noon, as the carrying parties were still losing many men, Colonel Cheape sent the Battalion bombers forward also. It was not, however, until the afternoon that a mixed party of the 6th and 7th Battalions The Black Watch, and 5th and 7th Battalions Gordon Highlanders succeeded in forcing an entrance into the ravine and in capturing the garrison. This done, the advance to the " green " line was completed on the whole front without further opposition.

The two platoons of the 7th attached to the 6th Battalion The Black Watch were engaged in this severe fighting and acquitted themselves well. D company's platoon, under Sergeant Jarvis—who had taken over command when Second Lieutenant Menzies was wounded—captured one German officer and 97 other ranks, taking 35 men from one dug-out alone. This was largely due to the gallant action of Private H. De Reuter, who went down a dug-out twenty feet underground and shouted in German for the defenders to come out. Receiving no reply, he threw two bombs round the corner of the staircase and, when they exploded, repeated the order. " One officer and thirty-five men," came the reply, and this time that number filed out. De Reuter's knowledge of German was useful later, when he compelled this officer to give orders to an isolated post containing about 60 Germans to stop firing and surrender, which they did.

The night of the 13th was spent in reorganizing and consolidating the captured area, four officers of the 7th and a number of Lewis guns being sent forward during the evening to assist the 6th Battalion, which had lost nearly all its officers. This ended the 7th's active part in the battle. The next day the attack was continued by other units of the Division, and on the 15th the 153rd Brigade was relieved, and returned to bivouacs near Mailly-Maillet. The total losses of the Battalion during this fighting were two officers killed and five wounded; 24 other ranks killed, 59 wounded and seven missing. Sergeant D. Jarvis was, later, awarded the D.C.M. for the gallantry and leadership he displayed during the fighting.

The Battalion remained at Mailly until the 18th, where it was employed on salvage and burial work. It was also visited by the Division Commander, General Harper, who congratulated the Battalion, especially the carrying parties, by whose efforts rations and battle stores reached the new front line as soon as it was established.

The three days spent in bivouacs in Mailly were rendered more unpleasant than usual by the weather, which was alternately wet and frosty, and no one was sorry when on November 18th orders were received that the Battalion would move that day to billets in Arquèves, about five miles behind the line. Nearly a year had now elapsed since the Division had been in rest and it was hoped that this was the beginning of a move to the back area, where Christmas and New Year could be spent in comfort. The reality proved somewhat different.

CHAPTER VII

NOVEMBER, 1916, TO JANUARY, 1917

Courcelette and a Rest in Millencourt

THE Division was now ordered to take over and consolidate the sector then held by the Canadians at Courcelette, about seven miles from Albert. On November 22nd the 7th started for the new area and reached Ovillers on the 26th, where it remained in Brigade reserve until the 30th. This was the Battalion's first experience of a completely devastated area. The villages of Ovillers, Pozières and Courcelette were in ruins. Many men of the Battalion could remember seeing them behind the German line during the summer of 1915, when they were almost untouched by shell fire and were half hidden by woods and copses. Now the whole area was desolate, the result of months of bombardment from both Allied and German artillery.

The site of Ovillers church was marked by a single piece of masonry about six feet high. Pozières was only distinguishable by the fact that in places the margin of the road was lined by fragments of the original curb stones. Later in the war scenes such as these were not uncommon, but none was so impressive as was this first realization of the power of modern artillery in the area round Courcelette.

Ovillers huts and Wolfe huts, the billets for the Battalion in Brigade reserve, were good types of such camps. They were situated just off the Albert–Bapaume road, which, being the main approach to the front line in that area, was crowded by day and night with lorries, cyclists, cars and infantry, in addition to which large labour parties and road rollers were constantly at work keeping the surface in repair.

On November 30th the Battalion moved into the line at Courcelette, where it relieved the 7th Battalion Gordon Highlanders. Weather conditions could not have been worse and the Division Commander issued orders that the kilt would be discarded and trews worn instead. Gum boots were also issued, and in this strange kit the 7th took over the front line, which proved to be a water-logged ditch.

Up to this time there had been many casualties throughout the whole force from " trench feet " and frost bite, although great care had been taken to guard against them. Special precautions were now taken and stringent orders issued on the subject. Every man was obliged to rub his feet daily with whale oil before proceeding to the trenches; and it became a point of honour that not a man in the Battalion should become useless through trench feet or frost bite.

THE SEVENTH BATTALION THE BLACK WATCH

Apart from the extreme discomfort of this tour, the days spent in the front line were uneventful. During the first tour in the line the Battalion snipers accounted for many of the enemy, who had the habit in this sector of leaving their trenches at certain places and running overland; one day eleven of them were shot in this way, the Germans coming out under a Red Cross flag and carrying away their bodies. The main work of the Battalion was consolidation of the position. The ground had recently been taken by the Canadians, and the position was a mere skeleton of trench system. There was no support line, no dug-outs or shelters of any kind and, as the half-finished communication trenches were filled with water and impassable, many positions in the front line were completely isolated by day.

At first it seemed impossible to carry out all the necessary work. Progress, of course, was slow, but by the time the 51st handed over the sector to the 2nd Division, early in January, a great change had taken place. Most of the front line posts contained iron shelters, each capable of holding a platoon, which served as protection from weather and kept the men's feet out of the water. The front was also protected by at least one belt of wire.

Owing to the fact that there were no communication trenches, and that all landmarks had been obliterated by shell fire, it was exceedingly difficult to find the way at night. Reliefs, ration parties and working parties frequently lost their way and more than once found themselves in No Man's Land, but no one made such a bad mistake as did a German machine gunner who had intended to go back to get an issue of hot coffee, and was eventually captured about a thousand yards inside the British line held by the 7th. On another occasion a young German, who had come up with a relief party, strayed into one of B company's posts.

One evening a large working party of four hundred men of the Battalion detailed to dig a communication trench under the supervision of the Royal Engineers failed to reach the rendezvous, although the ground had been reconnoitred by daylight, and wandered about in a circle most of the night. Such were the conditions under which the 7th spent the first few weeks of 1917. The battalions of the Brigade held the line for periods of four days. During the 7th's first tour in the line each company occupied it for four days, but even this was found to be too long a period, and the labour of carrying up rations absorbed too many men. Later, each man went into the line carrying forty-eight hours' rations, and at the end of that period an inter-company relief took place.

During the time the Division held this sector there was

TO CORPS RESERVE, JANUARY, 1917

usually one Brigade in reserve near Senlis-Bouzincourt, and twice the 153rd Brigade spent six days' rest in that area. One of these periods included Christmas Day, which was celebrated in the usual way, and in the evening the whole Battalion marched to Senlis and attended a performance of the " Balmorals " Concert Party.

New Year's Day was spent at Ovillers, but the large working parties required did not allow of any special celebration, with the exception of an entertainment given in the Scottish church's tent on December 29th. This institution will be ever gratefully remembered by all in the 51st Division; its little blue banner with St. Andrew's Cross became a familiar and welcome sight wherever the Division might be, but nowhere, perhaps, did it do better work than at Ovillers.

The bad weather and hard work experienced during the few weeks spent in the Courcelette area had reduced the strength of the Battalion considerably. Battle casualties had been comparatively few, but as the men became exhausted by the conditions of life in the forward area and as sickness consequently increased, the ranks were thinned. Fortunately, just as orders reached the Battalion that the Division was shortly going out to rest, a large draft of 282 other ranks from the Scottish Horse joined it. This draft consisted of a very fine type of men, who, although inexperienced in infantry work, soon learned their duties and were of great value to the Battalion.

The 7th began its march to the rest area on January 12th, 1917, and after halting successively at Puchvillers, Gézaincourt and Domquer arrived at its billets in Millencourt on the 16th. As the men had long been unused to marching they felt the strain after the mud of Courcelette, the marches being 13, 18 and six miles respectively. The rest area was not a good one. Millencourt, a small hamlet about four miles from Abbeville, was a poor village and its buildings gave but little shelter from frost and biting wind. This winter was the most severe of the whole war, and during the three weeks which the 7th spent in Millencourt the temperature never rose above freezing-point.

There was a good training area near the village, on which the Battalion carried out several attack practices over taped-out trenches. The Battalion was now brought up to nearly full strength by drafts, and platoon and company commanders had a good opportunity of exercising their men.

On January 22nd the Army Commander inspected the Battalion at training. It is interesting to note that the attack practice referred to above was evolved by General Harper, 51st Division Commander. The system he adopted was to attack in successive waves, each of which was given a definite objective. When the leading wave had taken the first objective, the one behind went through it to the second; the third wave would then go through the second and so on. It was understood that this method was first practised by the 51st Division when in this area.

The afternoons were chiefly given up to recreation of various kinds, especially in cross-country running, in which the Commanding Officer took a leading part. The usual inter-company and Battalion football matches were played and the Division held a boxing competition at Abbeville. The rest came to an end on February 5th, when the 51st moved off to join the Third Army at Arras, the Battalion strength on that day being 1180.

CHAPTER VIII

FEBRUARY TO JUNE, 1917

The Battle of Arras

THE move to Arras occupied a week. The weather continued bitterly cold and the roads were so slippery that progress was slow and irksome both for men and transport.

On its journey to the new area the 7th halted at the following places :—

February 5th, Domvast; 6th, Gapennes; 7th, Fillièvres; 8th, Beauvois; 9th, La Thieuloye; 10th, Bethonsart, and on the 11th the Battalion Headquarters and half A company reached Hermin. C and D companies, under Captain Munro, had left the Battalion at La Thieuloye and proceeded by motor omnibus to St. Vaast Bridge, north-west of Arras, to work on a broad-gauge railway which was then being laid out. B company and two platoons of A, under Captain Herd, were detached at Bethonsart and marched to St. Catherine, a suburb of Arras, where, for the next three weeks, they were employed under the IX Corps Signals in laying a buried telephone system linking up various battle headquarters.

Although nearly two months was to elapse before the Battle of Arras, there was much activity behind the line in preparation for it, and the greater part of the Battalion was employed for some time on this work. The remainder constructed large dug-outs for battle headquarters in and around the suburbs of Arras. On the whole, the work on which the Battalion was now engaged was not unpleasant. There were regular working hours and undisturbed rest. Definite tasks were allotted, and once these were finished the men were free to march off to their billets. For those employed at St. Catherine, Arras was near by, and the men were able to spend their evenings in the town.

On February 11th Lieutenant-Colonel Cheape proceeded to England for a month's leave, and a few days later Lieutenant-Colonel Allen, recovered from the wound received at High Wood, returned to the Battalion and resumed command. Under Lieutenant-Colonel Cheape the Battalion had acquitted itself right well at Beaumont Hamel, Courcelette, and elsewhere, a result largely due to his keenness and to his high capacity for command. This officer did not return to the 7th as, at the end of his leave, he was sent to another Division, and shortly afterwards was promoted Brigadier-General. Every officer and man welcomed the return of Lieutenant-Colonel Allen, who had done such splendid work for the welfare and for the training of the Battalion. At the same time the 7th greatly regretted the departure of Lieutenant-Colonel Cheape.

THE SEVENTH BATTALION THE BLACK WATCH

On February 21st the Battalion Headquarters and the details remaining with it moved to Bajus, where, on the 27th, C and D companies, having completed their work at St. Vaast Bridge, rejoined the Battalion, and steady work was continued with attack practices, musketry and the training of specialists. While this was going on B company had completed its cable-laying task and was engaged at Acq, Savy and St. Aubin in the formation of ammunition depots, upon which work it was retained until the 7th moved to Maroeuil on March 16th, when it rejoined the Battalion.

On March 17th the 7th moved from bivouacs in Maroeuil Wood and Bray to billets in Maroeuil itself. An unfortunate incident occurred at Bray; as a rule the village was not shelled by the enemy, but just before the 7th moved out on the 17th a shell from a high velocity gun struck one of C company's billets, killing four men and wounding five others.

The day after arriving in Maroeuil, Lieutenant-Colonel Allen left the Battalion to take up another appointment. His departure was a great loss. The difficulties which Lieutenant-Colonel Allen had to contend with during the training period were great, but in spite of all obstacles he laid down a solid foundation of discipline and set up an organization which stood the test of the whole war. His departure was very greatly regretted by all ranks. Lieutenant-Colonel H. H. Sutherland, D.S.O., a Regular Black Watch officer, now took over command. He had already seen much service in France, and before succeeding Lieutenant Colonel Allen had been in command of the 10th Service Battalion of the Gloucester Regiment.

After arriving in the forward area the 7th did two short tours of duty in the front line, holding the sector on the extreme left of the Division front in touch with the Canadians, the Arras–Lille road being the left boundary. Both tours were uneventful, although gradually the enemy seemed to show signs that he knew an attack was soon to take place, and became more and more active with his artillery. His fire, however, was chiefly directed on communication trenches, battery positions and billet areas behind the line. At this time the 154th Brigade was practising for the coming attack over model trenches in the Monchy–Breton area. Two companies of the 7th were detailed to assist that Brigade in the attack. A and D companies accordingly moved to La Comte and spent a week there with the 154th Brigade.

The attack on April 9th was to be made by the 34th Division, right; 51st Division, centre; and the Canadian Corps, left. The 51st Division attacked with the 152nd Brigade, right; the 154th, left; its objectives being the second and third German trench

BATTLE OF ARRAS, APRIL 9TH, 1917

systems. The area to be attacked was divided into three objectives, the "black," "blue" and "brown" lines respectively, the frontage at the final objective being a little over a mile, and the average depth about 3000 yards. For some days before the attack, British artillery and heavy trench mortar fire had increased in severity until it finally developed into intense bombardment at different hours of the day. During the assembly on the night of the 8th the guns concentrated on counter-battery work and for the time being reduced the enemy almost to silence. This was of great assistance to the infantry and enabled the movements to be carried out methodically and in good time.

On the 8th, Echelon B, consisting of six officers and 80 men under Major Milligan, moved to Savy, where it remained during the fighting as a nucleus on which the Battalion could draw in the event of severe battle casualties. The same evening the 7th moved into the trenches in "Abri central," with Headquarters in Grand Collectuer.

Zero had been fixed at 5.30 a.m. on April 9th, and at that hour the barrage opened. It consisted of a creeping barrage from 18-pounder guns, moving forward a hundred yards at a time, and a searching barrage covered the ground from 500 to 1000 yards in front of it. In addition, 4·5" and 6" howitzers and heavy guns were concentrated on the German battery positions and other points behind, while machine guns barraged the whole front to the Division.

The attack of the 154th Brigade reached the first objective, the "black" line, according to plan, but the progress towards the "blue" line was not made without considerable fighting. Here, as at Beaumont Hamel, isolated machine guns and snipers were the chief cause of delay; they were often difficult to locate, and even when found had to be dealt with by pressure from the flanks, as they seldom surrendered until almost completely surrounded. The machine gunners made the best use of their weapons, usually firing short bursts of about six shots, which proved very effective against the attackers as they advanced by rushes.

The task allotted to A and D companies was to follow the troops detailed for the capture of the final objective, the "brown" line, to stop midway between the "blue" and "brown" lines, and there to consolidate and form four strong points. By 12.30 p.m. A and D were moving up with the companies of the 7th Argyll and Sutherland Highlanders, when they overtook the troops then attacking the "blue line," and all entered the line about the same time. Here there was a pause in the barrage to allow troops to reorganize for the next advance and to enable the field guns to come forward.

THE SEVENTH BATTALION THE BLACK WATCH

When the barrage opened again the Argyll and Sutherland and Gordon Highlanders formed in waves, began their advance towards the "brown" line, and at about 1.40 p.m. they occupied, without serious opposition, a trench which they supposed to be the "brown" line, but which eventually turned out to be that allotted to A and D companies. Owing to this mistake the two companies began work on their strong points in a trench behind, known as "Allgoeur Weg." The error was eventually discovered, and the companies moved forward to their objective and set to work on the strong points whilst the attacking companies, the Argyll and Sutherland and Gordon Highlanders, advanced on the "brown" line.

This line had been evacuated by the enemy earlier in the day and had at one time been occupied by some of the Divisional machine gunners. But the enemy, finding that the advance had stopped, had returned to the trench, and when the 7th Argyll and Sutherland Highlanders tried to take it they found the Germans there in strength, sheltered behind a thick belt of wire which had not been destroyed by the British bombardment. They were thus forced to withdraw to the line held by A and D companies, and for the time being that became the front line on the 154th Brigade front, although the "brown" line was occupied by the 152nd Brigade on the right and the Canadians on the left. Bombing attacks from the flanks directed against the Germans still in possession of that part of the "brown" line failed to drive them out, and the position remained unchanged throughout the night of the 9th and through the whole of April 10th.

The weather, which had been cold throughout the attack, now changed to snow, so altering the appearance of the ground that some difficulty was experienced in recognizing landmarks, in addition to which all movements showed up clearly and brought down enemy fire. On the 11th, Battalion Headquarters and B and C companies joined A and D in the new front line—"Tommy trench."

It had been arranged that the 154th Brigade would attack the "brown" line again on the evening of the 12th, with the co-operation of a tank; but during the day scouts and patrols entered the "brown" line to find that the enemy had hurriedly evacuated the position, leaving much equipment and a newly delivered mail. The lights were still burning in their dug-outs. The "brown" line was thus occupied without further fighting, and patrols pushed forward to the railway line east of it.

The same night, 11th–12th, the 51st Division was relieved by the 4th, and the Battalion moved back in small parties to tents in Maroeuil Wood with Battalion Headquarters at Bray. There a message was received from Brigadier-General J. G.

SECOND PHASE, BATTLE OF ARRAS

Hamilton, commanding the 154th Brigade, thanking the Battalion for the assistance rendered to his Brigade in its attack on the 9th. The losses during the three days were light. One officer was wounded; six men killed, 12 wounded and one reported missing. In addition the Medical Officer, Captain E. J. Blair, was killed on the 11th; he had left Battalion Headquarters during the heavy bombardment to attend to a wounded man, and was killed by a shell as he came out of the dug-out. Captain Blair, a Fife man, was a most devoted medical officer; he had been attached to the Battalion since December, 1915, and had been previously wounded at Neuville-St. Vaast. His loss was keenly felt by all ranks.

Only three days' rest was allowed to the 7th. The Battalion was then called upon to take part in the second phase of the Arras battle. The 51st Division had been ordered to relieve the 9th (Scottish) Division on the right of the XVII Corps front, east of Fampoux, with the right of the Division resting on the Scarpe River, and on April 15th the 7th moved from Maroeuil Wood and marched to St. Laurent Blangy, where it halted for dinners, while advance parties proceeded to the line and arranged reliefs with the 8th Battalion The Black Watch, whose front it was to take over. In the evening the Battalion moved in by platoons, B and C companies occupying the front line with A and D in support in the Oppy line.

The front here had a character of its own in which there were three main features, namely, the village of Fampoux, the Scarpe River running through a swampy valley, and the embankment of the Arras-Douai railway, which ran north-east from Fampoux and through the southern slopes of Greenland Hill. The River Scarpe is about thirty feet broad at this part, and had only one practicable bridge south of Fampoux which made lateral communication difficult. Communication from front to rear had to be conducted by two well-defined routes, namely, by the Fampoux-Plouvain road and by a track along the river bank. In addition to these drawbacks the enemy on Greenland Hill, and their observers from the chimney of the Chemical Works at Roeux, were able to keep the whole Divisional area under observation. On the night of the relief the roads were heavily shelled with high explosive shells, and, there being much traffic with the ingoing and outgoing reliefs and transport, confusion resulted.

B company found its line, a shallow trench nearly three hundred yards in front and to the east of Fampoux; C on the right held the north side of the railway embankment facing south-east with its right on the Scarpe where the railway crosses the river. There were no dug-outs of any kind, but the men found some cover in holes cut in the embankment. The Battalion remained in the line three days and had to put up with constant shelling. There was no possibility of retaliation, and many men were wounded. The 7th was relieved on the 18th, and moved back to billets in Arras with Headquarters in the Rue des Agaches.

It had been decided to renew the attack on the Arras front on April 23rd, and the last tour had been for the purpose of familiarizing the troops with the nature of the ground and to enable preparations to be carried out. The next few days at Arras were therefore spent in reconnoitring overland routes to assembly positions, in issuing battle stores and in practising movements for the attack. While the 153rd Brigade and 154th Brigade were thus employed, the 152nd, then holding the line, had straightened out the front, and dug an assembly trench in No Man's Land, just east of a small wood on the front which had been allotted to the 7th.

General Harper had decided to attack with the 154th Brigade on the right and the 153rd on the left, while the 17th Division attacked south of the Scarpe River and the 37th on the left of the 51st. The 153rd Brigade attacked with the 7th Battalion The Black Watch on the right and 7th Battalion Gordon Highlanders on the left. The 6th Battalion Gordon Highlanders were in support on the right, and the 6th Battalion The Black Watch on the left. The front allotted to the 7th was that which it had held during its last tour in the trenches, the right flank resting on the railway embankment. The objectives allotted to the leading battalions were the "black" line, which corresponded with the enemy front line, and the "blue" line about a thousand yards beyond it, including the station buildings and chemical works of Roeux.

Zero hour was at 4.45 a.m. on the 23rd, and the Battalion left Arras the previous evening for its assembly positions. On the way up a halt was made at Hervin Farm near the embankment of the Arras-Lens railway, where a hot meal was served, and where the other three battalions of the Brigade were also assembled. The Battalion moved into position, and with the opening of the barrage the leading troops moved forward. A, B and C companies, each with a platoon of D attached to it, formed the first, second and third waves of the attack.

It was already daylight when the attack began, and almost before the British barrage had lifted off the German front line, the assaulting troops came under a murderous machine gun fire, and lost heavily. Several of the leading platoons reached the German wire, but it appeared to be undamaged, and in face of the heavy fire they were unable to advance further. The men,

SECOND PHASE, BATTLE OF ARRAS

consequently, were forced to lie down where they were and find what cover they could in shell-holes; time after time attempts were made to push forward through the wire but without success, each attempt being driven back with heavy loss. In these gallant and determined efforts the following platoon leaders were killed: Second Lieutenants Beatson, Nelson, Morris, Heard, Robertson, Allen and Wallace.

For four hours the position remained unchanged, the men lying with their dead and wounded comrades in shell holes unable to move. But about 9 a.m. a tank, which should have arrived at Zero hour, slowly approached across No Man's Land. Machine gun and rifle fire were useless against this, and as soon as the tank crossed the German wire and trench, the enemy in the front line put up their hands. A certain number were captured by the 7th, who had followed up the tank, and many more were killed.

A company thus gained its objective, the "black" line, although some hours late, and the survivors of B and C next pushed on towards the "blue" line accompanied by the tank, and advanced as far as the outbuildings of the Chemical Works. Many prisoners were taken during this advance, but in face of heavy fire from Greenland Hill and the Chemical Works further progress was held up. One or two posts were established, but the enemy now began to counter-attack fairly heavily and some of the ground had to be given up. These counter-attacks were carried out in mass with great determination. The British artillery and machine guns took advantage of the magnificent targets thus afforded, and their fire inflicted severe loss on the enemy, as most of the attacks were broken before they reached the line held by the 7th.

By that evening, after a day of confused and constant fighting, the Battalion had established itself in the enemy's support trenches on the west side of the Chemical Works. The attack had been similarly held up on either flank between the "black" and "blue" lines; but, although the final objective had not been reached, there had been substantial gains along the whole front, and practically all ground taken had been held and severe losses inflicted on the enemy.

The Battalion lost seven officers killed and five wounded; among the latter were Captain Cargill and Second Lieutenant Gowans, who died of their wounds; 64 other ranks were killed, 194 wounded and 65 missing.

The 7th held the new line all that night, and was relieved by the 27th Battalion Northumberland Fusiliers (103rd Brigade) on the morning of the 24th, when it moved back to the Oppy line, returning the next day to a factory in Arras. That afternoon the Battalion entrained and reached billets at Bailleul aux Cornailles late that night, where it remained resting and refitting until May 12th.

The men of the 7th will always remember this little French village. Situated about four miles from St. Pol, it was quiet, fresh and clean. Almost every billet had a shady orchard close by, and neither the village nor its inhabitants had been spoilt by constant contact with troops. The weather was delightful, and the three weeks spent resting were perhaps the most pleasant the Battalion experienced in France.

While at Bailleul, congratulatory messages were received from General Sir Charles Fergusson, commanding the XVII Corps, and from the Commander-in-Chief, who wired to General Harper:

"The fierce fighting of yesterday (23rd April) has carried us another step forward. I congratulate you on the results of it, and on the severe punishment you have inflicted on the enemy."

Brigadier-General D. Campbell, who had commanded the 153rd Brigade since it left Bedford over two years before, was now succeeded by Brigadier-General A. L. Gordon.

The training was varied by the usual football matches, and battalion sports were held on the 10th. Two days later the Battalion moved to Arras, and thence to "Fife Camp." Here two days were spent, but at 4 a.m. on the 16th a telephone message from the 153rd Brigade was received, stating that the enemy were counter-attacking the 152nd Brigade, and that two of its battalions had suffered severely from German bombardment. Orders were at once issued for the 7th to move by companies to the railway embankment between Blangy and Athies and there await instructions. Dawn was breaking as the Battalion moved off, and the German heavy artillery began to shell the area. B company, the last to start, lost Second Lieutenant Dunn killed and one or two men wounded from this fire.

The position in the front line was obscure. At first the enemy, advancing on either side of the railway embankment, succeeded in pushing their attack some way behind the front line, and for a time occupied Roeux Chemical Works. During the morning the Battalion Headquarters and A and B companies were ordered forward to the Oppy line, while C and D were placed under the orders of the 5th Battalion Gordon Highlanders, who had counter-attacked the enemy with the 152nd Brigade north of the railway.

Fighting went on all day, the Germans making several efforts to push forward their attack near the Chemical Works, but without success, and before nightfall the 152nd Brigade held its

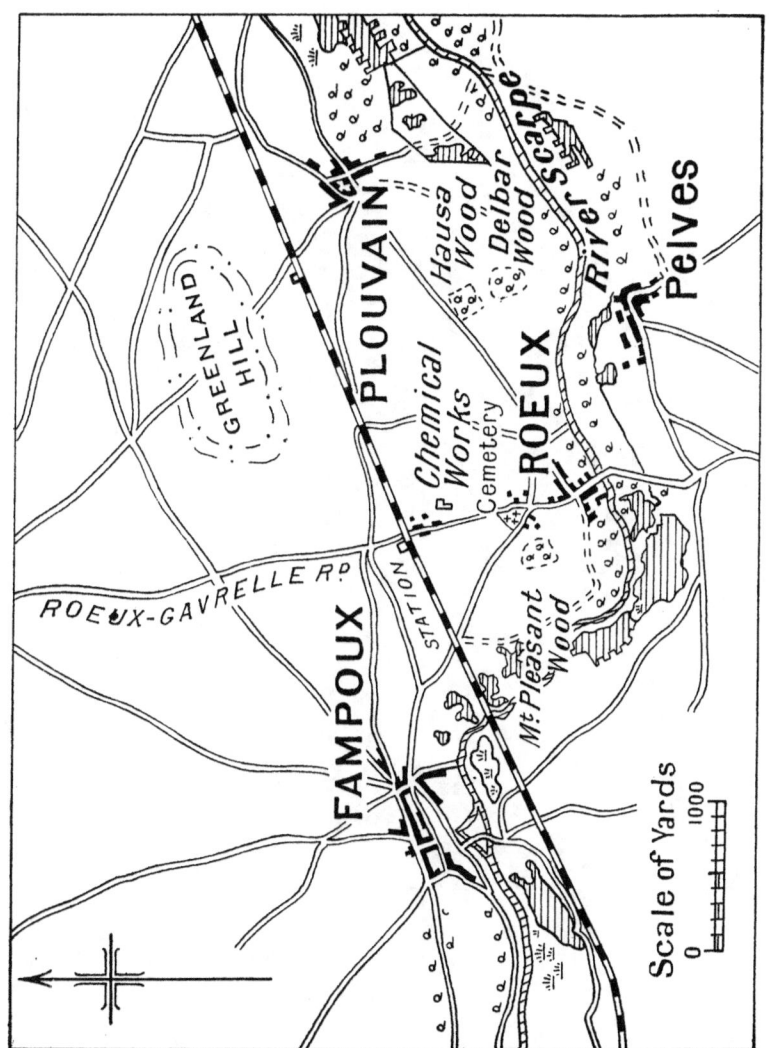

THE BATTLES OF ARRAS

Attack on the Chemical Works, Roeux, April, 1917. Attack on Greenland Hill, August, 1918

LEAVING THE ARRAS FRONT, MAY, 1917

original line, with the exception of a small part of an advance trench astride the railway. Consequently the 7th was not called upon to take action, and remained in support in the Oppy line. On the 19th the Battalion relieved the 6th Battalion The Black Watch in the front line, just east of the Chemical Works and astride the railway. The trenches in this sector were poor; some were only three feet deep, and in consequence the 7th—with the assistance of the 8th Battalion Royal Scots (Pioneers)—had hard work to make the line secure.

Throughout this tour the German artillery was fairly active, but no further infantry action took place and B company established a new post in a sunken road some two hundred yards in advance of the front line. During the night of the 25th the 7th was relieved by the 7th Battalion Gordon Highlanders. Unfortunately the trenches were heavily shelled and a number of men were wounded and Second Lieutenant Anderson killed. On relief the Battalion moved to Balmoral camp near St. Laurent Blangy, where it remained a few days. This proved to be the 7th's last experience of the Arras front for more than a year. The 51st Division was relieved, and on June 1st the Battalion, with the rest of the 153rd Brigade, set out by march route northwards to the Ypres sector.

Before leaving Arras, information was received that the M.C. had been awarded to Second Lieutenant W. Hopkins, and the D.C.M. to Company Sergeant-Major Raistick for gallantry during the attack on April 23rd. Lieutenant Hopkins had carried out a daring reconnaissance, advancing to within fifty yards of a number of German machine guns which were holding up the attack. Having thus located the position of these guns, he returned and led his company to the attack with complete success. Raistick, by his skilful use of rifle grenades, had silenced a German machine gun which was holding up the attack, and afterwards commanded his company with great success for twenty-four hours when all its officers had become casualties.

CHAPTER IX

JUNE TO SEPTEMBER, 1917

Ypres

THE move northwards occupied a full week, the Battalion sleeping in billets at La Thieuloye, Bailleul les Pernes, Bomy and Longuenesse. The weather was fine and the roads good. Moulle was reached on June 8th. This village, about four miles from St. Omer, was in the Second Army area, and the surrounding district was used as a training ground. It was well supplied with rifle ranges, and there were no restrictions as to moving over crops.

The Battalion spent a fortnight at Moulle practising attacks and carrying out general training and musketry. Leave, suspended during the Arras battles, was reopened and a liberal allotment given to the 7th. On June 12th the 51st Division was transferred to the XVIII Corps, General Sir F. I. Maxse, and three days later General Harper was informed that the Division would shortly take over a portion of the line in the Ypres salient and join in an impending attack. This proved to be the initial phase of the Third Battle of Ypres. On leaving Arras the 7th was under strength, but before going into the Ypres battle new drafts arrived, and when the fighting began the Battalion was almost up to strength.

The object of the forthcoming attack was to widen the Ypres salient, and capture the high ground which overlooked it; it was also hoped to carry the advance further towards the Houthulst Forest, should the attack prove successful.

The 153rd Brigade was allotted the left half of the Divisional front for this attack, and, to give the troops an opportunity of seeing the ground and becoming familiar with the local conditions, a week was spent in the trenches, from the 22nd to the 30th of June. During these eight days the 7th was in Brigade support, occupying shelters in the east bank of the Yser Canal, about two thousand yards behind the front line. Most of the water had been drained out of the canal, and its steep banks on both sides were honeycombed with dug-outs and shelters. Some of the dug-outs on the west bank were tunnelled, and lit by electric light.

As the preparations for the attack became more evident, the enemy artillery settled down to hinder the work, and, as the portion of the canal bank allotted to the 51st Division contained several well-marked routes across the canal, it appeared to be the object of every German artilleryman to smash these crossings. As time went on, the canal bank was more and more shelled, but the Battalion had but few casualties. It was chiefly employed in

THIRD BATTLE OF YPRES, JULY 31ST, 1917

constructing shelters near the canal to accommodate the troops when assembled for the assault, and in improving communication trenches.

On June 30th the Battalion was relieved by the 7th Battalion Gordon Highlanders, and after two days near Poperinghe, moved by train to St. Omer and marched to Marais and Nieurlet, two small villages north of St. Omer; here it received reinforcements and spent the next three weeks in steady training for the forthcoming attack. All ranks showed great keenness in the practice attacks and in learning and discussing the scheme of operations and the geography of the front line. In the training area a full-sized model of the German trench system and fortified farm houses was marked out. By constantly practising over this model course men soon became familiar with the ground and with the task allotted to them, and learnt how long it would take to reach their objectives and what had to be done to consolidate the position when won.

On July 17th a party of 30 men under Second Lieutenants Gerrard and Macgregor moved to the line to patrol the front over which the Battalion was to attack and to report on the progress the artillery had made in cutting the enemy wire. The Battalion observers also spent some days in the front trenches, making themselves familiar with the ground. On the 24th the Battalion, less Echelon B, moved by motor omnibus to Poperinghe and marched to Windmill Camp, about three miles nearer the front line, where it remained for four days. On the 28th A and D companies took over part of the front line, B and C remaining at Windmill Camp until the following day, when they also moved up. Both these moves were carried out after dark, in order that no hint of any concentration of troops should be given to the enemy.

The attack was timed to start at 3.50 a.m. on July 31st, and all troops had to be in assembly positions by two o'clock that morning. Overland tracks were clearly marked out with red lamps and arrows; and mounted police were stationed at every turn to regulate the traffic. During the assembly the German artillery was quiet, although there was some shelling at the crossings of the canal, where C company had lost 15 killed and wounded on the first night.

The frontage allotted to the Division was about 1500 yards, and ran from a point east of " Kempton Park " on the right, north-west to a point about 500 yards west of Hindenburg Farm. The objectives of the Division were: (1) The " blue " line which took in the whole of the German front system; (2) the " black " line, a supporting line of fortified farms roughly from Clark's Cottage to Jolle Farm; and (3) the "green" line, which was, practically, the line of the Steenbeek River.

On the right and left of the 51st Division were the 39th and 38th respectively. The Division attack was carried out on a two-Brigade front, the 152nd on the right and the 153rd on the left, each Brigade attacking on a two-battalion front. The leading battalions of the 153rd Brigade were the 7th Battalion Gordon Highlanders on the right and the 7th Battalion The Black Watch on the left. To these two battalions was given the task of capturing the first objective, namely, the "blue" line, after which the remaining battalions were to pass through them and go on to the "black" and "green" lines. The 7th attacked in four waves made up from A, C and D companies, B company being in Brigade reserve.

By 2 a.m. on the 31st the three leading companies were assembled in the front line, with Battalion Headquarters and B company in a large dug-out at Lancashire Farm, which also formed the battle Headquarters for the 153rd Brigade. Directly the leading companies got into position they set about cutting gaps in the wire, and, in order to give the correct direction for their advance, tapes were laid out by compass bearings through these gaps towards the German line. This work proved very useful, as at Zero hour, 3.30, the same morning, it was still dark, and had the tapes not been down, direction might easily have been lost.

Seldom has an attack been carried out with better artillery support. Every type and calibre of shell was used by the British batteries, and a new form of bombardment was introduced in the form of drums of burning oil projected on to the enemy's front line from trench mortars. The moral effect of these may have been considerable, and, to the attacking troops, the burning drums made a fine sight as they lit up the grey sky of that early morning.

The creeping barrage from the field guns moved forward at the rate of a hundred yards in four minutes and, except for one or two isolated German machine guns, it kept down all opposition, and C and D companies arrived in the "blue" line according to plan at 4.45 a.m. In the practice attacks this pace of a hundred yards in four minutes had seemed very slow, but on the actual day it was found that the ground was so badly cut up that the attackers could not have kept up with a faster barrage. So effective was this barrage that the whole enemy front system was taken with little opposition, and the few German machine guns which held out were quickly dealt with by rifle grenades and bombs, and their crews killed or captured.

WARRANT OFFICERS AND SERGEANTS OF THE SEVENTH BATTALION NEAR ST. OMER, JULY, 1917, BEFORE THE 3RD BATTLE OF YPRES

Top Row: Sergt. W. Moran, Sergt. A. Guthrie, Sergt. A. McKenzie, Sergt. A. Martin, Sergt. W. Byars, Sergt. Bogie, C.Q.M.S. Kirk, Sergt. D. O'Hare, Sergt. Thomas Malpas

Fourth Row: Sergt. D. Russell, Sergt. T. Gilzean, Sergt. G. Durham, Sergt. G. Tivendale, Sergt. McMillan, Sergt. Mortimer, Sergt. D. Murray, Sergt. A. Mitchell, Sergt. Horne, Sergt. Archibald Foster

Third Row: Sergt. N. McDonald, C.Q.M.S. D. Munnoch, Sergt. D. Jarvis, Sergt. R. R. Hughes, Sergt. Wilson, Sergt. Lumsden, Sergt. J. Wynd, Sergt. McCandlish, Sergt. D. Collier, Sergt. S. Brown, Sergt. Mollison, Sergt. Rennie, Sergt. Drum-Robertson

Second Row: C.Q.M.S. McKay, C.S.M. J. Logie, C.S.M. Cartwright, R.S.M. W. Ferrier, Lt. and Q.M.S. Watson, Lt.-Col. H. Sutherland, Lt. and Adjt. J. Reid, R.Q.M.S. A. McNab, C.S.M. G. Brown, C.S.M. Raistrick, C.Q.M.S. Gibson

Front Row: Sergt. James Inglis, Sergt. Thomas MacIntyre, Sergt. A. Farmer, Sergt. James McKinnie, Sergt. Thomas Stenhouse, Sergt. Bennett, Sergt. Cowie, Sergt. R. Adams, Sergt. G. Herron, Sergt. R. Thomson, Sergt. J. Rodgers, Sergt. Evans

THIRD BATTLE OF YPRES

The enemy front line had been almost wiped out, but the blockhouses, constructed of reinforced concrete, and fortified farms scattered between the front and support lines had successfully withstood the British artillery fire and it was at these points that resistance was met. The barrage paused for half an hour beyond the "blue" line while the other battalions of the Brigade got into position, after which it moved on and the supporting battalions passed through the 7th Battalion Gordon Highlanders and 7th Battalion The Black Watch and, although meeting with some opposition, reached all their objectives, the total depth of ground gained that day being over 2000 yards.

Directly they gained their objective, A, C and D companies started strengthening the "blue" line and constructing strong points, while in rear the field batteries were already moving up to position in the original No Man's Land. Roads were being made by the Pioneers and the Royal Engineers, and long lines of mule transport were bringing up rations and ammunition, in which work B company was employed most of the day. In the evening the weather, which had been fine, suddenly changed and the shell-torn area soon became a sea of mud, which greatly hindered the work of organizing the new line.

In this attack the 7th lost three officers wounded, 14 other ranks killed, 104 wounded and eight missing. All battalions of the 153rd suffered severely, and the day before the battle Brigadier-General A. Gordon, the Brigade Commander, and the Brigade Major, Captain H. Lean, were both killed by shell fire when walking round the trenches.

On August 1st the Battalion was relieved by one from the 154th Brigade and moved back to Siege Camp, near Brielen. It was not a comfortable resting-place, and was made worse by bad weather. The tents had been hurriedly pitched during heavy rain two days before, and the whole camp was a sea of mud. Unfortunately, the men were soaked to the skin, and although the Quartermaster did his best to fit up a drying shed, it was not until the Battalion moved back to another camp at St. Jan ter Biezin, two days later, that the men were able to dry their kits. In Roads Camp at St. Jan ter Biezin, the 7th spent three quiet and uneventful weeks, training and resting. During this period the Battalion football team, up till now unbeaten, received its one and only defeat from the Scots Guards, who won the match by two goals to one.

At this time the enemy were active in the salient with long range guns and with bombing raids. The latter were carried out with great daring by day and night, but fortunately Roads

THE SEVENTH BATTALION THE BLACK WATCH

Camp was too far to be visited by the raiders. Messages of congratulation on the result of the attack on July 31st were received from the Commander-in-Chief and General Maxse; Captain Mackintosh and Lieutenant Penney were awarded the M.C., and the M.M. was gained by 17 men of the Battalion. On August 30th the 7th again moved into the forward area, returning to Siege Camp, which now had been considerably improved. On September 12th it moved into shelters along the canal bank, in reserve to the 5th Gordon Highlanders, then holding the front line. On the 16th the 7th took over the front line from that battalion.

Conditions were just as bad in this part of the line as they had been at Courcelette. To reach the forward position it was necessary to march for about a mile along the duckboard track which, easily marked by German airmen, was generally under artillery fire. The actual front area was not much cut up by shell fire, and as the ground sloped down to the Steenbeek in rear it was comparatively dry. B and C companies held the front line with A and D in support. There were no trenches in the front line and no wire; the line consisted of isolated posts in shell holes, and as there were no communication trenches between these it was impossible to move by daylight.

Four days were spent in the line. There was considerable artillery activity on both sides, preparations being then made for an attack towards Poelcappelle on September 20th by the 154th Brigade. The plans for this could not be entirely hidden from the enemy, and in consequence the German guns put down a barrage each morning at dawn in the hope of catching assembling troops. As a rule this barrage fell behind the front line of posts and caused but few casualties.

On the night of the 19th the 9th Battalion Royal Scots (154th Brigade) came into its assembly positions in rear of B and C companies, who were then ordered to withdraw. A few hours before this took place a German ration party, which lost its way, blundered into one of B companies posts, one wounded German being captured. On relief the Battalion moved to Siege Camp, and two days later to Dirty Bucket Camp, where it spent a week cleaning and refitting. While here, General Gough, the Fifth Army Commander, attended Divine Service with the Battalion, and during the week messages of farewell were received from him and from General Maxse, the 51st Division being now bound for another part of the front. General Maxse wrote:—

". . . The Division fights with gallantry and can be de-
" pended upon to carry out any reasonable task allotted to it in

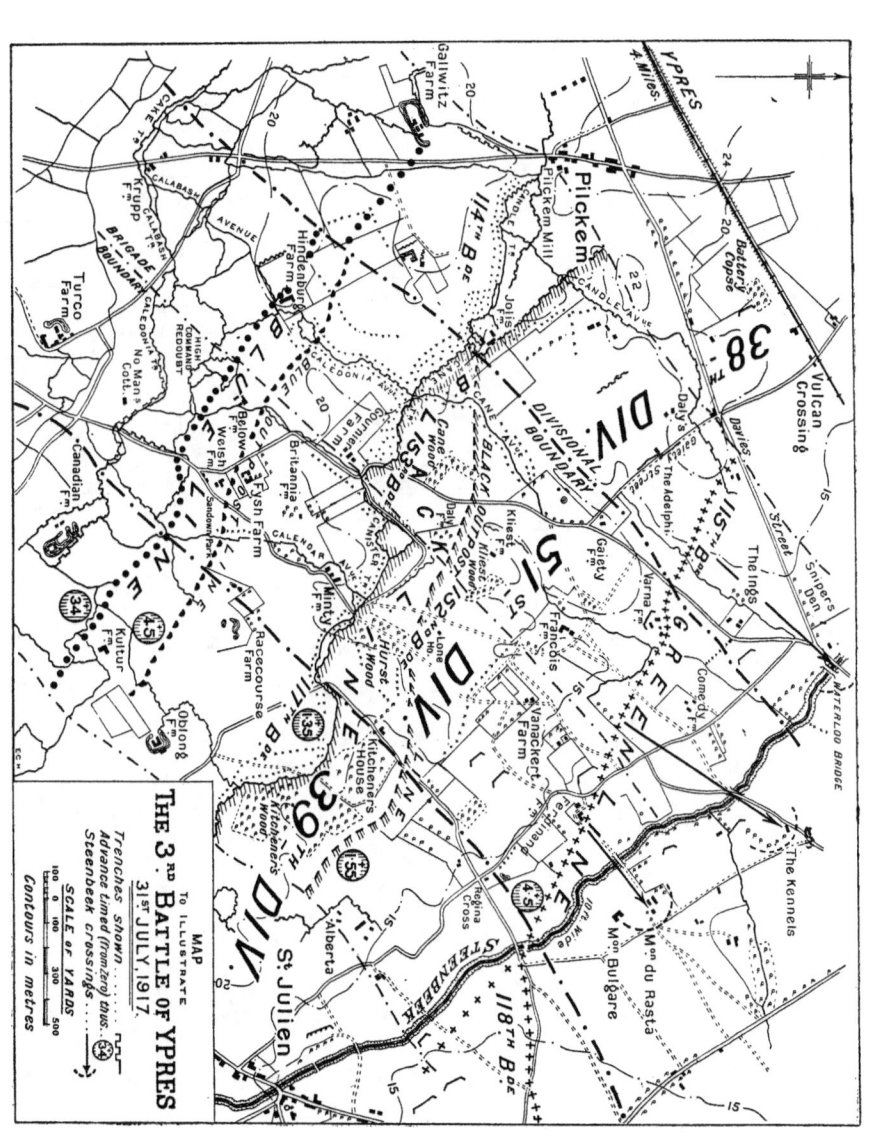

MOVE TO BAPAUME, SEPTEMBER 28TH, 1917

" any battle. For this reason I venture to place it among the
" three best fighting Divisions I have met in France during the
" last three years."

On September 28th the 7th entrained at Proven and arrived the following morning at Bapaume, marching from there to a camp at Gomiécourt about five miles away.

CHAPTER X

OCTOBER AND NOVEMBER, 1917

Attack on the Hindenburg Line

THE change from the Ypres salient to the fresh countryside round Bapaume was very marked, and although devoid of trees, houses and inhabitants, the change was refreshing after the mud of Flanders. On October 4th the Battalion moved into the line west of Cherisy, and on the 7th Colonel H. H. Sutherland took over temporary command of the Brigade, Captain H. C. Mackintosh assuming command of the Battalion. On the 28th the 51st Division left the Cherisy area and moved back for rest and special training, the Battalion marching to Wanquetin. During October only five men were wounded, and the strength at the end of that month was 49 officers and 1133 other ranks.

Colonel Sutherland returned to the Battalion on November 4th, Captain Mackintosh then becoming Second-in-Command. The Quartermaster, Lieutenant S. Watson, was promoted Captain about this time. Nothing could have been more popular with the 7th than this honour. " Sammy," like many others in the Regiment, had been promoted from the ranks in which he had served long and well. Genial and efficient, he was an outstanding personality not only in the Battalion, but in the whole Division.

During the three weeks spent at Wanquetin the weather was wet, but in addition to training, sports took up most of the afternoons, the Battalion winning a large share of the Brigade and Divisional competitions. Maps were issued showing a trench system but with no names whatever on them. For the sake of secrecy the instructions were vague, but it soon became common knowledge that the operation, wherever it was, would be carried out in conjunction with a large number of tanks.

On November 8th the first rehearsal with the tanks took place over a model course near Boyelles, and this exercise continued almost daily for a week; at the end of this time all ranks clearly understood what they had to do. In order to make co-operation still better, visits between the two arms were arranged and both officers and sergeants of the 7th dined with the Tank Battalion with whom they were to work. The secret regarding the point of attack was out on the 15th, when the Commanding Officer, Intelligence Officer and Company Commanders were taken to the sector from which the attack was to be launched. With the exception of the Commanding Officer, the rest of the party and Battalion Scouts remained in

CAPTURE OF FLESQUIÈRES, NOVEMBER 20TH, 1917

the area (Trescault) till the arrival of the Battalion four days later. This party discarded the Highland kit for that of a line regiment in order that the enemy might not by chance discover its presence in the front line.

On November 17th the 7th left Wanquetin for Bapaume, marching from there to Beaulencourt, where it spent that night and the following day. The next night the Battalion marched off after dark by companies to Rocquigny, where it spent the next day and received all stores necessary for the coming attack. At 11 o'clock on the night of the 19th the 7th entrained for Havrincourt Wood, where it was met by the Battalion Scouts, who led companies into their assembly positions, which were reached without incident.

The object of the forthcoming attack was the capture of the front and support portions of the Hindenburg line northeast of Havrincourt on a front of about 1500 yards at the start, but broadening at the third objective—north of the village of Fontaine Notre Dame—to just over 2000 yards, that village being some 5000 yards behind the enemy front line. This area was divided into three objectives, namely, the " blue," " brown " and " red " lines. The first included the Hindenburg front trenches and Chapel Trench, the second the village of Flesquières and the German support system, while the third was a sunken road running from Marcoing to Graincourt.

The 51st Division attacked on a two-Brigade front, the 152nd on the right, the 153rd on the left, each with two battalions in the front line and one in support. The 153rd Brigade attacked with the 6th Battalion The Black Watch on the right and 5th Battalion Gordon Highlanders on the left, the 7th Battalion being in support of the 6th, with the 7th Battalion Gordon Highlanders in support of their own 6th Battalion. The task of the leading Battalions was the capture of the German front trenches, that is, the " blue " line. After these had been taken, supporting battalions were to pass through and capture the " brown " and " red " lines. To assist this attack, seventy-two tanks were allotted to the Divisional front. These were allotted on a basis of three for every 150 yards and were to advance about 200 yards in front of the infantry. In order not to alarm the enemy, no artillery bombardment preceded the actual assault.

Zero hour was at 6.20 a.m. on the 20th, and by that time tanks, troops and guns were all in position. It speaks highly for the staff work of the Division that this concentration was carried out without a hitch and without the enemy having the faintest idea of what was taking place. Punctually at Zero hour the tanks began to move forward under artillery barrage, and thirty minutes later the 7th moved off behind those tanks which had been allotted to the second line.

The attack was a complete surprise, the enemy's counter-barrage was poor and little opposition was met with for some time. On reaching Havrincourt, however, the Division on the left was held up and the 5th Battalion Gordon Highlanders was delayed for a little time. During this period Chapel Trench was taken by C company of the 7th, which was immediately afterwards relieved by the Gordon Highlanders, who then continued their advance.

By this time C company had lost its tanks and had met with heavy machine gun fire, in spite of which Captain Beveridge, who was in command, gained Highland Cutting and the railway with little or no resistance, and at Cemetery Alley, near Flesquières, took 200 prisoners. At 10.35 a.m. the Hindenburg support line was reached and here the first set-back was met. In crossing the ridge to reach this line the surviving tanks came under the fire of a German field battery, very gallantly worked by an officer and two gunners. All the tanks received direct hits and were rendered useless. They were unable, therefore, to make gaps through the thick belt of wire in front of the German trenches. In addition to this bad luck the ground was swept by enemy machine gun fire from Flesquières, and the attack was thus held up on the whole Brigade front. During the afternoon Flesquières trench was taken, but no further advance was possible.

In this fighting one incident must be recorded. During the advance Second Lieutenant Clark's platoon was held up by machine gun fire and his Lewis gun section all became casualties. Lieutenant Clark himself then continued to work his gun in a most gallant style and succeeded in forcing the enemy to retire; unfortunately he was killed just as his efforts met with success.

That night patrols were sent out, and at 2 a.m. on the 21st reported that the Germans had evacuated Flesquières, and by 6 a.m. the final objective had been taken. Shortly after this the 5th Battalion Gordon Highlanders passed through the 7th and continued the advance. The following day the Battalion was attached to the 154th Brigade and moved to La Justice Farm, taking over the front line at Fontaine from the 7th Battalion Argyll and Sutherland Highlanders.

At dawn on the 23rd the 152nd Brigade attacked Fontaine Notre Dame, and the 7th then came under the orders of the Commander of the Brigade. The attack, which was pressed all day, was unsuccessful and the Battalion, which had not taken part in the operation, moved up that evening to meet an expected counter-attack. This, however, did not develop and the

MOVE TO FRÉMICOURT, DECEMBER, 1917

Guards' Division took over the line before dawn on the 24th, when the Battalion moved back to Trescault preparatory to leaving the area. The 7th's casualties in this battle were one officer and eight other ranks killed, one officer and 94 other ranks wounded and one missing.

Early on the 24th the Battalion left Trescault for Ytres, where it entrained for Acheux and marched from there to Hédauville. By this time the weather had broken and the march to Ytres was a trying one over country tracks inches deep in mud; train arrangements also failed and the Battalion spent a miserable night lying in the open. The next five days were spent resting and reorganizing at Hédauville. On the 30th the Battalion moved to Acheux, where it entrained and was rushed forward to help in stemming the German counter-attack at Cambrai. Detrainment was carried out at Bapaume and the Battalion marched from there to Léchelle, where it received its battle stores and stood by, ready to move at a moment's notice. The danger passed, however, and the Battalion was not engaged.

The weather was now bitterly cold and, as the huts at Léchelle were in bad repair and no blankets available, the time spent there was not agreeable. On December 2nd the 7th moved to Morchies and on the 5th to Frémicourt.

CHAPTER XI

DECEMBER, 1917, TO THE END OF APRIL, 1918

The German Offensives
(*See Map facing Page* 188.)

THE next three months were spent in the area in front of Bapaume, either in the line or in reserve positions behind it.

The 51st Division was now in the IV Corps, Third Army. The weather was dry and cold, but once the Battalion settled down conditions were not unpleasant. Many of the trenches in the area were old and in bad repair and no work had been done on defensive lines in rear. Much work on these defences and on the front line was therefore carried out by the whole Division during this period. The enemy counter-attack on December 1st had been successfully checked and no further trouble was met throughout the winter. At some places on the Divisional front the British and German lines were over a thousand yards apart and the enemy shelling was usually confined to areas behind the front and support lines. Patrolling was active, but there was little opposition. The enemy held his position with isolated posts well in front of the Hindenburg line and was content to remain behind the heavy wire entanglements of these posts.

As soon as the trenches had been put in good order work was begun on dug-outs. The old ones were improved and new ones constructed. Each battalion formed a mining platoon which went into the line with its battalion but did no ordinary duties. These were accommodated separately and worked in three shifts of eight hours in dug-outs in their battalion sectors. For the next three months the Battalion carried out alternate spells in the line and in billets or huts behind it, many of which were extremely uncomfortable and the weather was cold and snowy.

Early in February, owing to the shortage of men, all Brigades were reduced to three battalions and, in consequence, the 5th Gordon Highlanders left the 153rd Brigade. The farewell parade was an informal one, but the whole Battalion turned out, for all were sorry to say "Good-bye" to the Gordons, who had been with the Brigade ever since the formation of the Division.

Towards the end of February there were rumours of a coming German attack, and, in fact, the preparations which were then being made behind the German lines were obvious enough to support such stories. With the exception of these alarms and the preparations made to guard against any attack, the first weeks of March passed quietly. On March 1st Colonel Sutherland left the Battalion on being posted for six months' duty in England,

TRENCH WARFARE, JANUARY–MARCH, 1918

and the command passed to Lieutenant-Colonel S. R. McClintock, Gordon Highlanders. Colonel Sutherland had served for many years in the Regiment. His experience was wide, his judgment sure. No man loved The Black Watch more than he, and no man was held in higher esteem. No one had a greater regard for the traditions of The Black Watch than Harry Sutherland, and no one lived up to them more faithfully. His departure was deeply regretted by the whole Battalion.

The 7th took over the front line at Louverval on March 1st and much patrolling was carried out and a few skirmishes with German patrols took place. Several alarms caused the British artillery to open fire, but without drawing retaliation from the enemy. These alarms had one good effect, in that they kept everyone up to concert pitch; all ranks were now eager for a fight and it was in that spirit that the 7th met the German offensive on the 21st. There was now no doubt that the enemy intended to attack in the near future and, on the 20th, much movement behind the enemy lines seemed to point to an early attempt, although patrols which returned at 4 a.m. on the 21st reported everything normal.

An hour later, however, the enemy barrage fell with great violence and accuracy on the whole of the forward area as far back as Beugny. The two front line companies, C and D, were at once cut off, but resisted gallantly and were still holding out when the Battalion Headquarters were engaged with the enemy at Louverval. The intense bombardment entirely destroyed the front line trenches and few survivors of C and D were able to get back to Battalion Headquarters. The Germans had broken in on the left of the 6th Battalion and on the front of the 6th Division, and had thus outflanked the high ground around Louverval then held by the 153rd Brigade, which was thus compelled to retire.

The next stand was made at Louverval by B company and part of A, but by three o'clock in the afternoon this position also became untenable, the enemy threatening it from both flanks. It was here that Lieutenant Berry was captured. A buried cable ran from Brigade Headquarters direct to C company, and from his dug-out Berry was in communication with the Brigade right up to the moment of his capture and kept Headquarters informed of the progress of events. The final stand was made at Louverval by Second Lieutenant Cumming, who was last seen with a handful of men entirely surrounded and fighting gamely. All this garrison perished.

Meanwhile the Headquarters of the 7th and 6th Battalions came into action, occupying a trench just east of the Doignies road. Flanking fire from the left soon made this position

THE SEVENTH BATTALION THE BLACK WATCH

untenable, and after consultation Colonel McClintock and Major Campbell, Commanding the 6th Battalion, decided to withdraw to the reserve line, a movement which was carried out under heavy machine gun fire both from the left flank and front, and also from a low flying German aeroplane.

The next line taken up was along Beaumetz–Morchies road, which was held by the remainder of A company, about sixty strong, and by the remainder of the Battalion—some thirty all told, mostly men of B company. This position was held throughout the night and well into the afternoon of the 22nd, when the enemy, after several failures, pushed forward strongly from the front and also attacked on the flank from Morchies. During one of the attacks that morning the Germans actually got into the 7th Battalion line, but were thrown out again, leaving one prisoner. Late in the afternoon what was left of the Battalion took up a position in front of Lebucquière and south of the Bapaume–Cambrai road, passing north towards Morchies, under the personal command of Colonel McClintock, who, with the Adjutant, Captain Reid, were the only two officers remaining out of the nineteen who went into the line before the attack.

During the night the party was withdrawn and occupied the old German trenches in front of Bancourt, where they helped to form a continuous Divisional line. This was a support position to the 19th Division, which had now taken over the front line. The 23rd passed quietly, the main incident being the arrival of a German aeroplane which dropped pamphlets meant for their own troops stating the extent of their advance. It was here also that the famous German message was received by the Division which ran as follows: " Good old 51st. Still sticking it? "

On the morning of the 24th the 19th Division was gradually driven back, and by the afternoon the 7th was again directly facing the enemy. The line was held against constant pressure till 7 p.m., when a flank attack from the right turned the position. A withdrawal was made to Loupart Wood, where the remnants of the Battalion were joined by the officers and men from Echelon B.

The stand at Bancourt had been long enough to allow the 19th Division to take up another position, and the trenches in Loupart Wood again became the support line. The night passed quietly, but the enemy attack was resumed again in the morning of the 25th. Again the 19th Division held out until the afternoon, when, as before, the few survivors of the 7th, with what remained of the 51st Division, were again face to face with the Germans. Once more, with both flanks turned, the Division was obliged to withdraw and then took up a position on the ridge between Irles and Pys. The 7th then ceased to be a unit

THE GERMAN OFFENSIVE, MARCH, 1918

in itself, and became part of the composite "51st Division Force."

At dusk on the 25th a further withdrawal took place to a position in support of the 62nd Division, and here the composite force remained till midnight, when it was finally relieved and the survivors of the 7th marched back in two parties. The first under Major Keir, who had taken over command when Lieutenant-Colonel McClintock had been wounded, reached Hébuterne on the night of the 26th; the second party moved to Colincamps and then to Pas, where it spent the night of the 26th.

On the 27th the Battalion reassembled at Barly, where it was joined by the Quartermaster and transport, and reorganization was carried out, although by this time each company consisted of only a handful of men. On the 29th the Battalion entrained at Frévent for Lillers and marched from there to billets in Burbure.

Such is the story of the 7th during the great German offensive. The losses suffered by the Battalion were, as far as can be ascertained, 23 officers and 627 other ranks out of 39 officers and 941 other ranks. For their services during this fighting three officers and 13 other ranks received decorations.

The Battalion remained a week at Burbure, where several drafts arrived, and the time was spent in training and reorganization. For the first time in the history of the Battalion many of the men sent to the 7th belonged to other Highland regiments, though when it next moved into the line, the greater number were still Black Watch men; the Gordon Highlanders, Seaforth Highlanders and Argyll and Sutherland Highlanders contributing about one-eighth of the total strength. All difficulties, however, were soon overcome, thanks greatly to the untiring energy and unbounded enthusiasm of Major D. R. Keir, the Commanding Officer. Twice in 1918 Major Keir was called upon to command the Battalion in exceptionally difficult circumstances and each time he carried through successfully.

On April 8th the Battalion moved to Busnes, when the 51st Division came into the XI Corps area. Here it was inspected by the Corps Commander, who addressed the Battalion and said that he did not intend to call upon it for work until it had had a thorough rest. Little did his hearers think that within twenty-four hours the 51st Division would be engaged in another great battle. The strength of the Battalion was now 24 officers and 826 other ranks.

At dawn on the 9th the sound of an intense bombardment on the front held by the Portuguese was heard at Busnes, and at 10 a.m. it was reported that the enemy had broken through the line and that the 51st Division was to move up at once, each

THE SEVENTH BATTALION THE BLACK WATCH

company of the 7th to leave independently when it was ready. By 2 p.m. the Battalion was clear of Busnes and reached the point of assembly, Le Cornet Malo, about 5 p.m. in spite of the fact that it had to pass along roads crowded with French refugees and men of the shattered Portuguese Division. From here the 7th moved into Brigade reserve, taking up a position east of Pacault in the open country, while the 6th Battalion The Black Watch and 7th Battalion Gordon Highlanders held the front line along the west bank of the Lawe river from Fosse to Lestrem. Later that night C company moved up in support of the 6th Battalion.

On the 10th the 7th moved forward to support positions at 8.15 a.m., and an hour and a half later C company sent up a platoon to help the 6th Battalion, as the enemy had seized Lestrem post. With this exception the morning passed quietly, the time being spent in constructing breastworks as there were no defences of any kind. In the afternoon the situation north of Lestrem became obscure and C company moved forward into position astride the L'Epinette–Lestrem road. Four machine guns had been attached to this company and they, with the remainder of the Battalion, then moved forward north of their original positions. Just as the new area was occupied the 7th was ordered to send two platoons to the 6th Battalion, and in compliance with this Lieutenant Crosbie and two platoons of A company moved forward while C and D companies with the machine guns moved to the north of the L'Epinette–Lestrem road to clear up the situation and to prevent the enemy crossing the River Lawe. The last two platoons of A company then joined the 6th Battalion and filled a gap which had been made by the enemy between the 6th Battalion The Black Watch and the 7th Battalion Gordon Highlanders.

At 2 a.m. on the 11th A company was in position and in touch with the 6th Battalion on its left, but with its right flank exposed, as touch could not be gained with the 7th Battalion Gordon Highlanders.

An hour later D company was also in position with its left in touch with the 50th Division and its right with B company, but did not join up with the 6th Battalion on its right until 4.30 a.m. The delay was due to B company encountering the enemy, who were pressing forward their attack and had already crossed the River Lawe. At 6.15 a.m. C company was obliged to send a second platoon to support the 6th Battalion. The Germans had been pressing forward all night and at 6 a.m. increased their efforts, covered by heavy machine gun fire. To give them their due this enemy attack was magnificently led by their officers, and when dawn broke the Germans had already

WOUNDED MEN OF THE SEVENTH BATTALION WAITING TO BE TRANSFERRED TO HOSPITAL, MERVILLE, APRIL, 1918

THE GERMAN OFFENSIVE, MARCH, 1918

established themselves on the western bank of the Lawe. By 7 a.m. the right flank of B company was in the air, but a defensive flank was formed, and for an hour and a half B and D companies held their positions on the Lestrem–Beaupré line.

In this attack the Germans employed the same tactics which had been so successful in March. Forcing gaps through the line they pressed their advantage on each flank, bringing up machine guns to very advanced positions. Even light field guns came forward to within very short range—on one occasion the entire crew of one of these guns was killed by rifle fire from B company.

At 8.30 a.m. the enemy had broken through as far as the positions at L'Epinette held by the last two platoons of C company. Here they were checked until a continuous line was formed running back from D company's original position through B to C company's position in an extended defensive flank. From this point the 6th Battalion took up the line with what remained of A company, 7th Battalion, and with some of the 7th Battalion Gordon Highlanders.

In this way the 7th was heavily engaged all day helping to stop the enemy advance. The fighting was fierce and all battalions in the 153rd Brigade were more or less mixed up. It speaks well for the spirit of the Battalion that the men made such a stubborn resistance. It was almost entirely under the control of new and very junior officers and non-commissioned officers, the ranks being filled with young and inexperienced soldiers.

From this point the story of the Battalion can no longer be followed as a whole. The companies became more and more detached and were joined by men, not only of other regiments, but from other Brigades and Divisions. It could no longer be controlled from behind, and resistance depended entirely on those officers present in the line who were able to conform with the movements of the units on their right and left.

At midday men of the Battalion, chiefly survivors of A and C companies, and Battalion Headquarters were holding positions round La Bouzateux Farm with the 6th Battalion and the 7th Battalion Gordon Highlanders. On their left were the Duke of Cornwall's Light Infantry and beyond were B and D companies with part of the 6th Battalion and 8th Battalion Royal Scots, who held the line of the Merville–Estaires railway facing south.

In the afternoon the German efforts opposite the Battalion slackened, but La Bouzateux Farm was lost. Stragglers from various units of the Division were now formed into a reserve and moved up behind the Pacaut–Bouzateux Farm line under volunteer officers from the artillery. Two officers, Captain

Rickard and Lieutenant Seton, of the 12th Australians, were eventually attached to the Battalion and fought with it until the 13th. At 2 p.m. D company found that its left flank was in the air as the Duke of Cornwall's Light Infantry had been forced back, but it held its position until a fresh German battalion, attacking through Lestrem towards Paradis, forced it back. B and D companies then retired to the west of Merville, where they were reorganised and placed at the disposal of the 50th Division. These two companies then occupied the position north-west of the town, and here they held on throughout the night.

Earlier in the day part of A company under Lieutenant Menzies had formed a defensive flank at Bouzateux Farm, while Captain Beveridge and Lieutenant McCredie held a further position west of Paradis.

During the afternoon another party of men, who had been collected at Brigade Headquarters during the fighting, was sent up to reinforce the Battalion. This party was directed to a position near the Calonne–Merville–Pacaut cross roads, but, as this was found to be already held by the Duke of Cornwall's Light Infantry, a line some distance in rear was taken up.

That night the Battalion lay with companies scattered in the following order: On the left, and with the 50th Division, were B and D companies under Lieutenant Anderson. South of Merville, about Turbeauteau, were some of A and C companies under Lieutenants Crosbie and Gerrard, mixed up with men from the 8th Battalion Royal Scots. About Bouzateux Farm were other parties of A and C under Captain Beveridge and Lieutenants Kidd and Robertson-Reid, while Battalion Headquarters were at a farm on the outskirts of Calonne. During the night the Germans pressed forward, and the line thus held by the Battalion eventually became the front line.

At dawn on the 12th the enemy again attacked and occupied Merville, during which fighting Lieutenant Crosbie was killed, and the survivors of the Battalion fell back over the canal at Calonne. Unfortunately there was no time to demolish the canal bridges, with the result that they were captured by the enemy, who thus had no difficulty in crossing. A further stand was made on the north bank of the Lys in conjunction with the 9th Battalion Royal Scots, but a flank attack once again drove the 7th Battalion back, this time to the north-east of Calonne.

Here the 7th ceased for the time being to exist as an organised battalion, all available men being divided among the officers who remained. With detachments from the 50th and 61st Divisions they formed a line near the brickfields of La Corbie. B and D companies had become entirely separated and worked

REORGANIZATION, APRIL, 1918

with the 50th Division until it was relieved by the 5th north of Merville. During the afternoon the position at La Corbie had to be evacuated; Major Keir was wounded and the survivors of the 7th took up a position south of Bois Moyen about 8 p.m. An hour later the 7th Division counter-attacked and the Battalion was then withdrawn through St. Venant to Busnes, where it went into reserve.

The losses suffered by the 7th in the fighting between the 9th and 13th of April were one officer and seven other ranks killed; five officers and 660 other ranks wounded; and two officers and 162 other ranks missing. For gallantry during the action members of the Battalion received the following awards: one Bar to M.C., three M.C.'s, three D.C.Ms., and one Military Medal.

Reorganization was carried out at Busnes on the 13th, and the following day the Battalion took up a separate position along La Bassée Canal, and the same night Lieutenant-Colonel J. C. Millar, M.C., took over command. On the 15th the Seventh moved back to St. Hilaire-Cottes, where reorganization was completed and training of the new drafts was begun.

The Battalion was thus employed for the next nine days. On the 23rd it relieved the 4th Battalion Gordon Highlanders in the Robecq sector in support of the 61st Division and under the orders of the Officer Commanding 184th Infantry Brigade. Major Keir now returned from hospital and took over the duties of Second-in-Command. This period was marked by very heavy enemy shelling of the back areas. On April 28th the billets occupied by B and C companies in Busnes were so heavily shelled that the companies had to leave them, moving to the western outskirts of the town and, later, to La Pierrière. The night of the 29th was also marked by heavy shelling, which obliged A and D companies to withdraw to billets in Le Cornet Brassart and Battalion Headquarters moved to La Pierrière.

CHAPTER XII

MAY TO AUGUST, 1918

Roclincourt and Champagne

THE whole of May was spent in ordinary trench warfare and the Battalion had time to recover from the effects of the recent fighting. The 7th was now practically a new Battalion; the gaps caused by the recent losses were filled by young and inexperienced men, and few of the original non-commissioned officers had survived the two battles of March and April. Only six officers had come through the two battles unwounded, and many of those who now joined as reinforcements had never seen each other before.

The first five days of the month were spent training at La Pierrière, and on May 5th the Battalion moved to Ecoivres, taking over a sector of the line at Willerval from the 35th Canadian Infantry on the following day. June was a repetition of May, but there was more activity on the British side and a corresponding quietening down on the part of the enemy. Major Milligan left to take up an appointment at Corps Headquarters and Major Keir returned from the Divisional School to take his place. Captain F. I. Gerrard was appointed Adjutant in place of Captain Reid, who joined the Senior Officers' School at Aldershot.

The Battalion carried out a raid on the night of the 29th. The raiders entered the German front line, but found it unoccupied and no information was gained. The 7th remained in the Roclincourt area until July 8th, when it marched to Château de la Haie on relief by the 44th Canadian Infantry Battalion and, on the 12th, moved by light railway to billets in Maisnil and Neuville-au-Cornet. The 51st Division was now transferred to the XXII Corps, which was due to move to the French front in Champagne.

Entraining at Tincques at midnight on July 15th, the 7th detrained at Romilly in Champagne early the following morning and proceeded by motor 'bus to Avize. It thence marched to Monthelon, where, on the 18th, it was joined by its transport, which had moved by road. In this part of France the inhabitants had never before seen a Highlander, with the result that when the billeting officer arrived at dusk he found the doors of the houses slammed and locked as he approached them, the children flying shrieking before him. Accordingly the Battalion spent the night in the woods north-west of Monthelon, but managed to secure billets the following day, and by the end of their stay all ranks had become very popular with the inhabitants.

On July 19th the Commanding Officer and the Company

CHAMPAGNE, JULY, 1918

Commanders reconnoitred the line they were to take over from the French, while the Battalion marched through Pierry to Epernay, where it remained during the afternoon and where it received orders for an attack which was to take place the following morning. At 9 o'clock that night the Battalion again moved off and, led by French guides, arrived at its assembly position at 4 a.m. on the 20th, four hours late, due to the overcrowded routes and spasmodic shelling throughout the march.

The area over which the 51st Division was to attack was a difficult one. The line ran roughly north-east and south-west along the edge of the Bois des Éclisses, through which passed the German front line. It was known that the Germans were holding this line in strength, in fact there were three enemy Divisions in front of the 51st, namely, the 123rd (Saxon) Division on the German right, the 103rd (Hessian) in the centre, and the 22nd (Sachsen-Meiningen) on the left. The intention of the Divisional Commander was to penetrate deeply into the enemy line with the help of the 62nd Division on the right and the 14th (French) Division on the left. The attack was arranged to take place in three stages, the first objective being the " blue " line—roughly the original French front line—the second the " green " line—which ran from Chaumuzy on the right to the north-west edge of the Bois de Courton—and the third, the " brown " line some way further back. The operation was to be carried out on a two-Brigade front, the 154th on the right and the 153rd on the left, with the 152nd in reserve.

The attack of the 153rd Brigade was led by the 6th Battalion The Black Watch and 7th Battalion Gordon Highlanders, who were detailed to take the "blue" line. The 7th was directed to follow in support and continue the advance to the "green" line after the "blue" had been captured. At 8 a.m. the attack began with an artillery barrage, to which the enemy replied in thirteen minutes. Almost immediately after the infantry advance had started the leading battalions were held up by the thick woods in front of them, from which the enemy poured a heavy fire. The result was that the 7th, moving up in support, soon found itself involved in the fighting long before the leading battalions had reached their objective. The attack was now held up and the fire from German machine gun nests caused a gap in the Brigade line of attack. Colonel Millar observed what had happened and, realizing what the consequences might be, led one company up and filled the gap. His action, for which he received the D.S.O. later, is best described in the official account.

" Colonel Millar, seeing that his attacking waves had lost direc-
" tion owing to the gap made by the enemy barrage, pushed

"forward with his Intelligence Officer and passed through part
"of the heaviest of the barrage. He was thus able to direct a
"company from his rear wave to fill the gap. In passing through
"the barrage Colonel Millar lost his Intelligence Officer and both
"orderlies and was himself blown over by shells on more than
"one occasion."

Later on Colonel Millar sent for Battalion Headquarters to advance, but although they moved forward at once the Commanding Officer and Adjutant did not meet till noon. It was soon evident that the objectives would not be captured in the time allotted. The fighting throughout the day then resolved itself into surprise encounters and hand-to-hand fighting in the clearings and rides of the woods. Second Lieutenant McCorquodale's platoon of D company actually reached the final objective in the Bois des Eclisses, but being entirely unsupported, the position became untenable and he was obliged to come back.

During the day Second Lieutenant Cable also distinguished himself, and was later awarded the M.C. and Croix de Guerre. After his Company Commander had been wounded, he took command, and with two platoons captured a German officer and 25 prisoners. He then pushed forward and captured another 20 men. Subsequently, finding that his men were outflanked, he withdrew his company, but later in the day, on learning that the troops on his right flank were advancing, he again led his platoon forward and captured several machine gun nests.

By the afternoon all three leading battalions of the 153rd Brigade were mixed up and orders were issued for the line to be consolidated. The position won by the 153rd was well in advance of those on the right and left, but nevertheless the work was done. From the beginning of the attack the Germans in the village of Paradis, on the left, had repulsed all French attacks. In the evening about six o'clock they began a counter-attack on the 153rd Brigade front with the result that, as both its flanks were weak and unguarded, it was ordered to withdraw as far as the La Neuville-les-Haies road. Here the 6th Battalion Seaforth Highlanders came up and filled the gap on the left flank between the 6th Battalion and the French, and also took over the front line from the 7th who then moved back to reorganize.

On the 21st the 152nd Brigade was ordered to attack through the 153rd, while the 7th Battalion was directed to form a defensive flank on the left if required. The attack met with strong opposition and little ground was gained. Nothing happened on the 22nd until the afternoon, when the 7th was ordered to capture the position covering Paradis to give supporting fire to

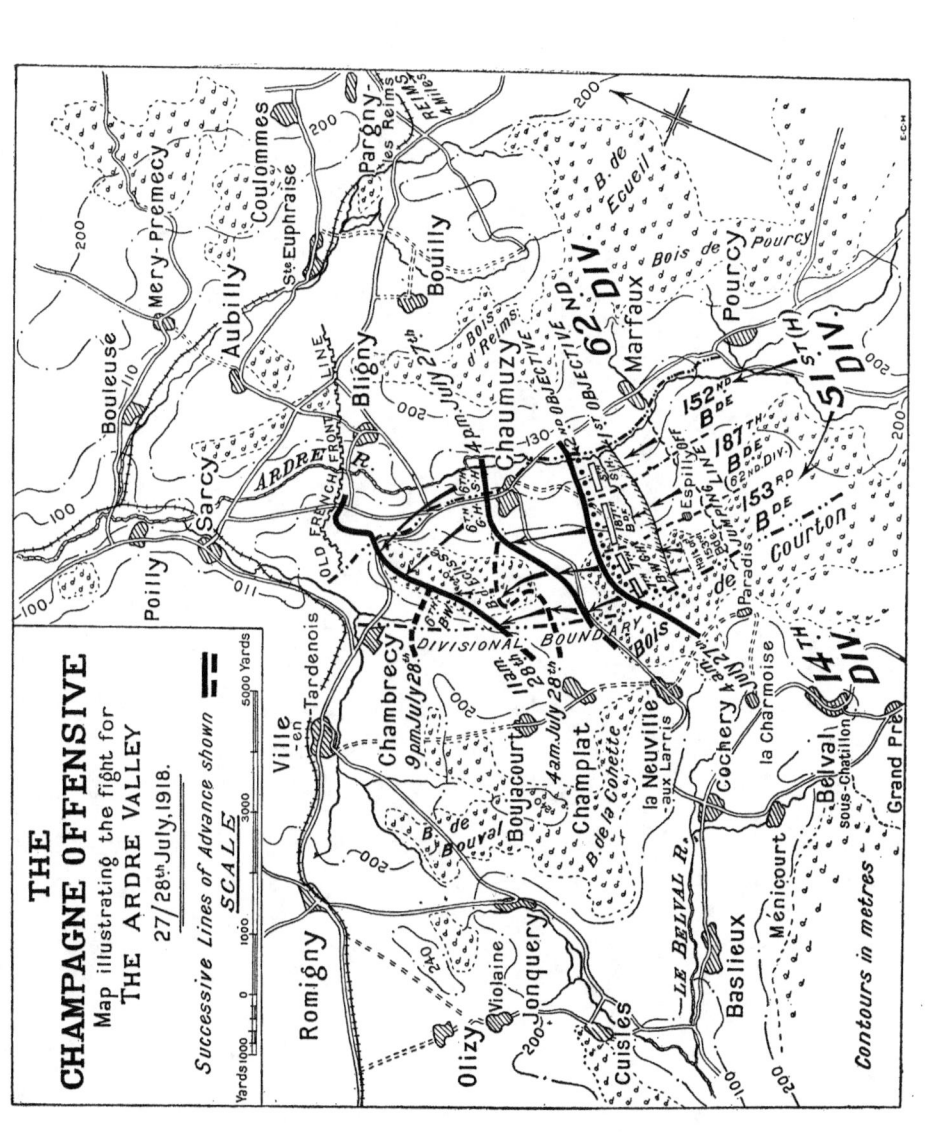

CAPTURE OF THE BOIS DE COURTON, JULY, 1918

another French attack on the village. The 6th Battalion was to co-operate by guarding the right flank of the 7th. Strong opposition was met with and at 5 p.m., when the French attack was launched, no progress had been made and their assault was repulsed with considerable loss.

Thus ended the first phase of the operations in Champagne. The Battalion casualties in the recent fighting were one officer and 20 other ranks killed; six officers and 171 other ranks wounded and 20 other ranks missing. The trench strength of the Battalion on the 20th was 12 officers and 249 other ranks, and on the 23rd, after having received reinforcements, it was 12 officers and 216 other ranks, a curious coincidence showing that nearly all the reinforcements received during the fighting were lost in the battle. The Battalion took four German officers and 169 other ranks prisoners, together with three heavy trench mortars and no less than thirty-seven machine guns.

The 23rd passed quietly and the Battalion was relieved the following day by a unit of the 35th (French) Division. It moved to huts near St. Imogé, where, on the 25th, it was visited by General Godley, the XXII Corps Commander, who congratulated the 7th on its action during the recent fighting.

The Battalion moved into the line once more on the 26th to take part in another attack arranged for the following day. This was to be carried out on a three-Brigade front, the 152nd on the right, the 187th (lent by the 62nd Division) in the centre, and the 153rd on the left, the 7th Battalion being in Brigade reserve on the Courton-Ruine road near Pourcy, detailed to capture the final objective after the leading troops had taken the first two.

This attack made a definite break in the German line. At 6 a.m. on July 27th the 51st and 62nd Division artillery, assisted by that of the French, put down a heavy barrage on the enemy trenches. Few German guns replied, and when the assault started it was found that the enemy had evacuated their positions. By 10 a.m. the 7th reached its objective, and D company captured Nappes an hour later without opposition. A further advance was then made, and the Battalion reached the north-west edge of the Bois de Courton by 2 p.m. and the western edge of the Bois des Eclisses by 9 p.m.

The Bois de Courton, which had caused so much trouble a few days before, thus fell without opposition, but the conditions during the fighting are never likely to be forgotten by those who took part in it. At places it was shambles. Broken trees, ruined houses, derelict transport wagons, motor lorries and guns (the last three almost all Italian) lay in confusion intermingled with other and more unpleasant signs of a big battle. On July 28th the Battalion remained in reserve at Chaumuzy, and that evening

THE SEVENTH BATTALION THE BLACK WATCH

the 153rd Brigade went into reserve under the orders of the General Officer Commanding 154th Brigade in the Bois de la Passe.

The next two days passed quietly and the 7th was relieved on the night of the 30th, when it moved to Nappes and bivouacked the following night in the woods east of Romery, where five men were killed and 14 wounded from enemy bombing. This ended the fighting of the 7th in Champagne. For services during the operations the following awards were given to officers and other ranks of the Battalion:—

One D.S.O., one Bar to M.C., three M.C.'s, one Bar to D.C.M., one D.C.M., three Bars to M.M., seven M.M.'s and four Croix de Guerre.

The casualties for July were one officer and 24 other ranks killed, seven officers and 191 other ranks wounded and 40 missing; but several drafts arrived during the last action, and the strength of the Battalion at the end of the month was 45 officers and 645 other ranks.

CHAPTER XIII

AUGUST, 1918, TO APRIL, 1919

The Final Offensive and Demobilization

ON the 1st of August the 7th marched to Moslins, where it was reviewed by the V (French) Army Commander; on the 2nd it entrained at Vertus, detrained at Pernes on the 4th and marched to Bouvigny, where it spent the following fortnight. By this time it was well known that German resistance had been broken, and all felt that the 51st Division had helped to bring this about. Officers and men were therefore in good trim and conscious of the fine spirit that, from the start to the end of the war, had animated the Battalion. The time spent at Bouvigny was taken up in training and recreation. Battalion sports were held on the 16th, and C company, who had won the title of "Best Company" at Wanquetin, was granted the right to hold the Battalion banner presented by Brigadier-General Cheape.

The great general offensive on the British front south of the River Scarpe had now begun, and the 51st Division was soon to be called upon to take part in it. On August 17th the Battalion, less B company, moved by road to Château de la Haie and thence by light railway to Ecurie, where it took over Wakefield Camp from the 1st Battalion Royal Munster Fusiliers, B company being in bivouacs in a sunken road near Roclincourt. Attacks were practised over a taped-out position by A and D companies, and by No. 10 platoon from C which had been detailed to carry out the attack. On the evening of the 23rd the attacking troops moved into the line followed by the remainder of the Battalion, the relief being complete by 12.30 a.m. on the 24th.

The task of the Division was to protect the left flank from the great attacks south of the Scarpe by capturing certain tactical features north of the river, namely, Greenland Hill and Hausa and Delbar Wood. The Battalion's objective included the famous Hyderabad Redoubt on the left of the 51st Division front. The assault took place at 4.30 a.m. on the 24th, and as A and D companies advanced on the left of the Division, No. 10 platoon formed a defensive flank, while on the right D company maintained touch with the 5th Battalion Seaforth Highlanders. The attack was successful in every way, the only check being on the left of Hyderabad Redoubt, where two officers of A company were killed. At the most easterly point of the Redoubt there was extremely heavy fighting in which Lieutenant Speid and Sergeants Greig and Adamson especially distinguished themselves.

Hyderabad Redoubt was a very strong point in the enemy

line. Perched on the summit of a crest it overlooked Arras and the country to the west, and its retention was of considerable importance to the enemy, who maintained a strong garrison in it and made more than one counter-attack to retake the Redoubt after the Battalion had captured it. Early in the morning of the 25th the Germans launched a very powerful counter-attack against the Redoubt, but met with the same lack of success as they had experienced the day before. An hour later the 6th Battalion, attacking on the left of No. 10 platoon, captured the only position which had withstood the assault the day before, and, although the Germans counter-attacked early the following day with a temporary success, the Battalion held on to what it had gained.

At 7 a.m. on the 26th B and C companies had moved up into the line to carry out a further attack which began at 10.30 a.m., the objectives being the front line known as Newton Trench, and, secondly, the support line known as Hoary, Haggard and Naval Trenches just west of the Fampoux–Gavrelle road. Each objective in turn was captured with very slight loss, and at seven o'clock that night two platoons of B and C companies continued the advance and also captured their objectives, the 7th Battalion Gordon Highlanders passing through to take the final one. The 7th suffered few losses during this fighting; three officers and six men were killed, 38 other ranks wounded and missing.

On the 28th the Battalion was relieved and moved to Athies, where it remained until September 4th, when it returned to the front line in the Greenland Hill sector, where it spent the remainder of the month. The Battalion Diary lays stress on the fact that during this period the German artillery fire was perhaps the heaviest and most prolonged that was experienced, except, of course, while attacking. The reason may have been that the Germans, having decided on a general retirement, were glad to fire off as much ammunition as they possibly could. The area round Greenland Hill was heavily shelled by day and night with "mustard gas" shells, which caused a good many casualties.

September passed uneventfully; constant pressure was kept on the enemy by means of strong fighting patrols and artillery fire to which there was a certain amount of retaliation, but on the whole the Germans showed no disposition to resume the offensive nor to oppose seriously the troops attacking them.

In October, while in reserve at Ecurie, the 153rd Brigade held a Highland Gathering, when the championship was won by the 7th Battalion Gordon Highlanders, the 7th being second and the 6th third. During these days—comparatively quiet as far as the Battalion was concerned—the constant pressure kept on

CROSSING THE ECAILLON, OCTOBER 24TH, 1918

the enemy was showing good results; all along the line the Germans continued to retire, and the subsequent fighting took the form of advanced and rear-guard actions.

On October 8th the Battalion moved by motor bus to Pronville, and two days later marched past His Royal Highness the Prince of Wales on the way to Tilloy. On the 12th the 7th moved to Thun-St. Martin, and on the 14th relieved the 4th Battalion Gordon Highlanders in the line at Lieu St. Amand, holding this line until the 19th when the advance was continued. Patrols kept constant touch with the enemy. On the 16th, when the 7th was in the line, reports were received that the Germans had retired on that part of the front; special patrols were at once sent out and proved that the news was false; unfortunately Lieutenant Dewar was killed while leading one of the patrols.

The advance began again on the 19th when B and D companies took Lieu St. Amand, and on the following day A company captured Neuville, entering Douchy later the same day. Here the wildest excitement prevailed. Civilians crowded into the main street almost before the Germans had left the village, and officers and men of the 7th were dragged into the houses and given coffee—the only drink that had been left behind by the retiring enemy. Three thousand civilians were liberated in Douchy alone and were evacuated at once, as at this time the Germans were putting up a considerable resistance. An attempt was made by C company to cut off a number of the enemy who were retiring from Rouvignies across the Canal de l'Escaut, but without success.

On the 24th the 7th took part in the crossing of the Ecaillon River. It was a difficult operation, particularly as few of the Battalion knew much about open warfare. A demonstration had been given the day before to one officer from each platoon on the method to be adopted. The crossing was a complete success. Bridges were brought up by the sappers, put together, and issued to companies, and at 4 a.m. on the 24th the crossing was achieved with very few casualties. Two German officers and 150 men with 22 machine guns were captured. The advance was held up eventually by machine gun fire directed on the Battalion when moving over some marshy ground. During this very successful operation the 7th lost two officers killed, four officers and 82 other ranks wounded, and captured two German officers, 167 other ranks, three trench mortars and 22 machine guns. This was the last battle in which the 7th took part.

The Battalion remained in reserve at Thaint until October 25th, when it was relieved by the 1/5th Battalion York and

THE SEVENTH BATTALION THE BLACK WATCH

Lancaster Regiment and moved back to Lieu St. Amand. On the 30th it moved to Iwuy, the strength of the Battalion being, on October 31st, 43 officers and 893 other ranks. On November 11th the 7th was addressed by the Commanding Officer, who announced the official signing of the Armistice. The rest of the day was declared a holiday, and passed off quietly.

The next few months were devoted to the difficult task of demobilization. Much salvage work was necessary, and this, combined with sports and recreational training, occupied the spare time. On November 14th the Commander-in-Chief established his advanced General Headquarters at Iwuy, and that day the Battalion formed part of a Guard of Honour when an American decoration was given by General Pershing to Sir Douglas Haig. The winter of 1918 passed quietly; many men left to be demobilized, and on January 9th, 1919, the Battalion moved by motor lorries to Familleureux in Belgium. Here the Colours were carred for the first time; the next two months were spent in this area, and much time was given to educational training.

Thirty officers and 706 other ranks, of whom a number were transferred to the 6th Battalion in Germany, were demobilized in February, and by the end of March the strength of the Battalion was reduced to 16 officers and 92 other ranks, and on April 6th the Battalion was reduced to Cadre strength. On the 7th the Cadre reached Dunkirk and embarking two days later arrived at Gailes on the 11th and Kirkcaldy on the 14th. The Battalion was disembodied at Kinross on the 15th of April, 1919.

This account of these four and a half years of constant training and hardships lightly borne, of stubborn defence and gallant attack, shows that the fine spirit which had led the first man to join the Battalion in 1914 animated all officers and men throughout the campaign, and gives to the 7th a high and honourable place among the Battalions of The Black Watch who served in the Great War.

APPENDIX I

Record of Officers' Services

Abbreviations :—"K."—Killed. "D. of W."—Died of Wounds. "W."—Wounded. "M."—Missing. "P. of W."—Prisoner of War.

THE SEVENTH BATTALION

Adamson, D. F. 2nd Lieut. Transferred to 153rd M.G. Coy. 16th Feb., 1916. Awarded M.C. 24th Aug., 1916.
Adamson, W. 2nd Lieut. Transferred to 153rd M.G. Coy. 12th Jan., 1916.
Adkins, R. E. W. 2nd Lieut. w. 16th Feb., 1918. Rejoined Battn. 26th Aug., 1918.
Aitken, G. Capt. Went out with Battn. May, 1915. w. 25th July, 1916.
Alexander, P. J. 2nd Lieut. Joined Battn. 1st July, 1915. w. 7th Nov., 1915.
Allan, J. 2nd Lieut. Joined Battn. 14th July, 1917. Transferred to 5th Gordon Highlanders 8th Sept., 1917.
Allen, H. C. 2nd Lieut. Joined 15th Feb., 1917. k. 23rd April, 1917.
Allen, H. M. Lieut.-Col. D.S.O. Went out with Battn. May, 1915. Mentioned in Despatches 1st Jan., 1916. To hospital 3rd May, 1916. Awarded C.M.G. 3rd June, 1916. Mentioned in Despatches 15th June, 1916. w. 28th July, 1916. Rejoined Battn. 16th Feb., 1917. Left Battn. 19th March, 1917.
Allison, C. L. 2nd Lieut. Joined Battn. 20th April, 1918. w. 26th April, 1918.
Anderson, J. Lieut. Joined 10th April, 1918.
Anderson, J. L. 2nd Lieut. Joined 9th Jan., 1917. k. 25th May, 1917.
Archibald, D. M. 2nd Lieut. Joined 21st Aug., 1916. Transferred to Brigade as Bombing Officer 24th Nov., 1916. w. 23rd April, 1917. Promoted Lieut. 25th Sept., 1917. Awarded M.C. 1st Jan., 1918. Transferred to 153rd T.M. Battery 21st Aug., 1918.

Badenoch, R. E. 2nd Lieut. Joined 21st Aug., 1916. w. 31st March, 1917.
Baird, W. 2nd Lieut. Joined 28th April, 1918. w. 22nd May, 1918. Rejoined 8th Nov., 1918.
Barclay, W. K. Lieut. Went out with Battn. May, 1915. w. 17th June, 1915.
Batchelor, F. C. 2nd Lieut. Joined 30th Aug., 1916. To U.K. 14th Jan., 1917.
Beatson, B. L. O. 2nd Lieut. w. 13th Nov., 1916. Rejoined 20th Jan., 1917. k. 23rd April, 1917.
Begg, A. C. 2nd Lieut. Joined 1st July, 1915. Promoted Lieut. 1st Jan., 1916. Appointed Adj. 16th Jan., 1916. To hospital 5th May, 1916. k. 30th July, 1916.
Berry, D. W. 2nd Lieut. Joined 3rd March, 1917. Promoted Lieut. 25th Sept., 1917. Rejoined Battn. w. March, 1918.
Beveridge, D. Capt. and Adj. Went out with Battn. May, 1915. To hospital sick 29th Aug., 1915. Promoted Major 1st Jan., 1916. Mentioned in Despatches 1st Jan., 1916. Relinquished appointment of Adj. 16th Jan., 1916. To hospital 4th May, 1916. To U.K. 1st June, 1916.

THE SEVENTH BATTALION THE BLACK WATCH

Beveridge, J. P. 2nd Lieut. Joined 21st Aug., 1916. Promoted Capt. Transferred to 7th Gordon Highlanders 20th May, 1918.

Beveridge, R. 2nd Lieut. Joined 9th Feb., 1916. Transferred to Labour Corps 14th September, 1917. Promoted Lieut. 25th Sept., 1917.

Blair, E. J. Capt. R.A.M.C. Joined 28th Dec., 1915. *w.* 2nd May, 1916. Rejoined Battn. Awarded M.C. 13th Nov., 1916. *k.* 11th April, 1917.

Blake, ———. 2nd Lieut. Joined 9th June, 1918.

Boase, E. L. Capt. From 1/4th Battn. 11th July, 1916. *k.* 30th July, 1916.

Boothby, G. A. 2nd Lieut. Joined 2nd Aug., 1915. *w.* 3rd Sept., 1915.

Boothby, J. V. Lieut. Joined 21st Nov., 1915. To hospital sick 23rd March, 1916. Rejoined Battn. *w.* 1st June, 1916.

Bracelin, D. 2nd Lieut. Joined 28th April, 1918. *k.* 20th July, 1918.

Brodie, W. F. 2nd Lieut. Joined 27th May, 1917. *w.* 31st July, 1917. To U.K. 12th Aug., 1917. Rejoined Battn. 25th July, 1918.

Brown, D. 2nd Lieut. Joined 26th Jan., 1916. *w.* 11th April, 1917. Promoted Lieut. 25th September, 1917.

Brown, J. 2nd Lieut. Joined 19th June, 1916. *w.* 30th July, 1916.

Brown, W. B. Lieut. Went out with Battn. May, 1915. *w.* 24th May, 1915. Promoted Capt. Rejoined 27th May, 1917. Appointed Comdt. Fifth Army Area 2nd Aug., 1917.

Burns, R. 2nd Lieut. Joined 10th Aug., 1916. Invalided to U.K. 27th Aug., 1916.

Cable, R. M. L. 2nd Lieut. Joined 10th May, 1918. Awarded M.C. 28th Aug., 1918. Awarded Croix de Guerre Dec., 1918.

Calderwood, W. M. 2nd Lieut. Joined 30th Aug., 1918. *w.* 24th Oct., 1918.

Campbell, J. W. G. 2nd Lieut.

Campbell, R. K. 2nd Lieut. Joined 30th May, 1916. Promoted Lieut. 25th Sept., 1917.

Cargill, J. 2nd Lieut. Joined 21st Aug., 1916. Promoted Capt. *w.* 23rd April, 1917.

Carmont, J. F. 2nd Lieut. Joined 26th Jan., 1917. To U.K. 7th July, 1917.

Carse, R. 2nd Lieut. Joined 7th July, 1917. Transferred Machine Gun Corps 20th March, 1918. Promoted Lieut. 8th July, 1918.

Carstairs, J. 2nd Lieut. Joined 28th April, 1918. To hospital 9th May, 1918. Rejoined Battn.

Carswell, W. A. 2nd Lieut. Joined 10th June, 1917. Promoted Lieut. 25th Sept., 1917. Awarded M.C. 23rd Nov., 1917. *w.* and *m.* March, 1918.

Cheape, G. R. H. Major. Joined 6th May, 1916. Promoted Lieut.-Col. Assumed temporary command of Battn 29th July, 1916.

Clark, W. L. 2nd Lieut. Joined 9th May, 1918. Promoted Lieut. 8th July, 1918. *w.* 22nd July, 1918.

Clark, W. M. 2nd Lieut. Joined 10th Oct., 1917. *k.* 20th Nov., 1917.

Craik, R. 2nd Lieut.

Crosbie, W. R. 2nd Lieut. Joined 3rd July, 1917. Promoted Lieut. 25th Sept., 1917. *m.* 11th April, 1918.

Cross, J. M. Capt. and Q.M. Joined 16th June, 1918.

Cumming, G. 2nd Lieut. Joined 3rd July, 1917. *w.* 22nd March, 1918.

Cuthbertson, A. A. Lieut. Joined 20th May, 1918. Awarded M.C. 14th Nov., 1918.

APPENDIX I

Dalrymple, W. E. 2nd Lieut. Joined 14th Oct., 1917. *w.* 11th April, 1918.
Daly, D. C. 2nd Lieut. Joined 29th April, 1918. Transferred to 1st. Battn. 10th May, 1918.
Davidson, H. C. 2nd Lieut. Joined 27th July, 1916. To U.K. sick 28th Nov., 1916.
Davies, C. F. 2nd Lieut. Joined 11th Nov., 1915. Transferred to R.F.C. 6th July, 1916.
Delahunt, P. G. 2nd Lieut. Joined 20th April, 1918. *w.* 1st June, 1918. Rejoined Battn. 20th June, 1918. *w.* 27th Aug., 1918. *d. of w.* 28th Aug., 1918.
Dempster, D. W. Capt. Awarded M.C. 23rd Nov., 1917. *w.* March, 1918.
Denovan, C. G. 2nd Lieut. Joined 17th June, 1918.
Dewar, J. M. Lieut. Joined 6th Oct., 1918. *k.* 16th Oct., 1918.
Dickson, D. E. Capt. R.A.M.C. Transferred to 1/3rd Highland F.A. 17th July, 1915.
Dickson, T. J. R. 2nd Lieut. To hospital sick 19th July, 1916. Rejoined Battn. 18th Feb., 1917. To U.K. sick 11th May, 1917. Promoted Lieut. Rejoined Battn. 28th April, 1918.
Donaldson, G. A. 2nd Lieut. Joined 21st April, 1916. *w.* 25th July, 1916.
Donaldson, G. V. 2nd Lieut. Joined 25th June, 1916. *w.* 29th June, 1916.
Donaldson, J. Capt. Went out with Battn. May, 1915. *w.* 17th June, 1915. Rejoined Battn. 17th March, 1916. To U.K. 27th June, 1916.
Doughty, A. G. Lieut. Joined 2nd Jan., 1918. *w.* March, 1918.
Duncan, J. O. Capt. Joined from 1/4th Battn. 11th July, 1916. To Base for duty 12th Nov., 1916.
Dunn, M. 2nd Lieut. Joined 22nd Jan., 1917. *k.* 16th May, 1917.

Edgar, J. 2nd Lieut. Joined 16th Feb., 1917. To U.K. 1st July, 1917.
Elder, J. 2nd Lieut. Joined 16th Oct., 1917. *m.* March, 1918.

Fleming, R. A. 2nd Lieut. Joined 22nd May, 1916. *w.* 30th July, 1916. *d. of w.* 31st July, 1916.
Foggie, J. K. 2nd Lieut. Joined 20th April, 1918. *w.* 22nd July, 1918.
Fraser, H. K. Lieut. Joined 6th Oct., 1918.
Fraser, J. H. Lieut. Joined 20th April, 1918. *w.* 16th Oct., 1918.
Fullerton-Carnegie, G. O. H. 2nd Lieut. Went out with Battn. May, 1915. *w.* 17th June, 1915. Rejoined Battn. 30th Dec., 1915. Mentioned in Despatches 1st Jan., 1916. Awarded M.C. 1st Jan., 1916. *w.* 20th June, 1916. Rejoined Battn. 9th July, 1916.
Fulton, L. A. 2nd Lieut. Joined 29th April, 1917.
Fulton, L. M. Joined 3rd July, 1917. Transferred to 5th Gordon Highlanders 8th Sept., 1917.

Gemmell, A. G. 2nd Lieut. Joined 9th June, 1918.
Gerrard, F. I. 2nd Lieut. Joined 7th July, 1917. Promoted Lieut. 9th Feb., 1918. Awarded M.C. April, 1918. Bar to M.C. 28th Aug., 1918. Promoted Captain. Awarded Croix de Guerre Dec., 1918.
Gibson, W. P. S. 2nd Lieut. Joined 21st Sept., 1915. To hospital sick 12th Feb., 1916.
Gillespie, J. Capt. Joined 28th July, 1915. *k.* 30th July, 1916.

THE SEVENTH BATTALION THE BLACK WATCH

Glen, J. F. Capt. Went out with Battn. May, 1915. *w.* 17th June, 1915.
Good, A. 2nd Lieut. Joined 14th Oct., 1916. To U.K. 12th May, 1917.
Gordon, J. R. 2nd Lieut. Joined 7th July, 1917. Promoted Lieut. 25th Sept., 1917. *m.* March, 1918. (*p. of w.*)
Gordon, R. G. Went out with Battn. May, 1915.
Gowans, A. D. S. 2nd Lieut. Joined from 6th Battn. 17th Feb., 1917. *d. of w.* 23rd April, 1917.
Graham, M. H. A. Lieut. Went out with Battn. May, 1915. *w.* 10th Nov., 1915.
Graham, H. B. 2nd Lieut. Went out with Battn. May, 1915. *w.* 20th Aug., 1915. Rejoined Battn. 18th Aug., 1916. Promoted Lieut. Transferred to 3rd Reserve Battn. 12th Sept., 1916.
Grant-Suttie, G. D. Major. Joined 22nd April, 1918. Transferred to Base 29th April, 1918.
Greig, D. W. 2nd Lieut. Joined 30th Aug., 1916. Promoted Lieut. 25th Sept., 1917. *w.* and *m.* March, 1918.
Guthrie, W. A. Major. Went out with Battn. May, 1915. To U.K. 4th April, 1916. Mentioned in Despatches 15th June, 1916.

Hallam, J. 2nd Lieut. Joined 26th Jan., 1916. *w.* 28th July, 1916.
Harley, D. P. 2nd Lieut. Joined 21st Aug., 1916. To Base 5th Oct., 1916
Harley, F. W. 2nd Lieut. Went out with Battn. May, 1915. *w.* 17th June, 1915. Rejoined Battn. 12th Oct., 1916. Promoted Lieut. 19th Nov., 1916. Transferred to R.F.C. 8th Dec., 1916. Promoted Capt. *k. in a.* 3rd June, 1917.
Heard, R. R. 2nd Lieut. Joined 12th Dec., 1916. *k.* 23rd April, 1917.
Herd, H. J. 2nd Lieut. Joined 24th Sept., 1915. Promoted Lieut. 1st Jan., 1916. Awarded D.S.O. 12th June, 1916. To hospital sick 19th July, 1916.
Higgie, C. J. Lieut. *w.* 13th Feb., 1918.
Hill, W. R. 2nd Lieut. Joined 9th Aug., 1918. *k.* 24th Aug., 1918.
Hislop, J. 2nd Lieut. To Third Army Rest Camp 20th Oct., 1917. Rejoined Battn. Feb., 1918. *m.* March, 1918.
Hog, R. D. 2nd Lieut. Joined 25th June, 1916. *w.* 30th July, 1916.
Honeyman, S. Lieut. R.A.M.C. Joined 7th Aug., 1915. Transferred to 1/4th L. N. Lancs 28th Dec., 1915.
Hopkins, W. 2nd Lieut. Joined 21st Aug., 1916. Awarded M.C. 5th June, 1917. Promoted Capt. 20th July, 1917. *w.* 20th Nov., 1917.
Horne, G. L. 2nd Lieut. Joined 20th April, 1918. *w.* 28th May, 1918.
Howard, C. N. 2nd Lieut. Joined 4th Nov., 1918.
Humphreys, H. J. 2nd Lieut. Went out with Battn. May, 1915. Transferred to 251st Tunnelling Coy., R.E. Promoted Lieut. Mentioned in Despatches 15th June, 1916. Awarded D.S.O. Awarded M.C. Promoted Major. Mentioned in Despatches 1st Jan., 1918.
Hunter, A. 2nd Lieut. Joined 26th Jan., 1916. Transferred to 417th T.M. Battery. 3rd March, 1916. Promoted Lieut. 25th Sept., 1917.
Hunter, F. J. W. Capt. Joined 15th April, 1918. To hospital 23rd May, 1918. Rejoined Battn. 8th June, 1918.
Hunter, J. M. Capt. C.F. Joined 9th Sept., 1916. To U.K. 12th May, 1917.

APPENDIX I

Jessop, J. C. 2nd Lieut. Joined 20th June, 1918. *w.* 24th Oct., 1918.
Johnstone, W. 2nd Lieut. Joined 22nd April, 1918. To hospital 22nd July, 1918. To U.K. 10th Aug., 1918.
Jones, N. M. 2nd Lieut. Joined 20th April, 1918. Promoted Lieut. 8th July, 1918.

Keir, D. R. Lieut. Went out with Battn. May, 1915. Promoted Capt. *w.* 30th July, 1916. Promoted Major. Rejoined Battn. 27th Dec., 1917. *w.* 11th April, 1918. Awarded D.S.O. Dec., 1918. Mentioned in Despatches.
Kerr, A. 2nd Lieut. Joined 27th May, 1917. *w.* and *m.* March, 1918.
Kidd, L. 2nd Lieut. Joined 3rd July, 1917. Transferred to R.F.C. 10th May, 1918.
Kilgour, A. 2nd Lieut. Joined 10th Feb., 1916.
Kinloch, G. N. 2nd Lieut. Joined 4th Nov., 1918.

Lang, D. 2nd Lieut. Joined 20th April, 1916. *w.* 28th July, 1916. Rejoined Battn. 29th Oct., 1917.
Law, G. 2nd Lieut. Joined 10th Aug., 1917. To U.K. 18th June, 1918.
Le Maitre, A. S. 2nd Lieut. Joined 27th July, 1916. Awarded M.C. 15th Sept., 1916. *w.* 15th Sept., 1916.
Levi, P. M. 2nd Lieut. Joined 9th May, 1918. Awarded M.C. 15th Oct., 1918. *k.* 24th Oct., 1918.
Lockhart, J. H. 2nd Lieut. Joined 22nd May, 1916. *k.* 30th July, 1916.
Lownie, J. W. 2nd Lieut. Joined 29th April, 1918. Awarded M.C. 28th Aug., 1918.
Lowson, W. D. 2nd Lieut. Joined 8th July, 1918.
Lyle, R. Lieut. Joined 30th April, 1918. Awarded M.C. 4th May, 1918. *w.* 21st July, 1918. Awarded Croix de Guerre Dec., 1918.

Macdonald, ——. Major. Joined 19th Jan., 1917.
Macdonald, C. 2nd Lieut. Joined 2nd June, 1917.
Macdonald, H. L. 2nd Lieut. Joined 27th May, 1917. To hospital 4th June, 1917. To U.K. 18th July, 1917. Rejoined Battn. 5th Aug., 1917.
Macdonald, P. 2nd Lieut. Joined 20th April, 1918.
MacDuff, P. Major. Joined 1st May, 1915. To U.K. 9th Nov., 1915.
MacGregor, J. G. 2nd Lieut. Joined 3rd July, 1917. Transferred to Tank Corps 26th Nov., 1917.
Mackintosh, H. C. Lieut. Went out with Battn. May, 1915. Promoted Capt. 1st Jan., 1916. To Base 30th Nov., 1916. Rejoined Battn. 16th Feb., 1917. Awarded M.C. 1st Sept., 1917. Promoted Major. To U.K. for duty 4th March, 1918. Rejoined Battn. 25th Oct., 1918.
Mackintosh, J. K. 2nd Lieut. Joined 3rd July, 1917. *k.* March, 1918.
Maclennan, I. 2nd Lieut. Joined 2nd Jan., 1918. *m.* March, 1918.
McArthur, M. 2nd Lieut. D.C.M. Joined 6th Oct., 1918. Awarded M.C. 14th Nov., 1918.
McClintock, S. R. Lieut.-Col. D.S.O. Joined Battn. and assumed Command 1st March, 1918. Awarded D.S.O. 1st Jan., 1918. *w.* March, 1918. Awarded Bar to D.S.O. March, 1918.
McCorquodale, R. 2nd Lieut. Joined 20th June, 1918. *w.* 13th Aug., 1918.

THE SEVENTH BATTALION THE BLACK WATCH

McCowan, D. 2nd Lieut. Joined June, 1918.
McCracken, J. 2nd Lieut. Joined 21st Oct., 1917. Transferred to 51st Div. 13th Nov., 1917.
McCredie, J. M. 2nd Lieut. Joined 1st June, 1916. To 2nd Australian Tunnelling Coy. 19th Aug., 1916. Transferred to 153rd T.M. Battery. 24th Nov., 1916. Rejoined Battn. Transferred to T.M. Battery. 26th June, 1917. Promoted Lieut. 25th Sept., 1917.
McDowall, D. Lieut. Joined 6th Oct., 1918.
McFarlane-Grieve, R. W. Lieut. Joined 29th April, 1918. Awarded M.C. 14th Nov., 1918.
McGregor, A. 2nd Lieut. Joined 16th Oct., 1917. *m.* 11th April, 1918.
MacIntosh, G. W. Capt. Went out with Battn. May, 1915.
McIntosh, I. K. 2nd Lieut. Joined 4th July, 1917. *k.* 31st March, 1918.
McLaren, D. B. 2nd Lieut. Joined 10th Oct., 1917. To hospital 4th Dec., 1917. To U.K. 11th Jan., 1918.
McLaren, H. Capt. M.C. Joined 6th Oct., 1918. *w.* 24th Oct., 1918.
McLaren, J. F. S. 2nd Lieut. Joined 29th April, 1918. *w.* 22nd July, 1918.
MacKie, J. S. 2nd Lieut. Joined 20th April, 1918.
MacKie, D. G. 2nd Lieut. Joined 15th Feb., 1917. *w.* 29th June, 1917. Rejoined 22nd April, 1918.
Marshall, J. 2nd Lieut. Joined 12th Dec., 1916. Left Battn. 12th March, 1917. Rejoined 25th Sept., 1917. To hospital 13th March, 1918. To U.K. 28th April, 1918. Rejoined Battn. *k.* 24th Oct., 1918.
Mathewson, W. G. Lieut. Went out with Battn. May, 1915. Promoted Capt. To Base for training course 15th Jan., 1916. Rejoined Battn. 3rd March, 1916. To hospital 23rd March, 1916.
Maxwell, C. H. Capt. Went out with Battn. May, 1915. To hospital 30th Aug., 1915. To U.K. 1st Nov., 1915.
Menzies, J. W. G. 2nd Lieut. Promoted Lieut. 25th Sept., 1917. *w.* March, 1918.
Menzies, R. M. 2nd Lieut. Joined 10th Feb., 1916. *w.* 25th July, 1916. Rejoined Battn. 3rd Aug., 1916. *w.* 13th Nov., 1916. Rejoined Battn. 4th April, 1918. Promoted Lieut. *w.* 11th April, 1918.
Menzies, T. A. 2nd Lieut. Joined Battn. 10th Aug., 1916. *w.* 14th Oct., 1916.
Millar, J. Lieut.-Col. M.C. Joined 14th April, and assumed command. To hospital 2nd July, 1918. Rejoined Battn. 11th July, 1918. To hospital 27th July, 1918. Awarded D.S.O. 28th Aug., 1918. To U.K. for three months' leave 14th Oct., 1918. Awarded Croix de Guerre Dec., 1918.
Miller, A. L. 2nd Lieut. Joined 1st July, 1915. Promoted Lieut. *w.* 23rd March, 1916. Rejoined Battn. 20th May, 1917. To Base for duty 1st Nov., 1917. Awarded M.C. 21st March, 1917. Rejoined Battn. 8th March, 1918. Missing March, 1918.
Miller, R. S. Lieut. R.A.M.C. Joined 17th July, 1915. To Field Ambulance 7th Aug., 1915.
Milligan, J. M. Major. Joined 10th Aug., 1916. Struck off strength of Battn. 12th Oct., 1917. Mentioned in Despatches 1st Jan., 1918. Rejoined Battn. 13th May, 1918.

APPENDIX I

Moir, J. Capt. Joined 21st Aug., 1916. Transferred to 5th Seaforth Highlanders 30th March, 1917.
Monkland, G. E. Lieut. Joined 21st Jan., 1916. *w.* 23rd April, 1917.
Moodie, A. M. 2nd Lieut. Joined 21st Aug., 1916. Promoted Lieut. 25th Sept., 1917. Promoted Capt. Awarded M.C. 23rd Nov., 1917. Missing March, 1918.
Moon, F. W. Capt. Joined from 4th Battn. 25th March, 1917. Left Battn. 11th July, 1918.
Morren, J. H. 2nd Lieut. Joined 30th Aug., 1916. Left Battn. May, 1917.
Morris, A. R. 2nd Lieut. Joined 10th Aug., 1916. *k.* 23rd April, 1917.
Muir, J. B. Capt. Joined 5th June, 1918.
Muir, J. M. Lieut. R.A.M.C. Joined 31st March, 1918.
Munro, R. M. Capt. Joined 21st Aug., 1916. To U.K. 9th June, 1917.
Murray, A. C. Capt. and Adj. *w.* 17th June, 1915.
Murray, J. A. C. Capt. C.F. Transferred to 15th Div. 5th Jan., 1918.

Nairn, R. S. Major. Joined 15th May, 1917.
Nelson, J. R. 2nd Lieut. Joined 6th Dec., 1915. To U.K. 23rd Jan., 1916. Rejoined 14th June, 1916. *k.* 23rd April, 1917.
Nelson, W. Lieut. Joined 30th April, 1918. *w.* 20th July, 1918.
Niven, W. F. 2nd Lieut. Joined 25th July, 1918.

Pagan, G. H. 2nd Lieut. Went out with Battn. May, 1915. *k.* 30th July, 1916.
Pattison, J. B. 2nd Lieut. Joined 12th Dec., 1916. To T.M. Battery 14th July, 1917. *w.* 4th Sept., 1917. Promoted Lieut. 8th July, 1918.
Paul, A. 2nd Lieut. Went out with Battn. May, 1915. To U.K. 28th Dec., 1915. Promoted Lieut. 1st Jan., 1916.
Penney, J. C. 2nd Lieut. Joined 11th May, 1917. Promoted Lieut. Awarded M.C. 1st Sept., 1917. To U.K. 3rd Sept., 1917.
Playfair, P. L. Capt. Joined 3rd March, 1917. *w.* 23rd April, 1917. Rejoined Battn. 4th April, 1918. *k.* 11th April, 1918.
Porter, W. 2nd Lieut. Joined 20th June, 1918.

Quekett, H. S. Lieut. Joined 27th May, 1917.
Quigley, J. E. Lieut. M.O.R.C., attached from U.S.A. Joined 1918. Missing March, 1918.

Ralston, C. G. Lieut. Joined 30th Dec., 1916. *w.* 23rd July, 1918.
Read, J. A. Lieut. Went out with Battn. 1st May, 1915. To U.K. 19th Dec., 1915. Rejoined Battn. 21st April, 1916. Promoted Capt. 19th Sept., 1916. Rejoined 20th April, 1918. To U.K. 8th Aug., 1918.
Reid, J. 2nd Lieut. Joined 10th April, 1916. Promoted Capt. Appointed Adjt. 11th June, 1917. Awarded M.C. 1st Jan., 1918. Awarded Bar to M.C. March, 1918. To U.K. 24th June, 1918.
Reid, J. R. 2nd Lieut. Joined 22nd April, 1918. Awarded M.C. April, 1918. To hospital 27th July, 1918. Rejoined 19th Sept., 1918. *w.* 27th Oct., 1918.
Reid, R. 2nd Lieut. Joined 25th June, 1916. *k.* 30th July, 1916.

THE SEVENTH BATTALION THE BLACK WATCH

Renny, A. B. 2nd Lieut. Joined 20th April, 1918. Transferred to T.M. Battery 24th May, 1918.
Richardson, D. A. 2nd Lieut. Joined 14th July, 1917. *k.* 21st–26th March, 1918.
Ritchie, ———. Lieut. To U.K. 5th May, 1917.
Robertson, F. M. B. Major. Joined from 2nd Battn. (Reg.) 23rd Oct., 1917, and assumed command of Battn. To hospital 24th Oct., 1917. Awarded D.S.O. 1st Jan., 1918. Mentioned in Despatches 1st Jan., 1918. To U.K. 9th Feb., 1918.
Robertson, J. C. 2nd Lieut. Joined from 2nd Battn. 25th July, 1918.
Robertson, J. W. 2nd Lieut. *k.* 23rd April, 1917.
Robertson, W. L. Capt. Joined 3rd June, 1918.
Ross, J. C. Capt. Joined 22nd April, 1918. Awarded M.C. 14th Nov., 1918.
Rowan, G. 2nd Lieut. Joined 2nd Aug., 1915. *w.* 3rd Aug., 1915. Awarded M.C. Mentioned in Despatches 7th Nov., 1917. To Tunnelling Coy. 26th Aug., 1918.
Rowan, J. G. Lieut. Joined 30th Dec., 1915. Promoted Capt. 31st June, 1916. *w.* 13th April, 1917. Mentioned in Despatches 1st Jan., 1918. Rejoined Battn. 4th April, 1918. *w.* 11th April, 1918. Awarded M.C. April, 1918.

Salmond, J. B. 2nd Lieut. Joined 30th Aug., 1916. To Town Major (Hermin) 18th Feb., 1917.
Scotland, R. J. 2nd Lieut. Joined 20th June, 1918.
Scott, W. D. 2nd Lieut. Joined 1st July, 1917. *w.* 31st July, 1917.
Scoular, J. G. 2nd Lieut. Joined 10th July, 1915. *w.* 30th July, 1916.
Sherwood, J. A. Lieut. Joined 21st Jan., 1916. *w.* 23rd April, 1917.
Simpson, D. M. 2nd Lieut. Joined 10th Oct., 1917. *m.* March, 1918.
Speid, W. W. 2nd Lieut. Joined 3rd July, 1917. To Third Army Rest Camp 12th Oct., 1917. Rejoined Battn. *w.* March, 1918. Rejoined Battn. 16th Aug., 1918.
Stein, J. M. 2nd Lieut. Joined 26th Jan., 1916. *w.* 30th July, 1916.
Stevenson, W. G. Lieut. Joined 2nd Jan., 1918. *w.* 16th Feb., 1918.
Stewart, J. R. 2nd Lieut. Joined 28th April, 1918.
Stuart, W. L. 2nd Lieut. Went out with Battn. May, 1915. Promoted Lieut. To U.K. 15th Dec., 1917.
Sutherland, H. H. Lieut.-Col. D.S.O. (Reg. from 1st Battn.). Assumed command of Battn. 17th March, 1917. Transferred to 153rd Infantry Brigade 7th Oct., 1917. Rejoined Battn. 4th Nov., 1917. Mentioned in Despatches 1st Jan., 1918. To U.K. for six months' duty 1st March, 1918.
Swinton, J. G. 2nd Lieut. Joined 3rd July, 1917. Missing March, 1918.

Taylor, W. S. 2nd Lieut. Joined 10th Oct., 1917. Promoted Lieut. 9th Feb., 1918.
Thomson, A. 2nd Lieut. Joined 29th April, 1917. Promoted Lieut. 25th Sept., 1917. *w.* 11th April, 1918.

APPENDIX I

Thomson, E. D. H. 2nd Lieut. Went out with Battn. May, 1915. *w.* 17th June, 1915. Promoted Lieut. Mentioned in Despatches 1st Jan., 1916. Promoted Capt. 10th June, 1916.

Thomson, H. McL. 2nd Lieut. Joined 20th April, 1918.

Thornton, W. T. 2nd Lieut. Joined 9th Dec., 1915. *k.* 30th July, 1916.

Tullis, G. S. Lieut. Went out with Battn. May, 1915. Struck off strength of Battn. 14th Dec., 1915.

Turner, P. S. 2nd Lieut. Joined 8th July, 1918.

Tovani, W. R. 2nd Lieut. Joined 12th Feb., 1916. To 1/1st Field Coy. R.E. 23rd Aug., 1916.

Valentine, A. Major. Joined 22nd Jan., 1917. Left Battn. 18th March, 1917.

Vassie, W. P. 2nd Lieut. Joined 7th Oct., 1916. To hospital sick 7th Nov., 1916. Rejoined Battn. 30th Dec., 1916. Promoted Lieut. 1st July, 1917. To U.K. 27th Oct., 1917. Rejoined 27th June, 1918.

Waddell, J. F. 2nd Lieut. Joined 21st Aug., 1916. To hospital 13th May, 1917.

Waddington, ——. Capt. Joined 17th April, 1918.

Walker, W. J. 2nd Lieut. Joined 20th June, 1918.

Wallace, F. T. Capt. Went out with Battn. 1st May, 1915. Appointed Adjt. 51st Div. Base Depot 16th July, 1915.

Wallace, J. K. 2nd Lieut. Joined 25th June, 1916. To hospital 19th Oct., 1916. Rejoined Battn. *k.* 23rd April, 1917.

Wallace, M. N. 2nd Lieut. Joined 1st July, 1915. Promoted Lieut. 1st Jan., 1916. Transferred to M.G. Coy. 12th Jan., 1916.

Watson, A. K. Capt. To hospital 20th Nov., 1916. Rejoined Battn. Left Battn. 21st March, 1917.

Watson, S. Lieut. and Q.M. Went out with Battn. May, 1915. Mentioned in Despatches 15th June, 1916. Promoted Capt. 1st Nov., 1917. Awarded M.C. April, 1918.

Welsh, A. 2nd Lieut. Joined 3rd July, 1917. Promoted Lieut. 8th July, 1918.

Westwood, A. C. Lieut. Went out with Battn. May, 1915. *k.* 17th June, 1915.

Wilkes, S. A. 2nd Lieut. Joined 9th June, 1918. *k.* 24th Aug., 1918.

Williamson, T. S. 2nd Lieut. Joined 14th Oct., 1917. Promoted Lieut. To U.K. 20th Dec., 1917.

Wilson, A. H. R. 2nd Lieut. Went out with Battn. May, 1915. *w.* 13th September, 1915. To U.K. 28th Dec., 1915.

APPENDIX II

Summary of Casualties. The Seventh Battalion

(*b*) The discrepancy between these figures and those given by the war diaries is accounted for by the fact that, save in the case of regular battalions, the diaries seldom give a record of casualties other than those suffered in main actions.

OFFICERS, 1914–18

Year.	Killed. D. of wounds. D. on service.	Wounded.	Missing.	Total.	Year.
1914	–	–	–	–	1914
1915	2	14	0	16	1915
1916	8	22	0	30	1916
1917	17	12	0	29	1917
1918	12	41	14	67	1918
Totals:	39	89	14	142	

OTHER RANKS, 1914–18

Year.	Killed. D. of wounds. D. on service.	Wounded.	Missing.	Total.	Year.
1914	–	–	–	–	1914
1915	16	81	4	101	1915
1916	61	177	21	259	1916
1917	86	392	74	552	1917
1918	67	513	532	1112	1918
Totals:	230	1163	631	2024	

TOTAL:

(*b*) Officers, 142.   Other Ranks, 2024.

APPENDIX III

Casualties—Officers

The Black Watch (Royal Highlanders)
7th (Fife) Battalion (Territorial)

* Killed in action.   † Died of wounds.   § Died.

Name.	Rank.	Date.
Aitken, J. H.	2nd Lieut.	§2.6.16.
Alexander, P. J.	Capt.	*12.10.17. M.C.
Allen, H. C.	2nd Lieut.	*25.4.17.
Anderson, J. L.	2nd Lieut.	†25.5.17.
Armstrong, W. W.	2nd Lieut.	27.12.17
Barclay, W. K.	Lieut.	†20.6.15.
Beatson, B. C. O.	2nd Lieut.	*23.4.17.
Begg, A. C.	T/Capt.	*30.7.16.
Cargill, J.	Capt.	†24.4.17.
Clark, W. M.	2nd Lieut.	*20.11.17.
Crosbie, W. R.	2nd Lieut.	*11.4.18.
Cumming, G.	2nd Lieut.	*22.3.18.
Darney, C. E.	2nd Lieut.	*2.9.18.
Dewar, J. M.	Lieut.	*16.10.18
Dunn, M.	2nd Lieut.	*16.5.17.
Donaldson, J.	Capt.	*23.8.17.
Fleming, R. A.	2nd Lieut.	31.7.16.
Gillespie, J.	Capt.	*30.7.16.
Gowans, A. D. S.	2nd Lieut.	†23.4.17.
Guthrie, H. S.	2nd Lieut.	§31.3.18. In German hands
Gyle, E. W.	2nd Lieut.	*18.10.18.
Harley, F. W.	2nd Lieut.	*3.6.17. R.F.C.
Heard, R. R.	2nd Lieut.	*23.4.17.
Kilgour, A.	Lieut.	*18.4.18.
Lockhart, J. H.	2nd Lieut.	*30.7.16.
McIntosh, J. R. H.	2nd Lieut.	*22.3.18.
Mitchell, J.	2nd Lieut.	§23.10.18. In German hands.
Morris, A. R.	2nd Lieut.	*23-25.4.17.
Nelson, J. R.	2nd Lieut.	*23.4.17.
Pagan, G. H.	Lieut.	*30.7.16.
Playfair, P. L.	Capt.	†11.4.18.
Pryde, J. W.	Lieut.	*5.5.18. K.A. Rifles.
Reid, R.	2nd Lieut.	*30.7.16.
Richardson, D. A.	2nd Lieut.	*21.3.18.
Robertson, J. W.	2nd Lieut.	*23.4.17.
Stevenson, R.	Capt.	*23.8.17.
Thornton, W. T.	2nd Lieut.	*30.7.16.
Wallace, J. K.	2nd Lieut.	*23.4.17.
Westwood, A. C.	Lieut.	*16.6.15.

APPENDIX IV

NOMINAL ROLL OF WARRANT OFFICERS, NON-COMMISSIONED OFFICERS AND MEN KILLED IN ACTION OR DIED OF WOUNDS OR DISEASE IN THE GREAT WAR, 1914–18

* Killed in action.   † Died of wounds.   ‡ Died at home.   § Died.

Abercrombie, B., Pte., 5532	†31.7.16	Bernard, H., Pte., S/16345	*26.3.18
Adam, A., Pte., 290368	*26.3.18	Beveridge, J., Sgt., 3336	§13.11.16
Adams, H. S., Pte., 291946	*25.4.17	Biggs, C., Pte., 5569	†20.11.16
Adams, J., Sgt., 292844		Binnie, W., Pte., 292508	*25.4.17
(M.M.)	*28.8.18	Bissett, T., Pte., S/16822	§15.7.18
Adams, J., Pte., S/41003	*24.7.18	Blackman, F. B., L/Cpl., S/41034	
Adamson, W., Pte., 240953	* 1.8.17		*24.7.18
Ainslie, J., Pte., S/21975	†21.7.18	Blackwell, J., Pte., 2425	*16.6.15
Aird, J., Pte., 267950	*26.3.18	Blake, G., Pte., 292589	†31.7.17
Aitken, J. M., Pte., 291604	*28.6.17	Blyth, D., Pte., 2188	*13.11.16
Allan, G., Pte., 201539	†11.8.17	Blyth, J., Pte., 1599	† 5.7.16
Allan, W. A., Pte., 292582	†30.7.17	Blyth, J., Pte., 1701	‡ 3.1.15
Allday, G., Sgt., 6934	†18.9.16	Boden, J. H., Pte., 292727	*26.3.18
Anderson, G., Pte., S/41407	*24.10.18	Bogie, G., Pte., 3259	‡ 5.5.16
Anderson, J. S., Pte., 241101	†20.3.18	Bogie, W., Sgt., 290206	*17.9.17
Anderson, J., Pte., 4224	*30.7.16	Boyter, A., Pte., 2205	*30.5.16
Anderson, J., Cpl., 350329	*24.10.18	Brady, J., Pte., 3/2800	† 8.6.17
Anderson, R., Pte., 292721	*23.4.17	Brand, T., Pte., 293037	§24.3.18
Anderson, S., Pte., S/3458	†16.8.18	Brash, D., Pte., 17590	*26.3.18
Anderson, T., Pte., 2376	*28.8.16	Bremner, A., Pte., 2426	‡15.5.16
Anderson, W., Pte., 267955	*26.3.18	Bremner, D., Pte., 290103	*23.4.17
Andrew, J. F., Pte., S/41404	*15.4.18	Britton, J. F. W., Pte., 10737	*26.3.18
Andrews, J., Pte., 292723	*17.9.17	Brodie, A., Pte., 1680	* 4.4.16
Angus, J., Sgt., 690	§ 5.7.15	Brown, A., Pte., 292247	*26.3.18
Angus, M., Pte., 292583	*26.3.18	Brown, A., Pte., 2291	* 3.6.15
Archer, G. W., L/Cpl., 292448		Brown, B. J., Pte., 292455	*23.4.17
	* 1.4.17	Brown, D. W., Pte., 292597	*25.4.17
Auchterlonie, A., Pte., 291694	†17.9.17	Brown, F., L/Sgt., 290563	*16.4.17
Aylott, W. T., Pte., 292725	†16.4.17	Brown, J., Pte., S/40135	*26.3.18
		Brown, J., Pte., 2465	*16.6.15
Baillie, J., L/Cpl., 290770	†30.3.18	Brown, J., Pte., 291866	† 1.4.18
Bain, J., Cpl., 292441	*20.11.17	Brown, M., Pte., 293110	*25.4.17
Bald, T., Pte., 3/2602	*26.3.18	Brown, R., Pte., 2135	*30.7.16
Balfour, G., Pte., 2751	*30.7.16	Brown, R., Pte., 290768	†3.11.18
Balmain, R., Pte., 292496	*25.4.17	Brown, S. W., Pte., 292516	*25.4.17
Band, A., Pte., 2339	*25.5.15	Brown, W., Pte., 290298	
Baptie, H., Sgt., 1571	*13.11.16	(M M. and Bar)	†31.3.18
Barbour, D., Pte., S/13411	*26.3.18	Brown, W., L/Cpl., 291138	*25.4.17
Barbour, D., Pte., 292730	*31.7.17	Bruce, E., Pte., S/12201	*24.10.18
Barclay, D., L/Cpl., 290350	†21.3.17	Bruce, G., Pte., S/41419	*15.4.18
Beckett, M., Pte., 2987	† 6.4.16	Bruce, W., Pte., S/40057	‡31.3.18
Bell, A. P., Pte., 310114	*26.3.18	Bryan, G., Pte., 292596	*25.4.17
Bell, J., Pte., 2421	*16.6.15	Buchanan, J., L/Cpl., 291671	
Bell, R., Pte., 2447	* 5.7.16	(M.M.)	*25.4.17
Bell, R., Pte., S/40981	†12.4.18	Buchanan, R., Pte., 4917	*26.7.16
Bell, T., Pte., 2321	‡ 4.1.16	Bulloch, J., Pte., 2749	*23.10.16
Bell, W., Pte., 292733	*23.4.17	Burke, T., Pte., 290672	†21.3.17

APPENDIX IV

Burness, R. A., Pte., 292592 *11.4.17
Burnett, G., Pte., 292593 *23.4.17
Burns, N., Pte., 292587 *15.4.17
Burns, W., Pte., 201548 *26.3.18
Butchart, J., Pte., 7023 *13.11.16
Butti, J. A., Cpl., S/6098 *24.10.18
Byars, W., Sgt., 241268
    (M.M.) *27.3.18

Calder, J., Cpl., 290230 *20.4.17
Cameron, H. W., Pte., 292744 *25.4.17
Cameron, J., Pte., 292827 *26.6.17
Campbell, A., Pte., 265670 *26.3.18
Campbell, A., Cpl., 292872 *26.3.18
Campbell, C. R., Pte., 292747 *31.7.17
Campbell, D., Pte., 374 * 6.8.15
Campbell, D., Pte., 5538 ‡31.8.16
Campbell, G., L/Cpl., 265124 *31.7.17
Campbell, J., Pte., S/17763 *12.12.17
Campbell, J., Pte., 291145 *20.4.17
Campbell, P., Sgt., 290410 †24.4.17
Campbell, T., Pte., 291588 *21.7.18
Cargill, W. C., Pte., 293105 † 1.8.17
Carlyle, T., Pte., 292112 *26.3.18
Carstairs, A., Pte., 5096 §30.12.16
Cavanagh, J., Pte., 2429 *30.7.16
Chalmers, J., Pte., 292599 *23.4.17
Chalmers, J., Pte., 290585 *25.4.17
Chapman, A., Pte., 292598 ‡30.1.18
Christie, W., Pte., 291436 *31.7.17
Clark, A., Pte., 4804 *30.7.16
Clark, B., A/Sgt., 2472 *30.7.16
Clark, C., Pte., 290299 *25.4.17
Clark, T., Pte., 313017 *23.9.18
Clunie, A., Pte., S/21918 *26.5.18
Cochrane, J., Pte., 292610 †23.4.17
Connell, H., Pte., 292601 * 4.4.17
Conway, W., Cpl., S/6003 *26.3.18
Cook, J., Pte., 6307 * 5.1.17
Cooper, J., Pte., 1804 *30.6.16
Cooper, J. W., L/Cpl., 292561
    *31.7.17
Cooper, J. J., L/Cpl., 291479 *23.4.17
Cornthwaite, A., Pte., 5128 *30.7.16
Coubrough, W., Pte., 292745
    (Italy) §15.11.17
Cowell, G., Pte., 291984 *26.3.18
Crabbe, T., Pte., S/41036 *24.7.18
Craen, J., Pte., 4383 *15.3.16
Craig, A., Pte., 292820 *25.4.17
Craig, A., Pte., 6306 * 5.1.17
Craigie, R., Cpl., 290228 *25.4.17
Crighton, G., L/Cpl., 2146 *16.6.15
Crombie, A., Pte., 203438 *20.8.18
Crombie, C., Pte., 5572 *31.10.16

Crombie, W., Pte., 3218 ‡ 9.5.15
Crone, P., Pte., 266744 *20.11.17
Cruikshanks, A., Pte., 6768 *15.10.16
Cruikshank, A., Pte., S/24021 †19.6.18
Cullen, G. C., Pte., 292748 *26.3.18
Culross, A., Pte., 292937 *26.3.18
Cumming, J., Pte., 268096 *26.3.18
Cunningham, G. M., Pte., 2476
    *30.7.16

Dalrymple, D., A/C.S.M., 369
    *16.6.16
Dalrymple, J., Pte., 4187 *30.7.16
Dalrymple, P., Pte., S/43285 *28.8.18
Dalrymple, R., Pte., 293155 *17.4.17
D'Arcy, W., Pte., 293039 ‡ 1.7.18
Davey, I., Pte., S/5059 †14.12.17
Davidson, A., Pte., 292617 *25.4.17
Davidson, W. T., Pte., 241086 *15.4.18
Davies, S., Pte., 291983 †27.9.17
Dawson, J. C., Pte., 292845 †16.4.17
Dear, J., Pte., 293122 *31.3.18
Deas, R., Pte., 1923 *19.8.15
Dempster, J., Cpl., 202245
    (M.M.) *24.7.18
Dempster, W., Pte., 2588 *30.7.16
De Reuter, H., Pte., 6928 *13.11.16
Devaney, F., Pte., 292960 *25.4.17
Dewar, T., Pte., S/12259 *21.3.18
Dick, H., Pte., 292884 *26.3.18
Dick, J. I., Pte., 4907 *25.10.16
Dickson, A., Pte., S/21622 † 2.5.18
Dickson, J., Pte., S/41378 *15.4.18
Dinwoddie, T. J., Cpl., 291246
    *26.3.18
Doig, G., L/Cpl., 290480 *25.4.17
Doig, W., Pte., 292426 *23.4.17
Don, J., L/Cpl., 292880 *25.4.17
Donaghy, J., Pte., 290474 †24.4.17
Donaldson, J., Pte., 2769 *15.10.16
Donoghue, D., Pte., S/17544 *26.3.18
Dougal, D., Pte., 293156 *23.4.17
Dowman, T. A., Pte., S/17081 *24.7.18
Downes, R., Pte., S/24427 *24.7.18
Drennan, F., Pte., 291079 †21.3.18
Drew, W., Pte., S/3415 *25.5.17
Driver, C. E., Pte., 292750 *26.3.18
Drummond, R., Pte., 4144 ‡20.7.15
Duff, A., Pte., 2477 *13.11.16
Duffy, W., Cpl., 290309 *31.7.17
Duncan, G., Pte., 292905 *25.4.17
Duncan, J. D., Pte., S/18407 *26.3.18
Duncan, J., Pte., 291563 *26.3.18
Duncan, P. McK., Pte., 291467
    †18.4.17

327

THE SEVENTH BATTALION THE BLACK WATCH

Duncan, R., Pte., 2922 *28.5.16
Dunlop, H., Pte., 292751 *24.11.18
Duthie, I. N., Pte., 293106 *25.4.17

Easton, C., Cpl., 290050 *23.4.17
Eddie, J., L/Cpl., 291390 *23.4.17
Edgar, T. J., Pte., 292566 *28.8.18
Elliot, D., Sgt., 292404 * 1.8.17
Elliot, W., L/Cpl., 291954 † 2.5.17
English, J., Pte., 2657 *26.3.18
Erskine, H., Cpl., 290419 *25.4.17

Fairweather, J., Pte., 292404 *25.4.17
Fairweather, J., Pte., 292924 *26.3.18
Falconer, J., Cpl., 3105 †28.7.16
Farrell, D., Pte., 292935 *23.4.17
Fenton, P., Pte., 2387 *13.11.16
Ferguson, A. B., Pte., 292821 *25.4.17
Ferguson, D., Pte., S/5596 *24.10.18
Ferguson, J., Pte., 267214 †3.10.17
Ferguson, J., Pte., 292482 *25.4.17
Ferguson, J., Pte., 5540 *15.10.16
Ferguson, P., Pte., S/17773 †22.3.18
Ferguson, R. S., Pte., 292630 *23.4.17
Ferguson, W., Pte., 292623 *11.4.17
Ferrier, W., Pte., 4168 † 7.7.16
Finlay, D., Pte., 292460 *26.3.18
Finlay, W. R., Pte., 292145 †9.12.17
Flannigan, J., Cpl., 290059 *20.4.17
Fleming, A., Pte., S/41394 †27.8.18
Fleming, W. P., L/Cpl., S/43384
 *26.3.18
Flockhart, M., Pte., 291008 †23.4.17
Fordyce, A. H., L/Cpl., 292868
 *26.3.18
Foreman, T., Pte., 293070 *20.11.17
Forrester, J., Sgt., 290690 †30.4.17
Forster, G., Pte., 202841 ‡27.7.17
Forsyth, J., Cpl., 2104 *16.6.15
Foster, A., Cpl., 3509 ‡22.10.15
Fowler, H., L/Cpl., 1984 *30.7.16
Fowler, W., Pte., 292529 *23.4.17
Fox, W., L/Cpl., S/43416 *21.3.18
Fraser, A., Pte., 266104 § 5.5.18
Fraser, J., Pte., 290314 *26.3.18
Fraser, W., Sgt., 328 †17.6.15
Frew, G., Pte., 291196 *25.4.17
Frew, J., Pte., 4108 † 7.5.16
Frew, W., Pte., 291197 *24.10.18
Fyfe, W., L/Cpl., 290614 *26.3.18

Galloway, D., Pte., 1826 *30.7.16
Galloway, J., Pte., 2279 * 3.6.16
Galloway, W., Pte., 537 *13.11.16
Gammage, J., Pte., 291641 †18.11.18

Ganly, A., Pte., 292761 *15.4.18
Gardner, T., Pte., 292760 *31.7.17
Gardiner, W. W., Pte., S/43409
 †24.11.17
Geddes, A. T., Pte., 2492 *15.4.18
Geekie, E., Pte., 25095 *31.7.18
Gentle, J., Pte., 291003 *23.4.17
Gibson, A., Pte., 2039 *31.7.16
Gibson, A., Cpl., 266326 †27.8.18
Gibson, T., Pte., S/12148 *31.7.17
Gilchrist, G., Pte., 5528 *15.9.16
Gilfillan, P., Pte., 291157 *26.3.18
Glen, P. J., Pte., S/25166 *24.10.18
Glendinning, J., L/Cpl., 292759
 *26.3.18
Goodwin, J., Pte., 2440 *16.10.14
Gordon, C., Pte., S/40121 *24.7.18
Gordon, J., Sgt., 290051 *31.7.18
Gourlay, A., Pte., 6229 †18.11.16
Gourlay, J., Pte., 2947 *30.7.16
Graham, A., Pte., 290449 §28.10.18
Graham, D. K., Pte., S/25084 *24.7.18
Grant, A., Pte., S/40966 *15.4.18
Grant, G. M., Pte., 2785 * 4.9.15
Grant, W. P., Pte., 5577 *2.12.16
Gray, A. McK., Pte., 310115 *21.3.18
Gray, G. H., A/Cpl., 292578 ‡ 7.5.17
Gray, J., Pte., 4073 *23.6.16
Gray, W., Pte., S/7984 †25.4.18
Gray, W., Pte., 291166 †31.11.18
Green, W. J., Pte., S/42004 *28.8.18
Greig, C. W., C.S.M., 292861 *23.4.17
Grey, W., Pte., 292532 *25.4.17
Grieve, J., Pte., S/43490 §18.5.18
Grieve, J., Pte., 291800 *26.3.18
Grieve, J., Pte., S/19959 *31.7.18
Griffin, R. A., Pte., S/5953 *31.7.17
Griffith, J. G., Pte., S/25092 *24.7.18
Grindell, E. C., Pte., 292483 †18.3.17
Guild, A., Pte., S/43032 *15.4.18
Guthrie, A., Sgt., 290540
 (M.M.) *26.3.18

Haddock, G., Pte., 203383 *26.3.18
Hamilton, W. G., Pte., 292638
 *25.4.17
Hampton, W., L/Cpl., 293104 *15.4.18
Hannan, H. G , Pte., S/24500 †21.7.18
Harley, W., Pte., 291224 *26.3.18
Harper, W., Pte., S/16846 *26.3.18
Harris, J., Pte., 292640 †29.4.17
Harris, W., Pte., 265495 §23.9.18
Harvey, A., Pte., 3034 *16.6.15
Hatrick, J., Pte., S/41012 † 8.6.18
Haxton, W., Pte., 4130 *23.1.16

328

APPENDIX IV

Hay, A., Pte., S/42007	*24.10.18	Keatings, J., Pte., 3913	*14.6.16
Henderson, A., Pte., 1634	*16.6.15	Keenan, J., Pte., 41016	*15.4.18
Henderson, D., Pte., 291803	*26.3.18	Keith, J. M., Pte., 268044	*20.11.17
Henderson, G. R., Sgt., 310155	*24.7.18	Kelly, H., Cpl., 269040	†20.7.18
		Kelly, J. E., Pte., 2643	† 4.7.15
Henderson, I., Pte., 235025	* 5.9.18	Kennedy, J., Pte., 351082	†24.7.18
Henderson, J., L/Cpl., 3290	*28.7.16	Kerr, T., Pte., S/4537	§2.11.18
Henderson, J., L/Cpl., 292454	*26.3.18	Kerr, W., Cpl., S/6523	†29.8.18
Hendry, M., L/Cpl., 292401	*23.4.17	Kerr, W. R., Pte., S/23126	*24.7.18
Hepburn, W., Pte., S/16332	‡18.2.18	Kidd, T., Pte., 291674	*26.3.18
Herd, J., Pte., 291380	*25.4.17	Kidston, P., Pte., 350943	§ 8.9.18
Hill, D. B., Pte., S/12760	*26.3.18	King, D., Pte., 290172	*25.4.17
Hogg, C., Pte., S/4958	*19.9.17	King, R., Pte., 290710	†28.4.17
Hollibon, W. J., Pte., 292468	*23.4.17	Kirk, R., A/Sgt., 283	† 9.9.15
Hollis, C. A. J., Pte., S/12782	*26.3.18	Kirk, W., L/Cpl., 290413	*30.7.16
Holmes, R. K., Pte., 292639	*25.4.17	Kirkcaldy, D., Pte., 290509	†26.3.18
Holt, C., Pte., 6926	† 4.1.17	Kirkcaldy, G., Cpl., 290624	†26.5.17
Hopkins, H. S., Pte., 291859	*25.4.17	Kirkpatrick, W., L/Cpl., 291163	†21.11.17
Honeyman, C., Pte., 2792	†19.6.15		
Hore, A., Pte., 4159	*13.11.16	Kirkup, S., Pte., 291460	*15.4.17
Horsburgh, A., Pte., 1549	* 5.1.17		
Hosie, A., Pte., 292641	†19.5.17	Lamb, J. R., Pte., S/20928	*26.3.18
Hosie, R., L/Cpl., 290697	†22.8.17	Lamb, W., L/Cpl., 290843	*26.3.18
Hughes, W., Pte., 2617	*30.7.16	Lamont, J., Pte., 292768	*26.3.18
Hunter, A. A., Pte., 290097	*23.4.17	Latto, A. F., Pte., 290161	*25.4.17
Hunter, A., Pte., 5543	*25.7.16	Lawrence, D., Pte., 291904	*25.4.17
Hunter, G., Pte., 291019	§22.10.18	Lawrie, W., Pte., 290311	*23.4.17
Hutchison, A., Sgt., 6866	*31.10.16	Lawrie, W., Pte., S/24612	†25.7.18
Hutchison, J., L/Sgt., 269015	*24.10.18	Learmouth, J. M., L/Cpl., 292649	*25.4.17
Hutton, A., Pte., 1625	*15.10.15		
		Leckie, W., Pte., 292652	*25.4.17
Imrie, J., Pte., 4116	*26.7.16	Lee, H., Sgt., S/40998	*15.4.18
Ireland, J., L/Cpl., 3277	‡14.5.15	Lee, J. D., Pte., 4918	* 9.6.16
Irvine, D., Pte., 4132	†31.7.16	Leighton, J., Pte., 292919	*25.4.17
		Leitch, J., Pte., 4852	†28.7.16
Jackson, D. N., Pte., 2638	*30.7.16	Lemon, J., Pte., 293094	†13.4.17
Jackson, G., Pte., S/42104	*28.8.18	Lennox, J., Pte., 241067	†16.5.17
Jackson, H., Pte., 292643	†20.4.17	Liddell, J., Sgt., 293027	*25.4.17
Jackson, J., Pte., 2637	†14.7.15	Lindsay, W., Pte., 6805	*13.11.16
Jamieson, J., Pte., 292307	*16.12.17	Lister, W. G., Pte., 290242	*23.4.17
Jamieson, J., L/Cpl., 290588	*19.9.17	Little, D., Pte., 290376	*25.4.17
Japp, D. L., Pte., 241106	*31.7.17	Little, P., Pte., 290315	†24.4.17
Jarvis, D., Sgt., 290341 (D.C.M.)	† 2.8.17	Livingston, J., Cpl., 632	*15.10.16
		Livingstone, W., Pte., 290080	‡ 9.2.17
Jephson, A., Pte., 5546	† 6.8.16		
Johnson, J., Pte., 292838	*23.4.17	Low, A. E., Pte., S/41619	†24.10.18
Johnson, J. J., Pte., 291930	*26.3.18	Low, G., Pte., 6968	*13.11.16
Johnston, J., Pte., 4470	* 8.1.17	Lowe, J., Pte., 292527	*25.4.17
Johnston, J., Pte., S/40820 (M.M.)	*15.4.18	Low, J., Pte., 290325	*25.4.17
		Lowson, G., Pte., S/41408	† 7.4.18
Johnston, J., Pte., 292562	*23.4.17	Lowson, J., Pte., 290441	†24.4.17
Johnston, R., Pte., 2016	*13.11.16	Lumsden, J., C.S.M., 125	†30.7.16
		Lumsden, W., Pte., 292509	*23.4.17
Kay, R. G., Pte., S/16610	*13.4.18	Lunn, A., Pte., 6389	† 4.1.17
Kaye, G. A., Pte., 293066	*23.3.18	Lyall, J., L/Cpl., 1600	* 5.6.15

THE SEVENTH BATTALION THE BLACK WATCH

MacDonald, C. R., Pte., 290464 *25.4.17
Mackie, W., Pte., 4566 * 3.6.16
Mackie, W., Pte., 1467 * 6.6.15
McAllister, W., Pte., S/41041 *24.10.18
McAlpine, D., Pte., 291744 *16.9.17
McAndrew, W., Pte., S/40020 *26.3.18
McArthur, J., Pte., 4633 *1.12.16
McArthur, J., Pte., 292851 *23.4.17
McBain, A. C. I., Pte., 201508 *19.9.17
McCall, W., Pte., 1795 †13.11.16
McCallum, J., A/Sgt., 290861 (D.C.M.) †22.5.18
McCarrick, W., Sgt., 292888 †17.3.17
McColl, J., Pte., 292784 *25.4.17
McCormack, T., Pte., S/16304 *26.3.18
McCowan, D., Pte., 292679 *25.4.17
McCrae, R., L/Cpl., 292665 † 5.5.17
McCulloch, A. H., Pte., S/11654 *24.10.18
McDermott, J., Pte., S/40056 *26.3.18
McDiarmid, M., Pte., 267184 *30.10.18
McDonald, A., Pte., 292977 * 4.9.18
McDonald, C., Pte., 292256 *26.3.18
McDonald, H., Pte., 292664 † 3.5.17
McDonald, J., Pte., 292538 †23.4.17
McDonald, J. M., Pte., 292526 *23.4.17
McEwan, W. D., Pte., 265490 *24.7.16
McEwan, J., Pte., 4961 * 1.9.16
McFarlane, J., L/Cpl., 5583 *13.11.16
McFarlane, J., Pte., S/25061 *24.7.18
McFarlane J., Pte., 290714 *25.4.17
McFarlane, R., Pte., S/11091 †23.11.17
McGill, J.,,Pte., 290129 *25.4.17
McGillivra y, D., Pte., 4569 *30.7.16
McGillivray, R. D., Pte., 290507 *28.7.16
McGowan, J., Pte., 5590 *13.11.16
McGregor, A., Pte., 293167 *23.4.17
McGregor, J., Pte., 2502 † 3.6.15
McGuire, J., Pte., 1998 *21.8.16
McIvor, J., Pte., 3880 ‡17.7.15
McInnes, A., Cpl., 292865 *16.4.17
McInnes, P., L/Cpl., 2055 *30.7.18
McIntyre, A., Pte., S/8505 *15.4.18
McIntyre, J. D., Pte., 202140 *26.3.18
McIntyre, N., L/Cpl., 290546 *23.4.17
McIntyre, R. C., Pte., S/9466 *15.4.18
McIntyre, W., A/Sgt., 291 *15.4.18
McKay, A. S., Pte., S/41424 *15.4.18
McKelvie, J., Pte., 292779 *20.11.17
McKenzie, R., Pte., 5549 *15.10.16
McKenzie, T. S., Cpl., S/5412 †24.10.18
McLaren, A., Pte., S/13471 *26.3.18
McLaren, F., Pte., S/41022 *15.4.18
McLaren, G., Pte., 6889 *13.11.16
McLaren, G., L/Cpl., 265922 * (M.M.) *26.3.18
McLaren, H., Pte., S/40773 *15.4.18
McLaren, W. H., Pte., 1673 †29.7.15
McLean, D., A/Cpl., 1615 *19.8.15
McLean, J., Pte., 351210 *24.7.18
McLean, W., Pte., 292395 *26.3.18
McLeish, A., A/Cpl., S/4324 *15.4.18
McLeod, H. W. D., Cpl., S/40991 *15.4.18
McLeod, J., Pte., 2654 *16.6.15
McLure, W., Pte., S/43239 *15.4.18
McMahon, S., Pte., 201062 *26.3.18
McMillan, A., Pte., 267142 *24.7.18
McNair, J., Pte., S/17568 *21.3.18
McNaughton, G., Pte., 6790 †3.12.16
McNaughton, R., Pte., 292676 †29.5.17
McNie, J. C., L/Cpl., 11605 † 1.8.18
McNiven, T., Pte., 293166 *23.4.17
McPherson, G., Sgt., S/41001 *15.4.18
McPherson, W. A., Pte., 350503 †20.7.18
McRae, J., Pte., 291593 §28.10.18
McVey, D., Pte., 292677 *23.4.17
McWhannell, J., Pte., 291665 *19.9.17
Mack, A., Pte., 1724 †28.7.16
Main, J., Pte., 292654 *25.4.17
Main, R. P., Pte., 291266 *30.7.16
Mangan, R. A., Pte., 6939 *13.11.16
Marcantonio, A., Pte., 267512 ‡ 4.2.18
Marnock, J., A/Sgt., 2355 *25.9.15
Marshall, R., Pte., 6865 *31.10.16
Martin, D., L/Cpl., 292445 *25.4.17
Martin, T., Pte., 291475 †30.4.17
Masson, B., Pte., S/25093 *26.5.18
May, A., Cpl., 292390 † 6.4.18
Meldrum, S., Pte., 267708 *26.3.18
Melville, G., L/Cpl., 290551 *25.4.17
Michie, D., Pte., 5516 *30.7.16
Michie, W., Pte., 291892 *23.4.17
Middleton, W., Pte., S/41182 *15.4.18
Miles, A., Pte., 6762 *13.11.16
Millar, R., Pte., 293030 *25.4.17
Millar, W., L/Cpl., 290580 *20.11.17
Millar, W. C., Pte., 3087 * 3.9.16
Miller, D., Pte., S/19582 §28.6.18
Miller, T., Pte., 291962 *23.4.17
Milne, F., Pte., 293107 § 2.9.18
Milne, G., Pte., 268070 *26.3.18

APPENDIX IV

Milne, G., Pte., 6951 — *15.10.16
Milne, J., Pte., 292656 — §20.9.18
Milne, T., Pte., 291007 — *18.9.17
Mitchell, G., Pte., S/23265 — *28.8.18
Mitchell, R., Pte., S/21751 — *21.3.18
Mitchell, T., Pte., 290577 — ‡15.9.17
Mitchell, W., Pte., 291464 — * 9.4.18
Moir, A. F., Pte., 292663 — *11.4.17
Mollison, J., Pte., 241018 — § 5.8.18
Monaghan, J., Pte., 310042 — *23.4.17
Moodie, A., A/Sgt., 290721 (M.M.) — †17.4.18
Morgan, D., Pte., 291301 — §5.11.18
Morrison, A., Pte., 291964 — *23.4.17
Morrison, C., Pte., 291253 — *30.7.16
Morrison, J., Pte., 290809 — ‡4.11.18
Morrison, W., Pte., 291796 — *15.4.18
Morrison, W. J. K., Pte., S/41191 — *24.7.18
Mortimer, P., Sgt., 292957 (M.M.) — *26.3.18
Morton, A., Pte., 292536 — *23.4.17
Muir, W., Pte., 3844 — *29.6.16
Muir, W., L/Cpl., 2416 — *13.11.16
Munn, W., Pte., 292773 — †30.4.17
Munro, J., Pte., 292946 — *31.7.17
Munro, W., Pte., S/41443 — *26.5.18
Murdoch, W., Pte., 310091 — *24.7.18
Murphy, P., Pte., 291298 — † 6.6.18
Murray, A., Pte., 292771 — *25.4.17
Murray, E., L/Cpl., 292477 — *25.4.17
Murray, J., Pte., 310154 — *15.4.18
Murray, W., Pte., 291130 — *25.4.17
Myles, A., Pte., 290510 (M.M.) — *25.4.17

Neave, D., L/Cpl., S/41379 — †16.10.18
Neil, R., Pte., S/7873 — *24.10.18
Neill, D., Pte., 290437 — § 1.7.18
Nicholson, B., Pte., 291798 — §14.7.18
Nicol, F., Pte., 3/8065 — *19.9.17
Nicol, J., Pte., 975 — *10.7.15
Nicoll, C. McD., Pte., 310095 — *31.7.18
Nicoll, G. R., Pte., 290730 — † 2.4.17
Nicoll, J., L/Cpl., 292986 — *26.3.18
Nicholl, J., Pte., 293058 — *15.4.18
Nicolson, T., Pte., 2517 — † 1.8.16
Nisbet, C., Sgt., 337 — †22.5.15
Noble, R. A., Pte., S/41198 — †25.7.18
Noble, W., Cpl., 350346 — †13.9.18
Nolan, F. A., Pte., S/25054 — *24/7/18

O'Brien, B., L/Cpl., 1524 — *30.7.16
Ogilvie, D., Pte., 268128 — §13.10.17
Oldman, J., L/Cpl., 290436 — *26.3.18
O'Neil, R., Pte., 291198 — *30.7.16
O'Shea, R., Pte., 292683 — *23.4.17
Paddock, A. J., Pte., S/40978 — *16.10.18
Palmer, F., Pte., 292402 — *24.5.17
Palmer, R., Pte., 5556 — *30.7.16
Panton, J., Pte., 203135 — *26.3.18
Parker, T., Pte., 291188 — *26.3.18
Parkin, C., Pte., 202547 — *23.4.17
Paterson, A., Pte., S/41544 — *24.10.18
Paterson, A., Cpl., 290065 — *25.4.17
Paterson, J., Pte., 2887 — *16.6.15
Paterson, J., Pte., 291582 — *21.3.18
Paton, W., Pte., 4832 — †22.4.16
Paton, W., Pte., 293010 — ‡20.5.17
Patterson, W., Pte., 290363 — *25.4.17
Paul, W., Pte., 3845 — *13.11.16
Peattie, T., Pte., 291449 (M.M.) — *19.9.17
Peebles, A., L/Cpl., 2270 — † 8.6.16
Penman, A., Pte., 1744 — *15.6.15
Penman, G., A/Sgt., 290936 — *21.3.18
Penman, P., Pte., 350171 — *26.3.18
Petrie, A., Pte., 2521 — *26.4.16
Petrie, J., Pte., 202815 — *20.11.17
Philip, A., Pte., 200781 — *26.3.18
Philip, J., L/Cpl., 2409 — ‡30.1.17
Philip, A., Pte., 291802 — *28.10.18
Picken, J., Pte., 292488 — *25.4.17
Pirrie, H., Cpl., 6918 — *13.11.16
Porteous, T., Pte., 291577 — *19.9.17
Potter, A., Sgt., 6863 — *31.10.16
Pratt, J., Pte., 2391 — *24.5.15
Pringle, G., Pte., 2678 — *9.12.15
Punler, D., A/Cpl., 291700 — ‡10.5.17

Quinn, J., Pte., 291871 — * 6.4.17

Rae, A., Pte., 1987 — *13.11.16
Rae, F., Pte., 4111 — *28.5.16
Ramsay, D. H., Cpl., 290860 — †17.3.17
Ramsay, J., Pte., 291968 — *26.3.18
Ramsay, J., Pte., 291509 — *16.9.16
Ramsay, J., Pte., 1626 — *31.10.16
Rankin, J., Pte., 266258 — *26.3.18
Reid, A., Pte., 3442 — *30.7.16
Reid, A. G., L/Cpl., 290346 — *26.3.18
Reid, H. G., Pte., S/24020 — *26.3.18
Reid, R., Pte., 2842 — *16.6.15
Reid, W., Pte., 1944 — † 2.8.16
Reilly, P., Pte., S/5032 — * 9.4.18
Rennie, W., C.S.M., 265679 — †10.5.18
Riach, G., Pte., S/41214 — *24.7.18
Richards, C., Pte., 292928 — * 7.4.17
Richmond, W., Pte., 4495 — *30.7.16

331

THE SEVENTH BATTALION THE BLACK WATCH

Ripley, W. E. S., L/Cpl., 292690 *23.4.17
Ritchie, J., Pte., 6746 †16.11.16
Ritchie, J. B., Pte., 203122 †24.11.17
Robb, A., Pte., 1703 †24.5.15
Robb, P., Pte., S/18767 *26.5.18
Robertson, A. W., Pte., S/41215 *15.4.18
Robertson, A., Pte., 2836 *16.6.15
Robertson, A., Pte., 291299 †31.10.18
Robertson, D., L/Cpl., 290398 *25.4.17
Robertson, E., L/Cpl., 290889 †14.4.18
Robertson, F., Pte., 292916 *30.7.16
Robertson, F. T., Pte., 290643 *25.4.17
Robertson, J., Pte., S/21630 §17.9.18
Robertson, J., L/Cpl., 291176 †29.3.18
Robertson, T., Pte., 4511 †17.6.16
Rodman, A., Sgt., S/7626 (M.M.) †25.3.18
Rose, J., Pte., 290539 * 8.1.17
Ross, C., Pte., 291072 *30.7.15
Ross, C. C., Pte., 203123 *24.7.18
Ross, R. S., L/Cpl., 292842 *25.4.17
Russell, J., Pte., 291637 *18.9.17

Sampson, B., Cpl., 292420 *23.4.17
Scanlan, R. J., Pte., S/8418 *15.6.17
Scobie, J., Pte., 292805 †17.3.17
Scott, A., Pte., 3329 ‡30.7.16
Scott, L. C., Pte., S/17737 * 1.8.17
Scullion, C., Pte., S/25083 †27.7.18
Shannon, I. H. C., Pte., 2713 *16.6.15
Sharp, A., Pte., 290255 *19.9.17
Shaw, A., Pte., 291838 †24.11.17
Shoolbraid, I. H., A/Sgt., 290479 †23.3.18
Simpson, D., Pte., 3599 ‡3.7.15
Simpson, D. T., Pte., S/41225 *15.4.18
Sinclair, D., L/Sgt., 1871 *23.10.16
Sinclair, T., Pte., 5632 *13.11.16
Skene, J. G., Pte., S/41227 *11.5.18
Slater, J. R., Pte., 293169 *23.4.17
Smallman, J., Pte., 241286 *21.3.18
Smith, A., Pte., 3372 *16.8.18
Smith, D. McA., Pte., 292697 *25.4.17
Smith, E., Pte., 3846 †3.12.16
Smith, G. L., Pte., S/41229 *15.4.18
Smith, J., Pte., 3330 *16.10.15
Smith, J., Pte., 3812 *13.11.16
Smith, J., Sgt., 290042 §26.8.18
Smith, J., Pte., 2537 *24.5.16
Smith, J., Pte., 292479 *17.3.17
Smith, W. C., L/Cpl., 291030 *11.4.18

Smith, W. P., Pte., 266891 * 6.3.18
Sneddon, W., Cpl., 2695 *1.12.16
Somerville, R., L/Cpl., 24000 *16.6.15
Speed, W. A., Pte., 290168 * 9.4.17
Spence, A., Pte., 2848 *31.7.16
Spence, T., Pte., 292702 † 2.4.18
Spink, J., Pte., 4211 §20.2.16
Spittal, J., Pte., 2349 *24.6.15
Stacey, I., Pte., S/41031 *15.4.18
Stafford, J., Pte., 3450 †24.12.16
Stainton, T. R., Pte., S/5166 *25.5.17
Stalker, G., Pte., S/16972 *25.6.17
Stanley, E., Pte., 290748 *23.4.17
Stark, W., Pte., 3038 †24.10.16
Stephen, J., A/Cpl., 292866 †25.4.17
Stewart, A., Pte., 292969 †14.4.17
Stewart, C., Pte., 293125 *25.4.17
Stewart, C., L/Cpl., 6922 *16.11.16
Stewart, J., L/Cpl., 1858 †29.7.16
Stirton, J., Pte., S/21698 *26.3.18
Stobie, J., Pte., 4264 *17.3.15
Stormouth, W., Pte., 241145 †26.3.18
Straiton, A., Pte., 292701 *23.4.17
Stuart, K., Pte., 291506 *29.7.17
Sturrock, G., Pte., S/40971 *24.10.18
Sumpter, W. H., L/Cpl., 292577 *26.3.18
Sturgeon, S., Cpl., 292459 *25.4.17
Swan, G., Pte., 204 †21.3.16
Swan, J., Pte., 5560 † 1.8.16
Swan, J., L/Cpl., 290385 *26.3.18
Syme, G. S., Pte., 291915 *26.3.18

Tait, A. W., Pte., 292708 *26.3.18
Taylor, A., Pte., 6868 ‡19.11.16
Taylor, A., L/Cpl., 292387 *23.4.17
Taylor, H., Pte., 292452 †10.4.17
Taylor, J., Pte., 290254 *30.7.16
Taylor, T. G., Pte., S/40098 *15.4.18
Thayne, J., Pte., 4349 *15.4.18
Thoms, A., Pte., S/9867 *15.4.18
Thomson, A., Pte., 4165 † 3.9.16
Thomson, A. McM., Pte., S/23715 *24.7.18
Thomson, A., Pte., 5102 *13.11.16
Thomson, C. R., Pte., S/41241 * 9.4.18
Thomson, J., Pte., 290306 * 2.7.17
Thomson, J. B., Pte., 290301 *26.3.18
Thomson, R., Pte., S/22017 *26.3.18
Thomson, W., Pte., 2347 *30.7.16
Thompson, W. S., Pte., 292709 *23.4.17
Thornton, J., Pte., 310032 *15.3.17
Tither, W., Cpl., S/7811 †20.10.18
Todd, J. D., L/Sgt., 2716 *13.11.16

APPENDIX IV

Todd, R., Pte., 290174	*25.4.17	Weir, J., Pte., 2871	† 3.6.16
Todd, T., Pte., 202429	*20.7.18	Weir, J. S., Sgt., 4225	*21.7.16
Torrance, J., Pte., 1837	*28.5.16	Whitecross, W., Pte., 290484	*26.3.18
Torrance, W., Sgt., 2003	*22.6.16	Whyte, A., Pte., S/12888	§ 9.8.18
Trayner, P., Pte., 293128	†11.4.17	Whyte, G., Pte., S/14047	*21.7.18
Tucker, D. M., Pte., S/23440	†26.4.18	Whyte, J., Pte., 293124	*25.4.17
Turner, J., Pte., 291973	§16.9.16	Wilkie, A., Pte., 1890	*16.6.15
Turner, R., Pte., 2715	†31.7.16	Williamson, J., Sgt., 3/1732	
Turner, R., Pte., 2860	†31.7.16	(M.M.)	*24.10.18
Turpie, J., Pte., 202839	*26.3.18	Wilson, A., Pte., 291115	*31.7.18
		Wilson, D., Pte., 290202	†25.4.17
Urquhart, D., Pte., 201514	*26.3.18	Wilson, D., Pte., 291423	*30.6.16
		Wilson, J., Pte., 1776	* 9.8.15
Verdon, J., Pte., S/41249	*15.4.18	Wilson, J., Pte., 310015	§ 4.3.17
		Wilson, J., Pte., 6834	*13.11.16
Walker, J., Pte., 1941	*16.6.15	Wilson, R., Pte., S/19493	§26.5.18
Walker, J., Pte., S/42116	†10.9.18	Wilson, W., Pte., 2728	*30.7.16
Walker, J. P., Pte., 293302	*24.7.18	Wilson, W., Pte., 4765	‡1.9.15
Walker, T., Pte., 2395	*16.6.15	Winton, J., Pte., 292379	*26.3.18
Wallace, A., L/Sgt., 2252	†23.12.16	Wishart, J., L/Sgt., 290656	*31.3.17
Wallace, A., Sgt., 454	*25.9.15	Wood, A., Pte., 310109	*26.3.18
Wallace, A. C., Pte., 2723	*14.3.16	Wood, H., Pte., 292815	*25.3.18
Wallace, G., Pte., 1718	*13.11.16	Wood, J. B., L/Cpl., 290433	*23.4.17
Walton, R., Pte., 2862	*31.10.16	Wotherspoon, G. R., Pte., S/25059	
Wands, W., Pte., 292715	*23.4.17		*28.5.18
Watson, G., Pte., 290839	*31.7.17	Wright, D., Pte., 290549	§16.8.18
Watson, J., Pte., S/18707	*26.3.18	Wright, W., Pte., 290105	† 3.6.17
Watson, J., Cpl., 292502	*23.4.17	Wright, W., Pte., 6794	†17.12.16
Watson, P., C.S.M., 492	*24.10.18	Wrigley, H., Pte., 292816	*31.7.17
Watson, R., Pte., 2551	‡19.4.15	Wyllie, D., Pte., 291977	†24.4.17
Watson, W., L/Cpl., 2200	*24.5.15		
Watt, D., Sgt., 292922	* 1.4.17	Yates, A., Pte., 351319	*24.7.18
Watt, D. L., Pte., S/43255	*21.3.18	Young, J., Pte., 2393	‡ 8.7.15
Watt, F., Dmr., 2234	*19.8.15	Young, J., Pte., 292718	†28.4.17
Watters, W., Pte., 292412	*26.3.18	Young, J. E. McI., Pte., S/41261	
Weatherhead, J., Pte., S/43534			*20.7.18
	†31.3.18	Young, W., Pte., S/22830	*26.5.18
Webster, D., Cpl., 268172	*20.3.18	Young, W., Pte., 291606	†13.5.17
Weir, J., Pte., 290415	*25.4.17	Young, W. A., Pte., S/41263	*15.4.18

APPENDIX V

HONOURS AND AWARDS

The First-Seventh Battalion

C.M.G.
Colonel H. M. Allen.

O.B.E.
Lieut. J. G. Rowan.

Bar to D.S.O.
Lieut.-Colonel S. R. McClintock, D.S.O.

D.S.O.
Lieut. H. J. Herd.
Major D. R. Keir.
Lieut.-Colonel J. Millar, M.C.
Lieut.-Col S. R. McClintock.
Major F. M. B. Robertson.

Bar to M.C.
Lieut. F. I. Gerrard, M.C.
Capt. J. R. Reid, M.C.
Capt. S. Watson, M.C.

M.C.
2nd Lieut. D. E. Adamson.
Lieut. D. M. Archibald.
Capt. D. Beveridge.
Capt. E. J. Blair.
2nd Lieut. R. M. L. Cable.
Capt. W. A. Casswell.
Capt. A. A. Cuthbertson.
Capt. D. W. Dempster.
2nd Lieut. G. D. H. Fullerton-Carnegie.
Lieut. F. I. Gerrard.
Capt. R. W. McF. Grieve.
Capt. W. Herd.
2nd Lieut. W. Hopkins.
2nd Lieut. A. S. Le Maitre.
Capt. P. M. Levi.
2nd Lieut. J. W. Lownie.
Lieut. R. Lyell.
Capt. H. C. Mackintosh.
Lieut. M. Menzies.
Lieut. A. L. Miller.
Capt. A. M. Moodie.
Lieut. M. MacArthur, D.C.M.
Capt. North.
Lieut. J. C. Penney.
Capt. J. R. Reid.
Capt. J. C. Ross.
Lieut. J. G. Rowan.
Capt. S. Watson.

Two Bars to D.C.M.
Sgt. A. Greig, D.C.M.

D.C.M.
Corpl. D. Brown.
R.S.M. A. Ferrier.
Sgt. A. Greig.
Pte. J. Hennessey.
Pte. Higgins.
Sgt. Jarvis.
Sgt. J. H. McIntosh.
L/Sgt. D. O'Hara.
Sgt. Patterson.
C.S.M. W. Raistrick.
Sgt. R. Wood.

M.S.M.
Pte. D. M. Mitchell.
L/Sgt. D. McBain.

APPENDIX V

Bar to M.M.

Sgt. A. Greig.
Pte. A. Jude.
Pte. J. Millar.
Sgt. J. Mitchell.
L/Corpl. J. McNeill.
Sgt. T. Stenhouse.

M.M.

Pte. Anderson.
L/Corpl. Adamson.
Pte. T. Beattie.
Dmr. H. Bowman.
Pte. A. Brown.
L/Corpl. D. Brown.
Pte. W. Brown.
Pte. Bruce.
Pte. Bunce.
Sgt. W. Byers.
L/Corpl. A. Campbell.
Pte. W. Christison.
L/Corpl. A. Cook.
Corpl. Demster.
Pte. R. Ewan.
Pte. Fairlie.
Pte. A. M. Fordyce.
Pte. Funkie.
Piper G. Galloway.
L/Sgt. Gilzean.
Pte. A. Grant.
Sgt. A. Greig.
Pte. Harvey.
Pte. J. Hennessey.
Pte. Hunt.
Pte. J. Hutt.
Pte. A. Jude.
Sgt. J. Lumsden.
Sgt. T. A. Malpas.
Pte. J. Millar.
Sgt. J. Mitchell.
Sgt. P. Mortimer.
L/Sgt. D. Murray.
Pte. W. McAndrew.
L/Corpl. McCabe.
Pte. J. McDill.
Sgt.-Piper T. McDonald.
Corpl. McKinley.
Pte. J. McNeill.
Pte. A. McPherson.
L/Corpl. J. Nicolson.
Pte. S. Normand.
Sgt. T. Penman.
L/Corpl. W. Robertson.
L/Sgt. Rodman.
Pte. Ross.
Pte. D. Simpson.
Pte. J. Small.
Pte. A. Stark.
Sgt. D. Stenhouse.
Pte. Swanson.
Sgt. D. Syme.
Pte. J. B. Torrance.
Pte. R. Wanless.
Sgt. A. Wilson.
Pte. Winton.
L/Corpl. A. Young.

Mentioned in Despatches

Lieut.-Colonel H. M. Allen.
Major D. Beveridge.
2nd Lieut. Bracelin.
Capt. D. Brown.
Lieut. Campbell.
2nd Lieut. G. D. H. Fullerton-Carnegie.
Major W. A. Gutherie.

Lieut. H. J. Humphreys (2).
Major J. M. Milligan.
Major F. M. B. Robertson.
Capt. J. Rowan.
Lieut.-Colonel H. H. Sutherland.
Lieut. E. D. H. Thomson.
Lieut. S. Watson.

Sgt. Carson.
L/Corpl. P. Drylis.
R.S.M. S. Ferrier.

L/Corpl. W. Halley.
Sgt. J. Lumsden.

THE SEVENTH BATTALION THE BLACK WATCH

FOREIGN DECORATIONS

Croix de Guerre

2nd Lieut. R. M. Cable.
Capt. F. I. Gerrard.

Lieut. R. Lyell.
Lieut.-Colonel J. Miller.

L/Corpl. R. Drummond.

Pte. Lumsden.

Military Croix de Guerre (Belgium)

C.S.M. Mitchell.

Bronze Medal for Valour (Italian)

Sgt. Jarvis.

APPENDIX VI

List of Actions and Operations

The Seventh Battalion

1915.   Landed in France. 2nd May.
   Trench warfare. Festubert, Indian Village, Laventie, Bécourt, Albert, Authuile and Aveluy. May–September.

1916.   Trench warfare. Maricourt, Neuville-St. Vaast, The Labyrinth and Maroeuil. January–July.

BATTLE OF BAZENTIN RIDGE. (High Wood.) 22nd July.

BATTLE OF POZIÈRES RIDGE. (Bazentin le Petit.) 30th–31st July.
   Trench warfare. Armentières Sector, Hébuterne, Anchonvillers and Beaumont Hamel. August–November.

BATTLE OF THE ANCRE (1916). (Beaumont Hamel.) 13th–14th November.
   Trench warfare. Courcelette Sector. November–December.

1917.   Trench warfare. Pys, Ecurie and Roclincourt. January–April.

FIRST BATTLE OF THE SCARPE. (Capture of Gavrelle.) 9th April.

SECOND BATTLE OF THE SCARPE. (Roeux.) 23rd–24th April.
   Trench warfare. Oppy Sector, Chemical Works, Ypres and Lancashire Farm. April–July.

BATTLE OF PILCKEM RIDGE. (Hindenburg Farm.) 31st July–1st August.
   Trench warfare. Ypres, Cherisy, Havrincourt Wood. July–November.

BATTLE OF CAMBRAI (1917). (Grand Ravine and Flesquières.) 20th–21st November.
   Trench warfare. Fontaine and Boursies. November–December.

1918.   Trench warfare. Boursies Area. January–March.

FIRST BATTLE OF BAPAUME. (Beaumetz, Morchies, Loupart Wood.) 21st–25th March.

BATTLE OF THE LYS. (Lestrem.) 9th April.
   Trench warfare. Lestrem, Robecq, Arleux, Bailleul and Gavrelle. April–July.

THE SEVENTH BATTALION THE BLACK WATCH

BATTLE OF TARDENOIS. (Bois de Courton.) 26th–31st July.

Trench warfare. Fampoux Sector. August.

SECOND BATTLE OF ARRAS (1918). (Hyderabad Redoubt.) 24th 26th August.

Trench–warfare. Greenland Hill and Plouvain. September–October.

BATTLE OF THE SELLE. (Crossing of the Ecaillon River.) 24th–25th October.

ADVANCE TO VICTORY. October–11th November.

THE BLACK WATCH
RESERVE BATTALIONS

OFFICERS OF THE BLACK WATCH (Territorial) BRIGADE, BRIDGE OF EARN, 1915

194 OFFICERS OF THE BLACK WATCH (TERRITORIAL) BRIGADE, BRIDGE OF EARN 1915.

Top Row.
1. Lieut. J. M. Mills
2. Lieut. J. Stewart
3. Lieut. J. Barr
4. Lieut. R. K. Mill
5. Lieut. Campbell
6. Lieut. W. P. Vassie
7. Lieut. A. S. Le Maitre
8. Lieut. T. A. Menzies
9. Lieut. J. Morris
10. Lieut. R. K. Campbell
11. Lieut. W. C. Reid
12. Lieut. J. H. B. Lockhart
13. Lieut. J. K. Wallace
14. Lieut. J. Reid
15. Lieut. R. M. Menzies
16. Lieut. H. L. C. Guthrie
17. Lieut. J. McCredie
18. Lieut. J. Anderson
19. Lieut. W. B. Brown
20. Lieut. G. S. M. Burton
21. Lieut. C. Taylor
22. Lieut. J. S. Nicoll
23. Lieut. S. Carr
24. Lieut. H. E. Wilkie
25. Lieut. G. G. C. Ralston
26. Lieut. A. Hunter
27. Lieut. A. C. Wallace
28. Lieut. D. Brown
29. Lieut. W. D. MacNaughton
30. Lieut. C. R. Brown
31. Lieut. W. H. Flett
32. Lieut. H. S. Wright
33. Lieut. H. W. W. Miller
34. Lieut. G. A. Ogg
35. Lieut. L. Mc L. Fulton
36. Lieut. F. Steele
37. Lieut. J. R. Nelson

Second Row.
1. Lieut. W. Nelson
2. Lieut. J. D. Stewart
3. Lieut. A. Mathewson
4. Lieut. F. Sheriff
5. Lieut. A. L. Edwards
6. Lieut. J. G. Rowan
7. Lieut. J. Lindsay
8. Lieut. W. Clark
9. Lieut. I. Heggie
10. Lieut. A. Kilgour
11. Lieut. R. Reid
12. Lieut. G. A. Donaldson
13. Lieut. W. D. Lang
14. Lieut. J. L. Scrymgeour
15. Lieut. N. Harley
16. Lieut. F. Kerr
17. Lieut. P. Watson
18. Lieut. D. Grant
19. Lieut. J. Geddes
20. Lieut. W. T. Thornton
21. Lieut. A. Morgan
22. Lieut. G. Paton
23. Lieut. P. Campbell

Third Row.
1. Lieut. W. T. Smith
2. Lieut. R. Cowan
3. Lieut. G. Burgess
4. Lieut. J. W. Fraser
5. Lieut. F. Batchelor
6. Lieut. S. Vair
7. Lieut. S. Thomson
8. Lieut. A. McLaren
9. Lieut. J. A. Watson
10. Lieut. R. H. Donald
11. Lieut. R. A. Fleming
12. Lieut. J. S. Finlayson
13. Lieut. B. C. O. Beatson
14. Lieut. R. W. Tovani
15. Lieut. C. L. Stewart
16. Lieut. D. P. Harley
17. Lieut. H. P. Henderson
18. Lieut. G. Fullerton-Carnegie
19. Lieut. G. H. Pagan
20. Lieut. W. Herd
21. Lieut. A. R. Davidson
22. Lieut. W. D. Berry
23. Capt. P. Moon
24. Lieut. J. Davidson
25. Surg.-Capt.R.V. Ash, R.A.M.C.
26. Lieut. J. Prosser
27. Lieut. J. G. M. Smith
28. Lieut. J. Young
29. Lieut. H. S. Roberts
30. Lieut. J. Duncan
31. Lieut. H. S. Greaves
32. Lieut. Allan
33. Lieut. J. Ritchie
34. Lieut. D. McEwan
35. Lieut. J. M. McCredie
36. Lieut. R. N. Keay
37. Lieut. H. B. Buchanan
38. Lieut. F. C. Hunter
39. Lieut. F. G. Shand
40. Lieut. R. E. W. Atkins
41. Lieut. F. M. Richardson
42. Lieut. F. W. J. Hunter

Fourth Row.
1. Lieut. W. K. Anderson
2. Lieut. A. G. Begg
3. Lieut. D. Wilson
4. Lieut. C. Butler
5. Lieut. A. Brown
6. Lieut. A. G. Laird
7. Lieut. H. S. Hunter
8. Lieut. R. Forbes
9. Lieut. J. W. Hay Robertson
10. Lieut. A. Watt
11. Lieut. B. Lawson
12. Lieut. J. Wighton
13. Lieut. J. Weir
14. Lieut. E. D. Nicoll
15. Lieut.
16. Lieut. R. E. Ferrier
17. Lieut. J. Hallan
18. Lieut. C. G. Kennaway
19. Lieut. Menzies
20. Lieut. J. N. Rose
21. Lieut. J. D. Ross Scott
22. Lieut. D. S. Gibson Turnbull
23. Lieut. F. E. Young
24. Lieut. A. D. S. Gowans
25. Lieut. & Q.M. J. Crerar
26. Lieut. W. Morris
27. Lieut. R. Campbell
28. Lieut. C. C. Penney
29. Lieut. J. H. Middleton
30. Lieut. R. B. Shaw
31. Lieut. J. A. Sherwood
32. Lieut. R. Sharp
33. Lieut. J. Pryde
34. Lieut. P. L. Forgan
35. Lieut. J. V. Boothby
36. Lieut. C. F. Davis
37. Capt. & Q.M. H. Studley
38. Lieut. & Q.M. A. McNab
39. Capt. R. L. Watson
40. Capt. W. Moir Scott

Fifth Row.
1. Capt. R. Harris
2. Capt. T. C. Crockett
3. Capt. E. Harrison
4. Capt. J. Rettie
5. Capt. K. G. McKenzie
6. Capt. G. W. McIntosh, R.A.M.C.
7. Capt. I. Keillor
8. Capt. & Hon. Chaplain D. Fraser,
9. Capt. T. H. B. Rorie
10. Major D. Wilkie
11. Capt. J. M. Doggart
12. Major A. Valentine
13. Major T. M. Guthrie
14. Major J. L. Macpherson
15. Col. Sir Ralph Anstruther, Bart.
16. Col. C. E. Colville
17. Col. D. Pirie
18. Col. A. W. H. Hay Drummond
19. Brig.-Gen. The Duke of
    Montrose, K.T., A.D.C.
20. Major T. K. Gardiner (Brigade
    (Major)
21. Col. P. S. Nicoll
22. Lieut. I. W. W. Shepherd
23. Col. H. K. Smith
24. Major Claude Hay
25. Capt. H. W. Laing, R.A.M.C.
26. Capt. R. Ferguson
27. Capt. D. Mackenzie
28. Capt. T. Hale
29. Capt. T. E. Young
30. Capt. S. E. R. Lane
31. Capt. J. B. Muir
32. Capt. F. W. L. May
33. Capt. J. M. Deuchars, R.A.M.C
34. Capt. J. M. Reid
35. Capt. A. K. Watson
36. Lieut. & Q.M. J. Marshall
37. Lieut. & Q.M. McCowan
38. Capt. W. R. Cable
39. Capt. E. A. Shepherd
40. Capt. F. McGrady
41. Col. J. B. Muir

Seated on the grass in front.

1. Capt. W. Reid 2. Capt. J. D. O. Coats 3. Capt. C. D. Smitton 4. Capt. H. J. Grierson 5. Capt. Canch Kavanagh

THE BLACK WATCH RESERVE BATTALIONS

THIS History of The Black Watch has been written to record the actions of those battalions who fought in the Great War. But to make no reference to the Reserve Battalions would be a grave omission. In these battalions were enlisted many officers and many thousands of men; there they began their training and there they were imbued with the spirit and tradition of The Black Watch.

The first duty of the Reserve Battalions was to enlist and train men, and so form organized units capable of taking an efficient part in Home Defence. The second, and latterly their main function, was to provide drafts for the battalions overseas.

The value of this early training was fully proved by the services of those officers and men who joined and fought with the various battalions of the Regiment overseas. To the labours of all those who took part in this training some measure of the success of these battalions is surely due.

On the outbreak of war, the 4th, 5th, 6th and 7th Territorial Battalions were mobilized, and the response to the call for recruits was so good throughout the Regimental District, that it was soon found necessary to form a Second or Reserve Battalion to each of these units.

It is worth noting as an example of the keen spirit and sense of duty that filled the country, that many local recruiting committees were formed throughout the Regimental District for the several Reserve Battalions. The work of the members of these committees was entirely voluntary, and proved most successful in maintaining the territorial character of the Reserve Battalions.

The responsibility for clothing and equipping the Reserve Battalions was readily undertaken by the County Territorial Associations and, after the difficulties which arose during the first few months of the war had been overcome, these duties were ably carried out.

Before the end of 1914, the 2/4th, 2/5th, 2/6th and 2/7th Reserve Battalions were all organized and fully equipped, and early in January, 1915, all four Battalions were assembled at Hawick and formed the 2/1st Infantry Brigade under the command of His Grace the Duke of Montrose.

This Brigade was one of several which later formed the 64th Reserve Highland Division under Major-General Bannatine-Allason. In the beginning of 1916 it was hoped that this Division would be sent overseas, but the demands from the 51st Highland Division to replace casualties in France were so heavy, that this proposal had to be given up. Consequently the duty—and none could be more important—of sending drafts to the first line battalions remained its chief function.

THE BLACK WATCH RESERVE BATTALIONS

In all battalions the men were of fine physique, and a spirit of keen enthusiasm filled the ranks. Officers devoted themselves to the training of their units; route marches were frequent, individual training was thorough, and among the hills surrounding Hawick attack and defence schemes were often practised.

In the spring of 1915, however, as the first line battalions were ordered to France, the second line battalions were called upon to take over different parts of the coast defences, and the accounts of the second line battalions from this time are best told separately.

2/4th Battalion

The 2/4th, which had been recruited mainly from Dundee, was ordered to that city and took over part of the Tay defences near Broughty Ferry. In the summer of 1915, the Battalion rejoined the 2/1st Black Watch Brigade at Bridge of Earn, but the winter was spent in Auchterarder, much time being given to training in position warfare and digging trenches near Glen-eagles.

In the spring of 1916, the 2/1st Black Watch Brigade was ordered to Norfolk, the 2/4th being billeted first in Norwich and later in Kelingheath. At Norwich a fine ceremonial parade was frequently seen. The drum and pipe bands of all the Highland Battalions, sometimes exceeding a hundred men, were massed in the square in front of the Cathedral, and played regimental marches and other pipe music before a large number of soldiers and civilians. The winter was spent in Cromer, after which the Battalion returned to Kelingheath, where it was disbanded in the autumn of 1917.

The Battalion was ably commanded by Colonel D. Pirie; Major T. Murray was Second-in-Command until he was given command of a battalion in France; Major Valentine served as Adjutant in 1914–15 and did much to add to the efficiency of the Battalion. Lieut. Prosser proved an able successor; he was subsequently killed when serving with the 8th Black Watch in France.

2/5th Battalion

The 2/5th Battalion, after leaving Hawick, moved to various stations of the Clyde defences in the spring of 1915. Later it moved to Dundee, when the officers and men selected for foreign service were separated from those for home defence; the Battalion then rejoined the 2/1st Black Watch Brigade at Bridge of Earn. At the end of the year the Battalion marched to Larbert, though now much reduced in strength owing to the despatch of drafts to France. Here the 2/5th was disbanded;

THE BLACK WATCH RESERVE BATTALIONS

officers and men of Class A joined the 3/5th Reserve Battalion at Ripon before being sent overseas; the few who were not of Class A were amalgamated with the 2/4th Battalion The Black Watch.

Colonel P. S. Nicoll, T.D., commanded the Battalion. His good services led to his appointment first as Officer Commanding a Reserve Battalion of the Gordon Highlanders, and finally as Officer Commanding British troops in Khartoum, 1918.

Major T. Maule Guthrie, T.D., served as Second-in-Command, and Major D. Wilkie, T.D., as Adjutant, both most efficient officers of the old 1/5th Battalion. Major Wilkie was killed in France when serving with the Naval Division.

2/6th Battalion

In April, 1915, the 2/6th moved to North Queensferry on the Firth of Forth, just opposite the village where the Battalion had been raised six months earlier, but rejoined the 2/1st Black Watch Brigade in camp near Bridge of Earn in May. The third line units joined in summer, the numbers in camp exceeding six thousand men.

The winter was spent first at Grangemouth and later at Blairgowrie. The Brigade moved to Norfolk in the spring of 1916, and was encamped at Taverham near Norwich during the summer. Here the first draft of nearly three hundred men, all thoroughly trained and of the finest physique, were sent to join the 51st Division in France.

In August the 2/6th furnished a guard for Her late Majesty Queen Alexandra at Sandringham House. Captains F. W. L. May and C. Willison and Lieutenants P. C. Hunter, G. S. M. Burton and R. B. Shaw were present with this guard.

In October, 1916, the Battalion was again billeted in Norwich. Much time was devoted to training, air raids were not infrequent, and many men who had been wounded in France joined the Battalion to take the place of those sent to France. But as the months passed the strength of the Battalion diminished, and neither the numbers nor the quality of the recruits could be maintained at the standard of the first years of the war. Consequently it became necessary to disband the 2/6th in September, 1917, at Norwich, after three years of continuous and excellent service.

Much credit for the efficiency of the 2/6th Battalion was due to the Commanding Officer, Colonel A. W. Hay-Drummond. He was ably supported by Major Claude Hay, first as Adjutant and later as Second-in-Command. Major Hay was succeeded as Adjutant by Captain H. J. Grierson, who did valuable work in training recruits and junior officers.

THE BLACK WATCH RESERVE BATTALIONS

2/7th Battalion

In April, 1915, the 1/7th was under orders to move to France. To replace this Battalion, the 2/7th was sent from Hawick, where it had been in billets for three months, to Kinghorn in Fife, in order to take over coast defence duties. In June the 2/7th rejoined the 2/1st Black Watch Brigade at Bridge of Earn, remaining there until October. The first draft—a very fine body of men—was sent to the 1/7th Battalion in France in September, and the Battalion continued to send drafts overseas until its disbandment in 1918.

From Bridge of Earn the 2/7th marched to Grangemouth, where it remained till January, 1916. After spending three months at Milnathort, the Battalion moved to Norwich where it rejoined the 2/1st Black Watch Brigade and formed part of the 64th Highland Division.

The Battalion had been recruited mainly from the mining districts of Fife where Lord Cochrane was well known, and he proved himself a most popular Commanding Officer. In 1917, however, he was appointed to the command of a composite battalion, but an able successor was found in Lieutenant-Colonel George Bower who commanded the 2/7th till its disbandment.

Major A. Lawson served as Second-in-Command and Major Bradbridge as Adjutant. Captain Russell Sharp and Captain C. D. Smitton, also old officers of the 1/7th, did excellent work in the training of recruits. It was thanks mainly to the persistent demands of Colonel Cochrane that the kilt was sanctioned as the dress of the Reserve Battalions of the 7th Black Watch.

Exact records concerning the Reserve Battalions have been difficult to obtain. But careful estimates show that the 2/4th, 2/6th and 2/7th each sent some 60 or 80 officers and about 2500 non-commissioned officers and men overseas. The 2/5th Battalion, which was disbanded earlier in the war than the others, sent some 50 officers and about 1500 men. The greater number of these officers and men served with the various battalions of The Black Watch in France and elsewhere.

These figures are in themselves sufficient to show some measure of the service rendered to the Regiment and to the country by the Reserve Battalions during the war.

Third Line Battalions

In the spring of 1915 recruiting in The Black Watch district had been so successful that the second line battalions were all well up to strength, consequently four new battalions were

THE BLACK WATCH RESERVE BATTALIONS

raised to form a third line. These units had two main duties: to send drafts to the oversea battalions, and to serve as depots which men, who had been sent from France when either wounded or sick, were able to join on leaving hospital.

These Battalions served at various stations in Scotland, and in 1915 were brigaded under the Duke of Montrose at Bridge of Earn. In the summer of 1916 the four third line battalions were amalgamated at Ripon and formed the 4th Reserve Battalion The Black Watch, under the command of Colonel Sir Robert Moncreiffe.

No records exist to show how many men passed through these four battalions, but certainly several thousands were sent to France. The accompanying photograph shows that 194 officers were serving in the second and third line battalions in June, 1915.

In the First and Third Volumes of this History short accounts of the 3rd and 11th Reserve Battalions are given. For the collection of material and many facts concerning the Reserve Battalions, the Editor is much indebted to the following officers: Colonel D. Pirie, Colonel P. S. Nicoll, C.B.E., Colonel A. W. Hay-Drummond, Colonel Lord Cochrane of Cults, Colonel H. K. Smith, Major R. Hoyer Millar, Colonel C. E. Colville, Colonel Sir Ralph Anstruther, Captain P. C. Hunter, Captain Russell Sharp and Captain G. S. M. Burton, M.C.

THE ROYAL
HIGHLANDERS
OF CANADA

"PIPES OF WAR"
After the painting by J. F. Beadle

CHAPTER I

AUGUST, 1914, TO AUGUST, 1916

Raising of 13th, 42nd and 73rd Battalions—13th embarks for England and then proceeds to France—Battle of Ypres—42nd arrives in France and takes over defence of part of Ypres Salient—73rd embarks for England and shortly afterwards lands in France.

UNDER the title of the 5th Militia Battalion of Canada, the Regiment now known as The Royal Highlanders of Canada was raised in 1816.

" As was the case with the gentlemen of The Black Watch
" in 1725, the original companies of the 5th Battalion Royal
" Light Infantry were organized and composed of gentlemen
" banded together to preserve peace. The title in subsequent
" years became the 5th Regiment The Royal Highlanders
" of Canada."*

Between 1866 and 1870 Fenian Raiders from the United States caused grave disorders in Canada, in the suppression of which the Battalion was actively employed. Again in 1882 men of the 5th Battalion served in the Nile Campaign, and also assisted in the quelling of the Canadian North-West Rebellion (Riel's); in 1899 it sent a contingent who took part in the Boer War in South Africa.

In 1904 the 5th Battalion Canadian Militia was affiliated to The Black Watch and since that date the bond of friendship between the two has been so strengthened that it is to-day, and has been for many years past, a real part of the regiment.

In August, 1914, when the call was made in Canada for men for service overseas, the response was great and the 5th was able to send three battalions in a short space of time. The first was numbered the 13th and, thanks to the special efforts of Colonel George Cantlie and Colonel Piers Davidson, the second and third battalions respectively were formed and given the titles and numbers of 42nd and 73rd. All three battalions were recruited from Montreal, but the 73rd enrolled some men from Quebec and Almonte regiments.

The 13th Battalion was the first to leave Canada. Embarking at Quebec on the *Alaunia* on September 26th, 1914, it arrived at Plymouth on October 14th and, after a short stay on Salisbury Plain, where it joined the 3rd Brigade, 1st (Canadian) Division, it eventually landed in France on February 16th, 1915.

* From *The Royal Highlanders of Canada*, published by Hugh Rees, 1918.

THE ROYAL HIGHLANDERS OF CANADA

Meanwhile the 42nd Battalion, which had been mobilized on February 8th, 1915, was being formed.

The 13th Battalion had only been a short time in France when it took part in one of the fiercest battles of the war—the Second Battle of Ypres, when it was engaged in repelling the German gas attack on April 22nd, and in the subsequent fighting round St. Julien from the 24th to the end of the month.

On the 22nd, the 13th occupied the front line north-east of St. Julien on the extreme left of the Canadian line. Nos. 1, 2 and 4 companies, left to right, were holding the front line, with two platoons of No. 3 company in support behind the right company, the remainder of No. 3 company being at Battalion Headquarters at St. Julien. At 3 p.m. a heavy bombardment of the French Moroccan troops on the immediate left of the Battalion line followed the gas attack, and at 1.5 p.m. the Germans assaulted these troops and forced them to withdraw, leaving the left flank of the 13th exposed. The two platoons of No. 3 company were sent up to reinforce the front line, while another formed a defensive flank covering the exposed flank of the Battalion, and in this position the enemy was held up throughout the night. History will give just credit to the Canadian troops for the part played by them in this battle but, posted as they were on the left flank of the Canadian Division, no praise can be too high for the gallant efforts of the 13th Battalion in this hard-fought action.*

In this action Lance-Corporal F. Fisher, who was awarded a posthumous Victoria Cross, was killed.

" Coming forward from St. Julien, Fisher discovered that
" some of the guns of Major W. B. M. King's field battery were
" being fought with the German infantry close on top of them.
" Capture of these guns seemed imminent, but Fisher set up
" his machine gun in advance of the Battery, and, with the
" assistance of a few men of the supports, held off the enemy
" till the guns got away. During this encounter Fisher's small
" section was under concentrated fire and four of his six men
" were killed. Returning to St. Julien, he got four men of the
" 14th Battalion and endeavoured once more to push up to the
" front line. In coming forward he lost these men and eventually
" reached the front line alone. Here he continued to render
" valuable service up to the moment of his death. For the valour

* During three days of continuous fighting the 13th had held their ground and repulsed all attacks. The Battalion was reduced to half its strength, having suffered 454 casualties. As Sir John French truly said, "the bearing and conduct of the splendid Canadian troops averted a serious disaster."

THE ROYAL HIGHLANDERS OF CANADA

Inspection by H.R.H. The Duke of Connaught on the Champ de Mars, Montreal, 28th May, 1915, before embarkation to France

MAY–JUNE, 1915

" he displayed on these occasions he was recommended for, and
" awarded, the coveted Victoria Cross, being the first Canadian
" to win this honour in the Great War."*

Having suffered heavy losses, the 13th was withdrawn to reserve trenches on the 24th and the next seven days were spent in support. In May the Battalion moved from Robecq to reserve trenches near Indian village in support of the 16th Canadian Battalion which attacked and captured The Orchard on the 19th. After the attack, at 9 p.m. that evening the 13th moved forward under heavy shell fire. It repulsed a strong German counter-attack, after which it was relieved and moved to Essars in Divisional reserve.

From this time until June, 1916, the 13th took part in no further operations of importance.

The 42nd Battalion had mobilized at Montreal, and embarked on the *Hesperian* on June 10th, 1915, and after a period of training at Shorncliffe, arrived in France on October 9th.

This Battalion was first employed as part of corps troops and later was brigaded with the Princess Patricia's Canadian Light Infantry (the first Canadian battalion to reach France), and with the Royal Canadian Regiment of the Canadian Permanent Force in the 7th Canadian Infantry Brigade. In January, 1916, the 7th Brigade formed part of the 3rd Canadian Division which was shortly afterwards organized in the field. The 42nd continued regular tours of duty in the line, and took over the defence of part of the Ypres salient.

Meanwhile, the 73rd Canadian Infantry Battalion, which had recruited and mobilized in Montreal, had left Halifax on the *Adriatic* on the 1st of April, 1916, and carried out four months' training in England.

On the 2nd of June the 13th was in Corps reserve near Lijssenthoek, about two miles south of Poperinghe, when the Germans opened a heavy bombardment on the front held by the 3rd (Canadian) Division which lasted for some time and culminated in a determined attack. At 7.30 p.m. that night the 13th was ordered to " stand to " and moved forward to a position near Zillebeke Lake, where it remained under heavy artillery fire until relieved by the 22nd (Canadian) Battalion on the 7th and proceeded to Dickebusch in Corps reserve.

On the morning of June 2nd, the 42nd Battalion was in 7th (Canadian) Infantry Brigade in the Hooge sector, disposed as follows: Headquarters and A and C companies in Zillebeke dug-outs, D company in Belgian Château, B company in Ypres ramparts. Shortly after 1 p.m. the Germans attacked

* From *The Royal Highlanders of Canada.*

the trenches held by the 7th and 8th Canadian Brigades, in consequence of which the Battalion carried out the following move:

A company was sent to reinforce the 5th (Canadian) Mounted Rifles, and with them was shelled out of Maple Copse, C went to man Zillebeke switch line, while B and later D moved up in close support of Princess Patricia's Light Infantry. Heavy enemy shelling continued throughout the night of the 2nd and the whole of the 3rd, and at 8 p.m. the 42nd received orders to relieve the front line troops, Princess Patricia's Light Infantry and the 49th (Canadian) Battalion who were then, together with B company of the 42nd and the 60th (Canadian) Battalion, busily engaged in repelling an enemy attack. This relief was carried out during the 4th, and the Battalion held the line until the evening of the 5th, when it was relieved by the 31st (Canadian) Battalion and moved into Divisional reserve at Renenghelst. On the 7th it went with the remainder of the 7th Brigade into Corps reserve and took no part in the second phase of the Battle of Mount Sorrel.

To return to the 13th Battalion. On June 12th it moved into assembly positions for an attack in front of Maple Copse. At 1.30 a.m. on the 13th, the Battalion advanced. The objective was the enemy position to the north of Hill 62, the attack being divided into four phases. The first objective was the enemy front line from Observatory Ridge to Vigo Street, the second was the enemy support line, the third the reserve line and the fourth a trench further back which had, at one time, been the British front line and was known as Vancouver Trench. The attack began and, although the weather and condition of the ground were bad, the Battalion waves had no difficulty in gaining the first three objectives. By this time, however, the enemy had brought up reserve troops and the fighting became severe. Undeterred by German resistance, the 13th pushed on and gradually forced its way to the final objective, Vancouver Trench, where the work of consolidating the position was at once commenced.

The following account of what took place is taken from *The Royal Highlanders of Canada.*

"The 13th Battalion carried out its allotted share in this
" attack. Zero hour was set for 1.30 a.m. June 13th. Through-
" out the night rain fell almost continuously, making the terrain
" difficult to cross, but notwithstanding the quagmire of mud
" and water-filled shell holes, upheaved defences and debris, the
" men went forward in the semi-darkness in an incredibly quick
" manner. During the assembly in the forward trenches, and

JULY–AUGUST, 1916

" pending the time to go ' over the top,' the Battalion was
" subjected to heavy shell fire and suffered a number of casual-
" ties; but there was no confusion or disorder. Patiently the
" attackers waited in the chilly cold until the moment our guns
" lifted, and in four lines they swept impetuously forward to
" their grim task, ejecting the enemy until their final objective—
" Vancouver Trench—was reached. All that morning and
" the following day the 13th Battalion held tenaciously to
" their trenches, which they consolidated under a gruelling
" bombardment, until relieved at dusk. It was through the
" medium of a carrier pigeon released by the late Lieutenant-
" Colonel Victor C. Buchanan, D.S.O., that the first message
" reached the anxious staff at Canadian Corps Headquarters.
" It gave the glad tidings of the rout of the enemy and the
" re-establishment of a part of our old front line trench system
" by the 13th Battalion. The Canadian supremacy, in the
" section they held in the salient, was never again seriously
" contested by the enemy."

After this fighting the 13th and the 42nd withdrew to Corps reserve and although they took part in trench warfare during July and August in the vicinity of Sanctuary Wood and Hill 60 were not again employed in any large operation until September.

During this time the 73rd (Canadian) Infantry Battalion completed its training and reached France on August 12th, 1916, forming part of the 12th Canadian Infantry Brigade, 4th Canadian Division. Like many other Canadian battalions, the 73rd had its first experience of trench warfare in the Ypres salient, where it was attached for training to the 58th Brigade, 19th Division. During this tour of instruction the Battalion was unfortunate, B and C companies coming under enemy artillery fire on the Ypres road and losing three officers and seven men killed, and 16 wounded.

CHAPTER II

AUGUST, 1916, TO APRIL, 1917

The Battle of the Somme

THE 13th Battalion with the 1st Canadian Division had left Belgium on the 11th of August, 1916, and arrived in the Somme area on September 1st. Three days later it supported an attack made by the 13th Australian Brigade on Mouquet Farm, the Battalion being at La Boiselle. At 9 a.m. on the 3rd, Nos. 1 and 2 companies moved to Pozières, where they took part in an attack made by the Australians and held a portion of the ground gained against heavy counter-attacks. Later in the day these two companies were joined by the rest of the Battalion and remained in the captured trenches that night and the following day.

Writing of this action, the Canadian historian states:

" Rain created most foul conditions and made progress well
" nigh impossible for our troops, in spite of courage and will
" power, reaching the height of human endurance. They
" advanced bombing and bayoneting down the German com-
" munication trench, and established blocks, dug in, and took
" over from the Australians that night. The next day and the
" following they bravely resisted furious counter-attacks en
" masse, flinging back the waves of Grey Coats with the greatest
" loss; and, though themselves suffering grievous casualties from
" the heavy shelling which the enemy concentrated on the
" captured position, they never budged an inch."

After several days march through Picardy, the 42nd arrived at the " Brick Fields," near Albert, the whole area being a vast concentration camp. Here the Battalion was under orders to stand in readiness to take part in the coming attack. The order for this came two days later with startling suddenness. Divine Service was being held about 9 a.m. on September 16th, 1916; in the middle of it orders arrived for the Battalion to proceed to assembly positions on Usna Hill, and half an hour later the 42nd was moving forward in battle order. Late that afternoon orders were received to attack, the objectives being a sunken road and Fabeck Graben Trench east of Pozières. By 5.50 p.m. the Battalion was in position with A company on the right, C on the left, B and D companies being held in support and in reserve. Zero was 6 p.m., and at that hour the 42nd, with the Princess Patricia's Canadian Light Infantry on its right, attacked the German position.

Though there had been no time for careful reconnaissance, and little for the issue of detailed operation orders, the attack

THE SOMME, SEPTEMBER, 1916

was carried out without a hitch. The official historian says, speaking of this action:

"The advance of the 7th (Canadian) Brigade into action on this occasion was accredited the finest performance of the Brigade that had taken place in the war up to that time."

The operation was completely successful, the final objective being captured with comparatively few losses. The position was at once consolidated and arrangements made for a further advance next day.

In the afternoon of the following day the officers commanding the front line companies were ordered to report to Captain E. C. Norsworthy, acting Second-in-Command, at a given point in the line. On arrival there they found him seated on the trench with a severe bullet wound in each leg. He had worked his way forward in this condition in order that he might make quite clear to the forward companies the orders for a further attack. Zero hour for the new advance was 5 p.m.; the objectives were the Zollern-Graben and the Redoubt of the same name, both heavily wired. Unfortunately the artillery preparation was insufficient and the barrage was incorrectly placed. As the leading companies left their trench, the enemy could be plainly seen standing breast high and almost shoulder to shoulder behind the parapet of the heavily fortified position. It was only then that the full danger of the situation was revealed. With adequate artillery preparation the attack might have been within the Battalion's power, but without that support success was almost impossible. There was, however, no alternative, and there can be no better example of the spirit of the Regiment than the manner in which all ranks of the 42nd went forward on that day, well knowing what they would undergo. Within a hundred yards of the " jumping off " trench, half the effective force had become casualties; little further progress could be made and, eventually, the survivors of the attacking companies—about a quarter of those who had started —returned to their original line. The losses of the 42nd in this action were 437 all ranks.

From information received later, it was found that at the actual hour of attack the Germans were massing in great forces in Zollern Trench preparatory to a counter-attack. It cannot, therefore, be said that the attack of the 7th Canadian Brigade was entirely useless, for it succeeded, at least, in disorganizing the German plans and stopped a determined enemy effort to recapture the positions which the Canadians had won the day before. Writing to the Commanding Officer, Colonel G. S. Cantlie, a few days later, General Macdonell, the Brigade Commander, said:

THE ROYAL HIGHLANDERS OF CANADA

"To-day I visited the Zollern Graben. I found some of the glorious dead of the 42nd Royal Highlanders of Canada quite near the trench, the nearest within thirty yards, head toward the enemy, ten or fifteen feet behind him a dead German, head toward his own trench.

"I proudly and reverently saluted the bodies of these heroes and I have given orders that they are to be buried by the Royal Canadian Regiment. Your splendid Battalion should know how near they were to the Zollern Graben. You may rightly be proud of such men. The old Highland saying— I will put it in English—'While the sun shines on the earth and the waves beat on the shore, victory now as ever follows in the wake of the kilt.' The 42nd R.H.C. are living up to it. I congratulate you and the Battalion."

The 42nd was relieved on the morning of September 17th and moved to Tara Hill, where, in the late evening of the same day, the Battalion met for a brief service.

"The old hymns 'Nearer my God to Thee' and 'Lead Kindly Light' had, that night, a new and deeper meaning for us all. There was hardly a man who had not lost a comrade or friend, and there, in the deepening twilight, while the guns roared and flashed in the valley beneath, we commended those who had gone to the keeping of God and covenanted to keep the faith."

Returning to the 13th Battalion. It was in support during the successful attack on Thiepval Ridge on September 26th. Here it had the misfortune to lose its Commanding Officer, Lieutenant-Colonel Victor C. Buchanan, D.S.O.

"While all ranks share in the sorrow and regret caused by the death of a beloved commanding officer, the sense of personal loss was accentuated in the case of those veterans, few in number by this time, who had sailed from Canada with the First Canadian Contingent almost exactly two years before. To them Colonel Buchanan had been more than a good commanding officer. They had served under him in times of peril and trusted and looked up to him in a manner that bore testimony, more eloquent than words, to the very definite affection that existed between them."

Colonel Victor Buchanan was succeeded by Major G. E. McCuaig.

After spending ten days in billets at Albert, the 13th returned to the front line north-east of Courcelette on the 7th before making an attack on Regina Trench the following day.

At 8.50 a.m. on the 8th of October, the Battalion moved forward to the attack in four lines; the first wave was formed

SEPTEMBER, 1916–MARCH, 1917

by No. 1 company; the second wave by No. 4; the third wave by No. 2, and the fourth wave by No. 3 company.

No Man's Land was crossed without incident, but, unfortunately, on reaching Regina Trench the assaulting troops encountered a mass of uncut wire which effectively stopped their advance. Terrific machine gun and rifle fire was brought to bear on the Highlanders who were struggling to get through this obstacle, with the result that nearly the whole of the attacking force was annihilated. On the right flank of the attack a party under Lieutenant Sykes managed to force its way into the trench, but owing to the failure of the main attack on the right, it was forced to withdraw.

" Of the 360 men making the Battalion attack, only a few
" succeeded in entering Regina Trench, whilst about 30 wounded
" made their way back. Of 17 officers, 10 were missing, three
" wounded (one died) and four returned."

The survivors of the Battalion held the "jumping off" trench during the whole of the 9th under heavy shell fire, and were relieved that night by the 2nd (Canadian) Infantry Brigade, after which they returned to billets at Albert—"So reduced
" was the unit that practically the whole Battalion rode back
" from Pozières on the limbers which the transport officer had
" sent forward."

Both the 13th and 42nd Battalions spent the remainder of 1916, and the first three months of 1917, in ordinary trench warfare and were not employed in any operation on a large scale. The 73rd, although it took part in no actual attack during that winter, carried out a great deal of work in providing carrying and other parties for battalions actively engaged, and during the fighting for, and capture of, Beaumont Hamel, from the 13th to the 18th of November it lost six officers wounded, 11 other ranks killed and 44 wounded. On the 29th it moved with its Brigade to the Somme, arriving there on December 4th.

A minor enterprise that brought much credit to the 42nd took place early in the morning of March 23rd, when the enemy exploded a series of mines on the Battalion front in La Folie sector. Owing to the action of the Highlanders, who rushed out and immediately occupied the highest point of the crater lips, the efforts of the enemy were useless.

The Brigadier, in commending the action of the 42nd, said:

" The courage and devotion to duty of all ranks of this fine
" Battalion has never been displayed to better advantage than
" in coping with the emergency created by the unexpected
" blowing of Longfellow Crater."

CHAPTER III

APRIL, 1917, TO NEW YEAR, 1918

Vimy Ridge—Passchendaele—Disbandment of 73rd Battalion— Gallant action at " Graf House "

IN April, 1917, all three Battalions were engaged in the operations on Vimy Ridge when, on the morning of the 9th of April, that magnificent assault was launched which brought victory to the Canadian Corps and made the capture of the ridge possible.

During this fighting the 13th provided many carrying and working parties. The 42nd, with Princess Patricia's Canadian Light Infantry on its right and the 102nd Canadian Battalion on its left, attacked the enemy positions on the ridge west of Bois de la Folie at 4 a.m. on the 9th. A and C companies led the assault, and gained their first objective without difficulty, taking many prisoners during the attack. B and D then passed through them and captured the final objective, namely, the crest of the ridge. The attack was successful in every way, and the result was due not only to the determination of all ranks, but also to the excellent barrage put down by the Canadian gunners. On reaching the final objective, the 42nd—the left battalion of the 3rd Canadian Division—found that the 4th Canadian Division, on its left, had been unable to reach its objective, a mound on the top of the ridge known as " Hill 145," with the result that the left flank of the 42nd Battalion was seriously exposed and suffered severely from enfilade machine gun fire and sniping from this mound. A defensive flank was immediately formed and the position was successfully held until the following afternoon, when the 4th Division, with fresh troops, was able to occupy " Hill 145."

The 73rd also took part in this fighting. Coming out of the line on March 30th, it spent a few days training at Château de la Haie. Early in the morning of April 4th, the Battalion commenced the relief of the 72nd Canadian Battalion in the front line. The relief was a long one and was not completed until 5.30 p.m., during which time the sector was heavily bombarded, the Battalion losing four other ranks killed and 10 wounded.

Early in the morning of the 9th the 73rd moved forward to its assembly position. At Zero hour, 5.30 a.m., mines were blown in " Gunner " and " Kennedy " Craters and the attack went forward, C company leading the Battalion. The advance was carried out in excellent order and with drill-like precision. Little opposition was met with, the enemy fleeing in disorder when they realized what was coming. The most serious resistance developed in the rear of " Kennedy " Crater, where the enemy attempted a counter-attack with bombs; this, however, was easily repulsed and the 73rd had no difficulty in gaining its objective. By 6 a.m. consolidation was well under way and the Battalion extended its line to the right, taking over the ground between "Gluck" and "Gunner" Craters from the 72nd Canadian Battalion.

On the 10th the 73rd pushed out posts in front and occupied "Clutch" Trench as a front line that night, the former German front line being turned into a support line. The next two days were spent consolidating and, on the evening of the 12th and early morning of the 13th, the Battalion pushed out patrols into Givenchy and established a post at the railway station. By 2 p.m. on the 13th another patrol was pushed further into Givenchy and B company advanced and occupied the Vimy–Ancres line from which the enemy had retired. The Battalion was then relieved and that evening marched back to Niagara Camp after a most successful operation. Between the 4th and 13th of April, the 73rd lost five officers wounded, 25 other ranks killed, 110 wounded and five missing.

This proved the last battle experience of the 73rd as a Battalion, for, on April 16th, 1917, orders were received that it was to be broken up, officers and men being sent to other battalions. All men from Nova Scotia were transferred to the 85th Canadian Battalion, some of the remainder to the 38th and 78th Canadian Battalions, and the rest were divided between the 13th and 42nd Battalions The Royal Highlanders of Canada, the 16th Canadian Machine Gun Company and other units. Neither the 13th nor the 42nd took an active part in any fighting on a large scale for some months after the capture of Vimy Ridge, but on June 8th the latter joined in a successful raid organized by its Brigade, in which 46 prisoners and three machine guns were captured; in addition, a large number of Germans were killed in hand-to-hand fighting.

The first of the two Battalions to be engaged was the 13th, on August 15th, when in conjunction with the 16th Canadian Infantry Battalion on the right and the 15th on the left, it attacked the enemy positions north-east of Loos, the object being to capture Hill 70. The attack of the 13th was carried out on a two-company front, B and D companies leading, A company in support, while C company was detailed to "mop up." Concerning this engagement, the 13th Battalion Diary limits itself to the following sentence:

"4.25 a.m. the Battalion attacked and gained its objective." That is all said about this highly successful action, but how well the Battalion fought is best expressed in the words of the 1st (Canadian) Division Commander. Addressing the 13th a few days after the battle he said: " Not only did you occupy the " German trenches, but you held on to them and successfully " repulsed all counter-attacks."

The following day was spent in consolidating the position, and early in the morning of August 17th the 13th was relieved by the 2nd and 3rd Canadian Battalions, after which it moved back to billets in Les Brebis, having lost nearly forty per cent of its fighting strength during the battle.

Both the 13th and 42nd were employed during the next two months in road making and supplying working and carrying parties during the fighting round Passchendaele, the 13th being attached to the 3rd Canadian Division and the 42nd being in Division reserve at Pommern Castle during the main attack.

During the night of November 2nd the 42nd made an attempt to advance its line along the Gravenstafel road, west of Passchendaele village. The force employed consisted of seven officers and 200 other ranks and was divided into several parties. Unfortunately the operation was not a success, but one incident must be mentioned. One of the parties consisting of 24 men under Lieutenant M. T. Cohen, M.C., successfully stormed and captured a German strong point, " Graf House." With equal bravery and determination, and against most heavy odds, this gallant band repelled for a long time every effort of the enemy to recapture the Post. Even after Cohen had been shot down, the five men who still remained unwounded fought on with unflinching courage. Only when ammunition and bombs were exhausted did Lance-Corporal Taylor, the one surviving non-commissioned officer, undaunted though not unwounded, withdraw the survivors of the twenty-four men who earlier in the day had stormed the " Graf House." This stubborn fight will ever be remembered in the history of the Regiment and was praised in the highest terms by the Division Commander. The remaining months of 1917 were spent by the two Battalions in ordinary trench warfare with the usual Brigade and Division rests.

In the material at the editor's disposal there are few official records regarding the movements of either the 13th or 42nd Battalions for the next few months. Two books, however, contain an interesting account of what occurred. Dealing with this period the history of *The Royal Highlanders of Canada* states:

" Numerous raids took place during the winter and spring " of 1918, with the object of capturing prisoners or posts. The " front was a very difficult one, consisting of a line of outposts, " scattered through the ruins of the city of Lens, and involving " patrol fighting of the most daring character. In all of the

MARCH, 1918

"operations the Battalion displayed brilliant initiative and
"resourcefulness. On May 1st the 42nd was relieved on this
"frontage, and concluded its longest tour, having spent fifty-
"seven days in the line."

In *Odds and Ends from a Regimental Diary*, by a Padre of the 42nd Battalion, the following account of a tour in the line is of interest:

"On March 1st, 1918, the Battalion marched from Villers
"au Bois to Neuville-St. Vaast preparatory to taking over the
"Avion sector of the line. Two platoons of B company were
"stationed in dug-outs near the barrier on the Arras–Lens road,
"and the other two were in the cellars of Vimy Ridge.

"On March 6th–7th, the 42nd took over the left sub-sector
"of the line from the 116th Battalion. Thus began the longest
"tour of the Battalion in the line. From March 6th until
"May 1st we were never withdrawn from the forward areas.
"These fifty-five days were marked with increasing vigilance.
"The last great attack of the German Army began on the front
"of the Fifth Army to the south. Every available unit was
"withdrawn from the north to stem the tide of German
"advance. From Arras to the sea our line grew thinner as the
"situation became more critical. The Canadian Corps was
"strung out over an immense front, but the morale and determi-
"nation of the men were never finer. We knew that a reserve
"line of trenches was being dug on Vimy Ridge and in the back
"areas, we had our instructions as to a possible withdrawal, but
"never for a moment did the men seriously contemplate
"leaving so hardly won a position. During this period the
"Battalion was, if possible, more on the offensive than ever.
"Repeated raids were made. It was at this time gallant Lieu-
"tenant Hugh Hoyles made his lone patrol across the waters
"of the embankment, swimming to the culvert, locating a post
"and returning unseen. Lieutenant Trout was on the warpath
"and raided a post at Tallow Trench. Lieutenant MacLachlan
"raided the embankment and though unsuccessful in his objective
"through the unexpected alertness of the enemy, effected his
"withdrawal without casualties. Lieutenant Cowing fought a
"desperate fight on the embankment at Lens with a strong
"German patrol, routed them and was brought in badly
"wounded by Private Mavor. And so the story runs, a record
"of unceasing activity, of courage and endurance.

"On April 4th, Lieutenant A. Scott, of D, was the leader
"of an expedition which was quite unique and afforded great
"delight to the troops. Lieutenant Hoyles having demon-

"strated that it was possible to cross the water front and reach
"the enemy's outpost line, it was resolved to make an attempt
"to secure a prisoner. Accordingly at 10.30 p.m. a select band
"of mariners entered the water towards the right of D company's
"frontage. They had with them rafts on which were placed
"bombs, ammunition, and not least in importance a bottle of
"rum to warm the chilled adventurers on landing. Major
"Grafftey stood on the shore and paid out after the expedition
"a long line, which was to be used as a tow rope to haul back
"the expected prisoner. Supporting him was the company
"Tug-of-War Team, very eager to demonstrate with what
"speed a foreign body could be propelled through the water
"and wire. All went well until one of the party was seized with
"the cramp. At this juncture, according to witnesses, sounds of
"distress came from the further side of the water. It appears
"that the victim was only rescued from drowning by the swift
"action of Private Dinesen (who afterwards at Parvillers won
"the V.C.). The party accordingly was forced to retire, without
"making a landing, which they did successfully. The most
"serious casualty of the night was the bottle of rum, which, in
"the excitement of saving life, was knocked off the raft to sink
"beyond recovery.

"On the night of May 1st the Battalion was relieved and
"went back to the Caucourt area to rest and the long tour came
"to an end. It was a period which proved the spirit of the
"Battalion in the most exacting way and the test was splendidly
"met. In the History of the Regiment it will not be forgotten
"how from March 6th to May 1st we were of the number of
"those who kept the Ridge."

Both Battalions were employed in the Ypres salient during the Second Battle of Passchendaele, although not actually engaged in the attack. The 1st Battalion The Black Watch, with the 1st Division, was also in this area during the autumn of 1917; several meetings among the officers took place, and in November the Battalions of the Canadian Black Watch received the right to wear the Red Hackle.

CHAPTER IV

JANUARY, 1918, TO MARCH, 1919

Preparations for German attack—Second Battle of Arras—Three Victoria Crosses awarded—Armistice—Demobilization

THE winter of 1917–18 passed quietly and the first part of the New Year was spent in preparing for the German attack which threatened every part of the Allied line, although it was not known where the actual attack would be launched. Every effort was made to strengthen the line, and in this both the 13th and 42nd were employed for some time before it took place. When the enemy attack was made on March 21st, both Battalions were in the Arras area, the Canadian Corps then holding the line north of the Scarpe.

Neither Battalion was engaged in any large operation until August, when both took part in the Battle of Arras, between the 8th and 11th of that month. The 13th, with a battalion on either flank, led the attack of the 3rd Canadian Brigade on Hangard Wood and Croates Trench, B company on the right and C on the left, with A and D companies in support. At Zero hour, 4.20 a.m., the Brigade advanced, the Battalion reaching Croates Trench, a thousand yards east of Hangard Wood West, with little opposition. The Germans, however, then fought more stubbornly and the final objective was not gained till 8 a.m. The operation was successful in every way: many prisoners were captured in addition to 19 field guns and howitzers, eight trench mortars and 31 machine guns, and the Brigade had forced its way five thousand yards into the enemy position. It was during this fighting that No. 445312 Private J. B. Croak won the V.C. (*London Gazette*, 27.9.18). The following is an account of the action for which the Cross was awarded:

" For most conspicuous bravery in attack when having
" become separated from his section he encountered a machine
" gun nest, which he bombed and silenced, taking the gun and
" crew prisoners. Shortly afterwards he was severely wounded,
" but refused to desist.

" Having rejoined his platoon, a very strong point containing
" several machine guns was encountered. Private Croak, how-
" ever, seeing an opportunity dashed forward alone and was
" almost immediately followed by the remainder of the platoon
" in a brilliant charge. He was the first to arrive at the trench
" line, into which he led his men, capturing three machine guns
" and bayoneting or capturing the entire garrison.

" The perseverance and valour of this gallant soldier, who

"was again severely wounded, and died of his wounds, were an
"inspiring example to all."

The next week the Battalion remained in reserve and, on August 17th, A and D companies advanced through La Chavatte and established a line on the eastern outskirts of the village.

The 42nd Battalion attacked Hill 102 and the enemy positions to the east of it on August 8th with the 7th Canadian Brigade. This successful attack ended with a fine bayonet charge against gun positions, from which the enemy fired on the advancing troops at point blank range. The day was marred, however, by the death of Lieutenant-Colonel Bartlett McLennan, D.S.O., who was killed by shell fire a few days before the attack. Colonel McLennan was one of the original officers of the 42nd, having gone to France with it as Second-in-Command. He was beloved by all, and his courage and devotion to duty during the entire campaign was an inspiration to all with whom he came in contact. During this fighting the right and centre companies, A and B, charged two hundred yards across the open against a battery of howitzers which continued firing until the moment of their capture. Two hundred prisoners, ten guns and many machine guns were taken.

After spending the next few days in reserve, the Battalion was employed near Damery, where, on August 12th, it attacked and captured the German trenches north of Parvillers, taking 60 prisoners and 20 machine guns but losing seven officers and 134 other ranks. It was in this fighting that No. 2075467, Private T. Dinesen won the Victoria Cross (*London Gazette*, 26.10.18). The following is the official account of his action:

"For most conspicuous and continuous bravery displayed
"during ten hours of hand-to-hand fighting, which resulted
"in the capture of over a mile of strongly garrisoned and
"stubbornly defended enemy trenches.
"Five times in succession he rushed forward alone, and
"single handed put hostile machine guns out of action, account-
"ing for twelve of the enemy with bomb and bayonet. His
"sustained valour and resourcefulness inspired his comrades at
"a very critical stage of the action, and were an example to all."

Both Battalions were engaged in the Arras area towards the end of the month, the 42nd taking part in the capture of Monchy le-Preux on the 26th. The objective was a line along Factory Trench and included a maze of other trenches south-east of Monchy. The Battalion attacked at 4.30 p.m., with A and B companies leading, and C and D in close support. The attack resulted in the capture of stubbornly defended enemy trenches

SEPTEMBER, 1918

to the depth of a thousand yards on a front of nearly a mile. A few prisoners and many machine guns were taken with comparatively slight loss—three officers and 42 other ranks.

The following day the 9th Canadian Brigade passed through the line held by the 42nd Battalion and advanced still further, and on the 29th the 42nd was relieved and moved back to Arras, and three days later to Hermaville.

The 13th took part in the attack on the Drocourt-Quéant switch line on September 2nd and 3rd. The attack was carried out on a two-brigade front. The 3rd Canadian Brigade attacked with the 16th (Canadian) Battalion on the right and the 13th on the left. The plan of attack was as follows: The leading battalions of the 3rd Brigade were to capture the Drocourt-Quéant line and consolidate it. The support battalions were then to pass through the Cagnicourt and Buissy switch line, while the 13th followed in support from the Drocourt-Quéant line. A and D companies led the assault of the 13th, with B and C in support. At 5 a.m. on the 2nd the attack commenced and the Battalion gained its objective with but little opposition, and established the new line in front and north-west of Cagnicourt. The 14th Battalion then passed through towards the final objective and, meeting with severe resistance from the German reserves, the 13th moved forward and took part in the further advance between the Bois de Louisin and Bois de Bouche. After this had been achieved the 13th moved back to the Drocourt-Quéant line in support and there assisted in the work of consolidation. The losses of the Battalion in this fighting were heavy, amounting in all to about 230, of which one officer and 32 other ranks were killed. But the success was far-reaching. The strong Drocourt-Quéant line had been definitely broken, thus making an attack on the Canal du Nord comparatively easy. In this manner the Canadian Corps, assisted by the 4th British Division, was the first of the Allied armies to breach the supposedly impregnable Hindenburg system of defences which, once broken, rapidly crumbled before the hammer strokes subsequently launched against it.

Both the 13th and 42nd were engaged in the fighting on the Canal du Nord between September 27th and October 1st. The former attacked the canal line from the south-west of Paviland Wood on the 27th. The 13th crossed the canal in rear of the 14th, and then passing through the 14th, gained its objective east of Sainsles Marquion though meeting with strong opposition.

During this fighting No. 445120 Corporal H. J. Good won the Victoria Cross (*London Gazette*, 27.9.18). The following is an official account of his action:

THE ROYAL HIGHLANDERS OF CANADA

"For most conspicuous bravery and leading when in attack his company was held up by heavy fire from three machine guns, which were seriously delaying the advance. Realizing the gravity of the situation, this N.C.O. dashed forward alone, killing several of the garrison and capturing the remainder.

"Later on, Corporal Good, while alone, encountered a battery of 5.9 in. guns, which was in action at the time. Collecting three men of his section, he charged the battery under point blank fire and captured the entire crews of three guns."

September the 28th and 29th were spent by the Battalion in Divisional support, and on the 31st the 13th moved into assembly positions for an attack south-west of Sancourt, with the object of capturing the villages of Sancourt and Blécourt. The attack of the 13th was a complete success, but the 14th and 16th battalions when continuing the advance met with such strong resistance that the line was withdrawn to a sunken road near Blécourt church, and here the Battalion was relieved on the 2nd of October.

From this date until the day of the Armistice the 13th pursued the retreating enemy. The Canadians were not engaged in any general action during the German retirement but took part in minor operations which harassed the retreating enemy, and on Armistice Day, November 11th, 1918, patrols of the 13th entered Mons.

This ends the story of the 13th in France. After the Armistice and for the first three months of the following year the Battalion was stationed in various parts of Belgium. On March 16th, 1919, it left France and arrived at Halifax, Nova Scotia, on April 18th and was demobilized at Montreal two days later. It is of interest to note that, when originally formed, the 13th was composed of drafts from the following Regiments:

	Officers.	Other ranks.
5th Regiment (Royal Highlanders of Canada)	30	966
78th Pictou Regiment (Highlanders)	10	117
93rd Cumberland Regiment	7	126
Totals	47	1209

To return to the 42nd. The Battalion was engaged in the operations which resulted in the crossing of the Canal du Nord and took part in the capture of Bourlon Wood on September 28th, 1918.

The task of the 42nd on the 29th was to capture the railway embankment north-west of Tilloy, advance and capture the high

ADVANCE TO VICTORY, OCTOBER–NOVEMBER, 1918

ground about 1500 yards due north of the village and then to swing south-east and seize the bridge head on the St. Quentin canal near Ramillies and Point d'Aire, in conjunction with the 49th Battalion on the right and one from the 4th Canadian Division on the left.

By 3 a.m. on the 29th the 42nd had reached its assembly positions in the low ground in rear of the Haynecourt–Cambrai road. The attack was launched at 8 a.m. and good progress was made until the leading troops reached a strong line of uncut wire in front of the Douai–Cambrai road from which accurate machine gun fire caused many casualties and checked the advance. In spite of this, however, the Battalion succeeded in crossing the road and established posts on the other side. In this position, owing to the heavy machine gun fire, the advance was definitely held up and the line consolidated west of the railway and about 1500 yards north-west of Cambrai.

The advance was continued at 6 a.m. on the following morning by the Princess Patricia's Canadian Light Infantry and Royal Canadian Regiment, but heavy resistance was met with and the attacking troops were compelled to dig in near the Tilloy–Blécourt road. That day the 42nd was in support, being posted along the railway embankment and in the sunken road north of Tilloy about 2500 yards west of Ramillies.

On October 1st the 9th Canadian Brigade and 4th Canadian Division continued the advance in conjunction with the 1st Canadian Division further north. The 42nd remained in support but a number of officers of the Battalion were sent up to help detachments of assaulting units on the left front, where a heavy German counter-attack was forcing them to withdraw across the front occupied by the 42nd; a platoon of the Battalion was also sent to help detachments of the 3rd and 11th Brigades and the Royal Canadian Regiment to garrison a captured position. At eight o'clock that night the Battalion was withdrawn and marched back to Quarry Wood. During this fighting the 42nd lost heavily, the casualties being 17 officers and 276 other ranks.

During the passage of the Grand Honelle between the 5th and 7th of November, the Battalion was not heavily engaged and lost four men only. On November 10th the 42nd relieved the Princess Patricia's Canadian Light Infantry and part of the line held by the Royal Canadian Regiment in the front line extending from the Condé–Mons canal to the Hyon–Quesmes road. On completion of this relief the Battalion pressed the attack on Mons from the western and eastern outskirts of the city and eventually occupied the railway station at 1 a.m. on the 11th. By daybreak Mons had been cleared of the enemy and posts established on its eastern outskirts.

THE ROYAL HIGHLANDERS OF CANADA

The first officers to enter the Hôtel de Ville were Lieutenants L. H. Biggar, M.C. and J. W. Cave, M.C.; the " Golden Book " was then taken from the vaults, where it had lain for over four years, and these two officers had the honour of being the first representatives of the British Army to sign it, the last entry being that of King Albert, who had signed the book in 1913 on his first visit to Mons as King of the Belgians. The keys of the City were subsequently presented by the Mayor to the General Commanding the 7th Canadian Infantry Brigade in honour of the capture of Mons by that Brigade; one company of the 42nd, together with representative detachments of other battalions of the 7th Brigade, took part in a march past, led by the 42nd Pipe Band. When King Albert visited Mons on November 27th, a Guard of Honour was formed by the 3rd Canadian Division, one battalion in each Brigade providing a hundred men; the 42nd represented the 7th Canadian Infantry Brigade.

The 42nd left France on February 7th, 1919, arrived in Canada on March 9th, and was demobilized at Montreal two days later.

Short as is this account of the actions of these three famous battalions, the 13th, 42nd and 73rd, it shows something of the bravery and endurance of the men, the power of leadership displayed by the officers and the gallant spirit—true to the finest traditions of the old " Forty-Twa "—that animated and inspired The Royal Highlanders of Canada throughout the Great War.

NOTE.—Since sending the above account to the Publishers I have been presented with a copy of the recently published *History of the 13th Battalion Royal Highlanders of Canada, 1914–1919."* This gives a most vivid account of the 13th Battalion, which will be of the greatest interest to all members of The Black Watch, and I am informed that a History of the 42nd Battalion will also shortly be published in Canada. —*Editor.*

APPENDIX I

SUMMARY OF KILLED. THE ROYAL HIGHLANDERS OF CANADA

Year.	13th Battn.		42nd Battn.		73rd Battn.	
	Officers	Other ranks	Officers	Other ranks	Officers	Other ranks
1915	6	242	1	5	–	–
1916	27	512	6	313	7	73
1917	5	212	13	258	9	168
1918–19	14	258	11	204	–	2
Grand total :	52	1224	31	780	16	243

APPENDIX II

HONOURS AND AWARDS

The Royal Highlanders of Canada

	13th Batt.	42nd Batt.	73rd Batt.
V.C.	5*	1	—
K.C.B.	1	—	—
C.M.G.	3	1	—
Bar to D.S.O.	4	1	—
D.S.O.	14	9	3
C.B.E.	1	1	—
O.B.E.	2	3	1
M.B.E.	1	—	—
Bar to M.C.	4	9	1
M.C.	39	37	11
Bar to D.C.M.	3	1	—
D.C.M.	44	24	5
2nd Bar to M.M.	—	1	—
Bar to M.M.	11	14	10
M.M.	184	169	33
M.S.M.	11	14	2
Brought to notice of Secretary of State for War	7	8	1
Mentioned in Despatches	64	45	12
Legion d'Honneur	1	1	—
Croix de Guerre (French)	4	5	—
Medaille Militaire (French)	1	1	—
Medaille de la Reconnaissance Francaise	—	1	—
Medaille d'Honneur	—	1	—
Order of Leopold (Belgian)	1	—	—
Croix de Guerre (Belgian)	3	2	—
Order of St. Ann (2nd Class with swords, Russian)	—	1	—
Cross of St. George (Russian)	4	3	4
Italian bronze medal for Military Valour	1	—	1
Order of the Rising Sun (Japan)	1	—	—
Czecho-Slovak War Cross	1	—	—

* Of the five Victoria Crosses won by the 13th Battalion, one was awarded to Lieut. Colonel W. H. Clark-Kennedy when serving with 24th Battalion V.R.C., and one to Lieutenant Milton F. Gregg when serving with R.A.F.

APPENDIX III

List of Actions and Operations

The Thirteenth (Canadian) Battalion

YPRES.
1915. THE GAS ATTACK. 22nd–23rd April.
    ST. JULIEN. 24th–30th April.
    Festubert. 19th–22nd May.

1916. MOUNT SORREL. 2nd–7th June. 11th–13th June.
SOMME.
    POZIÈRES RIDGE. 2nd–3rd September.
    Thiepval Ridge. 26th–27th September.
    REGINA TRENCH (ANCRE HEIGHTS). 8th–9th October.

1917.   Vimy Ridge. 9th–14th April.
    Arleux. 28th–29th April.
    Third Scarpe. 3rd–4th May.
    HILL 70. 15th–17th August.
    Second Passchendaele. 26th–28th October. 31st–10th November.

1918. AMIENS. 8th–11th August.
    DAMERY. 15th–17th August.
    Scarpe. 27th–30th August.
    DROCOURT-QUEANT LINE. 2nd–3rd September.
    CANAL DU NORD. 27th September–1st October.

The Forty-second (Canadian) Battalion

1916. MOUNT SORREL. 2nd–5th June.
SOMME.
    FLERS-COURCELETTE. 15th–18th September.
    Ancre Heights. 2nd–9th October.

1917. VIMY RIDGE. 9th–11th April.
    Arleux. 28th–29th April.
    SECOND PASSCHENDAELE. 26th October–5th November.

1918. AMIENS. 8th–11th August.
    DAMERY. 15th August.
    MONCHY-LE-PREUX. 26th–29th August.
    CANAL DU NORD. 27th October–1st November.
    Grand Honnelle. 6th–7th November.
    MONS. 11th November.

THE ROYAL HIGHLANDERS OF CANADA

The Seventy-third (Canadian) Battalion

SOMME.
1916.   Ancre Heights. 13th October–3rd November. 10th–11th November.

Ancre. 13th–15th November. 18th November.

1917.   VIMY RIDGE. 9th–13th April. (This Battalion was disbanded on 19th April, 1917.)

NOTE.—Battles in which the Battalions actually fought are shewn in capitals.

A SHORT NOTE ON THE SYDNEY SCOTTISH RIFLES

FOR MANY YEARS AFFILIATED TO THE BLACK WATCH

VOLUNTEER Corps were formed in Australia at the time of the Crimean War, but the Volunteer system did not prove successful in later years. The threat, however, of a Russian war in 1885 caused the formation of a number of Volunteer units, of which the Sydney Scottish Rifles was perhaps the best known. The Black Watch was accepted as its guide as regards uniform and equipment, and when it came about, the affiliation of the two corps was as popular in Sydney as it was throughout the Regiment.

Eighty-five officers and men of the Scottish Rifles took part in the South African War, among them being Lieutenant G. J. Grieve, who was attached to the 2nd Battalion The Black Watch, and killed at Paardeberg when helping a comrade in that battle.

In 1912 compulsory military training was adopted in Australia, and the Scottish Rifles was disbanded, though the majority of both officers and men joined other units. In the Great War many of these served overseas, and the following list of officers (prepared for this History by Colonel G. R. Campbell) give the names of those formerly of the Scottish Rifles, who fought with the Australian Imperial Force or the British Expeditionary Force:

Colonel (Hon. Brigadier-General) Gerald R. Campbell (Retired List)	Sea Transport Staff, A.I.F.
Colonel H. N. Machaurin	Commanding 1st Infantry Brigade, A.I.F. (killed 1915).
Brigadier-General A. Jobson, D.S.O.	Commanding 7th Infantry Brigade, A.I.F.
Colonel W. O. Watt, D.S.O.	Australian Flying Corps, A.I.F. (dead).
Colonel W. W. R. Watson, C.M.G., D.S.O.	
Lieutenant-Colonel W. K. S. Mackenzie, D.S.O.	Commanding 19th Infantry Battalion, A.I.F.
Lieutenant-Colonel D. A. Storey	A.I.F.
Lieutenant-Colonel E. C. Norrie	A.I.F.
Lieutenant-Colonel A. W. Ralston, C.M.G., D.S.O.	A.I.F.
Lieutenant-Colonel Humphrey Scott, D.S.O.	A.I.F. (killed).
Major Macnaghten, C.B., D.S.O.	A.I.F.
Major G. MacDonald	A.I.F.

THE SYDNEY SCOTTISH RIFLES

Captain J. L. Harcus	A.I.F. (killed).
Lieutenant I. Anderson	A.I.F. (killed).
Lieutenant Stewart Milson	A.I.F. (killed).
Lieutenant A. G. Ferguson	A.I.F. (killed).
Lieutenant C. T. Rennie	Leicester Regiment, B.E.F. (killed).
Captain Barrington Dickson	B.E.F. (killed).
Lieutenant A. W. Scott Skirving	A.I.F. (killed).
Lieutenant W. F. Crawford	Argyll and Sutherland Highlanders, B.E.F.
Lieutenant (now Lieutenant-Colonel) R. M. Sadler, D.S.O., M.C.	A.I.F.
Captain G. Sadler	A.I.F.
Captain Ross	A.I.F.
Captain W. MacDonald	A.I.F. (killed).
Major R. H. Jenkins	A.I.F. (killed).

Thus it may be seen that, although the Sydney Scottish Rifles did not take part in the war as a unit affiliated to The Black Watch, none the less many of its former members did gallant service and saw much hard fighting.

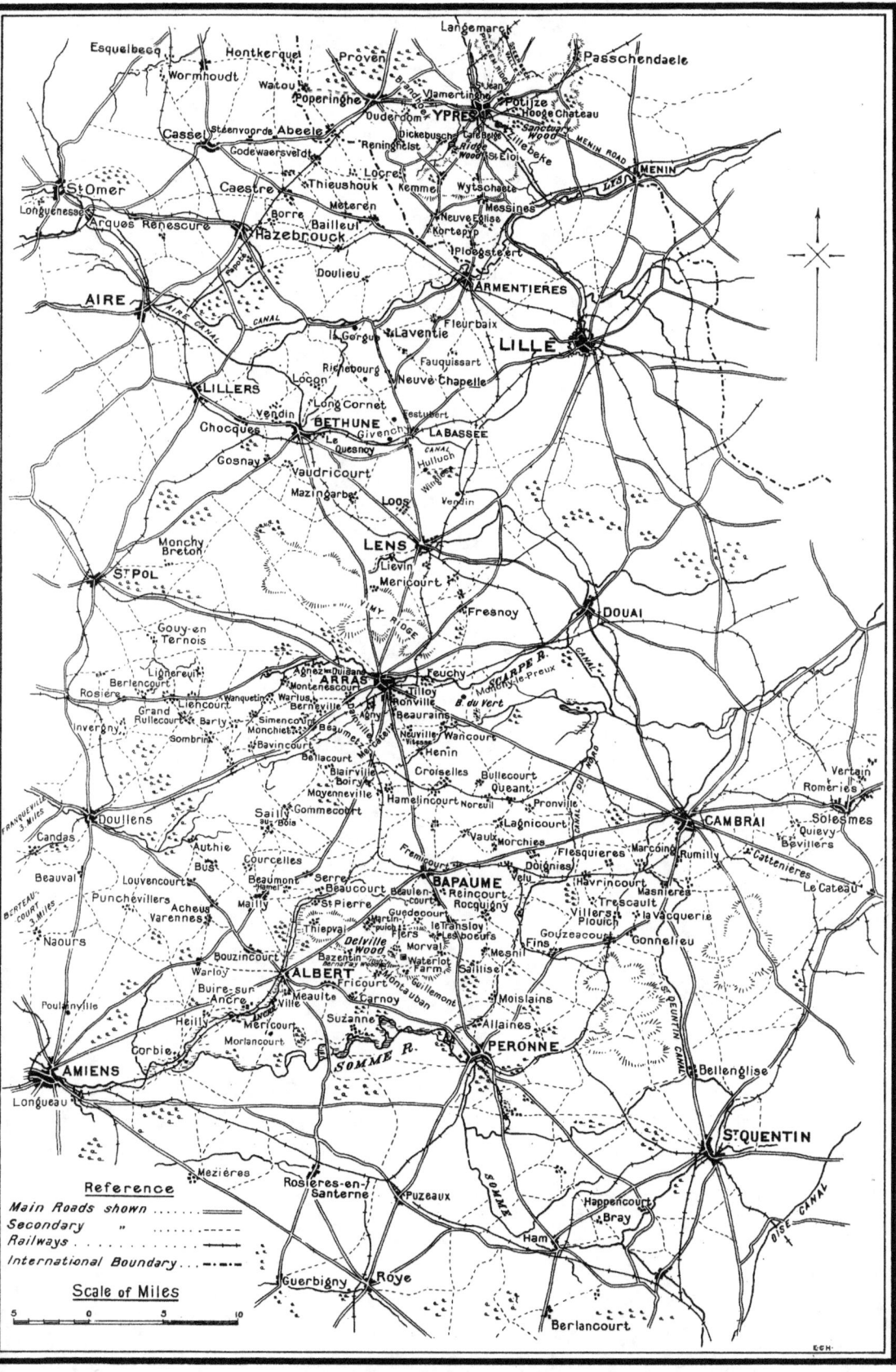

INDEX

The Roman numerals (IV), (V), (VI), (VII), after the entry, indicate the Battalion to which the entry refers

"Abri central," 281
Adam, L/Corpl., 69 (IV/V)
Adamson, Sergt., 311 (VII)
Adriatic, s.s., 351
Air, Captain C., 15, 19, 25 (IV)
Aitken, Captain G., 258 (VII)
Alaunia, s.s., 349
Albert, H.M. King, 368
Albert, 133, 356
Alexander, Captain W., 126, 128, Major, 133 (VI)
Alexandra, H.M. Queen, 343
Allan, Pte., 13 (IV)
Allen, Mrs., 243
Allen, Lieut.-Colonel H. M., 239, 242, 267, 279, 280 (VII)
Allen, 2nd Lieut., 285 (VII)
Allenby, General, 49
Allouagne, 23
Anderson, Lieut.-General C. A., 6, 10
Anderson, Capt. J. G. (R.A.M.C.), 179
Anderson, 2nd Lieut. J. L., 287 (VII)
Anderson, Lieut. T. H., 15
Anderson, Lieut. W. K., 193 (VI)
Andrews, Lieut. T. F., 25, 67, 69 (IV/V)
Angus, Pte., 13 (IV)
Anstruther, Lady, 243, 249
Anstruther, Colonel Sir R., 239, 345 (VII)
Antoing, 103
Argyll & Sutherland Highlanders, 6th Bn., 199, 7th Bn., 281, 296, 8th Bn., 145, 159, 168, 171
Armentières, 268
Arras, Battle of, 157 *sqq*., 279 *sqq*.
Athies, 312
Aubers Ridge, 11, 16
Aubertin, Captain T., 51, 68, 105 (IV/V)
Auchel, 70
Auchonvillers, 271

Authuile, 134
Aveluy, 155

Badenoch, Lieut., 98, 105 (IV/V)
Bailleul, 142, 269
Bailleul aux Cornailles, 286
Bain, Lieut. J. Mc P., 51, 68, 105 (IV/V)
Baird, Coy. Sergt.-Major, 51 (V)
Bajus, 280
Bancourt, 300
Bannatine-Allason, Major-General R., 128, 247, 256, 341
Baptie, Sergt. H., 273 (VII)
Barclay, Lieut., 251 (VII)
Barly, 301
Barr, Lieut., 150 (VI)
Battle Wood, 86
Bazentin-le-Grand, 139
Beatson, 2nd Lieut., 272, 285 (VII)
Beaumont Hamel, Battle of, 144 *sqq*., 271 *sqq*.
Beckwith, Brig.-General, 168, 184
Bécourt, 133
Bedford, 128, 129, 247
Bedfordshire Regt., 2nd Bn., 131, 257
Begg, Lieut., 147 (VI)
Begg, Lieut., 267 (VII)
Beel, 2nd Lieut., 83, 105 (IV/V)
Bellebuene, 89
Berdoulat, General, 98, 202
Berry, Lieut., 299 (VII)
Bethonsart, 70
Bethune-Duncan, Lieut., 67 (IV/V)
Beveridge, Captain D., 245, 257, 296 (VII)
Bewsher, Major F. W., 136, 160, 264
Biggar, Lieut. L. H., 367 (c)
Blackadder Trench, 12 (IV)
Black Watch, The
    1st Bn., 22, 249
    2nd Bn., 6, 7, 9, 10, 14, 16, 17, 21, 22, 23, 249
    4th Bn., 249
    5th Bn., 4, 14, 22, 24

375

INDEX

Black Watch, The (*contd.*)
  6th Bn. Pipers, 5
  8th Bn., 22, 104, 250, 283
  9th Bn., 22, 24, 97
Blair, Capt. (R.A.M.C.), 271, 283
Boase, Captain E. L., 5, 9, 13, 25 (IV)
Boesinghe, 78
Bois de Biez, 8 (IV)
Bois de Courton, 191, 194, 309
Bois de Pacaut, 130
Bois de Rheims, 190, 196
Bois d'Hartennes, 99
Bois Gerard, 98
Bombers, Battalion, 8, 17, 48, 148, 282
Booth, Lieut.-Colonel T. M., 144, 148, 150, 155, 156, 164–5–6, 168 (VI)
Boulogne, 129, 248
Bourgeon, 103
Bourlon Wood, 366
Bouvigny, 311
Bower, Lieut.-Colonel G., 344 (R)
Bowes-Lyon, Major G. F., 74, 75, 105 (IV/V)
Bowman, Sergt. T., 7 (IV), 11
Boyd, Lieut., 157 (VI)
Bradbridge, Major, 344 (R)
Brain-le-Comte, 104
Bray, 136, 262
Bresle, 132
Bresles, 254
Brigades
  Bareilly, 6, 10, 12, 13, 16
  Dehra Dun, 7, 12, 16, 18
  Garhwal, 13, 16
  Jullunder, 7
  Lancashire Territorial, 128, 130
  20th, 130
  60th, 16
  116th, 69, 70
  118th, 50, 68, 75
Bromielaw, Brig.-General, 68
Broughton Ferry, 3
Brown, Captain A., 173, 187 (VI)
Brown, Pte. W., 13 (IV)
Brown, Sergt. W. D., 13 (IV)
Bruce, Lieut. J. P., 15, 25 (IV)
Buchanan, Lieut.-Colonel Victor C., 353, 356 (c)

Buchanan, Pte., 259 (VII)
Buchanan, Lieut. F. H. H., 67, 105 (IV/V)
Buddon, 4
Bulloch, Lieut.-Colonel R. A., 97, 98, 105 (IV/V)
Burbure, 186, 301
Burgess, Coy, Sergt.-Major, 51 (IV/V)
Burnett, Sergt., 50 (V)
Burntisland, 240
Burton, Lieut. G. S. M., 343 (R), Captain, 345
Bus, 70
Busnes, 301, 305
Butler, Lieut.-General, 202
Butler, 2nd Lieut. C. H., 160 (VI)
Buzancy
  Attack on, 98
  Memorial, 100

Cable, Lieut. D., 158 179 (VI)
Cable, Lieut. J. B., 202, 308 (VII)
Cairns, Lieut., 147 (VI)
Cairns, Company Sergt.-Major, 140 (VI)
Cameron Highlanders, 24, 158
Campbell, Major-Gen. Carter, 178
Campbell, Brig.-General D., 128, 152, 161, 247, 286
Campbell, Lieut.-Colonel D. C., 126, 127 (VI)
Campbell, Captain E. V., 5, 15, 17, 25 (IV)
Campbell, Colonel G. R., 373
Campbell, Lieut.-Colonel N., 168, 171, 174, 176, 186, 187 (VI)
Campbell, Major W. P., 176–7, 179, 187, 300 (VI)
Cambrai, Battle of, 170 *et seq.*
Cambridgeshire Regt., 1/1st, 68, 75
Calonne, 6
Canadian Bns.
  13th, 359, 366
  16th M.G.C., 359
  38th, 359
  48th (Highlanders), 130
  72nd, 358
  73rd, 154

INDEX

Canadian Bns. (*contd.*)
  78th, 359
  85th, 359
  102nd, 358
  116th, 367
  Mounted Rifles, 351
  Royal Regt., 351–2, 356, 367
Canal du Nord, 365–6
Cane Wood, 165
Cantlie, Colonel G., 349 (C)
Cargill, Captain, 285 (VII)
Carnegie, 2nd Lieut., 252 (VII)
Carr, Captain Baker, 245 (VII)
Cassie, 2nd Lieut. J. R. B., 179, 182, 183 (VI)
Casualties
  Arras Offensive, 160, 283, 285
  Bazentin-le-Grand, 139
  Beaumont Hamel, 145, 150, 271, 274
  Busnes, 301
  Buzancy, 101
  Cambrai, 175
  Champagne, 196, 309–10
  Courcelette, 155
  Drucat, 156
  Drocourt-Quéant Line, 365
  Ecaillon River, crossing of, 313
  German Offensive, March–April, 1918, 186, 301, 305
  Greenland Hill, 198
  High Wood, 141, 265–6
  Hill 70, 360
  Hindenburg Line, 297
  Hyderabad Redoubt, 312
  Iwuy, 314
  Méaulte, 267
  Monchy-le-Preux, 355
  Mont Huoy, 201
  Neuville-St. Vaast, 263
  Regina Trench, 359
  Rue d'Ouvert, 252
  Schwaben Redoubt, 76
  Somme, Battle of the, 355
  Thiepval, 77
  Tower Hamlets, 87
  Vimy Ridge, 359
  Ypres, Third battle of, 86, 167, 291
  Zollern-Graben, 355

Caudescure, 68
Cave, Lieut. J. W., 367 (C)
Chambrecy, 195
Champagne, 16
Champagne Offensive, 306 *sqq.*
Chapelle d'Armentières, 142
Charles, Regimental Sergt.-Major, 4, 16, 18 (IV)
Château de la Haie, 198
Cheape, Major G.R.H., 260, Lieut.-Col, 267, 273, 279 (VII).
Cheshire Regt., 6th Bn., 68, 80
Chiévres, 104
Chivry Farm, 98
Chocolat Menier Corner, 130
Citation in French Army Orders, 196 (VI)
Clark, 2nd Lieut., 296 (VII)
Cochrane of Cults, Lord, 247, 344–5 (VII)
Coghill, Pte., 13 (IV)
Cohen, Lieut. M. T., 360 (C)
Coisy, 49
Coldstream Guards, 129
Colville, Lieut.-Colonel C.E., 126, 345 (VI)
Conder, 2nd Lieut., 149 (VI)
Congreve, General, 91
Corbie, 24, 135
Couper, Captain C. M., 5, 15, 17, 25 (IV)
Courcelles Le Comte, 175
Courcelette, 155, 275
Coutts, Captain, 179, 181 (VI)
Cowing, Lieut., 361 (C)
Cox, 2nd Lieut. G. W., 6, Lieut., 9, 25 (IV)
Cox, 2nd Lieut. W. A., 25, 67 (IV/V)
Craig, Sergt., 9, 19 (IV)
Cremarest, 89
Crescent Trench, 12 (IV)
Croix de Guerre, 202
Croak, Pte. J. B., 363 (C)
Croates trench, 363
Crosbie, Lieut., 302 (VII)
Cruickshank, Major, 51, 68, 94, 97, 106 (IV/V)
Cruickshank, Sergt., 24 (IV), 73, 90 (IV/V)

377

INDEX

Cumming, 2nd Lieut. D., 299 (VII)
Cunningham, Lieut. R. C., 15, 19–23, 25, 67, 71
Cunningham, 2nd Lieut. T. F., 25, 74 (M.G.C.)
Currey, Lieut. F. H., 25, 67 (IV/V)
Currie-Begg, Lieut., 257 (VII)

Davidson, Colonel Piers, 349 (C)
Davidson, Pte., 72 (IV/V)
Davies, Lieut., 259 (VII)
Deane, Pte., 131 (VI)
Dernamount, 264
Devlin, Pte., 157 (VI)
Dewar, Lieut., 313 (VII)
Diamond, Pte. J., 13 (IV)
Dick, Corpl. R., 7 (IV)
Dick, L/Corpl., 72 (IV/V)
Dickebusch, 351
Dickson, Capt. D. E. (R.A.M.C.), 243
Dickson, Lieut., 150 (VI)
Dickson, 2nd Lieut., 74, 75, 106 (IV/V)
Dineson, Pte., 362, 364 (C)
Divisions—
  1st Canadian, 354
  3rd   „   351
  4th   „   154, 358
  Guards, 296
  Lahore (3rd Indian), 7, 131
  Meerut (7th „) 6, 7, 16
  New Zealand, 268
  1st, 12
  2nd, 145
  3rd, 145
  4th, 162, 282, 356
  7th, 250
  8th, 48–9
  9th, 250, 283
  16th, 103
  17th, 284
  18th,
  19th, 300
  29th, 140
  30th, 136
  36th (Ulster), 171
  37th, 284
  38th, 164, 291
  39th, 50, 290
  44th, 23

Divisions—
  51st, 23
  57th, 198
  62nd, 194, 307, 309
  63rd, 145
  23rd (French), 358
  66th (French), 263
  3rd German Guards, 164
  103rd Hessian (German), 191, 307
  Sachsen-Meinigen, 191
  Saxon, 23rd, 164, 191, 307
  22nd (German), 307
Dobbie, 2nd Lieut. A. M., 182, 187 (VI)
Doe, 2nd Lieut., 160 (VI)
Dolan, Sergt., 86 (IV/V)
Dolan, Pte., 9 (IV)
Dollie's Brae, 70
Donaldson, Captain, 251, 253 (VII)
Donaldson, Piper, 9 (IV)
Donnachie, Pte., 13 (IV)
Douchy, 313
Dress—
  Khaki bonnets, 10
  Boots and half puttees, 10
  The Red Hackle, 362
Drocourt-Quéant switch, 365
Drucat, 156
Drummond, 2nd Lieut., 165, 166, 180 (VI)
Dudhope Castle, 4 (IV)
Duke, Lieut., A. W., 50 (V)
Duncan, Captain P. F., 15, 25 (IV)
Dundee, 3, 4 (IV)
Dunn, 2nd Lieut., 286 (VII)

Ecaillon River, crossing of, 313
Ecurie, 157
Edwards, 2nd Lieut., 71, 106 (IV/V)
Ellis, Captain, 148, 150 (VI)
Epernay, 190, 307
Essex Regt., 11th Bn., 175
Estaires, 14
Etinehem, 136

Fabeck Graben, 354
Famars, 200
Familleureux, 314
Fampoux, 158, 198, 283
Fauquissart, 131

INDEX

Ferguson, Captain T., 147
Fergusson, General Sir C., 161, 286
Festubert, 68, 129, 131, 251
Finlayson, Lieut. J. S., 260 (VII)
Fisher, L/Corpl F., 350 (C)
Fleming, Lieut.-Colonel C. R. E., 187
Flesquières, 174, 295
Flêtre, 129
Flett, Lieut., 137 (VI)
Foch, Marshal, 97, 195
Folkestone, 129, 248
Fontaine Notre Dame, 296
Fontenoy, 103
Forth Bridge, 126
France, arrival in, 6 (IV)
Francois Farm, 165
Frémicourt, 175, 182, 297
French Army Orders, citation in, 196 (VI)
French, Sir John, 10, 350
French Regt., 19th, 255
Fricourt, 23

Ganspette, 96
Gardiner, Company Sergt.-Major, 140 (VI)
Gardiner, Sergt., 19 (IV)
Garvie, 2nd Lieut., 160, 183 (VI)
Gas, first use of, 16
Gassouin, General C., 101
Gemmell, Colonel (R. Scots), 185
George V, H.M. King, 101, 133
German Offensives, 1918, 176, 298, 301
Germany, Crown Prince of, 69
Gerrard, Captain F. J., 306 (VII)
Gerrard, 2nd Lieut, 289 (VII)
Giant's Causeway, 70
Gibson, 2nd Lieut. C. M., 25, 67 (IV/V)
Gibson, Captain L., 126, 128, Major, 186 (VI)
Gilroy, Captain, 9, 10 (II)
Givenchy, 22, 68, 359
Gladstone, Lieut. B. H., 5 (IV)
Glass, 2nd Lieut, 160 (VI)
Glenday, Pte., 14 (IV)
Godley, Lieut.-General Sir A., 97, 190, 194, 309

Gomiecourt, 292
Good, Corpl. H. J., 365 (C)
Gordon, Brig.-Gen. A., 161, 164, 286
Gordon, Captain R. G., 126 (VI)
Gordon, Army Chaplain, 152 (VI)
Gordon Highlanders—
  2nd Bn., 130
  4th Bn., 148, 150, 194, 305, 313
  5th Bn., 98, 128, 146, 154, 162, 165, 252, 259, 286, 296
  6th Bn., 159, 284
  7th Bn., 128, 173, 179, 194-5, 263, 272, 284, 287, 289, 290, 295, 302
Gough, General, 91, 94, 292
Gournier Farm, 165
Gouzeaucourt, 92
Gowans, Captain S. B., 5, 16 (IV)
Gowans, 2nd Lieut., 285 (VII)
Grafftey, Major, 362 (C)
Grahame, Captain, 257 (VII)
Grant, Pte., 14 (IV)
Graves, Lieut., 172 (VI)
Gray, Lieut. W. B., 5, 9, 25 (IV)
Gray, Pte., 7 (IV)
Green, Colonel W., 202
Greenland Hill, attack on, 159
Greig, Sergt., 311 (VII)
Grierson, Captain H. J., 343 (R)
Grogan, Brig.-General, 250
Guedecourt, 91
Guillaumat, General, 196
Guoy en Terrois, 70
Gyle, 2nd Lieut., 160 (VI)
Guthrie, Major T. Maule, 260 (VII), 343 (R)

Habarcq, 168
Hackle, the Red, right to wear (Canadian Highlanders), 362
Hagan, Captain the Rev. E. J., 68, 107 (IV/V)
Haig, Sir Douglas, 10, 11, 97, 129, 190, 341
Haig, Major W. (R.A.M.C.), 128, 141
Haldane, Lieut. R. P., 130 (VI)
Hally, Captain J., 126, 140 (VI)
Ham En Antois, 187

INDEX

Hamel, 70
Hamilton, Lieut., 165 (vi)
Hamilton, Brig.-General J. G., 283
Hangard Wood, 363
Harper, Major-General Sir G. M., 23, 49, 156, 164, 177, 256, 274, 277, 284, 288
Harvey, 2nd Lieut., 97, 107 (iv/v)
Haut Deule Canal, 102
Havre, 6 (iv)
Havrincourt, 295
Havrincourt Wood, 171
Hay, Major C., 343 (R)
Hay-Drummond, Colonel A. W., 127, 343, 345 (R)
Heard, 2nd Lieut. R. R., 285 (vii)
Hébuterne, 73, 144, 185, 270
Hédauville, 297
Henderson, Major, 156 (vi)
Hénencourt, 133
Hepden, 2nd Lieut., 160 (vi)
Herd, 2nd Lieut, 260, Captain, 279 (vii)
Hermaville, 365
Herme, 189
Hertfordshire Regt., 1/1st, 68
Hesperian, s.s., 351
Hewat, Lieut. J. C. A., 182, 183, 187 (vi)
" Highland Gathering," 312
Highland Light Infantry, 134
Hill 60, 353
Hill 70, 359
Hill 102, 364
Hindenburg Farm, 165
Hindenburg Line, 168, 170, 295
Hislop, Lieut.-Colonel H. H., 164
High Wood, attack on, 139
Hooge, 351
Hopkins, 2nd Lieut., 287 (vii)
Horne, General Sir H. S., 100
Houplines, 141
Houtkerque, 82
Hoyles, Lieut. H., 361 (C)
Hudson, Major-General, 49
Huissignies, 104
Hulluch, 102
Humphreys, Lieut., 255 (vii)
Hunter, Army Chaplain, 152 (vi)

Hunter, Lieut. P. C., 343, Captain, 345 (R)
Hunter-Weston, General Sir Aylmer, 78
Husband, 2nd Lieut. J. W., 51, 54, 68, 107 (iv/v)
Hutton, Sergt., 75, 86, Company Sergt.-Major, 88, Regt. Sergt.-Major, 95 (iv/v)
Hyderabad Redoubt, 311

Ilot, 256
Imrie, Colonel Blair, 14, 49, 54
Indian Army Units—
    Dogras, 2/8th, 6, 8, 19
    Gurkhas, 2/3rd, 16
         „   2/8th, 6, 8, 19
    Punjabis, 33rd, 16
    Rifles, 58th, 6, 12, 16
Indian Village, 129
Inglebelmer, 70, 72
Innes, Captain A., 126, 133, 140, 142 (n.), 149, 156 (vi)
Irish Farm, 78, 89
Irish Guards, 202
Iwuy, 201, 314

Jacob, Major-General Claude, 16
Jacob's Horse, 36th, 256
James, Lieut. H., 25, 67, 69 (iv/v)
Jarron, Sergt. H., 14 (iv)
Jarvis, Sergt., 271, 273–4 (vii)
Jeffreys, Major, 250
Jenkins, Pte., 131 (vi)
Jenny, Lieut.-Colonel A. O., 138, 143 (vi)
Johnston, Captain Hamilton, 21 (iv)

Keay, Lieut., 150 (vi)
Keir, Major, 185, 301 305–6 (vii)
Kelman, Pte., 13 (iv)
Kennedy, Captain J., 26, 51, 67, 68 (iv/v)
Kennedy, Pte., 13 (iv)
King, Major W. B. M., 350 (C)
Kinghorn, 239
King's Liverpool, 8th Bn., 128, 252
King's Own R. Lancashire Regt., 128

INDEX

Kinross, 314
Kitson, Lieut., 50 (v)
Kliest Farm, 165
K.R.R.C., 16th Bn., 80

La Belle Hôtesse, 24, 50, 67
La Baisselle, 132, 255
La Brique, 83, 85
"Labyrinth," 136, 138, 258
La Chavatte, 364
La Comte, 280
Lacouture, 129
La Folie, 357
La Faulenic, 98
La Gorgue, 21
Laird, 2nd Lieut. G., 68 (iv/v)
Laird, Sergt., 72 (iv/v)
Lambert, Brig.-General, 202
La Miquellerie, 249
Lancashire Farm, 290
Lancashire Fusiliers, 2/5th Bn., 128
Lancashire Regt., 5th Bn., 81
Lancers, 19th, 256
La Neuville, 24
Lansdowne Post, 13 (iv)
La Pierrière, 129
La Raperie, 100
Laventie, 131, 253
Law, Lieut. I. H., 5, 16, 26 (iv)
Lawson, Major A., 344 (R)
Léalvillers, 271
Lean, Captain, 164
L'Ecuille, 103
"L 8," 130
Le Maitre, 2nd Lieut., 257, 269 (vii)
Le Poirier, 201
Les Brebis, 360
Leslie, 2nd Lieut., 148, 149, 150 (vi)
Le Touret, 129, 130
Lichelle, 297
Lieu St. Amand, 313
Lillers, 6 (iv)
Lindsay, 2nd Lieut. J., 147, 149, 150, Captain, 165
Locon, 251
Loftus, Sergt., 173 (vi)
Longairnes, 93
Loos, 15 *sqq.*

Louez, 156
Louvevral, 299
Low, Pte., 69 (iv/v)
Low, Pipe-Major, 9, 80 (iv)
Loyal N. Lancashire R., 4th Bn., 28, 181
Lucheux, 70
Lumsden, Sergt., 253 (vii)
Lyell, Captain T., 51, 68, 71, 72, 107 (iv/v)

Macdonald, Major, 159 (vi)
Macdonald, Sergt., 8, 11 (iv)
Macdonald, Pte., 131 (vi)
Macdonell, General, 355
MacDowell, Lieut.-Colonel, 127, 131 (vi)
MacDowell, Captain, 158 (vi)
MacGregor, 2nd Lieut., 289 (vii)
MacRosty, Captain, 179, 180 (vi)
Magnicourt, 70
Mailly-Maillet, 271
Mailly Wood, 72, 146
Maison Blanche, 136
Mametz Wood, 138, 139, 264
Mangin, General, 98
Maple Copse, 352
Mavais, 289
Maricourt, 135, 257
Maroeuil, 126, 138, 158, 262, 280
Marquay, 160
Marshall, Captain, 133 (vi)
Martin, Corporal, 181 (vi)
Martinsart, 73
Martinsart Wood, 76
Mavor, Pte., 361 (C)
Maxse, General Sir F. I., 163, 175, 288, 292
May, Captain F. W. L., 343 (R)
McAvoy, Pte., 13 (iv)
McBeth, 2nd Lieut., 160 (vi)
McClintock, Lieut.-Colonel, 179, 181, 184, 299, 300 (vii)
McCorquodale, Lieut., 192, 308 (vii)
McCririck, 2nd Lieut. C. S., 26, 68 (iv)
McCuaig, Major G. E., 356 (C)
McEwan, Lieut., 141 (vi)

381

INDEX

McIntosh, Captain G. W., 240, 292, 295 (VII)
McIntosh, Sergt., 261 (VII)
McIntosh, Pte., 14 (IV)
McIntyre, Captain R. W., 5, 15, 26 (IV)
McKerrell, Brig.-General, 5
McLachlan, Quartermaster and Hon. Lieut. J., 6, 16, 26 (IV) 68, 73, 89, 90 (IV/V)
McLachlan, Lieut., 361 (C)
McLaren, Lieut., 137, 144 (VI)
McLaughlan, Sergt., 79 (IV/V)
McLennan, Lieut.-Colonel B., 364 (C)
McLeod, Lieut., 147 (VI)
McLeod, Pipe-Major, 80 (IV/V)
McLiesh, L/Corpl., 72 (IV/V)
McNab, Sergt.-Major, 4 (IV)
McNeill, Company Q.M. Sergt., 202 (VI)
McNeill, Pte., 262 (VII)
McNicoll, Lieut. F. S., 182, 183 (VI)
Méaulte, 267
Mechernich, 201
Menzies, Lieut. R. J., 157, Captain, 166–7 (VI)
Menzies, 2nd Lieut. T. A., 272–3 (VII)
Menzies, L/Corpl., 157 (VI)
Méricourt, 138, 139
Merville, 10, 131, 254
Merzenich, 201
Meteren, 142
Methven, Lieut. C. M., 15, 26 (IV)
Metz, 171
Mill, 2nd Lieut. R. C. K., 50, 54, 68 (IV/V)
Millar, Lieut.-Colonel M. C., 305, 307 (VII)
Millar, Major R. H., 49, 345 (V)
Millar, Captain, 75 (R.A.M.C.)
Millar, Pte. P., 270 (VII)
Millencourt, 257, 277
Miller, Lieut. A. L., 259 (VII)
Miller, Lieut. K. L., 5 (IV)
Miller, Lieut. H. W., 141 (VI)
Milligan, Major J. M., 268, 281, 306 (VII)

Milne, Lieut. J. J., 81 (IV/V)
Milne, Sergt., 9 (IV)
Mitchell, Sergt. J. L., 262 (VII)
Mitchell, Sergt. W., 150 (VI)
Moated Grange, 68
Moffat, Captain A. J., 74, 75, 108 (IV/V)
Moislains, 92
Monchy-le-Preux, 364
Moncrieffe, Colonel Sir R., 125, 127, 131, 135, 201, 345 (VI)
Mons, first Officers to enter, 367
Montague, Pte., 13 (IV)
Monthelon, 306
Mont Huoy, 200
Montreal Camp, 81, 82
Montrose, His Grace the Duke of, 341, 345 (R)
Moodie, Captain O. S., 15, 17, 26 (IV)
Moon, Captain F. W., 5 (IV)
Morland, General, 81, 132
Morris, 2nd Lieut. A. R., 285 (VII)
Moslins, 311
Moulin de Piétre, 18
Moulle, 288
Muir, Major J. B., 5, 7, 12 (IV), 26 67, 69 (IV/V)
Mulligan, Corpl., 13 (IV)
Munro, General Sir C., 132, 255
Munro, Captain, 279 (VII)
Murray, Lieut. J. R., 51, 68, 70, 108 (IV/V)
Murray-Stewart, Major C., 126 (VI)
Murray, Captain A. C., 248 (VII)
Murray, Major T., 342 (R)
Murray, Colonel T. D., 73, 83, 90, 95, 108 (IV/V)

Naden, Major F., 92, 108 (IV/V)
Nappes, 309
Nelson, 2nd Lieut., 285 (VII)
Neuve Chapelle, 7, 9, 10 (IV)
Neuville, 313
Neuville-St. Vaast, 136
Neuville Vitasse, 101
Newell, Corpl., 131 (VI)
Newson, Major (Gordon H.), 185
New Zealanders, 141

INDEX

Nicoll, Lieut. E. D., 186 (vi)
Nicoll, 2nd Lieut. M. W., 68, 108 (iv/v)
Nicoll, Colonel P. S., 343, 345 (R)
Nicholson, Pte., 132 (vi)
Nieurlet, 289
Norie, Brig.-General Charles, 16, 18, 20
Northcote, Rev., 72 (iv/v)
Northumberland Fus., 27th Bn., 285
Norsworthy, Captain E. C., 355 (C)

" Oppy " line, 161, 283
"Orchard, The," 351
Osborne, Lieut. E. C., 26, 67 (iv/v)
Ovillers, 275
Oxley, Captain J. W., 126 (vi)

Pacaut, 130, 187, 251
Paradis, 10, 129
Paris, 202
Parvillers, 364
Passchendaele Ridge, 163
Paterson, 2nd Lieut. G. F., 90, 109 (iv/v)
Paterson, Lieut. I. S., 55, 68, 89, Captain, 90 (iv/v)
Paul, 2nd Lieut. W. B. D., 79, 109 (iv/v)
Peddie, Pte., 174 (vi)
Penin, 101
Penney, Captain, 95, 109 (iv/v)
Penney, Lieut., 292 (vii)
Peronne, 94
Pershing, General, 201, 314
Peterson, Captain, 88 (iv/v)
Petrie, Sergt., 18 (iv)
Petrie, Pte., 91 (iv/v)
Philip, 2nd Lieut. J. R., 6, 26 (iv), Lieut., 70, Captain, 92, 95 (iv/v)
Pierry, 190
Pirie, Colonel D., 342, 345 (R)
Plimpton, Lieut. R. A., 26, 67 (iv), Captain, 87, 88, 90 (iv/v)
Plumer, General, 142
Pont du Hem, 20 (iv), 21
Pont Riqueul, 129, 250

Port Arthur, 7, 9 (iv)
Poulainville, 136, 257
Pozières, 354
Princess Patricia's C.L.I., 351, 354, 358, 367
Proctor, Corpl., 19 (iv)
Puaux, Lieut. Rene, 100
Puisieux-au-Mont, 270
Pullar, Captain G. D., 126, 127, 133 (vi)
Pullar, 2nd Lieut. J. L., 6, Lieut., 16, 21, 23, 26 (iv)
Pyott, Sergt.-Major, 13 (iv)

Queensferry, 126
Queen's Westminster R., 2nd Bn., 138

Rafferty, Pte., 9 (iv)
Raincheval, 145, 152, 154
Rainneville, 23, 24 (iv)
Raistick, Comp. Sergt.-Major, 287
Red Hackle, issue of the, 260
Reed, General, 100, 102, 103
" Regina " trench, 154, 356
Reid, Captain J., 181, 185, 300, 306 (vii)
Reid, 2nd Lieut. J., 267 (vii)
Reigersburg Château, 86
Renenghelst, 352
Renescure, 24, 50
Renton, Lieut. H. W., 202 (vi)
Rettie, Captain J. L., 5, 26 (iv), 71 (iv/v)
Reuter, Pte. H. De, 273 (vii)
Richebourg-l'Avoné, 250
Richebourg St. Vaast, 6, 7, 11, 68
Riez de Vinage, 70
Rifle Brigade, 72
Ripley, Corpl. J., 249 (i)
Robb, Sergt. W., 9 (iv)
Robecq, 305
Robertson, Lieut. J.W.H., 5, 26 (iv)
Robertson, Lieut. W. L., 5, 26 (iv)
Robertson, Lieut. W. S., 5, 26, 67 (iv)
Robertson, Major, 242 (vii)
Robertson, 2nd Lieut., 285 (vii)
Robertson, Corpl., 156 (vi)
Roclincourt, 158, 199, 306

INDEX

Rogers, Major J. S. Y. (R.A.M.C.), 5, 13, 15, 20, 67, 72, 80, 87, 90, 95
Ross, Pte. J., 13, 14 (IV)
Ross, Regtl. Sergt.-Major, 202 (VI)
Rossetti, s.s., 6 (IV)
Rosyth, 126
Rouex, 159, 283
Rowan, Lieut. G., 255 (VII)
Roy, Lieut., 141 (VI)
Royal Fusiliers, 2nd Bn., 157
Royal Irish Rifles, 8/9th Bn., 171
Royal Munster Fusiliers, 1st Bn., 311
Royal Scots Fusiliers, 9th Bn., 158, 292, 8th Bn., 182, 287
Royal Sussex Regt., 11th Bn., 69, 70
Rudolph Farm, 165
Rue de Bruges, 49
Rue d'Ouvert, 252
Rutherford, Captain J., 156, 169 (VI)
Rutherford, Lieut. J. F., 137 (VI)

Sadler, Major B., 126 (VI)
Sailly-le-Sec, 135
Scouts, 100, 282, 361
Scrymgeour-Wedderburn, Lieut.-Colonel H., 39 (V)
St. Catherine, 279
St.-Hilaire-Cottes, 305
St. Imogé, 194
St. Jan Ter Biezen, 82, 83, 168, 291
St. Julien, 85
St. Laurent Blangy, 287
St. Pierre Divion, 77
St. Vaast Bridge, 279
Sanctuary Wood, 353
Sarton, 186
Savy, 281
Sceales, Lieut.-Col. G. McL., 23, 27 (IV), 51, 67, 72-4, 88, 90 (IV/V)
Schwaben Redoubt, 73
Scots Guards, 2nd Bn., 174, 291
Scott, Lieut. A., 361 (C)
Scott, Lieut. G., 157, 159 (VI)
Scottish Horse, 80, 156

Scratton, Lieut. G. H., 27, 67, 69, 86, 90 (IV/V)
Seaforth Highlanders—
  1st Bn., 22
  4th Bn., 24, 192, 265
  5th Bn., 145, 182
  6th Bn., 164, 165, 182, 201-2, 308
  8th Bn., 98
Selle, 89
Senegalese troops, 192
Senlis, 73, 76, 155
Serques, 163
Sharp, Captain R., 344-5 (R)
Shaw, Lieut. R. B., 180, 343 (VI)
Shepherd, 2nd Lieut. D. M., 5 (IV)
Shepherd, Captain E., 27, 67 (IV/V)
Sherriff, 2nd Lieut. C. B., 6, Lieut., 8 (IV)
Siege Camp, 168, 291
Simpson, Corpl., 173 (VI)
Skene, Colonel, 239 (VII)
Smart, Pte., 72 (IV/V)
Smeaton, L/Corpl., 181 (VI)
Smith, Colonel H. K., 345
Smith, L/Corpl., 14 (IV)
Smitton, Captain C. D., 344 (R)
Smoke clouds, first use of, 16
Somme, battle of, 69, 354
Southey, Brig.-General W. M., 6
Speid, Lieut., 311 (VII)
Spence, Sergt., 50 (V)
Steele, Sergt. N., 173 (VI)
Steenbeek River, 164
Steenbecque, 49
Steven, Lieut. Harvey, 21, 27 (IV)
Steven, Lieut. P. H., 5, 8, 11, 15, 22, 27 (IV)
Stevenson, 2nd Lieut., 6, Lieut., 22, 23, 27 (IV), Captain, 67, 69, 88, 90 (IV/V)
Stewart, Lieut. A. J., 5, 15, 17, 19, 27 (IV), Captain, 86, 90 (IV/V)
Stewart, Brig.-General Charles Edward, 24, 49
Stewart, Captain J. D., 93, 94, 109
Stewart, Sergt., 148 (VI)
Stewart, Corpl., 13 (IV)

384

INDEX

Steyn, Major (Gordon H.), 187
Stirling, Major R. (R.A.M.C.), 128
Stocks, Captain K. H. (R.A.M.C.), 88
Strathairn, Lieut., 150 (VI)
Strength, 4th Bn., 23, IV/V Bn., 68, 70, 81, 83, 88, 95, 97, 5th Bn., 49
Stuart, Captain J. O. G., 95, 109 (IV/V)
Studley, Captain H., 246 (VII)
Stuff Redoubt, 73
Sturrock, 2nd Lieut. B. S., 6, Lieut., 15, 27 (IV)
Suffolk Regt., 8th Bn., 133
Sutherland, Colonel H. H., 280, 294, 299 (VII)
Sutherland, L/Corpl., 202 (VI)
Swan, Pte., 259 (VII)
Sworder, Lieut.-Colonel F. R., 187
Sydney Scottish, Officers of, who served with A.I.F. or B.I.F., 373
Sykes, Lieut., 357 (C)

Tara Hill, 356
Tarleton, F. R., Captain, 4, 5, Major, 15, 17, 27 (IV), Lieut.-Colonel, 187, 193, 196, 203 (VI)
Tay defences, 3, 127
Taylor, L/Corpl., 13 (IV)
Taylor, L/Corpl., 360 (C)
Thaint, 313
Thiepval, capture of, 77 (IV/V)
Thiepval Spur, 73
Thieshouk, 86
Thomas, Lieut., 137 (VI)
Thompson, Brig.-General, 98, 103
Thomson, 2nd Lieut., 179 (VI)
Thun-St. Martin, 199
Tosh, Major E., 5, 15, 18, 27 (IV)
Tours-sur-Marne, 189
Tower Hamlets, 87
Trescault, 174
Troup, Drummer, 12, 13 (IV)
Trout, Lieut., 361 (C)

Truman, Lieut.-Colonel C. M., 135, 138 (VI)
Tunnelling Company, 22

Vancouver Trench, 352
Valentine, Major, 342 (R)
Victoria Cross, first Canadian to win, 350
Vaux-en-Amienois, 134
Villers Bretonneux, 95
Vimy Ridge, 136, 358
Violaines, 253
Vlamertinghe, 80, 82

Wailly, 169
Wales, H.R.H. The Prince of, 201, 313
Walker, Colonel H. W., 3, 4, 7, 10, 14, 15, 18–21, 27 (IV)
Walker, 2nd Lieut. J. M., 200 (VI)
Walker, Captain N. C., 5, 15, 17, 27 (IV)
Wallace, Major, 242 (VII)
Wallace, Sergt., 137 (VI)
Wanquetin, 294
Wardrecques, 141
Warloy, 77
Watson, Lieut. A. B., 15, 27 (IV)
Watson, Captain and Quartermaster, 246, 294 (VII)
Watson, Captain S. L., 15, 27 (IV)
Watson, Major (Tank Corps), 175
Watson, Pte., 91 (IV/V)
Watt, Captain J., 67, 69 (IV/V)
Watteau, 89
Wauchope, Major A. G., 10, Colonel, 14, 18, 21, 23
Waugh, Sergt., 81 (IV/V)
Wedderburn, Captain A. H., 51, 68, 110 (IV/V)
Weinberg, 2nd Lieut. P. D., 6, 13, 27 (IV)
Welsh Guards, 202
West, L/Corpl., 202
Westwood, Lieut., 252 (VII)
Whyte, L/Corpl., 13 (IV)
Wilkie, Major D, 343 (R)
Willard, Sergt., 131
Willcocks, Lieut.-General Sir J., 6, 10, 129

INDEX

Willerval, 306
Williamson, Lieut. T., 15, 27 (IV)
Willis, 2nd Lieut., 285 (VII)
Willis, Corpl., 131 (VI)
Willison, Captain, 193, 343 (VI)
Wilson, Sergt.-Major J., 126 (VI)
Wilson, Hon. Lieut. & Quartermaster J. C., 182 (VI)
Wilson, Lieut. L., 15 (IV)
Windmill Camp, 164, 289
Windy Corner, 7 (IV)
Wood, Sergt., 269 (VII)
Worcestershire Regt., 1st Bn., 46
Wormhoudt, 78
Wylie, Captain J., 126, 128, Major, 131, 133, Lieut.-Colonel, 143–4, 155–6

York & Lancashire Regt., 1/5th Bn., 313
Young, Captain T. E., 126–7, Major, 150 (VI)
Young, 2nd Lieut., 149 (VI)
Ypres Salient, 78 *sqq.*
Ypres, Second battle of, 350 (C)
Ypres, Third battle of, 84, 163, 288
" Y " Ravine, 145

Zillebeke Lake, 351
Zollern-Graben, 355

www.ingramcontent.com/pod-product-compliance
Lightning Source LLC
Chambersburg PA
CBHW070804300426
44111CB00014B/2419